ISBN 978-1-330-68546-4
PIBN 10092114

Similar Books Are Available from
www.forgottenbooks.com

Legal Maxims, Vol. 1
With Observations and Cases, by George Frederick Wharton

Readings on the History and System of the Common Law
by Roscoe Pound

A Handbook of Bankruptcy Law
Embodying the Full Text of the Act of Congress, by Henry Campbell Black

The Principles of Pleading and Practice in Civil Actions in the High Court of Justice
by W. Blake Odgers

Real Estate Principles and Practices
by Philip A. Benson

The New Law-Dictionary
by Giles Jacob

On Foreign Jurisdiction and the Extradition of Criminals
by George Cornewall Lewis

Principles of the Law of Contract
by William Reynell Anson

A Treatise of the Law Relative to Merchant Ships and Seamen, Vol. 1 of 4
by Charles Abbott

A Manual of Constitutional History, Founded on the Works of Hallam, Creasy, May and Broom
by Forrest Fulton

Patent and Trade Mark Laws of the World
by B. Singer

Thomas Aquinas
Treatise on Law (Summa Theologica, Questions 90-97), by Thomas Aquinas

A Treatise on the Conflict of Laws, and the Limits of Their Operation in Respect of Place and Time
by Friedrich Carl von Savigny

A Summary of the Law of Lien
by Basil Montagu

Introduction to Roman Law
In Twelve Academical Lectures, by James Hadley

The Science of Law
by Sheldon Amos

The Oldest Laws in the World
Being an Account of the Hammurabi Code and the Sinaitic Legislation, by Chilperic Edwards

The Law of Torts
by Francis M. Burdick

Cases on Criminal Law
by Jerome C. Knowlton

Constitution and Laws of the Cherokee Nation
by Cherokee Nation

A

SELECTION OF CASES

ILLUSTRATIVE OF

ENGLISH CRIMINAL LAW.

CAMBRIDGE UNIVERSITY PRESS
London: FETTER LANE, E.C.
C. F. CLAY, Manager

Edinburgh: 100, PRINCES STREET
London: STEVENS AND SONS, Ltd., 119 and 120, CHANCERY LANE.
Berlin: A. ASHER AND CO.
Leipzig: F. A. BROCKHAUS
New York: G. P. PUTNAM'S SONS
Bombay and Calcutta: MACMILLAN AND Co., Ltd.

A

SELECTION OF CASES

ILLUSTRATIVE OF

ENGLISH CRIMINAL LAW

BY

COURTNEY STANHOPE KENNY, LL.D.

DOWNING PROFESSOR OF LAW IN THE UNIVERSITY OF CAMBRIDGE.

THIRD EDITION.

CAMBRIDGE:

AT THE UNIVERSITY PRESS.

1912

First Edition 1901.
Second Edition 1907.
Third Edition 1912.

PREFACE.

THE increased attention which, of recent years, has been bestowed, both in England and in the United States, upon the methods of legal education, has caused a fuller recognition of the great value which case-law possesses for even the elementary student. Only by means of concrete cases can he give vividness and reality to the abstract principles which he learns from his text-books, or even form a clear idea of the way in which questions, whether of law or of fact, are handled in everyday practice by our courts of justice. But, valuable though this part of his legal training is, it is the part in which he most needs direction. Elementary students who read the Reports under their own guidance are prone to reverse the true order of things, by attending to the names of cases rather than to their facts, and to the facts rather than to the principles decided. Even when the principle itself is sought for, it is too often sought only by the compendious method of perusing nothing of the case beyond the head note ; a plan of study which combines the disadvantages of reading case-law with those of reading text-books. And even a student whose greater assiduity has saved him from these errors is often led, by a natural inclination for reading recent cases in preference to older ones, to waste his time upon the study of decisions that are concerned only with some refined limitation of a fundamental doctrine, when he has not yet become acquainted with the cases in which that broad doctrine itself is established.

K.   *b*

787806

These facts have often been forced upon my attention in the course of twenty-five years' experience as a law-lecturer at Cambridge; an experience which has also afforded me opportunities of observing what portions of our case-law are best adapted to arouse the attention and impress the memory of students in their early days of difficulty, when legal phrases and principles have not yet ceased to be unfamiliar and uninviting. In order to obtain such cases, I have gone to a variety of sources; not limiting myself to the decisions of the Courts of Criminal Appeal, or to modern decisions, or even to English ones. I have preferred short cases; any longer ones I have usually abridged. To beginners, at any rate, I hope the volume will be of service in affording brief and vivid illustrations of the practical working of the English Criminal Law.

The compilation of the book would have been impossible but for the permission which the Incorporated Council of Law Reporting generously conceded to me, to make use of their Reports; a permission for which my most cordial thanks are due. I must also thank the proprietors of the copyright of Mr Cox's Criminal Law Reports, for allowing me to take several cases from their series. To my friend and former pupil, Mr W. C. A. Landon, of Gray's Inn, I am indebted for assiduous assistance in preparing the volume and carrying it through the press. And to the kindness of Professor Maitland I owe the admirable English rendering in which the cases cited here from the Year Books—except one or two added by myself after he had gone abroad—are made acceptable to modern eyes.

1901.

IN this third edition I have introduced a few slight modifications; and added at the end an Index.

1911.

INDEX OF CASES.

Index of Cases.

CONTENTS.

PART I.

GENERAL PRINCIPLES OF CRIMINAL LIABILITY.

SECTION I.

THE DISTINCTION BETWEEN CIVIL AND CRIMINAL WRONGS.

SECTION II.

THE MENTAL ELEMENT IN CRIMINAL LIABILITY.

SECTION III.

MODES OF PARTICIPATION IN A CRIME.

SECTION IV.

INCHOATE CRIMES.

PART II.

DEFINITIONS OF PARTICULAR CRIMES.

SECTION I.

SUICIDE

SECTION II.

MURDER AND MANSLAUGHTER.

CHAPTER I. THE EXTERNAL ACT.

CHAPTER II. THE MENTAL STATE IN MURDER.

SECTION X.

LARCENY.

SECTION XI.

EMBEZZLEMENT.

SECTION XII.

FALSE PRETENCES.

SECTION XIII.

SECTION XIV.

HIGH TREASON.

SECTION XV.

SECTION XVI.

RIOT AND UNLAWFUL ASSEMBLY.

SECTION XVII.
CONSPIRACY.

SECTION XVIII.
PERJURY.

SECTION XIX.
BIGAMY . . . 423

SECTION XX.
LIBEL.

PART III.

MODES OF LEGAL PROOF.

SECTION I.
PRESUMPTIONS.

SECTION II.

THE BURDEN OF PROOF.

SECTION III.

EVIDENCE.

SELECT CASES ON CRIMINAL LAW.

PART I.

GENERAL PRINCIPLES OF CRIMINAL LIABILITY.

SECTION I.

THE DISTINCTION BETWEEN CIVIL AND CRIMINAL WRONGS.

[*Damnum sine injuria.*]

ANONYMOUS.

King's Bench.   1695.   3 Salkeld 187.

An indictment for scolding was quashed, because it was not said to have been *ad magnam perturbationem pacis.*

[*Breach of Contract.*]

REGINA *v.* NEHUFF.

Queen's Bench.   1706.   1 Salkeld 151.

Motion for a certiorari to remove an indictment found at the Old Bailey for a client.   The defendant had borrowed £600 from a feme covert, and promised to send her some fine cloth and gold dust as a pledge.   He sent no gold dust but some coarse cloth worth little or nothing....The Court granted a certiorari; because the fact was not a matter criminal (for it was the prosecutor's fault to repose such a confidence in the defendant), and it was an absurd prosecution.

K.   1

[*Breach of Contract.*]

REX *v.* WHEATLEY.

KING'S BENCH.   1760.   1 W. BL. 273.

The defendant was indicted for that he, being a common brewer, and intending to defraud one Richard Webb, delivered to him sixteen gallons (and no more) of amber beer for and as eighteen gallons [which latter quantity he had contracted to deliver]; and received 15s. for the same. He was convicted.

Morton moved in arrest of judgment. This was not an indictable offence; being merely a breach of civil contract, and not a selling by a false Measure, such as shows a general plan of imposing on the public.

DENNISON, J. ...What is it to the public whether Richard Webb has or has not his eighteen gallons of amber beer ?.

                                                     Judgment arrested.

[EDITOR'S NOTE.   Similarly in *Rex* v. *Bradford* (3 Salkeld 189, A.D. 1697), where the defendant had broken his contract to cure the prosecutor's ulcerated throat, it was held that, as no public interest was concerned, the only remedy was by civil action. Probably all these prosecutors were led to take criminal proceedings by the fact that in these they themselves would be admissible witnesses but not (as the law then stood) in civil proceedings. And in *Reg.* v. *Nehuff* the prosecutrix had the further disability of coverture.]

[*Tort.*]

REGINA *v.* DANIEL.

QUEEN'S BENCH.   1704.   3 SALKELD 191.

The defendant was indicted for enticing an apprentice to depart from his master and absent himself from his service....

HOLT, C. J., held that the seducing an apprentice to absent himself was not indictable, because it doth not affect the public....

[See also REG. *v.* CHEESEMAN, *infra*, p 85.]

[*Tort committed by many against many.*]

REX *v.* RICHARDS.

KING'S BENCH.   1800.   8 DURNFORD AND EAST 634.

This was an indictment against six defendants for not repairing a

private road constructed by virtue of an Act of Parliament for draining
and dividing a certain moor, called King's Sedgemoor, in the county of
Somerset....The defendants pleaded not guilty. On the trial at the
assizes at Bridgewater, before Grose, J., the jury found a special verdict,
in substance as follows :—That the commissioners named in the said
Act by their award set out the said private road and drove-way as
described in the indictment; that the commissioners directed that
it should be for the use of the several owners of the tenements of the
nine parishes mentioned in the indictment; and that it should be
repaired by the several owners of the tenements in six of those parishes.
That the said road was ruinous and out of repair : That the six defendants are severally and respectively owners of certain tenements in the
said several six parishes or hamlets....That the defendants had not
repaired the said drove-way....That there are five hundred tenements
in the said nine parishes, of which the owners are entitled to the use of
the said drove-way....And two hundred and fifty owners of tenements
in the said six parishes....That from the time of making the said
award, all persons willing to pass and repass over the said drove-way,
have at their free will and pleasure passed and repassed over the same
on foot, and with cattle and carriages : That the said drove-way com-
municates at both ends with the king's highway....

Praed, for the prosecutor, argued, That this, though a private
road, was set out by virtue of a public Act of Parliament, under which
the defendants were directed to repair it; that consequently the not
repairing was a disobedience to a public statute, and therefore the
subject of an indictment. That this non-repair might be considered to
a certain degree as concerning the public...because it appeared by the
special verdict that there were no less than 250 persons who were
liable to the repair of this road, and the difficulty of suing so many
persons together was almost insuperable.

BUT THE COURT interposed, and said that, however convenient it
might be that the defendants should be indicted, there was no legal
ground on which this indictment could be supported. That the known
rule was, that those matters only that concerned the public were the
subject of an indictment; and the road in question, being described to
be a private road, did not concern the public, nor was of a public
nature, but merely concerned the individuals who had a right to use
it. That the question was not varied by the fact that many individuals
were liable to repair ; or by the fact that many others were entitled
to the benefit of it, for each party injured might bring his action
against those on whom the duty was thrown. That the circumstance
of this road having been set out under a public Act of Parliament,

did **not** make the non-repair of it an indictable offence; for many public Acts are passed which regulate private rights, but it never was conceived that an indictment lay on that account for an infringement of such rights. That here the Act was passed for a private purpose, that of dividing and allotting the estates of certain individuals. That even **if** it were true that there was no remedy by action, the consequence would not follow that an indictment could be supported; but, **in** truth, the parties injured had another legal remedy [i.e. by action].

Judgment for the defendants.

[*Penalty sued for by a private informer.*]

ATCHESON *v.* EVERITT.

King's Bench.   1776.   1 Cowp. 382.

This was an action of debt to recover penalties, under the statute 2 Geo. II., c. 24, s. 7, against bribery[1]. Plea, not guilty. Verdict for the plaintiff. On behalf of the defendant, it was moved that there might be a new trial; because a Quaker had been received as a witness upon his affirmation, and it was objected that, this being a *criminal cause,* his evidence ought not to have been received.

Lord Mansfield. I wish that, when the Stat. 7 and 8 Wm. III., c. 34, was made, the affirmation of a Quaker had been put on the same footing as an oath, in all cases whatsoever: and I see no reason against it, for the punishment of the breach of it is the same. In this Act, however, there is an exception to their being admitted as witnesses in criminal causes. The question therefore is, What the statute means by the words "criminal causes"?...In cases where an action and an indictment both lie for the same act, as in assault, imprisonment, fraud, etc., a Quaker is an admissible witness in the action, though not on the indictment.

Actions for penalties are, to a variety of purposes, considered civil suits; *e.g.* they may be amended at common law. To be sure, the action in this case is not given only to recover a penalty but is attended likewise with disabilities. Therefore, it partakes much of the nature of a criminal cause. Moreover, the offence itself is not merely *malum prohibitum,* by statute, but it was indictable at common law.

---

[1] The bribed elector forfeiting £500 to *any one* who sued.

Morris, for defendant. Till the statute 7 and 8 Wm. III., there was no doubt about not receiving a Quaker's affirmation. But that statute, in compliance with the prejudices of this sect, broke in upon the rule of the common law, partly in favour to them, and partly for the general benefit of the subject. At the same time the legislature drew the line, by providing "that nothing should enable the affirmation of a Quaker to be received in any criminal cause": and another statute, 22 Geo. II., c. 30, sect. 3, says, "in any criminal case." But the Court has already decided that 'cause' and 'case' are the same. The question therefore is, Whether the present is a criminal case or not? Crimes and punishments are necessary attendants on each other. Punishment is a legal term, and is understood to be in consequence of some offence. The charge against the defendant is a charge of bribery. The statute upon which the action is brought, treats bribery as an 'offence,' throughout, and the person committing it is an 'offender.' Consequently it considers bribery as a crime. It will be said, on the contrary, that this action, to recover the penalty prescribed by the statute, is merely a civil action. That is not so. For bribery was a crime at common law: and the penalty given by the statute is only part of the fine due at common law to the public in satisfaction of the offence: besides which, the statute inflicts additional pains and penalties which are also incurred by the judgment.

With respect to indictments, and all prosecutions which upon the face of them are manifestly criminal suits, there can be no dispute. The question therefore is, Whether it is the form alone, or the substance, that constitutes a criminal action? There are two cases to this purpose. In 2 Str. 1219, a rule for quashing an appointment of overseers was held to be a civil action, and a Quaker's affirmation of service of the rule admitted accordingly. But in 2 Str. 856, which was the case of an appeal of murder, though the appellant had a right to release the appellee in every stage of the cause, a Quaker's evidence was rejected; because in substance it was a criminal prosecution. And it matters not whether the offence is of the greatest or least magnitude: If the end of the action is merely damages, a Quaker's affirmation is admissible: but wherever the end is punishment, as in this case, it is not. Here the penalty is not given as damages, but as part of the punishment; and even if it were, still this is a criminal action in respect of the additional pains and disabilities incurred by the judgment. And this is an answer to the objection, that if the party were arrested and imprisoned for the penalty, the action so much partakes of a civil suit, that the defendant might be discharged under an Act of insolvency. For, supposing he could be so discharged, the Insolvent

Act could not remove the further pains and disabilities. Therefore, both upon the reason of the thing, and the authorities in the books, this is a criminal action, and consequently a Quaker's affirmation is not admissible.

Rooke, for plaintiff. The great question is, Is this a criminal cause? The criterion of distinction between a criminal and a civil cause is, the form of the proceeding, not the offence which occasions it. An assault and nuisance may be prosecuted either by action or by indictment; in the one case, a Quaker's affirmation may be received; in the other, not. The offence of bribery may be prosecuted either by action or indictment. The plaintiff has chosen to prosecute by action, and in so doing he has proceeded civilly, not criminally. This cause is in its form an action of debt for a special cause, at the suit of a private subject. The plaintiff does not sue *tam pro rege quam pro seipso*; he sues in his own name only, and recovers the whole penalty. The declaration states, that the defendant owes the money; and that though often requested, he refuses to pay. The ground of complaint is, the non-payment of a debt. The action is founded upon that implied contract, which every subject enters into with the State to observe its laws. The plea is, *nil debet*; not that the defendant is not guilty. The judgment is to recover the debt; and the party imprisoned for non-payment may have the benefit of the Insolvent Act. Thus far, then, the whole is merely a civil proceeding. But it is said, there is a disability incurred by the judgment, and therefore it is a criminal proceeding. To this it may be answered, that the disability is no part of the judgment, but only a consequence of it: the form of the proceeding is not affected by it. The being restrained from suing for a debt beyond time of limitation, is as much a disability, as the being restrained from voting; yet there is no doubt but that a Quaker may give evidence to prove a debt to be above six years' standing.

LORD MANSFIELD....Is the present a criminal cause? A Quaker appears, and offers himself as a witness; can he give evidence without being sworn? If it is a criminal case, he must be sworn, or he cannot give evidence. Now there is no distinction better known, than the distinction between civil and criminal law; or between criminal prosecutions and civil actions. Mr Justice Blackstone, and all modern and ancient writers upon the subject, distinguish between them. Penal actions were never yet put under the head of criminal law or of crimes. To make this a criminal cause, the construction of the statute must be extended by equity. It is as much a civil action as an action for money had and received. The legislature, when they excepted to the evidence of Quakers in criminal causes, must be understood to mean causes technically criminal; and a different construction would not only be injurious to Quakers, but prejudicial to the rest of the King's subjects who may want their testimony....

No authority whatever has been mentioned on the other side; nor any case cited where it has been held that a penal action is a criminal case; and perhaps the point was never before doubted. The single authority mentioned against receiving the evidence of the Quaker in this case is, an appeal of murder[1]. But that is only a different mode of prosecuting an offender to death; instead of proceeding by indictment in the usual way, it allows the relation to carry on the prosecution for the purpose of attaining the same end which the King's prosecution would have had if the offender had been convicted, namely, execution. And therefore, the writers on the law of England class an appeal of murder in the books under the head of criminal cases. Co. Litt. 284, 287.

In the case of *Rex* v. *Turner*[2] on a motion to quash an appointment of overseers, the Court said, "though the prosecution is in the King's name, the end of it is a civil remedy," and very properly allowed the Quaker's affirmation to be read....

The three other Judges concurred.

Rule discharged

[*Penalty sued for by a public official.*]

THE ATTORNEY GENERAL v. BRADLAUGH.

COURT OF APPEAL. 1885.   L.R. 14 Q.B.D. 667.

Information in the Queen's Bench Division by the Attorney General to recover penalties of £500 each against C. Bradlaugh for voting as a member of the House of Commons without complying with the provisions of the Parliamentary Oaths Act, 1866[3].

---

[1] 2 Str. 856.   [2] 2 Str. 1219.

[3] 29 Vict. c. 19, sect. 3. "The oath hereby appointed shall in every Parliament be solemnly and publicly made and subscribed by every member of the House of Peers at the table in the middle of the said House before he takes his place in the said House, and whilst a full House of Peers is there with their Speaker in his place; and by every member of the House of Commons at the table in the middle

The information was tried at bar in the Queen's Bench Division, in June, 1884, before Lord Coleridge, C. J., Grove, J., and Huddleston, B., and a special jury....The jury found that the Speaker was sitting in the chair at the time when the defendant made and subscribed the oath ; but that he was sitting for the purpose of preparing or correcting notes which he was about to address to the defendant, and he had not resumed his seat for the purpose of allowing the defendant to make and subscribe the oath.   The jury further found that upon the 11th of February, 1884, the defendant had no belief in a Supreme Being, and was a person upon whose conscience an oath, as an oath, had no binding force; and, that the House of Commons had full cognizance and notice of these matters by reason of the avowal of the defendant.   The jury also found that the defendant did not take and subscribe the oath according to the full practice of Parliament; and that the defendant did not take and subscribe the oath as an oath.   Upon these findings the Queen's Bench Division, sitting for the trial at bar, ordered a verdict to be entered for the Crown upon the first, fourth, and fifth counts of the information, for separate penalties of £500....

The Court of Appeal granted a rule for a new trial or to enter judgment for the defendant, on the ground of misdirection and misreception of evidence..

Sir H. James, A.G., and *Sir H. Giffard, Q.C.* (*Sir F. Herschell, S.G.*, and *R. S. Wright*, with them), for the Crown.   There are two preliminary objections to the hearing of this appeal.   The first is, that the information is a "criminal cause or matter" within the meaning of the Supreme Court of Judicature Act, 1873, s. 47, and therefore that there can be no appeal to this Court.

This is an information filed by the Queen's Attorney General in order to recover a penalty; and the nature of informations of that

---

of the said House, and whilst a full House of Commons is there duly sitting, with their Speaker in his chair, at such hours and according to such regulations as each House may by its Standing Orders direct."

Section 5.   "If any member of the House of Peers votes by himself or his proxy in the House of Peers, or sits as a peer during any debate in the said House, without having made and subscribed the oath hereby appointed, he shall for every such offence be subject to a penalty of five hundred pounds, to be recovered by action in one of Her Majesty's Superior Courts at Westminster; and if any member of the House of Commons votes as such in the said House, or sits during any debate after the Speaker has been chosen, without having made and subscribed the oath hereby appointed, he shall be subject to a like penalty for every such offence, and in addition to such penalty his seat shall be vacated in the same manner as if he were dead."

kind was much discussed in *Attorney General* v. *Radloff*[1]. In that
case the Court of Exchequer was equally divided; two of the judges,
Platt and Martin, BB., holding that an information (which in that
case was for breach of the laws as to customs), was not a criminal
proceeding, and two of them, Pollock, C.B., and Parke, B., holding
that it was. It is true that in that case some stress was laid on the
fact that the offender might be summarily convicted before justices;
but this circumstance was really immaterial; under 11 and 12 Vict.
c. 43, justices have power to convict summarily for both civil and
criminal offences. It is submitted that the view of Pollock, C.B., and
Parke, B., was correct, and that informations filed by that Attorney
General in order to recover penalties are criminal proceedings. Moreover, to consider the question from a different point of view, although
the penalty imposed by the Parliamentary Oaths Act, 1866, s. 5,
might perhaps have been recovered by an action of debt, nevertheless
the wrongful act or offence, of which the defendant has been convicted, must be deemed to be of a criminal nature; for by s. 3 of
the Parliamentary Oaths Act, 1866, a member of Parliament is liable
to be indicted if he does not take the oath of allegiance, and the
remedy under s. 5 may be regarded as merely cumulative. Some
wrongs are both of a civil and criminal nature, such as libel and
assault, and it is erroneous to contend that the existence of a civil
remedy causes a wrongful act to become of a civil nature. There is
no distinction in principle between this case and *Mellor* v. *Denham*[2];
the only difference is that in that case the appeal was from the refusal
of justices to convict for contravention of the bye-laws of a school
board. *Mellor* v. *Denham* was followed by *Reg.* v. *Whitechurch*[3]. It
is true that the penalty is to be recovered "by action": Parliamentary
Oaths Act, 1866, s. 5; but the word "action" is of wide signification,
and includes even criminal proceedings; this is plain from Com. Dig.
Action (D. 1) Placita Coronae, and also from Bacon's Abridgment,
Actions in General (A.), where it is said that "actions are divided
into criminal and civil." These passages are cited and relied upon
by the Earl of Selborne, L.C., in *Bradlaugh* v. *Clarke*[4]. The Queen
by her prerogative can recover the whole of a penalty in any Court,
even although a moiety be expressly given to a common informer:
Rex v. *Hymen*[5]

BRETT, M. R. A majority of the Court are of opinion that the
present information is not a "criminal cause or matter" within the

[1] 10 Ex. 84.　　　　　　[2] 5 Q.B.D. 467.
[3] 7 Q.B.D. 534.　　　　　[4] 8 App. Cas. p. 362.
[5] 7 T.R. 536.

meaning of the Supreme Court of Judicature Act, 1873, s. 47....It has
been at different times during this argument contended before us on
both sides, for different purposes, that the 3rd section of the Parliamentary Oaths Act, 1866, imposes on every member a legal obligation
to take and subscribe the oath, and that, if a member does not take
and subscribe the oath in the manner therein set forth, an indictment
will lie against him on that section alone as for a misdemeanour, and
that the penalty in the 5th section is cumulative. That was at
one time argued by the Attorney General in order to shew that the
acts complained of in the information were criminal, and that no
appeal would lie. It was afterwards argued by the defendant in this
case that the same construction should be put upon the statute, for the
purpose of shewing, at all events, a great hardship, namely, that the
3rd section would put upon him an obligation to take the oath,
and that the 5th section, if construed in the way insisted upon by the
Crown, would inflict upon him a penalty of £500, for his voting after
he had then taken the oath thus forced upon him. I think that the
Act of Parliament must be read as a whole, and that the two sections
cannot be treated separately ; therefore it seems to me that the true
construction of the Act of Parliament is that it imposes a new obligation not known to the common law, and that with regard to a non-
performance of that obligation it enacts a certain consequence. Wherever an Act of Parliament imposes a new obligation, and in the same
Act imposes a consequence upon the non-fulfilment of that obligation,
that is the only consequence. Therefore, it seems to me that the only
consequence of voting as a member without having taken the oath in
the manner appointed is, that the member becomes liable to a penalty.
If that be so, no indictment will lie, and, as far as my judgment goes,
nothing in the nature of a criminal proceeding can be taken upon
this statute. The recovery of a penalty, if that is the only consequence,
does not make the prohibited act a crime. If it did, it seems to me
that that distinction which has been well known and established in
law for many years between a penal statute and a criminal enactment,
would fall to the ground, for every penal statute would involve a
crime, and would be a criminal enactment. In construing this Act of
Parliament I should on that ground alone say that no crime is enacted
by this Act. But there is more than that : this penalty of £500 is,
in the phraseology of this Act of Parliament, to be recovered "by
action in one of Her Majesty's superior courts at Westminster." Now,
it may be true to say, as appears from the passage cited from Comyn's
Digest (Action D. 1), that in some cases "actions" will include indictments or will include criminal informations. In some cases it may,

but the question is whether in this Act of Parliament it does, and when the legislature is found using the words, "by action," that word construed according to its ordinary meaning does not seem to me to include an indictment or a criminal information. But there is more than that. The words are "by action in one of Her Majesty's superior Courts at Westminster." Now, a criminal information never was moved except in the Court of Queen's Bench. An information by the Attorney General was also moved in the Court of Exchequer, but that was a procedure for the purpose of recovering a debt, or for the purpose of rectifying a trespass, or for the purpose of dealing with an injury to the Crown in its particular capacity, and not merely as the representative of the public. So that this argument seems to me to shew that by the use of the words "by action," and by the still stronger language "in one of Her Majesty's superior Courts" (which mean in any one of Her Majesty's superior Courts) at Westminster, this offence cannot be the subject matter of criminal information, and cannot be the subject matter of indictment; and that the only proceeding which can be brought upon the statute, as the House of Lords has now determined, is an information filed by the authority of the Attorney General, and in his name, such as was formerly brought generally on the revenue side of the Court of Exchequer. Now comes the question whether an information by the Attorney General on the revenue side of the Court of Exchequer is or is not a criminal proceeding in any sense. In order to answer this question, we must consider *Attorney General* v. *Radloff.* It is not binding on this Court; it is a case in the Court of Exchequer, and we are bound to exercise our own judgments upon it. It is a case in which the judges were equally divided in opinion, and, therefore, it could not bind any Court, but certainly could not bind this Court. Two of the judges were of opinion that unless there was something very peculiar in the Act of Parliament, such as that it in terms enacted that it was to be a criminal matter, the proceeding on the revenue side of the Court of Exchequer for the recovery of a penalty in the name of the Attorney General was not a criminal proceeding. The other two were of opinion that it was. I will not go into the reasons, but if I had been a member of the Court at that time, I should have been of opinion in that case that an information for a penalty on the revenue side of the Court of Exchequer could not at any time, unless there were special and clear words in an Act of Parliament saying it was so, be considered as a criminal proceeding [1]. If that be true, then it is said that we are met by the

---

[1] [EDITOR's NOTE. It is now clear that such proceedings are *not* criminal; *Rex* v. *Hausmann*, 3 Cr. App. B. 3.]

judgment of the House of Lords in *Bradlaugh* v. *Clarke*, and that the judgment of the House of Lords, particularly the judgment of Lord FitzGerald, seems to shew that in this Act of Parliament, even though we take the proceeding to be one which is the same as if it were brought on the revenue side of the Court of Exchequer, still it is a criminal matter. Now, that will partly depend on that judgment used as a binding authority, and partly on the argument which has been raised on the terms of this Act of Parliament itself. Reliance is placed on these words: "He shall for every such offence," and it is said that the use of the word "offence" shews that this is considered by the legislature as a crime. What is the offence? The offence is not a refusal to take the oath, it is not a declining to take the oath. What "offence" means in the statute is a voting or sitting without having taken or subscribed the oath. It is possible—I do not think it very probable—that at the beginning of a Parliament a member may sit or vote who from forgetfulness or ignorance has not taken the oath. I mean a member who is in every sense capable of taking the oath, but who accidentally, from forgetfulness or ignorance, sits or votes without taking the oath, without having any intention to break the Act, and without having any intention to do anything forbidden by law. I have no doubt that he would be liable to the penalty, for no question of intent is introduced into this Act of Parliament. Now, to my mind, it is contrary to the whole established law of England (unless the legislation on the subject has clearly enacted it) to say that a person can be guilty of a crime in England without a wrongful intent—without an attempt to do that which the law has forbidden....An act done without an evil intent must not be considered a crime, and therefore the forbidden act in this statute, made liable to a penalty whether done with or without an evil intent, is not to be a criminal act.

I am clearly of opinion that the proceeding under this Act of Parliament by the Attorney General, although it is a proceeding which could be taken only by him[1] and not by a private individual, is in the nature of a civil proceeding....

[1] [EDITOR'S NOTE. For, as no man can sue for matters in which he has no interest, a private person (*e.g.* a "common informer") cannot bring an action to recover a Penalty which has been imposed for the protection of the public, unless the Statute which created the penalty has said that he may do so. This Statute not having said so, only the Crown could sue.]

[*But for a crime* any one *may prosecute.*]

SMITH *v.* DEAR.

KING'S BENCH DIVISION.   1903.   88 L. T. 665.

[Prosecution at petty sessions, under s. 23 of the Larceny Act, 1861, for having unlawfully killed a pigeon.   Dear, after shooting the pigeon, found marked on its wing the name of a Mr Packman ; and then at once called on him and paid him 5s., the value of the bird. But the National Homing Union of pigeon-fanciers induced one of its members, Mr Smith, to prosecute Dear.   Packman gave evidence for the defence, saying that he had never complained of Dear's act and was quite satisfied with the 5s.   The magistrate held that a third party, who had no rights in the pigeon, could not prosecute the killer of it. Smith appealed.]

LORD ALVERSTONE, L.C.J....As there is nothing in the Act to limit to the owner of the bird the right to prosecute, any person can prosecute.

SECTION II.

THE MENTAL ELEMENT IN CRIMINAL LIABILITY.

[*Mens rea is essential to crime.*]

THE COMMONWEALTH *v.* PRESBY.

SUPREME COURT OF MASSACHUSETTS.   1859.   14 GRAY 65.

Indictment for assault and battery.

HOAR, J.   The defendant, a police-officer, arrested one Harford for being intoxicated in a highway ; and committed him to the watch-

house. For this arrest, he was indicted....Police officers are empowered
by a Massachusetts statute to arrest without a warrant for the offence
of intoxication in a public place. And at the trial, the presiding
judge was asked to instruct the jury that " If Presby had reasonable
cause to believe at the time of the arrest that Harford was intoxicated,
then he was authorised in taking and retaining him." But it was
argued, for the Commonwealth, that if Harford was not intoxicated,
the statute would afford no justification for his arrest; because the
fact of intoxication, and not a suspicion or belief however reasonable,
is requisite to such justification. This may be true in regard to the
civil rights of the person whose liberty is invaded; and in a civil
action, the wrongdoer must usually justify his act, or be held responsible....But to constitute a criminal act there must, as a general
rule, be a criminal intent. The general doctrine is stated in Hale's
Pleas of the Crown that "where there is no will to commit an offence,
there can be no transgression." And ignorance of fact, if unaccompanied
by negligence, is one of the causes of exemption from criminal responsibility. Hale gives (1 P. C. 42) the illustration of a sentinel
firing at his commanding officer (who advances towards his post), under
the reasonable belief that he is an enemy....Great caution should
certainly be used in admitting the excuse of ignorance or mistake;
so as to exclude from its protection those who do not exercise all
reasonable means to inform themselves before they commit an act
which is apparently an invasion of private rights and a breach of the
public peace....But in the present case, the duty is made imperative
upon the officer to make the arrest if he finds an intoxicated person in
the street....If the person whom he sees is really intoxicated, he must
arrest him or suffer the consequences of official misconduct. Now the
fact of intoxication, though usually easy to ascertain, is not in most
cases a fact capable of demonstration with absolute certainty. Suppose
a watchman to find a man in the gutter, stupefied and smelling very
strongly of spirituous liquors. The man may have fallen in a fit;
and some person may have tried to relieve him by the application of
a stimulant, and then have left in search of assistance. Or, in another
case, the person arrested may, for purposes of amusement or mischief,
have been simulating the appearance and conduct of drunkenness.
Is the officer to be held a criminal, if, using his best judgment and
discretion and all the means of information in his power, in a case
where he is called upon to act, he makes a mistake of fact and comes
to a wrong conclusion? It would be singular, indeed, if a man
deficient in reason should be protected from criminal responsibility,
but another, who was obliged to decide upon the evidence before him,

and used in good faith all the reason and faculties which he had, should be held guilty. We therefore feel bound to decide that... if the defendant acted in good faith, upon reasonable and probable cause of belief, without rashness or negligence, he is not to be regarded as a criminal because he is found to have been mistaken.

[*Mens rea is essential to crime.*]

THE QUEEN *v.* TOLSON.

CROWN CASE RESERVED.   1889.   23 Q.B.D. 168.

Case stated by Stephen, J., and reserved by the Court for the consideration of all the judges.

At the summer assizes at Carlisle in 1888 the prisoner Martha Ann Tolson was convicted of bigamy.

It appeared that the marriage of the prisoner to Tolson took place on September 11, 1880; that Tolson deserted her on December 13, 1881; and that she and her father made inquiries about him and learned from his elder brother and from general report that he had been lost in a vessel bound for America, which went down with all hands on board. On January 10, 1887, the prisoner, supposing herself to be a widow, went through the ceremony of marriage with another man. The circumstances were all known to the second husband, and the ceremony was in no way concealed. In December, 1887, Tolson returned from America.

Stephen, J., directed the jury that a belief in good faith and on reasonable grounds that the husband of the prisoner was dead would not be a defence to a charge of bigamy, and stated in the case that his object in so holding was to obtain the decision of the Court in view of the conflicting decisions of single judges on the point. The jury convicted the prisoner; stating, however, in answer to a question put by the judge, that they thought that she in good faith and on reasonable grounds believed her husband to be dead at the time of the second marriage. The judge sentenced her to one day's imprisonment.

The question for the opinion of the Court was whether the direction was right....

WILLS, J. The statute upon which the indictment was framed is the 24 and 25 Vict. c. 100, s. 57, which is in these words : " Whoever, being married, shall marry any other person during the life of the former husband or wife shall be guilty of felony, punishable with penal servitude for not more than seven years, or imprisonment with or without hard labour for not more than two years," with a proviso that "nothing in this Act shall extend to any person marrying a second time whose husband or wife shall have been continually absent from such person for the space of seven years last past, and shall not have been known by such person to be living within that time."

There is no doubt that under the circumstances the prisoner falls within the very words of the statute. She, being married, married another person during the life of her former husband, and, when she did so, he had not been continually absent from her for the space of seven years last past.

It is, however, undoubtedly a principle of English criminal law, that, ordinarily speaking, a crime is not committed if the mind of the person doing the act in question be innocent. "It is a principle of natural justice and of our law," says Lord Kenyon, C.J., "that actus non facit reum, nisi mens sit rea. The intent and act must both concur to constitute the crime:" *Fowler* v. *Paget*[1]. The guilty intent is not necessarily that of intending the very act or thing done and prohibited by common or statute law, but it must at least be the intention to do something wrong. That intention may belong to one or other of two classes. It may be to do a thing wrong in itself and apart from positive law, or it may be to do a thing merely prohibited by statute or by common law, or both elements of intention may co-exist with respect to the same deed. There are many things prohibited by no statute— fornication or seduction, for instance—which nevertheless no one would hesitate to call wrong; and the intention to do an act wrong in this sense at the least must as a general rule exist before the act done can be considered a crime. Knowingly and intentionally to break a statute must, I think, from the judicial point of view, always be morally wrong in the absence of special circumstances applicable to the particular instance and excusing the breach of the law, as, for instance, if a municipal regulation be broken to save life or to put out a fire. But to make it morally right some such special matter of excuse must exist, inasmuch as the administration of justice and, indeed, the foundations of civil society rest upon the principle that obedience to the law, whether it be a law approved of or disapproved of by the individual, is the first duty of a citizen.

Although primâ facie and as a general rule there must be a mind at fault before there can be a crime, it is not an inflexible rule, and

[1] 7 T. R. 509, 514.

a statute may relate to such a subject-matter and may be so framed as to make an act criminal whether there has been any intention to break the law or otherwise to do wrong or not. There is a large body of municipal law in the present day which is so conceived. Bye-laws are constantly made regulating the width of thoroughfares, the height of buildings, the thickness of walls, and a variety of other matters necessary for the general welfare, health, or convenience, and such bye-laws are enforced by the sanction of penalties, and the breach of them constitutes an offence and is a criminal matter. In such cases it would, generally speaking, be no answer to proceedings for infringement of the bye-law that the person committing it had bonâ fide made an accidental miscalculation or an erroneous measurement. The Acts are properly construed as imposing the penalty when the act is done, no matter how innocently, and in such a case the substance of the enactment is that a man shall take care that the statutory direction is obeyed, and that if he fails to do so he does it at his peril.

Whether an enactment is to be construed in this sense or with the qualification ordinarily imported into the construction of criminal statutes, that there must be a guilty mind, must, I think, depend upon the subject-matter of the enactment, and the various circumstances that may make the one construction or the other reasonable or unreasonable. There is no difference for instance in the kind of language used by Acts of Parliament which made the unauthorized possession of Government stores a crime, and the language used in bye-laws which say that if a man builds a house or a wall so as to encroach upon a space protected by the bye-law from building he shall be liable to a penalty. Yet in *Reg.* v. *Sleep*[1] it was held that a person in possession of Government stores with the broad arrow could not be convicted when there was not sufficient evidence to shew that he knew they were so marked; whilst the mere infringement of a building bye-law would entail liability to the penalty....

Now in the present instance one consequence of holding that the offence is complete if the husband or wife is de facto alive at the time of the second marriage, although the defendant had at the time of the second marriage every reason to believe the contrary, would be that though the evidence of death should be sufficient to induce the Court of Probate to grant probate of the will or administration of the goods of the man supposed to be dead, or to prevail with the jury upon an action by the heir to recover possession of his real property, the wife of the person supposed to be dead who had married six years and eleven months after the last time that she had known him to be alive would

---

[1] L. & C. 44; 30 L.J. (M.C.) 170.

be guilty of felony in case he should turn up twenty years afterwards. It would be scarcely less unreasonable to enact that those who had in the meantime distributed his personal estate should be guilty of larceny. It seems to me to be a case to which it would not be improper to apply the language of Lord Kenyon when dealing with a statute which literally interpreted led to what he considered an equally preposterous result, "I would adopt any construction of the statute that the words will bear in order to avoid such monstrous consequences[1]."

Again, the nature and extent of the penalty attached to the offence may reasonably be considered. There is nothing that need shock any mind in the payment of a small pecuniary penalty by a person who has unwittingly done something detrimental to the public interest. To subject him, when what he has done has been nothing but what any well-disposed man would have been very likely to do under the circumstances, to the forfeiture of all his goods and chattels, which would have been one consequence of a conviction at the date of the Act of 24 and 25 Vict., to the loss of civil rights, to imprisonment with hard labour, or even to penal servitude, is a very different matter ; and such a fate seems properly reserved for those who have transgressed morally as well as unintentionally done something prohibited by law..

CAVE, J. At common law a reasonable belief in the existence of circumstances, which, if true, would make the act for which a prisoner is indicted an innocent act has always been held to be a good defence. This doctrine is embodied in the somewhat uncouth maxim, "actus non facit reum, nisi mens sit rea." Honest and reasonable mistake stands in fact on the same footing as absence of the reasoning faculty, as in infancy, or perversion of that faculty, as in lunacy. Instances of the existence of this common law doctrine will readily occur to the mind. So far as I am aware it has never been suggested that these exceptions do not equally apply in the case of statutory offences unless they are excluded expressly or by necessary implication. In *Reg. v. Prince*[2] in which the principle of mistake underwent much discussion, it was not suggested by any of the judges that the exception of honest and reasonable mistake was not applicable to all offences, whether existing at common law or created by statute. As I understand the judgments in that case the difference of opinion was as to the exact extent of the exception, Brett, J., the dissenting judge, holding that it applied wherever the accused honestly and reasonably believed in the existence of circumstances which, if true, would have made his act not criminal,

---

[1] *Fowler v. Padget*, 7 T. R. 509, 514.   [2] *Infra*, p. 21.

while the majority of the judges seem to have held that in order to make the defence available in that case the accused must have proved the existence in his mind of an honest and reasonable belief in the existence of circumstances which, if they had really existed, would have made his act not only not criminal but also not immoral. Whether the majority held that the general exception is limited to cases where there is an honest belief not only in facts which would make the act not criminal, but also in facts which would make it not immoral, or whether they held that the general doctrine was correctly stated by Brett, J., and that the further limitation was to be inferred from the language of the particular statute they were then discussing, is not very clear. It is, however, immaterial in this case, as the jury have found that the accused honestly and reasonably believed in the existence of a state of circumstances, viz., in her first husband's death, which, had it really existed, would have rendered her act not only not criminal, but also not immoral.

STEPHEN, J. ...The definition of every crime contains expressly or by implication a proposition as to a state of mind. Therefore, if the mental element of any conduct alleged to be a crime is proved to have been absent in any given case, the crime so defined is not committed; or, again, if a crime is fully defined, nothing amounts to that crime which does not satisfy that definition. Crimes are in the present day much more accurately defined by statute or otherwise than they formerly were. The mental element of most crimes is marked by one of the words "maliciously," "fraudulently," "negligently," or "knowingly," but it is the general—I might, I think, say, the invariable—practice of the legislature to leave unexpressed some of the mental elements of crime. In all cases whatever, competent age, sanity, and some degree of freedom from some kinds of coercion are assumed to be essential to criminality, but I do not believe they are ever introduced into any statute by which any particular crime is defined.

The meanings of the words "malice," "negligence," and "fraud" in relation to particular crimes has been ascertained by numerous cases. Malice means one thing in relation to murder, another in relation to the Malicious Mischief Act, and a third in relation to libel, and so of fraud and negligence.

With regard to knowledge of fact, the law, perhaps, is not quite so clear, but it may, I think, be maintained that in every case knowledge of fact is to some extent an element of criminality as much as competent age and sanity. To take an extreme illustration, can anyone doubt that a man who, though he might be perfectly sane, committed what would otherwise be a crime in a state of somnambulism, would be entitled to be acquitted? And why is this? Simply because he would not know what he was doing....

The general principle is clearly in favour of the prisoners, but how does the intention of the legislature appear to have been against them? It could not be the object of Parliament to treat the marriage of widows as an act to be if possible prevented as presumably immoral. The conduct of the women convicted was not in the smallest degree immoral, it was perfectly natural and legitimate. Assuming the facts to be as they supposed, the infliction of more than a nominal punishment on them would have been a scandal. Why, then, should the legislature be held to have wished to subject them to punishment at all?

If such a punishment is legal, the following amongst many other cases might occur. A number of men in a mine are killed, and their bodies are disfigured and mutilated, by an explosion; one of the survivors secretly absconds, and it is supposed that one of the disfigured bodies is his. His wife sees his supposed remains buried; she marries again. I cannot believe that it can have been the intention of the legislature to make such a woman a criminal; the contracting of an invalid marriage is quite misfortune enough. It appears to me that every argument which shewed in the opinion of the judges in *Reg. v. Prince*[1] that the legislature meant seducers and abductors to act at their peril, shews that the legislature did not mean to hamper what is not only intended, but naturally and reasonably supposed by the parties, to be a valid and honourable marriage, with a liability to seven years' penal servitude.

....

Conviction quashed[2]

[*A slight mens rea suffices*]

ANONYMOUS.

KING'S BENCH.   1498.   YEAR BOOK 14 Hen. VII. f. 14. Hil. 5.

HUSSEY [C. J.] said that a question was asked of him, which was this:—A clerk of a church, being in a room, struck another with the

---

[1] *Infra*, p. 21.

[2] Nine of the judges held the conviction to have been wrong; five held it to have been right.

keys of the church. And by the force of the blow the keys slipped from his hand, and went through a window and struck out a woman's eye. Should this be called mayhem or no?—that was the question. And to him it seemed that it should; for at the beginning this man had a bad intent.

[*Mens rea may exist without any intention to do the criminal act which was done.*]

REG. *v.* PRINCE.

CROWN CASE RESERVED.   1875.   L.R. 2 C.C.R. 154.

Case stated by Denman, J.

At the assizes for Surrey, held at Kingston-upon-Thames, on the 24th of March last, Henry Prince was tried upon the charge of having unlawfully taken one Annie Phillips, an unmarried girl, being under the age of sixteen years, out of the possession and against the will of her father. The indictment was framed under s. 55 of 24 and 25 Vict. c. 100 [1]. He was found guilty.

All the facts necessary to support a conviction existed, unless the following facts constituted a defence. The girl Annie Phillips, though proved by her father to be fourteen years old on the 6th of April following, looked very much older than sixteen, and the jury found upon reasonable evidence that before the defendant took her away she had told him that she was eighteen, and that the defendant bonâ fide believed that statement, and that such belief was reasonable.

May 29. The case was argued before Cockburn, C.J., Kelly, C.B., Bramwell, Cleasby, Pollock, and Amphlett, BB., Blackburn, Mellor, Lush, Brett, Grove, Quain, Denman, Archibald, Field, and Lindley, JJ.

BRETT, J. ...Upon all the cases I think it is proved that there can be no conviction for crime in England in the absence of a criminal mind or "mens rea."

---

[1] By 24 and 25 Vict. c. 100, s. 55, "Whosoever shall unlawfully take or cause to be taken any unmarried girl, being under the age of sixteen years, out of the possession and against the will of her father or mother, or of any other person having the lawful care or charge of her, shall be guilty of a misdemeanor, and being convicted thereof shall be liable, at the discretion of the Court, to be imprisoned for any term not exceeding two years, with or without hard labour."

Then comes the question, what is the true meaning of the phrase? I do not doubt that it exists where the prisoner knowingly does acts which would constitute a crime if the result were as he anticipated, but in which the result may not improbably end by bringing the offence within a more serious class of crime. As if a man strikes with a dangerous weapon, with intent to do grievous bodily harm, and kills, the result makes the crime murder. The prisoner has run the risk. So, if a prisoner do the prohibited acts, without caring to consider what the truth is as to facts—as if a prisoner were to abduct a girl under sixteen without caring to consider whether she was in truth under sixteen—he runs the risk. So if he without abduction defiles a girl who is in fact under ten years old, with a belief that she is between ten and twelve. If the facts were as he believed he would be committing the lesser crime. Then he runs the risk of his crime resulting in the greater crime. It is clear that ignorance of the law does not excuse. It seems to me to follow that the maxim as to mens rea applies whenever the facts which are present to the prisoner's mind, and which he has reasonable ground to believe, and does believe to be the facts, would, if true, make his acts no criminal offence at all.

BRAMWELL, B. The question in this case depends on the construction of the statute under which the prisoner is indicted. That enacts that "whosoever shall unlawfully take any unmarried girl under the age of sixteen out of the possession and against the will of her father or mother, or any other person having the lawful care or charge of her, shall be guilty of a misdemeanour." Now the word "unlawfully" means "not lawfully," "otherwise than lawfully," "without lawful cause," such as would exist, for instance, on a taking by a police officer on a charge of felony, or a taking by a father of his child from his school. The statute, therefore, may be read thus: "Whosoever shall take, &c., without lawful cause." Now the prisoner had no such cause, and consequently, except in so far as it helps the construction of the statute, the word "unlawfully" may in the present case be left out, and then the question is, has the prisoner taken an unmarried girl under the age of sixteen out of the possession of and against the will of her father? In fact, he has; but it is not said within the meaning of the statute, and that that must be read as though the word "knowingly," or some equivalent word, was in; and the reason given is, that as a rule the mens rea is necessary to make any act a crime or offence, and that if the facts necessary to constitute an offence are not known to the alleged offender, there can be no mens rea. I have used the word "knowingly"; but it will, perhaps, be said that here the prisoner not only did not do the act knowingly, but knew, as he would have said, or believed, that the fact was otherwise than such as would have made his act a crime; that here the prisoner did not say to himself, "I do not know how the fact is, whether she is under sixteen or not, and will take the chance," but acted on the reasonable belief that she was over sixteen ; and that though if he had done what he did, knowing or believing neither way, but hazarding it, there would be a mens rea, there is not one when, as he believes, he knows that she is over sixteen.

It is impossible to suppose that, to bring the case within the statute, a person taking a girl out of her father's possession against his will is guilty of no offence unless he, the taker, knows she is under sixteen ; that he would not be guilty if the jury were of opinion he knew neither one way nor the other. Let it be, then, that the question is, whether he is guilty where he knows, as he thinks, that she is over sixteen ? This introduces the necessity for reading the statute with some strange words introduced ; as thus: "Whosoever shall take any unmarried girl, being under the age of sixteen, and not believing her to be over the age of sixteen, out of the possession," &c. Those words are not there, and the question is, whether we are bound to construe the statute as though they were, on account of the rule that the mens rea is necessary to make an act a crime. I am of opinion that we are not, nor as though the word "knowingly" was there, and for the following reasons : The act forbidden is wrong in itself, if without lawful cause; I do not say illegal, but wrong. I have not lost sight of this, that though the statute probably principally aims at seduction for carnal purposes, the taking may be by a female with a good motive. Nevertheless, though there may be such cases, which are not immoral in one sense, I say that the act forbidden is wrong.

Let us remember what is the case supposed by the statute. It supposes that there is a *girl*—it does not say a woman, but a girl— something between a child and a woman ; it supposes she is in the *possession* of her father and mother, or other person having lawful *care or charge* of her ; and it supposes there is a *taking*, and that that taking is *against the will* of the person in whose possession she is. It is, then, a *taking* of a *girl*, in the *possession* of some one, *against his will.* I say that done without lawful cause is wrong, and that the legislature meant it should be at the risk of the taker whether or no she was under sixteen. I do not say that taking a woman of fifty from her brother's or even father's house is wrong. She is at an age when she has a right to choose for herself; she is not a *girl*, nor of such tender age that she can be said to be in the *possession* of or under

the *care or charge* of anyone. I am asked where I draw the line;
I answer at when the female is no longer a girl in anyone's possession.

But what the statute contemplates, and what I say is wrong, is
the taking of a female of such tender years that she is properly called
a *girl*, can be said to be in another's *possession*, and in that other's *care
or charge*. No argument is necessary to prove this; it is enough to
state the case. The legislature has enacted that if anyone does this
wrong act, he does it at the risk of her turning out to be under sixteen.
This opinion gives full scope to the doctrine of the mens rea. If the
taker believed he had the father's consent, though wrongly, he would
have no mens rea; so if he did not know she was in anyone's possession, nor in the care or charge of anyone. In those cases he would
not know he was doing the *act* forbidden by the statute—an act which,
if he knew she was in possession and in care or charge of anyone, he
would know was a crime or not, according as she was under sixteen or
not. He would not know he was doing an act wrong in itself, whatever was his intention, if done without lawful cause.

In addition to these considerations, one may add that the statute
does use the word "unlawfully," and does not use the word "knowingly" or "not believing to the contrary." If the question was whether
his act was unlawful, there would be no difficulty, as it clearly was not
lawful.

This view of the section, to my mind, is much strengthened by
a reference to other sections of the same statute. Sect. 50 makes it
a felony to unlawfully and carnally know a girl under the age
of ten. Sect. 51 enacts when she is above ten and under twelve
to unlawfully and carnally know her is a misdemeanour. Can it be
supposed that in the former case a person indicted might claim to be
acquitted on the ground that he had believed the girl was over ten
though under twelve, and so that he had only committed a misdemeanour; or that he believed her over twelve, and so had committed
no offence at all; or that in a case under s. 51 he could claim to be
acquitted, because he believed her over twelve? In both cases the act
is intrinsically wrong; for the statute says if "unlawfully" done.
The act done with a mens rea is unlawfully and carnally knowing the
girl, and the man doing the act does it at the risk of the child being
under the statutory age. It would be mischievous to hold otherwise.
So s. 56, by which whoever shall take away any child under fourteen
with intent to deprive parent or guardian of the possession of the
child, or with intent to steal any article upon such child, shall be
guilty of felony. Could a prisoner say, "I did take away the child to
steal its clothes, but I believed it to be over fourteen"? If not, then

neither could he say, "I did take the child with intent to deprive the parent of its possession, but I believed it over fourteen." Because if words to that effect cannot be introduced into the statute where the intent is to steal the clothes, neither can they where the intent is to take the child out of the possession of the parent. But if those words cannot be introduced in s. 56, why can they be in s. 55?

The same principle applies in other cases. A man was held liable for assaulting a police officer in the execution of his duty, though he did not know he was a police officer[1]. Why? because the act was wrong in itself. So, also, in the case of burglary, could a person charged claim an acquittal on the ground that he believed it was past six when he entered, or in housebreaking, that he did not know the place broken into was a house? Take, also, the case of libel, published when the publisher thought the occasion privileged, or that he had a defence under Lord Campbell's Act, but was wrong; he could not be entitled to be acquitted because there was no mens rea. Why? because the act of publishing written defamation is wrong where there is no lawful cause.

As to the case of the marine stores, it was held properly that there was no mens rea where the person charged with the possession of naval stores with the Admiralty mark did not know the stores he had bore the mark: *Reg. v. Sleep*[2]; because there is nothing primâ facie wrong or immoral in having naval stores unless they are so marked. But suppose his servant had told him that there was a mark, and he had said he would chance whether or not it was the Admiralty mark? ...It seems to me impossible, where a person takes a girl out of her father's possession, not knowing whether she is or is not under sixteen, to say that he is not guilty ; and equally impossible when he believes, but erroneously, that she is old enough for him to do a wrong act with safety. I think the conviction should be affirmed[3].

DENMAN, J. ...In the present case the jury find the defendant believed the girl to be eighteen years of age; even if she had been of that age, she would have been in the lawful care and charge of her father, as her guardian by nature : see Co. Litt. 88, b, n. 12, 19th ed., recognized in *Reg. v. Howes*[4]. Her father had a right to her personal custody up to the age of twenty-one, and to appoint a guardian by deed or will, whose right to her personal custody would have extended up

---

[1] 10 Cox, Cr. C. 362.   [2] 8 Cox, Cr. C. 472.

[3] [EDITOR'S NOTE. Eight judges (including Bramwell B., and Denman J.) expressed concurrence in this judgment.]

[4] 3 E. and E. 332. Cf. *Evans* v. *Walton* (L. R. 2 C. P. 615) where damages were recovered for enticing away a girl of *nineteen*.

to the same age. The belief that she was eighteen would be no justification to the defendant for taking her out of his possession, and
against his will. By taking her, even with her own consent, he must
at least have been guilty of aiding and abetting her in doing an
unlawful act, viz. in escaping against the will of her natural guardian
from his lawful care and charge. This, in my opinion, leaves him
wholly without lawful excuse or justification for the act he did, even
though he believed that the girl was eighteen, and therefore unable to
allege that what he has done was not unlawfully done, within the
meaning of the clause. In other words, having knowingly done a
wrongful act, viz. in taking the girl away from the lawful possession of
her father against his will, and in violation of his rights as guardian
by nature, he cannot be heard to say that he thought the girl was of
an age beyond that limited by the statute for the offence charged
against him. He had wrongfully done the very thing contemplated by
the legislature : he had wrongfully and knowingly violated the father's
rights against the father's will. And he cannot set up a legal defence
by merely proving that he thought he was committing a different kind
of wrong from that which in fact he was committing.

Conviction affirmed [1]

[*Mistake of fact.*]

REX *v.* LEVETT.

NEWGATE SESSIONS.   1638.   CRO. CAR. 538.

JONES, J., said that there was resolved by the Chief Justice and
himself and the Recorder of London, at the last Sessions at Newgate,
the case of one William Levett, who was indicted of the homicide
of a woman called Frances Freeman. There it was found by special

[1] All the sixteen judges, except Brett, J., concurred, though not for identical
reasons, in affirming the conviction. When the Act of 1885 created the further
offence of "abducting a girl under *eighteen* with intent that she shall be carnally
known," it added a proviso that, if the accused had reasonable grounds to believe
her to be over eighteen, this *shall* be a sufficient defence ; thus preventing the
application of the rule in *Reg.* v. *Prince.*

verdict, That the said Levett and his wife being in the night in bed and asleep, one Martha Stapleton, their servant, having procured the said Frances Freeman to help her about the house-business, about twelve of the clock at night going to the doors to let out the said Frances Freeman, conceived she heard thieves at the doors offering to break them open. Whereupon she, in fear, ran to her master and mistress, and informed them that she was in doubt that thieves were breaking open the house door. Upon that he arose suddenly and fetched a drawn rapier. And the said Martha Stapleton, lest her master and mistress should see the said Frances Freeman, hid her in the buttery. And the said Levett and Helen his wife, coming down, he with his sword searched the entry for the thieves. And she the said Helen, espying in the buttery the said Frances Freeman, whom she knew not, conceiving she had been a thief, crying to her husband in great fear, said unto him, "Here they be that would undo us." Thereupon the said William Levett, not knowing the said Frances to be there in the buttery, hastily entered therein with his drawn rapier, and being in the dark and thrusting with his rapier before him, thrust the said Frances under the left breast, giving unto her a mortal wound, whereof she instantly died. And whether it were manslaughter, they prayed the discretion of the Court. And it was resolved that it was not ; for he did it ignorantly, without intention of hurt to the said Frances.

[Compare REG. *v.* ROSE, *infra*, p. 140.]

[*Mens rea may be excluded by Ignorance of Fact.*]

ANONYMOUS.

ASSIZES.   1745–63.   FOSTER'S CROWN LAW 265.

I once upon the circuit tried a man for the death of his wife by the like accident. Upon a *Sunday* morning the man and his wife went a mile or two from home with some neighbours to take a dinner at the house of their common friend. He carried his gun with him, hoping to meet with some diversion by the way; but before he went to dinner he discharged it, and set it up in a private place in his friend's house. After dinner he went to church, and in the evening returned home with his wife and neighbours, bringing his gun with him, which was carried into the room where his wife was, she having brought it part of the way. He taking it up touched the trigger, and the gun went off and killed his wife, whom he dearly loved. It came out in evidence, that, while the man was at church, a person belonging to the family privately took the gun, charged it and went after some game; but before the service at church was ended returned it *loaded* to the place whence he took it, and where the defendant, who was ignorant of all that had passed, found it, to all appearance as he left it. I did not inquire, whether the poor man had examined the gun before he carried it home; but being of opinion upon the whole evidence, that he had reasonable grounds to believe that it was not loaded, I directed the jury, that if they were of the same opinion they should acquit him. And he was acquitted.

[*But Ignorance of Fact does not excuse if it be careless and unreasonable.*]

REG. *v.* JOHN JONES.

SHREWSBURY ASSIZES. 1874.   12 Cox 628.

Prisoner was indicted before Mr Justice Lush for the manslaughter of Benjamin Jones.

The mother of the deceased said that he was eight years old; that she went upstairs leaving the prisoner downstairs and after a short time she heard the explosion of a gun. On coming down she saw that the boy's brains had been blown out. She said, "O Jack, you have shot the child." The prisoner did not speak. On a police constable arriving she repeated the expression, and the prisoner said, "He shot himself." The prisoner was always very kind to the boy. Another witness said that on the morning in question he (the witness) loaded the gun and went out with it, but did not discharge it, and on his return took off the cap and put it in a cap box in the cupboard in the house. He put the gun in a corner of the room. Being cross-examined, he said that he could not swear that he took the cap off. A police constable stated that the prisoner, when charged in his presence with shooting the boy, said, "Do you think I have no more sense? he did it himself"; but on the road to the police station said, "The boy was playing with it and I told him to put it down, and he did so, and

I picked it up and pointed it at him ; he ran into the pantry, and I
waited till he came out, then it went off."

It was contended for the defence that the gun went off by accident
as the prisoner was about to replace it in the corner.

LUSH, J., to the jury. No doubt the prisoner did not intend to
discharge the gun at the child. What he did was either an accident
or was negligence on his part. The charge is that he so carelessly
handled the gun as to occasion the death of the deceased. If a person
points a gun without examining whether it is loaded or not, and it
happens to be loaded and death results, he is guilty of negligence and
manslaughter. Can you come to any other conclusion than that the
prisoner did either in joke or otherwise point the gun at the boy?
[His LORDSHIP read the evidence.] If he held the gun pointed at the
boy, and so held it until the child came out of the pantry, and it went
off, what can that be but so improperly and carelessly handling the
gun as to be negligence, and therefore manslaughter?

Verdict: Guilty with a recommendation to mercy. Sentence: Two
months' imprisonment.

[N.B. If a man finds a pistol, *tries it with the rammer*, and
thinks it unloaded, carries it home, shews it to his wife, touches the
trigger, it goes off and kills her, ruled manslaughter; yet ought to have
been only accidental death. Per Holt, C. J., and Foster, J. (Foster's
Cr. Law, 263; Com. Dig. Tit. Justices, M. 18).]

[See also THE STATE *v.* HARDIE, *infra*, p. 123.]

[*Mens rea is not excluded by Ignorance of Law.*]

REX *v.* BAILEY.

ADMIRALTY SESSIONS. 1799.   RUSSELL AND RYAN 1.

The prisoner was tried before Lord Eldon, at the Admiralty
Sessions, December 1799, on an indictment for wilfully and maliciously
shooting at Henry Truscott.

It appeared in evidence, that on the 27th of June, 1799, the prisoner
was the captain of a vessel called the *Langley*, a letter of marque : that
about 130 leagues from Falmouth, on that day, he discovered in the
morning, and fell in with another vessel called the *Admiral Nelson*,
sailing at that time without colours hoisted, on board of which vessel

Henry Truscott, the person charged in the indictment to have been shot at, was a mariner.

This vessel was certainly so conducting herself, at that time, as to give the prisoner, the captain of the letter of marque, reasonable ground to think that she was an enemy....[But the jury were of opinion that the prisoner did subsequently satisfy himself that she was English. Still later, however, he fell into some altercation with her captain; after which, by prisoner's orders, three] guns were fired at the *Admiral Nelson*, one of which, loaded with grape-shot, wounded Henry Truscott severely in the arm

It was insisted that the prisoner could not be found guilty of the offence with which he was charged, because the Act of the 39 Geo. III. c. 37, upon which (together with the statute relating to maliciously shooting—9 Geo. I. c. 22) the prisoner was indicted at this Admiralty Sessions, and which Act of the 39 Geo. III. is entitled, "An Act for amending certain defects in the law respecting offences committed on the high seas," only received the royal assent on the 10th of May, 1799, and the fact charged in the indictment happened on the 27th of June, in the same year, when the prisoner could not know that any such Act existed (his ship, the *Langley*, being at that time upon the coast of Africa).

LORD ELDON told the jury that he was of opinion that he was, in strict law, guilty within the statutes, taken together, if the facts laid were proved, though he could not then know that the Act of the 39 Geo. III. c. 37 had passed ; and that his ignorance of that fact could in no otherwise affect the case, than that it might be the means of recommending him to a merciful consideration elsewhere should he be found guilty.

....

ALL THE JUDGES (except Mr JUSTICE BULLER) met at Lord Kenyon's chambers, and were of opinion that it would be proper to apply for a pardon, on the ground that the fact having been committed so short a time after the Act 39 Geo. III. c. 37 was passed, the prisoner could not have known of it.

[*Mens rea is not excluded by the prisoner's belief in a religious obligation
to commit the crime.*]

REYNOLDS *v.* THE UNITED STATES.

SUPREME COURT OF THE UNITED STATES.   1878.   8 OTTO 145.

In the District Court of the Territory of Utah, an indictment
for bigamy had been found against George Reynolds, a Mormon; who
had been convicted and sentenced thereon.

At the trial the prisoner requested the Court to direct the jury
that their verdict ought to be "Not Guilty" if they found that he
had married in pursuance of a belief that polygamy was a religious
duty. The Court declined to do so; and, in summing up, directed the
jury that if the prisoner deliberately married a second time, having
a first wife living, though under the influence of a religious belief that
polygamy was right, this want of consciousness of evil intent would not
excuse him....On this, and other grounds he sued out a writ of error
to the Supreme Court.

WAITE, C. J....As to the defence of religious belief. The accused
proved that at the time of his alleged second marriage, he was a
member of the Mormon Church and a believer in its doctrines. It is its
accepted doctrine that it is the duty of its male members, circumstances
permitting, to practise polygamy...and that a refusal to do so would be
punished...in the life to come....The question is raised whether religious
belief can be accepted as a justification of an overt act made criminal
by the law of the land....A criminal intent is a necessary element of
crime. But here every act necessary to constitute the crime was done
knowingly. Ignorance of a fact may sometimes be taken as evidence
of a want of criminal intent; but not ignorance of the law. And here
the only defence of the accused is his belief that the law ought not to
have been enacted. In *Reg. v. Wagstaffe* (10 Cox 531) the parents
of a sick child who omitted to call in medical attendance because of
their religious belief that what they did for its cure would be effective,
were held not to be guilty of manslaughter; but it was said the contrary would have been the result if the child had been starved to death
by them, under a notion that it was their religious duty to abstain
from giving it food. In that case WILLES, J., said, "There is a great
difference between neglecting a child in respect to food (with regard to
which, there can be but one opinion), and neglect of medical treatment.
as to which there may be many opinions." When the offence consists
of a definite positive act, which is done knowingly, it would be
dangerous to hold that the offender might escape punishment because

he religiously believed that the law which he had broken ought never to have been made. No case can be found, we believe, that has gone so far....

Judgment affirmed.

[EDITOR'S NOTE. Now, under the Prevention of Cruelty to Children Act, 1908, (8 Edw. 7, c. 67, s. 12) it is a statutory offence for a parent wilfully so to neglect a child as to cause unnecessary injury to its health. Accordingly, in such a case as that of *Reg.* v. *Wagstaffe*, the parent might now be convicted of manslaughter ; as, under an earlier Act, upon the prosecution of one of the "Peculiar People," in *Reg.* v. *Senior* (L. R. [1899] 1 Q. B. 283). In this case, some of the judges appear to have been prepared to hold, moreover, that the neglect would amount to manslaughter even at common law ; and thus to overrule *Reg.* v. *Wagstaffe.*]

[*In some exceptional crimes, less than the usual mens rea suffices.*]

SHERRAS v. DE RUTZEN.

QUEEN'S BENCH DIVISION.   1895.   **L. R. 1 Q.B.D. 918.**

Case stated by the chairman of quarter sessions for the county of London.

The appellant was the licensee of a public-house, and was convicted before a metropolitan police magistrate under s. 16, sub-s. 2, of the Licensing Act, 1872 [1], for having unlawfully supplied liquor to a police constable on duty without the authority of a superior officer of such constable for so doing.

It appeared that the appellant's public-house was situated nearly opposite a police-station, and was much frequented by the police

[1] By the Licensing Act, 1872 (35 and 36 Vict. c. 94), s. 16, "If any licensed person

"(1) Knowingly harbours or knowingly suffers to remain on his premises any constable during any part of the time appointed for such constable being on duty ...or

"(2) Supplies any liquor or refreshment whether by way of gift or sale to any constable on duty unless by authority of some superior officer of such constable, or

"(3) Bribes or attempts to bribe any constable,...
he shall be liable to a penalty...."

when off duty, and that on July 16, 1894, at about 4.40, the police
constable in question, being then on duty, entered the appellant's house
and was served with liquor by the appellant's daughter in his presence.
Prior to entering the house the police constable had removed his
armlet, and it was admitted that if a police constable is not wearing
his armlet that is an indication that he is off duty. The armlet is
removed at the police-station when a constable is dismissed, and
a publican seeing the armlet off would naturally think the police
constable off duty. The police constable was in the habit of using the
appellant's house, and was well known as a customer to the appellant
and his daughter. Neither the appellant nor his daughter made any
inquiry of the police constable as to whether he was or was not
on duty, but they took it for granted that he was off duty in consequence of his armlet being off, and served him with liquor under that
belief. The appellant and his daughter were in the habit of serving
a number of police constables in uniform with their armlets off each
day, and the question whether they were or were not on duty was
never asked when the armlet was seen to be off.

The appellant appealed to quarter sessions against the conviction,
contending that in order to constitute an offence under s. 16, sub.-s. 2,
of the Licensing Act, 1872, there must be shewn to be either knowledge that the police constable was on duty, or an intentional abstention
from ascertaining whether he was on duty or not. The Court of
quarter sessions, however, upheld the conviction, considering that
knowledge that the police constable, when served with liquor, was on
duty, was not an essential ingredient of the offence: but stated this
case for the opinion of the Court.

DAY, J. I am clearly of opinion that this conviction ought to
be quashed. This police constable comes into the appellant's house
without his armlet, and with every appearance of being off duty. The
house was in the immediate neighbourhood of the police-station, and
the appellant believed, and he had very natural grounds for believing,
that the constable was off duty. In that belief he accordingly served
him with liquor. As a matter of fact, the constable was on duty; but
does that fact make the innocent act of the appellant an offence? I do
not think it does. He had no intention to do a wrongful act; he
acted in the bonâ fide belief that the constable was off duty. It
seems to me that the contention that he committed an offence is
utterly erroneous. An argument has been based on the appearance of
the word "knowingly" in sub.-s. 1 of s. 16, and its omission in sub-s. 2.
In my opinion the only effect of this is to shift the burden of proof.
In cases under sub-s. 1 it is for the prosecution to prove the know-

K.   3

ledge, while in cases under sub-s. 2 the defendant has to prove that he did not know.

It appears to me that it would be straining the law to say that this publican, acting as he did in the bonâ fide belief that the constable was off duty, and having reasonable grounds for that belief, was nevertheless guilty of an offence against the section, for which he was liable both to a penalty and to have his licence indorsed.

WRIGHT, J. I am of the same opinion. There are many cases on the subject, and it is not very easy to reconcile them. There is a presumption that mens rea, an evil intention, or a knowledge of the wrongfulness of the act, is an essential ingredient in every offence; but that presumption is liable to be displaced either by the words of the statute creating the offence or by the subject-matter with which it deals, and both must be considered: *Nichols* v. *Hall*[1]. One of the most remarkable exceptions was in the case of bigamy. It was held by all the judges, on the statute 1 Jac. I., c. 11, that a man was rightly convicted of bigamy who had married after an invalid Scotch divorce, which had been obtained in good faith, and the validity of which he had no reason to doubt: *Lolley's Case*[2]. Another exception, apparently grounded on the language of a statute, is *Prince's Case*[3], where it was held by fifteen judges against one that a man was guilty of abduction of a girl under sixteen, although he believed, in good faith and on reasonable grounds, that she was over that age. Apart from isolated and extreme cases of this kind, the principal classes of exceptions may perhaps be reduced to three. One is a class of acts which, in the language of Lush, J., in *Davies* v. *Harvey*[4], are not criminal in any real sense, but are acts which in the public interest are prohibited under a penalty. Several such instances are to be found in the decisions on the Revenue Statutes, *e.g.*, *Attorney General* v. *Lockwood*[5], where the innocent possession of liquorice by a beer retailer was held an offence. So under the Adulteration Acts, *Reg.* v. *Woodrow*[6], as to innocent possession of adulterated tobacco; *Fitzpatrick* v. *Kelly*[7] and *Roberts* v. *Egerton*[8], as to the sale of adulterated food. So under the Game Acts, as to the innocent possession of game by a carrier: *Rex* v. *Marsh*[9]. So as to the liability of a guardian of the poor, whose partner,

---

[1] Law Rep. 8 C. P. 322

[2] R. & R. 237. [EDITOR'S NOTE. But this was a case of mistake of *law*; cf. p. 29 *supra*.]

[3] *Supra*, p. 21.   [4] Law Rep. 9 Q. B. 433.

[5] 9 M. & W. 378.   [6] 15 M & W. 404.

[7] Law Rep. 8 Q. B. 337.   [8] Law Rep. 9 Q. B. 494.

[9] 2 B. & C. 717.

unknown to him, supplied goods for the poor: *Davies* v. *Harvey*[1]
To the same head may be referred *Reg.* v. *Bishop*[2], where a person was
held rightly convicted of receiving lunatics in an unlicensed house,
although the jury found that he honestly and on reasonable grounds
believed that they were not lunatics. Another class comprehends
some, and perhaps all, public nuisances: *Reg.* v. *Stevens*[3], where the
employer was held liable on indictment for a nuisance caused by
workmen without his knowledge and contrary to his orders; and so in
Rex v. *Medley*[4], and *Barnes* v. *Akroyd*[5]. Lastly, there may be cases in
which, although the proceeding is criminal in form, it is really only
a summary mode of enforcing a civil right: see per Williams and
Willes, JJ., in *Morden* v. *Porter*[6], as to unintentional trespass in
pursuit of game; *Lee* v. *Simpson*[7], as to unconscious dramatic piracy;
and *Hargreaves* v. *Diddams*[8], as to a bonâ fide belief in a legally
impossible right to fish. But, except in such cases as these, there must
in general be guilty knowledge on the part of the defendant, or of
some one whom he has put in his place to act for him generally, or
in the particular matter, in order to constitute an offence. It is plain
that if guilty knowledge is not necessary, no care on the part of the
publican could save him from a conviction under s. 16, sub-s. 2, since
it would be as easy for the constable to deny that he was on duty
when asked, or to produce a forged permission from his superior officer,
as to remove his armlet before entering the public-house. I am, therefore, of opinion that this conviction ought to be quashed.

Conviction quashed.

See also COPPEN v. MOORE, infra, p. 454.

---

*[If a master has no mens rea, he is not liable criminally for his servant's
unauthorised act, even when liable for it civilly.]*

REX v. HUGGINS.

KING'S BENCH.   1730.   2 LORD RAYMOND 1574.

This was a special verdict found at the Old Bailey on an indictment
of murder against James Barnes and John Huggins, and removed into
the King's Bench by certiorari.

[1] Law Rep. 9 Q. B. 433.   [2] 5 Q. B. D. 259.   [3] Law Rep. 1 Q. B. 702.
[4] 6 C. & P. 292.   [5] Law Rep. 7 Q. B. 474.
[6] 7 C. B. (N.S.) 641; 29 L. J. (M.C.) 213.   [7] 3 C. B. 871.
[8] Law Rep. 10 Q. B. 582.

RAYMOND, C. J., delivered the opinion of the Judges. As to Huggins, the jury have only found these facts, viz. : That he had the office of Warden of the Fleet Prison granted to him by letters patent, to hold for his life, and to execute by himself or his deputy; that he on 1 September, 12 Geo. I. and before, and from thence to 1 January, 12 Geo. I., was Warden of the Fleet; that Thomas Gibbons was, and for all that time acted as, his deputy in that office; that James Barnes was for all that time servant of Gibbons, and acted under him about the care of the prisoners, and particularly about the care of Arne. Then they find that Barnes assaulted, and carried by force the said Arne into a room, and kept him there against his consent, as in the indictment, forty-four days. Then they find the situation and condition of the room, whereby it was very unwholesome, and dangerous to the life of any person kept therein; that Huggins, during the imprisonment of Arne in that room, viz. for fifteen days before Arne's death, knew that the room was then lately built, and that the walls were made of brick and mortar, and were then damp. But whether he knew it on the 7th of September they are ignorant. Arne on the 10th of September, 12 Geo. I., by duress of imprisonment became sick, and languished to the 20th of October, and then died by duress of imprisonment in the said room. During the imprisonment of Arne in that room, viz. for at least fifteen days before his death, Huggins was once present at that room, and then saw the said Arne in that room *sub duritie imprisonamenti praedicti, ac adtunc et ibidem se avertit,* and the said James Barnes, the same time as Huggins turned himself away, locked the door, the said Arne at the time when the said door was locked by Barnes being in the said room *sub duritie imprisonamenti praedicti.* And that Arne remained under that duress till his death: that Huggins acted sometimes as warden, during the time Gibbons was deputy; but it is not found that he acted as warden during the confinement of Arne.

The Judges are unanimously of opinion, that the facts found in this special verdict do not amount to murder in the prisoner at the bar.... Though he was warden, yet it being found that there was a deputy, he is not, as warden, guilty of the facts committed under the authority of his deputy. He shall answer as superior for his deputy civilly, but not criminally. It has been settled, that though a sheriff must answer for the offences of his gaoler civilly (that is, he is subject, in an action, to make satisfaction to the party injured), yet he is not to answer criminally for the offences of his under-officer. He only is criminally punishable who immediately does the act or permits it to be done. (Hale, P. C. 114.) So that if an act be done by an under-officer, unless it is done by the command or direction, or with the consent of the principal, the principal is not criminally punishable for it. In this case the fact was done by Barnes; and it nowhere appears in the special verdict that the prisoner at the bar ever commanded, or directed, or consented to this duress of imprisonment, which was the cause of Arne's death. No command or direction is found; and it is not found that Huggins knew of it. That which made the duress in this case was (1) Barnes carrying, and putting, and confining Arne in this room by force and against his consent; (2) the situation and condition of the room. Now it is not found that Huggins knew these several circum-stances which made the duress. It is not found that he knew anything of Barnes carrying Arne thither; nor that he was there without his consent or without proper support. As to the room it is found by the verdict:—(1) That the room was built of brick and mortar; (2) that the walls were *valde humidae*; (3) that the room was situate on the common sewer of the prison, and near the place where the filth of the prison and excrement of the prisoners were usually laid. *Ratione quorum* the room was very unwholesome, and the life of any man kept there was in great danger. But all that is found with respect to the prisoner's knowledge is, that for fifteen days before Arne's death he knew that the room was then lately built, that the walls were made of brick and mortar, and were then damp. But it is not found, nor does it appear, that he knew they were dangerous to a man's life or that there was a want of necessary support. Nor is it found that he directed or consented that Arne should be kept or con-tinued there. The chief thing relied upon is, that the verdict finds that once the prisoner at the bar was present at the room, and saw Arne *sub duritie imprisonamenti praedicti, et se avertit*; which, as was objected, made him an aider and abettor. But, in answer to this: (1) Being present alone, unless he knew all the circumstances, and directed that Arne should continue, or at least consented that he should, cannot make him an aider or abettor in the murder. Kelynge 113. A man may be present and be entirely innocent; he may be present casually. (2) The verdict is *vidit sub duritie imprisonamenti praedicti.* He might see him, and see him while he was *sub duritie imprisonamenti praedicti*, that is while he was in fact under the duress by Barnes; but it does by no means follow from thence that he knew that the man was under this duress, and it is not found that he did know it. It was objected, that if he saw the man under this duress he must know it; and it was his duty to deliver him. But we cannot take things by inference in this manner. The *vidit* does not imply a knowledge of the several facts that made the duress. If the nature of this duress be considered, it is impossible that it should be discovered by one sight of the man. It consists of several ingredients and circumstances, that are not necessarily to be discovered upon sight. For though he saw Arne in the room, yet by the view he could not tell that he was there without his consent, and by force, or that he wanted necessary relief. It is not found that the man made any complaint to him, or that any application was made to him on the man's behalf. If he was there with his consent it would take off the duress. His seeing is but evidence of his knowledge of these things at best, and very poor evidence too. And therefore the jury, if the fact would have borne it, should have found, that Huggins knew that Arne was there without his consent, and that he consented to and directed his continuance there; which not being done, we cannot intend these things nor infer them.

[*But a servant's authority to conduct a business may be so wide as to imply authority to conduct it in even a criminal way.*]

REX *v.* ALMON.

KING'S BENCH.   1770.   5 BURROW 2686.

The defendant having been convicted of publishing a libel (Junius's Letter to the King), in one of the magazines called *The London Museum*, which was bought at his shop, and even professed to be printed for him, his counsel moved, on Tuesday, 19th June, 1770, for a new trial, upon the foot of the evidence being insufficient to prove any criminal intention in Mr Almon, or even the least knowledge of their being sold at his shop. And they had affidavits [1] to prove, that it was a frequent practice in the trade, for one publisher to put another publisher's name to a pamphlet, as printed for that other, when, in fact, it was published for himself. That this was the fact in the present case; Mr Miller being the real publisher of this *Museum*, but having advertised it and published it as printed for Mr Almon, without consulting Mr Almon. That as soon as he saw his name put to it as being printed for him, he immediately sent a note to Mr Miller expressing his disapprobation. That he was not at home when

---

[1] [EDITOR'S NOTE. The student must observe that none of these assertions had been proved *at the trial*.]

they were sent to his shop. That the whole number sent to his shop was 300. That about 67 of them had been sold there by a boy in the shop, but without Mr Almon's own knowledge, privity, or approbation. That as soon as he discovered it he stopped the sale, ordered the remainder to be carried up into his garret, and took the first opportunity to return them to Mr Miller. That it was not proved, that the person who sold them was Mr Almon's servant or employed by him, or that Mr Almon was at all privy to the sale....

LORD MANSFIELD said that...buying the pamphlet in the shop of a professed bookseller and publisher of pamphlets, from a person acting in the shop, is primâ facie evidence of a publication by the master himself. But that it is liable to be contradicted, where the fact will bear it, by contrary evidence tending to exculpate the master, and to show that he was not privy nor assenting to it nor encouraging it. That this being primâ facie evidence of a publication by the master himself, it stands good till answered by him; and if not answered at all, it thereby becomes conclusive so far as to be sufficient to convict him. That proof of a public exposing to sale, and selling at his shop by his servant, was primâ facie sufficient; and must stand till contradicted or explained or exculpated by some other evidence; and if not contradicted, explained, or exculpated, would be in point of evidence sufficient or tantamount to conclusive.

ASTON, J....The bookseller has the profits of the shop, and is answerable for the consequences....If he had a sufficient excuse, he might have proved it.

The Court therefore unanimously discharged the rule.

[*If a servant has no mens rea, he is not liable criminally for a criminal act which he does in obedience to his master, even when liable for it civilly.*]

REGINA v. JAMES.

OXFORD CIRCUIT. 1837. 8 CARRINGTON & PAYNE 131.

Indictment on the statute 7 & 8 Geo. IV., c. 30, s. 6 for obstructing the airway of a mine

It was opened by *Ludlow, Serjt.* for the prosecution that a Mr Phelps's colliery...was adjacent to a colliery of Mr Protheroe's.

The two collieries, though adjacent, were not connected with each other; and belonging to Mr Phelps's mine, which ran more than a mile under ground, was an airway. In the coal mines there was a gas or vapour called the choke-damp, which was fatal to animal life, and to guard against the effects of this various contrivances had been resorted to. In the mine of Mr Phelps a long airway was constructed with a large fire near the end of it, and beyond that a pit called an air-pit; the effect of the fire being to create a strong draught of air, and thus draw off the choke-damp out of the mine; there being also side doors to close all the openings which led into other workings in the mines. Things were in this state till the 26th of May last, when the prisoners, headed by the prisoner James, who was a principal person in Mr Protheroe's colliery, proceeded to the place and pulled down the side doors and fire-grate, and also took down the side doors and built a wall across the airway. The effect of this would be to drive back the choke-damp into Mr Phelps's mine, and prevent the working.

LORD ABINGER, C.B. If a servant did this by his master's order, and supposed bonâ fide that the master had a right to order it to be done, would it not be too much to say that the servant is answerable as a felon for doing the thing maliciously, when the malice, if there is any, is his master's and not his own?

Ludlow, Serjt. Suppose that a master ordered his servant to shoot a man, that would be no excuse for the servant if he did it.

LORD ABINGER, C.B. That is an act which is malum in se. But if a master, having a doubt or no doubt of his own rights, sets his servants to build a wall in a mine, they would, if he proved to have no right, be all liable in an action of trespass, but it would not be felony in the servants. The rules respecting acts mala in se do not apply. If a master told his servant to shoot a man, he would know that that was an order he ought to disobey. But if the servant bonâ fide did these acts, I think they do not amount to an offence within this statute. If a man claims a right which he knows not to exist, and he tells his servants to exercise it, and they do so, acting bonâ fide, I am of opinion that that is not a felony in them, even if in so doing they obstruct the airway of a mine. What I feel is this, that if these men acted bonâ fide in obedience to the orders of a superior, conceiving that he had the right which he claimed, they are not within this Act of Parliament. But if either of these men knew that it was a malicious act on the part of his master, I think then that he would be guilty of the offence charged.

Verdict, Not Guilty.

INFANCY.

[*An infant if above seven, is capable of crime.*]

REX *v.* ALICE.

KING'S BENCH.   1338.   LIB. ASS. ANN. 12, f. 37, pl. 30;
Y.B. 11—12 EDW. III. (ROLLS SERIES) p. 627.

Alice of W., who was of the age of thirteen years, was burnt by judgment, because she had killed her mistress and because this was adjudged treason. And it was said that by the old law no one within age should be hanged or bear judgment of life or member &c., but it was found before Spigurnel[1], J., that an infant within age killed his comrade, and afterwards hid himself, and he was hanged forthwith. For he [Spigurnel] said that the hiding showed knowledge of right and wrong, *quia malicia supplet aetatem* &c.

[*But if he be under fourteen, mens rea must be proved expressly.*]

ANONYMOUS.

EXCHEQUER CHAMBER.   1488.   Y.B. 3 HEN. VII. f. 1, Hil. pl. 4.

Another matter debated [before all the Justices in the Exchequer Chamber] was, that an infant within the age of nine years slew an infant of nine years and confessed the felony. And it was also found that he hid him whom he had killed, and by way of excuse for the blood that was shed on himself, said that it came from his nose. And [the Justices] held that he should be hanged. And Fairfax [J.] said that it had been said by Sir John Fortescue [C. J.] that the cause why one shall be hanged for murder is the example which he sets to other men, but if an infant or a man without discretion kills, he shall not be hanged, for no example is set by him to those who have discretion.

---

[1] Henry Spigurnel sat in the King's Bench under Edw. I. and Edw. II.

[*Inadequate proof of mens rea.*]

REX *v.* OWEN.

OXFORD CIRCUIT.   1830.   4 CARRINGTON & PAYNE 236.

Indictment for stealing coals.   The prisoner was ten years of age,
and it was proved that, on the 28th of January, she was standing by
a large heap of coals belonging to Messrs Harford & Brothers, and
that she put a basket upon her head.   This basket was found to contain a few knobs of coal, which, in answer to a question put to her by
the witness for the prosecution, she said she had taken from this heap.

LITTLEDALE, J., was about to call upon the prisoner for her defence,
when

Carrington, *amicus curiae*, suggested that she was entitled to an
acquittal.   He submitted that a child under seven years of age could
not legally be convicted of felony; and that, in cases where the
accused was between the ages of seven and fourteen, it was incumbent
on the prosecutor to prove, not only that the offence was committed,
but also that the offender had, at the time, a guilty knowledge that he
or she was doing wrong.

LITTLEDALE, J.   I cannot hold that a child of ten years of age
is incapable of committing a felony.   Many have been convicted under
that age.

Carrington.—No doubt that is so.   A boy, named York, who was
only ten years old, was convicted of a murder; but in that case there
was the strongest evidence of guilty knowledge[1].

LITTLEDALE, J.—I think I must leave it to the jury.

The prisoner was then called on for her defence.

LITTLEDALE, J. (in summing up), said—In this case there are two
questions; *first*, did the prisoner take these coals; and, *secondly*, if she
did, had she at the time a guilty knowledge that she was doing wrong.
The prisoner, as we have heard, is only ten years of age; and, unless

[1] Fost. 70. [EDITOR'S NOTE.   He had killed a girl of five, mangled the dead
body, and buried it in a dung heap.   He was sentenced to death at Bury Assizes
in 1748, before Willes, L.C.J.; who referred the case to the whole of the judges.
They, upon consideration, unanimously agreed "That there are so many circumstances stated which are undoubtedly tokens of a mischievous disposition, that he
is certainly a proper subject for capital punishment, and ought to suffer.   For it
would be of very dangerous consequence to have it thought that children may
commit such atrocious crimes with impunity."   He received, however, several
successive reprieves; and ultimately, after being detained in prison nine years,
was pardoned on condition of entering the navy.]

you are satisfied by the evidence that, in committing this offence, she knew that she was doing wrong, you ought to acquit her. Whenever a person committing a felony is under fourteen years of age, the presumption of law is, that he or she has not sufficient capacity to know that it is wrong; and such person ought not to be convicted, unless there be evidence to satisfy the jury that the party, at the time of the offence, had a guilty knowledge that he or she was doing wrong[1].

> Verdict—Not Guilty; and the foreman of the jury added, "We do not think that the prisoner had any guilty knowledge."

See also REGINA *v.* MANLEY, *infra.*

INSANITY.

[Insanity may show absence of mens rea.]

ANONYMOUS.

KING'S BENCH.   1505.   Y.B. 21 HEN. VII. f. 31, Mich. pl. 16.

A man was arraigned for the murder of an infant. And it was found that at the time of the murder the felon was of non-sane memory. Therefore it was awarded that he should go quit. *Quod nota bene.*

[What forms of insanity will do this.]

REGINA *v.* DANIEL M'NAUGHTEN.

HOUSE OF LORDS.   1843.   10 CLARK AND FIN. 200.

[The prisoner had been indicted at the Central Criminal Court for the murder of Edward Drummond (Secretary to Sir Robert Peel),

---

[1] It is believed that the youngest person who was ever executed in this country, was a boy between eight and nine years old, named Dean, who was found guilty of burning two barns at Windsor, "and it appearing that he had malice, revenge, craft, and cunning, he had judgment to be hanged, and was hanged accordingly." This case was tried before Whitlock, J., at the Abingdon Assizes, 1629, and is reported in Emlyn's Edit. Hale's Pleas of the Crown, p. 25, n. (*u*).

by shooting him in the back, as he was walking up Whitehall, on 20th Jan. 1843. The prisoner pleaded Not Guilty. After evidence had been given of the shooting of Mr Drummond and of his death in consequence thereof, witnesses were called on the part of the prisoner, to prove that, at the time of committing the act, he was not in a sound state of mind. The medical evidence was in substance this:—That persons of otherwise sound mind might be affected by morbid delusions; that the prisoner was in that condition; that a person so labouring under a morbid delusion might have a moral perception of right and wrong, but that in the case of the prisoner it was a delusion which carried him away beyond the power of his own control, and left him no such perception; and that he was not capable of exercising any control over acts which had connection with his delusion; that it was of the nature of the disease with which the prisoner was affected, to go on gradually until it had reached a climax, when it burst forth with irresistible intensity; that a man might go on for years quietly, though at the same time under its influence, but would all at once break out into the most extravagant and violent paroxysms. Some of the witnesses, who gave this evidence, had previously examined the prisoner; others had never seen him till he appeared in Court, and they formed their opinions on hearing the evidence given by the other witnesses.

TINDAL, C.J., told the jury that the question to be determined was whether at the time the act in question was committed the prisoner had or had not the use of his understanding, so as to know that he was doing a wrong or wicked act.

The verdict of the jury was Not Guilty, on the ground of insanity. This verdict, and the question of the nature and extent of the unsoundness of mind which would excuse the commission of a crime, attracted great attention throughout England and became the subject of a debate in the House of Lords. The House determined to take the opinion of the Judges on the law. Accordingly, on June 19, 1843, all the Judges attended the House of Lords; when (no argument having been had) the following questions of law were propounded to them:—

"1st.—What is the law respecting alleged crimes committed by persons afflicted with insane delusion in respect of one or more particular subjects or persons; as, for instance, where, at the time of the commission of the alleged crime, the accused knew he was acting contrary to law, but did the act complained of with a view, under the influence of insane delusion, of redressing or revenging some supposed grievance or injury, or of producing some supposed public benefit?

"2nd.—What are the proper questions to be submitted to the jury when a person alleged to be afflicted with an insane delusion respecting one or more particular subjects or persons, is charged with the commission of a crime (murder, for example), and insanity is set up as a defence?

"3rd.—In what terms ought the question to be left to the jury as to the prisoner's state of mind at the time when the act was committed?

"4th.—If a person under an insane delusion as to existing facts commits an offence in consequence thereof, is he thereby excused?

"5th.—Can a medical man, conversant with the disease of insanity, who never saw the prisoner previously to the trial, but who was present during the whole trial and the examination of all the witnesses, be asked his opinion as to the state of the prisoner's mind at the time of the commission of the alleged crime, or his opinion whether the prisoner was conscious at the time of doing the act that he was acting contrary to law, or whether he was labouring under any and what delusion at the time?"

Mr Justice MAULE gave his own answers separately..

LORD CHIEF JUSTICE TINDAL.—"My lords, her Majesty's Judges, with the exception of Mr Justice Maule, who has stated his opinion to your lordships, in answering the questions proposed to them by your lordships' House, think it right in the first place, to state that they have forborne entering into any particular discussion upon these questions, from the extreme and almost insuperable difficulty of applying those answers to cases in which the facts are brought judicially before them. The facts of each particular case must of necessity present themselves with endless variety, and with every shade of difference in each case. As it is their duty to declare the law upon each particular case on facts proved before them, and after hearing argument of counsel thereon, they deem it at once impracticable, and at the same time dangerous to the administration of justice if it were practicable, to attempt to make minute applications of the principles involved in the answers given by them to your lordships' questions.

"They have, therefore, confined their answers to the statement of that which they hold to be the law upon the abstract questions proposed by your lordships; and as they deem it unnecessary, in this peculiar case, to deliver their opinions seriatim, and as all concur in the same opinion, they desire me to express such their unanimous opinion to your lordships.

"The first question proposed by your lordships is this: 'What is the

law respecting alleged crimes committed by persons afflicted with
insane delusion in respect of one or more particular subjects or persons;
as, for instance, where, at the time of the commission of the alleged
crime, the accused knew he was acting contrary to law, but did the act
complained of with a view, under the influence of insane delusion, of
redressing or revenging some supposed grievance or injury, or of producing some supposed public benefit?'

"In answer to which question, assuming that your lordships'
inquiries are confined to those persons who labour under such partial
delusions only, and are not in other respects insane, we are of opinion
that (notwithstanding the party accused did the act complained of
with a view, under the influence of insane delusion, of redressing or
revenging some supposed grievance or injury, or of producing some
public benefit) he is nevertheless punishable, according to the nature of
the crime committed, if he knew, at the time of committing such
crime, that he was acting contrary to law; by which expression we
understand your lordships to mean the law of the land.

"Your lordships are pleased to inquire of us, secondly: 'What are
the proper questions to be submitted to the jury, where a person
alleged to be afflicted with insane delusion respecting one or more
particular subjects or persons is charged with the commission of a
crime (murder, for example), and insanity is set up as a defence?'
And, thirdly: 'In what terms ought the question to be left to the jury
as to the prisoner's state of mind at the time when the act was
committed?' And as these two questions appear to us to be more conveniently answered together, we have to submit our opinion to be, that
the jury ought to be told in all cases that every man is to be presumed
to be sane, and to possess a sufficient degree of reason to be responsible
for his crimes, until the contrary be proved to their satisfaction; and
that, to establish a defence on the ground of insanity, it must be
clearly proved that, at the time of the committing of the act, the party
accused was labouring under such a defect of reason, from disease of
the mind, as not to know the nature and quality of the act he was
doing, or, if he did know it, that he did not know he was doing
what was wrong. The mode of putting the latter part of the question
to the jury on these occasions has generally been, whether the accused
at the time of doing the act knew the difference between right and
wrong; which mode, though rarely, if ever, leading to any mistake
with the jury, is not, as we conceive, so accurate when put generally,
and in the abstract, as when put with reference to the party's knowledge of right and wrong in respect to the very act with which he is
charged. If the question were to be put as to the knowledge of the

accused, solely and exclusively with reference to the law of the land, it might tend to confound the jury, by inducing them to believe that an actual knowledge of the law of the land was essential in order to lead to a conviction; whereas the law is administered upon the principle that every one must be taken conclusively to know it, without proof that he does know it. If the accused was conscious that the act was one which he ought not to do, and if that act was at the same time contrary to the law of the land, he is punishable. The usual course, therefore, has been, to leave the question to the jury, whether the party accused had a sufficient degree of reason to know that he was doing an act that was wrong; and this course we think is correct, accompanied with such observations and explanations as the circumstances of each particular case may require.

"The fourth question which your lordships have proposed to us is this:—'If a person under an insane delusion as to existing facts commits an offence in consequence thereof, is he thereby excused?' To which question the answer must of course depend on the nature of the delusion; but, making the same assumption as we did before, namely, that he labours under such partial delusion only, and is not in other respects insane, we think he must be considered in the same situation as to responsibility as if the facts with respect to which the delusion exists were real. For example, if, under the influence of his delusion, he supposes another man to be in the act of attempting to take away his life, and he kills that man, as he supposes, in self-defence, he would be exempt from punishment. If his delusion was that the deceased had inflicted a serious injury to his character and fortune, and he killed him in revenge for such supposed injury, he would be liable to punishment.

"The question lastly proposed by your lordships is:—'Can a medical man, conversant with the disease of insanity, who never saw the prisoner previously to the trial, but who was present during the whole trial and the examination of all the witnesses, be asked his opinion as to the state of the prisoner's mind at the time of the commission of the alleged crime, or his opinion whether the prisoner was conscious at the time of doing the act that he was acting contrary to law, or whether he was labouring under any and what delusion at the time?' In answer thereto, we state to your lordships, that we think the medical man, under the circumstances supposed, cannot in strictness be asked his opinion in the terms above stated; because each of those questions involves the determination of the truth of the facts deposed to, which it is for the jury to decide, and the questions are not mere questions upon a matter of science, in which case such evidence is admissible.

But, where the facts are admitted, or not disputed, and the question becomes substantially one of science only, it may be convenient to allow the question to be put in the general form; though the same cannot be insisted on as a matter of right."

[*How insanity is to be proved.*]

UNITED STATES *v.* GUITEAU.

U.S. COURT OF DISTRICT OF COLUMBIA, 1882.   10 FEDERAL REP. 161.

[Charles J. Guiteau was indicted for the murder, on July 2nd, 1881, of James A. Garfield, the President of the United States of America. The prisoner resided in Chicago; he was a lawyer, and had sought in vain to obtain a consulship. He attributed his failure to President Garfield's resolute abandonment of the policy which had led recent Presidents to give public appointments as rewards for electioneering services. As the President was entering a room in the railway station at Washington, Guiteau came behind him and fired two pistol-shots into his back. The President lingered several weeks; and died on Sept. 19th.]

Cox, J., in the course of his summing up to the jury, said:— Murder is committed when a person of sound memory and discretion unlawfully kills a reasonable creature, in being and in the peace of the United States, with malice aforethought. I apprehend that you will have little difficulty in reaching a conclusion as to all the elements which make up this crime, unless it be the one of 'sound memory and discretion' as it is called (which is only a technical expression for a sound mind). A man cannot commit murder if he is labouring under disease of his mental faculties to such an extent that he does not know what he is doing, or does not know that it is wrong. But the defence of insanity has been so abused as to be brought into great discredit. It has been the last resort in cases of unquestionable guilt; and has been the excuse of juries for acquittal when their own sympathy and that of the public have been with the accused. Nevertheless if insanity to the degree that I have already explained be established, it is a perfect defence to an indictment and must be allowed full weight. You must bear in mind that a man does not become irresponsible by the mere fact of being partially insane. Such a man may retain as much control over his passions as he had when in mental health. He may, too, commit offences with which his infirmity has nothing to do; be sane as to his crime, understand its nature, and be governed in regard to it by the same motives as other people, though on some other matter, having no relation whatever to it, he may be subject to delusions. In a case reported, a defendant was convicted of cheating by false pretences, and was not saved from punishment by his insane delusion that he was the lawful son of a well-known prince. The first thing, therefore, to be impressed upon you is, that wherever partial insanity is relied on as a defence, it must appear that the crime charged was the product of the morbid condition and connected with it as effect with cause; and was not the result of sane reasoning or natural motives, which the man may be capable of notwithstanding a circumscribed disorder of mind. Secondly, assuming that the infirmity has had a direct influence in producing the crime, we must fix the degree of disorder which will create irresponsibility in law. The judicial decisions on this subject have not always been entirely satisfactory. Courts in former times laid down a law of insanity in ignorance of the medical aspects of the subject; though it could only be properly dealt with through the concurrent light of the two sciences of law and medicine. Hence one theory after another was adopted and discarded by the judges in their efforts to find some common ground where they could combine a due regard for the security of society with humanity towards the afflicted. Nearly forty years ago, one MacNaughten was tried in England for killing Mr Drummond, the private secretary of Sir Robert Peel, mistaking him for the Premier himself. His acquittal on the ground of insanity caused so much excitement that the House of Lords addressed certain questions to the judges in regard to the law of insanity in certain cases. Their answers have been since regarded as settling the law on the subject in England; and, with some qualification, they have been approved in the United States.

It may be well to say a word as to the evidence by which juries are to be guided in this difficult inquiry. That subtle essence which we call "mind" defies, of course, ocular inspection and can only be known by its outward manifestations. By the language and conduct of the man, his thoughts and emotions are read. According as they conform to, or contrast with, the practice of people of sound mind, the large majority of mankind, we form our judgment as to his mental soundness. For this reason, evidence is admissible to shew that his conduct and language at different times and on different occasions indicated some morbid condition of his intellectual powers; and the more extended the view of his life, the safer is the judgment formed of him. Everything relating to his physical and mental history is relevant. Evidence as to insanity in his parents and immediate relatives may also be pertinent. It is never allowable to infer in-sanity in an accused person from the mere fact of its existence in his ancestors. But when testimony directly tending to prove insane conduct on the part of the accused himself has been given, evidence of his family antecedents is admissible as corroborative of that testimony.

The question for you to determine is, what was the condition of the prisoner's mind at the time when this tragedy was enacted? If he *then* was sufficiently sane to be responsible, it matters not to you what may have been his condition before or after. Yet evidence as to his previous and subsequent conditions is properly admitted; because it throws light, prospectively and retrospectively, upon his condition at the time of the crime. Inasmuch as mental disorders are of gradual growth and of indefinite continuance, if he is shown to have been insane shortly before or shortly after the commission of the crime, it is natural to at least conjecture that he was so at the time of it. But all the evidence must centre around the time when the deed was done. If you find from the whole evidence that at the time of the com-mission of the homicide, the prisoner, in consequence of disease of mind, was incapable of understanding what he was doing or of under-standing that it was wrong—as, for example, if he was under an insane delusion that the Almighty had commanded him to do the act, and in consequence of this delusion he was incapable of seeing that it was a wrong thing to do—then he was not in a responsible condition of mind, but was an object of compassion and not of justice, and he ought to be now acquitted.

Verdict, Guilty. Guiteau was executed.

[*Insane impulse is not, of itself, sufficient.*]

REGINA *v.* BURTON.

KENT ASSIZES. 1863. 3 FOSTER and FINLASON 772.

The prisoner, a youth of eighteen, was indicted for the murder of a boy. It appeared that the deceased boy had been playing on the Lines, a public place at Chatham, where the prisoner saw him, and was seen near him.

Some hours afterwards, the child's dead body was found on the Lines. The throat was cut and there were marks of a violent struggle. The police were engaged in prosecuting their inquiries, when the prisoner gave himself up, and admitted the act, recounting all the circumstances with perfect intelligence. He added, "I knew the boy, and knew his mother, but I had no particular ill-feeling against the boy; only I had made up my mind to murder somebody." He also said that he had wiped his hands and the knife. The Superintendent of Police in cross-examination admitted that when the prisoner said he had made up his mind to murder somebody, he said he was "tired of his life."...A person to whom the prisoner had been apprenticed stated that he had a very vacant look, and very often would drop his tools and run out of the shop and pace backwards and forwards as if absent in mind....Other witnesses deposed to his "vacancy of mind," and strange ways. He had been known to eat a piece of soap and a piece of a cat, and to bite a candle....On other occasions, however, he seemed sensible enough.

A doctor deposed that the prisoner's mother had twice been to a lunatic asylum and his brother was of weak intellect....The witness had attended the prisoner himself on two occasions, and believed he was labouring under what, in the profession, would be considered as "moral insanity," that is, he knew perfectly well what he was doing but had no control over himself. By the moral feelings he meant the propensities; which may be diseased while the intellectual faculties are sound.

Counsel for the prisoner proposed to ask the witness whether, having heard the evidence, he was of opinion that the prisoner was sane or insane at the time of the doing of the act; but the learned Judge would not allow the question to be put, as it was the very question the jury were to determine.

WIGHTMAN, J., in summing up the case, said: As there was no doubt about the act the only question was whether the prisoner, at the time he committed it, was in such a state of mind as not to be responsible for it. The *prisoner's* account of it was that he had done it from a morbid feeling; that he was tired of life and wished to be rid of it. No doubt prisoners had been acquitted of murder on the ground of insanity; but the question was what were the cases in which men were to be absolved from responsibility on that ground. Hatfield's case differed from the present, for there wounds had been received on the head which were proved to have injured the brain. In the more recent case of Macnaughten, the judges laid down the rule to be, that there must, to raise the defence, be a defect of reason from disease

4—2

of the mind, so as that the person did not know the nature and quality of the act he committed, or did not know whether it was right or wrong. Now to apply this rule to the present case would be the duty of the jury. It was not mere eccentricity of conduct which made a man legally irresponsible for his acts. The medical man called for the defence defined homicidal mania to be a propensity to kill; and described moral insanity as a state of mind under which a man, perfectly aware that it was wrong to do so, killed another under an uncontrollable impulse. This would appear to be a most dangerous doctrine and fatal to the interests of society and to security of life. The question is whether such a theory is in accordance with law. The rule laid down by the judges is quite inconsistent with such a view; for it was that a man was responsible for his actions if he knew the difference between right and wrong. It was urged that the prisoner did the act to be hanged, and so was under an insane delusion; but what delusion was he under? So far from it, it shewed that he was quite conscious of the nature of the act and of its consequences. He was supposed to desire to be hanged; and in order to attain the object committed murder. That might shew a morbid state of mind, but not delusion. Homicidal mania again, as described by the witnesses for the defence, shewed no delusion. It merely shewed a morbid desire for blood. Delusion meant the belief in what did not exist. The question for the jury was whether the prisoner at the time he committed the act was labouring under such a species of insanity as to be unaware of the nature, the character, or the consequences of the act he committed,—in other words whether he was incapable of knowing that what he did was wrong. If so, they should acquit him; if otherwise, they should find a verdict of guilty.

Guilty. Sentence, Death. The prisoner was executed.

[*Insane impulse.*]

REGINA *v.* HAYNES.

HAMPSHIRE ASSIZES.   1859.   1 FOSTER AND FINLASON 666.

MURDER. Insanity. The prisoner, a soldier, was charged with the murder of Mary MacGowan, at the Camp at Aldershot. The deceased was a woman with whom the prisoner had been on the most friendly terms up to the moment of the commission of the offence. No motive was assigned for the perpetration of the act. And general evidence was given that the prisoner having, while in Canada, seduced a young woman under a promise of marriage, had been unable to fulfil it by reason of his regiment having been ordered home, and his mind had been much affected by the circumstance...

BRAMWELL, B., in summing up to the jury, said :—As to the defence of insanity, it has been urged for the prisoner that you should acquit him on the ground that, it being impossible to assign any motive for the perpetration of the offence, he must have been acting under what is called a powerful and irresistible influence, or homicidal tendency. But I must remark as to that, that the circumstance of an act being *apparently* motiveless is not a ground from which you can safely infer the existence of such an influence. Motives exist unknown and in-numerable which might prompt the act. A morbid and restless (but resistible) thirst for blood would itself be a motive urging to such a deed for its own relief. But if an influence be so powerful as to be termed irresistible, so much the more reason is there why we should not withdraw any of the safeguards tending to counteract it. There are three powerful restraints existing, all tending to the assistance of the person who is suffering under such an influence—the restraint of religion, the restraint of conscience, and the restraint of law. But if the influence itself be held a legal excuse, rendering the crime dis-punishable, you at once withdraw a most powerful restraint—law, forbidding and punishing its perpetration. We must therefore return to the simple question you have to determine—did the prisoner know the nature and quality of the act he was doing[1] ; and did he know that he was doing what was wrong ?

Guilty. Sentence, Death. The prisoner was reprieved.

[NOTE. In the case of Mrs Brough, indicted in 1856 for murder, coram Erle, J., the law was laid down in precisely the same way as to homicidal impulse.]

REGINA v. TYLER.

[See this case, *infra* p. 57.]

[1] [EDITOR'S NOTE. The much later case of *Rex* v. *Hay* (A.D. 1911) would, as reported in 22 Cox 286, suggest that an uncontrollable homicidal impulse may now be a defence even for a man who knows his act to be wrong and knows its nature and quality. But a reference to the official report of the case (C. C. C. Sess. Pap. clv. 337) will show that Hay "knew the nature of the act *but he did not know the quality* " of it.]

INTOXICATION.

[*Drunkenness is compatible with mens rea.*]

REX *v.* MEAKIN.

OXFORD ASSIZES. 1836. 7 CARRINGTON AND PAYNE 297.

The prisoner was indicted for stabbing Benjamin Finney, with intent to murder him. There were also the usual counts laying the intent to do grievous bodily harm, &c.

It appeared that Benjamin Finney was a constable; and that the prisoner went into the house of Samuel Finney, where he was very abusive, and Samuel Finney desired Benjamin Finney to turn him out, which he did; and while he was taking him off the premises, the prisoner stabbed him with a fork. It was proved that the prisoner said he should not have done it if he had not been drunk, and it appeared that he was "something the worse for liquor."

ALDERSON, B. (in summing up).—It is my duty to tell you that the prisoner's being intoxicated does not alter the nature of the offence. If a man chooses to get drunk, it is his own voluntary act: it is very different from a madness which is not caused by any act of the person. That voluntary species of madness which it is in a party's power to abstain from, he must answer for. However, with regard to the intention, drunkenness may perhaps be adverted to according to the nature of the instrument used. If a man uses a stick, you would not infer a malicious intent so strongly against him, if drunk when he made an intemperate use of it....But where a dangerous instrument is used, which, if used, must produce grievous bodily harm, drunkenness can have no effect on the consideration of the malicious intent of the party.

Verdict, Guilty.

[*But it may cause such a Mistake of Fact as will excuse.*]

REGINA *v.* GAMLEN.

BRISTOL ASSIZES. 1858. 1 FOSTER AND FINLASON 90.

ASSAULT. The charge arose out of an affray at a fair; and there seemed some ground for supposing that the prisoner acted under apprehensions of an assault upon himself. All concerned were drunk.

CROWDER, J....Drunkenness is no excuse for crime. But in considering whether the prisoner apprehended an assault on himself you may take into account the state in which he was.

Verdict, Not guilty.

[*Or may disprove the presence of some* special *form of mens rea.*]

THE STATE *v.* BELL.

SUPREME COURT OF IOWA. 1870.   29 STILES 316.

The prisoner was indicted for a burglary in entering a house by night with intent to commit the crime of larceny. The evidence shewed that he had never before been charged with crime and was a man of good moral character. He had spent the evening of the night when the alleged burglary was committed (which was a New Year's Eve) in company with some friends; with whom he sat drinking until about 11 p.m. A few hours after, he was found in the house specified in the indictment; and was at once arrested. He was then in a state of intoxication.

At the trial before the District Court of Des Moines, the Judge was asked by defendant's counsel to tell the jury that if they should conclude from the evidence that the defendant entered the house through drunkenness, without knowing where he was and with no intent to steal or commit any felony, then they ought to acquit. He refused to do so. The prisoner was convicted. A motion was made in the Supreme Court of Iowa to reverse this conviction on the ground of mis-direction.

WRIGHT J. The offence here would not be complete unless the dwelling-house were broken with the intent to commit a felony. If that intent existed, it would make no difference whether the accused was drunk or sober. A criminal intent may exist in the mind of a man who is under the influence of intoxicating liquor: and if it do, the intoxication is no excuse. But if the defendant's drunkenness was such as to take away from his act all criminal intent, then the act was not criminal. The drunkenness is a proper circumstance to be weighed by the jury in determining whether there existed the intent to commit the specific felony charged. If, as he alleges, he blundered into this house through a drunken mistake, under such circumstances as indicate inability to form any definite purpose and especially to form the purpose of committing a larceny, then he is not guilty of the offence charged. If under such circumstances he had taken the property of another, it would not have been larceny; there being the absence of the requisite specific legal intent to steal. If so, the entering would not be burglarious.   Conviction reversed.

MISTAKE.

See Reg. *v.* Rose, *infra*, p. 140.

DURESS.

[Fear of death may excuse even Treason.]

REX *v.* M^cGROWTHER.

Special Commission.   1746.   Foster's Crown Law 13.

In the case of Alexander McGrowther, there was full evidence touching his having been in the rebellion; and his acting as a lieutenant in a regiment in the rebel army called the Duke of Perth's regiment. The defence he relied on was, that he was forced in.

And to that purpose he called several witnesses; who in general swore that on the 28th of August the person called Duke of Perth, and the Lord Strathallan, with about twenty Highlanders, came to the town where the prisoner lived; that on the same day three several summonses were sent out by the Duke, requiring his tenants to meet him, and to conduct him over a moor in the neighbourhood, called Luiny Moor; that upon the third summons the prisoner, who is a tenant to the Duke, with about twelve of the tenants appeared; that then the Duke proposed to them that they should take arms and follow him into the rebellion; that the prisoner and the rest refused to go; whereupon they were told, that they should be forced, and cords were brought by the Duke's party in order to bind them; and that then the prisoner and ten more went off, surrounded by the Duke's party.

These witnesses swore, that the Duke of Perth threatened to burn the houses, and to drive off the cattle of such of his tenants as should refuse to follow him.

They all spake very extravagantly of the power which lords in Scotland exercise over their tenants; and of the obedience (even to the joining in rebellion) which they expect from them.

Lord Chief-Justice Lee, in summing up, observed to the jury, that there is not, nor ever was, any tenure which obligeth tenants to follow their lords into rebellion.

And as to the matter of force, he said that the fear of having houses burnt or goods spoiled, supposing that to have been the case of the prisoner, is no excuse in the eye of the law for joining and march.ing with rebels[1].

The only force that doth excuse is a force upon the person and present fear of death; and this force and fear must continue all the time the party remains with the rebels. It is incumbent on every man who makes force his defence, to shew an actual force, and that he quitted the service as soon as he could; agreeably to the rule laid down in Oldcastle's case, that they joined *pro timore mortis*, and *recesserunt quam cito potuerunt*.

He then observed that the only force the prisoner pretends to was on the 28th of August; and that he continued with the rebels and bore a commission in their army till the surrender of Carlisle, which was on or about the 30th of December.

The jury without going from the bar found him guilty. But he was not executed.

N.B. All the Judges that were in town were present, and concurred in the points of law.

N.B. Many of the Scotch prisoners made force their defence, and produced the same sort of evidence as McGrowther did; and the same directions in point of law were given as in his case: and the matter of fact, whether force or no force, and how long that force continued, with every circumstance tending to shew the practicability or impracticability of an escape, was left to the jury on the whole evidence.

[*But not a fear of any lesser violence.*]

REGINA *v.* TYLER AND PRICE.

MAIDSTONE ASSIZES.   1838.   8 CARRINGTON AND PAYNE 616.

The prisoners were indicted for the murder of Nicholas Meares. The first count of the indictment charged that John Thom, otherwise called Sir William Courtenay, on the 31st day of May, 1838, at the ville of Dunkirk, had murdered the deceased by shooting him with a

[1] N.B. If threats of this kind were an excuse, it would be in the power of any leader in a rebellion to indemnify all his followers.

pistol, **and** that the prisoners were feloniously present, aiding and abetting. The second count charged the prisoners with the murder, as principals in the first degree.

John Thom, who called himself Sir William Courtenay, assembled a great number of persons, and led them about the neighbourhood of Canterbury, promising them plenty in this world and happiness hereafter. He asserted that he was above all earthly authority, **and** was the Saviour of the world....After Thom caused this assemblage, a warrant for his apprehension was placed in the hands of John Meares, a constable. He took with him the deceased (his brother) and one Edwards, as his assistants, and proceeded to a house at which Thom was. Some of the men who were with Thom were found placed as guards about the house, armed with bludgeons. On Thom being informed of the arrival, he said, "Are you constables?" The deceased replied, "I am"; upon which Thom shot him with a pistol....The prisoners and others, by the order of Thom, took the deceased, who was still alive, and threw him into a dry ditch....Thom afterwards killed Lieutenant Bennett; and was himself killed by the military.

Shee for the prisoners. Thom was insane; and, being so, could not be guilty of felony; so the prisoners could not be guilty of aiding and abetting him in felony. This disposes of the first count. As to the second count, which charges them as principals in the first degree, they did not fire the pistol; they can only be made liable if the act was done in the prosecution of some unlawful purpose in which all the parties were engaged. Now, here Thom and his followers are not shewn to have had any definite purpose of any kind; and, therefore, there could not be any community of purpose between Thom and the prisoners. I also submit that the prisoners acted from a fear of personal violence to themselves at the hands of Thom.

Lord Denman, C.J. (in summing up). In order to make out that part of the charge which imputes to Thom the act of murder, and that these persons were guilty of aiding and abetting him, it would be necessary to shew that Thom was a person capable of committing murder. In order to make out the malicious intention imputed in the indictment to the act of Thom, he must be shewn to have been of sound mind at the time when he committed it....Yet if Thom was on his trial, it could hardly be said, from the evidence, that he could be called on to answer for his criminal acts. That, therefore, simplifies the question you will have to decide, and confines it to the second count of the indictment. There these persons are charged with having committed the offence themselves. If they were aware of the malignant purpose entertained by Thom, and shared in that purpose, and were present assisting him in the commission of acts fatal to life, in the course of accomplishing this purpose, then no doubt they are guilty as principals on this second count....It seems wholly unimportant whether the parties had a well-defined particular mischief to bring about as the result of their combination.   For,...however blank might be the mind of Thom as to any ulterior purpose, and however unconscious the minds of the prisoners might be of any particular object, still if they contemplated a resistance to the lawfully constituted authorities of the country, in case any should come against them while they were banded together, there would be a common purpose; and they would be answerable..

You have heard that the prisoners were induced to join Thom from a fear of personal violence to themselves.   I am bound to tell you that where parties for such a reason are induced to join a mischievous man, it is not their fear of violence to themselves which can excuse their conduct to others.   You probably never saw two men tried at a criminal bar for an offence which they had jointly committed, where one of them had not been to a certain extent in fear of the other, and had not been influenced by that fear in the conduct he pursued.   Yet that circumstance has never been received by the law as an excuse for his crime, and the law is that no man, from a fear of consequences to himself, has a right to make himself a party to committing mischief on mankind....It cannot be too often repeated that the apprehension of personal danger does not furnish any excuse for assisting in doing an act which is illegal.

Verdict—Not guilty, on the first count.   Guilty on the second.

PUBLIC OFFICIAL SUBJECTION.

[*A crime is not* necessarily *excused by being committed in obedience to the command of a military supe*rior.]

REX v. THOMAS.

CROWN CASE RESERVED.   1816.   Ms of BAYLEY, J.[1]

[H.M.S. *Achille* lay in the Medway, and her crew were being paid off.   To avoid inconvenience from people coming to meet the departing sailors, one of her marines, named Thomas, was placed as sentinel

1 Cited in 3 Russell on Crimes 94; see also 4 M. and S. 111.

with orders to keep off all boats unless the officer on deck sanctioned their approach or officers in uniform were in them. A musket was given to him, with three blank cartridges and three bullets. Boats did approach; and Thomas repeatedly bade them keep off. One boat, however, persisted; and came close under the ship. He then fired at it, and killed a man who was in it. Thomas was tried before Bayley, J., for the murder of this man. The jury convicted him; but, in answer to a question from the judge, found that he fired under the (mistaken) impression that it was his duty to do so.

THE JUDGES held unanimously that his act was one of murder; (though they thought it a proper case for a pardon). They, however, added that the homicide would have been justifiable "if the act had been necessary for the preservation of the ship; as, for instance, if the deceased had been stirring up a mutiny."]

[*But it* probably[1] *will be excused thereby when the command is such as the soldier might reasonably—even by a mistake of* law—*suppose himself legally bound to obey.*]

REGINA *v.* SMITH.

SPECIAL COURT OF CAPE COLONY.   17 C.G.H. 561.

[Indictment for murder. In 1899, during the South African war, a party of British soldiers, of whom the prisoner was one, arrested a farmer's son who was suspected of being in communication with the Boer forces. It was necessary to remove him without delay. But a bridle, which was needed for his horse, was missing; and one of the farm-labourers, named Dolley, who appeared to know where it was, refused to fetch it. Capt. Cox, the officer in command, ordered Smith to shoot Dolley unless he produced the bridle promptly. Smith did so, and killed him.

Sir H. Juta, for prisoner. *R.* v. *Thomas* was not in time of war.

The Attorney-General, for the Crown. If an officer's order is not a lawful order, a soldier obeys it at his peril; for instance, if ordered to fire on an unoffending bystander. The principle remains, even in war;

---

[1] See the conflicting authorities cited in *Marks* v. *Frogley*, L.R. [1898] 1 Q.B. at pp. 890, 892; and the judgment of Kennedy, J., p. 396.

(though, of course, the state of war is a circumstance in the case). The test is, Could he fairly suppose that the order was reasonable and necessary? The shooting made it impossible to obtain the bridle.

Solomon, J.....It is not desirable to express an opinion as to whether the order was a lawful one—a matter which concerns Capt. Cox more than the prisoner. The point now is, whether, assuming the order to be unlawful, Smith is protected because he was carrying out the orders of his superior officer. Curiously enough, the point has never yet been decided in any English court....It is monstrous to suppose that a soldier would be protected where the order was grossly illegal...But that he is responsible whenever he obeys any order not strictly legal, is a proposition which the Court cannot accept;...immediate obedience is required, especially in time of war....I think it is safe to lay down that if a soldier honestly believes he is doing his duty in obeying, and if the orders are not so manifestly illegal that he ought to have known they were unlawful, he will be protected by the orders. We all are satisfied that the order here was not so plainly illegal that Smith would have been justified, under the circumstances, in refusing to obey it.   Acquittal.]

NECESSITY.

[*The necessity of avoiding starvation does not excuse Murder.*]

REGINA *v.* DUDLEY AND STEPHENS.

QUEEN'S BENCH DIVISION.   1884.   L.R. 14 Q.B.D. 273.

The master and mate of the yacht *Mignonette* were indicted at the Assizes at Exeter before Huddleston, B., for the murder of a cabin-boy named Parker. At the suggestion of the learned judge, the jury found the following special verdict, adding thereto a strong expression of compassion for the sufferings that the prisoners had undergone :—

"That on July 5, 1884, the prisoners, with one Brooks, all able-bodied English seamen, and the deceased, an English boy between 17 and 18, the crew of an English yacht, were cast away in a storm on the high seas 1600 miles from the Cape of Good Hope, and were compelled to put into an open boat; that in this boat they had no supply of water and no supply of food, except two 1 lb.-tins of turnips, and for three days they had nothing else to subsist on ; that on the fourth day they caught a small turtle, upon which they subsisted for a few days, and this was the only food they had up to the 20th day when the act now in question was committed; that on the 12th day the remains of the turtle were entirely consumed, and for the next eight days they had nothing to eat; that they had no fresh water, except such rain as they from time to time caught in their oilskin capes; that the boat was drifting on the ocean, and was probably more than 1000 miles from land; that on the 18th day, when they had been seven days without food and five without water, the prisoners spoke to Brooks as to what should be done if no succour came, and suggested some one should be sacrificed to save the rest, but Brooks dissented, and the boy, to whom they were understood to refer, was not consulted; that on the day before the act in question Dudley proposed to Stephens and Brooks that lots should be cast who should be put to death to save the rest, but Brooks refused to consent, and it was not put to the boy, and in point of fact there was no drawing of lots; that on that day the prisoners spoke of their having families, and suggested it would be better to kill the boy that their lives should be saved, and Dudley proposed if no vessel was in sight by the next morning the boy should be killed; that next day, no vessel appearing, Dudley told Brooks he had better go and have a sleep, and made signs to Stephens and Brooks that the boy had better be killed; that Stephens agreed to the act, but Brooks dissented from it; that the boy was lying at the bottom of the boat quite helpless, and extremely weakened by famine and by drinking sea water, and unable to make any resistance, nor did he ever assent to being killed; that Dudley, with the assent of Stephens, went to the boy, and telling him his time was come, put a knife into his throat and killed him; that the three men fed upon the boy for four days; that on the fourth day after the act the boat was picked up by a passing vessel, and the prisoners were rescued, still alive, but in the lowest state of prostration; that they were carried to the port of Falmouth, and committed for trial at Exeter; that if the men had not fed upon the body of the boy they would probably not have survived to be so picked up and rescued, but would within the four days have died of famine; that the boy, being in a much weaker condition, was likely to have died before them; that at the time of the act there was no sail in sight, nor any reasonable prospect of relief; that under these circumstances there appeared to the prisoners every probability that unless they then or very soon fed upon the boy or one of themselves they would die of starvation; that there was no appreciable chance of saving life except by killing some one for the others to eat; that assuming any necessity to kill any one, there was no greater necessity·

for killing the boy than any of the other three men ; but whether, upon the whole matter, the prisoners were and are guilty of murder the jury are ignorant, and refer to the Court."

The five senior Judges of the Queen's Bench Division sat as a Divisional Court to consider the effect of this verdict.

LORD COLERIDGE, in the course of delivering their judgment, said :

.We are dealing with a case of private homicide, not one imposed upon men in the service of their sovereign and in the defence of their country. Now it is admitted that the deliberate killing of this unoffend-ing and unresisting boy was clearly murder, unless the killing can be justified by some well-recognized excuse admitted by law. It is further admitted that there was in this case no such excuse, unless the killing was justified by what has been called "necessity." But the temptation to the act which existed here was not what the law has ever called necessity. Nor is this to be regretted. Though law and morality are not the same, and many things may be immoral which are not neces-sarily illegal, yet the absolute divorce of law from morality would be of fatal consequence ; and such divorce would follow if the temptation to murder in this case were to be held by law an absolute defence of it. It is not so. To preserve one's life is generally speaking a duty, but it may be the plainest and the highest duty to sacrifice it. War is full of instances in which it is a man's duty not to live, but to die. The duty, in case of shipwreck, of a captain to his crew, of the crew to the passengers, of soldiers to women and children, as in the noble case of the *Birkenhead*, these duties impose on men the moral necessity, not of the preservation, but of the sacrifice of their lives for others; from which in no country, least of all it is to be hoped, in England, will men shrink, as, indeed, they have not shrunk. It is not correct, therefore, to say that there is any absolute or unqualified necessity to preserve one's life. "*Necesse est ut eam, non ut vivam*," is a saying quoted by Lord Bacon himself with high eulogy, in the very chapter on necessity to which so much reference has been made. It would be a very easy and cheap display of commonplace learning to quote from Greek and Latin authors passage after passage in which the duty of dying for others has been laid down in glowing and emphatic language, as result-ing from the principles of heathen ethics. It is enough in a Christian country to remind ourselves of the example which we profess to follow. It is not needful to point out the awful danger of admitting the principle which has been contended for. Who is to be the judge of this sort of necessity? By what measure is the comparative value of lives to be measured? Is it to be strength, or intellect, or what? It is plain that the principle leaves to him who is to profit by it to determine the necessity which will justify him in deliberately taking another's life to serve his own.

> " So spake the fiend; and with necessity,
> The tyrant's plea, excused his devilish deeds."

In this case the weakest, the youngest, the most unresisting was chosen. Was it more necessary to kill him than one of the grown men? The answer must be "No." It is not suggested that in this particular case the deeds were devilish; but it is quite plain that such a principle once admitted might be made the legal cloak for unbridled passion and atrocious crime. There is no safe path for judges to tread but to ascertain the law to the best of their ability and declare it according to their judgment; and, if in any case the law appears to be too severe on individuals, to leave it to the Sovereign to exercise the prerogative of mercy which the Constitution has intrusted to the hands fittest to dispense it. It must not be supposed that in refusing to admit temptation to be an excuse for crime it is forgotten how terrible the temptation was; how awful the suffering; how hard in such trials to keep the judgment straight and the conduct pure. We are often compelled to set up standards we cannot reach ourselves, and to lay down rules which we could not ourselves satisfy. But a man has no right to declare temptation to be an excuse, though he might himself have yielded to it, nor allow compassion for the criminal to change or weaken in any manner the legal definition of the crime. It is therefore our duty to declare that the prisoners' act was wilful murder; and that the facts stated in the verdict are no legal justification[1]

COVERTURE.

[Husband's mere command, if he be present, raises a presumption of duress.]

ANONYMOUS.

King's Bench. 1353. Lib. Ass. Ann. 27, f. 137, pl. 40.

A woman was arraigned for that she had feloniously stolen two shillingsworth of bread. And she said that she did it by the commandment of him who was at that time her husband. And the

---

[1] [Editor's Note. Sentence of death was passed; but was commuted by the Crown to six months' imprisonment without hard labour.]

Justices for pity's sake would not hold her by her confession but took
an inquest. By which it was found that she did it by the coercion of
her husband and against her will. Therefore she went quit. An I
it was said that if she acted by the command of her husband, without
any coercion, it would be no felony.

[*Husband's command.*]

REGINA *v.* SAMUEL SMITH AND SARAH SMITH.

CROWN CASE RESERVED.   1858.   DEARSLY AND BELL 553.

The following case was reserved and stated by CHANNELL, B.

At the last Assizes for the county of Gloucester the said Samuel
Smith and Sarah Smith were jointly tried before me and found guilty
on a count charging them with feloniously wounding one John Leach
with intent to disfigure him, and in another count with intent to do
the said John Leach grievous bodily harm.

For the purposes of this case the conviction of Sarah Smith is to
be deemed and taken to be a good conviction, unless the same ought to
be reversed by reason of the facts following found by the jury, viz.
that the said Sarah Smith was at the time of the commission of the
offence the wife of the said Samuel Smith; that she acted under the
coercion of her husband; and that she herself did not personally inflict
any violence upon the said John Leach. A verdict of guilty was
entered against the husband and wife. I passed sentence on the said
Samuel Smith.

I reserved for the consideration of this Court the question whether
upon the aforesaid finding the conviction of the said Sarah Smith was
a good conviction; respiting the sentence upon her and taking bail for
her appearance hereafter to receive judgment if the conviction should
be affirmed.

The question for the opinion of the Court is, whether Sarah Smith,
the wife of the said Samuel Smith, having acted under his coercion,
and not having herself inflicted any violence on the said John Leach,
can be properly convicted of the offence before mentioned.

It appeared on the trial that the wife, acting, as the finding of the
jury established, under the coercion of her husband, wrote letters to
the prosecutor pretending that she had become a widow, and requesting a meeting at a distant place. The meeting was granted,

and the wife, dressed as a widow, met the prosecutor at a railway station, and induced him to go with her to a lonely spot where the husband fell upon him and inflicted the injuries alleged in the indictment.

This case was considered on the 24th April, 1858, by POLLOCK, C. B., WILLES, J., BRAMWELL, B., CHANNELL, B. and BYLES, J.

No counsel appeared.

POLLOCK, C. B. The jury have disposed of this case by their finding. They have found that Sarah Smith was a married woman; that she acted under the coercion of her husband; and that she herself did not personally inflict any violence upon the prosecutor. The conviction therefore, so far as it extends to her, must be reversed.

Conviction of Sarah Smith reversed.

[*Except in the gravest crimes.*]

ANONYMOUS.

CAMBRIDGE ASSIZES.   1664.   KELYNG 31.

It was propounded to all the Judges: If a man and his wife go both together to commit a burglary, and both of them break a house in the night and enter and steal goods; what offence is this in the wife? And agreed by all that it was no felony in the wife. For, the wife being together with the husband in the act, the law supposeth the wife doth it by coercion of the husband. And so it is in all larcenies. But as to murder; if husband and wife both join in it, they are both equally guilty. *Vide* the case of the Earl of Somerset and his lady, both equally found guilty of the murder of Sir Thomas Overbury by poisoning him in the Tower of London. (2 Howell's *State Trials*, 911.)

[*But the presumption may be rebutted by wife's activity in the crime.*]

REGINA *v.* THOMAS CRUSE AND MARY CRUSE.

CROWN CASE RESERVED.   1838.   2 MOODY 53; 8 C. AND P. 541.

The prisoners were tried at the Oxford Summer Assizes, 1838, before Mr JUSTICE PATTESON, on an indictment under 7 W. IV. and 1 Vict. c. 85, s. 2 which charged that the prisoner Thomas, on the 4th of

June at Thatcham, feloniously did assault Charlotte Heath, and that
he did cause unto the said Charlotte Heath a certain bodily injury
dangerous to life, by striking and beating her with his hands and fists
on her head and back, by kicking her on the back, by seizing and
lifting her and striking her head against a wooden beam of a ceiling,
by casting, throwing, and flinging her against a brick floor, with intent
feloniously to kill and murder her; by reason whereof the said
Charlotte Heath was grievously injured, and her life greatly endangered.

Mary Cruse was charged as being present, aiding and abetting.

It appeared by the evidence that both the prisoners in company
had ill-used Charlotte Heath, a girl of seven years of age, daughter of
Mary Cruse. Whereupon Mr Carrington for Mary Cruse contended
that she was entitled to be acquitted as having acted under the coercion
of her husband; and that the only excepted cases were treason and
murder. The learned Judge thought otherwise, and put the case to
the jury as to both. [Mary Cruse had taken an active part. She
ran after the child and gave her a blow on the head; and, subsequently,
said to the husband "Kill her, kill her."]

The jury acquitted both prisoners of the felony, not being satisfied
that they had any intent to murder; but found them guilty of the
assault.

The learned Judge respited the judgment; and requested the opinion
of the Judges on the point with regard to the wife being under the
coercion of her husband.

This case was argued before all the Judges (except LITTLEDALE, J.,
PARK, J., and BOLLAND, B.), in Michaelmas term, 1838.

Carrington for the prisoners.

The wife must be taken to be acting under the coercion of the
husband when present, and therefore is entitled to an acquittal; except
in cases of treason and murder, to which the presumption is held not
to apply.

TINDAL, C. J. Suppose the husband to be a cripple and confined to
his bed, his presence then would not be sufficient.

VAUGHAN, J. There was a case of arson before me on the Home
Circuit. The man and wife were tried together, and it appeared that
the man, though present, was a cripple and bedridden in the room, and
I held, after conferring with my Lord Chief Justice Tindal, that the
circumstances under which the man was, repelled the presumption of
coercion[1].

---

[1] This was a case of house-burning, with intent to defraud the insurance office.
Tried at Maidstone Spring Assizes, 1838; *Reg.* v. *Pollard.*

Carrington. In the case of *Rex* v. *Archer*, Moody's C. C. 143., it was held that the mere fact of the wife's being the more active of the two could not repel the presumption if the husband were actually present.

PARKE, B. An assault with an intent to commit murder may be within the exception of murder, but the difficulty does not arise here; it is sufficient to dispose of this case, that they are acquitted of the felony.

Carrington. The jury ought to have been told to acquit the wife, if they thought there was a felony committed. As to the text writers Lord Hale at first, 1 Hale, P. C. 45, 47., applies the presumption of coercion to all cases except treason and murder; but in later passages (vol. i. 434, 516), manslaughter is also excepted. In 1 Hawkins, c. i. p. 4, robbery is also introduced as excepted. But it was decided in Kel. 31, by the twelve Judges, that the presumption in favour of the wife applies to burglary. Blackstone in the first volume only excepts treason and murder: in the fourth volume he excepts crimes that are *mala in se* and prohibited by the law of nature, such as murder and the like.

ALDERSON, B. There was a case on the Northern Circuit in which Lord Chief Baron Thompson laid it down, that the presence of the husband raised only a primâ facie presumption that the offence was committed under coercion[1].

Carrington. It would appear from the case of *Rex* v. *Price*, 8 C. and P. 19, and *Rex* v. *Conolly* there cited, that the presumption is not limited to felony; as there the women were acquitted in misdemeanor for uttering counterfeit coin.

ALDERSON, B. It is decided in the case of *Regina* v. *Ingram*, 1 Salk. 384, that husband and wife may be jointly convicted of an assault; which is all these parties are convicted of.

LORD ABINGER. This case was one that must have been left to the jury. And they have convicted the parties of an offence of which they may be jointly guilty.

THE JUDGES held the indictment sufficient and the conviction good.

---

[1] *Rex* v. *Hughes*, 1 Russell on Crimes, 18.

CORPORATIONS.

THE QUEEN *v.* THE GREAT NORTH OF ENGLAND RAILWAY COMPANY.

QUEEN'S BENCH. 1846. 9 ADOLPHUS AND ELLIS. N. S. 315.

[Indictment for obstructing the Queen's highway. Plea, Not guilty. Issue thereon.]

On the trial, before WIGHTMAN, J., at the Durham Spring Assizes, 1845, evidence was given, on the part of the prosecution, to shew that the Company had cut through a carriage road with the railway ; and had carried the road over the railway by a bridge not satisfying the statutory provisions. For the defendants, it was objected that no indictment for a misfeasance could be maintained against a corporation.

A verdict was found for the Crown, leave being reserved to move to enter a verdict for the defendants or to arrest the judgment....

Granger, Otter and *Bovill* shewed cause. The dictum of Holt, C. J., in an *Anonymous*[1] case in *Modern Reports*, will be relied upon for the defendants. He is reported as saying : "A corporation is not indictable, but the particular members of it are." It does not appear what the facts there were, nor whether the indictment was for a misfeasance or a nonfeasance. [Lord DENMAN, C. J. referred to *Regina* v. *Birmingham and Gloucester Railway Company*[2].] It was there held that a corporation might be indicted for not obeying a statute : and this was assumed in *Rex* v. *The Severn and Wye Railway Company*[3]. These two cases, at least, shew that Lord Holt's dictum, as reported, is not now law : and by the judgment delivered in the former the dictum is distinctly overruled....It is not necessary for the prosecutors here to contend that an indictment would lie for any misfeasance involving a breach of the peace : a murder, for instance, could not be conceived to be authorised by the corporation seal. That is the distinction suggested in *Regina* v. *Birmingham and Gloucester Railway Company*[2], in the judgment of this Court, where Hawk. P. C. B. 1, c. 65. s. 13[4], is cited. But for that which is analogous to a mere trespass on land, an indictment may lie. The tendency of modern decisions has been to make corporations, criminally as well as civilly, amenable like indi-

---

[1] 12 Mod. 559. Case 935.
[2] 3 Q. B. 223.
[3] 2 B. and Ald. 646.
[4] Vol. II. p. 58, 7th ed.

viduals....And, in *Beverley* v. *The Lincoln Gas Light and* Coke Company[1]
and *Church* v. *The Imperial Gas Light and Coke Company*[2], it was held
that assumpsit, on a contract not under seal, might be maintained
against and by a corporation.   In the former of these two cases, the
Court expressed a readiness to sanction any decisions which they found
introducing a relaxation of "a rule established in a state of society
very different from the present, at a time when corporations were com-
paratively few in number ; and upon which it was very early found
necessary to engraft many exceptions."   In *Church* v. *The Imperial
Gas Light and Coke Company*[2] the Court said : " Wherever to hold the
rule applicable would occasion very great inconvenience, or tend to
defeat the very object for which the corporation was created, the exception has prevailed."   Here the corporation is a railway company, with
the ordinary powers of interfering with roads on certain conditions ;
and the offence charged is peculiarly one likely to be committed in the
performance of acts which the corporation may have occasion to do.
No difficulty exists as to connecting them with such acts.   *Rex* v.
Medley[3] shews that members of a company, who authorise their servants
to commit an act amounting to a nuisance, are liable to be indicted
with such servants : it follows that the corporate body, which has the
power of authorising an act under seal, is indictable for such act if it be
a breach of the law.   The common law punishment for a nuisance is
fine, or imprisonment, or both.   The first of these can be inflicted on
a corporation.   And the reasoning which the Court used in *Rex* v.
Trafford[4] seems applicable.   It was there said that an action on the
case would have lain ; and that it followed that an indictment lay.
Here trespass would lie.   That which, if committed against an individual, would be ground for an action, is ground for an indictment, if
committed against the public.   Reference may perhaps be made to *The
Case of Sutton's Hospital*[5], where it is said that a corporation aggregate
"cannot commit treason, nor be outlawed, nor excommunicate, for they
have no souls."   But that is met by the distinction already pointed
out : no actual breach of the peace, perhaps, can be the subject
of indictment against a corporation ; nor can the judgment proper to
treason or felony be executed upon them.   But they can, by their
servant, obstruct a highway ; and may be fined for doing so, or may be
compelled to abate....

Knowles, Bliss and Joseph Addison, contrà.   Admitting, for the
sake of the argument, that a corporation is liable to actions upon deeds
under the corporate seal, for acts authorised to be done under the corporate

---

[1] 6 A. and E. 829.   [2] 6 A. and E. 846.   [3] 6 C. and P. 292.
[4] 1 B. and Ad. 874, 886.   [5] 10 Rep. 1 a, 32 b.

seal, and for some acts of so ordinary a kind that they may be commanded without seal, and also that, according to *Regina* v. *Birmingham
and Gloucester Railway Company*[1], a corporation may be indicted for a
nonfeasance, it will not follow that an indictment lies against them for
a misfeasance. The prosecutors' counsel, in this last case, distinguished
expressly between a misfeasance and a nonfeasance, admitting that an
indictment would not lie for the former. That distinction appears to be
adopted by the Court; and there is good reason for it. For a non
feasance there would be no other remedy, except in the cases where
mandamus lies, inasmuch as the omission cannot be the omission of
any particular individual. But, where an indictable *act* is done, the
individual doing it may be indicted, and so may any individual
members of the corporation who have given the illegal command. But
suppose, after a corporation had been indicted for the act and punished,
such individuals were indicted. Could they support a plea of auterfois
convict by shewing the conviction of the corporation? Or are they to
be punished twice; once as individuals, and once as members of the
body corporate? It is admitted, on the other side, that the doctrine
stated in Hawkins, and sanctioned by this Court in *Regina* v. *Birmingham and Gloucester Railway Company*[2] excludes cases of violence : and
6 Vin. Abr. 309, *Corporations* (Z), pl. 2 is to the same effect. Yet
a road might be obstructed by violent means; and indeed it is impossible to charge an actual obstruction without alleging force, and it
must be supported by proof of what is legally a species of violence.
Nor, again, would it follow, from a civil action for trespass being maintainable, that an indictment for the same act is so. An injury committed out of the realm, an assault by an insane person, an assent to
a trespass previously committed for the defendant's benefit, would be
grounds for an action; but not for an indictment. The object of an
action is to give the injured party compensation; that of an indictment, to inflict punishment, for the sake of example, upon acts injurious
to the public.

Cur. adv. vult.

Lord DENMAN, C. J., now delivered the judgment of the Court.

The question is, whether an indictment will lie at common law
against a corporation for a misfeasance; it being admitted, in conformity with undisputed decisions, that an indictment may be maintained against a corporation for nonfeasance.

All the preliminary difficulties, as to the service and execution of
process, the mode of appearing and pleading, and enforcing judgment,
are by this admission swept away. But the argument is, that for

---

[1] 3 Q. B. 223.   [2] 3 Q. B. 232.

a wrongful act a corporation is not amenable to an indictment, though for a wrongful omission it undoubtedly is; assuming, in the first place, that there is a plain and obvious distinction between the two species of offence.

No assumption can be more unfounded. Many occurrences may be easily conceived, full of annoyance and danger to the public, and involving blame in some individual or some corporation, of which the most acute person could not clearly define the cause, or ascribe them with more correctness to mere negligence in providing safeguards or to an act rendered improper by nothing but the want of safeguards. If A. is authorised to make a bridge with parapets, but makes it without them, does the offence consist in the construction of the unsecured bridge, or in the neglect to secure it?

But, if the distinction were always easily discoverable, why should a corporation be liable for the one species of offence and not for the other? The startling incongruity of allowing the exemption is one strong argument against it. The law is often entangled in technical embarrassments; but there is none here. It is as easy to charge one person, or a body corporate, with erecting a bar across a public road as with the non-repair of it; and they may as well be compelled to pay a fine for the act as for the omission.

Some dicta occur in old cases: "A corporation cannot be guilty of treason or of felony." It might be added "of perjury, or of offences against the person." The Court of Common Pleas lately held that a corporation might be sued in trespass[1]; but nobody has sought to fix them with acts of immorality. These plainly derive their character from the corrupted mind of the person committing them, and are violations of the social duties that belong to men and subjects. A corporation, which, as such, has no such duties, cannot be guilty in these cases: but it may be guilty as a body corporate of commanding acts to be done to the nuisance of the community at large. The late case of *Regina* v. *Birmingham and Gloucester Railway Company*[2] was confined to the state of things then before the Court, which amounted to nonfeasance only; but was by no means intended to deny the liability of a corporation for a misfeasance.

We are told that this remedy is not required; because the individuals who concur in voting the order or in executing the work, may be made answerable for it by criminal proceedings. Of this there is no doubt. But the public knows nothing of the former; and the latter, if they can be identified, are commonly persons of the lowest rank, wholly

[1] *Maund* v. *The Monmouthshire Canal Company*, 4 M. and G. 452.
[2] 3 Q. B. 223.

incompetent to make any reparation for the injury. There can be no effectual means for deterring from an oppressive exercise of power for the purpose of gain, except the remedy by an indictment against those who truly commit it, that is, the corporation, acting by its majority. And there is no principle which places them beyond the reach of the law for such proceedings. The verdict for the Crown, therefore, on the first four counts, will remain undisturbed.

SECTION III.

MODES OF PARTICIPATION IN A CRIME.

[*Principals in first and second degree.*]

REGINA *v.* GRIFFITH.

SHROPSHIRE ASSIZES. 1553.   PLOWDEN 97.

At the Shropshire Assizes, persons of the county of Montgomery were indicted for killing Oliver David ap Hoel Vaughan, at Berriew, in the said county of Montgomery, of malice prepense; viz. some for giving the wounds whereof he died, and Griffith ap David ap John and others for that they were present, aiding, comforting and abetting the others to commit the said murder. And they who gave the wounds to the said Oliver, and killed him, had fled and escaped; and Griffith ap David ap John and the rest were brought to the bar. And whether they should be arraigned or no was a doubt.

BROMLEY, L.C.J. They who were present and abetting were principals, as well as they who struck the man and killed him, yet they are principals in only the second degree; in respect that the others, who struck the said Oliver and killed him, are principals in the first degree. These others, who abetted them and were present, are also principals; but in the second degree only, and in respect of the [strikers'] act. For if the [strikers] did not kill the man, then if the said Griffith and the rest, who were abettors and present, should be now arraigned, and found guilty, [and then the strikers and killers should be taken and arraigned and should be acquitted], I would know your opinions what should be done?

And all the other Justices above mentioned, after advising thereof for two days, held clearly enough that they might proceed with the prisoners now at the bar, without any inconvenience arising from it. For they said that when many come to do an act, and one only does it, and the others are present abetting him or ready to aid him in the fact, they are principals to all intents as much as he that does the fact. For the presence of the others is a terror to him that is assaulted, so that he dare not defend himself. For if a man sees his enemy and twenty of his servants coming to assault him, and they all draw their swords and surround him, and only one strikes him so that he dies thereof, now the others shall with good reason be adjudged as great offenders as he that struck him. For if they had not been present, he might probably have defended himself and so have escaped. But the number of the others being present and ready to strike him also, shall be adjudged a great terror to him, so as to make him lose his courage and despair of defending himself; and by this means they are the occasion of his death. And then inasmuch as both together, viz. the wounds and the presence of the others, who gave no wounds at all, are adjudged the cause of his death, it follows that all of them, viz. those that strike and the rest that are present, are in equal degree; and each partakes of the deed of the other. For which reasons it seemed to them that the prisoners now present might be arraigned. And afterwards BROMLEY and all the Court agreed to it. And therefore they were arraigned; and pleaded, not guilty.

And note (reader) that a case in 40 Ass. proves that the law anciently was that those who were present and abetting were not principals, but accessories; as the Lord Bromley said before. For the book is, that four were appealed as principals, and the others of Presence, Force and Aid. But of late time the law has been held contrary in this point; for now they are taken to be principals by all the sages of the law.

[*Principals in first and second degree.*]

REGINA *v.* SWINDALL AND OSBORNE.

STAFFORD ASSIZES.   1846.   2 CARRINGTON AND KIRWAN 230.

The prisoners were indicted for the manslaughter of one James Durose. The second count of the indictment charged the prisoners with inciting each other to drive their carts and horses at a furious

and dangerous rate along a public road, and with driving their cart
and horses over the deceased at such furious and dangerous rate, and
thereby killing him.   The third count charged Swindall with driving
his cart over the deceased, and Osborne with being present, aiding
and assisting.   The fourth count charged Osborne with driving his
cart over the deceased, and Swindall with being present, aiding and
assisting.

Upon the evidence, it appeared that the prisoners were each driving
a cart and horse, on the evening of the 12th of August, 1845.   The
first time they were seen that evening was at Draycott toll-gate,
two miles and a half from the place where the deceased was run over.
Swindall there paid the toll, not only for that night, but also for
having passed with Osborne through the same gate a day or two before.
They then appeared to be intoxicated.   The next place at which they
were seen was Tean Bridge, over which they passed at a gallop, the
one cart close behind the other.   A person there told them to
mind their driving : this was 990 yards from the place where the
deceased was killed.   The next place where they were seen was
forty-seven yards beyond the place where the deceased was killed.
The carts were then going at a quick trot, one closely following
the other.   At a turnpike gate a quarter of a mile from the place
where the deceased was killed, Swindall, who appeared all along to
have been driving the first cart, told the toll-gate keeper, "We have
driven over an old man"; and desired him to bring a light and look at
the name on the cart; on which Osborne pushed on his cart, and told
Swindall to "hold his bother," and they then started off at a quick
pace.   They were subsequently seen at two other places, at one of
which Swindall said he had sold his concern to Osborne.   It appeared
that the carts were loaded with pots from the potteries.   The surgeon
proved that the deceased had a mark upon his body which would
correspond with the wheel of a cart, and also several other bruises;
and, although he could not say that both carts had passed over his
body, it was possible that both might have done so.

Greaves, in opening the case to the jury, submitted that it was
perfectly immaterial in point of law, whether one or both carts had
passed over the deceased.   The prisoners were in company, and had
concurred in jointly driving furiously along the road ; that that was an
unlawful act, and, as both had joined in it, each was responsible for
the consequences, though they might arise from the act of the other.
It was clear that they were either partners, master and servant, or at
all events companions.   If they had been in the same cart, one holding
the reins, the other the whip, it could not be doubted that they would

be both liable for the consequences; and in effect the case was the same, for each was driving his own horse at a furious pace, and encouraging the other to do the like.

At the close of the evidence for the prosecution, *Allen*, Serjt., for the prisoners, submitted that the evidence only proved that one of the prisoners had run over the deceased, and that the other was entitled to be acquitted.

POLLOCK, C.B. I think that that is not so. I think that Mr Greaves is right in his law. If two persons are in this way inciting each other to do an unlawful act, and one of them runs over a man, whether he be the first or the last he is equally liable. The person who runs over the man would be a principal in the first degree, and the other a principal in the second degree.

Allen, Serjt. The prosecutor, at all events, is bound to elect upon which count he will proceed.

POLLOCK, C.B. That is not so. I very well recollect that in *Regina* v. *Goode* there were many modes of death specified, and that it was also alleged that the deceased was killed by certain means to the jurors unknown. When there is no evidence applicable to a particular count, that count must be abandoned; but if there is evidence to support a count, it must be submitted to the jury. In this case the evidence goes to support all the counts.

Allen, Serjt., addressed the jury for the prisoners.

POLLOCK, C.B. (in summing up). The prisoners are charged with contributing to the death of the deceased, by their negligence and improper conduct. If they did so, it matters not whether he was deaf, or drunk, or negligent, or in part contributed to his own death; for in this consists a great distinction between civil and criminal proceedings. If two coaches run against each other, and the drivers of both are to blame, neither of them has any remedy against the other for damages. So, in order that one ship-owner may recover against another for any damage done, he must be free from blame: he cannot recover from the other if he has contributed to his own injury, however slight the contribution may be. But in the case of loss of life, the law takes a totally different view—the converse of the proposition is true. For there each party is responsible for any blame that may ensue, however large the share may be; and so highly does the law value human life, that it admits of no justification wherever life has been lost, and the carelessness or negligence of any one person has contributed to the death of another person. Generally, it may be laid down that, where one by his negligence has contributed to the death of another, he is responsible; therefore, you are to say, by your verdict, whether you are of opinion that the deceased came to his death in consequence of the negligence of one or both of the prisoners. A distinction has been taken between the prisoners : it is said that the one who went tirst is responsible, but that the second is not. If it is necessary that both should have run over the deceased, the case is not without evidence that both did so. But it appears to me that the law as stated by Mr Greaves is perfectly correct. Where two coaches, totally inde-pendent[1] of each other, are proceeding in the ordinary way along a road, one after the other, and the driver of the first is guilty of negligence, the driver of the second, who had not the same means of pulling up, may not be responsible. But when two persons are driving together, encouraging each other to drive at a dangerous pace, then, whether the injury is done by the one driving the first or the second carriage, I am of opinion that in point of law the other shares the guilt.

Verdict, Guilty.

[*Principals in first and second degree.*]

REX *v.* WILLIAM MASTIN AND JOHN MASTIN

GLOUCESTER ASSIZES. 1834.   6 CARRINGTON AND PAYNE 396.

The first count of the indictment charged that the prisoner, William Mastin, rode against the horse of John Secker, the deceased, whereby he was thrown to the ground and killed ; and it then went on to charge John Mastin as a principal in the second degree. There was also a count charging that the prisoners were racing on the highway, and that the horse of the deceased thereby became frightened, and threw him.

It appeared that, on the evening of the 14th of September, the prisoners, who were brothers, were on horseback, and were riding at a very rapid pace along a rather unfrequented highway, leading from Burford to Widford, and that the deceased was also on horseback. It further appeared that the deceased drew off as far from the middle of the road as the situation of the place would allow ; and that John Mastin passed by him without any accident, but that the horse of William Mastin and the horse of the deceased came into collision, when both were thrown, and the deceased killed.

---

[1] See the next case, *Rex* v. *Mastin.*

Justice, for the prisoner John Mastin. I submit that the evidence does not affect my client at all. Two persons were riding, and at a rapid rate, and one goes by and does no mischief; he certainly cannot be guilty of manslaughter, because another, who comes up a little afterwards, kills a person. The aiding which is charged in this indictment is the aiding in some act which caused the death of the deceased.

Curwood, for the prosecution. As both the prisoners were racing, the act of one is the act of both.

PATTESON, J. I think that if two are riding fast, and one of them goes by without doing any injury to any one, he is not answerable because the other, riding equally fast, rides against some one and kills him.

His Lordship directed the acquittal of John Mastin.

[*Principal or Accessory before the fact.*]

THE QUEEN *v.* MANLEY.

SOMERSET ASSIZES.   1844.   1 Cox 104

Indictment for larceny. The facts, as proved by the prosecution, were, that the prisoner was an apprentice of the prosecutor: that he had induced the son of the prosecutor, a child of the age of nine years, to take money from his father's till, and give to him. On cross-examination, it further appeared that the child had done the like for other boys.

Cox, for the prisoner, submitted that the evidence did not sustain the indictment. The prisoner was charged with stealing money as principal,—the evidence showed him to be either an accessory or a receiver. If an offence be committed through the medium of an *innocent* agent, the employer, though absent when the act was done, is answerable as a principal. (*Rex* v. *Giles*, 1 Moody, C. C. 166; *Reg.* v. *Michael*, 2 Moody, C. C. 120; 9 C. and P. 356.) But if the instrument be aware of the consequences of his act, *he* is the principal in the first degree; and the employer, if he be absent when the fact is committed, is an accessory before the fact. (*Rex* v. *Stewart*, R. and R. 363.) In this case, the evidence had shewn, beyond doubt, that the child was of the age of discretion, and fully aware of the consequences of his act.

WIGHTMAN, J. What do you mean by an innocent agent, if this child be not one?

Cox. An agent who, from age, defect of understanding, ignorance of the fact, or other cause, cannot be *particeps criminis.*

WIGHTMAN, J. But though an act done through the medium of an innocent agent makes the prisoner a principal, how do you shew that he is *not* a principal where the act is done through the medium of a responsible agent?

Cox. Because, if the agent be responsible, he becomes the principal; and to constitute a principal, he must be the actor or actual perpetrator of the fact, or cognizant of the crime, and near enough to render assistance. Though there be a previous concerted plan, those not present or near enough to aid at the time when the offence is committed are not principals, but accessories before the fact.

WIGHTMAN, J. (to the jury). Apart from the consideration of the guilt or innocence of the prisoner generally, if you believe the story told by the child, you will have to determine whether that child was an innocent agent in this transaction; that is, whether he knew that he was doing wrong, or was acting altogether unconsciously of guilt and entirely at the dictation of the prisoner; for if you should be of opinion that he was *not* an innocent agent, you cannot[1] find the prisoner guilty as a principal under this indictment.

Verdict, Not guilty.

[EDITOR'S NOTE. A confederate, by being present at the commission of the offence, ceases to be an accessory before the fact, and becomes a principal. See *Rex* v. *Brown*, 14 Cox 144.]

[*Principal or Accessory before the fact.*]

ANONYMOUS.

KING'S BENCH. 1633. KELYNG 52.

MEMORANDUM. That my brother Twisden shewed me a report which he had of a charge given by Justice Jones to the grand jury at

1 [EDITOR'S NOTE.] For 24 and 25 Vict. c. 94, s. 1 (see p. 82 *infra*) was not yet enacted.

the King's Bench bar in Michaelmas Term 9 Car. I. In which he said, that...if one drinks poison by the provocation or persuasion of another, and dieth of it, this is murder in the person that persuaded it. And he took this difference : If A. give poison to J. S. to give to J. D.; and J. S., knowing it to be poison, give it to J. D., who taketh it in the absence of J. S. and dieth of it, in this case J. S. who gave it to J. D. is a principal. And A. who gave the poison to J. S. and was absent when it was taken is but accessory before the fact. But if A. buyeth poison for J. S., and J. S. in the absence of A. taketh it, and dieth of it; in this case A. though he be absent, yet he is principal. So it is if A. giveth poison to B. to give unto C. ; and B., not knowing it to be poison but believing it to be a good medicine, giveth it to C., who dieth of it. In this case, A. who is absent is principal; or else a man should be murdered and there should be no principal. For B. who knew nothing of the poison, is in no fault, though he gave it to C. So if A. puts a sword into the hand of a madman, and bids him kill B. with it; and then A. goeth away, and the madman kills B. with the sword as A. commanded him, this is murder in A. though absent, and he is principal. For it is no crime in the madman who did the fact; by reason of his madness. And he said that this case was lately before himself and Baron Trevor at the Assizes at Hereford. A woman, after she had two daughters by her husband, eloped from him and lived with another man. And afterwards one of her daughters came to her; and she asked her " How doth your father ?" To which her daughter answered that he had a cold ; to which his wife replied, " Here is a good powder for him, give it him in his posset." And on this, the daughter carried home the powder, and told all this that her mother had said to her, to her other sister ; who in her absence gave the powder to her father in his posset, of which he died. And he said that, upon conference with all the judges, it was resolved that the wife was principal in the murder ; and also the man with whom she ran away, he being proved to be advising in the poison. But the two daughters were in no fault, they both being ignorant of the poison. And accordingly the man was hanged and the mother burnt.

[*Principal or Accessory. Innocent agent.*]

REX *v.* SAUNDERS AND ARCHER.

FOSTER'S CROWN LAW, 371.

Saunders with intention to destroy his wife, by the advice of one Archer, mixed poison in a roasted apple, and gave it to her to eat. She, having eaten a small part of it, gave the remainder to their child. Saunders at this dreadful moment made a faint attempt to have saved the child; but, conscious of the horrid purpose of his own heart, and unwilling to make his wife a witness of it, desisted; and stood by and saw the infant he dearly loved eat the poison, of which it soon after-wards died. It was ruled, without much difficulty, that Saunders was guilty of murder of the child. [Cf. *Reg.* v. *Salisbury*, p. 102 *infra.*] With regard to Archer, it was agreed by the judges upon conference that he was not accessory to this murder, it being an offence he neither advised nor assented to. The judges however did not think it advisable to deliver him in the ordinary course of justice by judgment of acquittal: but, for example's sake, they kept him in prison by frequent reprieves from session to session, till he had procured a pardon from the Crown; a measure prudence will often suggest in cases of a doubtful or delicate nature.

[*Principal or Accessory.*]

THE QUEEN *v.* JAMES.

CROWN CASE RESERVED.　　1890.　　　　L.R. 24 Q.B.D. 439.

Case stated by STEPHEN, J.

On November 27, 1889, Nathan James was convicted at Gloucester for stealing a post-letter, the property of the Postmaster-General, from Edward Hopkins James, an officer of the Post Office, under the following circumstances. Nathan James was a servant of Messrs Burlingham & Co., and it was his duty to take orders and receive money on their behalf. Edward Hopkins James said, "The prisoner said to me, 'Will you retain certain letters that are coming through the post from Messrs Burlingham; as they are accounts that have been paid in to me,

K.　　　　　　　　　　　　　　　　　　　　　　　　6

and I don't want people to have them after they have paid their account ?' I said I thought it was wrong; and he afterwards said to me if anyone was to suffer he would, not me." In consequence E. H. James gave Shaw a good many of the letters in question instead of delivering them to the persons to whom they were addressed. The learned Judge directed the jury that if they believed this evidence it proved that both Nathan James and E. H. James were guilty of theft. If this direction was right, the conviction was to be affirmed ; if wrong, it was to be quashed.

LORD COLERIDGE, C.J. I can entertain no doubt in this case. Either the prisoner was a joint thief with the postman from whom he obtained the letter, or he was an accessory before the fact, in which case, by 24 and 25 Vict. c. 94, s. 1, he was liable to be convicted in all respects as if he were a principal felon. In either case, therefore, he was rightly convicted.

POLLOCK, B., concurred.

HAWKINS, J. The prisoner was a thief, either as principal felon at common law, or as accessory before the fact by statute, 24 and 25 Vict. c. 94, s. 1. In either case he was guilty.

GRANTHAM and CHARLES, JJ., concurred.

Conviction affirmed.

[*Accessory after the fact.*]

REGINA *v.* CHAPPLE AND OTHERS.

CENTRAL CRIMINAL COURT. 1840. 9 CARRINGTON AND PAYNE 355.

The indictment charged Thomas Chapple and Charles King with breaking and entering the dwelling of John Porter, on the 7th of September, at St Giles's in the Fields, and stealing therein fourteen silver spoons and various articles, the property of the said John Porter. It also charged Charles Chapple, Eliza Plant, Ann King, Henry Cox, and Sophia Cox, with feloniously receiving, harbouring, comforting, assisting, and maintaining the said Thomas Chapple and Charles King, well knowing that they had committed the felony.

It appeared that the various prisoners who were charged with the offence of harbouring the felons, had been found in possession of various sums of money derived from the disposal of the property stolen; but it did not appear, although they were in frequent communication with the persons charged with the felony, that they had received any of the stolen property itself, or had done any act to assist the felons personally.

At the close of the case for the prosecution,

LAW, Recorder, intimated an opinion that the offence charged, so far as Charles Chapple and the others not indicted for the stealing were concerned, was not made out by the evidence, as there was no act shewn to have been done by them to assist the felons personally. He referred to a case in which it had been held that writing letters, to intimidate the witnesses and prevent them from coming forward to give evidence, was not a harbouring and assisting of the felon. He then went into the adjoining Court for the purpose of consulting on the subject with Mr Justice Littledale and Mr Baron Alderson; and on his return said, "I have mentioned the case to the learned Judges as shortly as I could, so as not to cause an interruption of the public business, and the answer was what I expected, viz. that in their opinion the proof amounts to evidence of an imperfect receiving, and not to the offence charged in the indictment."

> Verdict—Thomas Chapple and Charles King guilty of breaking and entering, &c., and the other prisoners not guilty.

SECTION IV

INCHOATE CRIMES.

[*Incitements.*]

THE KING v. HIGGINS.

KING'S BENCH. 1801. 2 EAST 5.

The defendant was indicted for a misdemeanor at the Quarter Sessions for the county of Lancaster, and was convicted on the second count of the indictment, charging, "That he on, &c. at, &c. did falsely, wickedly, and unlawfully solicit and incite one James Dixon, a servant of J. Phillips, &c. to take, embezzle, and steal a quantity of twist, of the value of three shillings, of the goods and chattels of his masters, J. P., &c. aforesaid, to the great damage of the said J. P., &c. to the evil example, &c., and against the peace," &c. After judgment of the pillory and two years' imprisonment, a writ of error was brought....

For the defendant it was urged that the count in question contained no charge of any matter indictable at common law. It is not every act immoral in itself, or of evil example, which is indictable, although it may subject the party to find sureties of the peace. A bare solicitation or incitement of another to commit an offence is not indictable, unless it be accompanied by some overt act towards carrying the intent into execution; if no such act be done either by the inciter or the party solicited, it is nothing more, as Mr Justice Foster observes, than a mere fruitless ineffectual temptation....

On the part of the Crown it was contended that every attempt to commit a crime, whether felony or misdemeanor, is itself a misdemeanor and indictable; a fortiori in the former case. And if an act be necessary, the incitement or solicitation is an act: it is an attempt to procure the commission of a felony by the agency of another person. By the incitement the party does all that is left for him to do to constitute the misdemeanor; for if the felony be actually committed, he is guilty of felony as accessory before the fact....

Lord Kenyon, C.J....It is argued, that a mere intent to commit evil is not indictable, without an act done; but is there not an act done, when it is charged that the defendant solicited another to commit a felony? The solicitation is an act; and the answer given at the bar is decisive, that it would be sufficient to constitute an overt act of high treason. The case of *The King* v. *Vaughan*[1] was not passed over slightly. It was there attempted to be maintained, that an attempt to bribe the Duke of Grafton, then a cabinet minister and a member of the privy council, to give the defendant a place in Jamaica, was not indictable. Lord Mansfield rejected the attempt with indignation. It was a solicitation to the duke to commit a great offence against his duty to the king and the public. So it is here: and it would be a slander upon the law to suppose that an offence of such magnitude is not indictable

Lawrence, J....All such acts or attempts as tend to the prejudice of the community, are indictable. Then the question is, whether an attempt to incite another to steal is not prejudicial to the community? Of this there can be no doubt. The whole argument for the defendant turns upon a fallacy in assuming that no act is charged to have been done by him; for a solicitation is an act. The offence does not rest in mere intention; for in soliciting Dixon to commit the felony, the

[1] 4 Burr. 2494.

defendant did an act towards carrying his intent into execution. It is an endeavour or attempt to commit a crime....

LE BLANC, J. It is contended that the offence charged in the second count, of which the defendant has been convicted, is no mis. demeanor; because it amounts only to a bare wish or desire of the mind to do an illegal act. If that were so, I agree that it would not be indictable. But this is a charge of an act done; namely, an actual solicitation of a servant to rob his master, and not merely a wish or desire that he should do so.

[*Attempts.*]

REGINA *v.* CHEESEMAN.

CROWN CASE RESERVED. 1862.   LEIGH AND CAVE 140.

The following case was reserved by BLACKBURN, J.

Edwin Cheeseman was tried before me at the last Maidstone Assizes. The indictment contained three counts.

The first charged the prisoner with fraudulently keeping a false weight, and selling thereby to the Queen 467 lbs. of meat as $512\frac{1}{4}$ lbs.

The second count stated that Alfred Cheeseman was accustomed to furnish the Queen with large quantities of meat for the supply of soldiers, and that the prisoner, being his servant, fraudulently kept a false weight, &c., as in the first count.

The third count was for an attempt to steal 45 lbs of meat of Alfred Cheeseman.

On the trial it was proved that Alfred Cheeseman was the contractor who supplied meat to the Camp at Shorncliff.

On the 27th of June, the prisoner, who was a servant of the contractor, came down in charge of the meat; and he and the Quarter-Master-Serjeant proceeded to weigh out the meat to the different messmen with the Quarter-Master-Serjeant's weights, the prisoner being the person who put the weights in the scale. Before the weighing was complete, one of the messmen brought back his mess portion, with a complaint that it was short weight. It was discovered that the 14-lb. weight belonging to the Quarter-Master-Serjeant had been removed, and concealed under a bench; and that a false 14-lb. weight had been substituted for it, and used in weighing out the thirty-four messes; and that the prisoner had absconded on the commencement of the investigation. The messes were all brought back and re-weighed, and it was found that the weight delivered was 467¼ lbs., instead of being 512¼ lbs., as on the first weighing it had appeared to be ; and, after the true weight was supplied to the different messes, the surplus remaining to be taken by the contractor's men was about 15 lbs., instead of being about 60 lbs., as it had appeared to be.

The counsel for the prisoner objected that there was no case to go to the jury, inasmuch as the circumstances stated did not amount to a cheat at common law ; and there was no overt act so proximately connected with an act of stealing as to justify a conviction under the third count.

The jury, in answer to questions from me, found that the prisoner fraudulently substituted the false 14-lb. weight for the true weight, with intent to cheat ; that his intention was to carry away and steal the difference between the just surplus of about 15 lbs., for which he would have to account to his master, and the apparent surplus meat actually remaining after the false weighing ; and that nothing remained to be done on his part, to complete his scheme, except to carry away and dispose of the meat, which he would have done, had the fraud not been detected.

I directed a verdict of Not Guilty on the first count, and Guilty on the second and third counts, and reserved for this Court the question, whether on these facts and findings the prisoner was properly convicted on either of those counts.

The prisoner was admitted to bail.

This case was argued, on the 18th of January, 1862, before ERLE, C.J., BLACKBURN, J., WILDE, B., and MELLOR, J.

Ribton, for the prisoner, contended that the second count disclosed no offence indictable at common law, and that there was no evidence to support it. With regard to the third count, the jury found that the prisoner intended to steal the difference between the just and the ficti-tious surplus. A verdict of Guilty of an attempt to steal was not warranted by that finding of the jury. To constitute an attempt, there must be some overt act proximately connected with the offence charged. Here there was no overt act. Nothing was done by the prisoner with reference to stealing the meat ; all that he did was to put a false weight in the scale, and that act was too remote. There is a marked difference between attempting to attain an object, and the mere doing an act with intent to attain that object. A man may do an act with an intent to commit some crime anywhere ; for example, a man may buy a rifle in America with intent to shoot a man in England ; but the buying the rifle could not be construed into an attempt to shoot the

man[1]. Again, if a notorious burglar is seen to put a picklock key into
a door, the jury may assume that he is attempting to break into the
house. But, if he were found purchasing a picklock key ten miles from
the house in question, it would be impossible, without other evidence,
to say that it was bought with intent to break into that house

ERLE, C.J. I am of opinion that the prisoner was properly convicted. It is not necessary to decide whether the prisoner could be
convicted on the second count, for there is abundant evidence to
support the third. The prisoner, having charge of the meat, went
through the form of delivering it, but kept back part of what he ought
to have delivered. Now, if he had actually moved away with any part
of the meat, the crime of larceny would have been complete. It is
said, however, that the evidence here does not show any such proximate
overt act as is sufficient to support the conviction for an attempt to
steal the meat. In my opinion, there were several overt acts, which
brought the attempt close to completion. These were, the preparation
of the false weight, the placing it in the scale, and the keeping back
the surplus meat. It is almost the same as if the prisoner had been
sent with two articles, and had delivered one of them as if it had been
two. To complete the crime of larceny there only needed one thing,
the beginning to move away with the property. The meat was in the
prisoner's custody and under his control. He had almost the manual
comprehension of it, and had all but begun the asportation.

BLACKBURN, J. I am of the same opinion. There is, no doubt,
a difference between the preparation antecedent to an offence, and the
actual attempt. But, if the actual transaction has commenced which
would have ended in the crime if not interrupted, there is clearly an
attempt to commit the crime. Then, applying that principle to this
case, it is clear that the transaction which would have ended in the
crime of larceny had commenced here.

Conviction affirmed.

---

[1] See *Reg.* v. *Eagleton* (Dearsly, at p. 525).

[*An attempt to do what is* impossible *may be indictable.*]

THE QUEEN v. RING AND OTHERS.

CROWN CASE RESERVED. 1892.   61 L.J.R. (M.C.) 116.

This was a case stated by the learned Deputy-Chairman of the London County Sessions, held at Clerkenwell; before whom the prisoners were indicted for an attempt to steal.

The material evidence, given by an employé of the Metropolitan Railway Co., was as follows: "I was at King's Cross Station, on duty on the platform, when I saw the three prisoners....The 12.50 train came in. They closed up together. Some females were entering a third-class compartment. I saw the three prisoners get behind these women. I saw Atkins trying to find one woman's dress-pocket; the other two prisoners were hustling her. The woman looked up at Atkins. They then separated and got into different compartments of the train. I got in the same train. I jumped out at Gower Street. I saw the three prisoners get out. There were a lot of females getting in, and these men all closed round them just as before. I saw Atkins again trying to find a woman's pocket; the woman looked up at him. They separated; and again got into different compartments of the same train....At Baker Street all got out and were arrested." There was no evidence that there was anything in the pockets of the unknown females; no one having been in communication with them. The case was left to the jury by the learned Deputy-Chairman, who, having doubts whether *The Queen* v. *Collins*[1] had been overruled by *The Queen* v. *Brown*[2], reserved the question for the opinion of the Court. The jury found all three prisoners guilty. The question for the opinion of the Court is whether the learned Deputy-Chairman was right in leaving the case to the jury.

LORD COLERIDGE, C.J. I am of opinion that the conviction should be affirmed. The case was stated by the Deputy-Chairman to ascertain whether *The Queen* v. *Collins*[1] is still law. That case is no longer law. It was overruled by *The Queen* v. *Brown*[2], which was decided by five judges; and the present case is decided by five judges, one of whom was one of the judges in *The Queen* v. *Brown*[2]. Therefore, nine judges are of opinion that *The Queen* v. *Collins*[1] is no longer law.

HAWKINS, J. I unhesitatingly say that I am entirely of the same opinion.

WILLS, J., LAWRANCE, J., and WRIGHT, J., concurred.

Conviction affirmed.

[1] L. and C. 471; 33 L. J. R. (M. C.) 177.
[2] 59 L. J. R. (M. C.) 47; L. R. 24 Q. B. D. 357.

PART II.

DEFINITIONS OF PARTICULAR CRIMES.

SECTION I.

SUICIDE.

REX *v.* DYSON.

CROWN CASE RESERVED. 1823. RUSSELL AND RYAN 523.

The prisoner was tried before Mr JUSTICE BEST, at the Old Bailey Sessions, for the murder of Eliza Anthony. He had cohabited with the deceased for several months previous to her death, and she was with child by him. They were in a state of extreme distress. Being unable to pay for their lodgings they quitted them in the evening of the night on which the deceased was drowned, and had no place of shelter.

They passed the evening together at the theatre. After the performance was over, they called at a house in Sherrard Street, and from thence went to Westminster Bridge, to drown themselves in the Thames. They got into a boat, and from that into another boat. The water where the first boat which they entered was moored was not of sufficient depth to drown them. They talked together for some time in the boat into which they had last got, he standing with his foot on the edge of the boat, and she leaning on him. The prisoner then found himself in the water, but whether by actual throwing of himself in or by accident did not appear. He struggled to get back into the boat again, and then found that Eliza Anthony was gone.

He then endeavoured to save her, but he could not get to her, and she was drowned.

In his statement before the magistrates (which was read in evidence) he said, that he intended to drown himself, but dissuaded Eliza Anthony from following his example.

The learned Judge told the jury, that if they believed that the prisoner only intended to drown himself, and not that the woman should die with him, they should acquit the prisoner; but, that if both went to the water for the purpose of drowning themselves together, each encouraged the other in the commission of a felonious act, and the survivor was guilty of murder.

He also told the jury, that although the indictment charged the prisoner with throwing the deceased into the water, yet if he was present at the time she threw herself in, and consented to her doing it, the act of throwing was to be considered as the act of both, and so the case was reached by the indictment.

The jury told the learned Judge that they were of opinion that both the prisoner and the deceased went to the water together for the purpose of drowning themselves: and the prisoner was convicted. But the learned Judge thought it right to submit a question to the consideration of the Judges, namely, whether his direction was right.

In Michaelmas Term, 1823, the case was considered by nine of the Judges. They were clear that if the deceased threw herself into the water by the encouragement of the prisoner, and because she thought he had set her the example in pursuance of their previous agreement, he was a principal in the second degree, and was guilty of murder. But as it was doubtful whether the deceased did not fall in by accident, it was not murder in either of them; and the prisoner was recommended for a pardon.

[See also the cases of THE COMMONWEALTH *v.* BOWEN, and THE COMMONWEALTH *v.* MINK, *infra*, p. 91 and p. 110.]

SECTION II.

MURDER AND MANSLAUGHTER.

CHAPTER I. THE EXTERNAL ACT.

[*The deceased must be under the King's Peace ; but even a condemned criminal is under it.*]

THE COMMONWEALTH *v.* BOWEN.

SUPREME COURT OF MASSACHUSETTS. 1816. 13 MASS. 356.

Indictment for murder of Jonathan Jewett.

The evidence was that Jewett had been convicted of the murder of his father, and sentenced to suffer death. Bowen was a prisoner in the same prison ; confined in an apartment adjacent to that in which Jewett was, and in such a situation that they could freely converse together. Bowen frequently advised and urged Jewett to destroy himself, and thus disappoint the Sheriff and the people who might assemble to see him executed. In the night preceding the day fixed for his execution, Jewett put an end to his life, by suspending himself by a cord from the grate of the cell in which he was imprisoned.

PARKER, C.J., in the course of charging the jury, said :—It may be thought singular and unjust that the life of a man should be forfeited, merely because he has been instrumental in procuring the death of a culprit a few hours before his death by the sentence of the law. But the community has an interest in the execution of criminals ; and to take such an one out of the reach of the law is no trivial offence. Further, there is no period of human life which is not precious as a season of repentance. And a culprit, though under sentence of death, is cheered by hope to the last moment of his existence. Hence you are not to consider the atrocity of this offence as in the least degree diminished by the consideration that justice was thirsting for a sacrifice, and that but a small portion of Jewett's earthly existence could in any event remain to him.

[The jury acquitted the prisoner ; from a doubt whether the advice given by him was in any measure the procuring cause of Jewett's death.]

[The killing may be by a protracted chain of causation.]

ANONYMOUS.

KING'S BENCH.   1328.   YEAR BOOK, 2 EDW. III., f. 18, Hil. pl. 1.

One Thomas was indicted in the county of W. for that he took one Nicholas, his father, who was sick; and, against his will and desire, carried him from one town to another; and the weather was cold; so that the cold and the carrying hastened his death. Thomas sued that the indictment might be caused to come before the King a fortnight after St Hillary. And because in the indictment nothing was said of felony, the Justices would not arraign him; but made him find good mainprise to have his body before the King a fortnight after Easter, and in the meantime they would direct the sheriff and coroners to certify them whether there was another indictment or no.

[A similar chain of causation.]

THE HARLOT'S CASE.

CHESTER ASSIZES.   1560.   CROMPTON'S JUSTICE, 24.

A harlot woman was delivered of a child. She laid it away, alive, in an orchard; and covered it with leaves. A kite struck at it with his claws. In consequence of being thus stricken, the child died very soon afterwards. She was arraigned of murder; and was executed....For she had intended the child's death[1]; and *voluntas reputatur pro facto.*

---

1 [EDITOR'S NOTE. See Blackstone IV. ch. 14; and Stephen's *Digest*, art. 244. Sir James Stephen's note treats the case as one of gross negligence rather than of that express intention which the Reporter's language suggests. For it is not clear whether she meant the leaves to act as a concealment or as a protection. In either case, the woman's crime would be murder in that age; when, as Sir James points out, birds of prey were far more common than now.]

[Prisoner's act not the immediate cause of death.]

REX *v.* HICKMAN.

OXFORD ASSIZES.   1831.   5 CARRINGTON AND PAYNE 151

Indictment for Manslaughter....The prisoner and the deceased, being both on horseback, had a quarrel. The prisoner struck the deceased with a small stick, and he rode away along the Holyhead road, the prisoner riding after him; and on the deceased spurring his horse, which was a young one, the horse winced and threw him....

Mr Justice PARK....In the case of *Rex* v. *Evans* (see Russell on *Crimes* 6th Edn. p. 12) it was held that if the death of the deceased, who was the wife of the prisoner, was partly occasioned by blows, and partly by a fall out of a window, (the wife jumping out at the window from a well-grounded apprehension of further violence that would have endangered her life), the prisoner was as much answerable for the consequences of the fall as if he had thrown her out at the window himself.

Verdict, Guilty.

[Deceased's own omission the immediate cause of death.]

REGINA *v.* HOLLAND.

LIVERPOOL ASSIZES.   1841.   2 MOODY AND ROB. 351.

Indictment for Murder.

Deceased had been waylaid and assaulted by the prisoner; and among other wounds was severely cut across one of his fingers by an iron instrument. His surgeon urged him to submit to the amputation of the finger, telling him that unless it were amputated his life would be in great hazard; but he refused to allow the amputation. The deceased attended the infirmary from day to day to have his wounds dressed. At the end of a fortnight, however, lockjaw came on; induced by the wound on the finger. The finger was then amputated, but too late; and the lockjaw ultimately caused death. The surgeon deposed that, if the finger had been amputated in the first instance, he thought it most probable that the life of the deceased would have been preserved.

For the prisoner it was contended that the cause of death was not the wound inflicted by the prisoner, but the obstinate refusal of the deceased to submit to proper surgical treatment by which the fatal result would have been prevented.

MAULE, J., however, was clearly of opinion that this was no defence. He told the jury that if the prisoner wilfully, and without any justifiable cause, inflicted on the deceased the wound which was ultimately the cause of death, he was guilty of murder. And that for this purpose it made no difference whether the wound was instantly mortal in its own nature, or became the cause of death only by reason of the deceased's not having adopted the best mode of treatment. The real question was, whether in the end the wound was the cause of death.

Verdict, Guilty.

[See also REG. *v.* MARKUSS, *infra.*]

[Deceased's own act the immediate cause of death.]

REGINA *v.* SAWYER.

CENTRAL CRIMINAL COURT. 1887. SESSIONS PAPERS CVI.

John Sawyer was indicted for, and charged on the Coroner's Inquisition with, the manslaughter of Annie Sawyer.

Ann Joyce stated that she lived next door to the prisoner and his wife. She heard Mrs Sawyer say, through the window, to the prisoner, who was in the street, "I will shut the door." He said, "We will see," and he walked upstairs. Within five minutes after, she heard a loud scream. Then she heard a thud, and the window shut; she looked out and saw a dark figure in the street, as it lay. The prisoner came out at the door and stooped over the figure, took hold of it by the arm and said, "You are mad! what made you do it?" [In cross-examination, witness said "I do not think prisoner knew I was there when he used these words; and no one else was there, that I could see."] Witness then said, "Poor Mrs Sawyer, how did it happen?" She replied, "I jumped through the window." The prisoner was by, at the time she said it.

Alfred Humphreys stated that he was outside the house at the time. He heard a slight rattle of glass, the shaking of the window frame, then a slight scream, and a woman's voice directly after. She

said "Oh, don't." Then a prolonged scream and a thud on the pavement. Just before hearing the thud he saw something light pa s before
his eyes....

Geoghegan submitted that this evidence did not establish a case
of manslaughter. So far as the evidence went, the deceased might
have jumped out at the window because she was afraid the prisoner
might strike her ; and not because of any actual violence on his part.

Griffiths contended that there were questions for the jury,—viz.
whether the prisoner had actually thrown the deceased out ; and, if
not, whether he had used such violence to her as to cause her to throw
herself out. In either case it would amount to at least manslaughter.

Mr Justice STEPHEN decided to leave the case to the jury. He
directed them to say, if, in their opinion, either by actual violence, or
threats[1] of violence, on the part of the prisoner, the deceased was forced,
as her only means of escape, to jump from the window. In that case
it would be manslaughter. But if she did the act, constrained by
despair operating upon her mind, that would not be sufficient, and they
should acquit him.

Verdict, Not guilty.

[*Death from nervous shock.*]

REGINA *v.* TOWERS.

CARLISLE ASSIZES. 1874. 12 Cox 530.

Wilson Towers was charged with the manslaughter of John
Hetherington, on Sept. 6th, 1873.

The prisoner, who had been drinking, went on August 4th into
a public-house kept by the mother of the deceased. He there saw
a girl called Fanny Glaister, nursing the deceased child ; who was then
only about four months and a half old. The prisoner, who appeared
to have had some grievance against Fanny Glaister (about her hitting
one of his children), immediately on entering the public-house went
straight up to where she was, took her by the hair of the head, and hit

---

1 [EDITOR'S NOTE.] Similarly in *Reg.* v. *Parker*, [A.D. 1863], C.C.C. Sess. Pap.
LIX. 393, where "grievous bodily harm " was caused to a woman by her own act in
jumping out of a window, it was held that "If she threw herself out in the
immediate apprehension of the prisoner's violence, it is *his* act, and he is liable.'

her. She screamed loudly. This so frightened the infant that it became black in the face; and ever since that day, up to its death, it had convulsions, and was ailing generally, from a shock to the nervous system. The child was previously a very healthy one.

DENMAN, J., said that it might be that manslaughter had been committed. The prisoner committed an assault on the girl, which is an unlawful act; and if that act, in their judgment, caused the death of the child (*i.e.* if the child would not have died but for that assault), they might find the prisoner guilty of manslaughter. This was one of the new cases to which they had to apply old principles. If he were to say, that murder could not be caused by such an act as this, he might be laying down a dangerous precedent for the future; for, to commit a murder, a man might do the very same thing this man had done. They could not commit murder upon a grown-up person by using language so strong, or so violent, as to cause that person to die; therefore, mere intimidation, causing a person to die from fright by working upon his fancy, was not[1] murder. But there were cases in which intimidations had been held to be murder. If, for instance, four or five persons were to stand round a man, and so threaten him and frighten him as to make him believe that his life was in danger, and he were to back away from them and tumble over a precipice to avoid them, then murder would have been committed. Then did, or did not, this principle of law apply to the case of a child of such tender years as the child in question? For the purposes of the case he would assume that it did not; for the purposes of to-day he should assume that the law about working upon people by fright did not apply to the case of a child of such tender years as this. Then arose the question, which would be for them to decide, whether this death was directly the result of the prisoner's unlawful act—whether they thought that the prisoner might be held to be the actual cause of the child's death—or whether they were left in doubt upon that upon all the circumstances of the case. After referring to the supposition that the convulsions were brought on owing to the child's teething, he said that, even though the teething might have had something to do with it, yet if the man's act brought on the convulsions, or brought them to a more dangerous extent, so that death would not have resulted otherwise, then it would be manslaughter. If, however, the jury thought that the act of the

---

[1] [EDITOR'S NOTE.] But see now *Rex* v. *Hayward* (21 Cox 693), where Ridley, J., ruled that "No actual physical violence is necessary; death from Fright alone, if caused by an illegal act (such as Threats of violence), will suffice."

prisoner in assaulting the girl was entirely unconnected with the death, that the death was not caused by it but by a combination of [other] circumstances, it would be accidental death and not man. slaughter.

[*But prisoner's act must not be too remote a cause.*]

REX *v.* MACDANIEL.

OLD BAILEY SESSIONS.　　1756.　　　　　　　　　LEACH 44.

At the Old Bailey January Session 1754, one Joshua Kidden was tried before Mr Justice Foster, for robbing Mary Jones, Widow, on the highway, of one guinea, a half-crown, and two shillings and six-pence. The prosecutrix swore very positively to the person of the prisoner, and to the circumstances of the robbery, in which she was confirmed by one Berry. Thus Kidden, on the evidence of these two witnesses, was convicted and executed; and on the 1st of March following, the reward of forty pounds, given by 4 and 5 Will. and Mary, c. 8, to those who shall convict a highway robber, was divided between the prosecutrix Mary Jones, John Berry, Stephen Macdaniel, and Thomas Cooper. The history of this prosecution lay concealed until August, when...it was discovered to have been a conspiracy to obtain the reward [1].

Diligent search was accordingly made to apprehend the miscreants concerned in this extraordinary transaction. At the Old Bailey in June Session 1756, Stephen Macdaniel, John Berry, and Mary Jones, were indicted before Mr Justice Foster (present Mr Baron Smythe) for the wilful murder of Joshua Kidden, in maliciously causing him to be unjustly apprehended, falsely accused, tried, convicted, and executed, well knowing him to be innocent of the fact laid to his charge, with an intent to share to themselves the reward, &c. The prisoners were convicted, upon the clearest and most satisfactory evidence, of the fact; and a scene of depravity was disclosed, as horrid as it was unexampled. The judgment, however, was respited; upon a doubt whether an indictment for murder would lie in this case. The special circumstances were accordingly entered upon the record,

---

[1] [EDITOR'S NOTE.] Macdaniel and his confederates had made altogether some £1700 by rewards for procuring the convictions of about seventy persons. Cf. p. 259 *infra.*

K.

together with an additional finding of the jury, "That Justice-Hall, in the Old Bailey, is situated within the County of the City of London; yet that felonies committed in the County of Middlesex have from time immemorial been accustomed to be tried there"; in order that the point of law might be more fully considered upon motion in arrest of judgment. But Sir Robert Henley, the Attorney-General, declined to argue it; and the prisoners were, at a subsequent session, discharged from that indictment.

Sir William Blackstone however says (IV. 196) that there were grounds to believe it was not given up from any apprehension that the point was not maintainable, but from other prudential reasons [1].

In May Session, 1759, they were again put to the bar, upon an indictment for conspiring to defeat the public justice of the kingdom, in causing Joshua Kidden to be executed for a robbery which they knew he was innocent of, with intent to get into their possession the reward offered by Act of Parliament; but no evidence appearing, they were all three acquitted.

[*Prisoner's act too remote.*]

REGINA *v.* BENNETT.

CROWN CASE RESERVED. 1858.   BELL 1.

The following case was reserved by WILLES, J.

William Bennett was convicted before me of manslaughter.

The substantial question is whether a person who makes fireworks, contrary to the 9 & 10 W. III. c. 7 [2], is indictable for manslaughter if death be caused by a fire breaking out amongst combustibles in his possession, collected by him, and in the course of use, for the purpose of his business, but not completely made into fireworks at the time.

The prisoner had a firework shop where he openly carried on the business of selling fireworks....

---

[1] He probably means a fear that witnesses in capital cases (then so numerous) would be rendered afraid to give evidence. Sir Michael Foster, however (Crown Law 130), thinks such crimes are not homicide; for, if they were, Titus Oates would have been tried for murder.

[2] Which, under a penalty of £5, forbade the manufacture of fireworks. It was repealed by 23 & 24 Vict. c. 139.

On Monday the 12th of July, about six in the evening, the prisoner being out of the house and not personally interfering, a fire broke out in the red and blue fire which communicated to the fireworks, causing a rocket to cross the street and set fire to a house at the opposite side, in which the deceased Sarah Williams was, consequently, burnt to death.

The fire was accidental in the sense of not being wilful or designed. It did not happen through any personal interference or negligence of the prisoner; and he is entitled to the benefit of any distinction between its happening through negligence of his servants or by pure accident without any such negligence.

It was contended that there was no case against the prisoner, inas. much as the cases of red &c. fire were only parts of fireworks and not within the statute; and that it did not appear that it was by reason of making fireworks the mischief happened; and that, at all events, the death of the deceased was not the direct and immediate result of any wrong or omission on the prisoner's part: and there was cited a case from the *Sessions Reports* at the Old Bailey, in which Mr Baron Alderson is reported to have held that an indictment for manslaughter was not maintainable under such circumstances.

I, however, overruled these objections, holding that the prisoner was guilty of a misdemeanor in doing an act with intent to do what was forbidden by the statute; and that, as the fire was occasioned by such misdemeanor, and without it would not have taken place, or could not have been of such a character as to cause the death of the deceased, which otherwise would not have taken place, a case was made out.

COCKBURN, C. J. It appears that the prisoner kept in his house a quantity of fireworks, but that circumstance alone did not cause the fire by which the death was occasioned; but, the fireworks and the combustibles kept by the defendant for the purpose of his business being in the house, the fire was caused by the negligence of the defendant's servants. Can it be contended that, under such circumstances, the defendant is criminally responsible?

Martin, for the Crown. The explosive nature of these substances kept by the defendant in such a place is to be considered; and, if the keeping of the fireworks was unlawful, the prisoner would be responsible for all the consequences of that unlawful act.

COCKBURN, C. J. The keeping of the fireworks in the house by the defendant caused the death only by the superaddition of the negligence of some one else. By the negligence of the defendant's servants the fireworks ignited, and the house in which the deceased

7—2

was set on fire and death ensued. The keeping of the fireworks may be a nuisance; and if, from the unlawful act of the defendant, death had ensued as a necessary and immediate consequence, the conviction might be upheld. The keeping of the fireworks, however, did not alone cause the death: *plus* that act of the defendant, there was the negligence of the defendant's servants.

WILLES, J. The fire which caused the death did not happen through any personal interference or negligence of the defendant. The keeping of the fireworks in the house was disconnected with the negligence of the defendant's servants which caused the fire.

COCKBURN, C. J. The view which we all take of the case is, that the prisoner cannot be convicted upon these facts.

CHAPTER II.   THE MENTAL STATE IN MURDER.

(A)   AN INTENT TO KILL.

See REGINA *v.* TYLER AND PRICE *supra,* p. 57.

[*Persons with same intent do different acts.*]

REG. *v.* MACKLIN AND OTHERS.

DURHAM ASSIZES.   1838.   2 LEWIN 225.

The prisoner was indicted for murder.

It appeared that a body of persons had assembled together, and were committing a riot. The constables interfering for the purpose of dispersing the crowd and apprehending the offenders, resistance was made to them by the mob; and one of the constables was beaten severely by the mob. The different prisoners all took part in the violence used against him; some by beating him with sticks, some by throwing stones, and others by striking him with their fists. Of this aggregate violence the constable afterwards died.

ALDERSON, B. The principles on which this case will turn are these. If a person attacks another without justifiable cause, and from the violence used death ensues, the question which arises is, whether it be murder or manslaughter? If the weapon used were a deadly weapon, it is reasonable to infer that the party intended death ; and if he intended death, and death was the consequence of his act, it is murder. If no weapon was used, then the question usually is, was there excessive violence? If the evidence as to this be such as that the jury think there was an intention to kill, it is murder; if not, manslaughter. Thus, if there were merely a blow with a fist, and death ensued, it would not be reasonable to infer that there was an intention to kill; in that case, therefore, it is manslaughter. But if a strong man attacks a weak one, though no weapon be used—or if after much injury by beating, the violence is still continued—then the question is, whether this excess does not shew a general brutality, and a purpose to kill, and if so, it is murder. Again, if the weapon used be not deadly, *e.g.*, a stick, then the same question as above will arise for the determination of the jury, as to the purpose to kill. And in any case, if the nature of the violence, and the continuance of it be such as that a rational man would conclude that death must follow from the acts done, then it is reasonable for a jury to infer that the party who did them intended killing ; and to find him guilty of murder.

Again, it is a principle of law, that if several persons act together in pursuance of a common intent, every act done in furtherance of such intent by each of them is, in law, done by all. The act, however, must be in pursuance of the common intent. Thus, if several were to intend and agree together to frighten a constable, and one were to shoot him through the head, such an act would affect the individual only by whom it was done. Here, therefore, in considering this case, you, the jury, must determine, whether all these prisoners had the common intent of attacking the constables. If so, each of them is responsible for all the acts of all the others done for that purpose. And, if all the acts done by each, would, *if done by one man*, together shew such violence, and so long continued, that from them you would infer an intention to kill the constable, it will be murder in them all. If you would not infer such a purpose, you ought to find the prisoners guilty only of manslaughter.

Verdict, Manslaughter.

[*Persons with different intents concur in the same act.*]

[*Intent to kill one man results in the killing of a different one.*]

REG. *v.* SALISBURY,

George Salisbury, John Vane Salisbury, Richard Salisbury, one called Pigot, and another called Knowsley, were arraigned upon an indictment of murder, for killing in the county of Denbigh one who was servant to Doctor Ellis. At the end of the evidence, the Inquest demanded of the Court this question, viz. if so be in truth that John Vane Salisbury was in the company of them who, of their malice prepense, killed him that is dead; and when he saw them combating together, took part with them suddenly but had not malice prepense, and struck with the others him that is dead;—whether this be Murder or Manslaughter in John Vane Salisbury.

The Court answered that if John Vane Salisbury had not malice prepense, but suddenly took part with them who had malice prepense, this is Manslaughter in him, and not Murder; because he had not malice prepense.

Quod nota bene, Lector. For I have heard this greatly doubted, viz. if the master lies in wait in the highway to kill a man, and his servants attend upon him, and the master does not make his servants privy to his intent; and afterwards he, for whom the master lies in wait, comes, and the master attacks him; and his servants, seeing their master fighting, take his part, and all of them kill the man, whether or no this should be murder in the servants, as it shall be in the master, because they, without malice prepense, took part with him that had malice prepense. But this is by the above Rule of the Court put out of doubt; viz. it shall only be manslaughter in the servants.

And note that THE COURT said thus to the jury: You, jurors, have heard the evidence which has been given to prove the prisoners guilty of the murder whereof they are impeached. Which evidence proves that the conspiracy was to kill Doctor Ellis; and the malice prepense was against him, and not particularly against his servant who is killed. And therefore perhaps you will imagine that the evidence does not maintain the indictment; because no malice was against the servant, whom the prisoners perhaps did not know, nor ever heard of him before. We think it proper to tell you what the law is in this point, to the intent that you may not err in it. And, Sirs, we take the law to be, that the killing of him is murder in the prisoners, if they killed him upon the malice which they had against the master. So that if you shall find that they had malice against the Doctor, that malice does in the eye of the law make the killing of him that was killed, who was the doctor's servant and in his company, to be Murder.

[Cf. *Rex* v. *Saunders,* p. 81 *supra.*]

(B) INTENT TO DO AN UNLAWFUL ACT THAT IS DANGEROUS.

REX *v.* HALLOWAY.

NEWGATE SESSIONS.   1628.   CROKE, CAR. 131.

Halloway was indicted for murdering one Payne. The indictment was :—That he *ex malitia sua praecogitata* tied the said Payne at a horse's tail, and struck him two strokes with a cudgel, being tied to the said horse; whereupon the horse ran away with him and drew him upon the ground three furlongs, and thereby brake his shoulder, whereof he instantly died; and so murdered him. Upon this indictment, he being arraigned, pleaded Not guilty. Thereupon a special verdict was found :—That the Earl of Denbigh was possessed of a park called Austerley Park, and that the said Halloway was woodward of his woods in the said park. That the said Payne, with others unknown, entered the said park to cut wood there; and that the said Payne climbed up a tree, and with an hatchet cut down some boughs thereof. That the said Halloway came riding into the park; and seeing the said Payne on the tree, commanded him to descend, and he descending from thence, the said Halloway stroke him two blows upon the back with his cudgel. And the said Payne having a rope tied about his middle, and one end of the rope hanging down, the said Halloway tied the end of that rope to his horse's tail; and struck the said Payne two blows upon his back. Whereupon the said Payne, being tied to the horse's tail, the horse, running away with him[1], drew him upon the ground three furlongs, and by this means brake his shoulder, whereof he instantly

---

[1] [EDITOR'S NOTE. From this report, and still more clearly from the report of the same case in 1 W. Jones, 198, it appears that the horse set off, from spontaneous alarm—probably being startled by the sound of blows—and was not ridden away by the parkkeeper. The case is therefore one of less malice—and consequently is more instructive—than if Halloway himself had, as Blackstone (IV. ch. 14) represents it, "dragged the boy along the park."]

died; and the said Halloway cast him over the pales into certain
bushes. And whether upon all this matter found, the said Halloway
be guilty of the murder *pro ut*, they pray the discretion of the Court.
And if the Court shall adjudge him guilty of the murder, they find him
guilty of the murder. If otherwise, they find him guilty of manslaughter. This special verdict by certiorari was removed into the
King's Bench and defended three terms.

And the opinion of all the judges and barons was demanded, and
they all (besides Hutton, who doubted thereof) held clearly that it was
murder. For when the boy, who was cutting on the tree, came down
from thence upon his command, and made no resistance, and he then
struck him two blows, and tied him to the horse's tail, and then struck
him again, whereupon the horse ran away, and he by that means was
slain; the Law implies malice. And it shall be said in Law to be
prepensed malice; he doing it to one who made no resistance. And so
this term all the justices delivered the reason of their opinions; whereupon judgment was given, and he was adjudged to be hanged, and was
hanged accordingly.

REG. *v.* ERRINGTON AND OTHERS.

Newcastle Assizes.   1838.   2 Lewin 217.

The prisoners were charged with the murder of William Lee. It
appeared that the deceased, being in liquor, had gone at night into
a glass-house, and laid himself down upon a chest: and that while he
was there asleep the prisoners covered and surrounded him with straw,
and threw a shovel of hot cinders upon his belly; the consequence of
which was that the straw ignited, and he was burnt to death. There
was no evidence in the case of *express* malice; but the conduct of the
prisoners indicated an entire recklessness of consequences, hardly consistent with anything short of design.

Patteson, J., pointed the attention of the jury to the distinctions
which characterise murder and manslaughter. He then adverted to
the fact of there being no evidence of express malice; but told them
that if they believed the prisoners really intended to do any serious
injury to the deceased, although not to kill him, it was murder; whilst

if they believed their intention to have been only to frighten him in sport, it was manslaughter.

The jury took a merciful view of the case, and returned a verdict of manslaughter only.

(C.) UNLAWFUL AND DANGEROUS EXCESS IN LAWFUL ACT OF FORCE.

REX *v.* GREY.

NEWGATE SESSIONS. 1666.   KELYNG 64.

John Grey being indicted for the murder of William Golden, the jury found a special verdict to this effect:—"We find that John Grey, the prisoner, was a blacksmith, and that William Golden, the person killed, was his servant. Grey commanded him to mend certain stamps, being part belonging to his trade; which he neglected to do. The said Grey, his master, after coming in, asked the said Golden why he had not done it; and then the said Grey told the said Golden, that if he would not serve him he should serve in Bridewell. To which the said Golden replied, that he had as good serve in Bridewell as serve the said Grey, his master. Whereupon the said Grey, without any other provocation, struck the said Golden with a bar of iron, which the said Grey then had in his hand, and upon which he and Golden were working at the anvil. And with the said blow he broke his skull, of which he died. And if this be Murder," etc.

This case was found specially by my brother Wylde. I shewed the special verdict to all my brethren, judges of the King's Bench, and to my Lord Bridgman, Chief Justice of the Common Pleas. And we were all of opinion that this was Murder. For if a father, master, or schoolmaster will correct his child, servant or scholar, they must do it with such things as are fit for correction, and not with such instruments as may probably kill them. For otherwise, under pretence of correction, a parent might kill his child, or a master his servant, or a schoolmaster his scholar. And a bar of iron is no instrument for correction. It is all one as if he had run him through with a sword. And my brother Morton said he remembered a case at Oxford Assizes, before Justice Jones, then Judge of Assize, where a smith being chiding with his servant, upon some cross answer given by his servant, he, having a piece of hot iron in his hand, ran it into his servant's belly; and it was judged Murder, and the party executed[1].

And my Lord Bridgman said that in his circuit there was a woman indicted for murdering her child, and it appeared upon the evidence that she kicked her and stamped upon her belly, and he judged it Murder. And my brother Twisden said he ruled such a case formerly in Gloucester circuit; for a piece of iron or a sword, or a great cudgel, with which a man probably may be slain, are not instruments of correction. And therefore when a master strikes his servant willingly with such things as those are, if death ensue, the law shall judge it Malice prepense.

(D) INTENT TO COMMIT A FELONY.

REGINA v. SERNÉ AND GOLDFINCH.

CENTRAL CRIMINAL COURT.　1887.　　　　　16 Cox 311.

The prisoners Leon Serné and John Henry Goldfinch were indicted for the murder of a boy, Sjaak Serné, the son of the prisoner Leon Serné; it being alleged that they wilfully set on fire a house and shop, No. 274, Strand, London, by which act the death of the boy had been caused.

It appeared that the prisoner Serné with his wife, two daughters and two sons, were living at the house in question; and that Serné, at the time he was living there, in Midsummer, 1887, was in a state of pecuniary embarrassment, and had put into the premises furniture and other goods of but very little value, which at the time of the fire were not of greater value than £30. It also appeared that previously to the fire the prisoner Serné had insured the life of the boy Sjaak Serné, who was imbecile; and on the 1st day of September, 1887, had insured his stock at 274, Strand, for £500, his furniture for £100, and his rent for another £100; and that on the 17th of the same month the premises were burnt down.

---

[1] Vide Dalton, 278, a case cited to be before Justice Walmsley, 43 Eliz., at Stafford Assizes; where on words 'twixt husband and wife, he suddenly struck her with a pestle and killed her; and it was adjudged Murder. Yet a husband by law may correct; but the pestle is not an instrument to correct withal.

Evidence was given on behalf of the prosecution that fires were seen breaking out in several parts of the premises at the same time, soon after the prisoners had been seen in the shop together; two fires being in the lower part of the house; and two above, on the floor whence escape could be made on to the roof of the adjoining house, and in which part were the prisoners and the wife and two daughters of Serné, who escaped. That on the premises were a quantity of tissue transparencies for advertising purposes, which were of a most inflammable character; and that on the site of one of the fires was found a great quantity of these transparencies close to other inflammable materials. That the prisoner Serné, his wife and daughters, were rescued from the roof of the adjoining house, the other prisoner being rescued from a window in the front of the house; but that the boys were burnt to death.

STEPHEN, J. The definition of murder is unlawful homicide with malice aforethought; and the words malice aforethought are technical. You must not, therefore, construe them, or suppose that they can be construed, by ordinary rules of language. The words have to be construed according to a long series of decided cases, which have given them meanings different from those which might be supposed. One of those meanings is, the killing of another person by an act done with an intent to commit a felony. Another meaning is, an act done with the knowledge that the act will probably cause the death of some person. Now it is such an act as the last which is alleged to have been done in this case; and if you think that either or both of these men in the dock killed this boy, either by an act done with intent to commit a felony (that is to say, the setting of the house on fire in order to cheat the insurance company), or by conduct which, to their knowledge, was likely to cause death, and was therefore eminently dangerous in itself— in either of these cases the prisoners are guilty of wilful murder in the plain meaning of the word. I will say a word or two upon one part of this definition, because it is capable of being applied very harshly in certain cases, and also because (though I take the law as I find it) I very much doubt whether the definition which I have given, although it is the common definition, is not somewhat too wide. Now when it is said that murder means killing a man by an act done in the commission of a felony, the mere words are sufficient to cover a case where a man merely gives another a push with an intention of stealing his watch, and the person so pushed, having a weak heart or some other internal disorder, dies. To take another very old illustration; it was said that if a man shot at a fowl with intent to steal it, and accidentally killed a man, he was to be accounted guilty of murder.

because the act was done in the commission of a felony. I very much doubt, however, whether that is really the law, or whether the Court for the Consideration of Crown Cases Reserved would hold it to be so. The present case, however, is not such as I have cited, nor anything like them. In my opinion the definition of the law which makes it murder to kill by an act done in the commission of a felony might and ought to be narrowed; whilst that part of the law under which the Crown in this case claim to have proved a case of murder is maintained. I think that, instead of saying that any act done with intent to commit a felony and which causes death amounts to murder, it would be reasonable to say that any act known to be dangerous to life and likely in itself to cause death, done for the purpose of committing a felony, which caused death, should be murder. As an illustration of this, suppose that a man, intending to commit a rape upon a woman, but without the least wish to kill her, squeezed her by the throat to overpower her, and in so doing killed her, that would be murder. I think that everyone would say in a case like that, that when a person began doing wicked acts for his own base purposes, he risked his own life as well as that of others. That kind of crime does not differ in any serious degree from one committed by using a deadly weapon, such as a bludgeon, a pistol, or a knife. If a man once begins attacking the human body in such a way, he must take the consequences if he goes further than he intended when he began. That I take to be the true meaning of the law on the subject. In the present case, gentlemen, you have a man sleeping in a house with his wife, his two daughters, his two sons, and a servant, and you are asked to believe that this man, with all these people under his protection, deliberately set fire to the house in three or four different places, and thereby burnt two of them to death. It is alleged that he arranged matters in such a way that any person of the most common intelligence must have known perfectly well that he was placing all those people in deadly risk. It appears to me that if that were really done, it matters very little indeed whether the prisoners hoped the people would escape or whether they did not. If a person chose, for some wicked purpose of his own, to sink a boat at sea, and thereby caused the deaths of the occupants, it matters nothing whether at the time of committing the act he hoped that the people would be picked up by a passing vessel. He is as much guilty of murder, if the people are drowned, as if he had flung every person into the water with his own hand. Therefore, gentlemen, if Serné and Goldfinch set fire to this house when the family were in it, and if the boys were by that act stifled or burnt to death, then the prisoners are as much guilty of murder as if they had stabbed the

children.   I will also add, for my own part, that I think in so saying
the law of England lays down a rule of broad, plain, common sense.
Treat a murderer how you will, award him what punishment you
choose, it is your duty, gentlemen, if you think him really guilty of
murder, to say so.   That is the law of the land, and I have no doubt
in my mind with regard to it.   There was a case tried in this Court
which you will no doubt remember, and which will illustrate my
meaning.   It was the Clerkenwell explosion case in 1868, when a man
named Barrett was charged with causing the death of several persons
by an explosion which was intended to release one or two men from
custody.   And I am sure that no one can say truly that Barrett was
not justly hanged.

Verdict, Not Guilty

REGINA *v.* HORSEY.

KENT ASSIZES.   1862.   3 FOSTER AND FINLASON 287.

Indictment for murder of a person unknown.

The prisoner had wilfully set fire to a stack of straw in an enclosure in which also was an outhouse or barn, but not adjoining to
any dwelling-house.   While the fire was burning, the deceased was
seen in the flames, and heard to shriek, and his body was afterwards
found in the enclosure.   It did not very clearly appear whether
he had been in the outhouse or merely lying on (or by the side of)
the stack.   There was no evidence who he was...or how or when he
came there; nor any evidence that the prisoner had any idea that
any one was, or was likely to be, there.   On the contrary...when he
saw and heard the deceased he wanted to save him.   It did not
exactly appear how long after the fire had been kindled before it was
discovered; but very soon after it was discovered the deceased was
seen in the flames.

BRAMWELL, B., told the jury that the law, as laid down, is that
where a prisoner in the course of committing a felony, causes the
death of a human being, that is murder, even though he did not
intend it.   And although that may appear unreasonable, yet as it is
laid down as law, it is our duty to act upon it.   The law, however, is
that a man is not answerable except for the natural and probable
result of his own act; and therefore, if you should not be satisfied that

the deceased was in the enclosure *at the time* when the prisoner set fire
to the stack, but came in afterwards, then—as his own act intervened
between the death and the act of the prisoner—his death could not
be the natural result of the prisoner's act[1]. And in that view he ought
to be acquitted.

COMMONWEALTH *v.* LUCY ANN MINK.

SUPREME COURT OF MASSACHUSETTS. 1877.   9 LATHROP 422.

Indictment for the murder of Charles Ricker.

It was proved that Ricker came to his death by a shot from a
pistol in the hand of the defendant. The evidence for the defence
shewed that the defendant had been engaged to be married to Ricker.
An interview took place between them in the course of which he
expressed his intention to break off the engagement. She thereupon
went to a trunk, and took from it a pistol, with the intention of taking
her own life. Ricker then seized her, to prevent her from accomplishing
that purpose. A struggle ensued between them; and in this struggle
the pistol was accidentally discharged, and the fatal wound was thus
inflicted upon him. The jury returned a verdict of Guilty of Manslaughter. The defendant appealed.

GRAY, C.J. Suicide being criminal, any attempt to commit it is
likewise criminal. Hence every one has the same right and duty to
interpose to save a life from being taken thus criminally, that he
would have to defeat an attempt to unlawfully take the life of a third
person. Y.B. 22 Edw. IV. 45, pl. 10; *Marler* v. *Ayliffe,* Cro. Jac. 134.
And any person who in doing, or attempting to do, an act which is
criminal, kills another, is guilty of criminal homicide; and, at the least,
of manslaughter. The only doubt we entertain in this case is whether
the act of the defendant in attempting to kill herself was not so
malicious as to make the killing of Ricker a murder.

[See also REG. *v.* FAULKNER, *infra.*]

---

[1] [EDITOR'S NOTE. Similarly in cases of manslaughter by the omission to fulfil
a duty, the death must be the "immediate" result of that omission. *Reg.* v. *Pocock,*
(1851) 17 Q. B. 34.]

CHAPTER III. THE MENTAL STATE: IN MANSLAUGHTER.

(A.) INTENT TO KILL OR DO GRIEVOUS HARM BUT ON
SUDDEN PROVOCATION.

[A detected Adulterer.]

REX *v.* MADDY.

KING'S BENCH. 1672.   1 VENTRIS 158.

John Maddy was indicted, for that he of malice aforethought feloniously murdered Francis Mavers; upon which he was arraigned at the Assizes in Southwark, and pleaded Not Guilty. The jury found a special verdict, by the direction of Justice Twisden, then Judge of Assize there, which was to this effect:—That Maddy coming into his house, found Mavers in the act of adultery with his the said Maddy's wife, and he immediately took up a stool and struck Mavers on the head, so that he instantly died. They found that Maddy had no precedent malice towards him, and so left it to the judgment of the Court whether this were Murder or Manslaughter.

The Record was this Term removed into the King's Bench by certiorari, and Maddy brought by Habeas Corpus. And the Court were all of opinion that it was but Manslaughter, the provocation being exceeding great, and found that there was no precedent malice. It was taken to be a much stronger case than Royley's case[1] (Cro. Jac. 296): where, the son of Royley coming home with a bloody nose, and telling his father that such an one beat him in such a field, the father immediately ran to that field (which was a mile off) and found him that had beat his son there, and killed him; all which was found upon a special verdict, and resolved to be but Manslaughter.

But TWISDEN said there was a case found before Justice Jones, which was the same with this, only it was found that the prisoner being informed of the adulterer's familiarity with his wife, said he would be revenged of him, and after finding him in the act, killed him; which was held by Jones to be murder. Which the Court said might be so, by reason of the former declaration of his intent; but no such thing is found in the present case.

---

[1] [EDITOR'S NOTE. Sir Michael Foster (295) points out that in Royley's case "the provocation was not very grievous, as the boy had fought with one who happened to be an overmatch for him, and was worsted—a disaster slight enough, and very frequent among boys." On collating the various reports, it appears that the reason for Royley's crime being only manslaughter was not the provocation, but the triviality of the attack he made—a single blow with a mere wand.]

Sir T. Raymond's report (p. 212) adds :—'And he had his clergy at the bar, and was burned in the hand; and the Court directed the executioner to burn him gently, because there could not be greater provocation than this.'

[*An unpremeditated quarrel.*]

THE KING *v.* BROWN.

KENT ASSIZES. 1776.   1 LEACH 148.

John Brown was tried and convicted, before Mr Justice Gould, for the wilful murder of John Moncaster.

It had been argued by the prisoner's counsel that the offence was only manslaughter, and the learned judge concurring in that opinion had so directed the jury. But they thought fit to find the prisoner guilty of murder, and persisted in their verdict. Sentence of death was accordingly passed upon him; but he was reprieved from execution until the evidence which had been given against him was submitted to the consideration of the twelve judges. On the first day of the ensuing Michaelmas Term the case was stated at Serjeants' Inn Hall to the following effect:

The Case. The prisoner was a common soldier in a regiment of foot commanded by Captain Peter Hunter; and was, at the time mentioned in the indictment, on a recruiting party at Sandgate. In this character he had behaved during the course of five years with great propriety as a soldier, and with good nature and humanity as a man. On the 26th of June, 1776, he went with several of his comrades into a public-house in Sandgate, kept by one Meggison, to drink. This was between one and two o'clock in the morning. A quarrel arose soon after between the soldiers and a number of keelmen who were in the house. They went out into the street, and a violent affray ensued, which occasioned a tumult of men, women, and children. Between two and three o'clock one of the soldiers was seen stripped, and a party of five or six came up, fell upon him, and beat him cruelly. A woman called out from a window, "You rogues! you will murder the man!" The prisoner, who had before, with his sword in the scabbard, driven a part of the mob down the street, returned; when, seeing his comrade thus used, he drew his sword, which he brandished in the air, and desiring the mob to stand clear, said, "There it is, I'll sweep the street." The mob pressed in upon them, and he struck at them with the flat side several times. The mob then fled, and he pursued one of them down the street. The soldier who was stripped got up, and ran into a passage to save himself. The prisoner returned, and asked if they had murdered his comrade. The people came back and assaulted him several times, and then ran from him. He sometimes brandished his sword, and then struck fire with the blade of it upon the stones of the street, calling out to the people to keep off. At this time the deceased, who had a blue jacket on, and might be mistaken for a keelman, was going along about five yards from the soldier; but, before he passed, the soldier went to him, and struck him on the head with his sword. The deceased ran some paces and fell down, rose again, ran a few paces further out of the prisoner's sight, fell down again, and immediately expired. The soldier said he had been badly used; and it was the opinion of two witnesses, that, "if he had not drawn his sword, they would both of them have been murdered."

The JUDGES were clearly of opinion that it was only manslaughter.

[An unpremeditated quarrel.]

REX *v.* AYES.

EXETER ASSIZES. 1810. RUSSELL AND RYAN 167.

The prisoner was tried before Mr Baron Graham, at the Exeter Lent Assizes, in the year 1810, on an indictment charging him, the said Pierre Ayes (who was a French prisoner), with the murder of Jean Berjeant (a fellow prisoner), in the Mill Prison, at Plymouth, on the 12th of March, 1810, by throwing him on the ground, and stamping on his breast, belly, and loins, thereby, &c.

It appeared that some French prisoners were gambling in an upper room of the prison, and one of them whilst at play, feeling a man take a tin tobacco box out of his pocket, turned quickly round, and seeing the box in the hand of Jean Berjeant, the deceased, took it from him, gave him two slaps of the face, and bid him get away. The deceased went down stairs. But a clamour had been raised against him, and on coming down he was followed by several others. As he passed by the side of the beer table, the prisoner arose from the table, went up to the deceased, and with both his hands pushed against his breast with great force, and the deceased fell on his back to the ground. The deceased arose and struck the prisoner two or three times with his double fist in the face, and one blow on the eye. Then the prisoner being, as the witness expressed it, very drunk, pushed the deceased in the same manner a second time on the ground, and gave him as he lay on his back two or three stamps with great force with his right foot on the stomach and belly; the deceased cried out, "Helas! Helas! let me alone."...

The deceased was a small man, the prisoner stout, but, as all the witnesses agreed, much in liquor. The deceased after this went to his bed, and...died early on the 16th of March. The hospital surgeon opened the body. He described the whole of the intestines as in a state of excessive inflammation, the effects of the bruises, and he had no doubt that the stamps, such as he had heard described, and of which he saw the effects on the body before the deceased died, were the cause of his death.

The learned Judge observed to the jury that there was little doubt but that the evidence proved that the prisoner had caused the death of the deceased. If what he did was the effect of a sudden transport of passion beyond the control of reason, he was guilty of manslaughter; if done with malice, he was guilty of murder. This was not done of "malice" in its ordinary sense (a premeditated design of killing the deceased, or endangering his life); but malice, or great enmity far beyond the provocation, might still be implied from the circumstances of the case. The prisoner was the aggressor, and though he was assaulted and beaten by the deceased, he had provoked the assault; but although he was the aggressor, if his resentment had been confined to the second blow, by which the deceased was thrown to the ground and the death of the deceased had been the consequence, there would have been fair room to say it was done in heat of blood. But when the deceased was thrown upon the ground, incapable of further resistance, it was difficult to ascribe to the mere effect of sudden resentment the stamping upon his body in the manner described. With regard to the prisoner's defence, he told the jury that the law did not allow of the plea of drunkenness as an extenuation of the offence charged.

The jury, composed one half of foreigners, found the prisoner guilty of murder, and the learned Judge pronounced sentence upon him. But, thinking that the case required further consideration, particularly as there appeared to be no interval of time between the second blow which threw the deceased to the ground and the stamping on his body, he respited the sentence to take the opinion of the Judges whether upon the evidence this case was a case of murder, or manslaughter only.

In Easter term, 1810, all the JUDGES assembled, and were of opinion that the conviction was wrong, being only manslaughter.

[*Quarrel premeditated by part of the combatants but not by others.*]

See REGINA v. SALISBURY, *supra* p. 102.

[*But a lawful blow is no adequate provocation.*]

REX v. BOURNE.

OLD BAILEY.   1831.   5 CARRINGTON AND PAYNE 120.

Indictment for stabbing and wounding James Lightfoot with intent to murder him.

The prosecutor stated that the prisoner and his brother, who was a boy about six years younger than himself, were fighting on board the barge *Alfred*, which was lying in the West India Docks, and in which he (the prosecutor) also worked; that he laid hold of the prisoner to prevent him from beating his brother, and held him down on a locker, but did not strike him; and that the prisoner stabbed him with a knife just above the knee.

The prisoner in his defence said, that the prosecutor had knocked him down.

Mr Justice J. PARK (in summing up). The prosecutor states that he was merely restraining the prisoner from beating his brother, which was quite proper on his part; and he says that he did not strike any blow. If you are of opinion that the prosecutor did nothing more than was necessary to prevent the prisoner from beating his brother, the crime of the prisoner, if death had ensued, would not have been reduced to manslaughter; but if you think that the prosecutor did more than was necessary to prevent the prisoner from beating his brother, or that he struck any blows, then I think that it would. You will, therefore, consider whether anything was done by the prosecutor more than was necessary, or whether he gave any blows before he was cut.

(B)   INTENT MERELY TO HURT.

[In hostility.]

REGINA *v.* WILD.

LIVERPOOL ASSIZES.   1837.   2 LEWIN 214.

The prisoner was indicted for manslaughter. It appeared that the deceased had entered the prisoner's house in his absence. The prisoner, on returning home, found him there, and desired him to withdraw, but he refused to go. Upon this words arose between them, and the prisoner becoming excited proceeded to use force, and by a kick which he gave to the deceased, caused an injury which produced his death.

ALDERSON, B. A kick is not a justifiable mode of turning a man out of your house, though he be a trespasser. If a person becomes excited, and being so excited, gives to another a kick, it is an unjustifiable act. If the deceased would not have died but for the injury he received, the prisoner having unlawfully caused that injury, he is guilty of manslaughter.

[In a practical joke.]

REX *v.* SULLIVAN.

CENTRAL CRIMINAL COURT.   1836.   7 CARRINGTON AND PAYNE 641.

The prisoner was indicted for the manslaughter of Hugh Wood.

The deceased was a carman, and was loading a cart with potatoes; there were six sacks; they were put in front, three on each side; he was in the front part of the cart. There were two more sacks to come in, and when the first of the two was put in, the cart tilted up, in consequence of the trap-stick having been taken out, and the deceased was thrown out on his back on the stones, and the potatoes were shot out of the sacks, and fell on and covered him over. There was blood on the back of his head; he was taken to the hospital, and died soon after, from a fracture of the skull and concussion of the brain. The only evidence to connect the prisoner with the matter was, that, after the death of the deceased, the prisoner said that there were several persons he thought accused of pulling the trap-stick out, and he was the person who actually did do it; but not with intent to do him any harm, as he had seen it done several times before by others.

The prisoner, under the direction of the learned Judges, GURNEY, B. and WILLIAMS, J., was found guilty, but recommended strongly to mercy; and was fined 1*s.* and discharged.

[*In a dangerous tort.*]

REX *v.* FENTON AND OTHERS.

DURHAM ASSIZES.   1830.   1 LEWIN 179.

Indictment for manslaughter. The indictment charged that there was a scaffolding in a certain coal-mine, and that the prisoners, by throwing large stones down the mine, broke the scaffolding; and that, in consequence of the scaffolding being so broken, a corf, in which the deceased was descending into the mine, struck against a beam on which the scaffolding had been supported; and by such striking the corf was overturned, and the deceased precipitated into the mine, whereby he lost his life. It was proved that scaffolding was usually found in mines in the neighbourhood, for the purpose of supporting the corves and enabling the workmen to get out and work the mines. Evidence was given that the stones were of a size and weight sufficient to knock away the scaffolding; and that, if the beam only was left, the probable consequence would be, that the corf striking against it would upset and occasion death or injury.

TINDAL, C.J. If death ensues as the consequence of a wrongful act, an act which the party who commits it can neither justify nor excuse, it is not accidental death, but manslaughter. If the wrongful act was done under circumstances which shew an attempt to *kill*, or do any serious injury in the particular case, or any general malice, the offence becomes that of murder. In the present instance the act was one of mere wantonness and sport, but still the act was wrongful, it was a trespass. The only question therefore is whether the death of the party is to be fairly and reasonably considered as a consequence of such wrongful act; if it followed from such wrongful act as an effect,

from a cause, the offence is manslaughter; if it is altogether unconnected with it, it is accidental death.

The prisoners were convicted and sentenced to three months'
imprisonment.

[*But not in a tort which was unlikely to hurt*[1].]

REGINA *v.* C. H. FRANKLIN.

SUSSEX ASSIZES.   1883.   15 Cox 163.

Charles Harris Franklin was indicted, before FIELD, J., at Lewes,
for the manslaughter of Craven Patrick Trenchard.

The facts were as follows: On the morning of the 25th day of
July, 1882, the deceased was bathing in the sea from the West Pier, at
Brighton, and swimming in the deep water around it. The prisoner
took up a good sized box from the refreshment stall on the pier and
wantonly threw it into the sea. Unfortunately the box struck the
deceased, C. P. Trenchard, who was at that moment swimming underneath, and so caused his death.

Gore, for the prosecution, urged that, apart from the question of
negligence, it would be sufficient to constitute the offence of manslaughter that the act done by the prisoner was an unlawful act; which
the facts clearly shewed it to be. He cited the case of *Rex v. Fenton*
(*supra*, p. 117).

FIELD, J. The case must go to the jury upon the broad ground of
negligence, and not upon the narrow ground proposed by the learned
counsel. For it seems to me—and I may say that in this view my
brother Mathew agrees—that the mere fact of a civil wrong committed
by one person against another ought not to be used as an incident
which is a necessary step in a criminal case. I have a great abhorrence
of constructive crime. We think the case cited by the counsel for the
prosecution is not binding upon us in the facts of this case; and,
therefore, that the civil wrong against the refreshment-stall keeper is
immaterial to this charge of manslaughter. I do not think that the
facts of this case bring it clearly within the principle laid down by
Tindal, C.J., in *Rex v. Fenton*. And if I thought this case was in

---

[1] [EDITOR'S NOTE. This limitation of the rule seems not to have been accepted
by the late Mr Justice Stephen. See his *Digest of Criminal Law* (5th ed.), Art. 231.]

principle like that case I would (if requested) state a case for the opinion of the Court of Criminal Appeal.

Gill, for the prisoner, relied upon the point that there was not proved such negligence on the part of the prisoner as was criminal negligence.

FIELD, J., in summing up the case to the jury, went carefully through the evidence, pointing out how the facts, as admitted and proved, affected the prisoner upon the legal question as he had explained it to them.

The jury returned a verdict of guilty of manslaughter.

The prisoner was sentenced to two months' imprisonment.

[*Participation in unlawful act.*]

REGINA *v.* CATON.

STAFFORD SUMMER ASSIZES.   1874.   12 Cox 624.

Prisoner was indicted for the manslaughter of Henry Parker.

The deceased, a brewer's carter, was removing empty casks from a cellar of a beerhouse adjoining a public street. He rolled up a cask to his fellow carter above. It accidentally struck against the leg of one Allen, who was passing along the street. Thereupon Allen began to quarrel with the deceased, although the latter assured him that he had not intended to hurt him ; and soon Allen called the prisoner, who came out of a neighbouring house. Both went down into the cellar ; and beat the deceased with their fists. The other carter went down to his comrade's help. An affray ensued ; in the course of which the deceased received the fatal blow, struck with a heavy piece of timber which was in the cellar. The evidence was conflicting as to whether this blow was given by the prisoner or by Allen. The latter was tried before CLEASBY, B., at the last Spring Assizes, and convicted of the manslaughter.

At Caton's trial, on the close of the case for the prosecution,

LUSH, J., said that the only question for the jury was whether the prisoner struck the fatal blow. If two men concerted together to fight two other men with their fists, and one struck an unlucky blow causing death, both would be guilty of manslaughter. But if one used a knife, or other deadly weapon (such as this piece of timber), without the knowledge or consent of the other, he only who struck with the weapon would be responsible for the death resulting from the blow given by it.

McMahon. Allen called on Caton to do an unlawful act, viz., to assault Parker; and, after that call, a blow was given in furtherance of the common design. At the trial of Allen, who has been convicted, Cleasby, B., ruled that Allen, having invited Caton down into the cellar to beat Parker, was liable for whatever was done hereafter.

LUSH, J. That might be so. But the converse—viz., that Caton would be responsible for all that Allen did—is not a true proposition.

His Lordship, in summing up, told the jury that Caton was only answerable for his own acts, and not if the other man struck the fatal blow.

Verdict, Not guilty.

[Cf. REGINA *v.* SALISBURY, *supra*, p. 102.]

(C) MERE NEGLIGENCE.

[There must be not merely some negligence, but a high degree of it.]

REGINA *v.* FINNEY.

SHREWSBURY ASSIZES.   1874.   12 Cox 625.

Prisoner was indicted for the manslaughter of Thomas Watkins.

The prisoner was an attendant at a lunatic asylum. Being in charge of a lunatic, who was bathing, he turned on hot water into the bath, and thereby scalded him to death. The facts appeared to be truly set forth in the statement of the prisoner made before the committing magistrate, as follows: "I had bathed Watkins, and had loosed the bath out. I intended putting in a clean bath, and asked Watkins if he would get out. At this time my attention was drawn to the next bath by the new attendant, who was asking me a question; and my attention was taken from the bath where Watkins was. I put my hand down to turn water on in the bath where Thomas Watkins was. I did not intend to turn the hot water, and I made a mistake in the tap. I did not know what I had done until I heard

Thomas Watkins shout out; and I did not find my mistake out till I saw
the steam from the water. You cannot get water in this bath when
they are drawing water at the other bath; but at other times it
shoots out like a water gun when the other baths are not in use."...

[It was proved that the lunatic had such possession of his faculties
as would enable him to understand what was said to him, and to get
out of the bath.]

A. Young (for prisoner). The death resulted from accident. There
was no such culpable negligence on the part of the prisoner as will
support this indictment. A culpable mistake, or some degree of
culpable negligence, causing death, will not support a charge of manslaughter; unless the negligence be so gross as to be reckless. (*R.* v.
Noakes[1].)

LUSH, J. To render a person liable for neglect of duty there must
be such a degree of culpability as to amount to *gross* negligence on his
part. If you accept the prisoner's own statement, you find no such
amount of negligence as would come with this definition. It is not
every little trip or mistake that will make a man so liable. It was the
duty of the attendant not to let hot water into the bath while the
patient was therein. According to the prisoner's own account, he did
not believe that he was letting the hot water in while the deceased
remained there. The lunatic was, we have heard, a man capable
of getting out by himself and of understanding what was said to him.
He was told to get out. A new attendant who had come on this day,
was at an adjoining bath and he took off the prisoner's attention.
Now, if the prisoner, knowing that the man was in the bath, had turned
on the tap, and turned on the hot instead of the cold water, I should
have said there was gross negligence; for he ought to have looked to
see. But from his own account he had told the deceased to get out
and thought he had got out. If you think that indicates gross carelessness, then you should find the prisoner guilty of manslaughter.
But if you think it inadvertence not amounting to culpability—i.e.
what is properly termed an accident—then the prisoner is not liable.

Verdict, Not guilty.

---

[1] 4 F. and F. 920. [EDITOR'S NOTE. In *R.* v. *Noakes* the distinction between
the negligence which is sufficient ground for a civil action and the higher degree
which is necessary in criminal proceedings, is sharply insisted on. See similarly
per Stephen, J., in *Regina* v. *Doherty* (16 Cox, at p. 300); and *per* Willes, J., in
Hammack v. *White* (31 L.J.R., C.P., 131), and in *Regina* v. *Markuss, infra*, p. 124.]

[If such a degree of negligence might reasonably be inferred from the evidence, it is for the jury to decide whether or not to infer it.]

REX *v.* RIGMAIDON.

LANCASTER ASSIZES.   1833.   1 LEWIN 180

Prisoner, a wine merchant at Liverpool, was indicted for manslaughter, in having, by negligence in the manner of slinging a cask or puncheon, caused the same to fall, and to kill two females who were passing along the causeway.   It appeared in evidence that there were three modes of slinging casks customary in Liverpool : one by slings passed round each end of the cask; a second, by can-hooks; and a third, in the manner in which the prisoner had slung the cask which caused the accident, viz. by a single rope round the centre of the cask. The cask was hoisted up to the fourth story of a warehouse, and on being pulled end-ways towards the door, it slipped from the rope as soon as it touched the floor of the room.

PARK, J., to the jury.   The double slings were undoubtedly the safest mode.   But if you think the mode which the prisoner adopted, viz. that of a single rope, was reasonably sufficient, you cannot convict him.

Prisoner was convicted; and sentenced to a month's imprisonment.

ACTS OF NEGLIGENCE BY COMMISSION.

[Firearms.]

REX *v.* BURTON.

OLD BAILEY.   1721.   1 STRANGE 481.

The defendant came to town in a chaise; and before he got out of it, he fired off his pistols, which by accident killed a woman.

KING, C.J., ruled it to be but manslaughter.

[*Firearms.*]

THE STATE *v.* HARDIE.

SUPREME COURT OF IOWA.   1878.   10 RUNNELLS 617.

Indictment for manslaughter of Sarah Sutfen. The evidence shewed
that the deceased, whilst calling at the house of a Mr Gantz, where the
prisoner boarded, went into the yard to get a kitten. The defendant
said he would frighten her with a revolver as she came back. The
report of a revolver was soon afterwards heard, and the defendant
immediately thereupon came to Mrs Gantz and said, "My God! Come
Hannah, see what I have done." Mrs Sutfen was found in a dying
condition, with a gunshot wound in her head. It was proved that the
revolver had been found in the street, five years previously, with one
chamber loaded. Mr Gantz had tried to fire this charge, and afterwards
to hammer it out; but in vain. It had ever since been left about the
house in the same condition; and was regarded by all the family as
quite harmless.

The defendant was convicted of manslaughter. Against this he
appealed; contending that there was no evidence of such carelessness as
to render the act criminal, but that it was a homicide by misadventure.

ROTHROCK, C.J. That the revolver was in fact a deadly weapon is
conclusively shewn by the tragedy which occurred. Had it been unloaded, though no homicide would have resulted, yet the defendant
would have been justly censurable for a most reckless act in frightening
a woman by pretending that he was about to discharge it at her.
Human life is not to be sported with by the employment of firearms,
even though the person using them may have good reason to believe
that the weapon,....though loaded, will do no harm. When persons
indulge in such reckless sport, they should be held liable for the consequences of their acts.

                                           Conviction affirmed.

[See the ANONYMOUS case, *supra*, p. 27.]

[*Improper medical treatment; whether by inattention or by ignorance.*]

REGINA *v.* MARKUSS.

DURHAM ASSIZES.   1864.   4 FOSTER AND FINLASON 356.

Joseph Levy Markuss was indicted for the manslaughter of Jane Sumby.

The prisoner kept a shop in Sunderland, where he passed as a herb doctor....The deceased woman was shewn to have died from inflammation of the stomach, which the medical men who attended her attributed to an overdose of colchicum seeds, which she had taken by direction of the prisoner....Eighteen grains would be fatal, and the overdose administered contained eighty grains.

WILLES, J., said that every person who dealt with the health of others was dealing with their lives; and every person who so dealt was bound to use reasonable care, and not to be grossly negligent. Gross negligence might be of two kinds. In one, a man, for instance, went hunting and neglected his patient, who died in consequence. Another sort of gross negligence consisted in rashness; as where a person was not sufficiently skilled in dealing with dangerous medicines which should be carefully used, and was ignorant of their properties or of how to administer a proper dose. A person who with ignorant rashness, and without skill in his profession, used such a dangerous medicine, acted with gross negligence. It was not, however, every slip that a man might make that would render him liable to a criminal investigation. It must be a substantial thing. If a man knew that he was using medicines beyond his knowledge, and was meddling with things above his reach, that was culpable rashness. Negligence might consist in using medicines in the use of which care was required, and of the properties of which the person using them was ignorant. A person who so took a leap in the dark in the administration of medicines was guilty of gross negligence. If a man were wounded, and another applied to his wound sulphuric acid, or something else which was of a dangerous character and ought not to be applied, and which led to fatal results, then the person who applied this remedy would be answerable; and not the person who inflicted the wound, because a new cause had supervened. But if the person who dressed the wound applied a proper remedy, then if a fatal result ensued he who inflicted the wound remained liable. He left it to the jury to say whether on the evidence the deceased had died from natural causes, or from the supervening cause of the medicine prescribed for her by the prisoner, he being an irregular and apparently unskilled practitioner.

If from the latter cause, then had the prisoner prescribed this medicine (which was the cause of death) rashly, in the sense that he had explained?

Verdict, Not guilty.

[*Negligence in doing a lawful act which is dangerous.*]

REX *v.* HULL.

OLD BAILEY.   1664.   KELYNG 40.

John Hull was indicted for the murder of Henry Cambridge. The case was, that there were several workmen about building of a house by the horse-ferry; which house stood about 30 feet from any highway of common passage. Hull, being a master-workman, was sent by his master (about evening, when the master-workmen had given over work, and when the labourers were putting up their tools) to bring from his house a piece of timber which lay two stories high. He went up for that piece of timber; and before he threw it down, he cried out aloud, "Stand clear," and was heard by the labourers. All of them went from the danger but only Cambridge; and the piece of timber fell upon him and killed him.

And my Lord Chief Justice HYDE held this to be manslaughter. For he said he should have let it down by a rope; or else, at his peril, be sure that nobody is there. But my brother WYLDE and myself (KELYNG, C.J.) held it to be misadventure; he doing nothing but what is usual with workmen to do, and (before he did it) crying out aloud, "Stand clear," and so giving notice if there were any near they might avoid it. .And we put this case:—a man lopping a tree, when the arms of the tree were ready to fall, calls out to them below, "Take heed"; and then the arms of the tree fall and kill a man, this is misadventure. And we shewed him *Poulton de pace* 120, where the case is put, and the book cited, and held to be misadventure. And we said this case in question is much stronger than the case where one throws a stone or shoots an arrow over a wall or house, with which one is slain; which, in Keilwey 108 and 136, is said to be misadventure.

But we did all hold that there was a great difference 'twixt the case in question (the house from which the timber was thrown standing thirty feet from the highway or common foot-path) and the doing the same

act in the streets of London.   For we all agreed that in London, if one
be a cleansing of a gutter, and call out to stand aside, and then throw
down rubbish or a piece of timber, by which a man is killed, this is
manslaughter[1].   Being in London, there is a continual concourse of
people passing up and down the streets, and new passengers who did
not hear him call out; and therefore...if anyone be killed it is manslaughter.   Because, in common presumption, his intention was to do
mischief, when he casts or shoots anything, which may kill, among
a multitude of people.   But in case of a house standing in a country-
town, where there is no such frequency of passengers, if a man call out
there to "Stand aside, and take heed," and then cast down the filth of
a gutter, my brother Wylde and I held this a far differing case from
doing the same thing in London.   And because my Lord Hyde differed
in the principal case, it was found specially; but I take the law to be
clear that it is but misadventure.

[*Negligence as regards dangerous animals.*]

REGINA *v.* DANT.

CROWN CASE RESERVED.   1865.   LEIGH AND CAVE 567.

The following case was stated by MONTAGUE SMITH, J.

The prisoner was tried before me for feloniously killing and slaying
Mary Ann Papworth.

The deceased was a child about eight years old, and was killed by a
kick from a horse belonging to the prisoner.

The horse which caused the death of the child had been in the
possession of the prisoner about four years.   There was evidence that
it was a very vicious and dangerous animal; that it had kicked and
injured several persons; that some of these instances had been brought
to the knowledge of the prisoner; and that he otherwise knew the propensities of the horse.

There is a large common adjoining the town of Cambridge, between
Jesus College and the river, called Midsummer Common, on which the
ratepayers in the borough of Cambridge were accustomed to depasture

---

[1] [EDITOR'S NOTE.   Had the Londoner not taken the precaution of calling out
to the passers-by, his offence would amount to murder, according to Coke (3 Inst.
57).]

their horses. Through this common there are defined public foot paths, a yard wide or more, kept and gravelled by the Municipal Corporation of Cambridge. Two of these paths converge about twelve yards from a bridge over the river, and, from the point where they meet, form a broad pathway to the river; but the boundaries of the public foot-path from the said point to the river are ill-defined. These paths are all unfenced and open to the rest of the common. It was proved that the public have a right to use these foot-paths; but it was not proved that the public had a right to traverse the other parts of the common, although they often did traverse it. The prisoner claimed a right, as a ratepayer of the borough of Cambridge, to turn out his horses to depasture on this common; and it was not disputed by the Counsel for the prosecution that he had this right.

It appeared that the deceased, with some other children, was on the common; and, when she was either on or very near to the broad pathway above described, the vicious horse of the prisoner, which had been turned out loose on the common by him, and which was then on the common near the broad path, kicked at the deceased with his heels, struck her on the head, and killed her.

I left to the jury the question whether the death of the child was occasioned by the culpable negligence of the prisoner; and I told them they might find culpable negligence, if the evidence satisfied them that the horse was so vicious and accustomed to kick mankind as to be dangerous, and that the prisoner knew that it was so, and with that knowledge turned it out loose on the common, through which to his knowledge there were open and unenclosed paths on which the public had a right to pass and were accustomed to be.

I also asked the jury to find, as a separate question, whether the deceased, at the time she was kicked by the horse, was on the foot-path or beyond it.

The jury found the prisoner guilty of having caused the death of the child by his culpable negligence, but answered the last question by saying that the evidence did not satisfy them one way or the other—whether the child, at the time she was kicked, was on the pathway or beyond it....

Naylor (for the prisoner). For the purposes of this argument it must be taken that the child was off the path; and, if that was so, the conviction cannot stand. A man who puts a vicious horse into his own close would not be guilty of manslaughter if it killed a trespasser. So here, the child, being off the path, was a trespasser; and, if there was any neglect of duty, it was on the part of the corporation, the owners of the field, in neglecting to fence off the path. The prisoner could not erect a fence, for he had no right in the field except that of putting his cattle on it.

MONTAGUE SMITH, J. The path was unfenced; and he knew it to be so.

BLACKBURN, J. His negligence consisted in turning a vicious horse into a place where it might reasonably be expected that people would come.

Naylor. The negligence was rather that of the parent in suffering the child to go on a common where the paths were unfenced. If a man, having a field, digs a pit in it, and another, wandering from the path, falls into the pit, the owner of the field is not liable.

BLACKBURN, J. In *Barnes* v. *Ward*[1] it was held that an area dug so near to a public way as to be dangerous to the public unless fenced was a nuisance. Is not the letting a vicious horse come near a public way as bad as digging a pit near it?

Naylor. That might have been so, if the prisoner had been the owner of the field, and had had the power of fencing the path.

BLACKBURN, J. Not having that power, was it not his duty to clog or blind the horse?

MELLOR, J. The injury arose from turning the horse in. Is a man justified in turning a vicious horse into a field when there is an unfenced path? Would a commoner be justified in turning a bull he knew to be mischievous on to an unfenced common?

BLACKBURN, J. Surely it is his duty not to do anything in the use of his property which would be likely to endanger persons using the path.

ERLE, C.J. The corporation were not bound to fence the path. If the boon of walking over a man's land is given to the public, the public must take it as it is given.

Naylor. The child contributed to its death by its own negligence.

BLACKBURN, J. I have never heard that, upon an indictment for manslaughter, the accused is entitled to be acquitted because the person who lost his life was in someway to blame.

MELLOR, J. The only point reserved is whether the prisoner can be pronounced guilty of culpable negligence when the jury cannot say whether the child was on or off the path.

BLACKBURN, J. And whether the fact of the child's being on or off the path is material.

Naylor. If the child had been on the path, the accident might not have happened.

BLACKBURN, J. At any rate the child was close to the path; and

[1] 9 C. B. 392.

in *Barnes* v. *Ward*[1] the pit was not quite close to the footway, so that the deceased must have gone out of the way before she fell into the pit.

Naylor. In *Hardcastle* v. *The South Yorkshire Railway and River Dun Company*[2] it was held that an excavation near to a public highway was not a nuisance unless it, substantially, adjoined it.

MELLOR, J. Throwing stones off the top of a house by which persons passing below are killed is manslaughter or not, according as persons may or may not be expected to pass. As to the point that the child was guilty of contributory negligence; in *Regina* v. *Swindall*[3] Pollock, C. B., held that, where a man kills another by furious driving and running over him, it is no ground of defence that the death was partly caused by the negligence of the deceased himself.

BLACKBURN, J. The other day a man was very properly convicted of murder, because he aided and abetted another in committing suicide; yet he could not have been sued for so doing by the man who killed himself. In *Hammack* v. *White*[4] Willes, J., expresses an opinion that the question of negligence is not the same in an action as in an indictment for manslaughter.

MELLOR, J. Both *Barnes* v. *Ward*[5] and *Hardcastle* v. *The South Yorkshire Railway*[6] were considered in *Binks* v. *The South Yorkshire Railway*[7]; and the Court there adopted the distinction laid down in the second of those cases.

Naylor. In *Hounsell* v. *Smyth*[8] it was held that an owner of waste land, who had opened a quarry in his land near to and between two public highways leading over the waste, was not liable to an action at the suit of a man who had fallen into the quarry in crossing the waste by night to get from one road into the other.

MELLOR, J. Is there not a distinction between turning out cattle, which may roam about, and digging a pit, which is fixed and only dangerous to those who go out of their way to it?

Naylor. In this case the child had gone out of its way.

Markby, for the Crown, was not called upon.

ERLE, C.J. I am of opinion that this conviction should be affirmed. The defendant turned a dangerous animal on to a common where there was a public footpath. That has been found by the jury to be culpable negligence; and the child's death was caused by it. Ordinarily speaking, these are all the requisites of manslaughter. It is contended, however, that no offence was committed, because, as we must take it, the child was not on the path; the jury having found

---

[1] 9 C. B. 392.   [2] 4 H. and N. 67.   [3] *Supra*, p. 74.
[4] 31 L. J. C. P. 129, 131.   [5] 9 C. B. 392.   [6] 4 H. and N. 67.
[7] 32 L. J. Q. B. 26.   [8] 29 L. J. C. P. 203.

K.

that it was very near, but that they could not say whether it was on
or off. In my opinion, the defendant is responsible for having brought
so great a danger on persons exercising their right to cross the
common ; and it is not a ground of acquittal that the child had strayed
from the path. *Barnes* v. *Ward*[1] shews that a man is responsible for
making an excavation adjoining a highway, so as to render the way
unsafe to persons using it with ordinary care. In that case the
excavation was not on the highway ; and the plaintiff's wife had accidentally deviated on a dark night. The principle of that case applies
to this. I am of opinion that those who dedicate a road are not under
any obligation to fence it. When a right of way is granted, it must
be taken in the state in which it is granted ; but persons using it are
nevertheless to be protected from such danger as that in this case.
My judgment proceeds on the fact that the child was near the path ;
since the cases shew that persons trespassing a long way from the path
must take the chance of what may happen to them in consequence of
so doing, and cannot maintain any action against the owner of the
land for any damage they sustain thereby. Yet I do not say that,
because a man is not liable to an action in such a case, he is not liable
criminally. It is not necessary at present to embark on that question.

[The four other Judges delivered similar judgments.]

- - -

[*Driving.*]

[*Negligence in driving.*]

REX *v.* KNIGHT.

LANCASTER ASSIZES.   1828.   1 LEWIN 168.

Prisoner was indicted for manslaughter. The evidence was that,
being employed to drive a cart, he sat in the inside instead of attending
at the horse's head[2]. While he was sitting there, the cart went over a
child who was gathering up flowers on the road.

BAYLEY, J. The prisoner, by being in the cart, instead of at the
horse's head or by its side, was guilty of negligence. Death having
been caused by such negligence, he is guilty of manslaughter.

[In a similar case before Hullock, B., at York Assizes in 1829 a
similar judgment was delivered.]

- - -

[See also REG. *v.* DALLOWAY, *infra.*]

- - -

[1] 9 C. B. 392.

[2] [EDITOR'S NOTE. The cart evidently was one without driving-reins.]

[*Negligence in playing a lawful game.*]

REGINA *v.* BRADSHAW.

LEICESTER ASSIZES.   1878.   14 COX 83.

William Bradshaw was indicted for the manslaughter of Herbert Dockerty at Ashby-de-la-Zouch.

The deceased met with the injury which caused his death on the occasion of a football match played between the football clubs of Ashby-de-la-Zouch and Coalville, in which the deceased was a player on the Ashby side, and the prisoner was a player on the Coalville side. The game was played according to the "Association Rules." After the game had proceeded about a quarter of an hour, the deceased was "dribbling" the ball along the side of the ground in the direction of the Coalville goal, when he was met by the prisoner, who was running towards him to get the ball from him or prevent its further progress. Both players were running at considerable speed. On approaching each other, the deceased kicked the ball beyond the prisoner; and the prisoner, by way of "charging" the deceased, jumped in the air and struck him with his knee in the stomach. The two met, not directly but at an angle, and both fell. The prisoner got up unhurt, but the deceased rose with difficulty and was led from the ground. He died next day, the cause of death being a rupture of the intestines.

Witnesses from both teams were called whose evidence differed as to some particulars. Those most unfavourable to the prisoner alleged that the ball had been kicked by the deceased and had passed the prisoner before he charged; that the prisoner had therefore no right to charge at the time he did; that the charge was contrary to the rules and practice of the game, and made in an unfair manner, with the knees protruding. Those who were more favourable to the prisoner stated that the kick by the deceased and the charge by the prisoner were simultaneous; and that the prisoner had therefore, according to the rules and practice of the game, a right to make the charge; though these witnesses admitted that to charge by jumping with the knee protruding was unfair. One of the umpires of the game stated that in his opinion nothing unfair had been done.

BRAMWELL, L.J., in summing up the case to the jury said, "The question for you to decide is whether the death of the deceased was caused by the unlawful act of the prisoner. There is no doubt that the prisoner's act caused the death; and the question is whether that act was unlawful. No rules or practice of any game whatever can make that lawful which is unlawful by the law of the land; and the law of the land says you shall not do that which is likely to cause the death of another. For instance, no persons can by agreement go out to fight with deadly weapons (doing by agreement what the law says shall not be done), and thus shelter themselves from the consequences of their acts. Therefore, in one way you need not concern yourselves with the rules of football. But, on the other hand, if a man is playing according to the rules and practice of the game and not going beyond it, it may be reasonable to infer that he is not actuated by any malicious motive or intention, and that he is not acting in a manner which he knows will be likely to be productive of death or injury. But, independent of the rules, if the prisoner intended to cause serious hurt to the deceased—or if he knew that, in charging as he did, he might produce serious injury and was indifferent and reckless as to whether he would produce serious injury or not—then the act would be unlawful. In either case he would be guilty of a criminal act and you must find him guilty. If you are of a contrary opinion you will acquit him." His Lordship carefully reviewed the evidence, stating that no doubt the game was, in any circumstances, a rough one; but he was unwilling to decry the manly sports of this country, all of which were no doubt attended with more or less danger.

Verdict, Not guilty.

[EDITOR'S NOTE. In the similar case of *Reg.* v. *Moore*, also tried at Leicester Assizes (*Times*, Feb. 16, 1898), for manslaughter in a football match, but by charging from behind, which is contrary to the rules of the game, Hawkins, J., would not allow those rules to be put in evidence *by the Crown*, and said the only question for the jury was whether the prisoner used illegal violence.]

[*Negligence by mere omission.*]
REGINA v. SAMUEL LOWE.
WORCESTERSHIRE ASSIZES.   1850.   3 CARRINGTON AND KIRWAN 123.

The prisoner was indicted for the manslaughter of Thomas Tibbitts.

It appeared that he was an engineer, and that his duty was to manage a steam-engine employed for the purpose of drawing up miners from a coal-pit. When the skip containing the men arrived on a level with the pit's mouth, his duty was to stop the revolution of the windlass, so that the men might get out. He was the only man so employed on the premises. On the day in question he deserted his post, leaving the engine in charge of an ignorant boy, who, before the prisoner went away, declared himself to the prisoner to be utterly incompetent to manage such a steam-engine. The prisoner neglected this warning; and threatened the boy, in case he refused to do as he was ordered. The boy superintended the raising of two skips from the pit with

success. But on the arrival, at the pit's mouth, of a third, containing
four men, he was unable to stop the engine; and the skip being
drawn over the pulley, the deceased, who was one of the men, was
thrown down into the shaft of the pit and killed on the spot. It
appeared that the engine could not be stopped "in consequence
of the slipper being too low," an error which it was proved that any
competent engineer could have rectified, but which the boy in charge
of the engine could not.

Huddleston, for the prisoner, contended, that a mere omission or
neglect of duty could not render a man guilty of manslaughter, and he
cited the cases of *Rex* v. *Green* (7 C. and P. 156), and *Rex* v. *Allen*
(7 C. and P. 153).

LORD CAMPBELL, C.J. I am clearly of opinion that a man may, by
a neglect of [even an active] duty, render himself liable to be convicted of manslaughter, or even of murder.

[*But the omission must not be too remote a cause.*]

REGINA v. HILTON.

LIVERPOOL ASSIZES.   1838.   2 LEWIN 214.

The prisoner was indicted for manslaughter. It appeared that it
was his duty to attend a steam-engine; and that, on the occasion in
question, he had stopped the engine, and gone away. During his
absence, a person came to the spot, and put it in motion; and, being
unskilled, was not able to stop it again. It appeared, that in consequence of the engine being in motion, the deceased was killed.

ALDERSON, B., stopped the case, observing, "The death was the
consequence, not of the act of the prisoner, but of the person who set
the engine in motion after the prisoner had gone away. It is necessary,
in order to a conviction for manslaughter, that the negligent act
which causes the death should be that of the party charged."

[*Omission too remote.*]

REGINA v. REES.

CENTRAL CRIMINAL COURT.   1886.   SESSIONS PAPERS. CIV.

Frederick Samuel Rees was indicted for, and charged on the
coroner's inquisition with, the manslaughter of George Hill.

From *Poland's* opening of the case for the Crown, it appeared that
the prisoner was a fourth-class fireman in the London Fire Brigade,

having charge of a fire-escape; on the occasion in question he was absent from his post when a fire occurred in which the deceased lost his life. The allegation was that this death was caused by the prisoner's culpable neglect of his duty.

Besley, for prisoner. There was no direct connection between the prisoner's neglect of duty and the cause of death.

HAWKINS, J., concurring in this view, *Poland* offered no evidence, and the prisoner was acquitted.

[*Prisoner's negligence, however gross, will not render him responsible for a death which his diligence would not have averted.*]

THE QUEEN *v.* DALLOWAY.

STAFFORD ASSIZES.   1847.   2 Cox 273.

The prisoner was indicted for the manslaughter of one Henry Clarke, by reason of his negligence as driver of a cart.

It appeared that the prisoner was standing up in a spring-cart, and having the conduct of it along a public thoroughfare. The cart was drawn by one horse. The reins were not in the hands of the prisoner, but loose on the horse's back. While the cart was so proceeding down the slope of a hill, the horse trotting at the time, the deceased child, who was about three years of age, ran across the road before the horse, at the distance of a few yards; and one of the wheels of the cart, knocking it down and passing over it, caused its death. It did not appear that the prisoner saw the child in the road before the accident.

Spooner, for the prosecution, submitted that the prisoner, in consequence of his negligence in not using reins, was responsible for the death of the child. But

ERLE, J., in summing up to the jury, directed them that a party neglecting ordinary caution, and, by reason of that neglect, causing the death of another, is guilty of manslaughter; that if the prisoner had reins, and by using the reins could have saved the child, he was guilty of manslaughter; but that if they thought he could not have saved the child by pulling the reins, or otherwise by their assistance, they must acquit him.

[Contrast REX *v.* KNIGHT, *supra*, p. 130.]

[*But if prisoner's negligence formed even a part of the* proximate cause *of death, it is no defence that there was contributory negligence on the deceased's own part.*]

REGINA v. KEW AND JACKSON.

SUFFOLK ASSIZES. 1872. 12 Cox 155

The prisoners were indicted for manslaughter. It appeared that on the 2nd of June the prisoner Jackson, who was in the employ of Mr Harris, a farmer, was instructed to take his master's horse and cart, and drive the prisoner Kew to the Bungay railway station. Being late for the train, Jackson drove at a furious rate, at full gallop; and ran over a child going to school, and killed it. It was about two o'clock in the afternoon, and there were four or five little children, from five to seven years of age, going to school unattended by any adult.

Metcalfe and *Simms Reeve*, for the prisoners, contended that there was contributory negligence on the part of the child running on the road; and that Kew was not liable for the acts of another man's servant, he having no control over the horse, and not having selected either the horse or the driver.

BYLES, J., said :—Here the mother lets her child go out in the care of another child, only seven years of age. And the prisoner Kew is in the vehicle of another man, driven by another man's servant; so not only was Jackson not his servant, but he did not even select him. It has been contended that if there was contributory negligence on the children's part, then the defendants are not liable. No doubt contributory negligence would be an answer to an action. But who is the plaintiff here? The Queen, as representing the nation; and if they were all negligent together, I think their negligence would be no defence, even if they had been adults. If you are of opinion that the prisoners were driving at a dangerous pace, in a culpably negligent manner, then they are guilty. It is true that Kew was not actually driving; but still a word from him might have prevented the accident. If necessary, I will reserve for the Court of Criminal Appeal the question of contributory negligence as a defence.

The jury acquitted both prisoners.

[Compare REG. *v.* SWINDALL, *supra*, p. 74.]

SECTION III.

HOMICIDES THAT ARE NOT CRIMES.

[*Mere accident.*]

THE QUEEN *v.* BRUCE.

CENTRAL CRIMINAL COURT. 1847. 2 Cox 262.

The prisoner was indicted for manslaughter, under the circumstances detailed by one of the witnesses. He said the prisoner came into his master's shop; and pulled him, by the hair, off a cask where he was sitting, and shoved him to the door, and from the door back to the counter. That the prisoner then put his arm round his neck and spun him round, and they came together out of the shop; the prisoner kept hold of the witness when they were outside, and kept spinning him round; the latter broke away from him, and, in consequence and at the moment of his so doing, he (the prisoner) reeled out into the road and knocked against a woman who was passing and knocked her down. The prisoner was very drunk, and staggered as he walked.

The woman so knocked down died shortly afterwards of the injuries she had received; and it was for having caused her death that the prisoner was indicted.

Mr Justice ERLE inquired of the witness (a young lad) whether he resisted the prisoner during the transaction. The lad answered that he did not; he thought the prisoner was only playing with him, and was sure that it was intended as a joke throughout.

ERLE, J. (to the jury). I think, upon this evidence, you must acquit the prisoner. Where the death of one person is caused by the act of another, while the latter is in pursuit of any unlawful object, the person so killing is guilty of manslaughter, although he had no intention whatever of injuring him who was the victim of his conduct. Here, however, there was nothing unlawful in what the prisoner did to this lad, and which led to the death of the woman. Had his treatment of the boy been against the will of the latter, the prisoner would have been committing an assault—an unlawful act—which would have rendered him amenable to the law for any consequences resulting from it. But as everything that was done was with the witness's consent, there was no assault, and consequently no illegality. It is, in the eye of the law, an accident, and nothing more.

[*Mere accident.*]

REX *v.* MARTIN.

STAFFORD ASSIZES.   1827.   3 CARRINGTON AND PAYNE 211.

Manslaughter. The indictment charged the prisoner with giving
a quartern of gin to Joseph Sweet, a child of tender age, to wit, of the
age of four years; which caused his death. The indictment averred the
quantity of gin to be excessive for a child of that age. It appeared
that the father of the deceased kept a public-house at Wolverhampton,
and that the prisoner went there to drink, and having ordered a
quartern of gin, he asked the child if he would have a drop ; and that,
on his putting the glass to the child's mouth, with his left hand, as he
held the child with his right, the child twisted the glass out of his
hand, and immediately swallowed nearly the whole of the quartern of
gin. This caused his death a few hours after.

VAUGHAN, B. As it appears clearly that the drinking of the gin in
this quantity was the act of the child, the prisoner must be acquitted.
But if it had appeared that the prisoner had willingly given a child of
this tender age a quartern of gin, out of a sort of brutal fun, and had
thereby caused its death, I should most decidedly have held that to be
manslaughter ; because I have no doubt that the causing the death of
a child by giving it spirituous liquors, in a quantity quite unfit for its
tender age, amounts, in point of law, to that offence.

Verdict, Not guilty.

[EDITOR'S NOTE. In *Regina v. Packard and others* (C. and M. 236) where a
man of sixty died within two hours after being plied with spirits by the prisoners,
Parke, B., said, " The simple fact of persons getting together to drink, or even
of one pressing another to drink, is not an unlawful act, or, if death ensue, an
offence that can be construed into manslaughter. And if what took place in the
present instance was really and solely for making merry, this will not be a case
of manslaughter, though the act was attended with death. . . . . But a verdict
that the prisoners knew that the liquors were likely to cause the death of the
deceased would make the offence approach to murder."]

[*Self-defence.*]

ANONYMOUS.

1352.   LIB. ASS. ann. 26, f. 123, pl. 23.

Note that in an indictment for felony the defendant put himself
upon the country. And it was found that he was in his house; and the

man whom he killed and others came to his house in order to burn him, &c., and surrounded the house but did not succeed; and he leapt forth &c. and killed the other &c. And it was adjudged that this was no felony. Moreover it was adjudged by the whole Council that if a robber slays a merchant, and the merchant's lad then comes up in haste and kills the robber who robbed his master &c., this is not felony &c.

[*Self-defence.*]

REX *v.* COOPER.

SURREY ASSIZES. 1641. CROKE CAR. 544.

Cooper being indicted in the county of Surrey of the murder of W. L. in Southwark, with a spit, he pleaded not guilty. And upon his arraignment it appeared that the said Cooper, being a prisoner in the King's Bench, and lying in the house of one Anne Carricke, who kept a tavern in the Rules, the said W. L., at one of the clock in the night, assaulted the said house; and offered to break open the door and broke a staple thereof, and swore he would enter the house and slit the nose of the said Anne Carricke because she kept a house of ill-fame. And the said Cooper dissuading him from those courses, and reprehending him, he swore that, if he could enter, he would cut the said Cooper's throat: and he brake a window in the lower room of the house, and thrust his rapier in at the window against the said Cooper; who, in defence of the house and himself, thrust the said W. L. into the eye, of which stroke he died.

The question was, whether this were within the statute of 24 Hen. VIII.[1] The opinion of the Court was, that—if it were true he brake the house with an intent to commit burglary, or to kill any therein, and a party within the house (although he be not the master but a lodger or sojourner therein) kill him who made the assault and intended mischief to any in it—that is not felony, but excusable by the said statute of 24 Hen. VIII. c. 5, which was made in affirmance of the Common Law. Wherefore the jury were appointed to consider of the fact; and they found the said Cooper not guilty.

[1] [EDITOR'S NOTE.] This statute (c. 5) reasserts the common-law rule sanction-ing self-defence against robbers and burglars.

[*Self-defence.*]

REX *v.* SCULLY.

GLOUCESTER ASSIZES.   1824.   1 CARRINGTON AND PAYNE 319.

This prisoner was indicted for manslaughter, in shooting a man whose name was unknown.

It was proved that the prisoner had been set to watch his master's premises; and that he came to a constable to surrender himself. He said he had unfortunately shot a man; and that having seen the man on his master's garden wall in the night, he hailed him; and the man said to another, whom the prisoner could not see, "Tom, why don't you fire?" He hailed them again, and the same person said, "Shoot and be ——," whereupon he (the prisoner) fired at the legs of the man on the wall, whom he missed, and shot the deceased, whom he had not seen from his being behind the wall.

This confession was the only evidence against the prisoner; but it was proved that, when the deceased was found, he had three dead fowls, a housebreaker's crowbar, and a flint, steel, and matches.

GARROW, B. A person set by his master to watch a garden or yard, is not at all justified in shooting at, or injuring in any way, persons who may come into those premises, even in the night; and if he saw them go into his master's hen-roost, he would still not be justified in shooting them. He ought first to see if he could not take measures for their apprehension. But here the life of the prisoner was threatened; and if he considered his life in actual danger, he was justified in shooting the deceased as he had done; but if, not considering his own life in danger, he rashly shot this man, who was only a trespasser, he would be guilty of manslaughter.

[*Self-defence.*]

HOWEL'S CASE.

WORCESTERSHIRE EYRE.   1221.   MAITLAND'S SELECT PLEAS 94.

Howel the Markman, a wandering robber, and his fellows, assaulted a carter; and would have robbed him, but the carter slew Howel, and defended himself against the others, and escaped. And whereas it is testified that Howel was a robber, let the carter go quit thereof. And note that he is in the parts of Jerusalem; but let him come back safely, quit of that death.

[*Defence of near relation.*]

REGINA *v.* ROSE.

OXFORD ASSIZES. 1884.   15 Cox 540.

The prisoner was indicted for the wilful murder of his father John William Rose, at Witney.

The material facts proved were as follows :—The prisoner, a weakly young man, of about twenty-two years of age, was at the time of the alleged murder living with his father, mother, and sisters at Witney. The father, who was a very powerful man, had recently taken to excessive drinking, and while in a state of intoxication was possessed with the idea that his wife was unfaithful to him. He had on more than one occasion threatened to take away her life; and so firmly impressed was she with the idea that these were no idle threats, that the prisoner's mother had frequently concealed everything in the house which could be used as a weapon.

On the night in question the family retired to their bedrooms, which were situated adjoining to one another, about nine o'clock. The deceased man appears to have immediately commenced abusing and ill-treating his wife; accusing her of unfaithfulness to him, and threatening to murder her. On several occasions she retired for safety to her daughter's room; on the last occasion her husband pursued her, and, seizing her, dragged her towards the top of the stairs, threatening to push her down. He then said he would cut her throat; left her, saying he was going to fetch the knife, which all the family seem to have known was in his room; and then, rushing back, seized his wife and forced her up against the balusters, holding her in such a position that the daughters seem to have thought he was actually cutting her throat. The daughters and mother shouted "Murder," and the prisoner, running out of his room, found his father and mother in the position described. No evidence was given that the deceased man had any knife in his hand, and all the witnesses said that they did not then see or afterwards find his knife.

The prisoner (according to his own account) fired one shot to frighten his father, but no traces of any bullet could be found; and, immediately after, he fired another shot, which, striking his father in the eye, lodged in the brain, and caused his death in about twelve hours. On his arrest the prisoner said, "Father was murdering mother. I shot on one side to frighten him; he would not leave her, so then I shot him."

In cross-examination, the deceased man's employer said that the prisoner's father was the strongest man he had ever seen, and the prisoner would not have had the slightest chance in a hand to hand encounter with him.

LOPES, J. Homicide is excusable if a person takes away the life of another in defending himself, if the fatal blow which takes away life is necessary for his preservation. The law says not only in self-defence such as I have described may homicide be excusable, but also it may be excusable if the fatal blow inflicted was necessary for the preservation of life. In the case of parent and child, if the parent has reason to believe that the life of a child is in imminent danger by reason of an assault by another person, and that the only possible, fair, and reasonable means of saving the child's life is by doing something which will cause the death of that person, the law excuses that act. It is the same of a child with regard to a parent; it is the same in the case of husband and wife. Therefore, I propose to lay the law before you in this form: If you think, having regard to the evidence, and drawing fair and proper inferences from it, that the prisoner at the bar acted without vindictive feeling towards his father when he fired the shot, if you think that at the time he fired that shot he honestly believed, and had reasonable grounds for the belief, that his mother's life was in imminent peril, and that the fatal shot which he fired was absolutely necessary for the preservation of her life, then he ought to be excused from the consequences of the homicide. If, however, on the other hand, you are clearly of opinion that he acted vindictively and had not such a belief as I have described to you, or had not reasonable grounds for such a belief, then you must find him guilty of murder.

[*But violent self-defence is not permitted (except*[1] *to a person who has been purely passive) if retreat is possible.*]

ANONYMOUS.

NEWGATE SESSIONS. 1369. LIB. Ass. ann. 43, f. 274, pl. 31.

Note that at the delivery of Newgate, before Knivet and Ludlow, it was found that a chaplain *se defendendo* slew a man, and the justices asked how. And [the jurors] said that the man who was killed pursued the chaplain with a stick and struck him, and he struck back and so death was caused. And they said that the slayer, had he so willed,

----

[1] [EDITOR'S NOTE.] Some deny this exception; but the better opinion seems that Retreat is only required from persons who have taken some culpable share in the combat. See Foster 276.

might have fled from his assailant. And therefore the justices adjudged him a felon, and said that he was bound to flee as far as he
could with safety of life. And the chaplain was adjudged to the
ordinary [i.e. was handed over to his ecclesiastical superior as a clerk
convicted of crime.]

[*Unless retreat would involve letting a prisoner escape.*]

REX *v.* FORSTER.

LANCASTER ASSIZES.   1825.   1 LEWIN 187.

The prisoner was charged, on the coroner's inquisition, with murder.
The prisoner was an excise officer, and, being in the execution of his
office, had seized, with the assistance of another person, two smugglers
whom he detected in the act of landing whiskey from the Scottish
shore, contrary to law.

It appeared that the deceased had surrendered himself quietly into
the hands of the prisoner; but shortly afterwards, when the prisoner
was off his guard, he assaulted him violently with an ash stick, which
cut his head severely in several places. The prisoner lost much blood
from the wounds, and was greatly weakened in the struggle which
succeeded. Fearing the smuggler would overpower him, and having
no other means of defending himself, he discharged a pistol at the
deceased's legs, in the hope of deterring him from any further attack.
The discharge did not take effect, and the smuggler prepared to make
another assault. Seeing this, the prisoner warned him to keep off,
telling him he must shoot him if he did not. The smuggler disregarded
the warning, and rushed towards him to make a fresh attack. The
prisoner thereupon fired a second pistol and killed him.

HOLROYD, J. An officer must not kill for an escape where the
party is in custody for a misdemeanor. But if the prisoner had reasonable grounds for believing himself to be in peril of his own life or of
bodily harm, and if no other weapon was at hand to make use of or he
was rendered incapable of making use of any such weapon by the
previous violence that he had received, then he was justified. If an
affray arises and blows are received, and then weapons are used in heat
and death ensues, although the party may at the commencement have
been in the prosecution of something unlawful, still it would be manslaughter in the killer; though manslaughter only. In the present
case it is admitted that the custody was lawful. The jury are then to

say whether, under all the circumstances, the deceased being in the prosecution of an illegal act and having made the first assault, the prisoner had such reasonable occasion to resort to a deadly weapon, to defend himself, as any reasonable man might fairly and naturally be expected to act on.

Verdict, manslaughter.   Sentence one month's imprisonment.

[*Homicide in effecting arrest.*]

REX v. LEONIN AND JACOB.

WORCESTERSHIRE EYRE.   1221.   MAITLAND'S SELECT PLEAS 85.

Leonin, Philip's son, and Jacob his servant, slew John of Middleton in the forest of Kinfare.   Englishry is presented....

At Lichfield came Leonin and Jacob and put themselves upon their verdict as to when, where, and by whom the deed was done.   The jurors of the hundred of Seisdon say that, in the time of the war, John came with many others into the King's forest to offend in the forest, as was his wont, and was found seised of the whole body of a doe; and the King's servants and foresters could not take him alive, and he defended himself against our lord the King and cut off a forester's finger, and thus it was that he was slain.   And so it is considered that [Leonin and Jacob] be quit thereof.

[*Homicide in effecting arrest.*]

JOHN SMALL'S CASE.

NORTHAMPTON CORONER'S COURT.   1323.   SELECT CORONERS' ROLLS 79.

John Small, who had been arrested at Stoke Bruern for burglary at the house of Robert Gold, died in the prison of the castle of Northampton.   Inquest was taken by the oath of twelve [men], who say on their oath that, when the said John was arrested, he resisted the constable and frankpledges of the township of Stoke Bruern, and would not allow himself to be attached to the peace, until a certain unknown man of that township struck him in the left eye with an iron fork, and gave him a wound, half an inch wide and in depth penetrating to the brainpan; of which wound the said John died without the felony of anyone.

SECTION IV.

STATUTORY OFFENCES AGAINST THE PERSON.

[*In* statutory *wrongs of malice, there must be an intention to do the particular kind of harm that actually was done.*]

[See REGINA *v.* PEMBLITON, *infra*, p. 157.]

[*But it is sufficient if the harm done is of the* kind *intended, though it be produced in a* manner *or upon a* subject *that was not intended.*]

REGINA *v.* LATIMER.

CROWN CASE RESERVED.   1886.   L.R. 17 Q.B.D. 359.

Case stated by the Recorder of Devonport.

The prisoner was indicted and tried for unlawfully and maliciously wounding Ellen Rolston, and there was a second count charging him with a common assault. The evidence shewed that the prisoner, who was a soldier, and one Thomas Evan Chapple quarrelled in a public-house kept by the prosecutrix; and the prisoner was knocked down by Chapple. The prisoner went out into a yard at the back of the house, but about five minutes afterwards returned and passed hastily through the room in which Chapple was still sitting. The prisoner, as he passed, having in his hand his belt which he had taken off, aimed a blow with his belt at Chapple and struck him slightly; the belt, however, bounded off and struck the prosecutrix, who was standing talking to Chapple, in the face; cutting her face open and wounding her severely.

The Recorder left these questions to the jury :—

1. Was the blow struck at Chapple in self-defence to get through the room, or unlawfully and maliciously? 2. Did the blow so struck in fact wound Ellen Rolston? 3. Was the striking of Ellen Rolston purely accidental, or was it such a consequence as the prisoner should have expected to follow from the blow he aimed at Chapple?

The jury found: 1. That the blow was unlawful and malicious. 2. That the blow did in fact wound Ellen Rolston. 3. That the striking of Ellen Rolston was purely accidental, and not such a conse-quence of the blow as the prisoner ought to have expected.

Upon these findings the Recorder directed a verdict of guilty to be entered on the first count.

The question was, whether upon the facts and findings of the jury the prisoner was rightly convicted of the offence for which he was indicted?

Croft, for the prisoner, cited *Reg.* v. *Pembliton*[1]....The prisoner did not intend to strike the prosecutrix ; and the jury have found that the injury to her was purely accidental. Therefore there was no *mens rea*, and the wounding was not malicious....

LORD COLERIDGE, C.J. We are of opinion that this conviction must be sustained. It is common knowledge that a man who has an unlawful and malicious intent against another, and, in attempting to carry it out, injures a third person, is guilty of what the law deems malice against the person injured ; because the offender is doing an unlawful act, and has that which the judges call general malice, and that is enough. Such would be the case if the matter were *res integra* , and it is not so, for *Rex* v. *Hunt*[2] is an express authority on the point There a man intended to injure A, and said so, and, in the course of doing it, stabbed the wrong man, and had clearly malice in fact, but no intention of injuring the man who was stabbed....So, but for *Reg.* v. *Pembliton*[1], there would not have been the slightest difficulty. Does that case make any difference? I think not. It was quite rightly decided, but it is clearly distinguishable ; because the indictment in *Reg.* v. *Pembliton*[1] was on the Act making unlawful and malicious injury to property a statutory offence ; and the jury expressly negatived, and the facts expressly negatived, any intention to do injury to property ; and the Court held that under the Act making it an offence to injure any property there must be an intent to injure property. *Reg.* v. *Pembliton*[1] therefore, does not govern the present case ; and on no other ground is there anything to be said for the prisoner.

LORD ESHER, M.R. I am of the same opinion. The only case which could be cited against the well-known principle of law applicable to this case was *Reg.* v. *Pembliton*[1] ; but, on examination, it is found to have been decided on this ground, viz., that there was no intention to injure any property at all. It was not a case of attempting to injure one man's property and injuring another's ; which would have been wholly different.

BOWEN, L.J. It is quite clear that the act was done by the prisoner with malice in his mind. I use the word 'malice' in the common-law

[1] *Infra*, p. 157. [2] 1 Moo. C. C. 93.

sense, viz., a person is deemed malicious when he does an act which he knows will injure either the person or the property of another.... *Reg.* **v.** *Pembliton* might have been ground for an argument of some plausibility, here, if this prisoner had meant to strike a pane of glass and had hit a person; it might, in that case, have been that the malice was not enough. But...an intent to injure a person is proved; that is enough.

The other two Judges concurred.

Conviction affirmed.

SECTION V.

COMMON ASSAULTS.

[Force necessary to the discharge of a constable's duties does not amount to an assault.]

BEALE *v.* CARTER.

QUEEN'S BENCH. 1589. POPHAM 12.

In trespass of assault, battery and imprisonment,...the defendant saith that he was constable of a town, and that the plaintiff brought an infant not above the age of ten days in his arms, and left him upon the ground to the great disturbance of the people there being; and that he commanded the plaintiff to take up the said infant, and to carry it from there with him, which the plaintiff refused to do; for which cause he quietly laid his hands upon the plaintiff and committed him to the stocks in the same town; where he continued for such a time until he agreed to take up the infant again. Upon which the plaintiff demurred.

FENNER was of opinion that that which the constable did was lawful; and that it is hard that an officer shall be so drawn in question for it, for this shall be an utter discouragement to good officers to execute their offices as they ought to do.

POPHAM. A constable is one of the most ancient officers in the realm for the conservation of the peace, and by his office he is a conservator of the peace. If he sees any man breaking of the peace he may take and imprison him until he find surety by obligation to keep the peace. And if a man in fury be purposed to kill, maim or beat another, the constable seeing it may arrest and imprison him until his rage be passed ; for the conservation of the peace. And if a man lays an infant, which cannot help itself, upon a dunghill or openly in the field, so that the beasts or fowls may destroy it, the constable seeing it may commit the party so doing to prison. For what greater breach of the peace can there be than to put such an infant by such means in danger of its life? And what diversity is there between this case and the case in question? For nobody was bound by the law to take up the infant but he which brought it thither ; and by such means the infant might perish. The default thereof was in the plaintiff, and therefore the action will not lie.

And it was agreed that the plaintiff take nothing by his writ.

[*Force lawful in self-defence.*]

GREEN *v.* GODDARD.

QUEEN'S BENCH.   1704.   2 SALKELD 641.

Trespass by assault and battery on October 1st. The defendant as to *vi et armis* pleaded not guilty. And as to the residue says, That long before, viz., on the 13th of September, a stranger's bull had broke into his close ; that he was driving him out to put him in the Pound, and the plaintiff came into the said close, and with strong hand hindered him and sought to rescue the said bull ; and that, in order to prevent this, the defendant struck the plaintiff lightly with a small whip. The plaintiff demurred.

PER CURIAM. There is a force *in Law*, as in every trespass *quare clausum fregit*. As, if one enters into my ground. In that case the owner must request him to depart before he can lay hands on him to turn him out; for every *impositio manuum* is an assault and battery, which cannot be justified upon the account of breaking the close in law, without a request. The other is *actual* force, as in burglary, as breaking open a door or gate. In that case it is lawful to oppose force to force ; and if one breaks down the gate, or comes into my close *vi et armis*, I need not request him to be gone, but may lay hands on him immediately; for it is but returning violence with violence. So if one comes forcibly and takes away my goods, I may oppose him without any more ado, for there is no time to make a request.

10—2

POWELL, J., held that the attempt to take and rescue the bull was an assault on defendant's person, and a taking from his person. For if H is driving cattle on the highway, and one comes and takes them from him, it is robbery; which cannot be without a taking from his person.

[*Force lawful in removing persistent trespasser.*]

WHEELER *v.* WHITING.

HEREFORD ASSIZES.   1840.   9 CARRINGTON AND PAYNE 262.

Assault and false imprisonment. [The defendant was landlord of the Beaufort Arms Hotel, at Monmouth, and had given the plaintiff into custody for making a disturbance.]

PATTESON, J. The landlord of an inn, or the occupier of a private house, whenever a person conducts himself as the plaintiff did (even according to the evidence of his own witness), is justified in telling him to leave the house; and if he will not do so, he is justified in putting him out by force, and may call in his servants to assist him in so doing. He might also authorize a policeman to do it; but it would be no part of a policeman's duty as such, unless the party had committed some offence punishable by law. But, although it would be no part of a policeman's duty to do this, it might be better in many cases that a policeman should assist the owner of the house in a matter of this kind, as he would probably get the person out of the house with less disturbance than the owner himself could do. I think that the defendant was quite justified in having the plaintiff turned out of the house; but to give him in charge to a policeman "to be dealt with according to law," is a very different thing. Telling a policeman to take charge of him is the same as telling the policeman to keep him in custody. Now as to the imprisonment, the defendant pleads that the plaintiff was making a disturbance in the house and ready and desirous to commit a breach of the peace, whereupon he gave him in charge to the policeman, to be dealt with according to law. The policeman, however, was not justified in taking him, unless he saw some breach of the peace committed : on a charge of felony it would be different. There are several questions in this case :—1st, Did the defendant cause the plaintiff to be assaulted and turned out of the house? it is plain that he did; 2nd, Was the plaintiff conducting himself in an improper manner and disturbing the quiet of the house, and did the defendant desire him to leave, and on his refusal to do so put him out? On this question it is proved by the plaintiff's own witness that the plaintiff was so conducting himself; for even if the plaintiff had been ill-used by Mr Lawrence, he was not justified in saying he would follow him into every room in the house; and if he did so say, the landlord had a right to tell him to leave the house and insist on his doing so. Then, did the defendant request the plaintiff to depart before force was used? It is essential to the defence that that should be shewn; for although a person be in the house of another and misconducting himself, the owner has no right to turn him out by force, without first requesting him to depart.

[But not if greater than is necessary for defence.]

COCKCROFT *v.* SMITH.

QUEEN'S BENCH.   1705.   2 SALKELD 642.

In trespass for an assault, battery and mayhem, defendant pleaded *son assault demesne*; which was admitted to be a good plea in mayhem. But what assault was sufficient to maintain such a plea in mayhem?

HOLT, C.J., said:—That he did not think it reasonable that for every assault a man should be banged with a cudgel. The meaning of the plea was, That he struck in his own defence. If A strike B, and B strikes again, and they close immediately, and in the scuffle B mayhems A, that is *son assault*: but if upon a little blow given by A to B, B gives him a blow that mayhems him, that is not *son assault demesne*

[EDITOR'S NOTE.] "If the prosecutor aimed a blow at the defendant, and *missed* him, still the defendant is not limited to warding off the blow, but might be justified in striking the prosecutor...[if]...it was reasonably necessary for self-defence"; *Rex* v. *Carman Dearna*, 25 T.L.R. 399.

[*Excessive force in self-defence.*]

REGINA *v.* HEWLETT.

BRISTOL ASSIZES. 1858. 1 FOSTER AND FINLASON 91.

Wounding with intent. The prisoner was indicted for wounding with intent to do grievous bodily harm to the prosecutor. It appeared that the prisoner, with a knife, struck at one Witby. The prosecutor interfered, and caught on his arm the blow intended for Witby.

CROWDER, J. This will not sustain the charge of wounding with intent to do grievous bodily harm to the prosecutor[1], but he may be convicted of unlawful wounding.

It appeared that the prosecutor, Witby, and two women, who had been drinking together, met the prisoner at midnight on the highway. Some words passed between them, when Withy struck the prisoner. The prisoner then made the blow which was the subject of the charge. It was contended for him that, under the circumstances, he was justified in doing so.

CROWDER, J. Unless the prisoner apprehended robbery, or some similar offence, or danger to life or serious bodily danger (not simply being knocked down), he would not be justified in using the knife in self-defence.

Verdict, Not guilty.

[*Excessive force in self-defence.*]

OSBORN AND ANOTHER *v.* VEITCH AND ANOTHER.

MAIDSTONE ASSIZES. 1858. 1 FOSTER AND FINLASON 317.

Action for trespass and assault. Pleas: not guilty, and *son assault demesne.* Issue.

The plaintiffs were owners of a field in which the defendants were walking with loaded guns at the half-cock in their hands. The plaintiffs desired them to withdraw and give their names, and on their refusal, advanced towards them apparently as if to apprehend them. The defendants half raised their guns, pointed them towards the

---

[1] [EDITOR'S NOTE. It would be otherwise had the prisoner stabbed the prosecutor in consequence of a supposition that he was Withy. See *R. v. Smith*, Dearsly, 559.]

plaintiffs, and threatened to shoot them. The plaintiffs (one of whom was a constable) then gave them in charge to a policeman for shooting with intent. He, with plaintiffs' assistance, seized and handcuffed them

E. James, for the defendants, submitted that there was no assault. For, as the guns were only at half-cock, there was no "present ability" to execute the threat[1].

Sed per WILLES, J. Pointing a loaded gun at a person is in law an assault. It is immaterial that it is at half-cock; cocking it is an instantaneous act; and there is a "present ability" of doing the act threatened, for it can be done in an instant.

E. James. The assault was in self-defence; the defendants were only trespassers, so the attempt to apprehend them was unlawful. Excess is not even assigned[2].

WILLES J. It was not necessary that it should be. To shoot a man is not a lawful way of repelling an assault. No doubt the charge of shooting with intent was idle[3]; and the assault [i.e. the pointing of the guns] was only a misdemeanor. The handcuffing was utterly unlawful.

Verdict for the plaintiffs; damages one farthing.

[*Force must not be continued after self-defence has ceased to be necessary.*]

REGINA *v.* DRISCOLL.

CENTRAL CRIMINAL COURT. 1841. CARRINGTON AND MARSHMAN 214.

The prisoner was indicted for unlawfully, maliciously, and feloniously assaulting John Sullivan, on the 15th of August, and wounding him in and upon the left side of the neck and left cheek, with intent to do him some grievous bodily harm.

It appeared that the prosecutor and the prisoner had some dispute, in the course of which the prisoner called the prosecutor a liar; whereupon the prosecutor clenched his fist and was about to strike him, but the prisoner's wife interposed, and pushed him down, and the prisoner inflicted on him the injury stated in the indictment.

---

[1] *Read* v. *Coker,* 15 C. B. 850; 22 L. J. R., C. P. 201.
[2] *Broughton* v. *Jackson,* 18 Q. B. 378.
[3] See *Hogg* v. *Burgess,* 27 L. J. R. Exch.

COLERIDGE, J., in summing up, said—If one man strikes another a blow, that other has a right to defend himself, and to strike a blow in his defence. But he has no right to revenge himself: and if, when all the danger is past, he strikes a blow not necessary for his defence, he commits an assault and a battery. It is a common error to suppose that one person has a right to strike another who has struck him, in order to revenge himself; and it very often influences people's minds. I have, therefore, thought it right to state what the law upon the subject really is.

> Verdict, Guilty; sentence, transportation for fifteen years.

SECTION VI.

MALICIOUS OFFENCES AGAINST PROPERTY.

[Malice being necessary, the causing a fire unintentionally, even by a felony, is not arson.]

THE QUEEN *v.* FAULKNER.

IRISH CROWN CASE RESERVED.　1876.　　11 IRISH REP. C. L. 8.

Case reserved by Lawson, J., at the Cork Summer Assizes, 1876. The prisoner was indicted under the 24 and 25 Vict. c. 97, for arson of a ship, the "Zemindar." The indictment contained two counts; the first charged that the prisoner feloniously, unlawfully, and maliciously did set fire to the ship with intent thereby to prejudice the owners of the ship; the second was similar, but charged the intent to be to prejudice the owners of the goods and chattels on board the ship. It was proved that the "Zemindar" was on her voyage home with a cargo of rum, sugar, and cotton; that the prisoner was a seaman on board; that he went into the forecastle hold, opened the sliding door in the bulk-head, and so got into the hold where the rum was stored. He had no business there, and no authority to go there, and went for the purpose of stealing some rum. He bored a hole in the cask with a gimlet; the rum ran out; when trying to put a spile in the hole out of which the rum was running, he had a lighted match in his hand, and the rum caught fire. The prisoner himself was burned on the

arms and neck, and the ship caught fire and was completely destroyed.
...The Crown counsel conceded that the prisoner had no intention of
burning the vessel or of igniting the rum, and raised no question as to
prisoner's imagining or having any ground for supposing that the fire
would be the result or consequence of his act in stealing the rum....
I told the jury that, although the prisoner had no actual intention of
burning the vessel, still, if they found that he was engaged in stealing
rum, and that the fire took place in the manner above stated, they ought
to find him guilty. The jury convicted the prisoner on both counts, and
he was sentenced to seven years' penal servitude.

*   *   *

O'BRIEN, J. With respect to *The Queen* v. *Pembliton*[1], it appears
to me there were much stronger grounds in that case for upholding
the conviction than exist in the case before us. In that case, the
breaking of the window was the act of the prisoner. He threw the
stone that broke it. He threw it with the unlawful intent of striking
some one of the crowd about; and the breaking of the window was the
direct and immediate result of his act. Yet the Court unanimously
quashed the conviction ; upon the ground that, although the prisoner
threw the stone intending to strike some one or more persons, he did
not intend to break the window. The Court at the same time intimated their opinion that if the jury had found that the prisoner,
knowing the window was there, might have reasonably expected that
the result of his act would be the breaking of the window, then the
conviction should be upheld.

During the argument of this case, the Crown counsel required us to
assume that the jury found their verdict upon the ground that in their
opinion the prisoner may have expected that the fire would be the
consequence of his act in stealing the rum, but nevertheless did the
act recklessly, not caring whether the fire took place or not. But at
the trial there was not even a suggestion of any such ground. And
we cannot assume that the jury formed an opinion which there was no
evidence to sustain, and which would be altogether inconsistent with
the circumstances under which the fire took place. The reasonable
inference from the evidence is that the prisoner lighted the match for
the purpose of putting the spile in the hole to stop the further running
of the rum, and that while he was attempting to do so the rum came
in contact with the lighted match and took fire.

The recent case of *The Queen* v. *Welch*[2] has been also referred to ;
and has been relied on by the Crown counsel on the ground that,

---

[1] L. R. 2 C. C. R. 119. *Infra*, p. 157.   [2] 1 Q. B. D. 23.

though the jury found that the prisoner did not in fact intend to kill, maim, or wound the mare that had died from the injury inflicted by him, the prisoner was nevertheless convicted on an indictment charging him with having unlawfully and maliciously killed, maimed or wounded the mare, and such conviction was upheld by the Court. But on referring to the circumstances of that case it will be seen that it does not in any way conflict with the previous case of *The Queen* v. *Pembliton,* and furnishes no ground for sustaining the present conviction. Mr Justice Lindley, who tried that subsequent case, appears to have acted in accordance with the opinion expressed by the Judges in *The Queen* v. *Pembliton.* Besides leaving to the jury the question of prisoner's intent he also left them a second question, namely, whether the prisoner, when he did the act complained of, knew that what he was doing might kill, maim, or wound the mare, and nevertheless did the act recklessly, and not caring whether the mare was injured or not? The jury answered that second question in the affirmative; their finding was clearly warranted by the evidence; and the conviction was properly affirmed. By those two questions a distinction was taken between the case of an act done by a party with the actual intent to cause the injury inflicted; and the case of an act done by a party knowing or believing that it would or might cause such injury, but reckless of the result whether it did or did not. In the case now before us, there was no ground whatever for submitting to the jury any question as to the prisoner believing or supposing that the stealing of the rum would be attended with a result so accidental and so dangerous to himself.

[Nine Judges concurred in the decision; and one alone dissented from it.]

Conviction quashed.

[*Foresight of the probability of arson, if combined with recklessness as to that probability, will be sufficient malice.*]

REGINA *v.* HARRIS AND ATKINS.

Central Criminal Court. 1882.   Sessions Papers, xcv. 523.

James Harris and David Atkins were indicted for feloniously, unlawfully, and maliciously setting fire to the house of John Derby Allcroft with intent to injure him.

[Evidence was given by various witnesses, and amongst them by William Hearn, who said]:—"I am a builder and carry on business in Craven Terrace. In August last I was engaged by Mr Allcroft to do some work at his house, 108 Lancaster Gate. The prisoner Harris was in my employ as a painter. On the morning of 14th September I was called to a fire at 108 Lancaster Gate. I found that a picture known as "The Monarch of the Meadows" had been cut out of its frame. I had seen it on the previous afternoon, standing in the boudoir. The frame was partially burnt at the bottom, where it stood on the floor; there was oil on the canvas at the back of the frame, also some candle grease on the lower right-hand corner of the frame; and in front of the frame was this piece of one of my cloths, partially burnt, it is part of the covering that hung in front of the picture...I found nine of the joists of the floor nearly burnt through."

HAWKINS, J., in leaving the case to the jury, said, "If a man sets fire to a chattel[1] inside a house, and thereby accidentally and unintentionally sets fire to the house, this would not be arson (*Reg.* v. *Child*; L. R., 1 C. C. R. 307). But if the house was wilfully set fire to for the purpose of destroying the evidence of the picture having been stolen, and so leading to the supposition that it had been destroyed, that would amount to the crime of arson. Or again, if you should think that Harris set fire to the picture-frame, not with the purpose of setting fire to the house, but still with a knowledge that in all probability the house would be set fire to, and with a feeling of recklessness and indifference as to whether it caught fire or not, then (as the house was in fact set on fire though through the medium of the frame) there would be abundant evidence to justify a conviction for arson.

The jury, in reply to questions left to them, found—first, that the prisoner did not set fire to the house apart from the frame; secondly, that he did set fire to the frame; thirdly, that the probable result would be setting fire to the house; fourthly, that he did not intend to set fire to the house; fifthly, that he was not aware that what he did would probably set fire to the house; sixthly, that he was not reckless and indifferent as to whether it was set on fire or not. Upon these findings his Lordship directed a verdict of

Not guilty.

---

[1] [EDITOR'S NOTE. The statute (24 and 25 Vict. c. 97) contains no section making it a felony maliciously to set fire to *goods*; except when they are (s. 7) in a building under certain particular circumstances, as to which see *Reg.* v. *Child*, L. R. 1 C. C. R. 307.]

[But similar recklessness, without actual foresight, will not suffice.]

REGINA *v.* NATTRASS.

CENTRAL CRIMINAL COURT.   1882.   SESSIONS PAPERS, XCV. 520.

Maggie Nattrass was indicted, under 24 and 25 Vict. c. 97, s. 7, for feloniously, unlawfully and maliciously attempting to set fire to the dwelling-house of John Alexander by setting fire to certain things in the said dwelling-house under such circumstances that if the house had been set fire to, her act would have been felony. [Apart from this statute, the attempt would have been only a misdemeanor.]

[Evidence was given by various witnesses, and amongst them by Henry Brown, who said]:—"I am a friend of the prosecutor. I was at his house on Sunday evening January 15th about 7 o'clock. He shewed me some fires that had taken place. I went into the drawing-room. I there heard a cry of "Fire!" I directly rushed out with Mr Alexander into the nursery, and I assisted him to pull the things off the bed and put out the fire. The counterpane and two blankets were on fire and the spring mattress. The prisoner was in the room. There was no fire in the grate; the gas was alight; that was six or seven feet from the bedstead. I should not think the fire had been burning very long; it only took a minute or two to stamp it out with our feet. I think some things were in flames, the blankets were smouldering. I asked the prisoner why she did it, she said, 'I don't know how I did it; I did not do it willingly'."

HAWKINS, J. The mere setting fire to an article in the house, which might have set fire to the house itself, will not do. There must be an intent, or something from which we can infer an intent, to injure the house itself. A mere intent to injure the owner by destroying goods of his in the house is not sufficient.

Burnie, for Crown, submitted that such an intent to injure might, however, suffice, provided it were accompanied by some utterly reckless act which resulted in burning the house. Suppose the prisoner put coals on the bed and set fire to it, intending to injure the prosecutor, although not intending the house to catch fire.

HAWKINS, J. In my opinion even that would not suffice. If a person maliciously, with intent to injure another by merely burning his goods, sets fire to such goods in his house, that does not in my opinion amount to a felony, even though the house catches fire. Unless indeed the person setting fire to the goods knew that by so doing he would probably cause the house also to take fire; (in which latter case there would be strong evidence that he intended to bring about this probable consequence, viz., the burning of the house). If the prisoner put coals on the bed, but then called out "Fire!" immediately, so that there was little chance of the house being burnt—or if she spitefully set fire to the curtains, thinking that only the curtains would be burnt, and then against her wish the house caught fire—that would not be arson. In the present case the question for the jury is whether the facts do not rather shew a disposition to destroy the goods, but not the house. If so she might be punished for what she has done, but not upon this indictment.

Verdict, Not guilty.

[*In all* statutory *wrongs of malice, there must be intention to do the particular kind of harm that actually was done.*]

REGINA *v.* PEMBLITON.

CROWN CASE RESERVED.   1874.   L. R. 2 C. C. R. 119.

At the quarter sessions of the peace held at Wolverhampton, on the 8th of January, Henry Pembliton was indicted for that he "unlawfully and maliciously did commit damage, injury, and spoil upon a window in the house of Henry Kirkham," contrary to the provisions of the statute 24 and 25 Vict. c. 97, s. 51[1].

On the night of the 6th of December, 1873, the prisoner was drinking with others at a public-house called "The Grand Turk," kept by the prosecutor. About eleven o'clock, p.m., the whole party were turned out of the house for being disorderly, and they then began to fight in the street, and near the prosecutor's window, where a crowd of from forty to fifty persons collected. The prisoner, after fighting some time with persons in the crowd, separated himself from them and removed to the other side of the street, where he picked up a large

---

[1] This section of the statute enacts: "Whosoever shall unlawfully and maliciously commit any damage, injury, or spoil to or upon any real or personal property whatsoever, either of a public or a private nature, for which no punishment is hereinbefore provided, the damage, injury, or spoil being to an amount exceeding five pounds, shall be guilty of a misdemeanor; and being convicted thereof shall be liable at the discretion of the Court to be imprisoned for any term not exceeding two years, with or without hard labour."

stone and threw it at the persons he had been fighting with. The stone passed over the heads of those persons and struck a large plate-glass window in the prosecutor's house and broke it, thereby doing damage to the extent of £7. 12s. 9d. The jury, after hearing evidence on both sides, found that the prisoner threw the stone which broke the window, but that he threw it at the people he had been fighting with, intending to strike one or more of them with it, *but[1] not intending to break the window*; and they returned a verdict of "guilty." Thereupon the learned Recorder respited the sentence and admitted the prisoner to bail, and prayed the judgment of the Court for Crown Cases Reserved, whether upon the facts stated and the finding of the jury the prisoner was rightly convicted or not.

No counsel appeared for the prisoner.

Underhill, for the prosecution. The finding of the jury as to intent is surplusage; directly it is proved that he threw the stone which caused the damage without just cause, the offence is established.

[LUSH, J. That omits the word "maliciously."]

In this Act there are a number of sections in which intent is a necessary ingredient to the offence, and in all of them this is expressed. Thus a distinction is drawn by the legislature; and if intent had been necessary here, it would have been inserted. The common-law rule as to malice is applicable here, and the consideration arises whether "the fact has been attended with such circumstances as are the ordinary symptoms of a wicked, depraved, malignant spirit": Foster's *Crown Cases*, p. 256; *Russell on Crimes*, vol. I. p. 667 (4th ed.). And here the jury have found that the prisoner was actuated by malice.

[BLACKBURN, J. But only of a particular kind, and not against the person injured.]

In *Reg.* v. *Ward*[2] the prisoner was charged with wounding with intent, and convicted of malicious wounding, though his intention was to frighten, not to shoot the prosecutor.

[BLACKBURN, J. There was evidence of malice in that case, but here the express finding of the jury negatives malice.]

In *Rex* v. *Haughton*[3] the prisoner set fire to a cowhouse, not knowing a cow was in it, and was convicted of maliciously burning the cow. So in Hale's *Pleas*, p. 474, throwing a stone over a wall with intent to do hurt to people passing, and killing one of them, is murder.

---

[1] [EDITOR'S NOTE.] Cf. the similar finding in *Woodley* v. *Cork*, Irish L. R. [1910] 2 K. B. 29.

[2] Law Rep. 1 C. C. 356.

[3] 5 C. and P. 559.

[BLACKBURN, J. Lord Coke, 3 Inst., p. 56, puts the case of a man stealing deer in a park, shooting at the deer, and by the glance of the arrow killing a boy that is hidden in a bush, and calls this murder; but can anyone say that ruling would be adopted now?]

The test is whether the act is malicious in itself, as in the case of a person wilfully riding an unruly horse into a crowd: East, *Pleas of the Crown*, p. 231.

[BLACKBURN, J. I should have told the jury that if the prisoner knew there were windows behind, and that the probable consequence of his act would be to break one of them, that would be evidence for them of malice. The jury might perhaps have convicted on such a charge. But we have to consider their actual findings.]

LORD COLERIDGE, C.J. I am of opinion that the conviction should be quashed. The facts of the case are that there was fighting going on in the streets of Wolverhampton, near the prosecutor's house, and the prisoner, after fighting some time, separated himself from the crowd and threw a stone, which missed the person he aimed at, but struck and broke a window, doing damage to the extent of upwards of £5. The question is, whether under an indictment for unlawfully and maliciously injuring the property of the owner of the plate-glass window, these facts will support the indictment, when coupled with the other facts found by the jury, that the prisoner threw the stone at the people intending to strike one or more of them, but not intending to break a window. I am of opinion that the evidence does not support the conviction. The indictment is under the 24 and 25 Vict. c. 97. s. 51, which deals with malicious injuries to property, and the section expressly says that the act is to be unlawful and malicious. There is also the 58th section, which makes it immaterial whether the offence has been committed from malice against the owner of the property or otherwise, that is, from malice against some one not the owner of the property. In both these sections it seems to me that what is intended by the statute is a wilful doing of an intentional act. Without saying that if the case had been left to them in a different way the conviction could not have been supported, if, on these facts, the jury had come to a conclusion that the prisoner was reckless of the consequence of his act, and might reasonably have expected that it would result in breaking the window, it is sufficient to say that the jury have expressly found the contrary. I do not say anything to throw doubt on the rule under the common law in cases of murder which has been referred to, but the principles laid down in such cases have no application to the statutable offence we have to consider.

BLACKBURN, J. I am of the same opinion. We have not now to

consider what would be 'malice aforethought' to bring a given case within the common law definition of murder. Here the statute says that the act must be unlawful and malicious, and malice may be defined to be " where any person wilfully does an act injurious to another without lawful excuse." Can this man be considered, on the case submitted to us, as having wilfully broken a pane of glass? The jury might perhaps have found on this evidence that the act was malicious, because they might have found that the prisoner knew that the natural consequence of his act would be to break the glass, and although that was not his wish, yet that he was reckless whether he did it or not; but the jury have not so found. I think it is impossible to say in this case that the prisoner has 'maliciously' done an act which he did not intend to do.

*   *   *

The other three Judges were of the same opinion.

Conviction quashed.

[See REG. *v.* FAULKNER, *supra*, p. 152.]

SECTION VII.

BURGLARY.

CHAPTER I. THE PLACE.

[*Burglary can only be committed in a* dwelling-house.]

REX *v.* DAVIS AND ANOTHER.

CROWN CASE RESERVED. 1817.   RUSSELL AND RYAN 322.

The prisoners were tried before Mr JUSTICE ABBOTT (present Mr JUSTICE PARK), at the Old Bailey January Sessions, in the year 1817, upon an indictment which charged them with breaking and entering the dwelling-house of Thomas Porteous, Esq., in the day-time, certain persons named being therein, and stealing therein a silver candlestick of the value of fifty shillings.

The house was situate in Half-Moon Street, Piccadilly; and the evidence of breaking the house (upon which alone this case was reserved), was the opening of the area gate at the street with a skeleton key, and so descending the area steps, and entering the house by a door in the area, which did not appear to have been shut.

ABBOTT, J., having some doubt whether this was a breaking of the dwelling-house, told the jury he would reserve that point for the opinion of the Judges, if they should think the prisoners got into the house in the manner stated and stole the candlestick, and should think the candlestick of less value than forty shillings.

The jury said, they thought the candlestick was not worth forty shillings; and in other respects they thought the prisoners guilty.

ABBOTT, J., directed a minute to be made, that the verdict might afterwards be recorded according to the opinion of the Judges upon the point reserved; and the learned Judge directed, that if the Judges should be of opinion that this was a breaking, the verdict should be recorded as finding the prisoners guilty of the breaking and entering, &c., and stealing to the value of thirty-nine shillings. But if the Judges should be of opinion that this was not a breaking, then the verdict was to be recorded finding the prisoners not guilty of the breaking, but guilty of stealing to the value of thirty-nine shillings, in order that they might have the Benefit of Clergy.

In Hilary term, 1817, this case was considered by the Judges, when they were unanimously of opinion, that breaking the area gate was not a breaking of the dwelling-house, as there was no free passage, in time of sleep, from the area into the house.

[EDITOR'S NOTE. Even if the burglary were disproved, the charge of larceny remained; and in that charge, the value was a matter of importance. For though the Benefit of Clergy could be claimed in cases of simple larceny, it was taken away by 12 Anne, st. 1, c. 7 from larcenies which were aggravated by being committed in a dwelling-house to a value of 40s. or upwards. In burglary, the benefit had been taken away by 18 Eliz. c. 7.]

[*A building which, though occupied, is not slept in, is not a dwelling-house.*]

REX *v.* MARTIN.

CROWN CASE RESERVED.   1806.   RUSSELL AND RYAN 108.

The prisoners were tried before Mr BARON GRAHAM, at the Lent Assizes for the county of Northampton, in the year 1806, on an indictment for a burglary committed on the 19th of December, 1805, in the dwelling-house of one Samuel Clayson.

The house was to all intents and purposes a complete dwelling-house, if it could under the circumstances be considered as *inhabited*, upon which question the point arose.

The house stood in a street in Wellingborough, in the range of houses, the entry from the street being by a common door-way. The inside of the house consisted of a shop and parlour, from whence the goods were taken, and a staircase leading to a room over the shop in which there was bedding, but it was not fitted up. The prosecutor took it about two years before the offence was committed, and made several alterations in it, intending to have married and lived in it: but continuing unmarried, and his mother living in a house next door but one, he slept every night at her house. Every morning he went to his house, transacted his business in the shop and parlour, and dined and entertained his friends and passed the whole day there, considering it as his only home. When he first bought the house he had a tenant; who quitted it soon afterwards, and since that time no person had slept in it.

It appeared from the evidence, that the prisoners, and others connected with them, had broken open the house in the night and stolen drapery and hosiery goods to the amount of considerably more than £200. But an objection was taken that the shop from whence the goods were taken was not the dwelling-house of the prosecutor; and though the objection appeared to the learned Judge to have weight, he thought it proper, in a case attended with circumstances of considerable aggravation, to overrule it. The case being left to the jury, they found the prisoners guilty; and sentence of death was passed upon them; but the point was saved for the consideration of the Judges.

The question reserved for the opinion of the Judges was, whether this sort of inhabiting was sufficient to make the house the prosecutor's dwelling-house.

In Easter term 28th of April, 1806, at a meeting of all the Judges (except Lord Ellenborough) the conviction was held wrong, the house not being a dwelling-house.

[*Even though the tenant intend to sleep there soon.*]

REX *v.* THOMPSON.

SURREY ASSIZES.   1796.   LEACH 771.

Norreg Thompson was charged before Mr JUSTICE GROSE for burglariously breaking and entering the dwelling-house of Thomas Parry, at Stoke Newington, on the 9th of November preceding, and stealing two Brussels carpets, and a quantity of wearing apparel and other articles, the property of the said Thomas Parry.

It appeared in evidence that the prosecutor had recently before hired a house in the Apollo Plotts, in Walworth; that neither he nor any of his family or servants had ever yet slept therein; but that he had removed a great part of his household furniture into the house, which was locked up in the house after dark on the 9th of November. The door was broken open and the goods taken away before daylight the ensuing morning.

The Court was of opinion that this house, as no person had inhabited it, could not be considered as a dwelling-house so as to satisfy an indictment for burglary.

And the prisoner was accordingly acquitted.

[*Nor is it sufficient that persons do sleep there, unless they are members of the occupier's household.*]

REX *v.* HARRIS.

OLD BAILEY SESSIONS.   1795.   LEACH 701.

At the Old Bailey in October Session, 1795, John Harris was tried before the RECORDER of London for burglariously breaking and entering the dwelling-house of Henry William Dinsdale, on the 6th of October, and stealing therein a gold watch value £10, the goods of the said William Dinsdale.

It appeared in evidence, that Mr Dinsdale had lately taken the house in Queen Street, in Cheapside, but had never slept in it himself; but on the night of the burglary, and for six nights before, had procured two hair-dressers, of the names of Thomas Nash and James Chamberlain, who resided at St Ann's-lane, near Maiden-lane, in Wood-street, but in no situation of servitude to the prosecutor, to sleep in this house for the purpose of taking care of the goods and merchandize belonging to Mr Dinsdale, which were deposited in the house.

The Court was of opinion, that as the prosecutor had only so far taken possession of the house as to deposit certain articles of his trade therein, but had neither slept in it himself nor had any of his servants, it could not, in contemplation of law, be called his dwelling-house.

The jury, therefore, under the direction of the Court, found him guilty of the larceny only, but not guilty of stealing in a dwelling-house, or of the burglary; and he was sentenced to transportation for seven years.

[*But if occupied by a household habitually, it remains a dwelling-house even during their temporary absence.*]

A RESOLUTION.

1594.   POPHAM 52.

It was agreed by all the Justices and the Barons of the Exchequer (upon an assembly made at Serjeants' Inn), after search made for the ancient precedents, and upon good deliberation taken :—That if a man have two houses, and inhabit sometimes in one and sometimes in the other, if that house in which he doth not then inhabit be broken in the night, to the intent to steal the goods then being in this house, this is burglary, although no person be then in the house....For the house of every one is the proper place to preserve his goods, although no person be there.

REX *v.* NUTBROWN.

NEWGATE SESSIONS.   1750.   FOSTER'S CROWN LAW 76.

John Nutbrown and Miles Nutbrown were indicted for burglary in the dwelling-house of one Mr Fakney at Hackney, and stealing divers goods. It appeared by Mr Fakney's evidence, that he held this house for a term of years which is not yet expired, and made use of it as a country-house in the summer, his chief residence being in London. That, about the latter end of the last summer, he removed with his whole family to his house in the city, and brought away a considerable

part of his goods.   That in November his house was broke open before
and in part rifled : upon which he removed the remainder of his household furniture, except a clock, and a few old bedsteads, and some
lumber of very little value; leaving no bed or kitchen-furniture, nor
anything else for the accommodation of a family.   Mr Fakney being
asked whether at the time he so disfurnished his house he had any
intention of returning to reside there declared, that he had not come to
any settled resolution whether to return or not; but was rather inclined totally to quit the house, and to let it for the remainder of his
term.   It was not till January that the prisoners broke into it.

THE COURT was of opinion, that the prosecutor having left his house,
and disfurnished it in the manner before-mentioned, without any settled
resolution of returning, but rather inclining to the contrary, it could
not, under these circumstances, be deemed his dwelling-house at the
time the fact was committed ; and accordingly directed the jury to
acquit the prisoners of the burglary ; which they did ; but found them
guilty of felony in stealing the clock and some other small matters : and
they were ordered for transportation.

N.B.   Where the owner quitteth the house, *animo revertendi*, it
may still be considered as his mansion-house, though no person be left in
it ; many citizens, and some lawyers, do so from a principle of good
husbandry in the summer or for a long vacation....But there must be
an intention of returning, otherwise it will not be burglary.

CHAPTER II.   THE BREAKING.

[There must be a breaking.]

REGINA v. BAYNES.

NEWGATE SESSIONS.   1594.   POPHAM 84.

Indictment for burglary.   The case was this:—one Baynes, with
another, came in the night-time to a tavern, in London to drink.   And,
after they had drunk, the said Baynes stole, in a chamber of the same
house, a cup in which they drank....

Agreed by POPHAM, ANDERSON, and PERRIAM, with the Recorder
and Serjeants-at-law then being there, that this was not burglary.

[But either breaking in or (by Statute) breaking out will suffice.]

THE KING *v.* M'KEARNEY.

IRISH CROWN CASE RESERVED.   1829.   JEBB 99.

The prisoner was tried before M'CLELLAND, B., at the Spring Assizes
at Omagh in 1829, on an indictment for a burglary in the house of
Louis Davis.   There were three counts in the indictment; the first
for breaking and entering the house by night with intent to steal, &c.;—
the second for entering the house with intent to steal, &c., and breaking said house by night, and getting out of the same;—the third for
entering said house with intent to steal, &c., and by night breaking
out of said house.

It appeared on the trial that on the 8th of January, 1829, the
prisoner was, about 11 o'clock at night, discovered in the cellar of the
house hid under a heap of potatoes; he fled from the cellar into a room
in the house and locked himself in; this room had a shed roof and
a sky-light in the roof.   Davis, the owner of the house, heard the
sky-light breaking, and then ran round into his yard, when he saw the
prisoner with his head out of the sky-light endeavouring to escape,—
he struck the prisoner a blow on the head, when he fell down into the
room, where he was taken by a police constable immediately after, on
his breaking open the door which the prisoner had looked.   The jury
convicted the prisoner, but the learned Baron entertaining some doubts
whether there was a sufficient breaking out of the house to constitute
the crime of burglary, reserved the following question for the twelve
Judges: Whether, the prisoner having only got his head out of the
sky-light, this was a sufficient breaking out of the house to complete
the crime of burglary?

THE JUDGES unanimously ruled that the conviction was right.

[The breaking of even an inner door suffices.]

REGINA *v.* WENMOUTH.

BODMIN ASSIZES.   1860.   8 Cox 348.

Indictment for burglary.   The prisoner was in the service of
a carpenter and grocer; and was apprenticed to him in the business of
carpenter, and lived in his house.   The master, suspecting that he was
in the habit of robbing the till in the grocer's shop (which was

detached from the rest of the house, but connected with the passage and under the same roof) concealed himself there, having fastened the door. About 1 a.m. the prisoner burst open the door and entered the shop for the purpose of taking money from the till. He was stopped by his master. The prisoner had no business in the grocer's shop.

Cole, for prisoner, submitted that as the prisoner was domiciled in the house, his bursting open a door under the same roof could not be housebreaking.

KEATING, J. Even if the prisoner had opened the carpenter's shop, under these circumstances, I should be of opinion that it was house-breaking. I have no doubt that bursting open the door of the grocer's shop, in the manner described, was a sufficient breaking.

See also the ANONYMOUS case given below, p. 175.

[*Merely* moving *a closed window is a sufficient breaking.*]

REX *v.* HAINES.

CROWN CASE RESERVED.   1821.   RUSSELL AND RYAN 451.

The prisoners were tried and convicted before Mr JUSTICE RICHARD-SON, at the Old Bailey Sessions, February, 1821, for burglariously break-ing and entering the dwelling-house of Richard Plunkett, with intent to steal the goods and chattels in the same dwelling-house then being.

The evidence was satisfactory as to the fact; but a doubt arose whether the *breaking* was sufficient in point of law to constitute burglary.

The prisoners were found in the front parlour of the prosecutor's house, about a quarter-past five o'clock in the evening of the 16th of January, 1821. It was then quite dark. It appeared that they had entered through the upper part of the window, which the prose-cutor had closed a short time before, and which the prisoners had opened by pushing down the upper sash.

There was a fastening to the lower sash, but none to the upper sash, which, during the daytime, was usually kept closed by the pulley-weight only.

There was an outside shutter to this window, which was usually closed and fastened about dark by the sons of the prosecutor, on their return from school; but on the evening in question the closing the outer shutter was delayed, in consequence of the children returning later than usual from school.

The question was, whether the pushing down of the upper sash by the prisoners, in the manner stated, amounted to a sufficient breaking.

In Easter term, 1821, the Judges met, and considered this case. They were unanimously of opinion that the pulling down of the sash was a sufficient breaking, and the prisoner was rightly convicted.

[*But not moving a window which is* already *partly open.*]

REX *v.* SMITH.

CROWN CASE RESERVED.   1827.   1 MOODY 178.

The prisoner was tried before Mr JUSTICE HOLROYD, at the December Sessions at the Old Bailey, in the year 1827, for a capital felony, in breaking and entering a dwelling-house and committing larceny therein.

The housebreaking (if there was one by the prisoner) was by pushing up or raising the lower sash of the parlour window; which was proved to have been, at about eight or nine o'clock in the morning, in a close state and shut quite down, but to have been also seen about twelve o'clock at noon of the same day in an open state or raised about a couple of inches, with the prisoner very near it; but yet only so open and raised as that there was not room enough for a person to enter the house through that opening, and commit the larceny. On the evidence it was clear, that the prisoner immediately afterwards threw the sash quite up, and then having thus removed the obstruction to his entrance, entered through the enlarged aperture thus made, and committed the felony; but the jury declared their opinion to be that the prisoner did not open the window all the way, but only raised the sash a second time.

He was convicted of the full offence, on the authority of a similar case that had recently occurred at the Old Bailey, a note of which was furnished by Mr Baron Hullock: in which case similar circumstances had been held to amount to a felonious breaking of the house.

From doubts, however, that were understood to have been afterwards expressed upon the point, the learned Judge respited the judgment, in order to take the opinion of the Judges upon the propriety of the conviction, as to the capital part of the offence.

The question for the opinion of the Judges was, whether the prisoner was properly convicted of the house-breaking, or whether he should have been convicted of larceny only?

In Hilary term, 1828, the Judges met, and all thought there was no decision under which this could be held to be a breaking, and that they ought not to go beyond what had been decided, unless the case was within some settled principle, which this was not; and that the conviction for house-breaking was, therefore, wrong.

[*A mere entry, if obtained by deceit, is in law a* constructive *breaking.*]

LE MOTT'S CASE.

OLD BAILEY.   166–.   KELYNG 42.

At the Sessions I enquired of Le Mott's case, which was adjudged in the time of the late troubles. My brother WYLDE [the Recorder] told me, that the case was this: That thieves came with intent to rob Le Mott, and, finding the door locked up, pretended they came to speak with him. Thereupon a maid servant opened the door; and they came in and robbed him. And this being in the night-time, this was adjudged Burglary, and the persons hanged. For their intention being to rob, and getting the door open by a false pretence, this was *in fraudem legis.* So they were guilty of Burglary, though they did not actually break the house. For this was in law an actual breaking; being obtained by fraud to have the door opened. As, if men pretend a warrant to a constable, and bring him along with them, and under that pretence rob the house, this, if it be in the night, is Burglary.

[*Constructive breaking.*]

REX *v.* CASSY.

NEWGATE SESSIONS.   1666.   KELYNG 62.

Thomas Cassy and John Cotter were indicted for robbing William Pinkney, a goldsmith, in his house near the highway by the Temple Bar, in the night-time; and stealing several parcels of plate and other

things from him. They were also indicted for the same offence as
a burglary; for breaking his house in the night, and stealing his plate.
On both these indictments they were arraigned and tried. Upon
the evidence the case appeared to be, that Cotter was a lodger in the
house of the said Pinkney, and, knowing that he had plate and money
to a good value, he combined with the aforesaid Cassy, and one John
Harrington, and Gerard Cleasehard. They three contrived that one of
those three should come, as servant of the other, to hire lodgings there,
for his master and another gentleman. Cotter told them, that Pinkney
was one who constantly kept prayers every night; and they could not
have so good an opportunity to surprise him as to desire to join in
prayer with him, and at that time to fall on him and his maid, there
being then no other company in the house. Accordingly one of them
came on Saturday, in the afternoon, and hired lodgings there, pretending it to be for his master and another gentleman of good quality.
And about eight o'clock at night they all came thither; two of them
being in very good habits; and when they were in their chamber they
sent for ale, and desired Pinkney to drink with them, which he did.
While they were drinking, Cotter came in to his lodging; and they,
hearing one go upstairs, asked who it was, and Pinkney told them it
was an honest gentleman, one Mr Cotter, who lodged in his house.
They desired to be acquainted with him, and that he might be desired
to come to them. Thereupon Pinkney sent his maid to him, to let him
know the gentlemen desired to be acquainted with him. To which,
Cotter sent word it was late, the next day was the Sabbath, and he
desired to be private. Thereupon those persons told Pinkney they had
heard he was a religious man, and used to perform family duties; in
which they desired to join with them. At which Pinkney was very
well pleased that he had got such religious persons; and so called to
prayers. While he was at his devotion, they rose up, and bound him
and his servant; and then Cotter came to them and shewed them
where the money and plate lay. They ransacked the house, and broke
open several doors and cupboards fixed to the house. Upon this
evidence, myself, my brother Wylde (Recorder), and Mr Howell
(Deputy Recorder), (being all who were there present of the long robe),
were of opinion that the entrance into the house being gained by fraud,
with an intent to rob, and they making use of this entrance, thus fraudulently obtained in the night-time, to break doors open, this was
Burglary (agreeable to the case of Farr in this book, and the case of
Mr Le Mott in this book). Accordingly they were found guilty; and
had judgment; and were executed.

[*But not an entry which follows upon a mere* unsuccessful *attempt to deceive.*]

REGINA *v.* JOHNSON AND JONES.

CENTRAL CRIMINAL COURT.   1841.   CARRINGTON AND MARSHMAN 218.

Indictment for burglariously breaking and entering the house of Joseph Drake, [and also for a larceny therein.]

A lad named Cole, who was groom to Mr Drake, met with the prisoner Jones on Thursday the 26th of August, and they entered into conversation about the badness of trade. Jones said that he would not blame anybody who would rob another in these hard times, and asked the lad where his master kept his plate, and being told said, that if he would let him into the house he would give him £500. The lad, almost immediately, told a policeman what had passed; and, his master being out of town, agreed to act under the directions of the police, in order to detect the prisoner Jones. He accordingly met him on the Saturday, and arranged to meet him again on the Sunday, when they met with the other prisoner Johnson; and it was arranged that Cole should get the other servants out of the way and admit the two prisoners to the house on the Sunday evening. In the mean time several policemen were secreted in the prosecutor's house. The lad Cole, about a quarter past nine in the evening, went and fetched the prisoner Johnson to the house. Cole then lifted the latch of the stable-yard door and a little gate, and also the kitchen door, and let Johnson in, and followed him into the back kitchen. Johnson then went up-stairs, and, as he was about to open the door of the room in which the prosecutor's iron chest was deposited, the police seized him before he had done anything, and locked him up in one of the rooms of the house. A few minutes after he had been so locked up, Cole, who had been out to fetch the other prisoner Jones, brought him to the house and let him in in the same way as he had let in Johnson, viz. by opening the door for him. Jones went into the back kitchen, and took from it the plate-basket containing the articles of plate mentioned in the indict-ment.

MAULE, J., in summing up (ROLFE, B., being present), said—It appears to me that on the present occasion, according to the evidence, there was no such breaking as to constitute the crime of burglary. Cole, the groom, it is true, appeared to concur with the prisoners in the commission of the offence. But in fact he did not really concur with them; and he, acting under the directions of the police, must be taken to have been acting under the direction of Mr Drake the prosecutor.

Under the circumstances of this case the prisoners went in at a door which, as it seems to me, was lawfully open. Therefore neither of them was guilty of burglary. And the prisoner Johnson, if not guilty of burglary, was not guilty of anything that is charged in the indictment, because he was in custody at the time when the plate was taken.

> Verdict—Jones, guilty of stealing in a dwelling-house goods above the value of £5; Johnson, not guilty.

Johnson was detained to be indicted as an accessory before the fact to Jones' offence; and, at the following Sessions, was tried and convicted.

Chapter III.   The Entry.

[*Entry of any part, however small, of the* body *of the burglar suffices.*]

REX *v.* DAVIS.

Crown Case Reserved.   1823.   Russell and Ryan 499.

The prisoner was tried at the Old Bailey Sessions, in January, 1823, before the Chief Baron Richards, for burglary, in the dwelling-house of Montague Levyson.

The prosecutor Levyson, who dealt in watches and some jewellery, stated, that on the 2nd of January, about six o'clock in the evening, as he was standing in Pall Mall opposite his shop, he watched the prisoner, a little boy, standing by the window of the shop which was part of the prosecutor's dwelling-house; and presently observed the prisoner push his finger against a pane of the glass in the corner of the window. The glass fell inside by the force of his finger. The prosecutor added that, standing as he did in the street, he saw the forepart of the prisoner's finger on the shop side of the glass; and he instantly apprehended him.

The jury convicted the prisoner; but the learned Judge, having some doubt whether this was an entry sufficient to make the offence a burglary, submitted the case to the consideration of the Judges.

In Hilary term, 1823, the case was taken into consideration by the Judges; who held, that there was a sufficient entry to constitute burglary.

[*And the insertion of an instrument, if for the purpose of effecting
the* ulterior *felony aimed at, constitutes an Entry.*]

A RESOLUTION.

A.D. 1583.   1 ANDERSON 114.

All the Justices, assembled at Serjeants' Inn, agreed that if one
breaks the glass in a window in any one's dwelling and, with hooks,
drags the carpets out and feloniously takes them away, this, if done in
the night-time, is burglary, although the man who did it never entered,
or broke, the house in any further way....And an actual case was
mentioned; which was this:—in the night, one who meant to shoot
another, in a house, broke a hole through the wall of the house and
...shot at him through the hole with a gun, and missed him; which
was adjudged to be burglary. Just as where one broke a hole in the
wall; and, seeing one (who had a purse, with money in it, hanging at
his girdle) coming by the hole, snatched the purse and got it. This
also was agreed to be burglary; which happened in Essex.

REX *v.* HUGHES.

CROWN CASE RESERVED.   1785.   LEACH 406.

This was an indictment for burglary with intent to steal, tried
before Mr JUSTICE WILLES at the Old Bailey in December Session.

It appeared in evidence, that the prisoner had bored a hole, with
an instrument called a centre-bit, through the panel of the house-
door, near to one of the bolts by which it was fastened, and that some
pieces of the broken panel were found within-side the threshold of the
door; but it did not appear that any instrument, except the point of
the centre-bit, or that any part of the prisoners' bodies had been within-
side the house, or that the aperture made was in fact large enough to
admit a man's hand.

The Court was clearly of opinion, That this was a sufficient breaking; but the doubt was, Whether it could possibly be construed such
an entry as the law requires to constitute the crime of burglary?

Prisoner's counsel. Breaking without entering, or entering without
breaking, makes not burglary....It must be acknowledged that, from
an anxiety to preserve domestic security sacred and inviolate during
the hours of night, the ancient principles of the common law respecting

burglary have been construed with a latitude not usual in questions of life or death; and it has been held, that the smallest degree of entry whatever is sufficient to satisfy the law. Putting a hand, or a foot, or a pistol, over the threshold of the door, or a hook or other instrument through the broken pane of a window, have been decided to be burglarious entries; but the principle of all these new determinations is, that there has been such a previous breaking of the castle of the proprietor, as to render his property insecure, by affording to the burglar an opportunity to commit the projected felony, of whatsoever kind or description that felony may be. And in those cases where an instrument has formed any part of the question, it has always been taken to mean, not the instrument by which the breaking was made, but the instrument (as a hook, a fork, or other thing by which the property was capable of being removed) introduced subsequent to the act of breaking, and after that essential preliminary had been fully completed. Suppose the brick-wall of a house to be broken with a pickaxe, and that part of the pickaxe had in the violence of breaking been within-side of the house, could this have been held an entry to steal? In the present case, the introduction of the instrument is part of the act of breaking; it is impossible to conceive that it was introduced for the purpose of purloining property, for it is incapable of performing such an office. It was used for the purpose of breaking into the domicile of the proprietor; and if the breaking it effected had enabled the prisoners by any possible means to have taken goods through the aperture, that branch of the offence would most certainly have been complete; but as no property has been proved to lie near the hole, so as to be removed by means of a hand, hook, or other instrument, the degree of breaking seems insufficient for this.

The prisoners were acquitted of the felony.

[*But the insertion of an* instrument, *if for the mere purpose of* breaking, *does not constitute an Entry.*]

REX *v.* RUST' AND FORD.

CROWN CASE RESERVED. 1828.　　　　　　1 MOODY 183.

The prisoners were tried and convicted before Mr JUSTICE PARK at the April Old Bailey Sessions, 1828 (present Mr Baron Garrow), for burglariously breaking and entering the dwelling-house of John Roper with intent to steal.

Of the breaking there was no doubt; and the learned Judge left the intent to the jury, telling them if they thought the intent was to steal, to find the prisoners guilty; and he would take the opinion of the Judges upon the question of entering, the counsel for the prisoners having contended there was no sufficient proof of an entry. The jury having found the prisoners guilty, judgment was respited.

The facts as to the entering were these; the glass sash-window was left closed down, but was thrown up by the prisoners; the inside shutters were fastened, and there was a space of about three inches between the sash and the shutters, and the shutters themselves were about an inch thick. After the sash was thrown up, a crowbar had been introduced to force the shutters, and had been not only within the sash, but had reached to the inside of the shutters, as the mark of it was found on the inside of the shutters.

The inclination of the learned Judge's opinion at the trial, as well as that of Mr Baron Garrow, was that this was no burglary; as it did not nor could it appear whether any part of the hand was within the window, although the aperture was large enough to admit the hand. In Easter term, the learned Judges determined that this conviction was wrong, there being no proof that any part of the prisoner's hand was within the window.

Chapter IV. The Intent.

[*Though there must be an intent to commit some* ulterior *felony* inside *the house, it need not be actually committed.*]

[See Rex *v.* Davis, *supra*, p. 172.]

[*An intent to commit a* felony *of any kind will suffice.*]

ANONYMOUS.

OLD BAILEY SESSIONS. 1667. KELYNG 67.

A servant in the house, lodging in a room remote from his master, draweth in the night time the latch of a door, to come into his master's chamber, with an intent to kill him. This on a special verdict was agreed by all the Judges to be burglary.

[*But not an intent to commit a misdemeanor, or a* Tort, *e.g., a trespass to the person.*]

THE STATE *v.* COOPER.

SUPREME COURT OF VERMONT. 1844. 1 WASHBURN 551.

George Cooper was charged on two counts:—the first alleging that he burglariously and feloniously entered the dwelling-house of one Cyrus Marston, in the night-time, with intent to commit a rape; and the second count alleging that he burglariously and feloniously entered the same dwelling-house in the night-time with intent to commit adultery. The jury returned a verdict of guilty on the second count only.

He then, assigning as cause the insufficiency of the second count, moved the Supreme Court to arrest this judgment.

PER CURIAM. Adultery is not a felony nor even a crime at common law. It is merely a civil injury. 3 Bl. Comm. 139. Until the legislature think proper to declare the act, which the respondent was convicted of, to be a burglary, we cannot determine it to be so. The judgment is arrested.

[*Or a trespass to chattels.*]

REX *v.* DOBBS.

BUCKINGHAM ASSIZES. 1770. EAST'S PLEAS OF THE CROWN 513.

Prisoner was indicted for burglary in breaking and entering the stable of J. Bayley, part of his dwelling-house, in the night, with a felonious intent to kill and destroy a horse which was there. It appeared that the horse was to have run for a prize of forty guineas, and that the prisoner cut the sinews of his fore-leg to prevent his running. In consequence of which, he died.

PARKER, C.B., ordered him to be acquitted. For his intention was not to commit the [statutory] felony of killing and destroying the horse; but only a trespass[1], to prevent his running.

The prisoner was, however, subsequently indicted for killing the horse; and was convicted.

[*Trespass to chattels.*]

REX v. KNIGHT AND ROFFEY.

SUSSEX ASSIZES. 1781.   EAST'S PLEAS OF THE CROWN 510.

Indictment for burglary in breaking and entering the dwelling-house of Mary Snelling, at night, with intent to steal the goods of Leonard Hawkins. It appeared that Hawkins, being an Excise officer, had seized at the shop of a Mrs Tilt 17 bags of tea, which were entered in the name of Smith; in consequence of their being there without a legal permit. Hawkins removed the same to Mrs Snelling's house, where he lodged....At night the prisoners and divers other persons broke open the house, with intent to take this tea. It was not proved that Smith was in company with them; but the witnesses swore that they supposed the act was committed either in company with Smith or by his procurement. The jury were directed...to find, as a fact, with what intent the prisoners broke and entered the house. They found that they intended to take the goods on behalf of Smith.

ALL THE JUDGES held, in the Easter Term following, that the indictment was not supported; there being no intention to steal, however outrageous the behaviour of the prisoners was in endeavouring thus to get back the goods for Smith.

[*Intent to commit a breach of trust.*]

REX v. DINGLEY [OR BINGLEY].

KING'S BENCH. 1687.   SHOWER 53; LEACH 840.

By a special verdict, the jury found that the prisoner was a servant, employed to sell goods and receive the purchase-money for his master's

---

1 [EDITOR'S NOTE. But now under 24 and 25 Vic. c. 97, s. 40 it is a felony not only to kill but even to *maim* or *wound* horses or other cattle, maliciously.]

use. He sold a large parcel of goods; and received a hundred and
sixty guineas for them from the prosecutor. Ten of these he deposited
in a private place in the chamber where he slept. On being discharged
from his master's service, he took away with him the remaining hundred
and fifty guineas. But he afterwards, in the night-time, broke open
his master's house, and took away with him the ten guineas he had hid
privately in his bedchamber.

This was held by the Court of King's Bench to be no burglary.
For the taking away of the money was no felony; because, although it
was the master's money *in right,* it was the servant's money *in possession*[1]. And the first original act was no felony...when the prisoner,
who ought to have put the moneys into his master's till, instead of so
doing, hid them in his bedroom....If he had laid it underground in the
garden; and afterwards had come and taken it away, that taking
would have been no felony.

[The felonious intent must exist at the time of the breaking.]

OLD BAILEY.   1665.   KELYNG 46.

REX *v.* GARDINER.

Mr Martin Gardiner and other officers and their soldiers to the
number of nineteen were indicted for breaking open the house of
Jonathan Hutchinson in Cheapside in the day-time....Lord Arlington,
the King's Secretary made a warrant to apprehend certain dangerous
persons named in the warrant; and directed it to one of the King's
Messengers. He, having notice that the persons named were at a
meeting in Hutchinson's house, desired these soldiers to assist him.
Whereupon they came to the house and apprehended some of them.
But, in the doing of it, some of the common soldiers (without the
knowledge of their officers and against their command) took away
a cloak and some small things out of the house. But the witnesses
could not tell which of the soldiers they were..

I did to this effect declare the law. (1) That if several persons
come into a house together, with an intent to steal, if but one of
them steal goods, they all are equally guilty. (2) That this warrant

---

[1] [EDITOR'S NOTE. See below, Section x., that until the Statute of 1799,
embezzlement was not criminal.]

was not sufficient to justify the breaking open the doors of the house ...
(3) That this breaking of the door maketh them trespassers but can
never be interpreted to make them guilty of felony; for their design
[*then*] was not to commit felony....(4) If, after a door broken with
intent to apprehend a person any of the company take away any of
the goods from the house, this is felony in the person that did it, but
in none of the rest; unless...any of the rest were assenting to the
taking of the goods, and then it is felony in as many as consented.

SECTION VIII.

HOUSEBREAKING.

[The cases given above under BURGLARY, Chaps. II., III., IV. (to
explain what constitutes a sufficient Breaking, Entry, or Intent),
are equally applicable to HOUSEBREAKING.]

SECTION IX.

FORGERY.

CHAPTER I. THE INSTRUMENT.

[*It is a misdemeanor at common law to forge any kind of written
document.*]

REGINA *v.* RILEY.

CROWN CASE RESERVED.   L.R. [1896], 1 Q B 309.

Case reserved for the consideration of the Court by Kennedy, J.

The prisoner was indicted under s. 38 of 24 and 25 Vict. c. 98, for
that he "feloniously did cause and procure to be delivered and paid to
one Henry Dorber certain money, to wit, the sum of nine pounds, the
property and moneys of George Crompton and Samuel Radcliffe, under,

---

1 See Foster's Crown Law, 135, 320.   2 Hawkins P.C., chap. 14.

upon, and by virtue of a certain forged instrument, to wit, a forged telegram, that is to say, a forged message and communication purporting to have been delivered at a certain post office, to wit, at Royal Exchange, Manchester, for transmission by telegraph, and to have been transmitted by telegraph to a certain other post office, to wit, the head post office at Manchester, with intent thereby then to defraud, he the said Henry Riley then well knowing the same forged instrument to be forged against the form, &c."

It appeared that the prisoner was a clerk in the telegraph department of the head post office at Manchester. He had obtained from Dorber permission to make bets in his name with Messrs Crompton and Radcliffe, who were bookmakers, and with whom Dorber was in the habit of doing business. On June 27, 1895, the race known as the Newcastle Handicap was to be run at 2.45 p.m., and on that day the prisoner sent to Crompton and Radcliffe, in the name of Dorber, a telegram in these words—"Three pounds, Lord of Dale." The telegram purported to have been handed in at the Royal Exchange office at Manchester at 2.40 p.m., and to have been received at the head office at 2.51 p.m., from which office it was transmitted to Crompton and Radcliffe. In reality the telegram was not handed in at the Royal Exchange office at all, but it was despatched by the prisoner from the head office after the news had arrived there that the race had been won by Lord of Dale. Messrs Crompton and Radcliffe, acting on their usual practice, and believing that the bet was offered before the race was run, accepted it at the current odds of 3 to 1 against Lord of Dale, and in the result credited Dorber with £9, which in due course would be received by the prisoner.

No suggestion of fraud was made against Dorber.

The prisoner pleaded guilty.

The questions on which the opinion of the Court was asked by the learned Judge were—

(1). Whether the telegram was a forged instrument within the meaning of s. 38, and whether the prisoner could be convicted on the indictment..

HAWKINS, J....By the 24 and 25 Vict. c. 98, s. 38, "Whosoever with intent to defraud shall demand, receive, or obtain, or cause or procure to be delivered or paid to any person, or endeavour to receive or obtain, or to cause or procure to be delivered or paid to any person, any chattel, money, security for money, or other property whatsoever under, upon, or by virtue of *any forged or altered instrument whatsoever*, knowing the same to be forged or altered," shall be guilty of felony....

I proceed to discuss the question reserved for our consideration : whether the telegram described in the case constitutes a forged "instrument" in law ; and whether it is such an instrument as is contemplated by s. 38.

My answer to both these questions is in the affirmative.

In 4 Blackstone's *Commentaries*, 247, forgery at common law is defined as "the fraudulent making or alteration of a *writing* to the prejudice of another man's right." I seek for no other definition for the purposes of the present discussion. That a postal telegram is a writing is to my mind clear. It originates in a written message addressed and signed by the sender, and delivered by him into the post office of despatch for the express purpose that it shall, in the very words in which it is penned, be transmitted by means of an electric wire to another post office, which I will call the arrival office, and that it shall there again on its arrival be committed to writing verbatim et literatim, and that such last-mentioned writing shall be handed to the person to whom it is addressed. The writing delivered in at the office of despatch is the authority of the postmaster to transmit the message, and of the postmaster at the arrival office to commit it to writing and to deliver it to the addressee as the sender's written message to him. This message sent out from the arrival office is, in my opinion, as binding upon the sender as though he had written it with his own hand. If I am right in this, it follows that an offer by telegram accepted by telegram might well create a contract sufficient to satisfy the Statute of Frauds between the sender and the addressee, and a verbal offer accepted by telegram might create an ordinary contract. For this there is the authority of the Court of Common Pleas so long ago as 1870 : see *Godwin* v. *Francis*[1].

Assuming the telegram to be such a writing as I have stated, a bare reading of the contents of it, coupled with the admission of its falsity and of the purpose for which it was made, are overwhelming to establish that it was fraudulently made to the prejudice of another man's right, and thus a forgery at common law. For this I need only cite the judgment of Blackburn, J., in *Reg.* v. *Ritson*[2]: "When an instrument professes to be executed at a date different from that at which it really was executed, and the false date is material to the operation of the deed, if the false date is inserted knowingly and with a fraudulent intent, it is a forgery at common law."

In this case, unless the telegram was dated and despatched before the race was run, it would have been inoperative. The time of

---

[1] L. R. 5 C. P. 295.   [2] L. R. 1 C. C. 200, at p. 201.

despatch was therefore material : falsely to write the telegram so as to make it appear that it was sent in for despatch before the race was run, when it was not sent in till afterwards, was to make it appear on the face of it to be that which it was not.

The more vexed questions, however, are whether the writing can be treated as an instrument, and, if so, whether it is such an instrument as is contemplated by the 38th section, the contention for the prisoner being that it cannot properly be treated as an instrument at all, and that, even if it can, that the 38th section has reference only to such forged legal or commercial instruments as are mentioned (and the forgery of which is made felony) in the earlier sections of the statute. After much consideration, I have formed an opinion adverse to the prisoner on both these points.

Now, can this telegram properly be called an instrument? I am not aware of any authority for saying that in law the term "instrument" has ever been confined to any definite class of legal documents. In the absence of such authority, I cannot but think the term ought to be interpreted according to its generally understood and ordinary meaning. When applied to a writing, Dr Johnson defines it as "*a writing*—a writing containing any contract or order." Webster's definition is "a writing expressive of some act, contract, process, or proceeding." These definitions cover an infinite variety of writings, whether penned for the purpose of creating binding obligations or as records of business or other transactions.

Every one of the documents mentioned in the statute is unquestionably an instrument, and intended to be so treated. Throughout the statute it is evident the legislature attached no rigid definite meaning to the word, for it is used in a variety of senses, all falling within one or other of the definitions of Dr Johnson and Webster to which I have referred....

It will not, of course, be denied that there are very many instruments of an important character, commercial and otherwise, the forgery of which constitutes only offences at common law. I do not, for instance, find that the forgery of an ordinary written contract (not under seal or specially named in the statute) is a felony. So also a certificate of ordination, though the forgery of it is a mere common law offence, was nevertheless spoken of as an instrument by Blackburn, J., in *Reg.* v. *Morton*[1]....

In my view of the case, the telegram in question is an *instrument of contract* ; it is the instrument which completed the wager offered by Crompton and Radcliffe to those who were able and disposed to accept

[1] L. R. 2 C. C. 22.

it (see *Carlill* v. *Carbolic Smoke Ball Co., Limited*[1], and the cases there cited), and thenceforth an obligation was imposed upon each party in honour to fulfil it according to the result of the race. I say *in honour* because, though it was clearly not an illegal contract, it could not be enforced by any legal process. In virtue of it, and upon the assump tion that the telegram was what it purported to be, Messrs Crompton and Radcliffe paid the £9.

Assuming the document to be an "instrument," I come to the only remaining question, whether it is such within the meaning of s. 38 of the statute. Why should it not be so? It is contended that the section has reference only to such instruments as are mentioned in the earlier sections of the statute, and that s. 38 applies only to those forged instruments which are punishable as felonies. Such a construc. tion is, I think, erroneous. There is no definition of the word "instru. ment" in the statute to fetter us in giving to it the ordinary and general interpretation. It was clearly the intention of the legislature by s. 38 to create a new offence. If it had been the intention of the legislature to limit the operation of the section to felonious forgeries, how easy it would have been to use appropriate language for that purpose. So far from doing this, the legislature, having used the term "instrument" in a variety of senses all falling within one or another of the definitions I have above referred to, proceeds, in s. 38, to use language which read in its ordinary sense comprises *every description of written instrument.*

WILLS, J....The essence of this section appears to be, that where property has been obtained not merely by false pretences, but by false pretences into which forgery or its equivalent enters, the offence shall be constituted a felony, and may involve much severer punishment than either the mere obtaining of money by false pretences or a mere forgery at common law.

I cannot see anything in the nature of such a section which should make it necessary or desirable to restrict the application of the word "instrument" to writings of a formal character, and I think it is meant to include writings of every description if false and known to be false by the person who makes use of them for the purpose indicated....

No violence is done by this construction to the use of the word "instrument." In *Coogan's Case*[2] Buller, J., defined forgery at common law as the "making of a *false instrument* with intent to deceive." Blackstone, J., defines forgery as the "fraudulent making or alteration of a *writing* to the prejudice of another man's right": 4 *Comm.* 247.

---

[1] [1892] 2 Q. B. 484; [1893] 1 Q. B. 256.

[2] 1 Lea. 449; 2 East, P. C. c. 19, s. 43, p. 948.

It is plain that in these definitions "instrument" and "writing" are synonymous. East, himself a writer of considerable authority, defines forgery in one passage as " a false making—a making malo animo of any written *instrument* for the purpose of fraud and deceit" (2 *Pleas of the Crown*, 852); and in another paragraph as "the counterfeiting of any *writing* with a fraudulent intent whereby another may be prejudiced" (*ib.* 861). It is obvious that the writer in these passages treats "instruments" and "writings" as for the present purpose synonymous.

For these reasons I am clear that the conviction must be affirmed.

I think further that, even if the true construction of the word "instrument" required a more restricted meaning, the telegram in the present case would fall within it. It was a writing which, if accepted and acted upon, would establish a business relation and lead directly to business dealings with another person. It is true that the dealings were of such a nature that they led to no legal rights, and could not be made the foundation of an action ; but they were not forbidden by law, and in that sense and to that extent were legitimate. A post office telegram is issued by a public department in the course of business, and in the present case the telegram appears to me to have sufficient formality, both in its origin and in the use to which it was put, to deserve the name of an "instrument." The only hesitation I have in saying so is lest it should appear to imply any lingering doubt in my own mind as to the correctness of the wide meaning I have given in the principal part of my judgment to the word "instrument." I have no doubt or hesitation about the matter, and I notice the second point only because it was argued before us.

MATHEW, J., concurred.

[But LORD RUSSELL of Killowen, C.J., and VAUGHAN WILLIAMS, J., whilst concurring in the opinion that the defendant's act was a forgery at common law, entertained some doubt as to whether s. 38 of 24 and 25 Vict. c. 98 could be applied to any forgeries except those which had been made felonies in the preceding sections of that statute.]

REGINA *v.* CLOSS.

CROWN CASE RESERVED.   1858.   DEARSLY AND BELL 460.

[Indictment at the Central Criminal Court of a picture-dealer for procuring and selling a copy of one of the pictures of the artist John Linnell, on which copy "was unlawfully painted and forged the name of John Linnell." The prisoner was acquitted on the first count, which was for a verbal false pretence which the purchaser was found not to have relied on; but convicted on the second count, which was for a common-law cheat, and on the third count, which was for a cheat by forgery. His counsel objected, in arrest of judgment, that neither count disclosed sufficient circumstances to constitute the essentials of an indictable offence.]

McIntyre, for prisoner. To falsely pretend that a gun was made by Manton would be no offence at common law; and no case has gone the length of holding that to stamp the name of Manton on a gun would be forgery.

CROMPTON, J. That would be forgery of a trade-mark, and not of a name.

COCKBURN, C.J. Stamping a name on a gun would not be a writing, it would be the imitation of a mark, not of a signature.

McIntyre. The name put by a painter in the corner of a picture is not his signature. It is only a mark to show that the picture was painted by him. Any arbitrary sign or figure might be used for the same purpose instead of the name; it is a part of the painting, and every faithful copy would contain it....

Metcalfe, for the Crown. A false certificate in writing is the subject of an indictment at common law; *Regina* v. *Toshack* (1 Denison 492). I therefore contend that where, as here, the name of the artist is painted on the picture it is in the nature of a certificate, and the fact that the signature is on canvas, instead of being on a separate piece of paper, does not render the offence less indictable.

WILLIAMS, J. But it is consistent with all the allegations that the prisoner may have sold the picture without calling attention to the signature.

Metcalfe. The forging the name on a picture is in fact a forgery of the picture.

COCKBURN C.J. If you go beyond writing where are you to stop? Can sculpture be the subject of forgery?.

COCKBURN, C.J....As to the third count we are all of opinion that there was no forgery. A forgery must be of some document or writing, and this was merely in the nature of a mark put upon the painting with a view of identifying it, and was no more than if the painter put any other arbitrary mark as a recognition of the picture being his. As to the second count, we have carefully examined the authorities, and the result is we think if a person, in the course of his trade openly and publicly carried on, were to put a false mark or token upon an article, so as to pass it off as a genuine one when in fact it was only a spurious one, and the article was sold and money obtained by means of that false mark or token, that would be a cheat at common law. As. for instance, in the case put by way of example during the argument, if a man sold a gun with the mark of a particular manufacturer upon it, so as to make it appear like the genuine production of the manufacturer, that would be a false mark or token; and the party would be guilty of a cheat, and therefore liable to punishment if the indictment were fairly framed so as to meet the case; and therefore, upon the second count of this indictment, the prisoner would have been liable to have been convicted if that count had been properly framed. But we think that count is faulty in this respect, that, although it sets out the false token, it does not sufficiently show that it was by means of such false token the defendant was enabled to pass off the picture and obtain the money. The conviction, therefore, cannot be sustained.

REGINA *v.* SMITH.

CROWN CASE RESERVED.   1858.   DEARSLY AND BELL 566.

[The prisoner was indicted at the Central Criminal Court for forging certain documents, and with uttering them knowing them to be forged. It appeared that the prosecutor was in the habit of selling Baking Powders in packets, wrapped up in printed papers. The prisoner had 10,000 labels printed as nearly as possible like those used by the prosecutor (Borwick), except that the latter's signature was omitted. The jury found that the labels so far resembled those used by Borwick as to deceive persons of ordinary observation, and make them believe them to be Borwick's labels, and that they were made and uttered by him with intent to defraud the different parties by so deceiving them. It was objected on the part of the prisoner that the making or uttering such documents did not constitute forgery; and upon this question a case was stated by the Recorder of London.]

McIntyre, for the prisoner....A printed wrapper like this is not a document and is not the subject of forgery at common law....

POLLOCK, C.B. Suppose a man opened a shop and painted it so as exactly to resemble his neighbour's, would that be forgery?

McIntyre. No. The case of *Regina* v. *Toshack* (1 Denison 492) will perhaps be relied on by the other side. It was there held that a false certificate in writing of the good conduct of a seaman was the subject of an indictment at common law. But here there was no false certificate; and placing the powder within these wrappers was no more than asserting that the powder was manufactured by Borwick.

Huddleston, Q.C., for the prosecution. The labels...are false documents made and uttered by the prisoner with intent to defraud, and the prisoner is properly convicted of forgery. A printed document may be the subject of forgery as well as a written one.

POLLOCK, C.B. It is elevating a wrapper of this kind very much to call it a document or instrument.

Huddleston, Q.C. These labels are made to resemble Borwick's labels.....The wrapper in this case identifies the powder as having been manufactured by Borwick, and is as it were a certificate of the character of the article enclosed. The certificates in *Regina* v. *Toshack* (1 Den. 492), and *Regina* v. *Sharman* (Dearsley 285), certified that a man had done certain things. Here the wrapper is in effect a certificate that Borwick had put his powder in the packet.

POLLOCK, C.B. We are all of opinion that this conviction is bad. The defendant may have been guilty of obtaining money by false pretences; of that there can be no doubt: but the real offence here was the inclosing of the false powder in the false wrapper. The issuing of this wrapper without the stuff within it would be no offence. In the printing of these wrappers there is no forgery; nor could the man who printed them be indicted. The real offence is the issuing them with the fraudulent matter in them. I waited in vain to hear Mr Huddleston shew that these wrappers came within the principle of documents which might be the subject of forgery at common law. Speaking for myself, I doubt very much whether these papers are within that principle. They are merely wrappers, and in their present shape I doubt whether they are anything like a document or instrument which is the subject of forgery at common law. To say that they belong to that class of instruments seems to me to be confounding things together as alike which are essentially different. It might be as well said, that if one tradesman used brown paper for his wrappers, and another tradesman had his brown paper wrappers made in the same way, he could be accused of forging the brown paper.

BRAMWELL, B. I think that this was not a forgery. Forgery supposes the possibility of a genuine document, and that the false document is not so good as the genuine document, and that the one is not so efficacious for all purposes as the other. In the present case one of these documents is as good as the other—the one asserts what the other does—the one is as true as the other, but one gets improperly used.

Conviction quashed.

CHAPTER II. THE FORGING.

[It may be forgery even merely to antedate *a writing.]*

THE QUEEN *v.* WILLIAM RITSON AND SAMUEL RITSON.

CROWN CASE RESERVED. 1869.　　　　　　　L.R. 1 C.C.R. 200.

Case stated by Hayes, J.:

The prisoners were indicted at the last Manchester Assizes under 24 and 25 Vict. c. 98, s. 20, for forging a deed with intent to defraud J. Gardner.

W. Ritson was the father of S. Ritson. He had been entitled to certain land which had been conveyed to him in fee, and he had borrowed of the prosecutor J. Gardner, on the security of this land, more than £730, for which he had given on the 10th of January, 1868, an equitable mortgage by written agreement and deposit of title deeds.

On the 5th of May, 1868, W. Ritson executed a deed of assignment under the Bankruptcy Act, 1861, conveying all his real and personal estate to a trustee for the benefit of creditors; and on the 7th of May, 1868, by deed between the trustee and W. Ritson and the prosecutor, reciting amongst other things, the deed of assignment and the mortgage, and that the money due on the mortgage was in excess of the value of the land, the trustee and W. Ritson conveyed the land and all the estate, claim, &c., of the trustee and W. Ritson therein, to the prosecutor, his heirs and assigns, for ever. After the execution of this conveyance the prosecutor entered into possession of the land. Subsequently S. Ritson claimed title to the land, and commenced an action of trespass against the prosecutor. The prosecutor then saw the attorney for S. Ritson, who produced the deed charged as a forged deed, and the prosecutor commenced this prosecution against W. and S. Ritson.

This deed was dated the 12th of March, 1868, the date being before W. Ritson's deed of assignment and the conveyance to the prosecutor, and purported to be made between W. Ritson of the one part and S. Ritson of the other part. It recited the original conveyance in fee to W. Ritson, and that W. Ritson had agreed with S. Ritson for a lease to him of part of the land at a yearly rent, and then professed to demise to S. Ritson a large part of the frontage and most valuable part of the land conveyed to the prosecutor as mentioned above, for the term of 999 years from the 25th of March then instant.

The deed contained no notice of any title, legal or equitable, of the prosecutor, and contained the usual covenants between a lessor and lessee. It was executed by both W. and S. Ritson.

The case then stated evidence which shewed that the deed had in fact been executed after the assignment to W. Ritson's creditors and after the conveyance to the prosecutor, and that the deed had been fraudulently antedated by W. and S. Ritson for the purpose of over-reaching the conveyance to the prosecutor.

The counsel for the prisoners contended that the deed could not be a forgery, as it was really executed by the parties between whom it purported to be made. The learned Judge told the jury that if the alleged lease was executed after the conveyance to the prosecutor, and antedated with the purpose of defrauding him, it would be a forgery. The jury found both the prisoners guilty.

The question was, whether the prisoners were properly convicted of forgery under the circumstances.

The case was argued before Kelly, C.B., Martin, B., Blackburn, Lush, and Brett, JJ.

Torr, for the prisoners. The deed in this case was not forged, because it was really made between and executed by W. and S. Ritson, the persons by whom it purported to be executed, and between whom it purported to have been made. The date of the deed was false, but a false statement in a deed will not render the deed a forgery. If this deed were held to be a forgery, then any instrument containing a false statement made fraudulently would be forged.

[BLACKBURN, J. This is not merely a deed containing a false statement, but it is a false deed.]

There is no modern case to shew that a deed like this is a forgery. To constitute a forgery, there must be either, first, a false name, or, secondly, an alteration of another's deed, or, thirdly, an alteration of one's own deed. There is no modern authority to include any other kind of forgery. *Salway v. Wale*[1] appears an authority against the prisoners, but that was a decision upon 5 Eliz. c. 14, which is not worded in the same way as 24 and 25 Vict. c. 98, s. 20. The definitions of the text-writers, which may seem to include a case like the present, are not in themselves authorities. The decisions on which the definitions purport to be based, and not the definitions themselves, are the authorities which must be looked at.

Addison, for the prosecution. The deed in this case is a forgery because it is a false deed fraudulently made. Although there is

[1] Moore, 655.

no recent case where similar facts have been held to constitute a
forgery, yet such a state of facts comes within the definitions of forgery
given by the text-books: Russell, vol. ii. p. 709, 4th ed.; Hawkins,
P.C. bk. i. cap. 20, p. 263, 8th ed.; 3 Inst. 169; Bacon's Abr., tit.
Forgery, A.; Comyns' Dig., tit. Forgery, A.I. *Salway* v. *Wale*[1] is also
an authority for the conviction. The essence of forgery is the false-
making of an instrument: *Rex* v. *Parkes*[2].

BLACKBURN, J. By 24 and 25 Vict. c. 98, s. 20, it is felony to
"forge" any deed with intent to defraud. The material word in
this section is "forge." There is no definition of "forge" in the
statute, and we must therefore inquire what is the meaning of the
word. The definition in Comyns (Dig., tit. Forgery, A.I.) is "forgery
is where a man fraudulently writes or publishes a false deed or
writing to the prejudice of the right of another"—not making an
instrument containing that which is false, which, I agree with
Mr Torr, would not be forgery, but making an instrument which
purports to be that which it is not. Bacon's Abr. (tit. Forgery, A.),
which, it is well known, was compiled from the MS. of Chief Baron
Gilbert, explains forgery thus: "The notion of forgery doth not so
much consist in the counterfeiting of a man's hand and seal...but in
the endeavouring to give an appearance of truth to a mere deceit and
falsity, and either to impose that upon the world as the solemn act of
another which he is in no way privy to, or at least to make a man's
own act appear to have been done at a time when it was not done, and
by force of such a falsity to give it an operation which in truth and
justice it ought not to have." The material words, as applicable to
the facts of the present case, are "to make a man's own act appear to
have been done at a time when it was not done." When an instrument professes to be executed at a date different from that at which it
really was executed, and the false date is material to the operation of
the deed, if the false date is inserted knowingly and with a fraudulent
intent, it is a forgery at common law.

Ordinarily the date of a deed is not material, but it is here shewn
by extrinsic evidence that the date of the deed was material. Unless
the deed had been executed before the 5th of May, it could not have
conveyed any estate in the land in question. The date was of the
essence of the deed. and as a false date was inserted with a fraudulent
intent, the deed was a false deed, within the definition in Bacon's
Abridgement. This is a sufficient authority.

The other three Judges concurred.

[1] Moore, 655.   [2] 2 Leach, at p. 785.

[Or for an agent merely to exceed his authority in making a writing.]

THE QUEEN *v.* BATEMAN.

CENTRAL CRIMINAL COURT.   1845.   1 Cox 186.

The prisoner was indicted for forgery under the following circum-stances.   He was clerk to Messrs Sewell and Cross, and had been in the habit of getting blank cheques signed by the firm, and filling in the amount himself, to meet demands upon them.   It was proved that on a certain day he brought the cheque in question to one of the partners, and requested him to sign it, stating at the time that he had been told by Mr Sewell to pay certain rent which was due from Mr Sewell to a Mr Gardiner, but that the amount was not ascertained.   The cheque, when completed, was as follows :—

"No. 7476.   "London, Dec. 18th, 1844.
"London and Westminster Bank.   Pay to 1238 or bearer £100
                                          "Sewell and Co."

At the bottom was written "pay in notes": but neither this memorandum, nor the date, nor the amount, was filled in when it was signed.   The words "and Co." were across the cheque originally.   The name of the firm was written by the partner above mentioned, who stated that he never gave the prisoner any authority to receive cash for the cheque, or to appropriate it otherwise than for the rent.

Clarkson, for the prosecution, opened the case as clearly one of forgery.   That where a party had authority to fill up cheques under certain circumstances, and with certain limitations, and he chose to do so for purposes of his own, and quite beside such authority (which he was in a condition to prove was the case in the present instance), the offence was undoubtedly committed.

Before the evidence was gone into, *Ballantine* and *Wilkins*, for the prisoner, suggested that as there would be no question made as to the facts, it might be convenient at once to discuss the law of the case.

ERLE, J.   We cannot in a criminal case take any thing as admitted, and therefore the evidence must be gone into.

In addition to the testimony given by the partner above referred to, it was then proved that the amount of the cheque had been received by the prisoner ; and the notes were traced to the possession of parties to whom the prisoner had paid them on account of certain gaming debts of his own.   It was admitted by the prosecution that the rent due to Mr Gardiner was much larger in amount than the sum for which the cheque was filled up.   Neither Mr Sewell nor Mr Gardiner was called.

Ballantine, on the case for the prosecution being closed, contended that there was no evidence to sustain a charge of forgery. How could a party be charged with forging an instrument which he had a lawful authority to make? Admitting that such authority was limited, still in this instance it had not been exercised to its full extent; inasmuch as the amount actually filled in was less than he was permitted to insert. Of what part then of the cheque could the forgery be asserted? It is true that there might be a subsequent misappropriation of the proceeds, but that could not be adduced in support of the present charge, although it might be available under a different one. It is necessary to look to the precise period when the cheque was completed, and if the prisoner had authority at that time to act as he did, no subsequent conduct could make that a forgery which was not one in the first instance. Again, the evidence of Mr Sewell and of Mr Gardiner is absolutely essential to the support of any charge at all. We know nothing of what were Mr Sewell's directions to the prisoner, except as far as prisoner stated them to one member of the firm, and that statement is not at all inconsistent with his having implicitly obeyed his instructions in appropriating the money as he has done. Neither can the jury be satisfied in Mr Gardiner's absence that the rent has not in fact been paid.

ERLE, J., to Mr Clarkson. Without now expressing an opinion upon this point, I will ask you whether you are content to rest the case where it is, without calling these gentlemen?

Clarkson. I have sent for them, my lord, and expect them here every moment.

ERLE, J. I will wait then a short time for the chance of their arrival.

The witnesses, however, did not arrive.

ERLE, J., observed. I think the prisoner must be acquitted. It is clear that he had authority to fill up the cheque in some way or another; that was an authority derived from Mr Sewell, and there is no evidence to shew that his directions were not to get a blank cheque filled up for £100 and appropriate it as this has been. Moreover, it should have been shewn that Mr Gardiner did not authorize him to receive the money. He might, for anything that appears in evidence, have gone to that gentleman, have tendered him the cheque, and got it subsequently cashed by his directions. On this ground, therefore, the charge fails. But as some doubt appears to exist as to the law in cases of this sort, it is my duty to state, that I look upon the principle as laid down by the prosecution to be perfectly correct. If a cheque is given to a person with a certain authority, the agent is confined strictly within the limits of that authority, and if he choose to alter it, the crime of forgery is committed.   If the blank cheque was delivered to him with a limited authority to complete it, and he filled it up with an amount different from the one he was directed to insert (or if, after the authority was at end, he filled it up with any amount whatever), that too would be clearly forgery.

PATTESON, J.   I quite agree with my learned brother, that if the prisoner filled up the cheque with a different amount, and for different purposes than those which his authority warranted, the crime of forgery would be undoubtedly made out.   [Cf. *Reg.* v. *Wilson*, p. 209 *infra.*]

[EDITOR'S NOTE.   Yet though a duly appointed agent may thus commit forgery by making, in his principal's name, a writing different from that which he had authority to make, it was at common law no forgery for a man fraudulently to sign a writing as the (pretended) agent of another, though doing so without any authority from the supposed principal; for here the signature itself is genuine, though an untrue representation is made about it. (See *Reg.* v. *White*, 1 Denison 208.)   But s. 24 of the Forgery Act 1861 now renders it a felony, punishable with penal servitude for fourteen years, to make mercantile instruments in another person's name without his authority.   Even apart from this Statute, the false representation, though not a Forgery, would be an indictable False Pretence.]

[*Or to add, to the name of one of the parties to the writing, the address of a different person of the same name.*]

THE QUEEN *v.* BLENKINSOP.

CROWN CASE RESERVED.   1847.   2 CARRINGTON AND KIRWAN 531.

The prisoner was tried at York, before Mr Justice Coleridge, for.... uttering a forged bill, which was set out thus :—

"Leeds, October 22nd, 1847.

"No ———.   £148 7s. 9d.

"Three months after date pay to myself, or order, the sum of one hundred and forty-eight pounds, seven shillings, and ninepence.   Value received.

"ALEXANDER BLENKINSOP.

"To Mr W. Wilkinson, Halifax,

"Payable London."

It appeared that the prisoner had carried on business as a chemical manufacturer, and had two establishments, one at Leeds and the other

at Huddersfield.   He had in his employ at Leeds a man named William
Wilkinson, a mechanic, at weekly wages of 16s., and without any other
property.   This man was called, and he proved the acceptance to be of
his handwriting, so far as the mere name.   He stated that he wrote
that on a stamped paper, blank except some printed parts of a bill of
exchange, among which was the place of date—"Leeds"; that he
wrote it at the prisoner's house at Leeds.   The prisoner having called
him out of the yard, said to him : "I have some money to send up this
morning; there is no one about; you'll do as well as anyone else.
I want you to write your name here; I'll fill it up."   This witness said
that he knew what a bill of exchange was; that he left his master to
fill it up as he pleased ; and that he was at liberty to make it payable
at a banker's in London, if he liked, or anywhere else; that he himself
had never lived at Halifax, nor received authority from anyone there
to accept a bill for him.   And it was admitted that, at the time of the
acceptance being thus written, the prisoner intended to make the
drawing to be on a Mr William Wilkinson, of Halifax, and that there
were persons of that name resident there, from none of whom any
authority had been received.   It was proved that, when uttered by the
prisoner, the bill was drawn as it appears above set out, and accepted ;
and that over the acceptance were the words—"Payable at Smith,
Payne, & Co., bankers, London."

Overend, for the prisoner, contended that neither the bill nor the
acceptance was forged or altered ; and relied on *Webb's* case[1].

Coleridge, J., overruled the objection ; but reserved the point for
the opinion of the fifteen Judges.

Montagu Chambers, for the prisoner....This is no forgery of the bill
by alteration ; for if I get the signature, in London, of A. B., and then
address it to " A. B. of Liverpool," a non-existent person, that has been
held to be no forgery.   For in *Rex* v. *Webb*[1] a bill of exchange was
addressed "To Mr Thomas Bowden, baize manufacturer, Romford,
Essex"; and the prisoner uttered this bill, with the acceptance thereon
made by Thomas Bowden, who did not live at Romford, and was not
a baize manufacturer.   It was held, that the adopting a false description and addition where a false name was not assumed, and where
there was no person answering the description or addition, was not
a forgery.

Creswell, J.   There was a case at the Old Bailey, where, on the
trial of a person for forging a bill of exchange, purporting to be drawn
by Henry Bush, of Bristol, a witness named Henry Bush, not of

---

[1] R. and R. 405.

Bristol, came and stated that he drew the bill. It appeared that there was a Henry Bush of Bristol ; and Baron Rolfe (before whom the trial was) directed an indictment to be preferred against the witness, who was tried before me and convicted.

ALDERSON, B. Suppose, in the lifetime of the late Mr Coutts, a bill had been drawn upon "Thomas Coutts, banker," and accepted by a Thomas Coutts out of the streets?

*   *   *   *   *   *   *   *   *   *

The learned Judges present held the conviction right ; and that putting an address to the drawee's name, while the bill was in course of completion, with intent to make the acceptance appear to be that of a *different existing person,* was a forgery.

[Or to make a writing in the name of an imaginary person.]

REX *v.* LEWIS.

OLD BAILEY. 1754.   FOSTER'S CROWN LAW 116.

Anne Lewis was indicted under 2 Geo. II. c. 25 for feloniously uttering and publishing a certain false, forged and counterfeit deed, purporting to be a power of attorney from Elizabeth Tingle (administratrix of her father Richard Tingle deceased, late a marine belonging to his Majesty's ship, the *Hector*), to Frederick Predham of Barnard's-inn, gentleman, impowering the said Predham to demand and receive of the commissioners of his Majesty's navy, or whom else it may concern, all prize-money due unto her ; with intention to defraud Edmund Mason ; the said Anne knowing the said deed to be false, forged and counterfeit.

The prisoner was convicted upon very full evidence. But it appearing upon the trial that Richard Tingle, to whom administration had been taken in the name of Elizabeth his supposed daughter, died childless and unmarried, a doubt was conceived, whether, since there never was such person *in rerum naturâ* as Elizabeth the daughter of Richard, the counterfeiting a letter of attorney in that name and under that description be a forgery within the statute : and upon this doubt judgment was respited.

This doubt arose from what Chief-Justice Coke saith, speaking of forgery, in his 3 Inst. 169. "This," saith he, "is properly taken when the act is done in the name of another person."

From whence it was inferred, that, there never having been such person as Elizabeth Tingle the daughter of Richard, the counterfeiting a deed purporting to be executed by such person, cannot come within this definition of the offence; it is not an act done in the name of another person.

It was admitted by Sir Martin Wright who raised this doubt, that an alteration made in a deed really executed, in order to give it an operation different from the meaning of parties, if it be done *mala fide* and with an intention to defraud, will come within the legal notion of forgery; as antedating a deed of conveyance in order to overreach a former deed; an alteration in the name and description of the premises conveyed, or in the sum of money secured by bond or other deed, or in the estate intended to pass. These alterations and others of the like nature, made to the prejudice of a third person, and with a fraudulent intention, come within the Act on which the present prosecution is founded; in like manner as they have been holden to be within that of the 5th of Eliz. For in these instances there was a false-making, which is one of the words descriptive of the offence used in both the statutes; that is, the true deed was falsified; "but still," said he, "there was a real deed on which the forgery did operate."

So in the case of a deed or instrument totally forged, it was said by the same learned judge, that it must purport to be the deed of some person really existing, or that hath existed, whose deed by possibility might have been forged; otherwise it cannot be, according to Coke's description of the offence, "An act done in the name of another person."

But at a meeting of the Judges a few days after Trinity term 1754, at Lord Chief Justice Ryder's chambers, eleven Judges being present, ten of them were very clearly of opinion, that the prisoner's case is within the letter and meaning of the Act; and in that opinion Chief Justice Willes, who was absent, signified his concurrence by letter communicated at that meeting.

In support of this opinion it was argued, that Lord Coke's description of the offence on which the doubt is grounded, is apparently too narrow. It expresseth the most obvious meaning of the word, and taketh in that species of forgery which is most commonly practised; but there are other species of forgery which will not come within the letter of that description; the case of antedating, and the other cases which have been mentioned, and are admitted to come within the legal notion of forgery, are of that kind.

It may be said, *Cui bono*; to what purpose will it be to forge deeds or other instruments in the names of persons who never existed? The naked state of the present case answereth that question. Letters of administration to Richard Tingle had been taken out in the name of Elizabeth his supposed daughter; by these letters an existence in show and appearance is given to Elizabeth the daughter; and this was effected by a gross imposition on the Court, and by downright perjury. So that here is a title in show and appearance established by fraud and perjury in a fictitious person: this title is transferred in show and appearance by the deed stated in the case: and all this is done with intent to defraud an innocent person. Which clearly bringeth the prisoner's case within the letter and mischief of the Act. At the next Sessions at the Old Bailey (July 17th, 1754) the prisoner had judgment of death.

[*Or even to write* your own *signature that it may be taken for that of another person of the same name.*]

MEAD *v.* YOUNG.

KING'S BENCH.   1790.   4 DURNFORD AND EAST 28.

This was an action brought by the indorsee of a bill of exchange for £90 against the acceptor. The bill was drawn at Dunkirk by Christian, on the defendant in London, payable "to Henry Davis, or order"; and having been put into the foreign mail, inclosed in a letter from Christian, it got into the hands of another Henry Davis than the one in whose favour it was drawn. The defendant accepted the bill, and when Davis desired the plaintiff to discount it, the latter discounted it, not knowing the H. Davis from whom he took it. There was no ground to impute any fraud to the plaintiff. On the trial before Lord Kenyon, after the plaintiff had proved the defendant's handwriting and the indorsement by Davis, the defendant offered evidence to shew that the H. Davis, who indorsed to the plaintiff, was not the real H. Davis in whose favour the bill was drawn. But, Lord Kenyon being of opinion that such evidence was inadmissible, the plaintiff recovered a verdict. A rule had been obtained to shew cause why a new trial should not be granted on this misdirection.

Piggott, in support of the rule....There is also an objection to the plaintiff's recovery, because he claims through a forgery. For the Henry Davis who received the bill, inclosed in a letter from Christian, must have known that it was not intended for him. And the circumstance of his bearing the same name with the payee would be no defence to him on a prosecution for forgery; since he put a false signature to an instrument with intent to defraud.

✻   *   *   *   *

ASHHURST, J. In order to derive a legal title to a bill of exchange, it is necessary to prove the handwriting of the payee; and therefore though the bill may come by mistake into the hands of another person, even of the same name with the payee, yet his indorsement will not confer a title. Such an indorsement, if made with the knowledge that he is not the person to whom the bill was made payable, is in my opinion a forgery; and no title can be derived through the medium of a fraud or forgery....

BULLER, J. It is clear that the indorsement was not made by the same Henry Davis to whom the bill was made payable; and no indorsement by any other person will give any title whatever....I have no difficulty in saying that this Henry Davis, knowing that the bill was not intended for him, was guilty of a forgery. For the circumstance of his bearing the same *name* with the payee cannot vary this case, since he was not the same *person*.

GROSE, J....That this was a forgery cannot be doubted, if we consider the definition of it; which is "the false making of any instrument, with intent to defraud." It makes no difference whether the person making this false indorsement were or were not of the same name with the payee; since he added the signature of H. Davis, with a view to defraud, and knowing that he was not the person for whom the bill was intended.

[*But not merely to adopt, as a signature* for yourself,
an assumed name.]

THE QUEEN *v.* MARTIN.

CROWN CASE RESERVED.   1879.   L.R. 5 Q.B.D. 34.

Case reserved by COCKBURN, C.J.

The prisoner, Robert Martin, was convicted before me at the late
Assizes held at Maidstone, on an indictment which charged him in one
count with having forged, in another, with having uttered, a forged
order for the sum of £32, with intent to defraud.

The prosecutor, George Lee, is a horse dealer at Ashford, in Kent.
The prisoner Martin was well known to the prosecutor....The prosecutor
agreed to sell, and the prisoner to buy, a pony and carriage for £32.

The prisoner proposing to give his cheque for the amount, both
parties went into an adjoining inn, in order that the cheque might
be there drawn.   The prisoner then produced a printed form of
cheque of the bank of Messrs Wigan and Co.   This he filled up, in the
presence of the prosecutor, with the name of the latter as payee,
signed it in the name of *William* Martin, his name being *Robert*, and
delivered it to the prosecutor, who put it in his pocket without
further looking at it, or observing in what name it was signed; after
which he proceeded to give possession of the pony and carriage to the
prisoner....On the cheque being presented at Messrs Wigan's bank,
payment was refused, on the ground that the signature was not that
of any customer of the bank.   The prisoner had been a customer of
the bank, and had had an account there in his proper name of Robert
Martin; but...the account was then closed.   He had ceased to all intents
and purposes to be a customer of the bank, and must have been fully
aware that a cheque drawn by him on the bank would certainly be
dishonoured.   Under the circumstances there can be no doubt that the
prisoner had been guilty of the offence of obtaining the prosecutor's
goods by false pretences[1].   But the indictment being for forgery of the
cheque, and it appearing doubtful to me whether the charge of forgery
could upon the facts proved be upheld, I reserved the case.

The prisoner in drawing this cheque and delivering it to the
prosecutor did not do so in the name of, or as representing any other
person, real or fictitious.   The cheque was drawn and uttered as his
own, and it was so received by the prosecutor, to whom the prisoner

---

[1] See *Regina* v. *Hazelton, infra*, p. 336.

was perfectly well known as an acquaintance of twenty years' stand-ing, and by whom he was seen to sign it. The prisoner did not obtain credit with the prosecutor by substituting the Christian name of William for that of Robert. He would equally have got credit had he signed his proper name of Robert. The credit was given to the prisoner himself, not to the name in which the cheque was signed ; the cheque was taken as that of the individual person who had just been seen to sign it, not as the cheque of William Martin as distinguished from Robert Martin, or of any other person than the prisoner. On the contrary, if the prosecutor, who knew the prisoner's name to be Robert, had observed that the signature was in the name of William, he would in all probability have suspected something wrong, and would have refused to take the cheque.

There was nothing whatever from which the motive of prisoner in signing a wrong Christian name could be gathered....The only motive which has occurred to my mind as one which might have induced him to sign a false Christian name is, that he may have thought that by so doing he might avoid being liable on the cheque when payment had been, as it was certain to be, refused.

*   *   *   *   *   *   *   *   *   *   *

COCKBURN, C.J.   The case is concluded by authority. In *Dunn's* case[1] it was agreed by the judges that "in all forgeries the instrument supposed to be forged must be a false instrument in itself; and that if a person give a note entirely as his own, his subscribing it by a fictitious name will not make it a forgery, the credit there being wholly given to himself, without any regard to the name, or any relation to a third person." Upon authority as well as upon principle, it is clear that this conviction should be quashed.

LUSH, J., HUDDLESTONE, B., LINDLEY and HAWKINS, JJ., concurred.

Conviction quashed.

[*False* oral *representations about a writing cannot amount to a forgery.*]

REX *v.* JONES.

KING'S BENCH.   1779.   1 DOUGLAS 300.

[The prisoner had been indicted, as for a fraud, at Essex Assizes, before Blackstone, J. But as he entertained a doubt whether the

[1] 1 Leach 59.

offence was not, rather, a forgery, the prisoner was acquitted. At the next Assizes, he was indicted for forgery, before Lord Mansfield, who thought the case clear[1]; but, on account of the doubt which Blackstone, J., had felt, he directed this special verdict.]

This second indictment was made under 15 Geo. II. c. 13, s. 11[2] for uttering a certain forged paper writing purporting to be a bank-note, with intent to defraud James Rayner. The writing was

" No. F 946.

"I promise to pay John Wilson, Esq. or bearer Ten Pounds. London, March 4th, 1776.   For self and Company of my

£. Ten.   Bank in England."

"Entered, John Jones."

.The jury found by special verdict that this writing was not a note filled up by any of the officers of the Bank of England, but was forged ; that the prisoner, knowing the same, averred it to be " a good bank-note," and disposed of it as such to Rayner, with intent to defraud him ; and that Rayner, believing it to be a good bank-note, gave the prisoner the full value of it.   And further, that the Bank frequently pay bank-notes which are filled up by their officers and entered in their books, though they happen not to be signed.

Fielding argued that...from the finding, it appeared that to the man who received the note, it purported to be a bank-note ; and that, to constitute a forgery, a similitude is not at all necessary....

LORD MANSFIELD. The representation made by the prisoner to Rayner, after the note was made, could not alter the purport of the instrument ; which is what appears.   On the face of it, it does not purport to be a bank-note[3].   Such false representations might make the party guilty of a fraud or cheat, they could not make him guilty of a felony.

[EDITOR'S NOTE.   Sir James Mansfield, C.J., says of this case (in 4 Taunton 303), " Jones' crime was only that of telling a falsehood."]

---

1 [EDITOR'S NOTE.]   *I.e.* for acquittal.
2 [EDITOR'S NOTE.]   This statute made it a capital felony to forge the notes etc. *of the Bank of England.*
3 [EDITOR'S NOTE.]   *I.e.* of the Bank of England.

CHAPTER 3. THE INTENT.

[*In* all *common law forgeries, and in* most *statutory ones, an intent to defraud is necessary.*]

REGINA *v.* HODGSON.

CROWN CASE RESERVED. 1856.   DEARSLY AND BELL 3.

The following case was reserved and stated for the consideration and decision of the Court of Criminal Appeal by Mr Baron BRAMWELL, at the Staffordshire Spring Assizes, 1856.

Henry Hodgson was indicted at common law for forging and uttering a diploma of the College of Surgeons. The indictment was in the common form.

The College of Surgeons has no power of conferring any degree or qualification, but before admitting persons to its membership, it examines them as to their surgical knowledge, and if satisfied therewith, admits them, and issues a document, called a diploma, which states the membership. The prisoner had forged one of these diplomas. He procured one actually issued by the College of Surgeons, erased the name of the person mentioned in it, and substituted his own ; changed the date, and made other alterations to make it appear to be a document issued by the College to him. He hung it up in his sitting-room, and on being asked by two other medical practitioners whether he was qualified, he said he was, and produced this document to prove his assertion.

When a candidate for an appointment as vaccinating officer, he stated he had his qualification, and would shew it if the person inquiring (the clerk of the guardians who were to appoint to the office) would go to his (the prisoner's) gig. He did not, however, then produce or shew it.

The prisoner was found guilty ; the facts to be taken to be,—that he forged the document in question, with the general intent to induce a belief that the document was genuine, and that he was a member of the College of Surgeons ; and that he shewed it to two persons, with the particular intent to induce such belief in those persons; but that he had no intent in forging, or in the uttering and publishing (assuming there was one), to commit any particular fraud or specific wrong to any individual.

I reserved, for the opinion of the Court of Criminal Appeal, the question whether, on these facts, he ought to have been found guilty on any of the counts ?

Byrne, for the prisoner. No offence at common law was committed. The definition of forgery in 2 *Russell on Crimes and Misdemeanors*, p. 318, is said to be "the fraudulent making or alteration of a writing to the prejudice of another man's right"; and at p. 362 it is said, that the "fraud and intention to deceive constitute the chief ingredients of this offence." In order to support the conviction, it must be shewn that the prisoner had a definite object in view in the forgery, and intended to commit a fraud upon some individual. This case does not disclose any distinct intention to defraud; and the jury have negatived the intention to commit any particular fraud, or to deceive any individual. The other side will rely on *Reg.* v. *Toshack*[1]. There the prisoner forged a certificate of the master of a vessel, representing that the prisoner was an able seaman and had served on board a certain vessel.

ERLE, J. This seems very analogous to forging the certificate in that case. The prisoner used the diploma in his endeavours to get appointed to the poor house. If an incompetent man were appointed to such a situation, in consequence of his appearing to have this qualification, a large class of persons might suffer. I do not see any great distinction between the danger of loss of life at sea through the employment of an incompetent pilot, and the danger of loss of life on land through the employment of an incompetent surgeon.

Byrne. The Trinity House certificate of fitness to act as a pilot, which was the thing forged in *Toshack's* case, confers a distinct privilege, and is essential to the employment, and is that upon which those who employ the pilot rely; and in that case an intent to defraud particular persons was alleged, and proved. Here there is only a general intent; and the act is not done by the prisoner for the purpose of obtaining any particular benefit, but merely to induce the belief that he was qualified to act as a surgeon. There is an entire absence of intent to prejudice another person. Suppose a man was to concoct a pedigree, and hang it up in his room for the purpose of raising his credit, that would not be a forgery at common law.

JERVIS, C.J. One test is this, and it is in your favour. Suppose this had been an indictment before Lord Campbell's Act[2] had passed,

---

[1] 1 Den. 492.

[2] 14 and 15 Vict. c. 100. Section 8 is as follows:—"From and after the coming of this Act into operation it shall be sufficient in any indictment for forging, uttering, offering, disposing of or putting off any instrument whatsoever, or for obtaining or attempting to obtain any property by false pretences, to allege that the defendant did the act with intend to defraud *without alleging the intent of the defendant to be to defraud any particular person;* and on the trial of any of the

an intent to defraud some particular person must have been stated—
who could have been named? My brother Wightman suggests that the
intent was to defraud the guardians of the poor; but when the document was forged, it was not forged with that intent.

Byrne. No one could have been named as the person whom it was
intended to defraud. There was no intent, at the time when the
certificate was altered, to use it for the purpose of defrauding any
person....

Scotland, for the Crown...14 and 15 Vict. c. 100 not only dispenses
with the necessity of alleging an intention to defraud any particular
person, but also with the necessity of proving it.

Jervis, C.J. Formerly the indictment must either have alleged an
intent to defraud a person named, or have shewn that allegation
unnecessary on account of the public nature of the instrument forged.
Now, the *particular* person need not be named, but with that exception
the law is not altered. Before the new law, whom should you have
stated in the indictment the prisoner intended to defraud?

Scotland. Any one of the persons who might be defrauded by the
use of the pretended qualification at the time of the forgery; one of the
properly qualified practitioners in the immediate neighbourhood, or one
of the persons on whom the defendant attended professionally. If
necessary to allege and prove a particular intent to defraud, it would
be enough to allege any one who might be defrauded. The law infers
that a man intends the ordinary consequences of his act. A man may
be guilty of forging a bill of exchange, though not actually put in
circulation.

Jervis, C.J. I am of opinion that this conviction is wrong. The
recent statute for further improving the administration of criminal
justice[1] alters and affects the forms of pleadings only, and does not
alter the character of the offence charged. The law as to that is the
same as if the statute had not been passed. This is an indictment for
forgery at common law. I will not stop to consider whether this
is a document of a public nature or not, though I am disposed to think
that it is not a public document; but whether it is or not, in order to
make out the offence, there must have been, at the time of the instrument being forged, an intention to defraud some person. Here there
was no such intent at that time, and there was no uttering at the time
when it is said there was an intention to defraud.

offences in this section mentioned, it shall not be necessary to prove an intent on
the part of the defendant to defraud any *particular* person; but it shall be sufficient
to prove that the defendant did the act charged with an intent to defraud."

[1] 14 and 15 Vict. c. 100.

WIGHTMAN, J. I am entirely of the same opinion. Before the late statute it was necessary to allege an intent to defraud some one, and there must be an intention to do so now. In this case it does not appear that at the time when the forgery was committed there was an intention to defraud any one.

* * * * * * * * * * *

Conviction quashed.

[EDITOR'S NOTE. Now, by the Medical Act (21 and 22 Vict. c. 90, s. 40), it is made a specific offence, punishable, on summary conviction, by a fine not exceeding £20, falsely to pretend to be a legally recognised medical practitioner.]

[*Hence if prisoner knew that no one could be defrauded, there is no crime.*]

REGINA *v.* MARCUS.

YORK ASSIZES. 1846. 2 CARRINGTON AND KIRWAN 356.

The prisoner was indicted for having, on the 2nd of August, 1845, forged and uttered a deed of transfer of ten shares in the London and Croydon Railway (setting it out), with intent to defraud the London and Croydon Railway Company. In other counts the intent was laid to be to defraud Darnton Lupton, and to defraud William Booth. In another set of counts, the instrument was described as a deed, but not set out.

It was opened by *Hall*, for the prosecution, that the prisoner was a stock and sharebroker at Leeds, in partnership with Mr John Naylor, under the firm of Naylor and Marcus, and that Mr Darnton Lupton had employed the firm of Naylor and Marcus to a considerable extent, chiefly to buy scrip, and always for ready money; and that in the month of August, 1845, Mr Lupton went to the counting-house of Messrs Naylor and Marcus, and looked at his account in their books, and there found himself debited with a number of London and Croydon shares, for the purchase of which he had given no authority whatever. This led to inquiry; and it was ascertained that on the 28th of July, 1845, the London and Croydon Railway Company had received for registry, in the usual way, two deeds of transfer of shares, marked A. and B.; the deed marked A. purporting to be a deed for the transfer of eighty-seven shares in that Company from Ellithorpe Robinson to Darnton Lupton; the deed marked B. purporting to be a similar deed of transfer for thirteen shares from the same Mr Robinson to Mr Lupton, making in all 100 shares. These two deeds of transfer both purported to be executed by Mr Lupton, as vendee, and to be attested by the prisoner. It also would be proved, that, on the 9th of August following, the London and Croydon Railway Company received seven other deeds of transfer (marked from C. to I. inclusive), which purported to convey the whole of these 100 shares in the London and Croydon Railway to five different persons; one of these deeds (marked E.) purporting to convey ten of these shares to William Booth,—this deed, marked E., being the subject of the present indictment. All these deeds of transfer, marked from C. to I. inclusive, purported to be signed and executed by Mr Darnton Lupton, and his execution of them attested by the prisoner as the subscribing witness. And all these signatures, which purported to be signatures of Mr Lupton, would be proved to be forgeries, and to have been signed by the prisoner in Mr Lupton's name without his knowledge and without his authority; and one question for the jury would be, the intention to defraud, which was a necessary ingredient in the crime of forgery. It was not necessary that the party committing a forgery should contemplate a fraud on any particular person, as he must be taken to intend the necessary, and even the possible, consequences of his own act; and on this ground, a man who forged the name of another to a bill of exchange, though he himself might fully intend to take upon himself the providing for the bill when it came to maturity, would be held to intend the defrauding of the party whose name he so forged. In the present case an intent to defraud the Company was shewn, as they registered the new share-holder, and accepted him as a member of their Company on the faith of the supposed transfer: there was also a fraud on the transferee, who supposed that he had a transfer from a party who in truth did not convey anything, and who had no title to convey, and the transferee also would suppose that the supposed transferror had taken upon himself certain liabilities, among others, a covenant for his title to the shares which purported to be conveyed.

It was proved by Mr Raisbeck, a clerk of Messrs Naylor and Marcus, that the signature "Darnton Lupton," to the deeds of transfer marked A. and B., and also to the deeds of transfer marked from C. to I. inclusive, were all in the prisoner's handwriting, and were not an imitation of the handwriting of Mr Lupton, and that the attestation of each of those signatures purported to be the attestation of Mr Marcus, and was in his handwriting. In his cross-examination this witness stated, that, in the month of August, 1845, Mr Lupton came to the counting-house of Messrs Naylor and Marcus, and looked at his account in their books, which books were accessible to their clerks, and in which all the transactions to which the nine deeds of transfer (A. to I.) related, were entered ; and that Mr Lupton said, that these shares were not his : that there was a profit on them, but that the shares were certainly not his : that on the witness mentioning this to Mr Marcus, the latter replied, "If he won't have a profit, I cannot help it."

It was proved by Mr Lupton that he had never authorized Messrs Naylor and Marcus, or either of them, to buy any London and Croydon shares for him. That he never authorized or knew of the transfers mentioned in the deeds marked from A. to I., or in any of those deeds, and never signed any of those deeds, nor ever gave Mr Marcus, or any other person, any authority to sign any of them for him. Mr Lupton also stated that he had received a dividend-warrant from the London and Croydon Railway Company, and had put it into the fire.

Wilkins, Serjt., for the prisoner. There is, on the face of these transactions, a total absence of an intention to defraud. It is quite clear that the prisoner wished to make a good bargain for Mr Lupton, from whom he had received benefits for which he was grateful ; and the very mode in which these transactions were treated in the books of Messrs. Naylor and Marcus, open as they are to every one in the office, and even to Mr Lupton himself, shewed most clearly that these were fair bonâ fide transactions, by which it was not intended to defraud any one, and by which no one ever was, or ever could be, in fact, defrauded.

CRESSWELL, J. If, after hearing my opinion of the law of this case, Mr Hall wishes the case to go to the jury, I will leave it to them, reserving for the consideration of the Judges the question, whether, on this evidence, anything has been proved which shews an intent to defraud in point of law. At present, my view of the case is this :—It is not required certainly, to constitute in point of law an intent to defraud, that, in these cases, the party should have present in his mind an intention to defraud a particular person, if the consequences of his act would necessarily or possibly be to defraud some person ; but there must, at all events, be a possibility of some person being defrauded by the forgery ; and there does not seem to be any such possibility in the present case, either as regards Mr Lupton, Mr Booth, or the Company. With respect to Mr Lupton, the transfers were made to him in consequence of money actually paid, and the person who so procured the transfer got Mr Lupton's name into the list of proprietors in the Company, so as to entitle him to a dividend in their profits, there being, so far as appears, no call of which the Company could enforce payment ;

so that Mr Lupton might possibly receive money, but could not, under any circumstances, be required to pay any. Neither was there any possibility of the Company being defrauded, as it does not appear that they had any power to demand any further calls from shareholders; so that the substitution of Mr Lupton's credit for that of any other person, or the substitution of any other person's credit for his could do no injury to the Company.

Hall. I submit that there might be a fraud on Mr Lupton by the transfer of shares from him, which, in point of fact, stood in his name in the books of the Company.

CRESSWELL, J. It is merely taking from Mr Lupton something in which he never claimed any interest; and the person to whom the shares are transferred is not prejudiced, inasmuch as he has actually got the shares for which he has paid his money.

Hall. Might not Mr Lupton be liable on his covenants in the transfer? Every person executing a deed conveying property covenants that he has a right to transfer it.

CRESSWELL, J. But the shares actually are transferred. The purchaser has got them. How could the transferror be damnified by such a covenant, if there is no one in a position to gainsay it? By the Company's Act the register is the title.

* * * * * * * * * * *

CRESSWELL, J., directed an acquittal.

[*A sufficient intent to defraud may exist, even though the forger may intend to take steps to prevent any actual loss from arising.*]

REGINA *v.* HILL.

CROWN CASE RESERVED. 1837. 2 MOODY 30.

The prisoner was tried before Mr Baron ALDERSON at the Spring Assizes for the year 1838, at Shrewsbury, for uttering a forged bill of exchange, knowingly and with intent to defraud one Samuel Minor.

It appeared that the parties to the bill were all fictitious persons; and that circumstance was fully known to the prisoner at the time he uttered it to Samuel Minor; and no doubt existed therefore that the names were forged, and the bill was uttered by the prisoner with the full knowledge of that fact. There was, however, reason to contend that the prisoner, who had filled a respectable station in life as a farmer, and who had endorsed the bill to Minor, intended at the time he so uttered it to take up and pay the bill when it arrived at maturity. No such intention however, if it existed, was ever communicated to Minor.

Philips for the prisoner urged to the jury, that the existence of such an intention, if they believed it, was ground upon which they might properly negative the intention to defraud Samuel Minor as charged in the indictment; and a case was cited to the learned Judge at the bar (not reported), in which Lord Abinger at the previous Assizes for Shrewsbury had so decided.

In summing up the case, the learned Baron told the jury (after consulting Mr Baron Gurney), that if they were satisfied that the prisoner uttered the bill in payment of a debt due to Samuel Minor knowing at the time he so uttered it that it was a forgery, and meaning that Samuel Minor should believe it to be genuine, they were bound to infer that he intended to defraud Samuel Minor.

The prisoner was found guilty, and sentenced to be transported for life.

The learned Baron thought it proper, from respect to the opinion of Lord Abinger, to state a case for the opinion of the Judges, in order to know if the rule laid down by him in his summing up to the jury was correct.

In Easter term, 1838, Lord Denman, C.J., Tindal, C.J., Lord Abinger, C.B., Parke, J., Littledale, J., Parke, B., Bolland, B., Bosanquet, J., Alderson, B., Patteson, J., Coleridge, J., Coltman, J., met, and having considered this case, were unanimously of opinion that the conviction was right.

[*Or even though the money obtained by the fraud was legally due to the forger.*]

REGINA *v.* WILSON.

LIVERPOOL ASSIZES.   1847.   2 CARRINGTON AND KIRWAN 527;
1 DENISON 284.

The indictment charged that the prisoner did feloniously forge a certain warrant and order for the payment of money, which said warrant and order for the payment of money was as follows, that is to say—

"No.   Liverpool, Dec. 8th, 1847.

"To the Cashiers of the Liverpool Borough Bank.   Pay ——— or Bearer, Two Hundred and Fifty Pounds.

"£250.   JOHN M'NICOLL & CO."

with intent to defraud one John M'Nicoll.

It appeared that the prisoner was the clerk of John M'Nicoll, and that a bill for £156. 9s. 9d., for which Mr M'Nicoll was bound to provide, falling due on the 8th of December, Mr M'Nicoll on that day signed a blank cheque, with the signature "John M'Nicoll & Co.," and gave it to the prisoner, directing him to fill the cheque up with the correct amount due on the bill (which was to be ascertained by reference to the bill book), and the expenses (which would amount to about ten shillings), and after receiving the amount at the Liverpool Borough Bank, to pay it over to a Mr Williamson, in order that the bill might be taken up.   Instead of doing so, the prisoner filled up the cheque with the amount of £250, which sum he immediately received at the Bank, and without paying any part of the money over to Mr Williamson, retained the whole of it in his own possession, in satisfaction of a claim for salary which he alleged to be due to him, and in support of which he gave some evidence, but which his master on his cross-examination entirely denied to be due.   On the day after the receipt of the money on the cheque, he sent in an account of his claim, giving his master credit for the sum received on the cheque....

Edward James, for prisoner, objected..., that as the signature to the cheque was the genuine signature of M'Nicoll, and as the prisoner was entrusted to fill it up for a specified sum, the filling it up for a different sum, though it was a breach of trust, could not be considered as a forgery.

COLTMAN, J.   I think, on the authority of the cases of *Regina* v. *Minter Hart*, and *Regina* v. *Bateman*, that this is a forgery.

E. James further contended, that there was no proof of an intention to defraud M'Nicoll, but only to obtain from him a sum of money which the prisoner might honestly have supposed to be due to him.

With reference to this point,

COLTMAN, J. (in summing up), told the jury if they were satisfied that the prisoner was authorised only to fill up the cheque for the amount of the bill and expenses, and to pay the proceeds to William-son, and that he filled it up for a larger sum, and applied the money when received to his own purposes, that was evidence for their consideration of an intention to defraud Mr M'Nicoll, as alleged in the indictment.

                                        Verdict—Guilty.

COLTMAN, J., reserved the case for the opinion of the fifteen Judges.

On argument before the Judges, in the following term.

Brett, for prisoner, submitted...that this case was distinguishable from the cases of *Rex* v. *Minter Hart*[1] and *Regina* v. *Bateman*[2], as the prisoner in the present case had, to some extent, a discretion which did not exist in the case of *Minter Hart*, and which was the ground on which it was in that case held that the prisoner had committed a forgery. With respect to the intent to defraud, it appeared that the prisoner had a bonâ fide claim on the prosecutor for the larger amount; and if he really had such a claim, or bonâ fide believed that he had, that would entirely do away with any imputation of an intent to defraud.

The case was afterwards considered by the fifteen Judges, who held the conviction right. They agreed that whether he had a claim to the alleged amount of salary or not, there was no shadow of authority thereby given to draw a cheque for a larger sum than his master had expressly authorised; and the drawing a cheque to a larger amount, fraudulently, was forgery.

SECTION X.

LARCENY.

CHAPTER 1.　TAKING.

[There must be a Taking, *i.e. a change of* Possession.*]*

ANONYMOUS.

KING'S BENCH.　1584.　　　　　　　　CROMPTON 35 a.

A man cutteth my girdle privily, my purse hanging thereat, and the purse and the girdle fall to the ground; but he did not take them up (for that he was espied). This is no felony; for that the thief never had an actual possession thereof, severed from my person. But if he had holden the purse in his hand, and then cut the girdle (although it had fallen to the ground, and that he took it up no more), then had it been felony; [and capital] if above twelve pence in the purse.

---

[1] 1 Moody, 486.　　　　　　[2] *Supra*, p. 191.

14—2

For then he had it once in his possession. But these secret and privy takings from my person, are no robbery; for he neither assaulted me, nor put me in any fear.

And in antient time, the offender only lost his right thumb. See *Fitz. Cor.* 434.

[*An insufficient (and also fraudulent) Taking.*]

THE KING *v.* SHARPLESS AND GREATRIX.

CROWN CASE RESERVED.   1772.   LEACH 92.

At the Old Bailey in May Session, 1772, John Sharpless and Samuel Greatrix were convicted before Mr Justice GOULD, present Mr Baron ADAMS, of stealing six pair of silk stockings, the property of Owen Hudson.   But a doubt arising whether the offence was not rather a fraud than a felony, the judgment was respited, and the question referred to the consideration of the Judges upon the following case.

Case.   On the 14th of March, 1772, Samuel Greatrix, in the character of servant to John Sharpless, left a note at the shop of Mr Owen Hudson, a hosier in Bridge-street, Westminster, desiring that he would send an assortment of silk stockings to his master's lodgings, at the Red Lamp in Queen-square.   The hosier took a variety of silk stockings according to the direction.   Greatrix opened the door to him, and introduced him into a parlour, where Sharpless was sitting in a dressing-gown, his hair just dressed, and rather more powder all over his face than there was any necessity for.   Mr Hudson unfolded his wares, and Sharpless looked out three pair of coloured and three pair of white silk stockings, the price of which, Mr Hudson told him, was 14s. a pair.   Sharpless then desired Hudson to fetch some silk pieces for breeches, and some black silk stockings with French clocks. Hudson hung the six pair of stockings which Sharpless had looked out, on the back of a chair, and went home for the other goods; but no positive agreement had taken place respecting the stockings.   During Hudson's absence, Sharpless and Greatrix decamped with the six pair of stockings, which were proved to have been afterwards pawned by Sharpless and one Dunbar (an accomplice in some other transactions of the same kind for which the prisoners were indicted).

THE JUDGES were of opinion, That the conviction was right. For the whole of the prisoners' conduct manifested an original and preconcerted design to obtain a tortious possession of the property; the verdict of the jury imports that in their belief the evil intention preceded the leaving of the goods. But (independent of their verdict) there does not appear a sufficient delivery to change the possession.

[*A thief may take even by the act of the owner's own agent.*]

REX v. PITMAN.

GLOUCESTER ASSIZES.   1826.   2 CARRINGTON AND PAYNE 423.

The prisoner was indicted for stealing a mare, the property of Jonathan Blanch.

It was proved that the prisoner came to the George Inn, at Sodbury, on the fair day, and directed the ostler to bring out his horse. The ostler said he did not know which it was. The prisoner went into the stable, and pointing to the mare, said—"That is my horse; saddle him." The ostler did so, and the prisoner tried to mount the mare in the inn yard; but from the noise made by some music, the mare would not stand still. The prisoner then directed the ostler to lead the mare out of the yard for him to mount. The ostler led the mare out; and before the prisoner had time to mount her, a person who knew the mare came up, and the prisoner was secured.

Watson, for the prisoner, objected that this was not a felonious taking by the prisoner, as the mare was never in his possession. It all along remained in the possession of the ostler, who never parted with it; and if the mare was never in the possession of the prisoner, he could not be guilty of stealing it.

GARROW, B. If the prisoner caused the mare to be brought out of the stable, intending to steal her; and the animal being disturbed by the music, the ostler led her out of the yard, for his accommodation and by his procurement, that is a sufficient taking to constitute a felony.

The defence was that the prisoner was drunk, and took the mare by mistake; and the jury, on that ground, found him

Not guilty.

[*You cannot* take *what already is completely in your possession.*]

REX *v.* HARVEY.

CHELMSFORD ASSIZES. 1787.   LEACH 467.

[Prisoner was indicted for stealing a horse. The prosecutor had sent his servant with the horse to a fair to sell. The prisoner met the prosecutor, *to whom he was known,* and said—"You have a horse to sell: I think he will suit my purpose, and if you will let me have him a bargain I will buy him." The prosecutor said—"You shall have the horse for eight pounds"; and calling to his servant, he ordered him to deliver the horse to the prisoner. The prisoner mounted the horse, saying he would return immediately and pay him. The prosecutor replied, "Very well, very well." The prisoner rode away with the horse, and never returned.]

GOULD, J. It is impossible, by any construction, to make this case a felony. The case in Kelyng 82, where a man rides away on a horse which he had obtained on pretence of trying its paces, was a conditional delivery. Major Semple's case (1 Leach 420), was a contract [though] of unlimited duration. But, in this case, the delivery was unconditional, and the contract was completed. It was a sale; and the possession, as well as the property, was parted with. The prisoner has defrauded the prosecutor of the price of the horse, but not of the horse itself; and the only remedy the prosecutor has is by an action to recover the £8, but the prisoner cannot be indicted for a felony.

[EDITOR'S NOTE. Contrast with this the case of a purchase utterly fraudulent from the outset, and consequently entirely void; REX *v.* GILBERT, *infra,* p. 353, or REX *v.* SHARPLESS, *supra,* p. 212. Similarly contrast with the case of *Rex v. Jones* (4 Cr. App. R. 17) that of *Rex v. Fisher* (5 Cr. App. R. 102).]

[*No* taking *of what is already in your possession.*]

REGINA *v.* SMITH.

CROWN CASE RESERVED. 1852.   2 DENISON 449.

[Indictment at Glamorganshire Quarter Sessions for larceny of a piece of stamped paper.]

The prosecutor had been clerk to Isaac Powell, a railway contractor, from whom wages were still due to him. Prosecutor went to a public house where he saw the prisoner, who was a foreman in Powell's employ. They agreed upon between them the balance of wages due to prose. cutor which they fixed at £4. 11s. 1½d. Prisoner then took out of his pocket a slip of paper impressed with a sixpenny stamp, and put it on the table. Prosecutor took the stamp and pulled it towards himself, and asked the prisoner whether he (prosecutor) should write a receipt for the full sum of £10. 16s., or for the balance. Prisoner said "for the balance." While prosecutor was writing he observed the prisoner pull out a fist full of silver and turn it over in his hand. When prosecutor had written out the receipt, prisoner took it up and went out of the room. Prosecutor followed him and said, "Smith, you have not given me the money." Prisoner said, "It's all right." Prosecutor repeatedly asked prisoner for the money, but in vain....

The learned Chairman told the jury, after much doubt, that if they believed the evidence, the stamped receipt was the property and was in the possession of the prosecutor at and after the time of his writing the receipt; and that if they believed the prosecutor's statement, and should be of opinion that the prisoner took the receipt out of such possession with a fraudulent intent, they might convict him of larceny.

The jury returned a verdict of guilty, and the prisoner was sentenced to imprisonment for four calendar months with hard labour.

The counsel for the prisoner raised the following objections:—

1st. That there was not such a property and possession in the prosecutor as to support the charge laid in the indictment.

2nd. That there was no evidence of a felonious taking.

The Chairman thereupon reserved the case for the consideration of the Judges and begged their opinion thereon.

On the 24th of April, A.D. 1852, this case was considered by Pollock, C.B., Parke, B., Erle, J., Talfourd, J., and Crompton, J.

PARKE, B. The stamped paper never was in the prosecutor's possession, and the prisoner cannot be convicted of stealing it unless the prosecutor had such a possession of it as would enable him to maintain trespass. It was merely handed over for him to write upon it.

Terry. But it is found that it was obtained from the prosecutor by the prisoner with an intent to defraud.

PARKE, B. But there was never any property in the stamped paper in the prosecutor. It was never delivered to him to keep.

Terry. It is submitted that he had a property in it as a bailee?

PARKE, B. No. It was never intended that he should retain it It was merely handed to him to write upon it.

The Judges were all of opinion that this was not a case of larceny, and the conviction was ordered to be quashed.

[EDITOR'S NOTE. Contrast with the facts of this case, those of *Reg.* v. *Rodway* (9 C. and P. 784); where, upon an indictment for stealing a receipt, the prosecutor proved that he went to the prisoner's house to demand half-a-year's rent, and took with him a stamped receipt for it, written out and signed. The prisoner pulled out a bag of money, asking the prosecutor whether he had brought a receipt. The prosecutor said that he had, and the prisoner desired to look at it. The prosecutor gave him the receipt; the prisoner took it, put two sovereigns into the prosecutor's hand, and immediately went away. Upon the prosecutor afterwards asking him for the remainder of the money, he said "I have got my receipt, and I shall not pay." Coleridge, J., held this to be larceny.]

[*But if goods, though in your possession* physically, *are* constructively *in the owner's, any appropriation of them by you will be a sufficient* Taking]

[*Mere physical possession by* domestic servant *as custodian.*]

KING'S BENCH. 1506. Y.B. 21 HEN. VII. Hil. pl. 21.

Pigot, an apprentice-at-law, asked this question of *Cutler* (a Serjeant):—If I deliver a silver ring to my servant to keep, and he flees away from me and takes the ring, will this be a felony?

Cutler. It will. For so long as he is in my house or in my service, whatever I have delivered to him is held to be in my possession. Thus if my butler, who has my plate in his custody, goes off with it, this is felony. And the law is the same if he who has charge of my horse goes off with it. The reason is that the things continued, all the while, to be in my own possession. But if I deliver to my servant...a ring to take to London [1], and he goes off with it: there is no felony. For it was no longer in my possession and he came by it lawfully.

Pigot. A right distinction; for in the latter case the master has a good right of action against him, in detinue or in account.

[1] [EDITOR'S NOTE. See *The Carrier's Case*, at p. 225 *infra*, as to cases in which a man, although at the time your servant, is also employed by you in some particular transaction as a Bailee, being entrusted not merely with the Custody but with the legal Possession of an article.]

[*Mere physical possession;* by workman *as custodian.*]

ANONYMOUS.

OLD BAILEY SESSIONS.   1664.   KELYNG 35.

A silk throwster[1] had men come to work in his own house, and
delivered silk to one of them to work; and the workman stole away
part of it. It was agreed by HYDE, C.J. (myself and my brother
Wylde being there), that this was felony; notwithstanding the delivery
of it to the party. For it was delivered to him only to work; and so
the entire property remained only in the owner, like the case of a
butler who hath plate delivered to him; or a shepherd, who hath
sheep delivered; if they steal any of them, that is felony at the
common law.

[*Mere physical possession;* by customer.]

REX *v.* CHISSERS.

KING'S BENCH.   1678.   3 SALKELD 194; T. RAYMOND 275.

Where a person came to a seamstress's shop and asked her to shew
him some linen, which she did and delivered it into his hands, and
then he ran away with it, it was adjudged that this is felony. For
though the goods were delivered by the owner, yet they were never out
of her possession; because though the contract might be begun, by
asking and telling the price, yet it was not perfected. And the subsequent act of his running away doth plainly shew his intention to
take the goods feloniously before the property was altered. For which
he was indicted, convicted and executed.

[*For a custodian merely to* make *a false statement of accounts,
without handing it in, is not a sufficient Appropriation.*]

REGINA *v.* BUTLER.

LEICESTER ASSIZES.   1846.   2 CARRINGTON AND KIRWAN 340.

Butler was indicted for larceny. The prosecutors were spinners,
and the prisoner, who was in their employ, had been from time to

[1] To 'throw' raw silk is to clean it for weaving.

time intrusted by them with money for the purpose of paying the wages of their work-people. The duty of the prisoner was to keep an account in a book of the monies which he so disbursed. This book was produced at the trial; and on its being so produced, it was proved to contain three entries made by the prisoner, in each of which he had charged his employers with more money than he had paid on their account. The book had been balanced by the prisoner, but there was no evidence that he had actually accounted with his employers.

WIGHTMAN, J., stopped the case. The question here is, did the prisoner in fact deliver this account to his employers? True it is that here are certain entries, made by the prisoner, which are incorrect; but they are entries which, perhaps, he never intended to deliver, or, if he did deliver them, to deliver them with explanations. This was no accounting; and there must in this case have been an accounting, in order to fix the prisoner with the larceny.

The prisoner was acquitted.

CHAPTER 2. CARRYING AWAY.

[*The stolen article must be* entirely *removed.*]

REX *v.* CHERRY.

CROWN CASE RESERVED. 1781.   LEACH 236 AND 321.

The prisoner was indicted at the Oxford Assizes for larceny of a wrapper and four pieces of linen cloth. This bale, packed in the form of a long square, was in a waggon travelling the Acton Road; it lay lengthways in the waggon. The prisoner got into the waggon and raised the bale perpendicularly on its end for the greater convenience of taking the linen out, and cut the wrapper all the way down with the intent to take out the contents. But he was discovered by the waggoner and apprehended before he had taken anything out. The jury found him guilty, but Nares, J., reserved the case for the opinion of the Judges whether this was a sufficient carrying away to support the indictment.

THE TWELVE JUDGES were of opinion that it was not such a removal of the property as was necessary to constitute the offence of larceny.

For the carrying away must be a removal of the goods from the place where they were[1]....

[*But removal to another room in the* same house *suffices.*]

ANONYMOUS.

SURREY ASSIZES. 1353. 27 LIB. Ass. pl 39.

A man was arraigned, who had been arrested in possession of property he had stolen, viz. two sheets and a bundle of linen. He claimed his clergy. And it was found by the jury that he had been a guest in the house of a rich man, where he was allowed to sleep in the aforesaid sheets. They further found that he arose before day-break and took the sheets out of his chamber and carried them into the hall; and that he then went out to the stable to get his horse, but the ostler laid hands on him. Whereupon the question was put to the jury:—Did he carry the sheets into the hall with the intention of embezzling them? To which they answered, Yes. Thereupon he was adjudged a felon. But, as he was a clerk, he was delivered to the Ordinary.

[*Or even to another part of the* same room.]

REX *v.* SIMSON.

CAMBRIDGE ASSIZES. 1664. KELYNG 31.

Clement Simson was indicted for breaking an house in the day-time (nobody being in the house), and stealing plate to the value of £10. And upon the evidence it appeared that he had taken the plate out of a trunk in which it was, and laid it on the floor; but before he took it away he was surprised by people coming into the house. And the Chief Justice Hyde caused this to be found specially, because he doubted (upon the Stat. of 39 Eliz. cap. 15 that enacts, that if anyone be found guilty of the felonious taking away of any goods, &c., out of any house in the day-time, above the value of 5s. he should not have the benefit of his clergy), whether this were a taking away within the

---

[1] [EDITOR'S NOTE. *I.e.*, of every particle of the goods from the place where that particle was. Had this, instead of a flexible bale, been a solid box, the raising it from a horizontal to a perpendicular position would have constituted a sufficiently complete removal. See *Rex v. Thompson*, p. 221 *infra.*]

Statute. And on the 13th of June, ALL THE JUDGES being met together, this question was propounded to them. They agreed that clergy was taken away in this case; for the Stat. of 39 Eliz. does not go about to declare what shall be felony, but to take away clergy from that kind of felony...so that the felony is at common law. And by the common law, breaking the house and taking of goods, and removing them from one place to another in the same house, with an intent to steal them is felony; for by this taking of them he hath the possession of them, and that is stealing and felony.

[*Even though thief at once abandon the thing.*]

REX *v.* AMIER.

OXFORD ASSIZES. 1834.   6 CARRINGTON AND PAYNE 344.

Housebreaking, and stealing two half-sovereigns, the property of William Smith.

It appeared that the prisoner, after having broken into the house, took the two half-sovereigns from a bureau in one of the rooms, but that being detected, he threw them under the grate in that room.

PARK, J. If the half-sovereigns were taken with a felonious intent, this is a sufficient removal of them to constitute the offence.

Verdict, Guilty.

REX *v.* WALSH.

CROWN CASE RESERVED. 1824.   1 MOODY 14.

The prisoner was charged at the Old Bailey Sessions with stealing a leathern bag containing small parcels, the property of William Ray, the guard to the Exeter mail.

At the trial, it appeared that the bag was placed in the front boot, and the prisoner, sitting on the box, took hold of the upper end of the bag and lifted it from the bottom of the boot on which it rested. He then handed the upper part of the bag to a person who stood beside the wheel on the pavement; and both had hold of it together, endeavouring to pull it out of the boot, with a common intent to steal it. Before they were able to obtain complete possession of the bag, and while they were so engaged in trying to draw it out, they were interrupted by the guard and dropped the bag.

The prisoner was found guilty; but the facts above stated were specially found by the jury in answer to questions put to them by the Common-Serjeant. The Common-Serjeant entertaining some doubts whether the prisoner could be truly said to have "stolen, taken, and carried away" the bag, respited the judgment, in order that the opinion of the Judges might be taken on the case.

THE JUDGES met, and considered this case. They held the conviction right, being of opinion that there was a complete asportation of the bag.

REX *v.* THOMPSON.

CROWN CASE RESERVED. 1825. 1 MOODY 78.

The prisoner was tried before Mr Baron Garrow, at the Winter Assizes for the county of Sussex, 1825, for stealing from the person of John Hilman, a pocket-book and four promissory notes of £1 each.

The evidence of the prosecutor was this:—"I was at a fair at East Grinstead; I felt a pressure of two persons, one on each side of me; I had secured my book in an inside front pocket of my coat; I felt a hand between my coat and waistcoat; I could feel the motion of the knuckles; I was satisfied the prisoner was attempting to get my book out. The other person had hold of my right arm, and I forced it from him, and thrust it down to my book, in doing which I just brushed the prisoner's hand and arm; the book was just lifted out of my pocket; it returned into my pocket. It was out; how far I cannot tell; I saw a slight glance of a man's hand down from my breast. I secured the prisoner after a severe struggle and a desperate attempt at escape in which he was assisted by twenty or thirty persons." Upon cross-examination, the witness said, "My coat was open, the pocket was not above a quarter of an inch deeper than the book; I am satisfied the book was drawn from my pocket; it was an inch above the top of the pocket." Upon this evidence, it was insisted for the prisoner that the offence did not amount to a taking from the person.

The learned Judge recommended the jury, if they were satisfied that the prisoner removed the book with intent to steal it, to find him guilty. The jury found the prisoner guilty. But the learned Judge respited the execution of the sentence until the opinion of the Judges could be taken on the point.

THE JUDGES...were unanimously of opinion that the simple[1] larceny was complete.

REX *v.* LAPIER.

CROWN CASE RESERVED.   1784.   LEACH 320.

At the Old Bailey in May Session, 1784, James Lapier was indicted before Mr Baron PERRYN, for assaulting Albina Hobart, and taking from her person violently, and against her will, one gold ear-ring set with diamonds, value £150, the property of her husband George Hobart, Esq.

The circumstances of this case, as they appeared in evidence, were as follows: Mrs Hobart was retiring from the Opera-house, through the King's door, towards her carriage, which had drawn up close to the pavement of the street to receive her. Whilst she was preparing to step in, she felt a person, who was proved to be the prisoner, take hold of her ear, and pull her ear-ring as if endeavouring to pull it off. Her ear by this violence was torn entirely through; the ear-ring separated from the ear; and Mrs Hobart conceived it had been taken away: but on her arrival at home, it was found amongst the curls of her hair. There was no proof that the ear-ring was ever seen in the prisoner's hand; but his hand was seen elevated to her ear, and at that instant Mrs Hobart exclaimed, "I have lost my ear-ring."

Mr Baron PERRYN to the jury. Robbery is only an aggravated species of larceny; and to constitute a larceny, it is essential that there should not only be a taking, but a carrying away. The taking in the present case is very clearly proved; for the ear-ring was completely separated from the ear: but it seems questionable whether there has been a sufficient carrying away.

The jury found the prisoner guilty. But the judgment was respited and the case submitted to the consideration of the Judges.

THE TWELVE JUDGES were all of opinion that it was sufficient.

---

[1] [EDITOR'S NOTE. But not the aggravated: i.e. it was carried away, but not 'from' the prosecutor's person. Cf. *Rex* v. *Taylor*, L. R. [1911] 1 K. B. 674.]

CHAPTER 3. APPROPRIATION BY BAILEES.

[*But a* bailee *has legal as well as physical possession; and therefore an appropriation by him would not be a Taking.*]

[*Yet if he breaks bulk, he puts an end to his possession under the bailment, and so becomes capable of taking.*]

THE CARRIER'S CASE.

STAR CHAMBER. 1473. YEAR BOOK 13 EDW. IV. f. 9, Pasch. pl. 5.

In the Star Chamber before the King's Council this matter was shewn and debated. One had bargained with another to carry certain bales and other things to Southampton. He took and carried them to another place; and broke open the bales, and took the goods therein contained feloniously, and converted them to his own use, and disposed of them suspiciously. And the question was whether or no this could be called felony.

BRIAN [C.J., C.P.]. It seems to me that it cannot. For when he had possession lawfully by the bailment and delivery of the [other] party, it cannot afterwards be called felony or trespass: for no felony can be except with violence and *vi et armis*; and what he himself had he could not take *vi et armis* or *contra pacem*. Therefore it cannot be felony or trespass, for he [the bailor] can have no action for these goods except an action of detinue. Etc.

HUSSEY, *the King's Attorney.* It is felony where one feloniously claims the property without cause, with intent to defraud him in whom the property is *animo furandi*. And here, despite the bailment (as above), the property remained in him who made the bailment. Therefore he to whom the things were bailed can feloniously claim this property, just as a stranger can. So it may be felony well enough.

THE CHANCELLOR [*R. Stillington, Bp. of Bath*]. Felony depends on the intent, and his intent might be felonious in this case, just as if he had not had possession. Etc.

MOLINEUX to the same effect. A thing lawfully done can be called felony or trespass according to the intent, &c. Thus if he who does the act does not pursue the cause for which he took the goods; as, if a man distrains for damage feasant or for rent in arrear, and afterwards sells the goods or kills the beasts, this is now a tort, though it was good at the beginning. And so if a man comes into a tavern to drink, that is lawful; but, if he carries off the cup or does other trespass, then all is bad, &c. And so though the taking to carry (as above) was lawful; yet when he took the goods to another place (as above), he was not pursuing his carrying. And so, by reason of what he afterwards did, it can be called felony or trespass according to the intent. Etc.

BRIAN [C.J., C.P.]. Where a man does something of his own head, it can be made lawful or unlawful by what he does afterwards; as in the cases that you have put. For there his act shall be judged by his intent, &c. But where I have goods by your bailment, nothing that happens afterwards can make that taking bad. Etc.

VAVISOUR. Sir, it seems to me that our case is better than that of a bailment. For here the goods were not delivered to him; but there was a bargain that he should carry them to Southampton (as above). And then, if he took them to carry thither, he would take them warrantably. But, according to the case here set forth, his subsequent demeanour shews that he took them as a felon and with an intent other than that of carrying them (as above). And, in that case, he took them without warrant and cause; for he did not pursue his cause, and so it is felony. Etc.

CHOKE [J., C.P.]. It seems to me that when a man has goods in his possession by reason of a bailment, he cannot take them feloniously; they being in his possession. But yet it seems to me that in this case there is felony. For here the things that were within the bales were not bailed to him, but the bales were bailed to him as entire things (as above) to carry, &c. And in that case, if he had given or sold the bales, that would not have been felony. But when he broke them and took out what was therein he did this without warrant. As if one bails a tun of wine to be carried, if the carrier sells the tun, it is not felony or trespass, but if he takes what was inside, that is felony. And here the twenty pounds [the contents of the packages] were not bailed to him; and peradventure he knew not of them at the time of the bailment. And so if I bail the key of my chamber to one to keep my chamber, if he takes my goods out of my chamber, that is felony; for they were not bailed to him. Etc.

And it was submitted by some to the Chancellor that this matter ought to be determined at the common law and not here.

THE CHANCELLOR. This suit is brought by a foreign merchant, who is come here with a safe conduct. He is not bound to sue according to the law of the land and to tarry the trial by twelve men and other solemnities of the law of the land; but it shall be determined according to the law of nature in the Chancery. And there he can sue from day to day and hour to hour, for the speeding of merchants, &c. And the Chancellor said also that merchants are not bound by our statutes when they are introductive of new law; but only when they are declaratory of old law, to wit, the law of nature, &c.   And although they be come into the realm, so that the King has jurisdiction to make them stand to right, &c., that shall be according to the law of nature; which is called by some the law merchant, and which is universal throughout the world.   And he said that it had been adjudged, not-withstanding the statute [stat. 15 Hen. VI. c. 3; 18 Hen. VI. c. 8], which wills that safe conducts be enrolled and the number of sailors and the name of the vessel, &c., that if a foreigner has a safe conduct without these circumstances in it, still it shall be allowed.   For foreigners say that they are not bound to know our statutes, and they come here by virtue of the King's seal, to wit, the safe conduct.   And if that be not sufficient [to meet the terms of the statute], still it shall be received.

But some said that the statute forfeiting merchandise binds aliens as well as denizens.   And it was said that a denizen shall not sue an alien before the King's Council, but an alien may sue a denizen [there].   Some, however, said that this was by statute.

And afterwards the matter of the felony was argued before THE JUSTICES in the Exchequer Chamber.   And there it was held by all (except Needham [J., K.B.]) that when goods are bailed to a man he cannot take them feloniously.   But Needham held the contrary.   For he can just as well take them feloniously as can another.   And he said that it had been held that a man can take his own goods feloniously.   As if I bail goods to a man to keep, and I come privily with the intent to recover damages against him (in detinue, &c.) and take the goods privily, that is felony.   Etc.

And it was held that where a man has possession and that deter mines, he then can be a felon of the goods.   As if I bail goods to one to carry to my house; and afterwards he takes them out, this is felony; for his possession is determined when they are in my house, &c.   But if a taverner serves a man with a cup, and he carries it off, this is felony; for he had not possession of this cup, for it was put upon the table only to serve him to drink, &c.   And so it is of my butler or cook in my house; they are only ministers to serve me, and if they carry off, it is felony; for they have not possession, for the possession is always in me.   Otherwise would it be if peradventure the things were bailed to the servants, so that the servants were in possession of them, for then it would not be felony.   Etc.

Laken [J., K.B.].   There seems to me a difference between a bail-ment of goods and a bargain to take and carry them.   For by the bailment possession is delivered; but by the bargain he [the carrier]

K.   15

has not possession until he takes them, &c. And if he takes them to carry, then it is lawful, &c., but if he takes them with another intent than to carry them, so that he does not pursue the cause, then it seems to me that this may well enough be called felony. Etc.

BRIAN [C.J., C.P.]. It seems to me that it is all one, a bargain to carry them or a bailment of them. For in both cases he has authority from the very person in whom the property is; so that it cannot be called felony. In Michaelmas Term, 2 Edw. III. an indictment *quod felonice abduxit unum equum* was held bad, for it should have been *cepit*. The like in the Nottingham Eyre, 8 Edw. III. And in this case the taking cannot be felonious, for he had lawful possession, so that the breaking of the bales is no felony. [1]See a case in 4 Edw. II.: trespass for that the plaintiff had bought a tun of wine of the defendant, and this being in the defendant's possession, the defendant broke open the tun, took off part of the wine and filled up the tun with water, &c.; and, because it appeared that the defendant was in possession before this was done, objection was taken to the words *vi et armis* in the writ. But the writ was adjudged good, and the defendant then pleaded not guilty.

And afterwards THE JUSTICES made a report to the Chancellor in the Council, that in the opinion of most of them it was felony. Yet, though it was felony, still the goods could not be claimed as waif, for it appears here that he who sued for the goods is an alien, and the King has granted him *salvum et securum conductum tam in corpore quam in bonis*. And this is a covenant between the King and him, so that if a felon takes his goods it is not reason that this alien should lose them, or be put to suing against the felon; but he shall sue to the King on this covenant. And so it seems that the King cannot have such goods by way of waif, and for the same reason he cannot grant them to another, and no other can claim them by prescription. And note that the case was that the sheriff of London claimed the said goods as waif, &c., and alleged a prescriptive right to waif, &c.

[EDITOR'S NOTE. Modern statutory legislation has enlarged the definition of Larceny by making it possible for a bailee to commit this crime by a mere Appropriation, without any act of Taking, either real or constructive. For (originally by 20 and 21 Vict. c. 54, s. 4, and now by 24 and 25 Vict. c. 96, s. 3), "Whosoever, being a bailee of any chattel, money, or valuable security, shall fraudulently take or convert the same to his own use or the use of any person other than the owner thereof, *although he shall not break bulk or otherwise determine the bailment*, shall be guilty of larceny; and may be convicted thereof upon an indictment for larceny."]

---

[1] It is not clear whether this concluding reference comes from the Chief Justice, or is an interpolation by the reporter.

[*But this*[1] *statute only applies to such bailments as impose a duty of handing over the identical thing bailed.*]

REGINA v. HASSALL.

CROWN CASE RESERVED. 1861.   LEIGH AND CAVE 58.

The following case was reserved by the Chairman of Quarter Sessions for the West Riding of Yorkshire.

The prisoner was tried upon an indictment, under the 4th section of the 20 and 21 Vict. c. 54[2] (the Bailee Act), which charged him with stealing the sum of £2. 14s. 1d., the property of John Farrell.

It was proved that the prisoner and a man named Richard Shaw agreed, early in January, 1860, to start a Money Club. Shaw was secretary, the prisoner was treasurer; and they, together with one Bellhouse, formed the committee of management.

The rules of the Club were as follows :—Each member had to deposit weekly a sum of not less than threepence halfpenny nor more than thirteen pence halfpenny. Members omitting any weekly payment to be subject to a small fine; the odd halfpence to be expended, (1st) on a feast at the end of the year, and (2nd) in payment of the services of Shaw, the prisoner and Bellhouse. The prisoner alone had the custody of all moneys paid in by members; and had authority to lend out of the Club money in his hands, provided he first obtained the secretary's written consent to the loan, sums not exceeding £1, at the rate of 5 per cent. interest.

Each member was to receive back the exact amount he had paid in, less the odd halfpence and the amount of his fines, if any; he was also to receive, in addition to the sum he had deposited, an equal share of the total amount arising from fines and from interest on loans. The sum of £2. 14s. 1d. laid in the indictment was the exact amount paid by John Farrell, the prosecutor, into the prisoner's hands, no part of it being made up of interest or fines.

On the morning of the 24th of December, the day when the distribution of the Club money was to have taken place, the prisoner told Shaw that his house had been broken and robbed of the money belonging to the Club and of some of his own. The prisoner attended the Club the same evening, and said that, if time was given him, he could pay twenty shillings in the pound. The result of an examination of

---

[1] Now, however, the Larceny Act, 1901 (1 Edw. VII. c. 10), makes it a misdemeanour—not a Larceny—for an agent to misappropriate; even though he may *not* be bound to hand over the identical coins or things.

[2] That enactment is now replaced by s. 3 of 24 and 25 Vict. c. 96.

the prisoner's house by the police was that he was given into custody on a charge of stealing the Club money.

On the above facts it was contended by the prisoner's counsel :—

1st. That the prisoner was not a bailee of the sum of £2. 14s. 1d. within the meaning of the 20 and 21 Vict. c. 54 ; as this money had been paid into his hands by the prosecutor in small sums in silver and copper coins, which particular coins he was not bound to return.

2nd. That the prisoner was, together with the other members of the committee, trustee of the funds of the Club, and could not be indicted under section 4.

3rd. That the facts shewed a partnership existing between the prosecutor and the prisoner, who could not therefore be convicted.

I overruled the objections, and left the case to the jury, who found the prisoner guilty ; whereupon he was sentenced to twelve months' imprisonment with hard labour, until the opinion of the Court for the Consideration of Crown Cases Reserved could be taken, whether on the above facts the prisoner was rightly convicted.

Campbell Foster, for the prisoner. The evidence does not bring the case within the 20 and 21 Vict. c. 54, s. 4, which is a criminal enactment and must be construed strictly. The prisoner was not a bailee, inasmuch as he was not to return the specific coins. He had authority to lend out the money, and therefore was not a depositary, although that comes the nearest to his case. He is rather the banker of the Club ; and the money is not deposited with him, but lent to him, as was held in *Pott* v. *Clegg* [1] and *Tassell* v. *Cooper* [2]....

CROMPTON, J. The object of the statute was to defeat certain crotchets. If, for instance, I gave a pair of shoes to a man to carry, who did not happen to be my servant, and he appropriated them to his own use, an objection used to be taken that he could not be convicted of larceny, because the original taking was rightful and he was only a bailee.

WILLES, J. Here the circumstances shew that a debt was constituted between the prisoner and the prosecutor ; and the prisoner has not stolen the money but the debt. He is a trustee and not a bailee.

Hannay, for Crown. Unless this is held to be a bailment, there will be a failure of justice....

WILDE, B. Non-payment of debts, even if accompanied by fraud, is not criminal.

Hannay. It is impossible to use money unless it may be exchanged.

[1] 16 M. and W. 321.   [2] 9 C. B. 509.

COCKBURN, C.J. This conviction cannot be sustained. The prisoner is indicted, under the 4th section of the 20 and 21 Vict. c. 54, for larceny as a bailee. The word bailment must there be understood in its legal acceptation, viz., a deposit of something to be returned in specie; and does not apply to the receipt of money with an obligation to return the amount, where there is no obligation to return the identical coin. The present case is not a bailment of the ordinary kind, and so not within the statute, which must be construed in the usual way.

Conviction quashed.

[*Yet such a duty may be imposed by even a bailment of* cash.]

REGINA *v.* GOVERNOR OF HOLLOWAY PRISON.

QUEEN'S BENCH DIVISION. 1897.   18 Cox 631.

In this case a rule *nisi* had been obtained, calling upon the Governor of Holloway Prison to shew cause why a writ of *Habeas Corpus* should not issue directing him to bring up the body of one Emile George before the Court, to be dealt with as they should direct....This prisoner's extradition had been demanded by the French Government; and the magistrate at Bow Street had committed him for extradition for larceny by a bailee. The writ of *Habeas Corpus* was demanded on the ground that there was no evidence of any act which, if committed in England, would have constituted an offence according to English law....The deposition of the prosecutrix was as follows :—" George asked me for my daughter Martha in marriage. His references being excellent, I consented to the union. As it was necessary, in order to meet the expenses of the marriage, that I should get a certain sum of money, I entrusted George with a French 3 per cent. bond, the value of which was about 40,000 francs, on which he told me he had found the means of raising a loan;...and I gave him authority to borrow on it 10,000 francs, which he was to hand to me. But he only handed to me 5,000 francs....I consented at his request to negotiate on my bond a further loan of 6,000 francs; and gave him another authority to receive this money for me; which he did. But he kept the whole of it....After receiving peremptory notice to repay me, George ended by declaring that the marriage proposals which he had made were only conditional, and he disappeared."

Spencer Bower, for George. The money was received from the lender. Prisoner did not receive it from the prosecutrix at all. Nor did he appropriate the money actually advanced; for he was not bound to hand over those specific coins. There can be no larceny of these moneys, as there was no obligation to hand over the actual money received, but only an equivalent. See *Reg.* v. *Hassall (supra,* p. 227); *Reg.* v. *Brownlow,* 39 Law Times Rep. 479. [COLLINS, J., referred to *Reg.* v. *De Banks,* L.R. 13 Q.B.D. 29, and *Reg.* v. *Bunkall,* L. and C. 371 (*infra,* p. 231)].

LAWRANCE, J. I am of opinion that this rule must be discharged. The case of *Reg.* v. *De Banks* is on all-fours with the present, for, if you substitute a bond for the horse, the cases are one. It is said that the principle in *Reg.* v. *De Banks* is not in accord with *Reg.* v. *Hassall,* but the facts of the cases are entirely different. In *Reg.* v. *Hassall* a treasurer of a money club received small weekly payments from each member, and had authority with the secretary's consent to lend the club money to members. There was a periodical division of the funds and profits amongst the members. There it was held that the treasurer could not be indicted as a fraudulent bailee for larceny of moneys paid in by a member. Now, in *Reg.* v. *De Banks* the prisoner was employed by the prosecutor to take care of a horse for a few days, and afterwards to sell it and give him the money. He sold it, and absconded with the money. It was held that he was a bailee of the money, and could be convicted. That is practically what occurred here. It was like a person being sent to a bank to cash a cheque, who, after he had cashed it, absconded with the money. He would be a bailee, and could be convicted as such.

COLLINS, J. If Mr Spencer Bower's contention was a right one, it would shew a most lamentable deficiency in our criminal law. In these two transactions in this case there is abundant evidence of larceny by a bailee. In the first the bond was intrusted to George to obtain a loan, and in the second it was again intrusted to him to negotiate a further loan. It is contended that such transactions as took place in this case cannot be reached by the criminal law. But sect. 3 of the Larceny Act, 1861, is in these terms. [His Lordship read the section, and continued:] Now, the question is, was George a bailee? He undoubtedly converted this money. Why should he not be a bailee? There was a marked sum to be returned in this case, and unquestionably he was a mandatory, and, further, he was a depositary. It is said that *Reg.* v. *Hassall* bears on this case, but the facts there are altogether different, for obviously in that case there was a fund to be dealt with. He was not a bailee, but a trustee. That has no bearing on this. I think the rule must be discharged. *Reg.* v. *De Banks* is a clear authority for the principle in this case.

Rule discharged.

[*What circumstances suffice to create such a bailment.*]

REGINA *v.* BUNKALL.

CROWN CASE RESERVED. 1864.   LEIGH AND CAVE 371.

The following case was stated by the Chairman of Quarter Sessions for the county of Norfolk....

William Henry Bunkall was indicted for embezzling eight stones weight of coals, the property of his master, Henry Hart. In a second count of the indictment he was charged with the larceny of the said coals, which were therein also laid as the property of the said Henry Hart....

The prisoner had a horse and cart of his own, with which he was in the habit of carrying out his goods for sale. On the 31st of July the prosecutor requested the prisoner to fetch him, on the following day (August 1st), half a ton of coals from the said station, and on the next morning (August 1st) Robert Firman, a servant of the prosecutor, by his master's orders, took to and gave to the prisoner 8s. 6d. of his master's money to pay for the same. On the said 1st of August the prisoner proceeded to the *Dunham* Station with his own horse and cart, and there saw Rix, a person in Marriott's employ. Rix's evidence was as follows :—"The prisoner said, 'I want half a ton of blacksmith's coals.' I put nine hundred weight of coals in the cart and one hundred weight of coals in the sack. Bunkall asked me to put the hundred weight in the sack, as he said the cart would hang. He paid me 8s. for the coals. The price was 8s. 6d. He said he had not more money then. Bunkall has since paid the sixpence." In cross-examination the witness stated that he sold the coals to prisoner, and gave him credit for the balance of the price. Nothing was said as to the coals being for anybody else than Bunkall, nor was the prosecutor's name ever mentioned. Rix made out a receipt for the coals as bought by Bunkall. On the arrival of the prisoner with his cart at the prosecutor's house, the prosecutor immediately told the prisoner that he did

not think there was half a ton of coals in the cart. The prisoner said
there was full weight, for he had seen them weighed. The prosecutor
then said he should weigh them, and did so in the prisoner's presence,
and found them a hundred weight short....The prisoner confessed
taking the coals. On cross-examination the prosecutor stated that the
horse and cart in which the coals were brought from the station were
the property of the prisoner; that he was at liberty to fetch them
when and how he liked; and that, save as aforesaid, the prisoner had
never been in any way in the employment of or received any wages
from him.

Upon these facts it was objected by the counsel for the prisoner
that the prisoner could not be found guilty of larceny, as the goods in
question had never been in the possession, constructive or otherwise, of
the prosecutor, nor was the prisoner bound to deliver these specific
goods to the prosecutor; nor of embezzlement, inasmuch as he was not
employed in the capacity of a servant, nor were the goods delivered to
him on the account of the prosecutor as his employer within the meaning of the statute 24 and 25 Vict. c. 96.

The Court left the case to the jury, whether the prisoner (if guilty)
was guilty of embezzlement or larceny; and the jury found the prisoner
guilty of larceny upon the second count of the indictment.

Judgment was respited, and the prisoner discharged upon recognizance of bail to appear and receive judgment when called on.

The opinion of the Court for Crown Cases Reserved is requested,
whether upon the facts stated the prisoner was properly convicted of
larceny.

This case was argued, on the 23rd of January, 1864, before
COCKBURN, C.J., CROMPTON, J., WILLES, J., CHANNELL, B., and
KEATING, J.

Drake, for the prisoner. This conviction must be quashed. The
prisoner cannot be convicted of a larceny at common law, because the
prosecutor never was in possession of the coal. In *Reg.* v. *Reed*[1],
which is somewhat similar, the prisoner was sent by his master with
a cart to fetch coals, and was convicted of larceny in disposing of the
coals on the ground that the coals when placed in the master's cart
were in the master's possession. Here, on the contrary, the cart did
not belong to the prosecutor but to the prisoner, and, therefore, the
former never had possession of the coals. *Spears's Case*[2] is to the same
effect as *Reg.* v. *Reed*[1], and is so explained in *Rex* v. *Walsh*[3].

[1] Dears. C. C. 257.
[2] 2 Leach C. C. 825. See the judgment in *Reed's Case*, Dears. C. C. 263.
[3] 4 Taunt. 276.

COCKBURN, C.J. We are all of opinion that there was no larceny at common law.

Drake. Neither can the prisoner be convicted of larceny as a bailee, for the coals were not only never in the possession, but were not even the property of the prosecutor. Credit was given by the person who delivered the coals, not to the prosecutor, but to the prisoner; and the prisoner was at liberty, had he so pleased, to have kept these coals for himself, and to have fetched others for the prosecutor.

CROMPTON, J. Suppose I send bills to my agent abroad with directions to purchase goods and send them home to me, surely the cargo would be mine as soon as it was shipped, and it would make no difference if the agent chose to bring the goods home in his own ship There is some evidence that the prisoner had appropriated these particular coals to the prosecutor.

COCKBURN, C.J. The prisoner evidently meant to take these coals as part of the coals belonging to the prosecutor; and, if I had tried the case, I should have left that question to the jury.

WILLES, J. In *Taylor* v. *Plumer*[1]...it was held that the property of a principal entrusted by him to his factor for any special purpose belongs to the principal, notwithstanding any change which that property may have undergone in point of form, so long as such property is capable of being identified and distinguished from all other property. If I give a man money to buy a horse for me, and he buys a cow for himself with it, the cow is mine.

CROMPTON, J. In other words you may follow the money.

Drake. Suppose the prisoner had delivered no coals whatever to the prosecutor.

CROMPTON, J. In some cases, no doubt, he might have honestly done that; and not have been guilty of larceny, because of the absence of the felonious intent. Here, however, there was sufficient evidence of the existence of a felonious intent.

Drake. In the case of larceny by bailees, it is still necessary that the goods should have been at some time or other in the possession of the bailor. These coals never were in prosecutor's possession.

CROMPTON, J. If a man places debentures in the hands of a bailee and dies, the bailment continues, and the executors are entitled to them, although they have never had them in their possession. So again, in the case of a sale, before delivery there is a bailment between

[1] 3 M. and S. 562; where Lord Ellenborough accepted the proposition that "If A is *trusted by B with money* to purchase a horse for him, and he purchase a carriage *with that money*, B is entitled to the carriage."

the vendor and the vendee, though the latter has not yet obtained possession. It would be a very narrow construction to hold that the property must have been in the possession of the bailor.

Drake. There was no intention on the part of the coal owners to constitute a bailment. The duty of the prisoner would have been sufficiently fulfilled if he had delivered any other load of coals to the prosecutor, and therefore there was no bailment within the Act, for *Reg. v. Hassall*[1] shews that only those bailments are within the Act where the specific thing bailed is to be re-delivered.

COCKBURN, C.J. We are all of opinion that the conviction is good. The case turns on the construction of the 24 and 25 Vict. c. 96, s. 3, which enacts that "whosoever, being a bailee of any chattel, money, or valuable security, shall fraudulently take or convert the same to his own use, or the use of any person other than the owner thereof, although he shall not break bulk or otherwise determine the bailment, shall be guilty of larceny." In this case the prisoner was entrusted with money to buy coals, which he was to bring home to the prosecutor for remuneration in the prisoner's own cart. The prisoner, having bought the coals, abstracted a portion of them with the intention of appropriating such portion to his own use.

Some members of the Court are of opinion[2] that, even if there was no evidence of any specific appropriation of the coals by the prisoner to the prosecutor, yet, as they were bought with the prosecutor's money given by him to the prisoner for that purpose, that would ipso facto vest the property of the coals in the prosecutor, and so there would be a bailment within the terms of the statute.

Others are of opinion that a specific appropriation of the coals by the prisoner to the prosecutor was necessary; but that there was evidence of such specific appropriation. The prisoner went with the prosecutor's money to buy coals, put them into the cart, and took a portion for himself, pretending to the prosecutor that he had brought the whole of the coal to him. We are all of opinion that this was evidence of a specific appropriation sufficient to justify the jury in coming to the conclusion at which they arrived.

Conviction affirmed.

[1] *Supra*, p. 227; S. C. 30 L. J. R., M. C. 175.
[2] [EDITOR'S NOTE.] And, it would appear, rightly. See above, p. 233 *n.*

[*Only an act of* conversion quite inconsistent *with the bailment can amount to an* Appropriation.]

REGINA *v.* JACKSON.

SOMERSET ASSIZES. 1864.   9 Cox 505.

The prisoner was indicted for larceny of a coat of which he was the bailee. From the evidence it appeared that the prisoner lodged with the prosecutor, and on the 3rd of January borrowed a coat from the prosecutor for the day, and returned it. On the 10th of January he took the coat without the prosecutor's permission. He was seen wearing it by the prosecutor, who again gave him permission to wear it for the day. Some few days afterwards, he left the town ; and he was found, wearing the coat on his back, on board a ship bound for Australia[1].

MARTIN, B., stopped the case; stating that in his opinion there was no evidence of a conversion sufficient to satisfy the statute. There are many instances of conversion sufficient to maintain an action of trover, which would not be sufficient to support a conviction under this statute; the determination of the bailment must be something analogous to larceny, and some act must be done inconsistent with the purposes of the bailment. As, for instance, in the case of bailment of an article of silver for use, melting it would be evidence of a conversion. So, when money or a negotiable security is bailed to a person for safe keeping, if he spend the money or convert the security, he is guilty of a conversion within this statute. The prosecution ought to find some definite time at which the offence was committed ; *e.g.*, a taking the coat on board ship which was subsequent to the prisoner's going on board himself.

Edlin, for the prosecution, contended that there was evidence of a conversion sufficient to satisfy the statute; for the fact that the prisoner was taking the coat with him on a voyage to Australia was inconsistent with the bailment, it being a bailment to wear the coat for a limited period.

MARTIN, B., said that the case did not disclose such a crime as was contemplated by the statute. He refused the application of the prosecution that he would state a case.

---

1 [EDITOR'S NOTE.] But probably not about to sail so immediately as to leave him no opportunity of returning the coat.

[*But mere* pawning *may be such an act.*]

REGINA v. MEDLAND.

CENTRAL CRIMINAL COURT. 1851.   5 Cox 292.

The prisoner was indicted for larceny. It appeared that she had taken ready-furnished lodgings, and had pawned some of the property therein belonging to the landlord. It was proved that she had often pawned, and afterwards redeemed, portions of the same property.

Robinson, for the prisoner, submitted that if the jury were satisfied that the prisoner took the property for the purpose of pawning, but with the intention of redeeming it, she would be entitled to an acquittal, because the intent would not be permanently to deprive the owner of it.

The RECORDER, after consulting the judges in the adjoining court :— I have taken the opinion of Mr Justice Coleridge, and of Mr Baron Platt upon this case, and they both think with me that there is nothing in the evidence that will justify the jury in acquitting the prisoner on the ground that she took this property with the intention of redeeming it. It would be very dangerous to hold that the suggestion of such an intent would be sufficient to constitute a valid defence. A person may pawn property without the slightest prospect of ever being able to redeem it, and yet there may be some vague intention of doing so if afterwards the opportunity should occur, however improbable it may be that it will do so. But it can never be said that there is an intention to redeem, under circumstances that render it very improbable or at least uncertain that such ability will ever exist. A man may take my property, may exercise absolute dominion over it, may trade upon it and make a profit upon it for three months, and yet may say, when charged with stealing it, that he meant to return it to me at some time or another. I shall direct the jury that for such a defence to be at all available there must be not only the intent to redeem, evidenced by previous similar conduct, but there must be proof also of the power to do so, of which the evidence here seems rather of a negative character.

Verdict, Guilty.

[*Yet even* selling, *by a person who has* ceased *to be bailee or custodian, is not sufficient.*]

REGINA *v.* CHARLES JONES.

MONMOUTH ASSIZES. 1842. CARRINGTON AND MARSHMAN 611.

Indictment for stealing a pig. It appeared that on Dec. 18th the prosecutor had employed the prisoner to drive six pigs from Cardiff to Usk fair (which was on the 20th), for which he paid the prisoner six shillings. The prisoner had no authority to sell any of the pigs. On Dec. 19th, the prisoner left one of the pigs at Mr Matthews's, of Coedkernew, to be kept till the next night, saying that it was too tired to walk. On Monday, the 20th, the prisoner told the prosecutor at Usk that he had left the pig at Mr Matthews's because it was tired ; and the prosecutor then desired the prisoner to call at Mr Matthews's and ask him to keep the pig for him till the following Saturday, and he would pay him for the keep. On Tuesday, the 21st, the prisoner called at Mr Matthews's, and sold the pig to Mr Matthews for a guinea ; and on the 23rd, he told the prosecutor that he had seen Mr Matthews, and that Mr Matthews would keep the pig till Saturday.

Greaves, for the prosecution. The difficulty is, that the prisoner sold the pig when it was no·longer in his possession....He had merely the custody of the pigs, and if he had sold one of the pigs on the road it would have been larceny.

CRESSWELL, J. If a man is allowed to have the *possession* of a chattel and he converts it to his own use, it is not[1] larceny, unless he had an intention of stealing it when he obtained the possession of it. But if he has merely the *custody* of a chattel, he is guilty of a larceny if he disposes of it, although he did not intend to do so at the time when he received it into his custody. Here, it appears, that the prisoner left the pig on Sunday, the 19th ; and if nothing more had appeared, I should have held that Matthews kept it merely for the prisoner. But on Monday, the 20th, he told the prosecutor that he had left it there ; and the prosecutor told him to ask Matthews to allow the pig to remain there till the Saturday. The prosecutor thus consented to Matthews being the keeper of the pig for him (the prosecutor) ; and then the prisoner goes and sells the pig to Matthews. He must be acquitted.

[EDITOR'S NOTE. It was not until after the prosecutor had put an end to the prisoner's control over the pig, that the prisoner committed any act of dishonesty. Hence that act did not amount to a larcenous taking or appropriation.]

---

[1] [EDITOR'S NOTE.] At common law ; but see now the note on p. 226 *supra.*

CHAPTER 4.   PERSONAL CHATTELS.

[*There can be no larceny of* Real Property]

THE FORESTER'S CASE.

ASSIZES.   1338.   Y. B. 11 and 12 Edw. III. (Rolls Ser.) 641.

LIB. ASS. ann. 12, f. 37, pl. 32.

A forester was indicted for having feloniously cut down trees and carried them away.   The Justices would not arraign him; for the felling of trees which are so annexed to the soil cannot be called felony even if a stranger did it.   Besides here perhaps he himself had the keeping of them.   But because it was possible that the trees were first cut down by the lord, and then carried off by the forester, [the Justices] recalled the Inquest; who answered that he was forester when he felled them and carried them away.

SHARESHULL, [J.] to the Inquest.   Did the forester hide the trees from the lord?

The Inquest.   We do not know.

ALDEBURGH, [J.].   Assuredly we will not charge him, whether he concealed them or no.   We adjudge it no felony, for he was the keeper ; and a tree is part of the freehold.

[See also THE CASE OF PEACOCKS, *infra* p. 250.]

[*Even though the thing had originally been* Personal Property.]

CARVER *v.* PIERCE.

KING'S BENCH.   1648.   STYLE 66.

Carver brings an action upon the case against Pierce for speaking these words of him,—"Thou art a thief, for thou hast stolen my dung"; and hath a verdict.

The defendant moved in arrest of judgment, that the words were not actionable.   For it is not certain whether the dung be a chattel or part of the freehold; and if this, it cannot be theft to take it but a trespass; and then the action will not lie.

BACON, J. Dung is a chattel, and may be stolen.

But ROLLE, J., answered, Dung may be a chattel, and it may not be a chattel. For a heap of dung is a chattel, but if it be spread upon the land it is not. The word 'thief' here is actionable alone; and there are no subsequent words to mitigate the former words. For the stealing of dung is a felony if it be a chattel.

BACON, J., said, It doth not appear in this case of what value the dung was, and how shall it then be known, whether it be felony or petty larceny?

To this ROLLE answered, The words are scandalous and actionable, notwithstanding; though the stealing of the dung be not felony.

[See also REGINA *v.* EDWARDS, *infra* p. 247.]

[*Unless it has become identified with the land by mere legal fiction, without any physical attachment.*]

HOSKINS *v.* TARRANCE.

SUPREME COURT OF INDIANA. 1840. 5 BLACKFORD 417.

Appeal from the Montgomery Circuit Court.

DEWEY, J. This was an action of slander. The words laid in the declaration to have been spoken by the defendant of the plaintiff, are (amongst others), "He broke into my room and stole the key." Plea, not guilty. Verdict and judgment for plaintiff. There was evidence that the defendant said of the plaintiff, "He broke into a room of my house, and stole the key *out of the door.*" The defendant moved the Court to instruct the jury, "That the key in the lock of the door of a house, and belonging thereto, is part of the realty; and not the subject of larceny, unless the same is first severed from the realty by one act, and then stolen by another and distinct act." The Court refused to give this direction.

This refusal gives rise to a question not free from technical difficulties. It was anciently decided in England that charters and other assurances of real estate, and the chest in which they were kept, savoured so much of the realty that they could not be the subjects of theft. But it was held in a later case, that a window-sash, not hung or beaded into the frame, but fastened in only by laths so nailed across as to prevent it from falling out, was the subject of larceny. (*Rex* v. *Hedges*, 1 Leach 201). It is not easy, on principle, to reconcile these decisions. Clearly title deeds, and the trunk which contains them, are not fixtures, but are as moveable as any kind of personal property. But such papers descend to the heir, or pass to the purchaser, of the estate to which they belong; (and there is good reason why they should do so; for the safety of titles, of which they are the evidence, requires it). Yet would not the window-sash have taken the same course in the event of a descent or alienation of the house to which it was attached? I see no necessary or reasonable connection between the rule that title deeds shall pass with the estate, and the principle which has been made to exclude them from the possibility of being feloniously stolen. Indeed, the spirit of that very rule, having the security of title for its object, is violated by withholding from the evidences of title the protection of criminal justice. If all the technical consequences of considering charters and deeds as a part of the real estate were to be carried out, their owner, if dispossessed, would be obliged to resort to an action of ejectment, to recover them—a conclusion scarcely more absurd, than the doctrine that they cannot be the subjects of larceny (which is itself nothing but a technical deduction, and one not very fairly drawn, from the premises assumed as its foundation). There are, certainly, various purely personal chattels, which at common law go to the heir, with regard to which theft may be committed, namely, some species of heir-looms, and things in the nature of heir-looms— such as...coat-armour, and pennons, &c. On the contrary, there are things which go to the executor the taking of which (with whatever intent) is but trespass, and not larceny; emblements not severed from the ground are of this character. But a reasoning, analogous to that which excludes charters and deeds from being the subjects of larceny— because, though they have no actual connection with the freehold, they pass with the real estate—would include, within those larcenable subjects, emblements; for these follow the personalty, though they are attached to the soil.

It is true that the keys of a house follow the inheritance; and the writers who lay down this doctrine make no distinction between keys in the lock, and those in the pockets of their owners. They are, nevertheless, not fixtures; but a species of personal property, which, like title deeds, goes with the land, from a rule of law founded on public convenience. And as no decision, so far as we know, has as yet ranked them among the articles upon which larceny cannot be com_mitted, and as we see no good reason for carrying the doctrine of exemption farther than it has already gone, we feel at liberty, (upon the authority of *Rex* v. *Hedges*, as well as on principle), to decide that as "personal goods," they are within the purview of our statute relative to crime and punishment, and are the subjects of theft. Thus the Circuit Court committed no error in refusing the instruction to the jury which was asked for by the defendant. Its judgment is affirmed with damages and costs.

[*Even if the thief's act of Taking has rendered the thing* Personal Property *that act will not amount to Larceny.*]

[See REGINA v. TOWNLEY *infra*, p. 255.]

[*But if Things Real have been rendered Personal by* one *act of mine my subsequent taking of them, by an* entirely separate *act, may be Larceny.*]

THE QUEEN *v.* FOLEY.

IRISH CROWN CASE RESERVED.　　　　L.R. (Ir.) 1889. C.L. 299.

Case reserved by Mr Justice GIBSON.

The accused, Edward Foley, was tried before me at Maryborough Summer Assizes, for larceny of hay. The indictment was at common law.

Foley had been tenant of lands at Ballyadams. But his tenancy had been determined by a decree in ejectment, which was duly executed, and possession taken by the landlord on April 27th, 1888, when the house on the premises was levelled. On August 10th, the accused was seen by the police cutting a meadow on the said lands with a scythe. On the 11th he was again seen cutting there. A police constable went to him there and said, "I am glad someone will be responsible for the

cutting," when Foley replied, "I might as well have it as the landlord."
On August 13th, Foley proceeded to rake up the hay, which was then
lying scattered in the field, and put it into a cart. He took altogether
ten or twelve cwt., and brought it away.

Mr Leamy, counsel for the prisoner, contended that there was
no larceny, as the indictment was at common law, and the taking
was one continuous act: relying on *The Queen* v. *Townley*[1]. But
Mr Molloy, Q.C., for the Crown, contended that the hay was to be
deemed in the possession of the landlord at the time when the prisoner
removed it.

In reply to a question put by me the jury said that the prisoner did
not abandon possession of the grass cut between the time of cutting
and time of removing same.

Mr Molloy, Q.C., contended that there was no evidence to support
this special finding.

It must be taken that the landlord was in possession of the evicted
farm at the time when the grass was cut and removed. But there was
no evidence of any act done by him, or any person on his behalf, on the
evicted farm from the date of eviction until the removal of the hay;
nor was there any evidence of any act done by the prisoner in reference
to the farm or the grass cut, save as above stated.

I advised the jury to convict the prisoner, which they did. But
I did not sentence him, and he stands out on his own recognizance,
pending the decision of this case.

The question for the Court is, whether on these facts, the prisoner
was properly convicted of larceny?

*   *   *   *   *

HOLMES, J. The solution of this case depends upon whether there
is any evidence that the grass or hay was not in the possession of the
true owner in the interval between the severance and removal. When
the grass was growing, it belonged to the owner of the land; but,
although he was in possession of it as part of the land, he was not in
possession of it as a personal chattel. It first became capable of being
the subject of larceny when it was severed. It is, I think, clear that
where it is severed by a wrong-doer, and, as part of one continuous
transaction, it is carried away by him, there is no larceny. In such
a case it has never, as a personal chattel, been in the possession,
actual or constructive, of the true owner. It has been continuously in
the *actual*, though perhaps not always in the *physical*, possession of the
wrong-doer. In the case before us, the defendant, having cut the

---

[1] L. R. 1 C. C. R. 315; *infra* p. 254.

grass, left it on the land. Beyond the severance he did no act of any kind evidencing actual possession on his part, and for two days the owner of the land had, it seems to me, precisely the same kind of possession of it as he would have had if it had been cut and left there by his own servant.

There cannot, I conceive, be constructive (as distinguished from actual) possession by a wrong-doer; and when he returned, at the end of the period I have mentioned, he would be guilty of larceny, unless he was in actual possession in the interval. There is not, however, a particle of evidence of such actual possession, and therefore I hold the conviction right. This conclusion is in strict accordance with the authorities previous to *The Queen* v. *Townley,* referred to by Mr Molloy, and does not, I think, in any way conflict with that decision. In that case there was abundant evidence that the whole transaction was a continuous act; or, in other words, that the wrong-doer had never been out of actual possession, and under these circumstances the fact, upon the assumption of which the case was stated (that the poachers had no intention to abandon the wrongful possession of the rabbits which they acquired, but placed them in the ditch as a place of deposit till they could conveniently remove them), was decisive in the prisoner's favour. I consider, however, that that decision has no application to the present case.

Sir M. Morris, C.J. (*i. e.* Lord Morris). The question is—Was the possession of the hay in the prisoner at the time it was removed; or was it in the possession of the owner of the soil, in, that is, his constructive possession? Upon the decision of this question it depends whether the prisoner was or was not guilty of larceny. If the cutting and taking away were one continuous act the prisoner is not guilty. That question would have to be found in the prisoner's favour, to entitle him to an acquittal; but the jury have not so found. They have, no doubt, found that the prisoner did not abandon the possession of the grass; but that was a finding upon a question of law. Furthermore, the jury have found the prisoner guilty. There is no finding that the cutting and removing was *one continuous act.*

In this case the prisoner cut the grass on the 10th and 11th August, and was then seen doing so by a policeman. He came again three days after, on the 13th August, and removed the hay. Can it be said that the hay was, during all that interval, in the prisoner's possession, and not in the possession of the owner of the soil? I do not think it can, or that such removal can be said to be a continuous act with the original taking....

The Queen v. *Petch* (14 Cox 116) went on the same ground—the continuity of the act. Mr Justice Field says (at p. 119): "But it is said that the *continuity of the possession* by the prisoner was broken by the act of the keeper in going to the trap and nicking the rabbits"; the learned Judge, by the use of the words "continuity of possession," shewing the grounds upon which the Court decided the case.

The Court in *The Queen* v. *Townley* decided that the prisoner was not guilty; on the ground that the hiding in the hole in the ground of the dead rabbits was the same as if they had remained in the prisoner's possession.

On these grounds I consider that these cases of *The Queen* v. *Townley* and *The Queen* v. *Petch* are authorities in favour of the Crown in this case. For these reasons I am of opinion that the conviction should be sustained.

* * * * *

Eight Judges were of this opinion ; though PALLES, C.B., dissented.

Conviction affirmed.

CHAPTER V. THE VALUE.

[Some things are regarded by law as of so little value that there can be no larceny of them.]

REX *v.* SEARING.

CROWN CASE RESERVED. 1818. LEACH 350.

The prisoner was tried before Mr Baron WOOD, at the Lent Assizes for Hertfordshire, for larceny, in stealing "five live tame ferrets confined in a certain hutch," of the price of fifteen shillings, the property of Daniel Flower.

It appeared in evidence that ferrets are valuable animals, and that those in question were sold by the prisoner for nine shillings.

The jury found the prisoner guilty. But on the authority of 2 East's Pleas of the Crown 614, where it is said that ferrets (among other things) are considered of so base a nature that no larceny can be committed of them, the learned Judge respited the judgment until the opinion of the Judges could be taken thereon.

THE JUDGES met and considered this case. They were of opinion that ferrets (though tame and saleable) could not be the subject of larceny; and that judgment ought to be arrested.

[See also THE CASE OF PEACOCKS, p. 250; and REGINA *v.* ROBINSON, *infra*, p. 357. But remember sec. 21 of the Larceny Act 1861, making it a petty offence, summarily punishable with six months' imprisonment with hard labour, to steal any bird or animal ordinarily kept in a state of confinement or for any domestic purpose.]

[*Yet even a small slip of paper is of sufficient value.*]

REGINA *v.* PERRY.

CROWN CASE RESERVED. 1845. 1 CARRINGTON AND KIRWAN 725; 1 DENISON 69.

The prisoner, in one count of the indictment, was charged, as a servant of the Great Western Railway Company, with stealing an order for the payment of money, to wit, an order for the payment of £13. 9s. 7d., the property of the Great Western Railway Company; in another count the thing stolen was described to be "one piece of paper of the value of one penny," of the goods and chattels of the Great Western Railway Company. In other counts, the property was laid in different ways.

It appeared that the Great Western Railway Company being indebted for poor-rates to the overseers of the parish of Taunton St James in the sum of £13. 9s. 7d., a cheque for that amount was by the proper authority drawn at Paddington upon their London bankers, and then transmitted through the hands of various officers of the company to the superintendent at the Taunton station. He received it on Saturday, the 1st of March; and at the time when the prisoner, the chief clerk there, was going into the town to his dinner, placed it in his hands, ordering him to pay it to the overseer, and to bring him a stamped receipt on his return. On his return, the superintendent asked the prisoner if he had paid the overseer; he answered, "Yes"; and being asked for the receipt, said, that the overseer, not having one by him, had promised to forward it to a certain inn in the town for him. In truth, the prisoner had not paid it, and on Monday morning got it changed by a tradesman in Taunton, and applied the proceeds to his own use.

W. C. Rowe and *Edwards*, for the prisoner, objected that the cheque being void for want of a stamp was not a valuable security, and could not be used in evidence. They cited the stat. 55 Geo. III., c. 184, s. 13.

COLERIDGE, J. overruled the objection, and reserved the case for the opinion of the fifteen Judges.

Verdict. Guilty.

W. C. Rowe. I submit that this cheque was void, and that the prisoner could not be properly convicted of stealing it.

Lord DENMAN, C.J. Is it not a piece of paper of the value of one penny?

ALDERSON, B. There is no difference in the offence of stealing a cheque and stealing a piece of paper, and the count which states this to be a piece of paper puts an end to all question.

W. C. Rowe. The only two cases at all resembling the present case are *Rex* v. *Clark*[1] and *Rex* v. *Bingley*[2]. In the former of these cases it was held, that a person who stole re-issuable notes after they had been paid might be convicted of larceny, in stealing the piece of paper bearing the stamps; and in the latter, that a piece of paper on which the prosecutor had written a memorandum as to some money due to him was the subject of larceny. In those cases the paper might be of some value to the owner; but it is here rendered valueless by a void security being written on it. Mr Serjeant Hawkins, in treating of those things which are the subject of larceny, says[3], "They ought to have some worth in themselves, and not to derive their whole value from the relation they bear to some other thing which cannot be stolen, as paper or parchment on which are written assurances concerning lands, or obligations, or covenants, or other securities for a debt, or other chose in action."

WIGHTMAN, J. Not as valuable securities. But are they not pieces of paper?

CRESSWELL, J. If a blank cheque had been stolen, would that be a larceny?

W. C. Rowe. I think it would.

CRESSWELL, J. Would it be worse for being filled up? In *Rex* v. *Clark* bankers' paid notes were held to be the subject of larceny of the stamps and paper. The paper was held to be "of some value"; and I do not see how the stamps carry the thing further, except by making the paper of greater value.

TINDAL, C.J. There are two charges here—the one a charge of stealing a valuable security; the other a charge of stealing a piece of

[1] R. and R. C. C. 181. [2] 5 C. and P. 602.
[3] 1 Hawk. P.C.; Bk. I., ch. 33, s. 22.

paper. You may get rid of the first by its being a bad cheque; but how can you get rid of the other ?

W. C. Rowe. It appeared to me that the effect of converting the paper into a cheque was to make it valuable, if at all, as a security for money; and that, the moment the paper had a cheque written upon it, it became[1] a chose in action, which is not the subject of larceny.

ALDERSON, B. The nature of the paper is not so wholly absorbed in the chose in action as you put it.

W. C. Rowe. If the paper is not wholly absorbed in the chose in action, I should submit that it was of so infinitesimal value as to fall within the rule (de minimis non curat lex).

Lord DENMAN, C.J. Your client got £13. 9s. 7d. for it.

W. C. Rowe. This cheque never could fulfil any good purpose, for want of a stamp. I submit, therefore, that it was valueless, and not the subject of larceny.

The case was considered by the Judges, who held the conviction right, as, at all events, there was a stealing of a piece of paper which was sufficient to sustain a count for larceny.

[*Or mere carrion.*]

REGINA *v.* EDWARDS AND ANOTHER.

CROWN CASE RESERVED. 1877.   13 Cox 384.

The prisoners were tried at the West Kent Quarter Sessions, held at Maidstone, on the 5th January, 1877, on an indictment charging them with stealing three dead pigs, the property of Sir William Hart Dyke, Bart.

The evidence was to the following effect: The three pigs in question having been bitten by a mad dog, Sir William Hart Dyke, to whom they belonged, directed his steward to shoot them. The steward thereupon shot them each through the head, and ordered a man named Paylis to bury them behind the barn. The steward stated that he had no intention of digging them up again, or of making any use of them. Paylis buried them, accordingly, in a place where a brake stack is usually

---

[1] [EDITOR'S NOTE.] See *Reg.* v. *Watts,* Dearsly 334.

placed. The hole in which the pigs were buried was three feet or more deep; and the soil was trodden in over them. The prisoner Edwards was employed to help Paylis to bury the pigs. Edwards was seen to be covering the pigs with brakes; and in answer to Paylis's question why he did so, said that it would keep the water out, and it was as well to bury them "clean and decent." The two prisoners went the same evening and dug up the pigs; and took them to the railway station, covered up in sacking, with a statement that they were three sheep; and sent them off for sale to a salesman in the London Meat Market, where they were sold for £9. 3s. 9d., which was paid to the prisoners for them.

The counsel for the prisoners submitted that there was no evidence in support of the charge to go to the jury; on the following grounds Firstly, that the property was not proved as laid in the indictment, as Sir William Hart Dyke had abandoned his property in the pigs; secondly, that under the circumstances the buried pigs were of no value to the prosecutor; and thirdly, that under the circumstances the buried pigs were attached to the soil, and could not be the subject of larceny.

The Chairman, however, thought that the case was one for the jury; and directed them as to the first point that in his opinion there had been no abandonment, as Sir William's intention was to prevent the pigs being made any use of, but that if the jury were of opinion that he had abandoned the property they should acquit the prisoners. He also told the jury that he thought there was nothing in the other two objections.

The jury found the prisoners guilty.

The question for the consideration of the Court is, whether, having reference to the objections taken by prisoners' counsel, there was evidence on which the jury were justified in convicting the prisoners of larceny.

No counsel appeared to argue on either side.

By the COURT: Conviction affirmed.

CHAPTER VI. THE OWNERSHIP.

[*There can be no larceny of things that have no owner.*]

A RESOLUTION.

1348.   22 LIB. Ass. 95 99

Nota. For killing doves or fishes or other wild things, taken whilst still wild, no man must suffer death ; unless they were feloniously taken out of some dwelling-house or mansion;

Nota. That punishment for taking and carrying away treasure trove or wrecks or waifs must be by imprisonment and fine ; and must never be of life and limb.

[*And the ownership of living things depends on the control of them.*]

ANONYMOUS.

KING'S BENCH. 1478.   Y.B. 18 EDW. IV., fo. 8, pl. 7.

A man was indicted for having with force and arms broken into a dovecote, and taken twenty young pigeons which could not fly. It was adjudged a good indictment, notwithstanding the objection of the taker of the said pigeons. Because the property in such pigeons must always be in the person to whom the dovecote belongs, so long as they cannot get out of it and he can take them whenever he likes. It is otherwise if he were indicted for taking old pigeons ; because the law considers the property in them to belong to no one ; for they go about the country and so he cannot take them at his pleasure, &c.[1] If a man be indicted for feloniously taking pike or tench out of a pond or trunk, the indictment is good for the aforesaid cause ; but otherwise if they were taken out of a river. The law as to young goshawks which cannot fly or go, hatched in my own park, is that it is felony[3] ; but otherwise as to other goshawks. So note the difference according as the property can or cannot be taken by him at pleasure.

[1] *I.e.* After the capturing of them has created ownership.

[2] But the law now holds even old pigeons to be larcenable if *tame*, in spite of their being thus able to fly freely ; *Reg.* v. *Cheafor*, 2 Den. 361.

[3] But in *Rex* v. *Stride*, L. R. [1908] 1 K.B. 617, this old doctrine, that a mere property *per impotentiam* can be protected by the law of Larceny, was overthrown.

[*And the animal's habits determine what degree of physical control is necessary.*]

THE CASE OF PEACOCKS.

KING'S BENCH.   1526.   Y.B. 18 HEN. VIII., pl. 11.

A question was proposed to all the Judges by the Chancellor: If a man feloniously appropriates peacocks which are tame and domestic, is this felony or not?

FITZHERBERT and ENGLEFIELD [JJ.] replied that it is no felony, for they are of wild nature, just as are doves in a dovecote....The law is the same with regard to...swans taken, or a buck or hind; or to hares taken otherwise than in a walled garden. It is the same, again, with regard to a mastiff, a hound, or a spaniel, or a tamed goshawk; for these are more properly things for pleasure than for profit. And similarly the peacock is rather a bird of pleasure than of profit; for it often kills all its chickens except one. And it was agreed that carrying off apples from my orchard which were growing on the trees at the time of the taking, or trees themselves which were growing at the time of the taking, or reaping corn and carrying it away, is no felony, even when the taking is with a felonious intent; for, at the time of the taking, these things were part of the freehold. But if I cut my trees or reap my corn, and then another person takes them away, with a felonious intention, this is felony.

But FITZJAMES [C.J.] AND ALL THE OTHER JUDGES said that peacocks are usually of the same habits as are hens and capons and ducks and geese; they have an animus revertendi, and the owner has a true property in them. They are not fowls of warren, like pheasants and partridges, whereof the taking, even with felonious intent, is not felony.

And at last ALL THE JUDGES agreed that such a taking of peacocks was felony, for the reason aforesaid. *Quod nota.*

REX *v.* ROUGH.

CROWN CASE RESERVED.   1779.   2 EAST P.C. 607.

At the Surrey Lent Assizes, John Rough was convicted on an indictment for stealing a pheasant of the value of forty shillings, of the goods and chattels of H. S.

ALL THE JUDGES on a conference in Easter Term agreed (after much debate and difference of opinion) that the conviction was bad. For in cases of larceny of animals ferae naturae the indictment must shew that they were either dead, tamed, or confined. Otherwise they must be presumed to be in their original state.

[See also REX v. EDWARDS *supra*, p. 247.]

[*But even a temporary ownership* during helplessness *suffices.*]

THE QUEEN v. SHICKLE.

CROWN CASE RESERVED.   1868.   L.R. 1 C.C.R. 159.

The following case was stated by COCKBURN, C.J.:—

James Shickle was tried before me at the last Assizes for the county of Suffolk on an indictment for larceny, for stealing eleven tame partridges.

There was no doubt that the prisoner had taken the birds animo furandi; but a question arose whether the birds in question could be the subject of larceny; and the prisoner having been convicted, I reserved the point for the consideration of the Court.

The birds in question had been reared from eggs which had been taken from the nest of a hen partridge, and which had been placed under a common hen. They were about three weeks old, and could fly a little. The hen had at first been kept under a coop in the prosecutor's orchard, the young birds running in and out, as the brood of a hen so confined are wont to do. The coop had, however, been removed, and the hen set at liberty, but the young birds still remained about the place with the hen, as her brood, and slept under her wings at night.

It is well known that birds of a wild nature, reared under a common hen, when in the course of nature they no longer require the protection and assistance of the hen and leave her, betake themselves to the woods or fields; and after a short time differ in no respect from birds reared under a wild hen of their own species.

The birds in question were neither tame by nature **nor** reclaimed. If they could be said to be tame at all, it was only that their instinct led them during their age of helplessness to remain with the hen. On their attachment to the hen ceasing, the wild instincts of their nature would return and would lead them to escape from the dominion and neighbourhood of man.   On the other hand, from their instinctive attachment to the hen that had reared them, and from their inability to escape, they were practically in the power and dominion of the prosecutor.   The question is, whether under the circumstances, there can be such property in birds of this description as can be the subject matter of larceny.

Douglas, for the prisoner. These birds are ferae naturae, and unless reclaimed are not the subject of larceny.   The case finds that they were not tame nor reclaimed, that they were restrained by their instinct only from betaking themselves to the woods or fields; not being confined in any way. They could not, therefore, be the subject of larceny.

No counsel appeared for the Crown.

BOVILL, C.J.   I am of opinion that, upon the facts stated, the question asked of us must be answered in the affirmative, and that the conviction is right.   The case states that "from their inability to escape, they were practically in the power and dominion of the prosecutor."   That is sufficient to decide the point.   In *Reg.* **v.** *Cory*[1] the law on the subject is very clearly laid down by my brother Channell.   He there says, speaking of pheasants hatched under circumstances similar to those here: "These pheasants, having been hatched by hens, and reared in a coop, were tame pheasants at the time they were taken, whatever might be their destiny afterwards.   Being thus, the prosecutor had such a property in them that they would become the subject of larceny, and the inquiry **for** stealing them would be of precisely the same nature as if the birds had been common fowls or any other poultry; the character of the birds in no way affecting the law of the case but only the question of identity."   In that statement of the law we all concur.   The question here is, were these birds the subject of property?   They were so when first hatched, and they remained so at the time they were taken by the prisoner, though it might be that at a later period they would become wild and cease to have an owner.   The prisoner, therefore, was rightly convicted.

CHANNELL, B., concurred.

BYLES, J.   I am of the same opinion.   The usual cases of larceny of animals are those of animals which, being at first wild, have become

[1] 10 Cox C. C. 23.

tame and reclaimed. In this case the only difference is that the birds are tame and have been so from their birth, though they may become wild at a future time.

BLACKBURN and LUSH, JJ., concurred.

Conviction affirmed.

[*Or a mere right to the* possession *of the Thing.*]

ANONYMOUS.

1429.   Y.B. 7 HEN. VI., fo. 43, pl. 18.

It was said that if I deliver to you certain goods to take care of, and then I retake them with felonious intent, I shall be hanged for it, although the ownership was in me. And Norton agreed that this was good law. [Cf. p. 225 *supra.*]

[See also the cases suggested in REX v. MACDANIEL, *infra,* at p. 261.]

[*Right to Possession.*]

REX v. NOWELL WILKINSON AND JOSEPH MARSDEN.

CROWN CASE RESERVED. 1821.   RUSSELL AND RYAN 470.

[The prisoners were indicted at the Old Bailey for stealing thirty bales of nux vomica.

A duty of 2s. 6d. on the pound weight was leviable on all nux vomica imported for consumption in England; though no duty was levied on any that was brought here for re-exportation. To cheat the Government of this import duty, William Marsden, the owner of these bales, induced a merchant named Cooper to allow his name to be employed for passing them through the Custom House (where they then lay in

bond) as if intended for exportation to Amsterdam. Cooper accordingly
employed a firm of lightermen, Messrs Marsh and Co., to effect the
actual passing of the bales. Messrs Marsh, in all good faith, entered
them at the Custom House for a vessel called the *York Merchant,* about
to sail for Amsterdam ; and gave a bond to Government, in which they
bound themselves so to export them. They then employed the prisoner
Wilkinson, as their servant, to convey the bales in their boat from the
Customs' warehouse to the *York Merchant.* Having obtained the
goods, Wilkinson took them in Messrs Marsh and Co.'s boat (not to
the ship but) to a warehouse which had been hired by William
Marsden. There the bales were unpacked by the two prisoners and
William Marsden ; the nux vomica was taken out and sent off to
London. The bales were repacked with cinders and other rubbish ;
and were then put by Wilkinson on board the *York Merchant.* The
fraud was not discovered by the Customs authorities until two or three
days afterwards.

The jury convicted the prisoners ; and found that the goods
belonged to William Marsden. PARK, J., reserved for the Judges the
question whether an owner commits larceny by taking his own goods
from a bailee who has made himself responsible that a given thing
shall be done with the goods, the doing of which the owner, without
the knowledge or consent of the bailee, entirely prevents by his taking
of the goods.]

Four of the Judges, viz. RICHARDSON, J., BURROUGH, J., WOOD, B.,
GRAHAM, B., doubted whether this was larceny, because there was no
intent to cheat Messrs Marsh and Co., or to charge them; but only to
cheat the Crown. Seven of the Judges, viz. GARROW, B., HOLROYD, J.,
PARK, J., BAYLEY, J., RICHARDS, C.B., DALLAS, C.J., ABBOTT, L.C.J.,
held it a larceny; because Marsh and Co. had a right to the possession
until the goods reached the ship ; and had also an interest in that
possession ; and the intent to deprive them of this possession, wrongfully and against their will, was a felonious intent as against them,
because it exposed them to a suit upon the bond. In the opinion of
part[1] of these seven Judges, there would have been a larceny, even
though there had been no felonious intent against Marsh and Co.,
but only an intention to defraud the Crown.

---

[1] [EDITOR'S NOTE.] Russell, who had before him the MS notes of Bayley, J.,
says "*most*" of the seven.

[*The ownership must exist* before *the act of theft, and* **not** *merely to* created by it.]

THE QUEEN *v.* TOWNLEY.

CROWN CASE RESERVED. 1871.   L.R. 1 C.C.R. 315.

Case stated by BLACKBURN, J.

The prisoner and one George Dunkley were indicted at the North-ampton Spring Assizes for stealing 126 dead rabbits. In one count they were laid as the property of William Hollis, in another as being the property of the Queen. There were also counts for receiving.

It was proved that Selsey Forest is the property of Her Majesty. An agreement between Mr Hollis and the Commissioners of the Woods and Forests on behalf of Her Majesty was given in evidence, which the learned Judge thought amounted in legal effect merely to a licence to Mr Hollis to kill and take away the game; and that the occupation of the soil, and all rights incident thereto, remained in the Queen. No point, however, was reserved as to the proof of the property as laid in the indictment.

The evidence shewed that Mr Hollis' keepers, about eight in the morning on the 23rd of September, discovered 126 dead and newly-killed rabbits and about 400 yards of net concealed in a ditch in the forest, behind a hedge close to a road passing through the forest. The rabbits were some in bags, and some in bundles strapped together by the legs, and had evidently been placed there as a place of deposit by those who had netted the rabbits. The keepers lay in wait, and at about a quarter to eleven on the same day Townley, and a man who escaped, came in a cab driven by Dunkley along the road, Townley and the man who escaped left the cab in charge of Dunkley, and came into the forest, and went straight to the ditch where the rabbits were concealed, and began to remove them.

The prisoners were not defended by counsel.

It was contended by the counsel for the prosecution that the rabbits on being killed and being reduced into possession by a wrong-doer became the property of the owner of the soil, in this case the Queen : *Blades* v. *Higgs*[1]; and that even if it was not larceny to kill and carry away the game at once, it was so here, because the killing and carrying away was not one continued act. Hale's Pleas of the Crown, vol. i, p. 510, and *Lee* v. *Risdon*[2], were cited.

---

[1] 11 H. L. C. 621; 34 L. J. (C.P.) 286.   [2] 7 Taunt. 189, at p. 191.

The jury, in answers to questions from the learned Judge, found that the rabbits had been killed by poachers in Selsey Forest, on land in the same occupation and ownership as the spot where they were found hidden. That Townley removed them knowing that they had been so killed, but that it was not proved that Dunkley had any such knowledge.

The learned Judge thereupon directed a verdict of not guilty to be entered as regarded Dunkley, and a verdict of guilty as to Townley, subject to a case for the Court of Criminal Appeal.

It was to be taken as a fact that the poachers had no intention to abandon the wrongful possession of the rabbits which they had acquired by taking them; but placed them in the ditch as a place of deposit till they could conveniently remove them. The question for the Court was, whether on these facts the prisoner was properly convicted of larceny.

BOVILL, C.J....The first question is as to the nature of the property in these rabbits. In animals ferae naturae there is no absolute property. There is only a special or qualified right of property—a right ratione soli to take and kill them. When killed upon the soil they become the absolute property of the owner of the soil. This was decided in the case of rabbits by the House of Lords in *Blades* v. *Higgs* [1]. And the same principle was applied in the case of grouse in *Lord Lonsdale* v. *Rigg* [2]. In this case therefore the rabbits, being started and killed on land belonging to the Crown, might, if there were no other circumstances in the case, become the property of the Crown. But before there can be a conviction for larceny for taking anything not capable in its original state of being the subject of larceny, as for instance, things fixed to the soil, it is necessary that the act of taking away should not be one continuous act with the act of severance or other act by which the thing becomes a chattel, and so is brought within the law of larceny. This doctrine has been applied to stripping lead from the roof of a church, and in other cases of things affixed to the soil. And the present case must be governed by the same principle. It is not stated in the case whether or not the prisoner was one of the poachers who killed the rabbits. But my brother Blackburn says that such must be taken to be the fact. Under all the circumstances of the case I think a jury ought to have found that the whole transaction was a continuous one; and the conviction must be quashed.

MARTIN, B. I am of the same opinion. I think it is of the

[1] 11 H. L. C. 621; 34 L. J. (C.P.) 286.
[2] 1 H. and N. 923; 26 L.J. (Ex.) 196.

utmost importance that the criminal law should rest upon plain and
simple principles. Now if a man kills a rabbit and carries it away at
once, it is clearly not larceny. But it is said that if he leaves it
for a little time before carrying it away, it is. And in support of this
view a passage from Hale's Pleas of the Crown, p. 510, is relied on,
where he says, "If a man come to steal trees, or the lead of a church
or house, and sever it, and after about an hour's time or so come and
fetch it away, this hath been held felony, because the act is not
continuated but interpolated; and so it was agreed by the Court of
King's Bench, 9 Car. 2, upon an indictment for stealing the lead of
Westminster Abbey." A dictum of Gibbs, C.J., in *Lee* v. *Risdon*[1] to
the same effect is also cited. Those statements may be perfectly
correct, and ought perhaps to be followed in cases exactly similar in
their facts, where there has been an actual abandonment of possession
of the things taken. But here it is expressly found that there was no
abandonment. And where the act is merely interrupted I think it
more reasonable to hold that there is no larceny.

BRAMWELL, B. I am of the same opinion. And I think our
decision is consistent with the passage cited from Hale, and the
dictum of Gibbs, C.J., referred to, which appear to me quite correct.
If a man were unlawfully to dig his neighbour's potatoes; and from
being disturbed in his work, or any other cause, were to abandon
them at the place where he had dug them; and were afterwards, with
a fresh intention, to come back and take them away, I think the case
would be the same as if during this interval of time the potatoes had
been locked in a cupboard by the true owner. Wherever, in such
cases, the goods may be said to have been in the possession of the true
owner in the interval between the severance and the removal, I think
the removal is larceny. But is that so in this case? If the poachers
had taken these rabbits to their own house, or to a public-house, can it
be supposed that the subsequent removal of them from there would
have been larceny? And if the case be varied by supposing them to
have placed them upon land adjoining that on which they were killed,
can that make any difference? And if so, how can it be otherwise,
because the place of deposit chosen is upon the land of the same owner
on whose grounds the rabbits were killed. The case seems to me not
to fall within the rule laid down by Hale; for, to use his words, the act
here was "continuated."

BYLES, J. I am of the same opinion, though I have entertained
some doubts. It is here proved as a fact that the possession of the
poachers was never abandoned; and, in fact, the rabbits from the

[1] 7 Taunt. 188, at p. 191.

time they were taken remained, in part at least, in the bags of the poachers. I think, therefore, the whole transaction must be regarded as one continuous transaction.

BLACKBURN, J. I am of the same opinion. To constitute larceny at common law it was necessary that the thief should both take and carry away. And it was early settled that in the case of a thing like a tree, for instance, when the very act which converted it into a chattel was accompanied by the taking of it away, there was no larceny. Almost all the cases falling within this rule have since been made larceny by statute; but the common law rule remains the same. Even in the case of *Blades* v. *Higgs*[1], in which it was held that game when killed becomes the property of the owner of the land upon which it was raised and killed, it was expressly pointed out that it by no means followed that an indictment for larceny would lie. The doctrine is a very early one; see Book of Assizes, 12th year, par. 32, where it was applied to the case of trees[2]. The result is, that while taking away dead game is larceny, it is otherwise where the killing and taking away are one continuous act.

Now, to apply these principles to the present case, I do not think it makes any great difference that the prisoner was himself one of the poachers; I think the result would be the same if he had been the servant of a dealer with knowledge of the circumstances under which the rabbits had been killed. But then there is the fact that the rabbits after being killed were left for nearly three hours. I should myself have thought that that made no difference in the case; but a passage has been cited from Lord Hale in which he says, that if you strip lead from a church, "and after about an hour or so come and fetch it away," this is larceny; and he speaks of this as decided law, citing Dalton as his authority. A dictum of Gibbs, C.J., to the same effect has also been referred to. If we are to understand these passages in the sense put upon them by my brother Bramwell, as applying only to a case in which the wrongdoer has abandoned and lost all property and possession in the things in question, I have no quarrel with them, and they do not apply to the present case. But if those passages mean that the mere cessation of physical possession is sufficient to make the subsequent act of removal larceny, then they do apply to the present case. And in that case, great as is my respect for Lord Hale, I cannot follow him. I cannot see that it makes any difference whether those who have taken game hide it in one place or hide it in another.

Conviction quashed.

[See REGINA v. FOLEY, *supra*, p. 241.]

---

[1] 11 H. L. C. 621; 34 L. J. (C.P.) 286.   [2] *The Forester's Case, supra*, p. 238.

CHAPTER VII. THE CLAIM OF RIGHT.

[To constitute larceny, the thing must be taken not only without a **right** *but without even a mistaken claim of right.]*

[The owner's consent to transfer the possession excuses a Taking]

REX *v.* MACDANIEL.

OLD BAILEY SESSIONS. 1755.   FOSTER 121.

[The indictment charged Macdaniel, Berry, Egan, and Salmon, as accessories before the fact to a felony and robbery committed by Peter Kelly and John Ellis in the king's highway in the parish of Saint Paul, Deptford, in the county of Kent, upon the person of James Salmon one of the present prisoners at the bar.]

On this indictment the prisoners have been tried, and the jury have found a special verdict to this effect:—That Kelly and Ellis were by due course of law convicted of the said felony and robbery. That before the robbery all the present prisoners and one Thomas Blee, did feloniously meet at the Bell Inn in Holborn; and did then and there agree [cf. p. 97 *supra*] that the said Thomas Blee should procure two persons to commit a robbery on the highway in the parish of Saint Paul, Deptford, upon the person of the prisoner Salmon. That in pursuance of this agreement, and with the privity of all the prisoners, the said Blee did engage and procure the said Ellis and Kelly to go with him to Deptford in order to steal linen ; but did not at any time before the robbery inform them or either of them of the intended robbery.

That in consequence of the said agreement at the Bell, and with the privity of all the prisoners, the said Ellis and Kelly went with the said Blee to Deptford.

That the said Blee, Ellis, and Kelly being there, and the prisoner Salmon being likewise there waiting in the highway in pursuance of the said agreement, the said Blee, Ellis and Kelly feloniously assaulted him, and took from his person the money and goods mentioned in the indictment....

As to the prisoner Salmon, THE JUDGES upon consideration of this special verdict were unanimously of opinion, that he cannot be guilty within this indictment. For unless he was party to the agreement at the Bell, there can be no colour to involve him in the guilt of Ellis and Kelly. And on the other hand, if he did part with his money and

17—2

goods in consequence of that agreement, it cannot be said that in legal construction he was robbed at all : since it is of the essence of robbery and larceny, that the goods be taken against the will of the owner.

It hath been holden, and I think rightly, that a man may make himself an accessory after the fact to a larceny of his own goods, or to a robbery on himself, by harbouring or concealing the thief, or assisting in his escape. And under some circumstances a man may be guilty of larceny in stealing his own goods, or of robbery in taking his own property from the person of another. A. delivereth goods to B. to keep for him, and then stealeth them, with intent to charge B. with the value of them ; this would be felony in A. Or A., having delivered money to his servant to carry to some distant place, disguiseth himself and robbeth the servant on the road, with intent to charge the hundred ; this, I doubt not, would be robbery in A. For in these cases the money and goods were taken from those who had a special temporary property in them, with a wicked fraudulent intention ; which is the antient known definition of larceny, fraudulenta contractatio rei alienae invito domino. But I never did hear before this time of any attempt to charge a man as accessory before the fact to a robbery committed on his own person.

[*But merely* facilitating *the taking, for purposes of* detection, *is not a consent.*]

THE KING *v.* EGGINTON AND OTHERS.

Crown Case Reserved. 1801.   Leach 913.

Indictment for burglary [at the factory of the celebrated James Watt and Matthew Boulton at Soho, near Birmingham]. The prisoners had applied to one Joseph Phillips, who was employed as watchman to the manufactory, to assist them in robbing it....He informed his employer who told him to carry the affair on, and consented to his opening the door and to his being with the prisoners the whole time.... At about 1 a.m. the prisoners came ; and Phillips and they broke open the counting-house, which was locked, and took from thence ingots of silver and guineas...and went down into the middle yard, where they were taken by the persons placed to watch. On this case two points were made for the prisoners ; the first of which was that no felony was proved, as the whole was done with the knowledge and consent of Matthew Boulton and all the acts of the watchman were his acts....The jury found the prisoners guilty; but LAWRANCE, J., reserved the objections for the opinion of the twelve Judges.

Clifford, for the prisoners....The whole criminality is done away by the consent and assistance which Matthew Boulton gave to the perpetration of the offence. Suppose Phillips the watchman had been indicted for the burglary, what could have prevented his being convicted of the crime but the assent of the prosecutor?...The offence could not possibly have been perpetrated if it had not been for the assistance afforded to the prisoners. He referred to *Rex* v. *Macdaniel* (*supra*, p. 259).

Manley, for the Crown....Matthew Boulton did not stand in a similar situation with Salmon in *Rex* v. *Macdaniel*; for he cannot in any view of his conduct be considered particeps criminis; inasmuch as his consent was only given for the purpose of detecting the prisoners, and the only business to which that consent applied was *that* which the prisoners themselves had originally contrived and proposed to Phillips to join in executing. Neither the prosecutor nor the watchman did any act to invite or induce the prisoners to commit the offence....A hop-dealer was suspected of having robbed an inn at Worcester. The landlord, with a view to detect him, hung up a great-coat in the yard, with a handkerchief hanging partly out of the pocket; and the man, being watched, was detected in the very act of stealing the handkerchief. On his trial before Mr Baron Thompson at the ensuing Worcester Assizes, I took the objection that the landlord had voluntarily suffered the property to be taken, and by this contrivance had induced the prisoner to commit the offence; but the objection was overruled and the prisoner convicted. There is a case in Fitzherbert (31 b) which is precisely in point. The servant of an alderman of London agreed with strangers to steal his master's plate, and procured a false key of the place where the plate was kept in the house; but the servant afterwards revealed the design to his master, who, on the appointed night, had men ready to apprehend them; the strangers afterwards came and entered into the said place with intent to steal the plate and were taken, and being tried for the burglary they were found guilty and executed.

A majority of THE JUDGES held that the prisoners were guilty of the larceny, for, although Matthew Boulton had permitted or suffered the meditated offence to be committed, he had not done anything originally to induce it; that his object being to detect the prisoners, he only gave them a greater facility to commit the larceny than they otherwise might have had; and that this could no more be considered as an assent than if a man, knowing of the intent of thieves to break into his house, were not to secure it with the usual number of bolts; that there was no distinguishing between the degrees of facility a thief might have given to him; that Boulton never meant that the prisoners should take away his property; that the design originated with the prisoners; and that all Boulton did was to prevent their design being carried into undetected execution; which differed the case greatly from what it might have been if he had employed his servant to suggest the perpetration of the offence originally to the prisoners.

[EDITOR'S NOTE. In America, two similar cases have very recently been similarly decided against the prisoner; *The State* v. *Abley* (80 N. W. Rep. 225; Iowa), *Alexander* v. *The State* (12 Texas 540). In 1907, in the West Australian case of *Rex* v. *Hansen,* the prisoners had suggested to a watchman a robbery of the warehouse. By his master's advice, he agreed with them as to a time when he should unlock the gate for them. On his doing so, they entered and took goods. They were convicted; the Court distinguishing Macdaniel's case, because in it all was arranged before the robbers had any idea of robbing.]

[*And a consent obtained by* intimidation *is no consent.*]

THE QUEEN *v.* McGRATH.

CROWN CASE RESERVED.   1869.   L.R. 1 C.C.R. 205.

P. McGrath was charged with feloniously stealing 26*s.*, the money of Peter Powell.

Jane Powell, the wife of the prosecutor, passed a sale room, and on being invited to enter, did so. There were about a dozen persons in the room. After two table cloths had been sold, a cloth was put up for sale by auction, the prisoner acting as auctioneer. A man bid 25*s.* for it, when another man standing between Jane Powell and the door said to the prisoner that she had bid 26*s.* for it, upon which the prisoner knocked it down to her. The witness Jane Powell said: "I had not bid for it, nor made any sign. I told the prisoner I had not bid. He said I did. I said I did not, and would not pay for it: I said this several times. I went to go out. The prisoner said I had bid for it, and must pay before I would be allowed to go out. I was then prevented going out by the man who had said I had bid for it. He stood between me and the door, and said I must pay for it. I wanted to go out and the man prevented me. I then paid 26*s.* to the prisoner: I paid the money because I was afraid. The piece of cloth was then given to me, and I took it away." In about an hour after she returned and saw the prisoner, and told him she could not keep the cloth, as she had not bid for it. He told her he could not give the money back, but if she came the following week he would exchange it. The next day the place was closed.

The counsel for the prisoner objected that the facts did not prove a larceny.

The jury were directed that if the prisoner had the intention to deprive Jane Powell of her money, and in order to obtain it was guilty of a trick and artifice, by fraudulently asserting that she had made a bid, when she had not, as he well knew, and that he obtained the money by such means, he was guilty of the offence charged.

The jury found that no bid had been made by Jane Powell, which the prisoner knew, and that he obtained the money from her by the trick and artifice mentioned above. A verdict of guilty was taken.

The questions were, first, whether the facts proved a larceny; secondly, whether the jury were rightly directed.

The case was argued before Kelly, C.B., Martin, B., Blackburn, Lush, and Brett, JJ.

Commins, for the prisoner....Jane Powell gave the money to the prisoner. The jury were not asked whether the money was obtained against the will of Jane Powell, yet this is a necessary ingredient in the crime of larceny. The facts of the case shew clearly that the money was not obtained by a trick, because Jane Powell was not deceived. The money, therefore, was given either willingly or through fear. The jury have not found that the money was given through fear, and therefore it cannot be assumed against the prisoner that it was not given willingly.

*   *   *   *   *

BLACKBURN, J. To constitute a larceny there must be an animus furandi, i.e. a felonious intent to take the property of another against his will. The essence of the offence is knowingly to take the goods of another against his will. The goods may be obtained in various ways. If by force, then a robbery is committed. This would include larceny, but force is not a necessary ingredient in larceny. It is sufficient to constitute a larceny if the goods are obtained against the will of the owner. It would be a scandal to the law if goods could be obtained by frightening the owner, and yet that this should not constitute a taking within the meaning of the definitions of larceny. The material ingredient is that the goods should be obtained against the will of the owner. The other ingredients of larceny undoubtedly existed here, as appears from the evidence in the case.

There is ample evidence that the money was obtained against the will of Jane Powell. If there had been any doubt upon the point the jury should have been asked the question; but it is clear that Jane Powell did not part with her money of her own free will. This is, in effect, stated in the case. There was evidence that the money was obtained by the prisoner with a felonious intent and against the will of Jane Powell. The jury have, in effect, found these facts against the prisoner, and these facts constitute larceny. Even if a robbery had, in fact, been committed, that does not preserve the prisoner from the liability to be convicted of larceny. A robbery includes a larceny. There may be some doubt whether a robbery was committed in this case; but it is not necessary to consider that question.

* * * * *

Brett, J. The question is, whether there was a sufficient taking of the money. If the matter rested on the trick alone that might be insufficient, as it is rather evidence of the prisoner's motives than the means by which he obtained the money. I had some doubt also whether the fear of a temporary imprisonment, not accompanied by any personal violence, rendered the taking in this case a robbery. Upon consideration, however, I think that as the threat was capable of being executed, and Jane Powell really parted with her money against her will, that is sufficient to constitute a larceny. There was evidence of such a taking, and the jury have found, in effect, that the money was obtained under a fear sufficient to make the giving of it an unwilling act. Consequently the taking was against the will of Jane Powell, and was therefore a larceny.

The other Judges concurred. Conviction affirmed.

[*Nor a consent obtained by a trick.*]

REX *v.* HENCH.

Crown Case Reserved. 1810. Russell and Ryan 163.

The prisoner was tried at the Old Bailey for larceny of a chest of tea....It appeared that Layton and Co., who were tea brokers, purchased the chest of tea in question, No. 7100, at the East India House, but did not take it away.

It was proved by a witness, a labourer in the service of the East India Company, that on the 5th of October, 1809, he had the care of the request notes, and that on that day he saw the prisoner go to the Excise box, the place where they were kept, and take out a handful and select one of them. The prisoner then went with the paper in his hand to look for the chest, No. 7100. The witness went up to him and asked him what he wanted ; he then took the paper out of the prisoner's hand, and seeing the number 7100 he pointed to a chest with a corresponding number, and said that was the chest he wanted ; he then returned the request paper to the prisoner in order that he might go to the permit office and get a permit. The prisoner went to the permit office and returned with the permit. The witness then took the permit out of his hand, and asked him whose porter he was, and the prisoner said Noton's. The witness returned him the permit and entered the name of Noton in the book, and the prisoner took away the chest of tea.

It was proved that the prisoner was not employed by Layton and Co., and that he had no authority from them to demand the chest.

The jury found the prisoner guilty.

An objection was taken by prisoner's counsel, that as the possession of the property was obtained by a regular request note and permit, it could only be considered as a misdemeanor.

The Recorder was of a different opinion, but respited the judgment in order to take the opinion of the Judges, Whether the facts above stated did or did not amount to a felonious taking.

In Hilary term, 27th of January, 1810, all the Judges met (except Heath, J.) and held this conviction to be right.

[*Larceny by a trick.*]

REX *v.* WILLIAMS.

MONMOUTH ASSIZES. 1834. 6 CARRINGTON AND PAYNE 390.

The prisoner was indicted for stealing a half-crown, two shillings, and six penny pieces. It appeared that the prisoner went to the shop of the prosecutor, and asked the prosecutor's son, who was a boy, to give him change for a half-crown. The boy gave him two shillings and six penny pieces, and the prisoner held out a half-crown, of which the boy caught hold by the edge, but never got it. The prisoner then ran away.

Talbot, for the prosecution, cited the case of *Rex* v. *Oliver* (2 Leach 1072).

PARK, J. (in summing up). If the prisoner had only been charged with stealing the half-crown I should have had great doubt. But he is indicted for stealing the two shillings and the copper. He pretends that he wants change for a half-crown; gets the change, and runs off. I think that is a larceny.

Verdict, Guilty.

[*But if the owner consent to a transfer of the ownership, as well as of the possession, it is doubtful whether his* Spontaneous Mistake (*even though sufficient to invalidate the transfer*) *will prevent the consent from excusing the Taking.*]

THE QUEEN v. MIDDLETON.

CROWN CASE RESERVED. 1873.   L.R. 2 C.C.R. 38.

At the Session of the Central Criminal Court, held on Monday, the 23rd of September, 1872, George Middleton was tried for feloniously stealing certain money to the amount of £8. 16s. 10d. of the moneys of the Postmaster-General.

The ownership of the money was laid in other counts in the Queen and in the mistress of the local post office.

It was proved by the evidence that the prisoner was a depositor in a Post Office Savings Bank, in which a sum of 11s. stood to his credit.

In accordance with the practice of the bank, he duly gave notice to withdraw 10s., stating in such notice the number of his depositor's book, the name of the post office, and the amount to be withdrawn.

A warrant for 10s. was duly issued to the prisoner, and a letter of advice was duly sent to the post office at Notting Hill to pay the prisoner 10s. He presented himself at that Post Office and handed in his depositor's book and the warrant to the clerk, who, instead of referring to the proper letter of advice for 10s., referred by mistake to another letter of advice for £8. 16s. 10d., and placed upon the counter a £5 note, three sovereigns, a half sovereign, and silver and copper, amounting altogether to £8. 16s. 10d. The clerk entered the amount paid, viz., £8. 16s. 10d. in the prisoner's depositor's book and stamped it, and the prisoner took up the money and went away.

The mistake was afterwards discovered, and the prisoner was brought back, and upon being asked for his depositor's book, said he had burnt it. Other evidence of the prisoner having had the money was given.

It was objected by counsel for the prisoner that there was no larceny, because the clerk parted with the property and intended to do so, and because the prisoner did not get possession by any fraud or trick.

The jury found that the prisoner had the animus furandi at the moment of taking the money from the counter, and that he knew the money to be the money of the Postmaster-General when he took it up.

A verdict of guilty was recorded, and the learned Common Serjeant reserved for the opinion of the Court for Crown Cases Reserved the question whether under the circumstances above disclosed, the prisoner was properly found guilty of larceny.

[The case came on in the ordinary course before five Judges; but on the argument, they were not agreed, and the case was adjourned to be re-argued before a fuller Court. Fifteen Judges sat to hear it. Eleven of them were of opinion that the conviction ought to be affirmed, but four were of a contrary opinion. Judgment was given in accordance with the opinion of the majority.

Martin, Bramwell and Cleasby, B.B., and Brett, J., held that as the clerk delivered the money with the intention of passing the property in it, there was no trespass and therefore no larceny.

Three of the remaining eleven Judges (Bovill, C.J., Kelly, C.B., and Keating, J.) agreed that this would have been so if the clerk had had full authority to dispose of the money, but held that his act was unauthorised; and the prisoner's taking was therefore a larceny. The other eight Judges (Cockburn, C.J., Blackburn, Mellor, Lush, Grove, Denman, and Archibald, JJ., and Pigott, B.) held that the clerk's mistake defeated the effect of his intention to pass the property, and that consequently, irrespectively of the question as to how far his authority extended (which they left undecided), there was a larceny. And one of the eight (Pigott, B.) held that, irrespectively of the mistake, the manual acts of the clerk had not amounted to even a physical delivery.]

Cockburn, C.J., Blackburn, Mellor, Lush, Grove, Denman, and Archibald, JJ., concurred in the following judgment....The finding of the jury, that the prisoner at the moment of taking the money, had the animus furandi and was aware of the mistake, puts an end to all objection arising from the fact that the clerk meant to part with the possession of the money.

On the second question, namely whether, assuming that the clerk was to be considered as having all the authority of the owner, the intention of the clerk (such as it was) to part with the property prevents this from being larceny, there is more difficulty, and there is, in fact, a serious difference of opinion, though the majority, as already stated, think the conviction right. The reasons which lead us to this conclusion are as follows:—At common law the property in personal goods passes by a bargain and sale for consideration, or a gift of them accompanied by delivery; and it is clear, from the very nature of the thing, that an intention to pass the property is essential both to a sale and to a gift. But it is not at all true that an intention to pass the property, even though accompanied by a delivery, is of itself equivalent to either a sale or a gift. We will presently explain more fully what we mean, and how this is material. Now, it is established that where a bargain between the owner of the chattel has been made with another, by which the property is transferred to the other, the property actually passes, though the bargain has been induced by fraud. The law is thus stated in the judgment of the Exchequer Chamber, in *Clough* v. *London and North Western Railway Co.*[1], where it is said, "We agree completely with what is stated by all the judges below, that the property in the goods passed from the London Pianoforte Co. to Adams by the contract of sale; the fact that the contract was induced by fraud did not render the contract void, or prevent the property from passing, but merely gave the party defrauded a right, on discovering the fraud, to elect whether he would continue to treat the contract as binding, or would disaffirm the contract and resume his property....We think that so long as he has made no election, he retains the right to determine it either way, subject to this, that if in the interval, whilst he is deliberating, an innocent third party has acquired an interest in the property; or if, in consequence of his delay, the position even of the wrongdoer is affected, it will preclude him from exercising his right to rescind." It follows obviously from this that no conversion or dealing with the goods, before the election is determined, can amount to a stealing of the vendor's goods; for they had become the goods of the purchaser, and still remained so when the supposed act of theft was committed. There are, accordingly, many cases, of which the most recent is *Reg.* v. *Prince*[2],

---

[1] Law Rep. 7 Ex. 26, at pp. 34, 35. [2] Law Rep. 1 C. C. 150.

which decide that in such a case the guilty party must be indicted for obtaining the goods by false pretences, and cannot be convicted of larceny. In that case, however, the money was paid to the holder of a forged cheque payable to bearer, and therefore vested in the holder subject to the right of the bank to divest the property.

In the present case, the property still remains that of the Post-master-General, and never did vest in the prisoner at all. There was no contract to render it his which required to be rescinded; there was no gift of it to him, for there was no intention to give it to him or to anyone. It was simply a handing it over by a pure mistake, and no property passed. As this was money, we cannot test the case by seeing whether an innocent purchaser could have held the property. But let us suppose that a purchaser of beans goes to the warehouse of a mer. chant with a genuine order for so many bushels of beans, to be selected from the bulk and so become the property of the vendee, and that by some strange blunder the merchant delivers to him an equal bulk of coffee. If that coffee was sold (not in market overt) by the recipient to a third person, could he retain it against the merchant, on the ground that he had bought it from one who had the property in the coffee, though subject to be divested? We do not remember any case in which such a point has arisen, but surely there can be no doubt he could not; and that on the principle enunciated by Lord Abinger, in *Chanter v. Hopkins*[1], when he says, "If a man offers to buy peas of another, and he sends him beans, he does not perform his contract, but that is not a warranty; there is no warranty that he should sell him peas; the contract is to sell peas, and if he sends him anything else in their stead, it is a non-performance of it."

We admit that the case is undistinguishable from the one supposed in the argument, of a person handing to a cabman a sovereign by mistake for a shilling; but after carefully weighing the opinions to the contrary, we are decidedly of opinion that the property in the sovereign would not vest in the cabman, and that the question whether the cab-man was guilty of larceny or not, would depend upon this, whether he, at the time he took the sovereign, was aware of the mistake, and had then the guilty intent, the animus furandi.

But it is further urged that if the owner, having power to dispose of the property, intended to part with it, that prevents the crime from being that of larceny, though the intention was inoperative, and no property passed. In almost all the cases on the subject, the property had actually passed, or at least the Court thought it had passed; but

[1] 4 M. and W. at p. 404.

two cases, *Rex* v. *Adams*[1], and *Rex* v. *Atkinson*[2], appear to have been decided on the ground that an intention to pass the property, though inoperative, and known by the prisoner to be inoperative, was enough to prevent the crime from being that of larceny. But we are unable to perceive or understand on what principles the cases can be supported if *Rex* v. *Davenport*[3] and the others involving the same principle are law; and though if a long series of cases had so decided, we should think we were bound by them, yet we think that in a Court such as this, which is in effect a Court of error, we ought not to feel bound by two cases which, as far as we can perceive, stand alone, and seem to us contrary both to principle and justice.

*   *   *   *   *

KELLY, C.B.....If the money had belonged to the clerk, and the clerk had intended to pass the property in the money from himself to the prisoner, or if the money belonging to the Postmaster-General or the Queen, the clerk had been authorised to pass the property in that money to the prisoner, the case might have been different; but this money did not belong to the clerk, and he had no authority to pass the property in that money to the prisoner.

Reg. v. *Prince*[4] was cited, where a banker's clerk to whom a forged cheque was presented paid the money in ignorance of the forgery, and the receiver, who intended to defraud the banker of the money, was acquitted of larceny, on the ground that the clerk had authority to receive the cheque, and to dispose of the money which he had paid to the prisoner, and was the agent of the banker in so doing, so that the case was the same as if the banker himself, who was the owner of the money, had delivered it to the prisoner. There, however, the clerk was not only the agent of the banker, but he acted strictly in the discharge of his duty, for he had not only the authority of his employer to pay the money, but in the absence of any suspicion or reason to suspect that the cheque was forged, it was his duty to pay it, as he did pay it, with the banker's money. And there are other cases where the owner of a chattel delivers it to another, with the intent to pass the property, and the receiver has been acquitted of larceny.

But in this case the post office clerk was not the owner of the £8, and had no authority whatever to deliver that sum of money to the prisoner. The case appears to me to be the same, as indeed I suggested during the argument, as if the prisoner had left a watch at a watchmaker's to be repaired, and afterwards goes to the watchmaker's, sees his watch hanging up behind the counter and another watch of greater

---

[1] 2 Russell on Crimes, 6th ed. at p. 145.   [2] 2 East, P. C. 673.
[3] 2 Russell on Crimes, 4th ed. at p. 201.   [4] Law Rep. 1 C. C. 150.

value and belonging to another person hanging beside it, and upon his asking for his watch the shopman by mistake hands him the watch belonging to another; he sees his own watch, he knows that the watch handed to him does not belong to him, but is the property of another, and the shopman has no authority whatever to deliver the watch of another to him. I have no doubt, therefore, that one who had so received and taken away another man's property would have been guilty of larceny; that the shopman in such a case, and the clerk in this case, is in the condition of a mere stander-by who, without authority and by mere mistake, hands to him a chattel which he sees before him.......

*　　*　　*　　*

BRAMWELL, B....The taking must be *invito domino.* (That does not mean *against* his will, but *without* it. All he need be is *invitus*; this accounts for how it is that a finder may be guilty of larceny)....But where the dominus has voluntarily parted with the possession, intending to part with the property in the chattel, it has never yet been held that larceny was committed (whatever fraud may have been used to induce him to do so, nor whatever may be the mistake he committed), because in such case the dominus is not invitus.

...A point is made for the prosecution on which I confess I have had the greatest doubt. It is said that here the dominus was invitus; that the dominus was not the post office clerk, but the Postmaster-General or the Queen; and that therefore it was an unauthorised act in the post office clerk, and so a trespass in Middleton invito domino. I think one answer to this is, that the post office clerk had authority to decide under what circumstances he would part with the money with which he was intrusted. But I also think that, for the purposes of this question, the lawful possessor of the chattel, having authority to transfer the property, must be considered as the dominus within this rule, at least when acting bonâ fide. It is unreasonable that a man should be a thief or not, not according to his act and intention. but according to a matter which has nothing to do with them, and of which he has no knowledge.

According to this, if I give a cabman a sovereign for a shilling by mistake, he taking it animo furandi, it is no larceny; but if I tell my servant to take a shilling out of my purse, and he by mistake takes a sovereign, and gives it to the cabman, who takes it animo furandi, the cabman is a thief. It is ludicrous to say that if a man, instead of himself paying, tells his wife to do so, and she gives the sovereign for a shilling, the cabman is guilty of larceny, but not if the husband gives it. It is said that there is no great harm in this; that a thief in mind

and act has blundered into a crime.   I cannot agree.   I think the
criminal law ought to be reasonable and intelligible.   Certainly a man
who had to be hung owing to this distinction might well complain, and
it is to be remembered that we must hold that to be law now which
would have been law when such a felony was capital.   Besides, juries
are not infallible, and may make a mistake as to the animus furandi,
and so find a man guilty of larceny when there was no theft and no
animus furandi.   Moreover, *Reg.* v. *Prince*[1] is contrary to this argument, for there the banker's clerks had no authority to pay a forged
cheque if they knew it; they had authority to make a mistake, and so
had the post office clerk.   And suppose in this case the taking had
been bonâ fide—suppose Middleton could neither write nor read, and
some one had made him a present of the book without telling him the
amount, and he had thought the right sum was given him—would his
taking of it have been a trespass?   I think not, and that a demand
would have been necessary before an action of conversion could be
maintained.......

✿   ✴   ✸

CLEASBY, B.......The cases establish, first, that where delivery is
fraudulently obtained from any person having no authority to deal
with the property, it is a taking from the owner.   The instances of
this are obtaining delivery from a mere servant by a false representation of the master's orders : obtaining delivery from a carrier whose
only authority is to change the possession from A. to B., by a false
representation of being B.   Another instance, more like the present,
because there is a mistake, where a person leaves his umbrella, or
cloak, or watch, with any person to be returned on application, and he
afterwards fraudulently identifies as his own a more valuable umbrella
or cloak belonging to another person.   This would be a taking, because
the parties had no transaction or dealing connected with property, the
person in charge having only an authority to return to each person his
chattel.

Secondly, the cases establish that, when the owner himself delivers
them, but only for the purpose of some office or custody, as of a man
delivering sheep to his shepherd (an instance put by Coke), if the shepherd who has them in his charge fraudulently converted them to his
own use, it would be a taking, because the right of possession (much
less of property) was not for an instant changed.

But the cases also establish that, where there is a complete dealing
or transaction between the parties for the purpose of passing the

---

[1] Law Rep. 1 C. C. 150.

property, and so the possession parted with, there is no taking, and the case is out of the category of larceny.

Considering what the penalty was, there was nothing unreasonable or contrary to the spirit of our laws in drawing a dividing line, and holding that, whenever the owner of property is a party to such a transaction as I have mentioned, such serious consequences were not to depend upon the conclusion which might be arrived at as to the precise terms of the transaction, which might be complicated, and uncertain, and difficult to ascertain.

.I believe the rule is as I have stated, and that it is not limited to cases in which the property in the chattel actually passes by virtue of the transaction. I have not seen that limitation put upon it in any text book on the criminal law, and there are, unless I am mistaken, many authorities against it. The cases show, no doubt, beyond question, that where the transaction is of such a nature that the property in the chattel actually passes (though subject to be resumed by reason of fraud or trick), there is no taking, and therefore no larceny. But they do not show the converse, viz., that when the property does not pass, there is larceny. On the contrary, they appear to me to show that where there is an intention to part with the property along with the possession, though the fraud is of such a nature as to prevent that intention from operating, there is still no larceny. This seems so clearly to follow from the cardinal rule that there must be a taking against the will of the owner, that the cases rather assume that the intention to transfer the property governs the case, than expressly decide it. For how can there be a taking against the will of the owner, where the owner hands over the possession, intending by doing so to part with the entire property?

As far as my own experience goes, many of the cases of fraudulent pretences which I have tried have been cases in which the prisoner has obtained goods from a tradesman upon the false pretence that he came with the order from a customer. In these cases no property passes either to the customer or to the prisoner; and I never heard such a case put forward as a case of larceny. And the authorities are distinct, upon cases reserved for the judges, that in such cases there is no larceny ; *Reg.* v. *Adams*[1].

With those authorities before me, I cannot accept as the proper test, not the intention of the owner to deliver over the property (which is a question of fact), but the effect of the transaction in passing the property, which might raise in many cases a question of law.

[1] 1 Den. Cr. C. 38.

This appears to me to be a novelty ; at variance with the definition of larceny, which makes the mind and intent of the owner the test; and irreconcileable with the manner in which these cases have always been dealt with.

[*Consent of owner's wife excuses a taking*]

THE KING *v.* HARRISON.

OLD BAILEY SESSIONS.   1756.   LEACH 47.

At the Old Bailey in February Session, 1756, Nathaniel Harrison was tried before Mr Baron ADAMS, present Mr Justice Denison and Mr Justice Bathurst, for stealing a silver tankard and three silver castors, the property of James Cobb.

The prisoner was an apprentice to the prosecutor. The prosecutor's wife had continual custody of the key of the closet where her husband's plate was usually locked up. It appeared that she had pawned some articles of it, in order to supply the prisoner with pocket money ; but the articles she pawned were not those mentioned in the indictment. The prisoner confessed that he took the articles mentioned in the indictment from the closet; and a pawnbroker proved that he received them in pledge from the prisoner ; but it did not appear by what means the prisoner had gained access to the closet from which they were taken.

THE COURT held, That the prosecutor's wife having the constant keeping of the key of the closet where the plate was usually locked up, and it appearing that the prisoner could not have taken it without her privity or consent, it might be presumed that he had received it from her. He was accordingly acquitted.

[*But not where she gives this consent to her* adulterer.]

REGINA *v.* FEATHERSTONE.

CROWN CASE RESERVED.   1854.   DEARSLY 369.

The prisoner, George Featherstone, was tried at the Spring Assizes, 1854, holden at Worcester. The indictment charged him with stealing twenty-two sovereigns and some wearing apparel.

It appeared that the prosecutor's wife had taken from the prosecutor's bed-room thirty-five sovereigns and some articles of clothing, and that when she left the house she called to the prisoner, who was in a lower room with the prosecutor and other persons, and said, "George, it's all right, come on." Prisoner left in a few minutes after.

The prisoner and the wife were afterwards seen together at various places, and eventually were traced to a public-house where they passed the night together. When taken into custody the prisoner had twenty-two sovereigns upon him.

The jury found the prisoner guilty, stating that they did so "on the ground that he received the sovereigns from the wife, knowing that she took them without the authority of her husband."

Whereupon the Judge respited the judgment, admitted the prisoner to bail, and reserved for the opinion of the Court of Criminal Appeal the question whether a delivery of the husband's goods by the wife to the adulterer, with knowledge by him that she took them without the husband's authority, was sufficient to maintain the indictment for felony against him?

*   *   *

LORD CAMPBELL, C.J. We are of opinion that this conviction is right. The general rule of law is, that a wife cannot be found guilty of larceny for stealing the goods of her husband, and that is upon the principle that the husband and wife are, in the law, one person. But this principle is, properly and reasonably, qualified when she becomes an adulteress. She thereby determines her quality of wife, and her property in her husband's goods ceases. The prisoner was her accomplice; and the jury find that he assisted her, and took the sovereigns, knowing that she had taken them without the husband's consent. It is said, in 1 Russell on Crimes (p. 23), that a stranger cannot commit larceny of the husband's goods by the delivery of the wife; but a distinction is pointed out where he is her adulterer. In Dalton, p. 353, it is said, " but it should be observed that if the wife should steal the goods of her husband, and deliver them to B., who knowing it carries them away, B. being the adulterer of the wife, this, according to a very good opinion, would be felony in B.[1]; for in such case no consent of the husband can be presumed." That case is identical with the present. The prisoner knew that it was without the consent of the husband. We think the conviction was clearly right.

The other learned Judges concurred.

Conviction affirmed.

1 [EDITOR'S NOTE. And, by virtue of ss. 12 and 16 of the Married Women's Property Act 1882, the *eloping* wife herself also may be convicted of larceny.]

[Finding a lost article, with no likelihood of discovering its owner, gives a sufficient Claim of Right.]

REGINA v. THURBORN.

CROWN CASE RESERVED. 1849.   1 DENISON 387.

The prisoner was tried before PARKE, B., at the Summer Assizes for Huntingdon, 1848, for stealing a bank note.

He found the note; which had been accidentally dropped on the high road. There was no name or mark on it, indicating who was the owner; nor were there any circumstances attending the finding which would enable him to discover to whom the note belonged when he picked it up; nor had he any reason to believe that the owner knew where to find it again. The prisoner meant to appropriate it to his own use, when he picked it up. The day after, and before he had disposed of it, he was informed that the prosecutor was the owner, and had dropped it accidentally; he then changed it, and appropriated the money taken to his own use. The jury found that he had reason to believe, and did believe, it to be the prosecutor's property, before he thus changed the note.

The learned Baron directed a verdict of guilty, intimating that he should reserve the case for further consideration. Upon conferring with MAULE, J., the learned Baron was of opinion that the original taking was not felonious, and that in the subsequent disposal of it, there was no taking; and he therefore declined to pass sentence, and ordered the prisoner to be discharged on entering into his own recognizanee to appear when called upon.

On the 30th of April, A.D. 1849, the following judgment was read by PARKE, B....To prevent the taking of goods from being larceny, it is essential that they should be presumably lost; that is that they should be taken in such a place and under such circumstances, as that the owner would be reasonably presumed by the taker to have abandoned them, or at least not to know where to find them. Therefore if a horse is found feeding on an open common or on the side of a public road, or a watch found apparently hidden in a hay stack, the taking of these would be larceny; because the taker had no right to presume that the owner did not know where to find them, and consequently had no right to treat them as lost goods. In the present case there is no doubt that the bank note was "lost." The owner did not know where to find it; the prisoner reasonably believed it to be lost; he had no reason to know to whom it belonged; and therefore, though he took it with the intent of taking not a partial or temporary but the entire dominion over it, the act of taking did not, in our opinion, constitute the crime of larceny. Whether the subsequent appropriation of it to his own use by changing it, with the knowledge at that time that it belonged to the prosecutor, does amount to that crime, will be afterwards considered.

It appears, however, that goods which do fall within the category of lost goods, and which the taker justly believes to have been lost, may be taken and converted so as to constitute the crime of larceny, when the party finding may be presumed to know the owner of them, or there is any mark upon them, presumably known by him, by which the owner can be ascertained. There are many reported cases on this subject. Some where the owner of the goods may be presumed to be known, from the circumstances under which they are found; amongst these are mentioned the cases of articles left in hackney coaches by passengers, which the coachman appropriates to his own use, or a pocket book, found in a coat sent to a tailor to be repaired, and abstracted and opened by him. In these cases the appropriation has been held to be larceny. Perhaps these cases might be classed amongst those in which the taker is not justified in concluding that the goods were lost; because there is little doubt he must have believed that the owner would know where to find them again, and he had no pretence to consider them abandoned or derelict..

The appropriation of goods by the finder has also been held to be larceny where the owner could be found out by some mark on them; as in the case of lost notes, checks, or bills, with the owner's name upon them.

This subject was considered in the case of *Merry* v. *Green*, 7 M. and W. 623.

The result of all the authorities is, that the rule of law on this subject seems to be, that if a man find goods that have been actually lost, or are reasonably supposed by him to have been lost, and appropriates them with intent to take the entire dominion over them, really believing when he takes them that the owner cannot be found, it is not larceny. But if he takes them with the like intent, but reasonably believing that the owner can be found, it is larceny. In applying this rule, as indeed in the application of all fixed rules, questions of some nicety may arise. But it will generally be ascertained whether the person accused had reasonable belief that the owner could be found, by evidence of his previous acquaintance with the ownership of the particular chattel, by the place where it is found, or by the nature of the marks upon it. In some cases it would be apparent, in others would appear only after examination. It would probably be presumed that the taker would examine the chattel as an honest man ought to do, at the time of taking it; and if he did not restore it to the owner, the jury might conclude that he took it, when he took complete possession of it, animo furandi. The mere taking it up to look at it, would not be a taking possession of the chattel.

To apply these rules to the present case. The first taking did not amount to larceny; because the note was really lost, and there was no mark on it or other circumstance to indicate then who was the owner, or that he might be found, nor any evidence to rebut the presumption that would arise from the finding of the note as proved, that he believed the owner could not be found, and therefore the original taking was not felonious. If the prisoner had changed the note or otherwise disposed of it, before notice of the title of the real owner, he clearly would not have been punishable. But after the prisoner was in possession of the note, the owner became known to him, and he then appropriated it, animo furandi; and the point to be decided is whether that was a felony.

Upon this question we have felt considerable doubt.

If he had taken the chattel innocently, and afterwards appropriated it without knowledge of the ownership, it would not have been larceny ; nor would it, we think, if he had done so, knowing who was the owner ; for he had the lawful possession in both cases, and the conversion would not have been a trespass in either. But here the original taking was not innocent in one sense; and the question is, does that make a difference? We think not. It was dispunishable as we have already decided ; and though the possession was accompanied by a dishonest intent, it was still a lawful possession and good against all but the real owner ; and the subsequent conversion was not therefore a trespass in this case more than the others, and consequently no larceny.

We therefore think that the conviction was wrong.

[*But not finding a lost article with likelihood, from the outset
of discovering its owner.*]

REGINA *v.* PETERS.

The prisoner was indicted for stealing a golden chain, one breast
pin, and one eye-glass and pin, the property of Henry Bulkeley.

It appeared that Mrs Bulkeley went into her garden, adjoining to
the house, to walk; and, on her return into the house, missed the articles
in question, which had been upon her dress when she went out walking.
The prisoner was employed about the premises on the day in question;
and, by the direction of the prosecutor, had walked through the
garden, in company with the gardener, immediately after Mrs Bulkeley
had returned into the house....Mr Bulkeley caused the loss to be cried
the same evening and the following morning, and offered £2 reward to
any person who had found the articles. On the following morning,
the prisoner went to the crier and stated that he knew a person
who had found the things; and took the crier to his house, fetched
them down stairs and gave them to the crier, with directions to go to
Mr Bulkeley's with them, but not to deliver them up unless the reward
of £2 was paid. His wife, in his presence, said that she found them
in a street in Cheltenham, a quarter of a mile from the prosecutor's;
and the prisoner, on two subsequent occasions, stated that he found
them in two other places, neither being the garden....

ROLFE, B. ...If I drop a thing where there is no reasonable
means of finding out that it belongs to me, then, though I am
found out to be the owner, the party finding it would not be guilty
of felony if he converted it to his own use; though he would be liable
to an action of trover. But it is perfectly well known that, if a
person leave anything in a stage coach, if the owner can be found
by inquiry, the party finding the thing, and appropriating it to his
own use, is guilty of larceny. So if it is found in a street, and there
is any mark by which the owner can be discovered. So, in the
case where a gold ornament is found at the door of a house, it is
ridiculous to say that any person picking it up would not suppose that
it belonged to the owner of the house. There are two questions here.
First, did the prisoner pick the things up? Secondly, with what
intention did he take up the chain and take it to his own house? The
picking it up might be the most innocent act in the world; but
what does he do with it? He takes it home. Did he or not take
it home with the intention of appropriating it to his own use?

Or did he take it home with the intention of finding the true owner? If the latter, he is not guilty. If he took it up, and did not immediately bring it to the prosecutor, in the hopes that, by coming next day, he would get a present of £5, perhaps it might not amount to a larceny. If he took it away with the intention to appropriate it, and only restored it because the reward was offered, it is clear that he is guilty of felony. Are you satisfied that he took it home, either intending to sell it, or to get a reward if one was offered? If so, he is guilty of larceny.

Verdict, Guilty.

[*Taker claims the thing as* his own.]

REX *v.* HALL.

GLOUCESTER ASSIZES. 1828. 3 CARRINGTON AND PAYNE 409.

Indictment for robbing John Green, a gamekeeper of Lord *Ducie*, of three hare-wires and a pheasant. It appeared that the prisoner had set three wires in a field belonging to Lord *Ducie*, in one of which this pheasant was caught; and that Green, the gamekeeper, seeing this, took up the wires and pheasant, and put them into his pocket. And it further appeared that the prisoner, soon after this, came up and said: "Have you got my wires?" The gamekeeper replied that he had, and a pheasant that was caught in one of them. The prisoner then asked the gamekeeper to give the pheasant and wires up to him, which the gamekeeper refused; whereupon the prisoner lifted up a large stick, and threatened to beat the gamekeeper's brains out if he did not give them up. The gamekeeper, fearing violence, did so.

Maclean, for the prosecution, contended, that, by law, the prisoner could have no property in either the wires or the pheasant; and, as the gamekeeper had seized them for the use of the lord of the manor, under the statute 5 Ann. c. 14, s. 4, it was a robbery to take them from him by violence.

VAUGHAN, B. I shall leave it to the jury to say whether the prisoner acted on an impression that the wires and pheasant were his property. For, however he might be liable to penalties for having them in his possession, yet, if the jury think that he took them under a bonâ

fide impression that he was only getting back the possession of his own
property, there is no animus furandi and I am of opinion that the
prosecution must fail.

Verdict, Not guilty

[See also REX *v.* KNIGHT, *supra*, p. 177.]

[*Taker claims the thing as* his own.]

CAUSEY *v.* STATE.

SUPREME COURT OF GEORGIA. 1887.   79 GEORGIA 564.

Indictment for stealing a bell.

Causey had been employed by a Mr Gunn to drive a milk-cart.
He bought a bell to be used in attracting customers; and, upon being
discharged by Mr Gunn, he left this bell. Mr Gunn engaged a successor to drive the cart; and this successor used the bell for some time.
On one occasion he left the cart in the street; and Causey went to it
to get his bell. Not finding the driver, he took the bell and rang it
loudly for some time. No one came; and Causey then requested a
by-stander to tell the driver, when he came, that Causey had taken the
bell. The message was never delivered. Causey was prosecuted for
stealing the bell, and convicted....He moved for a new trial.

BLECKLEY, C.J. The evidence was that Causey had left the bell as
the property of his employer Mr Gunn; and that Mr Gunn had
accounted to him for the value of it in settling their accounts for milk-
money. The question was whether that accounting really took place.
Causey had submitted at the trial an account book, kept in his way;
but it seems not to have been very intelligible. Mr Gunn thought
he had accounted for the price of the bell to Causey; but he may have
been mistaken.

The authorities are abundant that when one takes property under
a fair claim of right, it is not larceny; and publicity in the taking is
very powerful evidence to establish the bona fides of a claim of right.
There could hardly have been greater publicity than here; because
this was done in an open street near the heart of the city, and the
ringing of the bell was loud enough to be heard in adjacent streets.
He made a sort of bell-ringing proclamation that he was about to
resume his ancient possession, and he seemed to desire it to be known
and observed of all men. That is a very strong circumstance in
favour of the man's innocence....We direct that the case be tried again.

[*Taker claims thing as* an equivalent *for his own.*]

REGINA *v.* BODEN.

STAFFORD ASSIZES.   1844.   1 CARRINGTON AND KIRWAN 395.

Assault with intent to rob.   The prisoner was indicted for assaulting one Thomas Simcocks, with intent to rob him, on the 27th of
December, 1843, at Leek.   It appeared that the father of the prosecutor had been at a fair at Congleton, some days before the day of the
alleged offence charged in the present indictment; and that a person
had there come up to him and given him eleven sovereigns into his
hand, for the purpose of buying a horse, and that the prosecutor's
father had put the money into his pocket and refused to give it back.
The person who gave him the money followed him to an entry in the
town of Congleton; and there, in company with the prisoner, assaulted
him, and endeavoured to get the money out of his (the father's)
pocket.   The prosecutor came up and interfered; and on his saying
that the person who had given his father the money was the man that
had robbed Cotterell at Leek fair, that person ran away.   It further
appeared that the prisoner called at the prosecutor's father's house the
next morning, and demanded the eleven sovereigns; but the prosecutor's
father refused to give them to him, at the same time saying that he
would give the money to the man from whom he had received it, if he
would come and ask for it.   It was proved that at Leek fair, on the
27th of *December,* 1843, the prisoner saw the prosecutor receive seven
sovereigns for a cow that he had sold; and followed the prosecutor, and
said, "Pay me the eleven sovereigns you owe me."   He then knocked
the prosecutor down, and put his hand into the pocket of the prosecutor, where he had seen the sovereigns placed, but was prevented
from getting them, and the parties were separated.

Greaves, for the prosecution, in opening the case, stated that it was
well settled that if a party, under an honest impression that he was
entitled to anything, took that thing away from another, it would not
amount to larceny, although, in reality, he had no right to it; and he
conceived that the same rule might apply to robbery.   And therefore, if
the prisoner assaulted the prosecutor with the honest impression and
real belief that he had a right to get the sovereigns from him, he would
not be guilty of the offence charged; although it was clear that, as the
prosecutor never received the sovereigns, and the sovereigns were not
the property of the prisoner, he had no real right at all to them.   At
the conclusion of the evidence for the prosecution,

PARKE, B., said, I think that there was too much semblance of a right to claim the sovereigns, to justify our proceeding with the case for the felony. But there remains the assault.

[*Taker claims a* lien *on the thing.*]

REGINA *v.* WADE.

BURY ST EDMUNDS ASSIZES.   1869.   11 Cox 549.

John Wade was charged with larceny under the following circum-stances. The prosecutor was a labouring man, and the prisoner a travelling umbrella mender; and it appeared that on the 18th of November he accosted the wife of the prosecutor, asking her if she had any umbrellas to mend. She replied she had; and he said he would do it cheap—for two or three halfpence.

Accordingly he repaired it, and when done demanded ninepence for his labour. The umbrella had then been re-delivered to the prose-cutor's wife, who refused to pay the demand. The prisoner declined to take 2*d.*, which was offered to him, but rushed upstairs, where the umbrella had been deposited, and took it away with him.

[In reply to the prisoner, the wife denied that he offered to restore the umbrella to its original condition.]

The prisoner, in defence, stated that he had no intention of stealing it, but merely took it to secure being paid.

BLACKBURN, J., to the jury. The prisoner had a right to keep the umbrella until he had been paid for the trouble he had been put to in repairing it. The question for them to consider was, was he honestly claiming his right when he removed it from the house? If it was honestly done, that would not be stealing; but, on the other hand, if they were of opinion that it was a mere colourable pretence to obtain possession, then it would be larceny. It did not matter whether any-thing was due to him, if, at the time he took it, he honestly intended to hold it as a security for his alleged lien.

Not guilty.

CHAPTER VIII. THE INTENTION.

[*An intention to deprive the owner of the possession* only temporarily *is not sufficient.*]

ANONYMOUS.

OLD BAILEY.   1698.   EAST'S PLEAS OF THE CROWN   662.

Before Holt, C.J., and other Judges, it was found that A. assaulted B. on the highway, with a felonious intent, and searched the pockets of B. for money.   But, finding none, A. pulled off the bridle of B.'s horse, and threw it—and also some bread which B. had in panniers—about the highway.

Upon conference with ALL THE JUDGES, it was resolved that this was no robbery.

[*Stealing a ride is not stealing a horse.*]

REX *v.* CHARLES CRUMP.

WORCESTER ASSIZES.   1825.   1 CARRINGTON AND PAYNE 658.

Indictment for stealing a horse, three bridles, two saddles, and a bag, the property of Henry Bateman.

It appeared that the prisoner got into the prosecutor's stable, and took away the horse and the other property all together ; but that, when he had got to some distance, he turned the horse loose, and proceeded on foot to Tewkesbury, where he was stopped whilst attempting to sell the saddles.

GARROW, B., left it to the jury to say whether the prisoner had any intention of stealing the horse.   For if he intended to steal the other articles, and only used the horse as a mode of carrying off the other plunder more conveniently—and as it were, borrowed the horse for that purpose—he would not be, in point of law, guilty of stealing the horse.

Verdict, Not guilty of stealing the horse, but guilty
of stealing the rest of the property.

[*There must be an intention to appropriate the thing in a manner wholly
inconsistent with the rightful possessor's interest in it.*]

REGINA *v.* HOLLOWAY.

CROWN CASE RESERVED.   1848.   1 DENISON 370.

The prisoner, William Holloway, was indicted at the General
Quarter Sessions, holden in and for the borough of Liverpool, for
stealing within the jurisdiction of the Court, one hundred and twenty
skins of leather, the property of Thomas Barton and another.

Thomas Barton and another were tanners, and the prisoner was
one of many workmen employed by them at their tannery, in Liverpool,
to dress skins of leather.   The skins, when dressed, were delivered to
the foreman, and every workman was paid in proportion to and on
account of the work done by himself.   The skins of leather were afterwards stored in a warehouse adjoining to the workshop.   The prisoner,
by opening a window and removing an iron bar, got access clandestinely
to the warehouse, and carried away the skins of leather mentioned in
the indictment, which had been dressed by other workmen.   The
prisoner did not remove these skins from the tannery, but they were
seen and recognized the following day at the porch or place where he
usually worked in the workshop.   It was proved to be a common
practice at the tannery for one workman to lend work, that is to say,
skins of leather dressed by him, to another workman; and for the
borrower in such case to deliver the work to the foreman, and get paid
for it on his own account, as if it were his own work.

A question of fact arose as to the intention of the prisoner in
taking the skins from the warehouse.   The jury found that the prisoner
did not intend to remove the skins from the tannery, and dispose of
them elsewhere; but that his intention in taking them was to deliver
them to the foreman, and to get paid for them as if they were his own
work, and in this way he intended the skins to be restored to the
possession of his masters.   They convicted him, under the direction of
the Court; but a case was reserved on the question whether, on the
finding of the jury, the prisoner ought to have been convicted of
larceny.

Lowndes, for the Crown....Here the skins were taken wrongfully;
and though with a view of returning them to the master, it was not
until they had been first made the means of defrauding him; therefore
they cannot be said to have been returned to him in the same state as
when taken.   They had other incidents attached to them by the
wrongful act of the prisoner, which incidents carried with them an

intent to deprive the owner of his property. The taking was clearly a trespass; it therefore was such a taking as to support a charge of larceny, provided the object of the taker was to convert them to his own use wrongfully. It clearly was so. The old authorities shew that where there has been a fraudulent taking, and an intention on the part of the taker to use the thing taken as his own and so wrongfully to assert an entire dominion over the thing pro tanto, there is no necessity that he should also intend to deprive the owner wholly of his property for ever. It is true that where such intention exists, coupled with a taking, every such act is a larceny; but there may be a larceny without such intention. Surely it would be a larceny to take a horse out of A.'s stable with a view of using him for six months, and then returning him to A. If it be not, what length of user on the part of the taker will make the taking felonious?...

ALDERSON, B. If a servant takes a horse out of his master's stable, and turns it out into the road with intent to get a reward the next day by bringing it back to his master, would that be larceny?

PARKE, B. cited *R.* v. *Phillips*, 2 East, Pl. C. ch. 16, s. 98, as shewing that a wrongful taking for a temporary user was not larceny, even though the takers there were found by the jury to be *perfectly indifferent* whether the owner ever recovered his property or no, and certainly to have had no intention of returning it to him themselves[1].

*　　　*　　　*　　　*　　　*

PARKE, B. We are bound to say that this is no larceny. The books do not give a full definition of that crime; East, P. C. ch. 16, s. 2, defines it with perhaps more accuracy than other writers to be "the wrongful or fraudulent taking and carrying away by any person of the mere personal goods of another from any place with a felonious intent to convert them to his (the taker's) own use, and make them his property, without the consent of the owner." But this definition needs some addition; the taking should be not only wrongful and fraudulent, but should also be "without any colour of right." All the cases shew that if the intention were not to take the entire dominion over the property, that is no larceny. *R.* v. *Phillips and Strong*, 2 East, Pl. Cr.

---

[1] [EDITOR'S NOTE. The judge directed them to consider whether the prisoners intended to make any further use of the horse than to ride it to the place whither they were going (33 miles from its stable), and then leave it "to be recovered by the owner or not, as it might turn out"; and they found that no further use was intended. One judge thought it nevertheless a larceny; because there was no intention to return the horse to the owner, but rather, so far as the prisoners were concerned, to deprive him of it. But the others were unanimous that, on the intent as found, there was only a trespass; though the facts would legally have warranted the jury in finding a larcenous intent.]

ch. 16, s. 98, is the earliest case on the subject, and there are others to
the same effect. Then there is the case of *R.* v. *Webb*, 1 Moo. C. C.
431, which is precisely the same as the present case. Therefore the
essential element of larceny is here wanting, viz., the intention to
deprive the owner wholly of his property.

The four other Judges concurred.

[*Ignorance of law, though it does not prevent an* ordinary *mens rea, may
prevent this* complex *mens rea from arising.*]

REGINA v. REED.

Taunton Assizes.   1842.   Carrington and Marshman 306.

The prisoner, Elizabeth Reed, was indicted for stealing a five-pound
note, and her husband for receiving it.

The daughter of the prisoners and another little girl, while walking
in the street at Taunton, saw a small piece of paper lying on the
ground, and the other girl directed the prisoners' daughter to pick it
up; which she did, and gave it to her companion. It was a five-pound
note. The prisoners' daughter, on returning home, told her mother
of the circumstance, who thereupon went to the house where the other
girl lived, and said to her, " Where is that note which our Mary picked
up?" Upon its being given to her, she went away with it, and gave it
to her husband, who converted it at once into money. When the note
was missed, and inquiry was made for it, both the prisoners denied all
knowledge of any of the above circumstances.

     *   *   *   *   *

Coleridge, J....Ignorance of the law cannot excuse any person;
but, at the same time, when the question is with what intent a person
takes, we cannot help looking into his state of mind; as, if a person
take what he believes to be his own, it is impossible to say that he
is guilty of felony. Elizabeth Reed might think that she had a right
to the note, in consequence of her daughter having picked it up; and
if she have acted openly, you must say that she took the note from the
other little girl in ignorance of the continuing rights of the owner. It
is almost impossible to think that she supposed the owner to have
intentionally abandoned the note; but yet she might have thought that
her daughter, having first picked it up, had a right to it, and a right

prior to that of the other girl who first saw it; and, thinking so, she might have gone and made the demand for it, as if she had said, "You have Mary's note, give it up." Under these circumstances, she could not be guilty of larceny. But then, the conduct of the parties subsequently to this is to be considered. His Lordship went through the facts subsequent to the taking.

Verdict, Guilty.

[Contrast this case with REX *v.* BAILEY, *supra*, p. 29.]

[*A* wrongful *intention must exist at the time of the taking.*]

REX *v.* HOLLOWAY.

AYLESBURY ASSIZES. 1833. 5 CARRINGTON AND PAYNE 525.

The prisoner was indicted for stealing a gun from the prosecutor, who was one of the gamekeepers of the manor of Beaconsfield.

The prosecutor met the prisoner and another man, whom he knew to be poachers, on a part of the manor, and seized the prisoner; his companion came up and rescued him. The prisoner, on getting free, wrested the gun from the prosecutor, and ran off with it. It was proved that the next day the prisoner said he should sell the gun. It was not afterwards found.

VAUGHAN, B., in summing up, said that the prisoner might have imagined that the prosecutor would use the gun so as to endanger his life; and, if so, his taking it under that impression would not be felony. But if he took it, intending at the time to dispose of it, it would be felony.

The jury said that they did not think that the prisoner, at the time he took the gun, had any intention of appropriating it to his own use.

VAUGHAN, B. Then you must acquit him. It is a question peculiarly for your consideration. If he did not, when he took it, intend its appropriation, it is not a felony; and his resolving afterwards to dispose of it will not make it such.

Verdict, Not guilty.

[*But it is not necessary that the full* larcenous *intention should exist then.*]

REGINA *v.* RILEY.

CROWN CASE RESERVED.　1853.　　　　　DEARSLY 149.

At the General Quarter Sessions of the peace for the county of Durham, held at the city of Durham before Rowland Burdon, Esquire, chairman, on the 18th day of October, 1852, the prisoner was indicted for having on the 5th of October, 1852, stolen a lamb the property of John Burnside.

On the trial it was proved that on Friday, the 1st day of October, 1852, John Burnside, the prosecutor, put ten white-faced lambs into a field in the occupation of John Clarke, situated near to the town of Darlington. On Monday, the 4th day of October, the prisoner went with a flock of twenty-nine black-faced lambs to John Clarke, and asked if he might put them into Clarke's field for a night's keep, and upon Clarke's agreeing to allow him to do so for one penny per head, the prisoner put his twenty-nine lambs into the same field with the prosecutor's lambs.

At half-past seven o'clock in the morning of Tuesday, the 5th day of October, the prosecutor went to Clarke's field, and in counting his lambs he missed one. The prisoner's lambs were gone from the field also. Between eight and nine o'clock in the morning of the same day, the prisoner came to the farm of John Calvert, at Middleton Saint George, six miles east from Darlington, and asked him to buy twenty-nine lambs. Calvert agreed to do so and to give eight shillings apiece for them. Calvert then proceeded to count the lambs, and informed the prisoner that there were thirty instead of twenty-nine in the flock. and pointed out to him a white-faced lamb, upon which the prisoner said, 'If you object to take thirty, I will draw one.' Calvert, however, bought the whole of them, and paid the prisoner twelve pounds for them.

One of the lambs sold to Calvert was identified by the prosecutor as his property, and as the lamb missed by him from Clarke's field.

There was evidence in the case to shew that the prisoner must have taken the lambs from Clarke's field early in the morning, which was thick and rainy....

The jury returned the following verdict:—"The jury say that at the time of leaving the field the prisoner did not know that the lamb was in his flock, and that he was guilty of felony at the time it was pointed out to him."

The prisoner was then sentenced to six months' hard labour.

K.　　　　　　　　　　　　　　　　　　　　　　　　　19

Liddell, for the prisoner. The conviction is wrong on three grounds. First, the original taking being when the lamb left the field, the question for the jury was whether the lamb was taken by the prisoner animo furandi, or by mistake; the verdict of the jury amounts to a finding that it was taken by mistake. Secondly, the chairman misdirected the jury. He told them, that though they might be of opinion that the prisoner did not know that the lamb was in his flock until it was pointed out to him, yet in point of law the taking occurred when it was so pointed out to the prisoner, and sold by him, and not at the time of leaving the field. But in order to constitute larceny he should have told the jury that something more was necessary; and the jury not having found it the Court will not now intend it. Thirdly, the finding of the jury does not amount to a verdict of guilty.

POLLOCK, C.B. Suppose a traveller at an inn in packing up six pieces of anything packed up a seventh with it by mistake in his portmanteau. He does not find out the mistake till he goes to a distance, and then converts it to his own use. When does he take it? Surely when he discovers his mistake and resolves to appropriate it to himself animo furandi.

Liddell. Here the prisoner had the lamb in his possession before the time of the alleged taking.

POLLOCK, C.B. What do you mean by the term "possession"?

Liddell. He had such a possession as would have enabled him to maintain trespass. If it be said that the prisoner took the lamb when it was pointed out to him on the road, then the jury have not found that he knew, or had the means of knowing, at the time, who the true owner was. The lamb was, in fact, animal vagrans, without an owner, and within the rule laid down by Parke, B., in *Reg.* v. *Thurborn,* 1 Den. C. C. 388. It was without an owner;—it had no mark upon it to indicate the owner's name; for it was marked T., while the initial of the prosecutor's name was B. It was an estray, to take which at common law was no larceny. The law in cases of taking by mistake is stated in 1 Hale P. C. 505. If the sheep of A. stray from his flock to the flock of B., and B. drive them along with his own flock, and by mistake and without knowing it or taking heed of the difference, shear them, it is no felony. But if B. knew them to be the sheep of another person, and tried to conceal the fact; if, for instance, finding another's mark upon them, he deface it, and put his own mark upon them, this would be evidence of a felony. When then was the felony committed here? Was it when the lamb left the possession of the true owner? It is submitted that the question here is, what was the prisoner's intent when the lamb left the field. His subsequent conduct is only evidence of that intent....It is quite evident that before the sale of the lamb the prisoner might have maintained an action of trespass, upon his possessory title, although the property was in the true owner. If the lamb had strayed and mixed with the lambs of the prisoner, he would be in the innocent possession of it while he drove it six miles along the road; and then the rule laid down in *Thristle's case*, 1 Den. C. C. 502, would apply "that where a chattel comes into the possession of a party without the animus furandi, in the first instance, the subsequent appropriation is no larceny."

WILLIAMS, J. Suppose no animus furandi, and that a civil action is brought for the trespass. The whole would form a continuous transaction. In the first instance take it that here there is no animus furandi when the lamb is taken from the field; but the trespass continues, and then there is the animus furandi; does it not then become felony?

POLLOCK, C.B. The difficulty in the case is, *when* can it be said that there was a taking?

PARKE, B. The prisoner must have driven them away. In doing so he committed a trespass; which began when he left the field....He became a trespasser, though not a felonious trespasser; but when he afterwards sold the lamb the trespass became a felony.

Liddell. Is not this like the case where the prisoner had possession of a chattel dispunishably?

PARKE, B. No. That was not a case of trespass. That was a case where trover might have been maintained; where the chattel was 'found,' and the person who found it had a good title against all the world....

POLLOCK, C.B. We are all of opinion that the conviction in this case is right. The distinction between this and the case of *Reg.* v. *Thristle*, 1 Den. C. C. 502, is this. If a man rightfully gets possession of an article without any intention at the time of stealing it, and afterwards misappropriates it, the law holds it not to be a felony. In that case a man had delivered his watch to a watchmaker to regulate it, and the watchmaker afterwards disposed of it for his own use....It may reasonably be said not to be a violation of any social duty for a man who finds a lost article to take it home for the purpose of finding out the true owner; and if he does this honestly in the first instance, and afterwards, though he may have discovered the true owner, is seduced into appropriating it to his own use, he is not guilty of larceny, though he does wrong. So in *Leigh's case*, 2 East P. C. 694, it appeared that the prosecutor's house was on fire, and that the prisoner assisted in saving some of his goods, and took some of them home to her lodgings, but next morning denied that she had them in her possession. It was suggested that she originally took the goods with an honest intent, that of assisting in saving her neighbour's property from the fire. She was found guilty; but the judges, as it appeared that she originally took the goods merely from a desire of saving them for and returning them to the prosecutor, and that she had no evil intention till afterwards, held that the conviction was wrong. There the original taking was not wrongful; indeed it was right, for she took possession of the goods under the authority of the true owner. In all these cases the original possession was not wrongful. But in the case now before the Court the prisoner's possession of the lamb was from the beginning wrongful. Here the taking of the lamb from the field was a trespass; or if it be said that there was no taking at that time, then the moment he finds the lamb he appropriates it to his own use. The distinction between the cases is this: if the original possession be *rightful*, subsequent misappropriation does not make it a felony; but if the original possession be *wrongful*, though not felonious, and then a man disposes of the chattel, animo furandi, it is larceny.

[The other four Judges concurred.]

Conviction affirmed.

[*Where a thing is delivered under a* Mutual Mistake, *it is not yet settled whether the time of* physical delivery, *or that of the* discovery of the mistake, *is to be legally regarded as being the* time of taking.]

REGINA *v.* ASHWELL.

CROWN CASE RESERVED.   1885.   L.R. 16 Q.B.D. 190.

Case stated by Denman, J.

At the Assizes for the county of Leicester in January, 1883, Thomas Ashwell was tried for larceny of a sovereign, the moneys of Edward Keogh.

Keogh and Ashwell met in a public-house on the evening of the 9th of January. At about 8 p.m., Ashwell asked Keogh to go into the yard, and when there requested Keogh to lend him a shilling, saying that he had money to draw on the morrow, and that he would then repay him. Keogh consented, and putting his hand in his pocket pulled out what he believed to be a shilling, but what was in fact a sovereign, and handed it to Ashwell, and went home leaving Ashwell in the yard.   About 9 the same evening, Ashwell obtained change for the sovereign at another public-house.

At 5.20 the next morning, Keogh went to Ashwell's house and told him that he had discovered the mistake, whereupon Ashwell falsely denied having received the sovereign, and on the same evening he gave false and contradictory accounts as to where he had become possessed of the sovereign he had changed at the second public-house on the night before.   But he afterwards said, "I had the sovereign, and spent half of it, and I shan't give it him back because I only asked him to lend me a shilling".

The jury found that the prisoner did not know that it was a sovereign at the time he received it; but said they were unanimously of opinion that the prosecutor parted with it under the mistaken belief that it was a shilling; and that the prisoner having, soon after he received it, discovered that it was a sovereign, could have easily restored it to the prosecutor, but fraudulently appropriated it to his own use and denied the receipt of it, knowing that the prosecutor had not intended to part with the possession of a sovereign but only of a shilling.   They added that if it were competent to them consistently with these findings and with the evidence to find the prisoner guilty, they meant to do so.

Sills, for the prisoner.... Admitting that if the prisoner had known at the time it was handed to him that the coin was a sovereign there would be a larceny (for in such case trespass would lie), that is not the present case, for some time elapsed before he discovered what the coin was.   A necessary ingredient of the crime of larceny at common law, is that there must be a taking invito domino.   If the prisoner induces the delivery by trick or otherwise, then there is such a taking, but it is otherwise if the mistake as to what is delivered is common to both : *Reg.* v. *Prince*[1]; *Reg.* v. *Middleton*[2].   The case of giving a cabman a sovereign by mistake for a shilling, which was much argued there, is exactly the present case.   There was here an intention to deliver the particular coin which the prosecutor held in his hand, although he did not before handing it over ascertain its value.   A mere mistake as to value does not make any difference in the delivery.   There can have been no finding here, because there was no loss; and there was no bailment, because there was no mandate.

A. K. Lloyd, for the prosecution.   Where property comes into the hands of a transferee by mistake as to the subject-matter transferred, there is no delivery which will prevent a subsequent appropriation of it from being a felonious taking; and a trespass is committed when, on

---

[1] Law Rep. 1 C. C. 150.   [2] Law Rep. 2 C. C. 38.

the discovery of the mistake, the holder of the chattel wrongfully appropriates it to himself. The delivery which can be set up as an answer to a charge of larceny must be a delivery with intention to pass the property. Delivery induced by fraud, by threats, or by accident, could not be so set up....

If a delivery under a mistake as to the subject-matter is of any validity, it can only be treated as delivery for a limited purpose. When the coin delivered turned out to be something else than a shilling, the identical coin should have been returned..

* * * * * * * * * * *

CAVE, J. It is, undoubtedly, a correct proposition, that there can be no larceny at common law unless there is also a trespass, and that there can be no trespass where the prisoner has obtained lawful possession of the goods alleged to be stolen; or, in other words, the thief must take the goods into his possession with the intention of depriving the owner of them. If he has got the goods lawfully into his possession before the intention of depriving the owner of them is formed, there is no larceny. Applying that principle to this case, if the prisoner acquired lawful possession of the sovereign when the coin was actually handed to him by the prosecutor, there is no larceny, for at that time the prisoner did not steal the coin; but, if he only acquired possession when he discovered the coin to be a sovereign, then he is guilty of larceny, for at that time he knew that he had not the consent of the owner to his taking possession of the sovereign as his own, and the taking under those circumstances was a trespass.

It is contended that, as the prosecutor gave and the prisoner received the coin under the impression that it was a shilling and not a sovereign, the prosecutor never consented to part with the possession of the sovereign, and consequently there was a taking by the prisoner without his consent. But to my mind it is impossible to come to the conclusion that, at the time when the sovereign was handed to him, the prisoner, who was then under a bonâ fide mistake as to the coin, can be held to have been guilty of a trespass in taking that which the prosecutor gave him. It seems to me that it would be equally logical to say that the prisoner would have been guilty of a trespass if the prosecutor, intending to slip a shilling into the prisoner's pocket without his knowledge, had by mistake slipped a sovereign in instead of a shilling. The only point which can be made in favour of the prosecution, so far as I can see, is that the prisoner did not actually take possession until he knew what the coin was of which he was taking possession, in which case, as he then determined to deprive the prosecutor of his property, there was a taking possession simultaneously with the formation of that intention. Had the coin been a shilling, it is obvious that the prisoner would have gained the property in and the possession of the coin when it was handed to him by the prosecutor. As there was a mistake as to the identity of the coin no property passed, and the question is whether the possession passed when the coin was handed to the prisoner, or when the prisoner first knew that he had got a sovereign and not a shilling.

There are cases which it is important to consider. The first is *Cartwright* v. *Green*[1], which, however, differs slightly from the present, because in that case there was no intention to give the defendant Green either the property in or the possession of the guineas, but only the possession of the bureau, the bailor being unaware of the existence of the guineas. If the bailee in that case had, before discovering the guineas in the secret drawer, negligently lost the bureau with its contents, it is difficult to see how he could have been made responsible for the loss of the guineas. In *Merry* v. *Green*[2] the facts were similar to *Cartwright* v. *Green*[1], except that the bureau had been sold to the defendant. In that case Baron Parke says, that though there was a delivery of the bureau to the defendant, there was no delivery so as to give a lawful possession of the purse and money in the secret drawer.

If these cases are rightly decided, as I believe them to be, they establish the principle that a man has not possession of that of the existence of which he is unaware. A man cannot without his consent be made to incur the responsibilities towards the real owner which arise from even the simple possession of a chattel without further title; and if a chattel has, without his knowledge been placed in his custody, his rights and liabilities as a possessor of that chattel do not arise until he is aware of the existence of the chattel, and has assented to the possession of it....

In my judgment a man cannot be presumed to assent to the possession of a chattel; actual consent must be shewn. Now a man does not consent to that of which he is wholly ignorant; and I think, therefore, it was rightly decided that the defendant in *Merry* v. *Green*[3] was not in possession of the purse and money until he knew of their existence. Moreover, in order that there may be a consent, a man must be under no mistake as to that to which he consents; and, I think, therefore, that Ashwell did not consent to the possession of the sovereign until he knew that it was a sovereign. Suppose that, while still ignorant that the coin was a sovereign, he had given it away to a third person who had misappropriated it, could he have been made responsible to the prosecutor for the return of 20*s.*? In my

---

[1] 8 Ves. 405.   [2] 7 M. and W. 623.

judgment he could not. If he had parted with it innocently, while still under the impression that it was only a shilling, I think he could have been made responsible for the return of a shilling and a shilling only, since he had consented to assume the responsibility of a possessor in respect of a shilling only. It may be said that a carrier is responsible for the safe custody of the contents of a box delivered to him to be carried, although he may be ignorant of the nature of its contents; but in that case the carrier consents to be responsible for the safe custody of the box and its contents whatever they may happen to be; and, moreover, a carrier is not responsible for the loss of valuable articles, if he has given notice that he will not be responsible for such articles unless certain conditions are complied with, and is led by the consignor to believe that the parcel given to him to carry does not contain articles of the character specified in the notice: *Batson* v. *Donovan*[1]. In this case Ashwell did not hold himself out as being willing to assume the responsibilities of a possessor of the coin whatever its value might be; nor can I infer that at the time of the delivery he agreed to be responsible for the safe custody and return of the sovereign. As, therefore, he did not at the time of delivery subject himself to the liabilities of the borrower of a sovereign, so also I think that he is not entitled to the privileges attending the lawful possession of a borrowed sovereign. When he discovered that the coin was a sovereign, he was, I think, bound to elect, as a finder would be, whether he would assume the responsibilities of a possessor; but, at the moment when he was in a position to elect, he also determined fraudulently to convert the sovereign to his own use; and I am therefore of opinion that he falls within the principle of *Regina* v. *Middleton*[2] and was guilty of larceny at common law.

For these reasons I am of opinion that the conviction was right.

* * *

STEPHEN, J....Ashwell received the sovereign innocently; though he dealt with it fraudulently an hour afterwards, when he became aware of its value. The inference that he committed no felony at common law appears to me to follow of necessity.

There are two ways in which it is sought to avoid this inference. It is said, first, that the delivery, being made under a mistake, passed neither the property in the sovereign nor the right to a possession of it; and that the prisoner must be regarded as having taken it, not when he accepted it under a mistake as to its value, but when knowing its value he determined to appropriate it to himself, or when he did so appropriate it by getting it changed and keeping the change. It is

[1] 4 B. and A. 21.　　　　[2] Law Rep. 2 C. C. 45.

also said that even if no offence at common law was committed, the prisoner was guilty of larceny as a bailee under the 3rd section of the Larceny Act. I am unable to concur with either of these views.

The first view is, I think, contrary to principle, because it evades by a legal fiction the principle that a fraudulent appropriation consequent upon an innocent taking is not larceny. The guilt of the prisoner would follow easily and immediately from the principle that such a taking is larceny, and this second principle is in effect substituted for the first by an artificial interpretation either of the word "possession," or of the word "taking." If the word "possession" is chosen to be interpreted, this is done by explaining it to mean something beyond actual control over the thing possessed, namely, control coupled with knowledge, which may or may not exist. If the word "taking" is chosen to be interpreted, it is in this case interpreted to mean not an actual physical taking, but a subsequent change of mind relating back to such physical taking. I know of no authority for either of these fictions. The word "possession" is indeed used in many senses, some of them highly artificial, but this is a bad reason for adding a new artificial meaning to it. Its plain meaning in this case is the reception of the coin by Ashwell from Keogh. The interpretation suggested appears to me to be one against which there is express authority, which I now proceed to examine.

The cases which set the matter in the clearest light are those which relate to the finding of lost property, particularly those which have been decided in modern times....

If the present case is to be decided against the prisoner, we shall have the following result: If A. finds a sovereign in the road not knowing to whom it belongs, and appropriates it to himself after discovering the owner, he is not guilty of theft; but if A. innocently receives a sovereign from the owner believing it to be a shilling, and appropriates it to himself after discovering its value, he is guilty of theft. This can hardly be the law.

When Ashwell received the coin and put it in his pocket, and for an hour afterwards, he did not know that Keogh was the owner of it in any sense whatever. He believed it to be his own, and this on the reasonable ground that Keogh had lent it to him, thereby passing to him an absolute property in the coin itself. When he discovered its value he had the lawful possession of it, at all events as against every one except Keogh; and if his subsequent conversion of it to his own use amounted to a felonious taking, *Regina* v. *Thurborn*[1] was wrongly decided....

[1] 1 Den. C. C. 387.

The question, therefore, reduces itself to this : What difference
was there between the taking by a finder and the reception by Ashwell
ot the coin given him by Keogh ? Whatever difference there was
appears to me both in law and in common sense to be in Ashwell's
favour. A finder must know that the property he finds is not his,
whoever may be the owner of it. Ashwell for an hour after he
received it reasonably believed that the coin which he received was his
own. I cannot see how any taking could be more innocent, and to say
that for the first hour his possession was Keogh's possession, and that
when he determined to convert it he was guilty of a felonious taking,
is expressly to contradict *Regina* v. *Preston*[1], and is, I think, inconsistent with the reasons for all the other decisions referred to....

I may here notice one point which was raised in argument. It
was said that the actual time of taking could not be the point at
which the guilt or innocence of a finder must be determined, because
in most cases a short time must elapse between the actual taking of
a note or coin, the discovery of its nature or value, and the determination consequent upon that discovery to appropriate it; and this, it
was said, shews that the time to be considered is the time of acquiring
knowledge of the property taken, and not the time of taking. If a
man picks up a purse containing money, some seconds must usually
pass before he can open the purse and discover, and determine to
appropriate, the money. I think, however, that for legal purposes it
is neither possible nor desirable to attempt to go into such a refine-
ment as this. If a man finds a purse, picks it up, opens it, finds
money in it, and thereupon determines to keep it for himself, it
appears to me that the whole process ought to be regarded as one
action, taking place at one time; as for many purposes the fractional
parts of a day are not regarded by the law. If the examination were
delayed for a substantial time, I think the question for the jury would
be whether at the time of the taking the prisoner intended to keep
what he had found, conditionally upon its turning out upon examination to be worth his while to do so, and whether at the time of taking
the goods he had the means of knowing the owner.

Suppose, for instance, a man found a bank-note bearing the owner's
name indorsed on it; suppose he put it in his pocket without examination, and ten minutes afterwards examined it, and after that kept it, it
might be a fair inference that when he took it up he meant to examine
it and to keep it if it was worth keeping. If by any means he could
convince the jury that he took it up only to look at it, and changed his
mind ten minutes afterwards, he would, I think, be entitled to be

[1] 2 Den. C. C. 353.

acquitted; but a jury would be likely to require strong evidence to induce them to believe in such a change of mind. In the present case it is admitted that the reception of the coin was quite innocent, and that the dishonest change of mind occurred upon the discovery by Ashwell of the mistake which was common to himself and Keogh.

The case of *Merry* v. *Green*[1] seems to suggest the possibility of a kind of double finding; for instance, a man finds a pocket-book on one day, and some days afterwards examines it and finds in it a bank-note with the owner's name. The judgment in *Merry* v. *Green* seems to suggest that the finding of the bank-note would take place when the pocket-book was opened, not when it was found, and that though the possession of the pocket-book might be innocent the appropriation of the note might be felonious. However this may be, it has no application to the present case.

*　　*　　*　　*　　*
*　　*　　*　　*　　*

LORD COLERIDGE, C.J....I assume it to be now established law that where there has been no trespass, there can at common law be no larceny. I assume it also to be settled law that where there has been a delivery—in the sense in which I will explain in a moment—of a chattel from one person to another, subsequent misappropriation of that chattel by the person to whom it has been delivered will not make him guilty of larceny, except by statute, with which I am not now concerned. But then it seems to me very plain that delivery and receipt are acts into which mental intention enters; and that there is not in law any more than in sense a delivery and receipt, unless the giver and receiver intend to give and to receive respectively what is respectively given and received. It is intelligent delivery, as I think, which the law speaks of; not a mere physical act from which intelligence and even consciousness are absent. I hope it is not laying down anything too broad or loose, if I say that all acts, to carry legal consequences, must be acts of the mind; and to hold the contrary, to hold that a man did what in sense and reason he certainly did not, that a man did in law what he did not know he was doing and did not intend to do—to hold this is to expose the law to very just but wholly unnecessary ridicule and scorn. I agree with my brother Stephen that fictions are objectionable, and I desire not to add to them. But it seems to me, with diffidence, that he creates the fiction who holds that a man does what he does not know he does and does not mean to do; not he who says that an act done by an intelligent being for which he is to be responsible is not an act of that being unless it is an act of his

[1] 7 M. and W. 623.

intelligence. In this case, therefore, it seems to me, there was no delivery of the sovereign to the prisoner by Keogh, because there was no intention to deliver, and no knowledge that it had been delivered....

[Seven Judges were for affirming the conviction, and seven for quashing it : accordingly, the rule of the Court being 'praesumitur pro negante,' the conviction stood affirmed.

Three months later, in the case of *The Queen* v. *Flowers*, L.R., 16 Q.B.D. 646, it was stated, on behalf of the seven judges who had affirmed the conviction, that they did so on the ground that the facts of Ashwell's case did not shew an innocent reception of the sovereign; but they had no intention of questioning the rule of law that, when a chattel has been innocently received, the subsequent fraudulent appropriation of it will not amount to larceny.]

REGINA v. HEHIR.

IRISH CROWN CASE RESERVED.   1895.   IRISH L.R. '95, 2 Q.B. 709.

Denis Hehir was tried before Palles, L.C.B. and a common jury for the larceny of a ten-pound note, of the goods and chattels of one John Leech. It was shewn at the trial that Leech owed Hehir for work done the sum of £2. 8s. 9d. For the purpose of paying this sum, Leech handed the prisoner nine shillings in silver and two bank-notes, each of which both Leech and the prisoner believed at the time to be a £1 note. One of those notes was in fact a £10 note. The prisoner left, taking away the two notes with him. Within twenty minutes afterwards, Leech discovered his mistake, and went in search of the prisoner; whom he found within half an hour after he had given him the notes. Leech told the prisoner that he had given him a £10 note instead of £1. The prisoner alleged that he had already changed both the notes. There was evidence that, at the time when the prisoner first became aware that the note was for £10 (which was a substantial period after it had been handed to him by Leech), he fraudulently and without colour of right, intended to convert the said note to his own use, and to permanently deprive the said John Leech thereof; and that to effectuate such intention the said prisoner shortly afterwards changed the said note and disposed of the proceeds thereof.

The Judge requested the opinion of the Court upon the question, " Whether he ought to have directed a verdict of acquittal by reason of the prisoner not having had the animus furandi when Leech handed him the £10 note?"

MADDEN, J....If the handing of the note by Leech to the prisoner, under the circumstances of this case, amounted to a delivery, transferring legal possession, no fraudulent intention on the part of the prisoner, subsequently formed, although carried into effect by actual conversion of the note to his own use, would suffice to constitute the crime of larceny at common law....Was there, then, a delivery to which any legal consequences can be attached? There was a physical transfer of a certain chattel from Leech to the prisoner; and the ordinary transactions of mankind could not be carried on if such a transfer were not primâ facie a delivery of the chattel, with a consequent change of legal possession. But although men are presumed to know what they are doing, and intend the consequences of their acts, the contrary may be proved; and we must deal with this case on the assumption that when Leech transferred this chattel to the prisoner they both believed it to be something different from what it actually was, and that their intention was to transfer a piece of paper representing one sovereign, not a piece of paper representing ten times that amount of gold....

I am of opinion that a transfer made under such circumstances can pass neither property nor legal possession. I do not mean to say that in all cases where delivery of a chattel is made under a mistake common to both parties to the transaction it is inoperative to transfer legal possession; for example...A. may deliver to B., in discharge of a trifling obligation, an old battered copy of Shakspeare printed in 1623, both innocently believing at the time that being old, full of errors and misprints and badly spelled, it would only fetch a couple of shillings at an auction. Suppose B. to sell it to a collector for several hundreds of pounds and to appropriate the proceeds, he would not be guilty of larceny, inasmuch as there was an intelligent delivery of the chattel, as such, though under a mistake as to its value....But the mistake in the present case—(and in *The Queen* v. *Ashwell*)—was one not of value but of identity. Here the chattel transferred had no intrinsic value. What is present in the mind on the delivery of a bank-note is not the paper, *per se*, but the money which it represents, and into which it is convertible. It would take some argument to persuade me that one sovereign is the same identical thing *in rerum natura* as a pile of ten sovereigns, and I think the notes by which they are represented are essentially different also. The case would appear plainer if exchange were carried on here, as in some countries, by means of shells or precious stones, each essentially different in nature as well as in conventional value, and if one of these stones had been mistaken for another. But, looking at the substance and reality of the transaction as present to the minds of both parties, I think mistake between a £10 note and a £1 note is one of precisely the same character.

If I am right in regarding the mistake as one of identity, and not merely of value, it appears to me clear upon the general principles of our law, and indeed of all jurisprudence, that a consent given, a contract entered into, or an act done, under, and in consequence of, such a mistake can have no legal consequences whatever. This would clearly be the law with regard to a contract for sale of a chattel, where a mistake occurred as to the identity of the purchaser: *Cundy* v. *Lindsay*[1]; and to import a different principle into our criminal law would, in my opinion, instead of tending to simplification, introduce confusion and contradiction into the administration of justice....There can be no intelligent delivery of a chattel or consent to its transfer when both parties either are ignorant of its existence or believe it to be something different from what it is in fact. In either case the *dominus* remains *invitus,* for the element of intelligent volition is wanting.

The question remains, assuming the *dominus* to be *invitus,* and the delivery to be inoperative to effect a change of legal possession, was there any felonious taking, or any taking at all, having regard to the circumstance that such taking, if it had any existence, occurred while the note was in the physical possession of the prisoner ?...

In *The Queen* v. *Ashwell* the circumstance that the alleged felonious taking was not contemporaneous with the actual physical taking, appears to have largely affected the judgment of Mathew, **J.** He says: "The argument on behalf of the Crown means that though the defendant did not take in point of fact, he ought by a fiction to be treated as having done so in point of law, in order that he may be punished as a thief" (p. 205). But this is not the only instance in which a felonious taking, amounting to a trespass, may be effected by a person already in physical possession of a chattel. It is sufficient to instance the case of a servant feloniously appropriating an article which is in his custody under circumstances sufficient to render his possession the legal possession of his master. The taking in such a case appears to partake quite as much of a legal fiction as in *The Queen* v. *Ashwell,* and in the present case. But, if we are to disregard legal subtleties, would it not, to the ordinary mind, savour even more of legal fiction, and appear less consonant with common sense, to say that Hehir *never* took £10 without the consent of Leech, than to say that he took £10 when he conceived and carried into effect the idea of fraudulently appropriating the note to his own use ?

[1] 3 A. C. 459.

It is well said by Mathew, J., that it is desirable that the rules by which guilt and innocence are to be determined should be susceptible of ready comprehension and easy exposition. The rule in accordance with which the present case ought in my opinion to be decided is certainly capable of easy exposition, and I believe of ready comprehension. It may be thus stated : A man to whom a chattel is delivered under a mistake as to its identity, does not thereby acquire legal possession : and if he subsequently discovers the mistake, and thereupon fraudulently misappropriates it to his own use, he is guilty of larceny. A rule so short and simple appears to me to be equally adapted to the comprehension of the average thief and to the moral sense of the honest citizen : and believing it to be in accordance with principle and authority, I am of opinion that the conviction should stand.

ANDREWS, J. In my opinion the conviction ought to be quashed. The two independent questions of the property in the £10 note, and the possession of it, ought to be carefully kept distinct. No doubt the property did not pass to the prisoner; but we have to deal with an entirely distinct question, viz. the possession of it. Now, it appears to me manifest that when the owner of the £10 note handed it to the prisoner, he intended to give the prisoner the possession of the thing he handed him. If he had known it was a £10 note, doubtless he would not have given it; but in my opinion, that only shews that his intention arose from a mistake, and does not shew that the intention did not exist. He, in fact, openly and visibly, handed the actual paper to the prisoner, knowing that he was handing it to him; and the prisoner took it, knowing that he was taking it. In neither case can the fact of the knowledge which existed be annihilated by the absence of the knowledge that it was a £10 note, or by the mistaken belief that it was a £1 note. I am wholly unable to agree with the proposition that a man cannot take, and be in lawful possession of, a thing which he believes to be of a different quality or value from its real quality or value. His acceptance of the possession is entirely distinct from his acceptance of the property, and may obviously exist without any acceptance whatever of the property. Nor can I at all agree that if a man takes into his possession, without reservation, a chattel openly handed to him, the quality and value of which he believes to be different from what they really are, his possession can in any rational sense be said to commence only when, at some subsequent time (to which no limit is assigned), he becomes aware of its quality and value. In the interval the taker is, in fact, knowingly in possession of the chattel, and why if he received it innocently from the owner, is not that a legal possession? Unquestionably it is not an unlawful possession, and therefore it must come to this that, though he received it unconditionally and had lawfully retained it in his sole custody in the interval, he was not in possession of it at all—a strange proposition, as it seems to me, to find anywhere, but passing strange in the criminal law in which, above all, words ought not to be divorced from their natural and proper meaning, nor refinements adopted which fritter that meaning away....I think it would be a fiction, such as should have no place in the criminal law, to ignore the actual taking, and to make (in the language of Mr Justice Talfourd) "a mere movement of the mind" amount to a taking. I think that the note in question was both given to the prisoner, and taken by him, *intelligently*, in the only sense in which that word is material to the question before us, (which does not at all necessarily include a knowledge of the actual quality or value of the thing which was in fact given); and that at the time the prisoner received the note he got lawful possession of it innocently, in the largest sense of the word, and without anything in the remotest degree resembling a trespass;...by the voluntary act of the owner, not feloniously and without the consent of the owner....

[Judgments were delivered by all the nine Judges present; five holding that the conviction should be quashed, and four upholding it. The conviction was accordingly quashed.]

SECTION XI.

EMBEZZLEMENT.

[The common law rule which, by regarding an act of Taking as essential to larceny, rendered it impossible to take criminal proceedings against a Possessor who dishonestly appropriated the thing bailed to him (see above, p. 222), applied not only to Bailees, strictly so-called, but even to servants who, on behalf of their masters, had received goods from third parties. The criminal lawyers refused to adopt in such cases the rule of the commercial lawyers which treated the servant's possession as being, constructively, the master's possession.]

[See REX v. DINGLEY, *supra*, p. 177.]

REX *v.* BAZELEY.

CROWN CASE RESERVED. 1799.   LEACH 835.

At the Old Bailey, Joseph Bazeley was tried for feloniously stealing a banknote for £100. [He was a cashier in the bank of Messrs Esdaile and Hammett, his duty being to receive and pay at the counter. A customer paid in £137, to his own account, in cash and notes, including a £100 note. The prisoner received from him the £137, placed £37 of it in the proper receptacles, but put the £100 note into his pocket. Later in the day, he paid away this note in discharge of an acceptance of his own. The jury convicted the prisoner. The Court reserved for the opinion of the Judges the question whether the act amounted in law to a larceny or was merely a fraudulent breach of trust.]

Const, for the prisoner. Bazeley received this note, by the permission of the prosecutors, whilst it was passing from the customer's possession into theirs; and, having been thus intercepted in transit, it is clear that it never came into the possession of the prosecutors.... The law will not, under such circumstances, consider the master to have a 'constructive' possession of the property, in a *criminal* case; for such a possession arises by a mere implication of law, and it is an established rule that no man's life shall be endangered by any implication....

Fielding, for the Crown, insisted...that as the customer paid the notes at the counter in the banking house of the prosecutors, of which Bazeley was merely one of the servants, the payment to him was in effect a payment to them, and his receipt vested the property *eo instanti* in their hands, and gave them the legal possession of it....He cited *Rex* v. *Abrahat,* Leach 824, and *Rex* v. *Spears,* Leach 825, to shew that a servant may be guilty of larceny, upon the principle that the possession of the servant is to be considered as the possession of the master.

On consultation among THE JUDGES some doubt was at first entertained. But at last all assembled agreed that it was not felony, inasmuch as the note was never in the possession of the prosecutors: though it would have been otherwise if the prisoner had deposited it in the drawer, and had afterwards taken it (*Chipchase's case,* Leach 699), and they thought that this was not to be differed from the cases of *Rex* v. *Waite,* Leach 28, and *Rex* v. *Bull,* Leach 841, which turned on this consideration—that the thing was not taken by the prisoner out of the possession of the owner; and here it was delivered into the possession of the prisoner. That although to many purposes the note was in the actual possession of the masters, yet it was also in the actual possession of the servant, and that possession not to be impeached, for it was a lawful one.

[In consequence of this case the statute 39 Geo. III. c. 85 was passed, which is now replaced by s. 68 of the Larceny Act, 1861 (24 and 25 Vict. c. 96), viz.—"Whosoever, being a clerk or servant (or being employed for the purpose or in the capacity of a clerk or servant) shall fraudulently embezzle any chattel...which shall be...taken into possession by him for, or in the name, or on the account of, his master... shall be deemed to have feloniously stolen the same from his master although such chattel...was not received into the possession of such master...otherwise than by the actual possession of...the person so employed."]

CHAPTER I. WHO IS A SERVANT?

[See the ANONYMOUS case, *supra*, p. 216.]

[*If an agent is not bound to obey the principal's orders, he is not his servant.*]

THE QUEEN *v.* NEGUS.

CROWN CASE RESERVED.   1873.   L.R. 2 C.C.R. 34.

Case stated by the Assistant Judge of the Middlesex Sessions.

The prisoner was indicted for embezzling £17 as clerk and servant to Roape and others.

The prisoner was engaged by the prosecutors to solicit orders for them, and he was to be paid by a commission on the sums received through his means. He had no authority to receive money; but if any was paid to him he was forthwith to hand it over to his employers. He was at liberty to apply for orders whenever he thought most convenient, but was not to employ himself for any other persons than the prosecutors.

Contrary to his duty he applied for payment of the above sum, and having received it he applied it to his own use, and denied, when asked, that it had been paid to him.

The prisoner's counsel contended that the prisoner was not a clerk or servant within the statute, but the learned Judge refused to stop the case, and directed the jury to find him guilty.

F. F. Lewis, for the prosecution. *Reg.* v. *Bowers*[1] somewhat resembles the present case, and is an authority in favour of the prisoner; but there the commission agent carried on a retail trade for himself at a shop, and so could not be deemed a clerk or servant of the merchants who supplied coal for him to sell.

[BOVILL, C.J. And here the prisoner might apply for orders whenever he thought most convenient.]

So might the traveller in *Reg.* v. *Bailey*[2]; he was nevertheless held to be clerk or servant of his employers.

[BLACKBURN, J. For he was under their control, having to devote his whole time to the service.]

The stipulation that the prisoner was not to employ himself for any other persons than the prosecutors shews that they had control over him.

[BOVILL, C.J. Not at all. He might go away to amuse himself whenever he liked.]

BOVILL, C.J....Generally speaking, I should say that the question whether a person is a clerk or servant depends on so many considerations that it is one to be left to the jury, as it is extremely difficult for the Court to come to a satisfactory conclusion upon such a matter. Much depends on the nature of the occupation in which the individual is engaged, and the kind of employment. But we have to see if there was enough evidence to shew that the prisoner here was a clerk or servant. I think that that fact is not sufficiently made out. What is a test as to the relationship of master and servant? A test used in many cases is, to ascertain whether the prisoner was bound to obey the *orders* of his employer, so as to be under his employer's *control*; and on the case stated there does not seem sufficient to shew that he was subject to the employers' orders, and bound to devote his time as they should direct. Although under this engagement with them, it appears he was still at liberty to take orders, or to abstain from doing so, and the masters had no power to control him in that respect. Where there is a salary, that raises a presumption that the person receiving it is bound to devote his time to the service; but when money is paid by commission a difficulty arises, although the relationship may still exist where commission is paid, as in ordinary cases of a traveller, and in *Reg.* v. *Tite*[3], and the other case cited. But in either case there may

[1] Law Rep. 1 C. C. 41. [2] 12 Cox Cr. C. 56.
[3] Leigh and Cave, Cr. C. 29; 30 L. J. (M.C.) 142.

be no such control, and then the relationship does not exist. All the authorities referred to seem to shew that it is not necessary that there should be a payment by salary—for commission will do—nor that the whole time should be employed, nor that the employment should be permanent,—for it may be only occasional, or in a single instance—if, at the time, the prisoner is engaged as servant. The facts before us do not make out what the prosecution was bound to prove, viz., that the prisoner was clerk or servant.

BRAMWELL, B. This conviction ought to be quashed unless we can see that the prisoner, on the facts stated, must have been clerk or servant within the meaning of the Act of Parliament. I am of opinion that on the facts we cannot do so. Looking to principle we find that the statute was intended to apply—not to cases where a man is a mere agent, but—where the relationship of master and servant, in the popular sense of the term, may be said to exist. Erle, C.J., in *Reg.* v. *Bowers* says, the cases decide " that a person who is employed to get orders and receive money, but who is at liberty to get those orders and receive that money when and where he thinks proper, is not a clerk or servant within the meaning of the statute." I think that is perfectly good law, consistent with all the authorities, and, applied here, it shews that the prisoner was not clerk or servant within the definition there given.

BLACKBURN, J. I am of the same opinion. The test is very much this, viz., whether the person charged is under the control and bound to obey the orders of his master. He may be so without being bound to devote his whole time to this service; but if bound to devote his whole time to it, that would be very strong evidence of his being under control. This case differs in nothing from the ordinary one of a commission agency, except in the sole statement that the prisoner was not to work for others. But I do not think that circumstance by itself alone enables us to say that he was a servant of the prosecutor.

ARCHIBALD, J., concurred.

HONYMAN, J. I agree. The question was not left to the jury to decide, and I cannot satisfy myself that the relationship of masters and servant certainly existed between the prosecutors and the prisoner. It does not appear that the prisoner was bound to obey every single lawful order. Possibly the masters might tell him to go somewhere, and he might justly refuse.

Conviction quashed.

[*But a man may be a servant though he is* under no contract
that binds him to continue serving.]

THE QUEEN *v.* FOULKES.

CROWN CASE RESERVED.	1875.	L.R. 2 C.C.R. 150.

[Indictment for embezzlement of two sums of £100 each; for each
sum there was a count describing it as the property of his employers,
the Local Board of Whitchurch, and a further count describing it as
the property of his master, Charles Foulkes.]

Charles Foulkes was the prisoner's father; and was the salaried
clerk of the Whitchurch Local Board....In the absence of his father,
the prisoner acted for him at the meetings of the Local Board; and
assisted him when present at them. Prisoner was not appointed or
paid by the Local Board. There was no evidence that he was paid any
salary by his father....Money was raised by the Board on mortgage of
the local rates....The course of business was, that prisoner received at
his father's office the money from the mortgagees, in exchange for the
mortgages, and paid it into the Whitchurch and Ellesmere Bank (who
were the treasurers of the board) to an account called the "market
account." In the course of this employment he embezzled and appropriated to his own use the two sums of money mentioned in the indictment.
It was objected by counsel for the prisoner that he could not be convicted on the first two counts of the indictment, as he was not a clerk
or servant of the board, nor employed by the board in that or any
other capacity; and that he could not be convicted on the third or
fourth counts, as there was no evidence that he was the clerk or
servant of his father, or was employed by him in that capacity, beyond
the fact that he assisted his father, and as the moneys embezzled were
not the moneys of Charles Foulkes, but of the Local Board. The
prisoner was convicted and sentenced, but the learned Judge respited
the execution of the sentence till after the decision of the Court on
this case.

Rose, for the prisoner. The prisoner could not properly be convicted of embezzlement. To constitute embezzlement by a person
"being a clerk, or servant, or being employed for the purpose or in the
capacity of a clerk or servant" there must be a contract of service of
some kind express or implied. In the present case there was none;
for the prisoner was in no sense in the employment of the Local Board,
and the services he rendered to his father were mere voluntary services,

not rendered in pursuance of any contract.   [He cited *Rex* v. *Burton*[1];
Rex v. *Nettleton*[2]; *Reg.* v. *Bowers*[3]; *Reg.* v. *Tyree*[4]; *Reg.* v. *Turner*[5];
Reg. v. *Cullum*[6]; *Reg.* v. *Negus*[7].]

No counsel appeared for the prosecution.

COCKBURN, C.J.   I think there was evidence on which the jury
might well find that the prisoner either was a clerk or servant, or
was employed as a clerk or servant.   The father held various offices;
and the prisoner, his son, in consequence of his father's illness, or for
other reasons, did the duties which the father would otherwise have
had to do himself or to employ a clerk to do.   It is true there was no
contract binding him to go on doing those duties.   But the relation of
master and servant may well be terminable at will; and while the
prisoner did act he was a clerk or servant.   The second question is,
whether there was an embezzlement.   I think there was.   The money
was to be received by the father, though received for the Local Board.
He was the proper custodian of the money, and the son received it for
him.   There was, therefore, evidence upon both points.

BRAMWELL, B.   I am of the same opinion.   If the prisoner had not
been the son of the man for whom he acted, and had not lived with
him, it is abundantly evident that he would have been a clerk or
servant, and would have been entitled to payment upon a quantum
meruit.   Then what difference can his being a son make?   It may
affect the nature of his remuneration; but nothing else.   With regard
to the money, the father might have had to account for it; but he was
entitled to receive it from the son.   Therefore there was an embezzlement.

*   *   *   *   *

BRETT, J.   The prisoner undertook to do things for his father
which a clerk does for his master, and to do them in the way a clerk
does them.   Now, assuming that there was no contract to go on doing
those things, still as long as he did them with his father's agreement,
he was bound to do them with the same honesty as a clerk, because he
was employed as a clerk.

POLLOCK, B.   If it had been necessary to say absolutely that the
prisoner was a clerk or servant, I should have hesitated.   But I think
the words "employed as a clerk or servant," are wider, and that there
is evidence to bring the case within them.

Conviction affirmed.

---

[1] 1 Moo. Cr. C. 237.   [2] 1 Moo. Cr. C. 260.   [3] Law Rep. 1 C. C. 41.
[4] Law Rep. 1 C. C. 177.   [5] 11 Cox Cr. C. 551.
[6] Law Rep. 2 C. C. 28.   [7] *Supra*, p. 306.

CHAPTER II.   WHAT CAN BE EMBEZZLED.

[*A servant can embezzle only what he has received* as servant.]

[*See* REGINA *v.* FOULKES, *supra*, p. 309.]

[*Not what he has merely earned with* master's tools.]

REGINA *v.* CULLUM.

CROWN CASE RESERVED.   1873.   L.R. 2 C.C.R. 28.

Case stated by the Chairman of the West Kent Sessions.

The prisoner was indicted, as servant to George Smeed, for stealing £2, the property of his master.

The prisoner was employed by Mr Smeed, of Sittingbourne, Kent, as captain of one of Mr Smeed's barges.

The prisoner's duty was to take the barge with the cargo to London, and to receive back such return cargo, and from such persons, as his master should direct....By direction of Mr Smeed, the prisoner took a load of bricks to London. In London he met Mr Smeed, and asked if he should not on his return take a load of manure to Mr Pye, of Caxton.   Mr Smeed expressly forbade his taking the manure to Mr Pye, and directed him to return with his barge empty to Burham. Notwithstanding this prohibition, the prisoner took a barge load of manure from London down to Mr Pye, at Caxton, and received from Mr Pye's men £4 as the freight.   It was not proved that he professed to carry the manure or to receive the freight for his master.   The servant who paid the £4 said that he paid it to the prisoner for the carriage of the manure, but that he did not know for whom....In answer to the manager's inquiries, the prisoner stated that he had not brought back any manure in the barge from London, and he never accounted for the £4 received from Mr Pye for the freight for the manure.   The jury found the prisoner guilty, as servant to Mr Smeed, of embezzling £2.   The question was whether, on the above facts, the prisoner could be properly convicted of embezzlement.

No counsel appeared for the prisoner.

E. T. Smith (with him *Moreton Smith*) for the prosecution. The prisoner received this freight either "for," or "on account of," his master or employer, and therefore is within the terms of 24 and 25 Vict. c. 96, s. 68[1]. The words, "by virtue of such employment," which were in the repealed statutes relating to the same offence, have been advisedly omitted, in order to enlarge the enactment and get rid of the decisions on the former enactments.

[BLACKBURN, J. How can the money here be said to have been received into the possession of the servant so as to become the property of the master?]

The prisoner was exclusively employed by the prosecutor. With his master's barge he earned, and in the capacity of servant received, £4 as freight, which, on receipt by him, at once became the property of his master: *Rex* v. *Hartley*[2].

[BLACKBURN, J. But in this case the servant was disobeying orders. Suppose a private coachman used his master's carriage without leave, and earned half-a-crown by driving a stranger, would the money be received for the master, so as to become the property of the latter?]

Such coachman has no authority to receive any money for his master; the prisoner, here, was entitled to take freight.

[BOVILL, C. J. He was expressly forbidden to do so on this occasion.]

Can it be said that he may be guilty of embezzlement, if, in obedience of orders, he receives money, and yet not guilty of that crime if he is acting contrary to his master's commands?

*   *   *   *   *

BRAMWELL, B. The wrong committed by the prisoner was not fraudulent or wrongful with respect to money, but consisted in the improper use of his master's chattel. The offence is, as I pointed out during argument, only that which a barge-owner's servant might be guilty of, if, when navigating the barge, he stopped it, allowed persons to stand upon it to view a passing boat-race, charged them for so doing, and pocketed the money they paid to him. There is no distinction between that case and this, save that the supposititious case is more evidently out of the limits of the statute....

BLACKBURN, J....I cannot see how this was the master's property, or that the servant had authority to carry anything in this barge but the cargo he was directed to convey. He was actually forbidden to load this barge on the return voyage; he did load it, and very improperly earned money by the use of it; but in what sense he can be said to have received this sum for the use of his master I cannot understand. The test of the matter would really be this—if the person

---

[1] *Supra*, p. 306.   [2] Russ. and Ry. 139.

to whom the manure belonged had not paid for the carriage, could the master have said, "There was a contract with you, which you have broken, and I sue you on it"? There would have been no such con. tract, for the servant never assumed to act for his master; and on that ground his act does not come within the statute. I think that in no case could he have been properly convicted under the Act unless the money became that of the master.

* * * * *

Conviction quashed.

[*Or by selling* master's property *without authority.*]

REGINA *v.* WILSON.

CENTRAL CRIMINAL COURT.   1839.   9 CARRINGTON AND PAYNE 27.

Indictment for embezzlement of 4s. 6d., the property of William Phillipps.

It was the duty of the prisoner to go round and take orders from customers, and to enter them, on his return to the shop in the evening, in the day or order book, and also to receive moneys in payment of such orders; but he had no authority whatever to take, or to direct the delivery of, any goods from the shop. On the 20th of March, Mr William Crachnell, one of Mr Phillipps's customers, gave the prisoner, Edmund L. Wilson, an order for two gallons of mixed pickles, and 14 lb. of treacle, which order was entered by him in the order book as for the pickles only. An invoice for the pickles, pursuant to the entry, was made out by Mr Phillipps's brother, and given to the carman Michael; but he delivered Mr Crachnell the pickles, and 14 lb. of treacle. The sum charged for the pickles was 6s. 6d.; and Michael entered the treacle at the foot of the invoice at 4s. 6d. The prisoner Edmund afterwards received the whole amount, viz. 11s.; but paid over to Mr Phillipps 6s. 6d. only.

THE RECORDER. I have conferred with Mr Justice PATTESON, who concurs with me in the opinion I was inclined to entertain of this question; and, on his suggestion, I may put the case in this form,—that the prisoner, Edmund Wilson, does not receive the 4s. 6d. for or on account of his master, but contrary to, and in breach of, his duty towards that master. I may also liken the case to that of two servants —one of whom has authority to sell, and the other not, but merely to receive money ; if the one who has no authority to sell introduces himself behind the counter, and sells his master's goods, putting the money into his own pocket, that is clearly a stealing, for he sells and receives the money contrary to his authority; and he cannot be said to have been employed and intrusted as clerk and servant, and to have received the money by virtue of such employment, where the act is done contrary to that employment. In this case, the servant having authority to send out goods to the amount of 6s. 6d., puts up goods to the amount of 11s., his intention being to put 4s. 6d. into his own pocket. The time never arrives when he receives that "on account of" his master, for all that he does is adverse to, and in fraud of, the interest of his master.

Verdict, Not guilty.

[*It is otherwise if the sale, though dishonest, was* authorised.]

REX *v.* HOGGINS.

CROWN CASE RESERVED.   1809.   RUSSELL AND RYAN 145.

The prisoner was tried before Mr JUSTICE BAYLEY, at the Lent Assizes, for the borough of Leicester, in the year 1809, on an indictment on the 39 Geo. III. c. 85, for embezzlement.

The prisoner worked for Burbidge and Co., who were turners; and was paid according to what he did. It was part of his duty to receive orders for jobs, to take the necessary materials from his master's stock, to work them up, to deliver out the articles, and to receive the money for them ; and then his business was to deliver the whole of the money to his masters, and to receive back at the week's end a proportion of it for working up the articles. The jobs were commonly paid for as soon as they were executed, it being a ready money part of the business.

On the 27th of January, 1809, the prisoner received an order from one Jonathan Mallett for six dozen of coffee-pot handles. The order was given to him in his character of servant to Burbidge and Co. He took the wood for the handles from their stock, and turned them on their premises, and with their machinery. He then delivered them to Mr Mallett, and received the price, which was three shillings, but he concealed the whole transaction from Burbidge and Co. and kept the whole money.

His own share of the price would have been a third, viz. one shilling.

The learned JUDGE doubted whether this was within the Act, or whether it was not rather a case of fraudulently concealing the order, and embezzling the masters' materials and using their machinery to execute it; but as the point was considered of extensive importance, he did not state his doubts to the jury. They found the prisoner guilty; but the prisoner was let out on bail, and judgment was respited till the following Assizes.

In Easter term, 29th of April, 1809, at a meeting of THE JUDGES, they all agreed that the conviction was right.

[*Not money which he has obtained by cashing master's forged cheque.*]

REGINA *v.* AITKEN.

CENTRAL CRIMINAL COURT. 1883. SESSIONS PAPERS XCVII. 336.

[Indictment for embezzling three several sums of £16. 19s. 5d., £6. 10s. 11d., and £11. 15s. 2d., the property of Sarah Berry.

The prisoner acted as book-keeper to the prosecutrix, who carried on the business of an engraver.

The prosecutrix usually paid the petty disbursements of the business out of its current earnings; but when these were not sufficient she then made the payments out of her banking account, and told Aitken of them, that he might enter them in a day-book, which also recorded the receipts. This book was made up once a week. When signing cheques she sometimes left the amounts blank, and Aitken then filled them up, and entered the amounts in the day-book. The prisoner was proved to have filled up three cheques for the sums specified in the indictment, without being authorised by his mistress to do so; though it did not clearly appear whether she had previously signed them, or whether he had forged the signatures. He cashed them; but he never entered them in the day-book; and he did not hand over the money to his mistress.]

THE RECORDER (Sir Thomas Chambers, Q.C.) considered that as the prisoner did not receive the money from the bank in his capacity of a servant, but on forged cheques, there was no embezzlement.

Not guilty.

[*It is otherwise if he obtained the money by cashing master's* stolen *cheque.*]

REGINA *v.* GALE.

CROWN CASE RESERVED. 1876. L.R. 2 Q.B.D. 141.

At the Quarter Sessions for the borough of Liverpool, James Edward Gale was tried upon an indictment consisting of two counts, in the first of which the prisoner was charged with having, on the 19th of May, 1874, when a clerk and servant to the London and Lancashire Fire Insurance Company, Limited, embezzled £400, the property of his said masters ; and in the second of which he was charged with having, when in the same capacity, and on the same day, embezzled £200, also the property of his said masters.

The evidence in support of the charge, so far as the same is material, was as follows : The said Company's head office is in Liverpool. There are branch offices at Manchester, Glasgow, and elsewhere. The prisoner was the head manager of the Company, and was their clerk and servant. In ordinary course he opened all letters and received all remittances sent to the head office, and handed the remittances to the cashier, who kept the ordinary books under the superintendence of the prisoner as manager ; and those books were from time to time submitted to, and checked by, Mr Blenham, the Company's accountant at Liverpool. It frequently happened that the managers of the provincial offices remitted cash or cheques to the prisoner as chief manager, which it was the duty of the prisoner to hand on receipt to the cashier, and in the case of cheques it was the duty of the prisoner to indorse them if they were payable to his order, and they were then paid into the Company's bankers by the cashier, and accounted for in the books.

On the 19th of May, 1874, the prisoner received on account of the Company by post from Glasgow a cheque dated the 18th of May, 1874, for £400, drawn by the manager of the Glasgow branch upon the Commercial Bank of Scotland, payable to the prisoner's order. On the same day the prisoner also received on account of the Company, by post from Manchester, a cheque for £200, dated the 19th of May, 1874, drawn by the manager of the Manchester branch upon the Manchester and County Bank, Limited, payable to the prisoner's order.

The prisoner did not hand over either of these cheques to the cashier, or inform him or anyone else of their receipt, except that he acknowledged the receipt of them to the Glasgow and Manchester managers respectively.

On the same day, the 19th of May, the prisoner indorsed and cashed both the cheques through private friends of his own, who gave him the cash and paid the cheques into their own banks. Later in the day, the prisoner paid £600 in bank notes and gold, which was probably the produce of the cheques, to the cashier of the Company, saying that he wished it to go against his salary, which was then overdrawn to that amount. The cashier, supposing the money to be the prisoner's own, received it for him, and handed back to the prisoner I. O. U.s for the amount which he had received from the prisoner in respect of the overdraft

The prisoner never accounted for either the cheques or the money.

At the close of the case for the prosecution, counsel for the prisoner submitted that the prisoner could not be properly convicted of embezzling either of the sums charged in the indictment, inasmuch as the cheques were sent to the prisoner payable to his order and required his indorsement, and the prisoner was entitled to cash the cheques and receive the cash which was paid to him in respect of them ; and, therefore, there was no embezzlement by him of the said sums or either of them. It was also submitted that there was no embezzlement, because the identical money received for the cheques was paid to the cashier, although it was so paid as the prisoner's own money, and in discharge of so much of his own overdraft....

The jury convicted the prisoner. The question for the Court was whether there was evidence of embezzlement which the Recorder was justified in leaving to the jury.

Torr, for prisoner....Secondly, there is no embezzlement unless the money be received "for, or in the name of, or on account of, the master." That must at least mean that the servant purports to receive it on account of the master; which was not so here. Thirdly, there must be an intention to deprive the master of the money permanently. Here the prisoner paid it over to the cashier.

COCKBURN, C.J....The difficulty arises from the fact that, instead of cashing the cheques at the bank, the prisoner obtained money for them from friends of his own, who, having given him the money, paid the cheques to their own bankers. Now, the prisoner is liable under the statute if he received the money on account of his masters. Mr Torr ingeniously suggests that he cannot have done so, because the persons who gave him the money knew nothing of his masters. But the question is not whether those persons paid on account of his masters, but whether he received on account of his masters. And he did so because it was his duty to pay over the proceeds at once, in whichever way he received them. It is the same case as if, being on his way to cash the cheques, he had met a friend in the street who cashed them for him, to save him the trouble of going to the bank. The prisoner, then, having received the money on account of his masters, and having dealt with it as he did, with the intention of appropriating it to his own use, was rightly convicted of embezzlement.

The other four Judges concurred.

Conviction affirmed.

[*And it must not be* from his master, *directly or indirectly, that he has received it.*]

[*Receipt through fellow-servant from* master.]

REX *v.* MURRAY.

CROWN CASE RESERVED. 1830.   1 MOODY 276.

The prisoner was tried before T. DENMAN, Esq., Common Serjeant, at the Old Bailey Sessions in June 1830.

The indictment stated that the prisoner, being a clerk in the employ of A., did, by virtue of such employment, receive and take into his possession the sum of £3 for and on account of the said master, and did afterwards fraudulently and feloniously embezzle 10s., part of the sum above mentioned; and further stated that the prisoner did feloniously steal, take, and carry away from the said A. the said sum of 10s. of the moneys of the said A. The prisoner was proved to be a clerk in the employ of A.; he received from another clerk £3 of A.'s money that he might pay (among other things) for inserting an advertisement in the Gazette. The prisoner paid 10s. for the insertion; and charged A. 20s. for the same, fraudulently keeping back the difference, which he converted to his own use.

The prisoner's counsel contended that this evidence did not support the indictment.

The learned Common Serjeant directed the jury to find the prisoner guilty, if they thought the evidence proved the facts above set forth, which they did; and he therefore now respectfully requested the opinion of the learned Judges, whether the facts sustained the indictment.

At a meeting of the Judges after Trinity term, 1830, at which all the learned Judges were present, this case was considered. They thought the case not within the statute, because A. had had possession of the money by the hands of his other clerk; and that the conviction was therefore wrong.

[*Receipt through fellow-servant from* stranger.]

REGINA *v.* MASTERS.

CROWN CASE RESERVED.   1848.   1 DENISON 332.

Orlando Masters, a clerk in the employment of William Holliday, was tried at the Michaelmas Quarter Sessions, A.D. 1848, for the borough of Birmingham, on an indictment charging him with embezzling three sums of money received by him for and on account of his master, the prosecutor.

It appeared in evidence, that the course of business adopted by the house was for the customers to pay moneys into the hands of certain persons, who paid them over to a superintendent; he accounted with the prisoner, and paid over such moneys to him; and the prisoner, in his turn, accounted with cashiers, and paid over the moneys to them; he having no other duty to perform with respect to such moneys than to keep an account which might act as a check on the superintendent and the cashiers, their accounts being in like manner checks upon him. These four parties to the receipt of the moneys were all servants of the prosecutor.

With respect to the three sums in question, it was proved that they passed in due course from the customers, through the hands of the immediate receivers and the superintendent, to the prisoner; who wilfully and fraudulently retained them.

On behalf of the prisoner it was objected, on the authority of *Rex* v. *Murray* (*supra*, p. 318), that the moneys having, before they reached the prisoner, been in the possession of the prosecutor's servants, did in law pass to the prisoner from his master; and that consequently the charge of embezzlement could not be sustained

For the Crown it was answered, that the prisoner having intercepted the moneys in their appointed course of progress to the master, this case was not governed by that of *Rex* v. *Murray*, where the prior possession of the master having been as complete as it was intended to be, the money might reasonably be considered as passing from the master to the prisoner, whereas, in the present case, it was in course of passage through the prisoner to the master.

The Recorder left the case to the jury, reserving the point.

The prisoner was convicted and sentenced to twelve months' imprisonment, with hard labour.

This case was argued before Pollock, C.B., Patteson, J., Maule, J., Cresswell, J., Erle, J., on the 11th of November, 1848, at the first sitting of the Court created by stat. 11 and 12 Vict. c. 78.

Miller, for the prisoner. It seems clear that there was no tortious taking by the prisoner: his taking was lawful in the first instance. His duty was to receive the money and pass it on to his master.

*   *   *   *   *

POLLOCK, C.B. The Court are unanimously of opinion that no further argument is necessary. This case is quite different from that of *Rex* v. *Murray*. Because there the master had had possession of the money by the hands of another servant; and when it was given to the prisoner by that servant to be paid away on account of the master, it must be deemed in law to have been so given to the prisoner by his master: the fraudulent appropriation of it, being thus a tortious taking in the first instance, was not embezzlement but larceny. But here the money never reached the master at all: it was stopped by the prisoner on its way to him. The original taking was lawful, and, therefore, the fraudulent appropriation was embezzlement.

[*And he must not yet have delivered it over to his master.*]

REX *v.* SULLENS.

CROWN CASE RESERVED. 1826.   1 MOODY 129.

[Indictment at Essex Assizes. The first count charged the prisoner with larceny of a £5 note; the second, with larceny of £5 worth of silver coin.]

It appeared in evidence that Thomas Nevill, the prisoner's master, gave him a £5 country note, to get change, on the said 25th of September; that he got change, all in silver, and on his obtaining the change he said it was for his master, and that his master sent him. The prisoner never returned.

The jury found the prisoner not guilty on the first count, but guilty on the second count.

In Easter term, 1826, THE JUDGES met and considered this case, and held that the conviction was wrong; because, as the master never had possession of the change, except by the hands of the prisoner, he was only amenable for Embezzlement.

[*No* embezzlement *of things which prisoner had already delivered to his master.*]

REGINA *v.* HAYWARD.

SHREWSBURY ASSIZES. 1844. 1 CARRINGTON AND KIRWAN 518.

[The indictment contained a count for embezzlement of forty pounds weight of straw, and a further count for the larceny of the same.]

It was proved that, previously to the 24th of July, 1844, Allen Boyd, the prosecutor, had ordered some straw of Messrs Morris, and was to send for it; and that, on the 24th of July, he sent the prisoner (whom he then employed at 20*d.* a day) to Messrs Morris's to fetch it. The straw was then delivered by Mr John Morris to the prisoner, who took it into the prosecutor's court-yard, and put it down at the stable-door; and the prisoner then went to the prosecutor to ask him to send some one to open the hay-loft, which was over the stable, that the straw might be put in. The prosecutor sent his niece, who opened the hay-loft, and saw the prisoner put a part of the straw into the hay-loft, and take the rest away in a direction towards the Plough public-house at Whitchurch; where it was proved that the prisoner sold it.

TINDAL, C.J. (in summing up). If the prisoner took away this straw to the public-house with a felonious intent, it was a stealing of it from his master, Allen Boyd. His putting the whole quantity of straw at the stable-door, on his master's premises, was a delivery of it to his master; and his taking a part of it away afterwards, if it was done with a felonious intent, would be a larceny of the property of his master, and not an embezzlement. The only question, therefore, is, whether you think there was a felonious intent.

[EDITOR'S NOTE. The weight being so light, Hayward doubtless took it on his back. Had he taken it home in a vehicle *belonging to his master*, it would have been larcenable even during the journey.]

K. 21

CHAPTER III.   PROOF OF APPROPRIATION.

[*What may suffice.*]

[See REGINA *v.* GALE, *supra*, p. 316.]

REX *v.* SARAH WILLIAMS.

PEMBROKE ASSIZES.   1836.   7 CARRINGTON AND PAYNE 338.

Embezzlement.   The prisoner was indicted for embezzling the money of her master Nathaniel Phillips.   It appeared that the prisoner, who was a servant of Mr Phillips, was sent by his daughter to receive rent which was due from Mr Gwynne Harries, one of Mr Phillips's tenants; and that the prisoner on having received the rent went off to Ireland, and never returned to her master's service.

COLERIDGE, J. (in summing up).   I think that the circumstance of the prisoner having quitted her place, and gone off to Ireland, is evidence from which you may infer that she intended to appropriate the money; and if you think that she did so intend, she is guilty of embezzlement.

Verdict, Guilty.

[*What may not suffice.*]

REX *v.* JONES.

GLOUCESTER ASSIZES.   1837.   7 CARRINGTON AND PAYNE 833

Embezzlement.   The prisoner was indicted for embezzling a sum of £6. 13*s.* 7*d.*, received on account of George Bettis, his employer, from George Linsley Walker.   There was another count as to a sum of £19. 4*s.*, received from Benjamin Smith.

It appeared that Mr Bettis was a slate merchant at Carnarvon, who, by means of the prisoner as his clerk, carried on the slate trade at a wharf at Gloucester.   It further appeared that the course of business was for the prisoner to sell the slates, and to convey them to the customers in his own boats, as Mr Bettis had no boats; the prisoner being also a coal merchant on his own account. It was proved that these sums had been received by the prisoner; but it further appeared that the prosecutor and prisoner had had no adjustment of accounts for two years, and that, on Mr Bettis calling for the prisoner's books, he could not find these sums entered. It was stated by Mr Bettis that he had never specifically asked the prisoner to account for either of these two sums, and that the accounts of the prisoner for these two years amounted to ten or twelve thousand pounds.

BOLLAND, B. Mr Francillon, you can make nothing of this case; there is not a felonious conversion. I will take it that the prisoner put the money into his own pocket, and has made no entry; that is not sufficient. Had he denied the receipt of the money, the case might have been different. If the mere fact of not entering a sum was enough to support an indictment for embezzlement, every clerk who, through carelessness, omitted an entry, would be liable to be convicted of felony. The prisoner must be acquitted.

Verdict, Not guilty.

SECTION XII.

FALSE PRETENCES.

[By section 88 of the Larceny Act, 1861 (24 and 25 Vict. c. 96), "Whosoever shall, by any false pretence, obtain from any other person any chattel, money, or valuable security, with intent to defraud, shall be guilty of a misdemeanor."]

CHAPTER I. THE MERE PRETENCE.

[It must be a representation about an existing fact, not about some merely future event.]

REGINA v. LEE.

CROWN CASE RESERVED.   1863.   LEIGH AND CAVE 309.

[The prisoner was indicted at the Devonshire Quarter Sessions for obtaining £10 by the false pretence that he (the said Lewis Lee) had to

21—2

pay his rent to the squire, meaning thereby Richard Sommers Gard, on the first of March then next, but as that day was Sunday he had to pay the said rent on the Monday then following; and that he (the said Lewis Lee) wanted ten pounds to make up his said rent.

The prosecutor proved that the prisoner had said to him, "I am going to pay" (or "I've got to pay") "my rent to the squire on the first of March; but as that is Sunday, I am going to pay it the next day. Will you advance ten pounds for your father-in-law on the rent of the flax field?" The rent was in truth due on March 1.

Prosecutor thereupon lent him £10 on his promissory note. Prisoner did not say that he required the sum of £10 to make up his rent; but the prosecutor believed that he wanted the money for that purpose; and he would have refused to lend it him but for his statement that he was going to pay his rent. The jury found the prisoner guilty, and stated their opinion that the prisoner's statement that he was going to pay his rent on the Monday was a false pretence, and that the money was advanced on the credit of that false pretence.

The Court reserved the question as to whether the prisoner's statement as shewn in evidence amounted to an indictable false pretence.]

COCKBURN, C.J. We are all agreed that the case proved against the prisoner will not warrant the conviction. There is no false pretence of any existing fact. The pretence alleged is that he was going to pay his rent, while in fact he had no intention of paying it but meant to appropriate the money to his own purposes. That is not a false pretence of an existing fact[1].

Conviction quashed.

[Pretences *or* Promises.]

REGINA *v.* JENNISON.

CROWN CASE RESERVED. 1862.   LEIGH AND CAVE 157.

The following case was reserved by COCKBURN, C.J.

John Jennison was indicted and tried before me, at the last Assizes for the county of Derby, for obtaining £8 of one Ann Hayes by false pretences.

---

[1] Mr C. S. Greaves, Q.C., the learned editor of Russell on Crimes (n. 16 *n.*), points out the difference between the representation alleged in this indictment, and a representation that "rent is due." Cf. the report of this case in 9 Cox 304.

The prisoner, who had a wife living, had represented himself to the prosecutrix, who was a single woman in service, as an unmarried man ; and, pretending that he was about to marry her, induced her to hand over to him a sum of £8 out of her wages received on leaving her service; representing that he would go to Liverpool, and with the money furnish a house for them to live in, and that having done so he would return and marry her. Having obtained the money, the prisoner went away, and never returned.

The prosecutrix stated that she had been induced to part with her money on the faith of the representations of the prisoner that he was a single man; that he would furnish a house with the money; and would then marry her.

There was no doubt that these representations were false, and that, morally, the money had been obtained by false pretences. But it was contended on the part of the prisoner that, as the prosecutrix had been induced to part with her money by the joint operation of the three representations made by the prisoner—that he was unmarried ; that he would furnish a house with the money ; and that he would then marry her,—and as only the first of these pretences had reference to a present existing fact, while the others related to things to be done in futuro, the indictment could not be maintained.

I reserved the point, and, the prisoner having been convicted, have now to request the decision of the Court upon the question.

This case was considered, on the 26th of April, 1862, by ERLE, C.J., MARTIN, B., CHANNELL, B., BLACKBURN, J., and KEATING, J.

No counsel appeared on either side.

ERLE, C.J. In this case we are all of opinion that the prisoner was properly convicted. He was indicted for obtaining money by false pretences, the false pretences being, that he was an unmarried man, that he would marry the prosecutrix, and that with the money she was to give him he would furnish a house for them to live in. Now, it is clear that a false promise cannot be the subject of an indictment for obtaining money by false pretences. Here, however, we have the pretence that he was an unmarried man. This was false in fact, and was essential, for without it he would not have obtained the money. Then this false fact by which the money is obtained will sustain the indictment, although it is united with two false promises, neither of which alone would have supported the conviction.

Conviction affirmed.

[Can a mere state of mind (e.g. Intention) be a sufficient Fact?]

THE QUEEN v. GORDON.

CROWN CASE RESERVED.   1889.   L.R. 23 Q.B.D. 354.

[The prisoner, Isaac Gordon (the well-known money-lender), was tried before Lord COLERIDGE, C.J., at Worcester Assizes, for obtaining money by false pretences, on an indictment containing five counts.] The charges were,—first, on June 5, 1889, with intent to defraud, obtaining from Richard Summers Brown 10s. 6d. by false pretences that he was prepared to advance £100 to him "at lower interest than was charged to others," and that all advances were repayable by easy instalments, to suit applicants; second count, on January 9, 1889, with like intent, obtaining from Richard Summers Brown and Richard Brown a promissory note for £100 by false pretences "that he was prepared to pay them or one of them by way of loan £100"; third count, same date, with like intent, obtaining from them the said note for £100 by false pretences "that a document then presented for signature was a mere receipt for moneys advanced"; fourth count, same date, with like intent, inducing them to make said promissory note for £100 by false pretence "that he was prepared to pay to them or one of them £100"; fifth count, same date, with like intent, fraudulently inducing them to execute said note for £100 by false pretence "that he had agreed with said Richard Summers Brown to lend and was ready to pay over £100."...

The Lord Chief Justice, after setting out the evidence in the case, stated. "I told the jury that if they were of opinion that the prisoner obtained the promissory note for £100 from the two Browns, or either of them, by falsely pretending to them that he was ready to pay and would then pay to them, or one of them, £100 on their signing the note, they might find him guilty. I explained to them that a false pretence must be the representation of an existing fact untrue in fact, false to the knowledge of the person making it, and that the money or other subject-matter must be obtained or procured by means of it. I had great doubts as to the validity of counts 1, 2, and 4, and I withdrew count 3 from their consideration, as I thought it bad in law, and that there was no evidence of it, in fact. I was not free from doubt as to count 5; and I directed the jury to find separately on each count. They found the prisoner guilty on counts 1, 2, 4, and 5, and not guilty on count 3.

"I have to request the opinion of the Court of Criminal Appeal whether the conviction upon all or any of the four counts on which a verdict of guilty was entered can be sustained. If it can be sustained on any of those counts the conviction is to be affirmed ; if not it is to be quashed."

Lockwood, Q.C. (Harington, with him), for the defendant.

[THE COURT intimated that the argument might be limited to the fourth count.]

First, no false pretence of an existing fact is alleged in the fourth count. The meaning of it is only that the defendant said, "If you will give me a promissory note for £100 I will lend you £100"—that is a mere promise to do something in the future, such as would be in the case of a purchaser saying to a tradesman, "If you will send goods to my house I will pay for them."

[WILLS, J. Suppose the defendant said, "I have the intention of advancing £100," and he, in fact, had no intention of the kind.]

That would not be a sufficient false pretence. It would be impossible to prove that his intention was not that stated at the time, although it might have been changed afterwards. The defendant was undoubtedly in a position and able to advance £100, and therefore literally "was prepared to do so."...

WILLS, J. I am glad that it is possible to support the conviction without venturing on the somewhat dangerous ground to which I referred in the course of the argument, and rendering it necessary to distinguish between a promise to do something, and a statement of intention. I find it difficult to see why an allegation as to the present existence of a state of mind *may* not be under some circumstances as much an allegation of an existing fact as an allegation with respect to anything else. For example, suppose that by an arrangement for the settlement of litigation, a man was to pay a sum of money ; and when the time came he said : "I shall not pay until I know that A. has the intention of acceding to this arrangement. I do not insist upon having his promise. I shall be content if I know what his present intention is. Otherwise I shall not pay." Suppose B., who was to get the money, then told him that A. had that intention, and he believed B. and paid the money upon the faith of B.'s assurance; and all the while B. knew that A.'s intention was exactly the contrary to what he had stated. I should have thought that the allegation as to A.'s intention was one of an existing fact, capable of supporting an indictment for obtaining money by false pretences. But I am very sensible that in such an inquiry there must always be a danger of confounding intention with a representation or a promise as to something future ;

and I am very glad that it is possible, for the reasons given by my
Lord, to affirm this conviction without approaching any such debate-
able ground.

*   *   *   *   *

[The other FOUR JUDGES concurred.]

Conviction affirmed.

[EDITOR'S NOTE. In *Rex* v. *Bancroft* (A.D. 1909, 26 T. L. B. 10), and in later
cases, the Court of Criminal Appeal has favoured the doctrine that a statement of
Intention *is* a statement of existing Fact.]

[*Statements as to matters of* mere opinion (*e.g. expressions of indefinite
praise*) *do not amount to Representations of* Fact.]

REGINA *v.* JOHN BRYAN.

CROWN CASE RESERVED.   1857.   DEARSLY AND BELL 265.

The following case was reserved and stated for the consideration
and decision of the Court of Criminal Appeal by the Recorder of
London.

John Bryan was tried for obtaining money by false pretences.

There were several false pretences charged in the different counts of
the indictment, to which, as he was not found guilty of them by the
jury, it is not necessary to refer. But the following pretences were
among others charged. That certain spoons produced by the prisoner
were of the best quality; that they were equal to Elkington's A (meaning spoons and forks made by Messrs Elkington, and stamped by them
with the letter A); that the foundation was of the best material; and
that they had as much silver upon them as Elkington's A. The prosecutors were pawnbrokers; and the false pretences were made use of by
the prisoner for the purpose of procuring advances of money on the
spoons in question, offered by the prisoner by way of pledge; and he
thereby obtained the moneys mentioned in the indictment by way of
such advances. The goods were of inferior quality to that represented
by the prisoner; and the prosecutors said that, had they known the real
quality, they would not have advanced money upon the goods at any
price. They moreover admitted that it was the declaration of the
prisoner as to the quality of the goods, and nothing else, which induced
them to make the said advances. The moneys advanced exceeded the

value of the spoons. The jury found the prisoner guilty of fraudulently representing that the goods had as much silver on them as Elkington's A, and that the foundations were of the best material, knowing that to be untrue; and that in consequence of that he obtained the moneys mentioned in the indictment. The prisoner's counsel claimed to have the verdict entered as a verdict of Not Guilty, which was resisted by the counsel for the prosecution; and, entertaining doubts upon the question, I directed a verdict of Guilty to be entered, in order that the judgment of the Court for the Consideration of Crown Cases might be taken in the matter.

*   *   *   *   *

G. Francis, for the Crown. This is in fact a misrepresentation of quantity, and substantially the same as *Reg.* v. *Sherwood.* (D. and B. 251.)

LORD CAMPBELL, C.J. Of the quantity of the silver?

G. Francis. Yes. Elkington's A is an article of ascertained manufacture; and by representing the spoons to be equal to Elkington's A, the prisoner represented that they were covered with the same quantity of silver as Elkington's spoons would be covered with. The money was therefore obtained by a false representation that there was a greater weight of silver than there really was, and therefore there was a false pretence of an existing fact within the statute. Secondly, if the representation was of quality merely, it is within the statute; the money was obtained by the representation, and the jury have found the representation was made with intent to defraud.

*   *   *   *   *

POLLOCK, C.B. There may be considerable difficulty in laying down any general rule which shall be applicable to each particular case; but I continue to think that the statute[1] was not meant to apply to the ordinary commercial dealings between buyer and seller; still I am not prepared to lay down the doctrine in an abstract form, because I am clearly of opinion that there might be many cases of buying and selling to which the statute would apply—cases which are not substantially the ordinary commercial dealings between man and man. I think if a tradesman or a merchant were to concoct an article of merchandize expressly for the purpose of deceit, and were to sell it as and for something very different even in quality from what it was, the statute would apply. So, if a mart were opened, or a shop in a public street, with a view of defrauding the public, and puffing away articles calculated to catch the eye but which really possessed no value, there, I think, the statute would apply. But I think the statute does not apply to the

[1] 7 and 8 Geo. IV. c. 29, s. 53; almost identical with 24 and 25 Vict. c. 96, s. 88.

ordinary commercial transactions between man and man ; and certainly, as has been observed by the Lord Chief Justice, if it applies to the seller it equally applies to the purchaser, although it is not very likely that cases of that sort would arise.   It would be very inconvenient to lay down a principle that would prevent a man from endeavouring to get the article cheap which he was bargaining for, so that if he was endeavouring to get it under the value he might be indicted for obtaining it for less than its value.   And there is this to be observed, that if the successfully obtaining your object, either in getting goods or money, is an indictable offence, any attempt or step towards it is an indictable offence as a misdemeanor ; because any attempt or any progress towards the completion of the offence would be the subject of an indictment. And then it would follow from that, that a man could not go into a broker's shop and cheapen an article but he would subject himself to an indictment for misdemeanor in endeavouring to get the article under false pretences.   For these reasons I think it may be fairly laid down that any exaggeration or depreciation in the ordinary course of dealings between buyer and seller during the progress of a bargain is not the subject of a criminal prosecution.   I think this case falls within that proposition, and I therefore think this conviction cannot be supported.

*   *   *   *   *

ERLE, J.   I am also of opinion that this conviction cannot be sustained; not on the ground that the falsehood took place in the course of a contract of sale or pawning, but on the ground that the falsehood is not of that description which was intended by the legislature.   It is a misrepresentation of what is more a matter of opinion than a definite matter of fact

No doubt it is difficult to draw the line between the substance of the contract and the praise of an article in respect of a matter of opinion ; still it must be done.   The present case appears to me not to support a conviction, upon the ground that there is no affirmation of a definite triable fact in saying the goods were equal to Elkington's A ; but the affirmation is of what is mere matter of opinion, and falls within the category of untrue praise in the course of a contract of sale where the vendee has in substance the article contracted for, namely, plated spoons.

*   *   *   *   *

[Judgments were delivered by all the twelve Judges.   Ten of them held that the conviction was wrong; Willes, J., dissented; and Bramwell, B., expressed a doubt.]

[*What is matter of* Fact *and not of* Opinion.]

THE QUEEN *v.* ARDLEY.

CROWN CASE RESERVED.   1871.   L.R. 1 C.C.R. 301.

Case reserved by the learned Chairman of the Court of Quarter Sessions for the county Palatine of Durham.

John Ardley was tried before me on the 2nd of January, 1871, for obtaining £5 and an albert chain of the value of 7*s.* 6*d.* by false pretences....

The prisoner went into the shop of the prosecutor, who was a watchmaker and jeweller; and stated that he was a draper, and was £5 short of the money required to make up a bill, and asked the prosecutor to buy an albert chain which he (the prisoner) was then wearing. The prisoner said, "It is 15-carat fine gold, and you will see it stamped on every link. It was made for me, and I paid nine guineas for it. The maker told me it was worth five pounds to sell as old gold."

The prosecutor bought the chain, relying as he said, on prisoner's statement, but also examining the chain; and paid £5 for it, and gave also to the prisoner in part payment a gold albert chain valued at 7*s.* 6*d.*

The prisoner's chain was marked "15-carat" on every link....It was proved that 15-carat was a Hall mark used in certain towns of England, and placed on certain articles made of gold of that quality; and that chains when assayed are generally found to be 1 grain less than the mark—exceptionally 2 grains.

The chain bought by the prosecutor was assayed and found to be of a quality a trifle better than 6-carat gold, and of the value in gold of £2. 2*s.* 9*d.*....There were no drapery goods or anything connected with such trade found on the prisoner....

I was asked by counsel for the prisoner to stop the case on the authority of *The Queen* v. *Bryan* (*supra*, p. 328). This I declined to do and left the case to the jury; who found the prisoner guilty, and in answer to me said they found that the prisoner knew he was falsely representing the quality of the chain as 15-carat gold.

The question for the opinion of this honourable Court is, whether or not the prisoner was rightly convicted of obtaining money under false pretences.

BOVILL, C.J....Looking at the whole evidence the jury found the prisoner guilty; and there is sufficient ground on which the finding of the jury may be supported and the conviction sustained.

But the jury have further found that the prisoner, when he represented the chain to be 15-carat gold, knew this representation to be false. And the question whether the conviction can be supported upon that finding alone stands upon a somewhat different footing. The cases have drawn nice distinctions between matters of fact and matters of opinion, statements of specific facts and mere exaggerated praise. It is difficult for us, sitting here as a Court, to determine conclusively what is fact and what is opinion, what is a specific statement and what exaggerated praise. These are questions for the jury to decide. And the prisoner has this additional security, that the jury have to consider not only whether the statements made are statements of fact, but also whether they are made with the intention to defraud..

The statement here made is not in form an expression of opinion or mere praise. It is a distinct statement, accompanied by other circumstances, that the chain was 15-carat gold. That statement was untrue, was known to be untrue, and was made with intent to defraud. How does that differ from the case of a man who makes a chain of one material and fraudulently represents it to be of another? Therefore, whether we look at the whole of the evidence, or only at that which goes to the quality of the chain, the conviction is good. The case differs from *Reg.* v. *Bryan*[1], because here there was a statement as to a specific fact within the actual knowledge of the prisoner, namely, the proportion of pure gold in the chain.

WILLES, J. I am of the same opinion. In *Reg.* v. *Bryan*[1] Erle, J., and several other judges said that if the prisoner had said that the spoons were Elkington's A., instead of that they were equal to Elkington's A., the conviction would have been good. Here the prisoner stated that the chain was 15-carat gold.

Conviction affirmed.

[EDITOR'S NOTE. A contrast, analogous to that presented by the two preceding cases, may be obtained by comparing *Reg.* v. *Crab* (11 Cox 85) with *Reg.* v. *Williamson* (11 Cox 328); the former of which decides that false representations as to the successfulness of a business establishment are indictable if there was no establishment at all, whilst the latter shews that they *may* be mere unindictable exaggerations of praise if the establishment did actually exist.]

---

[1] Dearsly and Bell, C. C. 265, *supra*, p. 328.

[*The representation may be made by mere silent conduct.*]

REX *v.* BARNARD.

OXFORD ASSIZES.   1837.   7 CARRINGTON AND PAYNE 784.

False pretences. The indictment charged that the prisoner falsely pretended that he was an undergraduate of the university of Oxford, and a commoner of Magdalen College ; by means of which he obtained a pair of boot-straps from John Samuel Vincent.

It appeared that Mr Vincent was a boot-maker, carrying on business in High Street, Oxford; and that the prisoner came there, wearing a commoner's cap and gown, and ordered boots, which were not supplied him, and straps, which were sent to him. He stated he belonged to Magdalen College.

It was proved by one of the butlers of Magdalen College that the prisoner did not belong to that college, and that there are no commoners at Magdalen College.

BOLLAND, B. (in summing up). If nothing had passed in words, I should have laid down that the fact of the prisoner's appearing in the cap and gown would have been pregnant evidence from which a jury should infer that he pretended he was a member of the university; and if so, would have been a sufficient false pretence to satisfy the statute. It clearly is so, by analogy to the cases in which offering in payment the notes of a bank which has failed, knowing them to be so, has been held to be a false pretence without any words being used.

[*Or by words which do not* express *but only* imply *it.*]

THE QUEEN *v.* COOPER.

CROWN CASE RESERVED.   1877.   L.R. 2 Q.B.D. 510.

Case stated by the chairman of the Quarter Sessions for the West Riding of Yorkshire, holden at Wakefield.

The indictment charged that William Cooper did falsely pretend to one John Gellatly that he the said William Cooper then was a dealer in potatoes, and as such dealer in potatoes then was in a large way of business, and that he then was in a position to do a good trade

in potatoes, and that he then was able to pay for large quantities
of potatoes as and when the same might be delivered to him; by means
of which said false pretences the said William Cooper did then unlawfully obtain from the said John Gellatly eight tons fifteen hundred-
weights and two quarters of potatoes of the goods and chattels of the
said John Gellatly, with intent thereby then to defraud. The indictment then negatived the pretences.

In support of the prosecution the following letter, addressed to
John Gellatly, was given in evidence:—

"Sheffield, Jan. 17th, 1876.

"Dear Sir,—Please send me one truck of regents and one truck of
rocks as samples, at your prices named in your letter; let them be good
quality, then I am sure a good trade will be done for both of us.
I will remit you the cash on arrival of goods and invoice. Yours truly,

William Cooper."

"P.S.—I may say if you use me well I shall be a good customer.
An answer will oblige saying when they are put on."

It was amply proved in evidence that the prisoner when he ordered
the regents and rocks (which are kinds of potatoes) had no intention of
paying for them; that he held from time to time a stall in the public
market for which he paid by the day, and also dealt as a huckster,
carrying about fruit in a small cart drawn by a donkey; and several of
the witnesses, though very well acquainted with him and his trade,
were ignorant of his dealing in potatoes.

The potatoes were sold by the prisoner in part at the railway
station, at a less cost than they would have stood to him; and as to the
other part, when, on receipt of a telegram from the seller, inquiries were
made by the railway people, the prisoner, who was at the station filling
his sacks, left the potatoes and his sacks, and could not be heard of for
several weeks though the police were in active search of him.

It was contended by the prosecution that the letter or order of
the prisoner amounted to a representation that he was a person trading
in a considerable way, and that the order given was on a scale consistent with his ordinary transactions; whereas his ordinary dealings
were on a very small scale, to which the large order for potatoes was
disproportionate; and that consequently the prisoner had misrepre-
sented his real character and position, and thereby had made the false
pretence alleged in the indictment.

The falsehood of the pretence, supposing this construction to be
correct, being amply proved by the evidence, I left the case to the jury,
holding that the contention of the prosecution was consistent with law;

but leaving it to them, that if they thought the letter did not prove
the false pretence as alleged in the indictment the prisoner should be
acquitted. The jury convicted; and the prisoner was admitted to bail
to appear to receive sentence at the next Quarter Sessions.

The question was whether upon the facts proved the defendant was
properly convicted upon this indictment.

S. Tennant, for the prisoner. The letter is perfectly consistent
with the position of the writer being that of a man who has just
begun, or who is just about to begin, to trade largely in potatoes.
The expression "as samples" in the letter is consistent with this view.
The letter does not contain any statement as to the writer's past
position, or as to his then position, but merely statements of what the
writer intends or hopes to do in the future. Even if the letter is
capable of the interpretation sought on the part of the prosecution
to be placed upon it, yet it is at least as capable of an innocent inter
pretation. It contains no express statement of existing facts, and it
does not, by necessary implication, contain any such statement.

[LUSH, J. I do not think the inference need be a "necessary"
inference, it must be a natural and reasonable inference.]

A promise to pay has never been held to imply a statement of
present ability to pay, and the letter contains no statement of ability to
pay, unless it is to be inferred from the words "I will remit you cash
on arrival of goods and invoice."...

*   *   *   *   *

LUSH, J. The question for our consideration is, was there evidence
on which the jury could reasonably convict the prisoner of the offence
charged? The pretences charged are that "he then was a dealer in
potatoes, and as such dealer in potatoes then was in a large way of business"; that he "then was in a position to do a good trade in potatoes";
and that he "then was able to pay for large quantities of potatoes as and
when the same might be delivered to him." The pretence, in order to
justify a conviction, must be of existing facts. It may be made either by
words or by acts. It is sufficient if it can be reasonably and naturally
inferred from the words, or from the acts, in order to raise a question
for the decision of the jury. It is not necessary that the words or
that the acts should be capable, only, of the meaning charged by the
indictment. If the words in the letter written by the prisoner in the
present case were intended to mean, and are fairly capable of meaning,
that which is charged, and if they were so understood, then there was
as much a pretence as though the letter had contained a definition of
their meaning. The words here are capable of supporting the pretences charged. Without further explanation this large quantity is

asked for as a sample; and then the prisoner says he will remit, and talks of the trade to be done. The letter is fairly capable of representing and conveying to the mind of the reader that the defendant was a man dealing largely, and in a position to do a good trade and remit at once on delivery. The jury have adopted this construction, and have found that the prosecutor did so read the letter, and that the prisoner intended it to be so read. I therefore think the conviction right.

* * * *

Four other Judges concurred.

Conviction affirmed.

[See also REGINA *v.* CLOSS, *supra*, p. 184.]

[*What representations are implied in* drawing a cheque.]

THE QUEEN *v.* HAZELTON.

CROWN CASE RESERVED. 1874. L.R. 2 C.C.C.R. 134.

Case stated by the common serjeant of London.

At the Central Criminal Court, the prisoner was tried on an indictment for obtaining goods by false pretences with regard to cheques for £5 and £8. 8s. given in payment for those goods. It was proved in evidence that the prisoner opened an account at the Birkbeck Bank on the 30th of June, 1873, with a payment to his credit of £22. 10s., and had a cheque book given to him for his use, containing fifty blank cheques. That on the 9th of December, 1873, the balance in his favour in the Birkbeck Bank was five shillings and three pence; and the account remained unaltered up to the 27th of June, 1874, when he applied to the Birkbeck Bank for a new cheque book, which they refused; and then he withdrew 5s. He could have had the 3d. That thirty-three of his cheques were honoured and about seventeen refused by the Birkbeck Bank. That he would not have been allowed to overdraw his account at the Birkbeck Bank.

Evidence was given that in April, 1874, the prisoner drew the two cheques on the Birkbeck Bank for £5 and £8. 8s., and gave them in payment for goods bought by him (which goods he pawned immediately afterwards). On presentation at the Bank, the cheques were dishonoured; his balance in the bank at that time being only 5s. 3d.

The common serjeant doubted whether, in point of law, a man who gives a cheque in payment, under the circumstances before mentioned, does by the mere fact of giving the cheque, without saying more than that he wishes to pay ready money, make either of the false pretences alleged in the indictment, viz.:—1. That he then has money to the amount of the cheque in the bank upon which it is drawn. 2. That he then has authority to draw upon the bank for that sum. 3. That the cheque which he gives is a good and valid order for the payment of its amount. 4. That he then has a banking account with the bank upon which his cheque is drawn and where his account is overdrawn. He summed up the case to the jury; and they found that the prisoner did not intend, when he gave the respective cheques mentioned in the indictment, to meet them, and that he intended to defraud. A verdict of "guilty" was thereupon recorded; and the learned common serjeant reserved for the opinion of this Court the question, whether there was any evidence to go to the jury of the prisoner having made any of the false pretences mentioned in the indictment. If there was, the conviction was to be confirmed. If there was not, it was to be reversed.

KELLY, C.B. There are two questions in this case; first, whether the prisoner has expressly or impliedly made a representation upon the faith of which goods have been obtained; and, secondly, whether that representation was false.

Several representations are laid in the indictment, and are proposed to us in the case as arising from the conduct of the prisoner in the present case. It is suggested that a person acting as the prisoner did represents that he then has money, to the amount of the cheque which he tenders, in the bank upon which it is drawn. If this had been the only representation suggested there would have been great difficulty in upholding the conviction. The giving of a cheque does not necessarily imply any such representation. Not only may a banking account be kept under a guarantee upon the express terms that it may be overdrawn, but, without any such arrangement, a person of position may often overdraw an account in perfect good faith and with the tacit sanction of his bankers.

Then it is suggested that the conduct of the prisoner amounted to a representation that he had authority to draw upon the bank for the sum for which he drew. I think that representation does arise. I do not see how it can but be implied.

But as to the third representation there can be no doubt, namely, that the cheque is a good and valid order for the payment of its amount. The case which has been cited, *Reg. v. Parker*[1], is

---

[1] 7 C. and P. 829; 2 Moo. Cr. C. 1.   34 L. J. (M.C.) 50.

express upon the point; and that the goods were obtained upon the faith of the representation admits of no question.

It remains to consider whether the representation made was untrue. If a man's account were overdrawn, and he had reason to suppose that his cheque would still be honoured, this might be consistent with his having authority to draw and with his cheque being a good and valid order. But, in the present case, it is quite clear that the prisoner knew that his account at the bank was virtually closed, and that he knew this cheque would not be paid. He had, therefore, no authority to draw. And his cheque was not a good and valid order, that is to say, one which might be cashed.

BRETT, J....I think there also is evidence of the fourth false representation charged.

*

Conviction affirmed.

[Or in sending a half of a bank-note.]

THE QUEEN *v.* MURPHY.

IRISH CROWN CASE RESERVED. 1876.   IRISH REPORTS 10 C.L. 508.

[The prisoner was indicted for obtaining certain quantities of tea and sugar from J. O'Connor, with intent to defraud, by falsely pretending that she then had in her custody the proper halves corresponding to the halves of two bank-notes which accompanied her order for the said goods, and that the same would in due course be sent by her to him. In other counts she was similarly indicted in respect of half-notes sent to other persons.

Evidence was given by several witnesses that the prisoner had written letters to them inclosing half-notes, and requesting that goods should be forwarded to her ; that the goods were sent, but the prisoner did not send the second halves of the notes. In some cases, one half of a note had been sent to one witness, and the other half of the same note to another. Counsel for the prisoner contended that the indictment could not be maintained ; as the false pretence should be of an existing fact, and here the goods had been obtained upon a mere promise to send the other half notes.

The jury found the prisoner guilty, but a case was reserved for the opinion of the Court for Crown Cases Reserved upon the point thus raised.]

O'Moore, for the prisoner....The test to apply is, was the sending of the half-notes merely a promise to pay in the future? If so, it is not a false pretence; it was merely a security. It is not a false pretence on the face of it, like a flash note. It is quite possible that the prisoner made a mistake in sending the half-notes....

O'BRIEN, J. You say, Mr Murphy, that the mere act of sending the half-notes was a representation that the prisoner had the corresponding halves?

James Murphy, Q.C., for the prosecution. Yes; upon the authority of *R.* v. *Giles* (L. and C. 205).

MORRIS, C.J., stated that the Court were unanimously of opinion that the conviction should be affirmed.

CHAPTER II. THE OBTAINING.

[*The Pretence must have been followed by an Obtaining.*]

REGINA v. MARTIN.

SUSSEX ASSIZES. 1859.   1 FOSTER AND FINLASON 501.

False Pretences. The indictment charged that the prisoner, by falsely pretending to one Cloke that he was authorised by F., obtained from the said Cloke certain hop-poles, the property of the said Cloke, with intent to defraud him.

The prisoner, hearing that one F., who lived at M., wanted hop-poles, went to him and agreed to sell him a number, at 16s. 9d. per hundred, to be delivered at M. station. He then went to Cloke, who had hop-poles, and said he was commissioned by F. to buy them, promising that F. would send a cheque for the price. A cheque was sent; but it did not appear by whom. Cloke sent the poles to the station, by his own team, consigned to F. The bill was made out to F., who paid the carriage, and got the poles. Then the prisoner got the purchase money from him.

Roupell, for prisoner. The prisoner never got the *poles*. He pretended to sell, or sold, goods he had not got (*Kingsford* v. *Merry*,

1 H. and N. 503); Cloke ratified the contract between F. and the prisoner. If the prisoner was indictable at all, it was for obtaining money from F., not goods from Cloke.

WIGHTMAN, J., so held, and directed an acquittal.

[*And this Obtaining must have been actually caused by the Pretence.*]

REGINA *v.* MILLS.

CROWN CASE RESERVED.   1857.   DEARSLY AND BELL 205.

At the General Quarter Sessions of the Peace, holden for the County of Cambridge on the 9th of January, 1857, William Mills was tried and convicted upon the following indictment, for obtaining money under false pretences :—" Cambridgeshire, to wit. The jurors for our Lady the Queen upon their oath present, that William Mills, on the 14th day of November, 1856, did falsely pretend to one Samuel Free that the said William Mills had cut sixty-three fans of chaff for him the said Samuel Free; by which said false pretence the said William Mills then unlawfully did obtain from the said Samuel Free certain money of him the said Samuel Free, with intent to defraud; whereas in truth and in fact the said William Mills had not cut sixty-three fans of chaff, as he the said William Mills did then so falsely pretend to the said Samuel Free, but a much smaller quantity (to wit) forty-five fans of chaff. And the said William Mills, at the time he so falsely pretended as aforesaid, well knew the said pretence to be false, against the form of the statute," &c. It appeared from the evidence that the prisoner was employed to cut chaff for the prosecutor, and was to be paid twopence per fan for as much as he cut. He made a demand for 10s. 6d., and stated he had cut sixty-three fans; but the prosecutor and another witness had seen the prisoner remove eighteen fans of cut chaff from an adjoining chaff-house and add them to the heap which he pretended he had cut; thus making the sixty-three fans for which he charged. Upon the representation that he had cut sixty-three fans of chaff, and notwithstanding his knowledge of the prisoner having added the eighteen fans, the prosecutor paid him the 10s. 6d., being three shillings more than the prisoner was entitled to for the work actually performed.

It was objected, on behalf of the prisoner, first, that this was simply an overcharge, as in the case of *Reg.* v. *Oates*[1]; and secondly, that, as the prosecutor, at the time he parted with his money, knew the facts, the prisoner cannot be said to have obtained the money by the false pretence. Judgment was postponed; and the prisoner was discharged upon recognizances to appear at the next Quarter Sessions. The opinion of the Court of Criminal Appeal is requested, whether the prisoner was rightly convicted of misdemeanor under the foregoing indictment.

Thos. St Quinton,
Chairman.

Orridge, for the Crown. I submit that this conviction was right.

COLERIDGE, J. How do you say the money was obtained by the false pretence?

Orridge. When the owner of goods knows that a thief is coming, and does not prevent him from taking the goods, the offence of larceny is as complete as it would have been if the owner had known nothing about it. *Reg.* v. *Egginton*[2].

WILLES, J. But in larceny the question does not turn on the belief of the prosecutor.

Orridge. In *Rex* v. *Adey*[3], Patteson, J., says:—"If the defendant did obtain the money by false pretences, and knew them to be false at the time, it does not signify whether they intended to entrap him or not[4]"

COCKBURN, C.J. The test is, what was the motive operating on the mind of the prosecutor which induced him to part with his money? Here the prosecutor knew that the pretence was false; he had the same knowledge of its falseness as the prisoner. It was not the false pretence, therefore, which induced the prosecutor to part with his money; and if it is said that it was parted with from a desire to entrap the prisoner, how can it be said to have been obtained by means of the false pretence?

COLERIDGE, J. In *Rex* v. *Adey* it is said that the prosecutor believed the false statement.

CROWDER, J. It is always a question whether the prosecutor was induced to part with his money by the false pretence.

WILLES, J. The prosecutor handed the money over to the prisoner with a full knowledge of the true state of the circumstances.

---

[1] Dearsly, C. C. 459.   [2] 2 B. and P. 508.   [3] 7 C. and P. 140.

[4] Patteson, J., also said to the jury, "If you believe any one of the pretences was false, *and that the mind of the prosecutor was operated upon by it*, then you will find him guilty."

BRAMWELL, **B.** The prosecutor paid the money with a knowledge
of the facts. I doubt if he could get it back in a civil action.

COCKBURN, **C.J.** The case is very clear. The conviction is wrong.

Conviction quashed.

[*And the Pretence must not have been* too remote *a cause.*]

THE QUEEN *v.* BUTTON.

CROWN CASE RESERVED.   1900.   EDITOR'S MS. NOTE[1]

At the Lincoln City Quarter Sessions on July 3, 1900, the defendant was indicted for attempting to obtain goods by false pretences.
At the Lincoln Athletic Sports in August, 1899, the defendant came
forward as a competitor in a 120 yards race and a 440 yards race, for
each of which there was a ten guinea prize. He presented entry forms
which purported to be signed by "O. Sims, Thames Ironworks Athletic
Club"; and which contained a statement as to the last four races in
which Sims had run, and also a statement that he had never won
a race. These statements were true; but Sims had not signed them,
and he knew nothing of them. In consequence of what appeared in
them the handicapper of the Lincoln Sports allowed Sims a start of
eleven yards in the 120 yards race, and 33 yards in the 440 yards
race. At the time of the sports, Sims was at his home at Erith. The
defendant, who was a good runner and had won a race in his own
name, personated Sims; and easily won the two races. The suspicions
of the handicapper were aroused after the first of these races; and he
questioned the defendant as to whether he really was Sims and really
had never previously won a race. The defendant answered in the
affirmative. The handicapper swore at the trial that he should not
have given the defendant such favourable starts if he had known his
true name and performances. The defendant never applied for the
prizes, and never received them. It was suggested for the defence
that the defendant might have acted as he did merely for "a lark," or
for the purpose of keeping himself in training. The Recorder of
Lincoln directed the jury that if the defendant did it "for a lark,"
with no criminal intent, and without intending to get the prizes, they

---

[1] A report of this case will also be found in L. R. [1900] 2 Q. B. 597.

ought to find him not guilty: but that if he made the false representations wilfully and fraudulently, with intent to obtain the prizes, they
ought to find him guilty of attempting to obtain them by false
pretences.　The jury found him guilty.　The Recorder reserved a case
for the consideration of the Court; the questions to be decided
being (1) whether the Recorder had rightly directed the jury; and
(2) whether the attempt to obtain the prizes was too remote from the
pretence.

Hughes, for defendant.　The false representation is not sufficiently
proximate.　In *Reg.* v. *Larner* (14 Cox 497) it was held by the
Common Serjeant, after consulting Stephen, J., that where after a
similar false entry, a competitor received 25 seconds start in a swimming match and won the cup, what he obtained by the false pretence
was not the cup itself, but only the ticket permitting him to compete.
In the present case he has not even received the prize, as Larner did.
By the false entry he obtained nothing beyond an advantage in running in the race.　The winning was not the effect of the entry, but of
his actual skill in running; he might or might not have won.　And
even the winning gave only an optional right to the prizes, a right
which he might or might not have enforced; so something remained
still to be done by him.　There is no true indictable attempt until a
defendant has performed the final act that it depends on himself to
perform.　In *Reg.* v. *Eagleton* (6 Cox 559) Parke, B., said, "If any
further step by defendant had been necessary, we should have thought
it not sufficiently proximate."　Accordingly, in the present case, there
would be no indictable attempt until he made actual application for the
prizes.　The case falls within the principle of *Reg.* v. *Burgess* (7 Cox
136) where a false pretence by which lodgings had been obtained was
held not to extend to the board which had been supplied in them.

Shearman and *Walker* for the Crown were not called upon.

MATHEW, J.　We are all agreed that the conviction must be
upheld.　*Reg.* v. *Larner* is a decision on the particular facts; no
reasons are given for it.　It has been differed from by Lord Lindley;
and we think his Lordship was right.　What was intended by the
defendant when he entered his name for the races?　Was it to obtain
the prizes?　If it were, was that entry too remote from the obtaining?
He falsely represented himself as a man who had never won a race;
and he was accordingly handicapped as such.　Did he do this merely
"for a lark"?　The jury have negatived that view of his intention.
It is argued that his winning was due to his own athletic powers; but it
was due also to his false representations.　It is argued that his criminal
intention was exhausted before the final act that remained to be done

by him was reached. But the jury have found that he had a fraudulent intention, and made false representations. They were not too remote.

WRIGHT, J. If he had merely entered for the races, probably that act alone would not have been sufficiently proximate to be indictable. But here he actually ran; and, even when the running was over, he repeated the lie. If so, there is an indictable attempt; for *Reg.* v. *Larner* is not to be recognised as an authority.

The other three Judges concurred.

[*But mere* lapse of time *does not necessarily make the causation too remote.*]

THE QUEEN v. MARTIN.

CROWN CASE RESERVED. 1867.　　　　　　　L.R. 1 C.C.R. 56.

[The prisoner was indicted at the Quarter Sessions for the county of Warwick for obtaining a spring van with intent to defraud, by falsely representing that he was "the agent to the Steam Laundry Company, of which some of the leading men in Birmingham were at the head," and that, as such agent, he was desired by the company to procure a spring van for the use of the company. It was shewn that the prisoner, when ordering the van, had made the representation set out in the indictment. And the prosecutor stated that he supplied the van to the prisoner solely as agent of the company, and on the faith of his representation that the company consisted of the leading men in Birmingham; though he admitted that he had taken the prisoner's representation about the company without inquiring who the leading men of Birmingham at the head of it were, and without requiring any reference. The prosecutor had built the van and lettered it as directed, when the prisoner wrote countermanding the order. The van was nevertheless delivered, in pursuance of the original order; and at prisoner's request some boards were afterwards put in it. Subsequently the prosecutor received notice of a meeting of prisoner's creditors, which he was invited to attend as a creditor. This he declined to do; and on his protesting to the prisoner that it was the company he had made the van for, the latter replied, "I am the company; there is no company but only me." The prisoner was convicted; but a case was stated for the opinion of the Court of Criminal Appeal whether a verdict of Guilty was a right verdict upon the evidence.]

Kennedy, for the prisoner. In order to support an indictment for obtaining by false pretences, the thing obtained must be in existence when the false pretence is made. A man cannot be indicted for obtaining by false pretences an agreement to make something. The old law contemplated the existence of something of which there could be an owner; and although now, by the 24 and 25 Vict. c. 96, s. 88, ownership need not be alleged, yet the nature of the thing to be obtained is not altered. Section 90 of that act applies to the case of valuable securities not in existence when the false pretence is made; but there is no offence in ordering a chattel to be made. A man cannot be convicted of obtaining a dog by false pretences, because a dog is not the subject of larceny: *Reg.* v. *Robinson*[1]. Neither is that the subject of larceny which is not in existence when the false pretence is made.

[WILLES, J. The law did not condescend to take notice of base animals. A dog was not the subject of larceny at common law, because, as it was said, a man shall not hang for a dog[2].]

In *Douglass's Case*[3] it was held that money obtained from a servant cannot be described as the property of the master because the master afterwards reimburses the servant. In *Wavell's Case*[4] where a man induced a banker to honour his cheques by false pretences, the conviction was held bad, because what was obtained was credit on account.

[BLACKBURN, J. There the prisoner never obtained the money at all. The question here is, whether the van, when built, was obtained by a continuing false pretence.]

The doctrine of a continuing pretence is not to be found in the statute. In *Gardner's Case*[5] the prisoner obtained a contract for lodging by false pretences, and afterwards obtained food under that contract; but it was held that the getting the food was too remotely the result of the false pretence. So here the false pretence was exhausted in obtaining the contract to build the van. *Bryan's Case*[6] is still more strongly in favour of the prisoner.

[LUSH, J. In *Gardner's Case*[5] the prisoner did not contemplate obtaining the food when he made the false pretence.

BLACKBURN, J. It is not everything obtained subsequently that is obtained by the false pretence. I should have said that even in *Gardner's Case*[5] the question of remoteness was one for the jury. Here, however, the delivery of the van was the very object and aim of the false pretence.]

No counsel appeared for the Crown.

---

[1] Bell, C. C. 34; 28 L. J. (M.C.) 58.   [2] See 7 Rep. 18 a.   [3] 1 Camp. 212.   [4] 1 Moo. C. C. 224.   [5] Dearsly and Bell, C. C. 40.   [6] 2 F. and F. 567.

BOVILL, C.J. The question asked of us is, whether the verdict was right upon the evidence. This we understand to mean whether there was evidence to go to the jury; and so understanding it, we are all of opinion that there was. The objection urged upon us has been answered by my brothers Willes and Blackburn in the course of the case; and it is obvious that there are many cases within the mischief of the statute where the thing obtained is not in existence when the false pretence is made. Thus a man, by false pretences, may induce a tailor to make and send him a coat, or a friend to lend him money which may consist of bank-notes not printed when the false pretence was made on which the loan was granted. So also a man might obtain coals which were not got (and therefore not a chattel in the eye of the law) at the time of making the pretence. It is absurd to say that the chattel obtained must be in existence when the pretence is made. The pretence must, indeed, precede the delivery of the thing obtained; but at what distance of time? What is the test? Surely this, that there must be a direct connection between the pretence and the delivery—that there must be a continuing pretence. Whether there is such a connection or not is a question for the jury. In *Gardner's Case*[1] the prisoner obtained, at first, lodgings only; and, after he had occupied the lodgings more than a week, he obtained board; and it was held that the false pretence was exhausted by the contract for lodging; the obtaining board not having apparently been in contemplation when the false pretence was made. It is true that in *Bryan's Case*[2] the contract was for board as well as lodging: but there the indictment was for having obtained sixpence as a loan some time after the contract for board and lodging had been entered into; and it is clear that the obtaining the loan was as remote from the false pretence under which the contract for board and lodging had been entered into, as the obtaining of the board was from the false pretence made in *Gardner's Case*[1]. In the present case, when the false pretence was made and the order given, it was never contemplated that the matter should rest there; and we have no difficulty in holding that there was a continuing pretence, and a delivery obtained thereby.

*   *   *   *   *

Conviction affirmed.

[See REGINA v. CLOSS, *supra*, p. 184.]

---

[1] Dearsly and Bell C. C. 40.   [2] 2 F. and F. 567.

CHAPTER III.   THE RIGHT OBTAINED.

[*Obtaining a mere* right to possession, *and not* ownership, *does not suffice.*]

THE QUEEN *v.* KILHAM.

CROWN CASE RESERVED.   1870.   L.R. 1 C.C.R. 261.

Case stated by the Recorder of York.

Indictment under 24 and 25 Vict. c. 96, s. 88, for obtaining goods by false pretences. The prisoner was tried at the last Easter Quarter Sessions for York. The prisoner, on the 19th of March last, called at the livery stables of Messrs Thackray, who let out horses for hire, and stated that he was sent by a Mr Gibson Hartley to order a horse to be ready the next morning for the use of a son of Mr Gibson Hartley, who was a customer of the Messrs Thackray. Accordingly, the next morning, the prisoner called for the horse, which was delivered to him by the ostler. The prisoner was seen, in the course of the same day, driving the horse, which he returned to Messrs. Thackray's stables in the evening. The hire for the horse, amounting to 7*s.*, was never paid by the prisoner. The prisoner was found guilty.

The question was, whether the prisoner could properly be found guilty of obtaining a chattel by false pretences within the meaning of 24 and 25 Vict. c. 96, s. 88.

*   *   *   *   *

BOVILL, C.J. To constitute an obtaining by false pretences it is equally essential, as in larceny, that there shall be an intention to deprive the owner wholly of his property; and this intention did not exist in the case before us. In support of the conviction the case of *Reg.* v. *Bolton*[1] was referred to. There the prisoner was indicted for obtaining, by false pretences, a railway ticket with intent to defraud the company. It was held that the prisoner was rightly convicted, though the ticket had to be given up at the end of the journey. The reasons for this decision do not very clearly appear; but it may be distinguished from the present case in this respect: that the prisoner, by using the ticket for the purpose of travelling on the railway, entirely converted it to his own use for the only purpose for which it was capable of being applied. In this case the prisoner never intended to deprive the prosecutor of the horse or the property in it, or to

[1] 1 Den. C. C. 508; 19 L. J. (M.C.) 67.

appropriate it to himself, but only intended to obtain the use of the horse for a limited time.   The conviction must therefore be quashed.

Conviction quashed.

[*But if* ownership *be criminally obtained, the crime is False Pretences* (*and cannot be Larceny*).]

[See REX *v.* HARVEY, *supra* p. 214.]

REGINA *v.* WILSON AND MARTIN.

STAFFORD ASSIZES.   1837.   8 CARRINGTON AND PAYNE 111.

Larceny.   The prisoners were indicted for stealing a £5 note and two sovereigns, the property of Robert Parker.

Mr Robert Parker said, "I am a farmer.   I was, on the 20th of June, walking towards Walsall, when I saw the prisoner Peter Wilson. He pointed to the ground and said, 'There is a purse.'   He picked it up.   I said, 'We had better have it cried; as some one may own it.' He replied, 'Some one to whom it does not belong may say it is his, and get it from us.'   We walked on, and I said, 'We had better see what the purse contains.'   He replied, 'Not here, as there are men at work who will see us.'   We went about twenty yards further, and the prisoner Wilson opened the purse and took out what appeared to me to be a gold watch chain, and two seals.   He said he did not know the value of them, but there was a gentleman on the other side of the road who could probably tell us.   This was the prisoner Ambrose Martin. The things were shewn to him; and he said he was in the trade, and asked how we came by the articles.   I said we had found them.   The prisoner Martin then said it was a very prime article, and worth £14, and that we should divide it between us; and he added that, as we found it on the road, it belonged to us and no one else.   The prisoner Wilson said he would take the things to his master; but the other prisoner said he had no right to do so; and he also said, that if I would

buy the other man's share he would give me £18 for the articles, and
get a good profit for himself besides.   He added that he was the
brother of Mr Dutton, the watch-maker, whom I knew.   The prisoner
Wilson had gone on a little way, when he was called back by the other
prisoner, who asked him if he would take £7 for his share.   This he
agreed to do.   I gave him a £5 note and two sovereigns, and took the
chain and seals.

Evidence was given to shew that the prisoners were connected
together, and that the supposed valuable articles were worth only a few
shillings.

COLERIDGE, J.   Is this a larceny?

Beadon, for the prosecution, cited the case of *Rex* v. *Moore* (1 Leach
314).

COLERIDGE, J.   In that case nine of the judges thought that the
money charged to have been stolen was given as a pledge; so that the
possession of it only was parted with by the prosecutor, and the
property not.   In this case the prosecutor intended to part with the
money for good and all, and to have the articles.   If the party meant
to part with the property in the money as well as the possession of it, I
am of opinion that it is no larceny.   Here the prosecutor meant to
part with his money for ever.

Beadon cited the case of *Rex* v. *Robson* (R. and R. 413).

COLERIDGE, J.   The party there had only the possession of the
money given to him as a stakeholder.   When this prosecutor parted
with his £7, he never intended to have it back again, but meant
to sell the chain and seals for himself.   The prisoners must be
acquitted.

Verdict, Not guilty.

The prisoners were afterwards tried again, the offence being then
laid as a conspiracy to defraud the prosecutor; and were convicted.

[*There is no sufficient* Obtaining, *if the ownership was only to pass*
conditionally, *and the condition has not been fulfilled.*]

THE QUEEN *v.* RUSSETT.

CROWN CASE RESERVED.   1892.   L.R. [1892] 2 Q.B.D. 313.

Case stated by the deputy-chairman of the Gloucestershire Quarter
Sessions.

The prisoner was tried and convicted upon an indictment, charging him with having feloniously stolen, on March 26, 1892, the sum of £8 in money, of the moneys of James Brotherton. It appeared from the facts proved in evidence that on the day in question the prosecutor attended Winchcomb fair, where he met the prisoner, who offered to sell him a horse for £24. He subsequently agreed to purchase the horse for £23, £8 of which was to be paid down; and the remaining £15 was to be handed over to the prisoner either as soon as the prosecutor was able to obtain the loan of it from some friend in the fair (which he expected to be able to do) or at the prosecutor's house at Little Hampton, where the prisoner was told to take the horse if the balance of £15 could not be obtained in the fair. The prosecutor, his son, the prisoner, and one or two of his companions, then went into a public-house, where an agreement in the following words was written out by one of the prisoner's companions, and signed by prisoner and prosecutor: "26th March, G. Russett sell to Mr James and Brother (sic) brown horse for the sum of £23. 0s. 0d. Mr James and Brother pay the sum of £8, leaving balance due £15. 0s. 0d. to be paid on delivery." The signatures were written over an ordinary penny stamp. The prosecutor thereupon paid the prisoner £8. The prosecutor said in the course of his evidence: "I never expected to see the £8 back, but to have the horse." The prisoner never gave the prosecutor an opportunity of attempting to borrow the £15, nor did he ever take or send the horse to the prosecutor's house; but he caused it to be removed from the fair under circumstances from which the jury inferred that he had never intended to deliver it.

It was objected on behalf of the prisoner that there was no evidence to go to the jury; on the ground that the prosecutor parted absolutely with the £8, not only with the possession, but with the property in it; and, consequently, that the taking by the prisoner was not larceny, but obtaining money by false pretences, if it was a crime at all. The objection was overruled. In summing up, the deputy-chairman directed the jury that if they were satisfied from the facts that the prisoner had never intended to deliver the horse, but had gone through the form of a bargain as a device by which to obtain the prosecutor's money, and that the prosecutor never would have parted with his £8 had he known what was in the prisoner's mind, they should find the prisoner guilty of larceny.

The question for the Court was whether the deputy-chairman was right in leaving the case to the jury.

Gwynne James, for the prisoner. The conviction was wrong. The only offence disclosed was that of obtaining money by false pretences. There was no evidence to go to the jury upon a charge of larceny. The property in the money passed to the prisoner at the time when it was handed to him by the prosecutor, who admittedly never expected to see it again ; the receipt given for the money is strong evidence of the change of property.

The case is distinguishable from *Reg.* v. *Buckmaster*[1] ; for in that case the question was whether the prosecutor expected to have his money back. There is in the present case a breach of contract, for which the prosecutor has a civil remedy ; and it is immaterial that the prisoner in making the contract had a fraudulent intent: *Rex* v. *Harvey*[2].

*   *   *

POLLOCK, B....The rule of law has long been acted on, that where the prosecutor has intentionally parted with the property in his money or goods as well as with their possession, there can be no larceny. My mind has therefore been directed to the facts of the case, in order to see whether the prosecutor parted with his money in the sense that he intended to part with the property in it. In my opinion, he certainly did not. This was not a case of a payment made on an honest contract for the sale of goods, which eventually may, from some cause, not be delivered, or a contract for sale of a chattel such as in *Rex* v. *Harvey*[2]. From the first the prisoner had the studied intention of defrauding the prosecutor. He put forward the horse and the contract ; and the prosecutor, believing in his bonâ fides, paid him £8, intending to complete the purchase and settle up that night. The prisoner never intended to part with the horse, and there was no contract between the parties. The money paid by the prosecutor was no more than a payment on account.

HAWKINS, J. I am entirely of the same opinion. In my judgment the money was merely handed to the prisoner by way of deposit, to remain in his hands until completion of the transaction by delivery of the horse. He never intended, or could have intended, that the prisoner should take the money and hold it, whether he delivered the horse or not. The idea is absurd ; his intention was that it should be held temporarily by the prisoner until the contract was completed, while the prisoner knew well that the contract never would be completed by delivery. The latter therefore intended to keep and steal the money. Altogether, apart from the cases and from the principle which has been so frequently enunciated, I should not have a shadow of doubt that the conviction was right.

A. L. SMITH, J. The question is whether the prisoner has been guilty of the offence of larceny by a trick or that of obtaining money

---

[1] 20 Q. B. D. 182.   [2] 1 Leach, 467; *supra*, p. 214.

by false pretences; it has been contended on his behalf that he could only have been convicted on an indictment charging the latter offence; but I cannot agree with that contention. The difference between the two offences is this. If possession only of money or goods is given, and the property is not intended to pass, that may be larceny by a trick; the reason being that there is a taking of the chattel by the thief against the will of the owner. But if possession is given and it is intended by the owner that the property shall also pass, that is not larceny by a trick, but may be false pretences; because in that case there is no taking, but a handing over of the chattel by the owner. This case, therefore, comes to be one of fact; and we have to see whether there is evidence that, at the time the £8 was handed over, the prosecutor intended to pass to the prisoner the property in that sum, as well as to give possession. I need only refer to the contract, which provides for payment of the balance on delivery of the horse, to shew how impossible it is to read into it an agreement to pay the £8 to the prisoner, whether he gave delivery of the horse or not; it was clearly only a deposit by way of part payment of the price of the horse, and there was ample evidence that the prosecutor never intended to part with the property in the money when he gave it into the prisoner's possession.

WILLS, J. I am of the same opinion. As far as the prisoner is concerned, it is out of the question that he intended to enter into a binding contract; the transaction was a mere sham on his part. The case is not one to which the doctrine of false pretences will apply; and I agree with the other members of the Court that the conviction must be affirmed.

Conviction affirmed.

[EDITOR'S NOTE. The ruling in this case, that Russett never became the owner of the eight pounds, and therefore never "obtained" them, may be supported on either (or on both) of two grounds:—(1) that the arrangement between the parties included an implied agreement that the instalment of £8, though placed in the prisoner's hands, should not become his property until delivery of the horse; (2) that the arrangement (whatever its terms) was, in law, wholly void—inasmuch as there was no *consensus voluntatum*, the prisoner never having any genuine intention to contract—and it therefore could confer on the prisoner no rights whatever (though he himself would be estopped from denying its validity). This latter ground, which is suggested by Pollock, B., and Wills, J., has the advantage of involving no conjectural assumption as to the prosecutor's intentions with regard to a contingency which possibly never occurred to his mind at all. Having been present at the hearing, I may mention that these two learned judges emphasized this latter ground in their actual words still more distinctly than appears from the printed report. My notes shew that Pollock, B., said, "There was no honest contract. And where one contracting party has no intention of ever performing his contract, the other party is entitled to treat it as null, and to bring trover for anything which he has delivered under it." And Wills, J., said, "He falsely represented that he had a contracting mind. This was a false pretence, not as to a merely extraneous fact, but as to one which goes to the root of the contract; so that it prevented it from ever becoming a contract at all." As to this principle, the student may refer to *Reg.* v. *Buckmaster* (L. R., 20 Q. B. D. 182) and to the judgment of Mathew, L.J., in *Cavalier* v. *Pope* (L. R., 1905 2 K. B. 757).

The case is closely parallel to that of *Rex* v. *Pratt*, (1 Moody 250).

The judges who decided *Reg.* v. *Russett* did not express themselves as over-ruling *Rex* v. *Harvey* (*supra*, p. 214); and the two cases are clearly distinguishable. For, of the two grounds on which the decision in Russett's case may be supported, the former is not applicable to Harvey's, inasmuch as Harvey clearly bought the horse on credit, though only a short credit; and the latter is not applicable, inasmuch as there was no finding by the jury that Harvey, from the outset, had never had any intention of paying the purchase-money.

The following old case, that of *Rex* v. *Gilbert*, is curiously similar to Russett's case—except that in it, the fraudulent party is not the vendor but the purchaser.]

REX *v.* GILBERT.

BEDFORD ASSIZES. 1828.   1 MOODY 185.

Indictment for stealing four oxen.

It appeared that one Baker, a servant of the Marquis of Tavistock, had four oxen to sell at Ampthill Fair, and the prisoner agreed to purchase them for £48. 10*s.*, and to pay ready money for them. Baker proposed to mark the oxen, but the prisoner opposed it, and said he would pay for them by-and-bye, at the King's Arms. Baker went to the King's Arms at the appointed time, but the prisoner was not there; and on going back to the market he found that the prisoner had driven away the oxen and sold them, and he could not be found till some time after, when he was apprehended. Baker, on the trial, swore that he did not consider the oxen to have been sold and delivered to the prisoner until the money should be paid.

GARROW, B., left it to the jury to say if they believed the prisoner originally intended to convert the oxen to his own use without paying for them; and they returned for answer that they believed he never had any intention of paying for them.

The Judges were unanimously of opinion, that, under these circumstances, the prisoner was properly convicted, the jury having found that the prisoner never meant to pay for the oxen.

[*And there is no sufficient obtaining if possession is given by an Agent
who, though intending to pass the ownership, has no authority
to do so.*]

THE QUEEN *v.* STEWART AND WIFE.

KENT ASSIZES.　1845.　1 Cox 174.

The prisoners were indicted for larceny, under the following circumstances. They passed for husband and wife; and had so taken
a house at Tunbridge Wells. Mrs Stewart went to the shop of the
prosecutor, selected the goods in question to the amount of £10, and
ordered them to be sent to her home. The prosecutor accordingly
despatched the goods by one Davies, and gave him strict injunctions
not to leave them without receiving the price. Davies, on arriving at
the house, told the two prisoners he was instructed not to leave the
goods *without the money or an equivalent.* After a vain attempt on the
part of Mr Stewart to induce Davies to let him have the property on
the promise of payment on the morrow, he, Stewart, wrote out a
cheque for the amount of the bill and gave it to Davies, requesting
him not to present it until the next day. It was drawn on the London
Joint Stock Bank, Prince's-street, London. Davies having left the
goods, returned with the cheque to his employers. It was presented
at the Bank, in London, the next morning, when it was dishonoured
for want of effects. It was also proved that, although the prisoner
had opened an account at the said Bank, it had been some time before
overdrawn, and several of his cheques had been subsequently dishonoured.

Jones, Serjt., for prisoners, submitted that against the male
prisoner the charge of larceny could not be sustained. The shopman
parted not only with the possession of the goods, but also with the
property in them. Nor was any false representation made to him to
induce him so to do. The prisoner requested that the cheque might
not be presented until the next day; but it was presented on the next
morning, and had never been taken to the banking-house since.
Although there were no funds there in the morning, it did not follow
that provision might not have been made for the cheque in the course
of the day. This is like the case of *Rex* v. *Parker* (7 C. and P. 825),
where the prisoner was charged with falsely pretending that a post-
dated cheque, drawn by himself, was a good and genuine order for £25,
whereby he obtained a watch and chain: there the prisoner represented
as here, that he had an account with the bank, and had authority to

draw the cheque, both which were proved to be false, and the Court held the case one of false pretences.

ALDERSON, B. It is for you to shew that the prisoner had reason. able ground for believing that the cheque would be paid. The case seems to me to approach more nearly to *Rex* v. *Small* (8 C. and P. 46) than to *Rex* v. *Parker*. In the former, a tradesman was induced to send his goods by a servant to a place where he was met by the prisoner, who induced the servant to give him the goods in exchange for a counterfeit crown piece; and it was held to be larceny. If, in consequence of a fraudulent representation of the party obtaining them, the owner of goods parts with the possession, he meaning to part also with the property, it is not larceny, but a mere cheat. But if the owner does not mean to part even with the possession, except in a certain event which does not happen, and the prisoner causes him to part with them by means of fraud, he, the owner, still not meaning to part with the property, then the case is one of larceny. Here, if the owner had himself carried the goods and parted with them as the servant did, no doubt it would have been a case of false pretences : or if the servant had had a *general* authority to act, it would have been the same as though the master acted. But in this instance he had but a limited authority, which he chose to exceed. I am of opinion, as at present advised that if the prisoner intended to get possession of these goods by giving a piece of paper, which he had no reasonable ground to believe would be of use to anybody, and that the servant had received positive instructions not to leave the articles without cash payment, the charge of larceny is made out.

CHAPTER IV. THE SUBJECT-MATTER OF THE RIGHT.

[*It must be* personal *property.*]

REGINA *v.* PINCHBECK

CENTRAL CRIMINAL COURT.   1896.   SESSIONS PAPERS CXXIII. 205.

[Kent Pinchbeck was indicted, in the first four counts, for unlaw-fully obtaining from Charles Eames a large quantity of bricks and other building materials, and other property from other persons, by false pretences, with intent to defraud. There were four further counts, for obtaining credit by fraud.

The prosecutor's evidence was as follows. "I am a builder at Watford. On Sept. 28th, 1894, I received this letter with the prisoner's signature (I have seen him write); and with the address 'York Buildings, Adelphi.'" (The letter stated that the writer was desirous of obtaining tenders for the erection of several pairs of villas at Northwood, and that information could be obtained at York Buildings.) "Before I received that letter I had had no dealings with the prisoner and did not know him. The prisoner, in an interview, told me that the houses were to be erected for a client of his, Miles Atkinson, of Blackheath, a gentleman with a lot of money; and that as soon as we had pressed far enough with the work the money would be paid by him. I believed in, and relied on, his statement about Miles Atkinson at the time....It was agreed that I should build a pair of villas for £1030 to be paid by instalments....As the work went on, I made efforts from time to time to obtain payment, with the result that I received altogether £460."

Evidence was also given that Miles Atkinson (otherwise Wells) was a man who was employed as a collector by the Singer Machine Company, and who gave Kent Pinchbeck as a reference when he applied for that situation.]

Rooth, for the prisoner, submitted that the first four counts of the indictment should be withdrawn from the jury, upon the ground that what was alleged by the indictment to be obtained by false pretences was real property; and, as real property could not be the subject of larceny, it could not be the subject of an indictment for obtaining it by false pretences. The prisoner had not obtained anything in the form of a chattel which he could carry away; for no property passed to him in any of the building material until it became part of a house, and it could not be said that the labour which was exerted for him was either "a chattel, or money, or valuable security."

HAWKINS, J., in leaving the case to the jury, directed them to return a verdict of Not guilty upon the first four counts.

Verdict, Guilty upon the last four counts for obtaining credit by fraud.

[*And of sufficient* value *to be larcenable.*]

REGINA *v.* ROBINSON.

CROWN CASE RESERVED.　1859.　　　　　　　BELL 35.

The following case was reserved by the Recorder of Liverpool.

The prosecutor, who resided at Hartlepool, was the owner of two dogs, which he advertised for sale. The prisoner, Samuel Robinson, having seen the advertisement, made application to the prosecutor to have the dogs sent to him at Liverpool on trial, falsely pretending that he was a person who kept a man-servant. By this pretence the prosecutor was induced to send the dogs to Liverpool, and the prisoner there obtained possession of them with intent to defraud, and sold them for his own benefit. The dogs were pointers, useful for the pursuit of game, and of the value of £5 each.

At the Liverpool Borough Sessions, holden in December 1858, the prisoner was indicted, convicted, and sentenced to seven years' penal servitude, under the statute 7 and 8 Geo. IV. c. 29, s. 53.

On behalf of the prisoner a question was reserved and is now submitted for the consideration of the Justices of either Bench and Barons of the Exchequer, viz., whether the said dogs were chattels within the meaning of the said section of the statute, and whether the prisoner was rightly convicted.

Littler, for the prisoner. A dog is not "a chattel" within the meaning of the statute. At common law no larceny could be committed of a dog. It is laid down (Lambard's *Eirenarcha,* 267) that "it is felonie to steale any the moveable goods of any person; but because it may in some cases bee doubted whether the things so taken are to be numbered amongst moveable goods or no I will proceed in particularitie"—then he says, "to take dogges of any kind, apes, parats, singing birds or such like, though they be in the house, is no felonie"; and Dalton adds (*Country Justice,* 372): "No, not by taking a blood-hound or mastiff; although there is good use of them, and that a man may be said to have a property in them so as an action of trespass lieth for taking them." And by statute it is not to this day made larceny to steal a dog. For, by section 31 of the very same statute under which the prisoner has been convicted, the *stealing* of a dog was made punishable by fine only, and by a three months' imprisonment in default; and yet, if the intention of the legislature were that section 53 should be applicable to dogs, the obtaining a dog by *false pretences* would involve, as in this case, penal servitude.

The present Dog Stealing Act, 8 and 9 Vict. c. 47, by section 1, repeals the provisions of 7 and 8 Geo. IV. c. 29 so far as it relates to dog stealing; and, by section 2, enacts that to steal a dog shall be a misdemeanor, for which the offender shall be liable, on summary conviction, to imprisonment and hard labour not exceeding six months: and the same statute enacts that a second offence shall be an indictable misdemeanor. [8 and 9 Vict. c. 47 ss. 1, 2 are now reincorporated in 24 and 25 Vict. c. 96 s. 18.]

Brett, for the Crown. It cannot be disputed that for some purposes dogs are chattels. They are chattels which pass to the executor, and for which trover will lie; 1 *Williams on Executors, Com. Dig. Action sur Trover, Ireland* v. *Higgins*[1]*, Wright* v. *Ramscott*[2]*, The Case of Swans*[3]; but it is said they are not chattels within this section, because they are not the subject of larceny at common law. The statute relating to false pretences was passed to provide a remedy in cases of cheating. The reason which is assigned why dogs should not be the subject of larceny at common law is, not that they were not always considered to be chattels, but because "they are of so base a nature that a man shall not die for them"; but death never was the punishment for cheating; and, therefore, the reason why dog stealing should not be a larceny does not apply.

LORD CAMPBELL, C.J. It is admitted that dog-stealing is not larceny at common law, and a specific punishment of a milder character has been enacted by the later statute, which makes the offence a misdemeanor. That being so, it would be monstrous to say that obtaining a dog by false pretences comes within the statute 7 and 8 Geo. IV. c. 29 s. 53, by which the offender is liable to seven years' penal servitude. My brother Coleridge used to say that no indictment would lie under that section unless, if the facts justified it, the prisoner could be indicted for larceny, and that is now my opinion.

The other four Judges concurred.

Conviction quashed.

[See THE CASE OF PEACOCKS, *supra*, p. 250.]

---

[1] Cro. Eliz. 125.   [2] Wms. Saund. 83.   [3] 7 Rep. 15 *b.*

SECTION XIII.

RECEIVING STOLEN GOODS.

[*The goods must* already *have been stolen.*]

REGINA *v.* GRUNCELL AND HOPKINSON.

CENTRAL CRIMINAL COURT. 1839. 9 CARRINGTON AND PAYNE 365.

The prisoner Gruncell was indicted for stealing a quantity of hay, the property of his master; and the prisoner Hopkinson with receiving it, well knowing it to have been stolen.

It appeared that the prisoner Gruncell, who was a carter and was allowed by his master a small quantity of hay for the use of the horses on their journey to and from London, on the day mentioned in the indictment took from his master's stables two trusses of hay above the quantity which was allowed for the horses; and that the prisoner Hopkinson, who was the ostler at a public-house where the waggon stopped on the journey, came to the tail of the waggon, and received the two trusses of hay from the other prisoner, and carried them from the waggon to the stable.

Adolphus submitted that the indictment was wrongly framed as to the prisoner Hopkinson in charging him with being a receiver. Because, if he had committed any offence at all, it was that of stealing; as the hay, being in the master's waggon, was in the master's possession in point of law, and the act of the prisoner, in removing it from the waggon, constituted a larceny, and not a receiving.

MIREHOUSE, Common Serjeant, thought the indictment properly framed, but said he would consult Mr Baron Parke, who was in the adjoining Court. He accordingly did so, and, on his return, said—"The learned Judge has gone very carefully, with me and Mr Clark, through the cases on the subject, and he is clearly of opinion with me, that the indictment is properly framed; and he is so on this ground, that, as the hay was not hay appropriated by the master for the horses, the larceny was complete the moment it got into the cart animo furandi. If it had been hay allowed for the horses, which had been stolen, it would have been otherwise."

Verdict, Guilty.

[*And must not have been* subsequently returned *to the owner.*]

REGINA *v.* VILLENSKY.

CROWN CASE RESERVED. 1892.   L.R. [1892] 2 Q.B. 597.

Case stated by the Chairman of the County of London Sessions, from which the following facts appeared :—

Jacob Villensky and Mark Villensky were tried on an indictment charging them with having feloniously received two dozen night-gowns, the goods of Carter, Paterson and Co., before then feloniously stolen by one George Clark.

The goods in question were packed in a parcel consigned by Messrs McIntyre, Hogg, Marsh and Co. of the City of London, to Messrs Crisp and Co. of Holloway, and the parcel was delivered by the consignors to Carter, Paterson and Co., who are common carriers, for the conveyance of the consignees. In the ordinary course it arrived at the Goswell Road depôt of Carter, Paterson and Co., and there, also in the ordinary course, it was (together with many other parcels) unloaded from the van in which it had been brought. George Clark, who pleaded guilty, was a carman in the employ of Carter, Paterson and Co., and took part in the unloading. His conduct in reference to this particular parcel excited the suspicion of a fellow-servant named Roberts, by whom he was seen to remove it from that part of the platform appropriated to Holloway parcels, and transfer it to the part appropriated to Spitalfields parcels. On examining the parcel, Roberts found on it a label addressed to "Jacobs and Co., Hanbury Street, Spitalfields." The prisoner, Jacob Villensky, resided and carried on business there as a chandler with the other prisoner, Mark Villensky (his son), and they were known by the name of Jacobs. Roberts reported to Mr Waters, the superintendent of Carter, Paterson and Co., the finding of the parcel thus addressed.

The superintendent, having inspected the parcel, gave directions that it should be replaced in the Spitalfields part of the platform where Roberts had found it; and that a special delivery-sheet should be made out according to the label "Jacobs and Co., Hanbury Street, Spitalfields," and that the parcel should be forwarded in a van to that address; and by his further directions two detectives travelled in the van to Hanbury Street. It did not appear that either Mr Waters or Roberts knew at this time who were the consignees to whom the parcel had been addressed, and neither the consignors nor the consignees were informed of the substitution of the false address, nor of the consequent action of Mr Waters, nor was Clark, the thief, informed of it. The parcel

was received by both the Villenskys in Hanbury Street under circumstances pointing clearly to the conclusion of complicity with Clark, and
knowledge on their part that it had been stolen. Upon that point no
question arose.

At the conclusion of the evidence, the learned Chairman offered to
amend the indictment by substituting the names of the consignees,
Crisp and Co., as the owners of the property, for those of the bailees,
Carter, Paterson and Co.; but the prosecution declined to ask for any
amendment. It was then objected by counsel for the defence that
there was no case to go to the jury; inasmuch as at the time the parcel
was received by the Villenskys it had ceased to be stolen property, the
bailees, Carter, Paterson and Co., having resumed actual possession of
it. He cited in support of his contention *Reg.* v. *Dolan*[1] and *Reg.*
v. *Schmidt*[2]. The learned Chairman overruled the objection, and the
prisoners were convicted of felonious receiving, but were admitted to
bail pending the decision of the present case....

LORD COLERIDGE, C.J. There is no doubt that Clark stole these
goods and the other two prisoners intended to receive them; but the
carriers, in whose name those responsible for the prosecution insisted
on the case going on, had in the meantime, before its receipt by the
prisoners, got hold of the property, which, by their special directions,
was sent off to the prisoners' house in a special van accompanied
by two detectives.

POLLOCK, B. It is, of course, frequently the case that when it is
found that a person has stolen property he is watched; but the owner
of the property, if he wishes to catch the receiver, does not resume
possession of the stolen goods; here the owners have done so, and the
result is that the conviction must be quashed.

＊　　　＊　　　＊　　　＊　　　＊

The other Judges concurred.

[*And must have reached* prisoner's possession, *actual or constructive.*]

REGINA v. WILEY.

CROWN CASE RESERVED.　1850.　　　2 DENISON 37.

At the General Quarter Sessions for the county of Northumberland,
holden at Newcastle-upon-Tyne, on the 26th of February, A.D. 1850,
Bryan Straughan, George Williamson, and John Wiley, were jointly

[1] Dearsly. 436.　　　　[2] Law Rep. 1 C. C. 15.

indicted under stat. 7 and 8 Geo. IV. c. 29 s. 54, for stealing and receiving five hens and two cocks, the property of Thomas Davidson. It was proved that, on the morning of the 28th day of January, in the same year, about half-past four, Straughan and Williamson were seen to go into the house of John Wiley's father with a loaded sack that was carried by Straughan. John Wiley lived with his father in the said house, and was a higgler, attending markets with a horse and cart. Straughan and Williamson remained in the house about ten minutes; and then were seen to come out of the back door, preceded by John Wiley, with a candle, Straughan again carrying the sack on his shoulders, and to go into a stable belonging to the same house, situated in an enclosed yard at the back of the house, the house and stable being on the same premises. The stable door was shut by one of them, and on the policemen going in they found the sack on the floor tied at the mouth, and the three men standing round it as if they were bargaining, but no words were heard. The sack had a hole in it, through which poultry feathers were protruding. The bag, when opened, was found to contain six hens, two cocks, and nine live ducks. There were none of the inhabitants up in the house but John Wiley, and on being charged with receiving the poultry, knowing it to be stolen, "he said that he did not think he would have bought the hens."

The jury found Straughan and Williamson guilty of stealing the poultry laid in the indictment, and John Wiley guilty of receiving the same, knowing it to be stolen.

The Court told the jury that the taking of Straughan and Williamson with the stolen goods as above by Wiley into the stable, over which he had control, for the purpose of negotiating about the buying of them, be well knowing the goods to have been stolen, was a receiving of the goods by him within the meaning of the statute.

The question for the opinion of the Court was, whether the conviction of Wiley was proper....

[The case was argued before five Judges, constituting the Court of Criminal Appeal, created by 11 and 12 Vict. c. 78; but as the Court was not unanimous, the case was re-argued before the twelve Judges.]

Otter, for the prisoner. The question is as to the meaning of the word *receiving*. The statutes taken together shew that it is no longer an offence merely to buy; therefore the mere fact of admitting the goods with a view to buying them is not a receiving....There must be a willing parting with the possession by the thief, and a willing taking on the part of the receiver.

Lord CAMPBELL, C.J. Can there not be a joint possession between a receiver and a thief?...

ALDERSON, B. Suppose there was a large halo ; and A. a thief, had hold of one end of it, and B. a receiver, had hold of the other end, there would be actual possession in both. Here the question is only as to the *actual* possession ; that may be in two persons. *Reg.* v. *Parr* (2 M. and R. 346).

We have to decide whether the direction to the jury is right. It is consistent with that direction that the thieves alone had actual possession at the time of going into the stable. For all the circumstances set out in the case are not to be taken as incorporated into the direction by the words "as above."

Liddell, for the Crown. The direction to the jury must be taken to incorporate all the circumstances set out in the case. On the other side the fallacy has been to confound *constructive* with *joint actual* possession. Here the prisoner had the latter with the thieves....They are all treating it as a chattel in their possession and power ; they were only undecided as to the mode of partition.

LORD CAMPBELL, C.J. If a man receives stolen goods for any purpose malo animo, knowing them to be stolen, is he not a receiver? Supposing the prisoner to have carried the sack, then he would have been a receiver ; supposing him to have carried the candle, in order to aid one of the thieves in carrying the sack, where is the legal difference? The act was a joint act. It is difficult to see why the prisoner had not joint possession of the sack as much as the other thief, who is not said to have had the manual possession....

*　　　*　　　*　　　*　　　*

V. WILLIAMS, J. I think the conviction right. I think the case made out against the prisoner, if he is proved to have had possession of the goods malo animo knowing them to be stolen. Here the knowledge and the animus are clear. The only question is as to the possession. I think it was only necessary for one of the party to have possession of the goods ; the prisoner was proved to have had a common purpose with the thieves, although he had not the manual possession. They were all agents for each other, and the possession of the thieves was, therefore, in law, the possession of the prisoner.

PLATT, B. I think the conviction wrong. It seems to me that the goods must have been in such a condition as to be under the dominion of the prisoner, and exclusive of that of the thief. If they all are to be deemed in joint possession of them, the possession of the thieves would be different in kind from that of the receiver ; for in him it would be treated as a receiving, and in them as an asportation. I think that the thieves here retained the control and possession, and never intended to part with it until after their bargain was concluded.

*　　　*　　　*　　　*

PATTESON, J. I think the conviction wrong. I don't consider a manual possession or even a touch essential to a receiving. But it seems to me that there must be a control over the goods by the receiver, which there was not here. How far the other circumstances stated in this case might affect the question, I don't think we need inquire, for, in my opinion, they are not brought before us for consideration. The case as submitted to us, does not put the matter on that ground. However, though I entertain some doubts on that point, I am inclined to think that those additional facts would make no difference.

* * * * *

PARKE, B. I think the conviction wrong. We have only to consider the precise point submitted to us in the case reserved. The taking "as above" was said by the Chairman to amount to a receiving; that only incorporates so much of the transaction as relates to the taking of the goods into the stable. We must not therefore speculate on the question whether the three prisoners were all participating in the wrongful act, or what would be the legal consequences to each of their so doing. Receiving must mean a taking into possession actual or constructive, which I do not think there was here. The prisoner took the thieves into the stable, but he never accepted the goods in any sense of the word except upon a contingency, which, as it happened, did not arise. I think the possession of the receiver must be distinct from that of the thief; and that the mere receiving a thief with stolen goods in his possession would not alone constitute a man a receiver.

* * * *

[Four of the Judges were for affirming the conviction, and seven for quashing it. The conviction was therefore quashed.]

[*And have been* received *by him with* guilty knowledge.]

REGINA *v.* WOODWARD.

CROWN CASE RESERVED. 1862.   LEIGH AND CAVE 122.

The following case was stated by the Chairman of Quarter Sessions for the county of Wilts.

At the Quarter Sessions of the Peace for the county of Wilts, held at Marlborough, on the 16th day of October, 1861, before me,

Sir John Wither Awdry, Knight, and others my fellows, Benjamin Woodward, of Trowbridge, in the county of Wilts, dealer, was found guilty of receiving stolen goods, knowing them to have been stolen, and was thereupon sentenced to nine calendar months' imprisonment with hard labour in the county gaol, where the prisoner now is, undergoing his sentence.

The actual delivery of the stolen property was made by the principal felon to the prisoner's wife in the absence of the prisoner, and she then paid sixpence on account; but the amount to be paid was not then fixed. Afterwards the prisoner and the principal met, and agreed on the price, and prisoner paid the balance.

Guilty knowledge was inferred from the general circumstances of the case.

It was objected that the guilty knowledge must exist at the time of receiving, and that this was the time of the delivery to the wife; and that, when the wife received the stolen property, guilty knowledge could not have come to the prisoner.

The Court overruled the objection; and directed the jury that, until the subsequent meeting, when the act of the wife was adopted by the prisoner, and the price agreed upon, the receipt was not so complete as to exclude the effect of guilty knowledge acquired at that meeting.

If the Court shall be of opinion that the above direction was correct, the conviction to stand confirmed; but if the Court should be of a contrary opinion, then the conviction to be quashed.

This case was argued, on the 18th of January, 1862, before ERLE, C.J., BLACKBURN, J., KEATING, J., WILDE, B. and MELLOR, J.

Brodrick, for the prisoner....There is no proof of a guilty knowledge in either the wife or the husband at the time when each respectively received the goods. Further, there is no proof that the wife ever gave the goods over to her husband at all. Receipt imports a transfer of possession, and there is no proof of such transfer.

BLACKBURN, J. We do not require proof of transfer. That was for the jury; and they have found that he received the goods. The only question for us is, whether he received them with a guilty knowledge.

Brodrick....It is plain that in the Chairman's mind the receipt was simultaneous with the payment of the balance. In *Reg.* v. *Button*[1], Lord Denman says, "The receipt of stolen goods knowingly does not of necessity comprise any series of acts: on the contrary, that offence is not committed at all unless the receipt and the knowledge are

[1] 11 Q. B. 929.

simultaneous." It is absurd to say that payment of the balance constituted a receipt, or was evidence of a receipt then taking place. If
it is anything, it is evidence of a receipt having previously taken place;
and, if that was so, the guilty knowledge was subsequent to the
receipt. It is quite consistent with the case that the goods never came
into the prisoner's possession at all, but were disposed of by the wife
before he came into the transaction....Upon one of three grounds,
therefore; either that the wife's receipt was presumably innocent, and
that a guilty receipt by the husband cannot be founded on it; or,
secondly, that there may have been no receipt by the husband, and
that the goods may never have come into his possession; or, thirdly,
that, if they did, his receipt may well have been complete before the
guilty knowledge was acquired; I submit that the conviction should be
quashed.

No counsel appeared for the Crown.

ERLE, C.J. The argument for the prisoner has failed to convince
me that the conviction was wrong. The thief brought the goods to
the prisoner's house, and left them there, receiving sixpence on
account. That was no complete receipt. Subsequently the thief found
the husband, who then acquired a guilty knowledge, and with such
knowledge struck a bargain with the thief, and paid for the goods. If
the offer had not been satisfactory, the thief might have reclaimed the
goods.

KEATING, J. The agreement for the sale of the goods was not
complete, until the husband met the thief. Then the transaction was
complete. What took place then amounted to a receipt by the
husband with a guilty knowledge. If that were not so, it would be
almost impossible to convict any receiver who was absent at the time
when the goods were actually delivered.

*   *   *   *   *

[The remaining three Judges also upheld the conviction.]

[*The offence is now a* felony *whenever the original taking was felonious either at common law or by the Larceny Act* 1861.]

REGINA *v.* STREETER.

CROWN CASE RESERVED. 1900. EDITOR'S MS.[1]

At the West Sussex Quarter Sessions on June 28, 1900, William Streeter and Ellen Tickner were tried under an indictment; the first count of which charged them jointly with larceny in a dwelling house, and the second count charged them jointly with feloniously receiving goods and £27 in money knowing them to be stolen.

Ellen Tickner had been married for twenty-six years, and resided with her husband at Stammerham. Streeter came to lodge with them; and remained there until on April 21 Mr Tickner turned him out of the house. On May 11, Ellen Tickner packed up two boxes, and labelled them with Streeter's name, and handed them to a carrier. He delivered them to Streeter, at Horsham. She then left her home during her husband's absence, and joined Streeter. The husband, finding that money and other articles of his were missing, gave information to the police. It was found that the two defendants were living together as man and wife, at Farnham; and in their house the missing articles were found in the boxes which Tickner had sent to Streeter on May 11; and in another box, which belonged to Streeter but the key of which was in Ellen Tickner's purse, there was found a sum of £27.

The jury convicted Ellen Tickner on the count for larceny, and Streeter on the count for receiving. Streeter's counsel objected that, as the stealing of a husband's goods by his wife (though now made felonious by the Married Women's Property Act) was not a felony either at common law or under the Larceny Act 1861, the receiving of goods so stolen did not come within that section of the Larceny Act which renders the receiving of stolen goods, in certain cases, a felony.

The Chairman accordingly reserved the point for the opinion of the Judges.

Raven (with him *Humphreys*) for prisoner. At common law, a wife did not commit larceny by taking her husband's goods even when she went to join an adulterer; and therefore the receiving of them by the adulterer was not a receiving of stolen goods. And though the wife's taking is now made a larceny by secs. 12 and 16 of the Married Women's Property Act 1882, yet the adulterer's receiving is still not felonious. For the Larceny Act 1861 (24 and 25 Vict. c. 96 s. 91)

---

[1] A report of this case will also be found in L.R. [1900] 2 Q.B. 601.

makes the receiving stolen goods with guilty knowledge a felony only in cases where the original stealing "shall amount to a felony either at common law or by virtue of this Act." And the stealing here is one which only became felonious by a statute long subsequent to the Larceny Act.

MATHEW, J. The case of *Reg.* v. *Smith* (L.R. 1 C.C.R. 266) is in point; where it was decided that though stealing by a partner had been made a felony under an Act of 1868, yet the receiving of goods so stolen would not be within the Larceny Act.

Graham Campbell (with him *Hurst*) for the Crown. The point has hitherto been treated in the text-books as an open one; for though Archbold thinks the adulterer cannot be indicted for a felonious receiving, an opposite view is expressed by the latest editors of Roscoe's "Criminal Evidence" and of Russell on Crimes. The decision in *Reg.* v. *Smith* was spoken of by the late Mr Justice Stephen, in his Digest of Criminal Law, as "instructive but most unfortunate."

[MATHEW, J. Mr Justice Stephen did not mean that the decision was an unsound construction of the statute; but that it shewed an unfortunate defect in the statute.]

Graham Campbell. Even if it be a valid decision, it is certainly not one to be extended. Moreover it can be distinguished from the present case. For the Larceny by Partners Act 1868 altered the very definition of larceny; the Married Women's Property Act merely removed a technical disability peculiar to the wife, arising from her unity of person with her husband.

Moreover, apart from the substantive offence of receiving, Streeter was an accessory to the larceny by Mrs Tickner; and, as the Accessories Act (24 and 25 Vict. c. 94) makes it possible to indict an accessory as if he were a principal, Streeter could be validly convicted on the present indictment. *Reg.* v. *Caspar* (9 C. and P. 289).

WRIGHT, J. Probably that is not so; but even if it were, such a conviction must have been on the first count, whereas the present conviction is on the second.

MATHEW, J. We are agreed that the case is determined by *Reg.* v. *Smith.* Formerly there were two cases in which stealing did not amount to larceny;—where a partner stole from his partner, or a wife from her husband. The legislature has now passed statutes which correct these two defects, and make these persons criminally responsible. But both statutes are subsequent to the Larceny Act. Now section 91 of that Act is clear in its language, and it is limited to the receiving of property the stealing whereof was a felony "either at common law or by virtue of this Act." It was in neither way, but under a statute passed long after the Larceny Act, that a wife became indictable for stealing her husband's goods.

Wʀɪɢʜᴛ, J.   In future cases of this kind there might, it seems, be an indictment at common law for the receiving.   But that was not the form of the indictment here.

[Eᴅɪᴛᴏʀ's Nᴏᴛᴇ.   By common law, receivers of stolen goods are guilty of a misdemeanor, punishable with fine and imprisonment.   The Larceny Act 1861 (24 and 25 Vict. c. 96 s. 91) makes it a felony to receive goods which have been feloniously stolen.]

SECTION XIV.

HIGH TREASON.

[Constructive *compassing of the King's death.*]

REX *v.* Dʀ FLORENCE HENSEY.

Kɪɴɢ's Bᴇɴᴄʜ.   1758.   1 Bᴜʀʀᴏᴡs 642.

[In 1758 the defendant was committed by warrant under the hand and seal of the Earl of Holderness, one of His Majesty's principal Secretaries of State, for high treason.

At the trial on June 12th, 1758, the evidence for the Crown consisted chiefly of letters to and from the prisoner, which were alleged to be a proof of overt acts of two different sorts of high treason, viz. of compassing and imagining the death of the King, and also of adhering to the King's enemies.]

Lᴏʀᴅ Mᴀɴsғɪᴇʟᴅ, in summing up the evidence, said :—As to the law, levying war is an overt act of compassing the death of the King. Any overt act of the intention of levying war, or of bringing war upon the kingdom, is settled to be an overt act of compassing the King's death.   Soliciting a foreign prince, even in amity with this Crown, to invade this realm, is such an overt act; and so was *Cardinal Pole's* case.   And one of these letters is such a solicitation of a foreign prince to invade the realm.   Letters of advice and correspondence and intelligence to the enemy, to enable them to annoy us or defend themselves, written and sent in order to be delivered to the enemy, are, though intercepted, overt acts of both these species of treason that have been mentioned.   And this was determined by all the Judges of

ᴋ.   24

England in *Gregg's* case: where the indictment (which I have seen) is much like the present indictment. There, the only doubt arose from the letters of intelligence being intercepted and never delivered: but they held that that circumstance did not alter the case.

As to the facts, in the present case, the jury are to consider whether the letters were written by the prisoner at the bar, in order to be delivered to the enemy, and with intent to convey to the enemy such intelligence as might serve and assist them in carrying on war against this Crown or in avoiding the destinations of our enterprises and armaments against them.

[Constructive *levying of war against the King.*]

THE QUEEN *v.* DAMAREE AND PURCHASE.

OLD BAILEY. 1709.   FOSTER 213; 15 HOWELL'S STATE TRIALS 521.

The indictments charged, that the prisoners withdrawing their allegiance &c. and conspiring and intending to disturb the peace and public tranquillity of the kingdom, did traitorously compass, imagine, and intend to levy and raise war, rebellion, and insurrection against the Queen within the kingdom; and that in order to complete and effect these their traitorous intentions and imaginations, they on the —— day of —— at —— with a multitude of people, to the number of 500, armed and arrayed in a warlike manner &c., then and there traitorously assembled, did traitorously ordain, prepare, and levy war against the Queen, against the duty their allegiance &c.

It appeared upon the trial of these men, which I attended in the students' gallery at the Old Bailey, that upon the 1 March 1709, during Dr Sacheverell's trial, the rabble, who had attended the doctor from Westminster to his lodgings in the Temple, continued together a short space in the King's Bench Walks, crying, among other cries of the day, "Down with the Presbyterians."

At length it was proposed, by whom it was not known, to pull down the meeting-houses, and thereupon the cry became general, "Down with the meeting-houses!"; and some thousands immediately moved towards a meeting-house of Mr Burges, a Protestant dissenting minister;

the defendant Damaree, a waterman in the Queen's service and in her livery and badge, putting himself at the head of them, and crying, "Come on, boys, I'll lead you. Down with the meeting-houses!" They soon demolished Mr Burges's; and burnt the pews, pulpit, and other materials in Lincoln's-inn-fields. After they had finished at that place, they agreed to proceed to the rest of the meeting-houses; and hearing that the guards were coming to disperse them, they agreed, for the greater dispatch, to divide into several bodies, and to attack different houses at the same time: and many were that night in part demolished and the materials burnt in the street.

The prisoner Damaree put himself at the head of a party which drew off from Lincoln's-inn-fields and demolished a meeting-house in Drury-lane, and burnt the materials in the street; still crying that they would pull them all down that night.

While the materials of this house were burning, the prisoner Purchase, who had not, for aught appeared, been before concerned in the outrages of that night, came up to the fire very drunk; and, with his drawn sword in his hand, encouraged the rabble in what they were doing, and incited them to resist the guards, who were then just come to the fire in order to disperse the multitude. He likewise assaulted the commanding officer with his drawn sword, and struck several of their horses with the same weapon; and then, advancing towards the guards, cried out to the rabble behind him, "Come on, boys, I'll lose my life in the cause; I will fight the best of them."

Upon the trial of Damaree, all the Judges present were of opinion that the prisoner was guilty of the high treason charged upon him in the indictment: for here was a rising with an avowed intention to abolish all meeting-houses in general; and this intent they carried into execution as far as they were able. If the meeting-houses of Protestant dissenters had been erected and supported in defiance of all law, still a rising in order to destroy such houses in general would fall under the rule laid down in Kelyng 70 with regard to the demolishing all disorderly houses. But since the meeting-houses of Protestant dissenters are, by the Toleration Act, taken under the protection of the law, the insurrection in the present case was to be considered as a public declaration by the rabble against the Act, and an attempt to render it ineffectual by numbers and open force.

Accordingly Damaree was found guilty, and had judgment of death as in cases of high treason.

With regard to the case of Purchase, there was some diversity of opinion among the Judges present at the trial; because it did not appear upon the evidence, that he had any concern in the original rising, or was present at the pulling down any of the houses, or any way active in the outrages of that night; except his behaviour at the bonfire in Drury-lane, whither he came by mere accident, for aught appeared to the contrary.

The jury therefore by the direction of the Court found a special verdict to the effect already mentioned.

Upon this special verdict, which in substance took in the whole transaction on the first of March, the Judges unanimously resolved that for the reasons mentioned at Damaree's trial, he and the others concerned with him in demolishing and rifling the meeting-houses were guilty of high treason in levying war against the Queen.

As to the case of Purchase, Chief Justice TREVOR, Justice POWELL and Baron PRICE were of opinion that, upon the facts found, he was not guilty of the charge in the indictment. But all the rest of the Judges differed from them; because the rabble was traitorously assembled, and in the very act of levying war, when Purchase joined them, and encouraged them to proceed, and assaulted the guards, who were sent to suppress them. All this, being done in defence and support of persons engaged in the very act of rebellion, involved him in the guilt of that treason in which the others were engaged.

[*What does* not *amount to War against the King.*]

REX *v.* THISTLEWOOD AND OTHERS.

OLD BAILEY SESSIONS.   1820.   33 STATE TRIALS 381.

[Arthur Thistlewood, John Thomas Brunt, and nine others were indicted for high treason. The principal overt act assigned was the compassing a levying of war against the King, in the "Cato Street Conspiracy"; a plot to assassinate the King's cabinet ministers when assembled at dinner at Lord Harrowby's house in Grosvenor Square. Another indictment charged them with the murder of a constable, who was shot by them in resisting their arrest at their place of assembly in Cato Street (now Horace Street), Edgware Road.

The prisoners severed in their challenges; and accordingly had to be tried separately.]

On the trial of Brunt, RICHARDS, C.B., in summing up, said : ...It is admitted distinctly by the learned counsel for the prisoner, and by the prisoner himself—it is admitted, and it is also proved, that it was a conspiracy formed for a most nefarious purpose. It is admitted that it was a conspiracy founded in the diabolical intention to destroy His Majesty's Cabinet Council ;—fifteen of those persons who transacted the principal affairs of Government, against whom there had been no personal indignation on the part of any body. If, however, this terrible purpose was the only purpose which this conspiracy embraced, there is no high treason in it, because the object is confined to the destruction only of those fifteen noble Lords and Gentlemen, so there is a particular purpose only to be answered. But it is said on the other side that this particular purpose is only intended as one of the steps to the general purpose of subverting the constitution..

The object of the prisoner and his associates was to destroy fifteen of the King's Ministers as they sat at dinner in the unsuspecting hour of cheerfulness, by a degree of violence, and in the prosecution of a plan, which one cannot think of without shuddering ; that is admitted. Is that all the purpose? If that is all the purpose of these men, the prisoner is not guilty of high treason. But you are to ask yourselves, gentlemen, whether that could be the sole purpose ; why are the fifteen principal Ministers of the King to be destroyed in this way? If you attend to the evidence of Adams, and many of the others, there is no question at all that there was an ulterior plan and intention ; and that ulterior plan and intention, beyond all question, proves directly, if you believe the evidence, the treason charged against the prisoner at the bar. It is stated that it was an absurd project ; so absurd, that it is not only improbable, but impossible that it should be ascribed to any reasonable being. It has been said, very truly, that the attempt or the project to destroy the King's Ministers is such that one knows not how to deal with the supposition of it. But it is proved—it is true ; the prisoner has stated it, and his counsel are obliged, by the force of evidence, to admit it. But then they contend, that it was for no other project : you will judge whether that is the case.

Verdict, Guilty.

[*What does* not *amount to War against the King.*]

REGINA *v.* JOHN FROST AND OTHERS.

MONMOUTHSHIRE SPECIAL COMMISSION.   1839.

4 STATE TRIALS (N.S.) 85.

[Indictment for high treason by levying war against the Queen.
The evidence showed that Frost, in command of a body of some 5000
persons, many of whom were armed, had entered Newport; and had
fired upon, and broken into, the Westgate Inn, which was occupied by
a detachment of soldiers. A conflict took place, in which several of
the rioters were killed.]

TINDAL, C.J., in the course of his summing up, said: ...The learned
Attorney General stated the case on the part of the Crown against the
prisoner to be this—that the prisoner at the bar had brought down to
the town of Newport a very large multitude of persons, armed and
arrayed in a warlike manner ; and that the plan was to get possession of
the town of Newport, to break down the bridge, and stop the mail, so
that, the mail not arriving at Birmingham for some time, it would be a
signal for a general rising in Birmingham and Lancashire

On the part of the prisoner, the learned counsel who appear for him
state, and I think are justified in so stating, that they are not bound
to shew what was the object or purpose or intent of the acts that were
undoubtedly done by the prisoner at the bar. His counsel say the
offence charged against him must be proved by those who make the
charge; that he stands only to hear the evidence that is given against
him, and therefore he is not bound to shew at all, or in any way
whatever, what his real object or design was. Undoubtedly the
proof of the case against the prisoner must depend for its support, not
upon the absence or want of any explanation on the part of the
prisoner himself, but upon the positive affirmative evidence of his guilt
that is given by the Crown. It is not, however, an unreasonable thing,
and it daily occurs in investigations, both civil and criminal, that if
there is a certain appearance made out against a party, if he is
involved by the evidence in a state of considerable suspicion, he is
called upon for his own sake, and his own safety, to state and to bring
forward the circumstances, whatever they may be, which might reconcile such suspicious appearances with perfect innocence. And therefore
the learned counsel of the prisoner, although he entered his protest
against his being necessarily required to make such a statement, proceeds to say, that the case of the prisoner at the bar was one that was

perfectly innocent, that is, perfectly innocent so far as regards the crime of high treason. He stated that it was never intended by the prisoner either to take the town, or to attack the military, which latter act was purely accidental; that all that was intended was, to make a demonstration to the magistracy of ·Newport and the county, of the strength of those persons who were called Chartists, for the single purpose and design of inducing the magistrates either to procure the liberation of one Vincent and three other persons, who had been convicted of some political offences and were then confined in Monmouth gaol, or, at all events, to procure a mitigation in their mode of treatment whilst under imprisonment.

Gentlemen, if that outline which is made by the officers of the Crown is filled up by evidence, there is no doubt whatever that the guilt of the party accused amounts to high treason; and on the other hand, if falling short of that offence, it amounts to no more than the description which has been given of it by the counsel for the prisoner, although it would be a most grievous offence as a misdemeanor, involving the security of the property, and perhaps of the lives, of many persons in the town of Newport. Yet it would be deficient in the main ingredient of the offence of levying war against the Queen within her realm; it would want the compassing and designing to put down the authority and government of the Queen; it would amount to no more than a very aggravated misdemeanor; and upon that supposition and state of facts the prisoner would be entitled to an acquittal upon the present indictment....

Verdict, Guilty.

[*Adhering to the King's enemies.*]

REX *v.* VAUGHAN.

OLD BAILEY SESSIONS.   1696.   2 SALKELD 634

The defendant was indicted for treason in adhering to the King's enemies *cum plurimis subditis Gallicis inimicis Domini Regis*; and that they did navigate a certain vessel, called *The Clancarty*, with a design to destroy the King's ships.

At the trial, it was held by HOLT, C.J., and the other justices that an indictment for adhering to the King's enemies generally, without

shewing particular acts or instances, is not good. For the words of
the Statute are, "And thereof be proveably attainted by some overt
deed."...

And if it be not a good indictment without special acts, the
question is whether [when it does set out special acts] only those
that are alleged ought to be proved, and no others.

Per HOLT, C.J. A distinct overt act cannot be given in evidence
unless it relate to that which is alleged, or conduce to the proof of it.
But if it conduce to prove an overt act alleged, 'tis good evidence. If
consulting to kill the King be alleged, any acting or doing in
pursuance of that consultation may be proved; for it proves their
agreement and consent, and is a further manifestation of the act
alleged in the indictment.

It was also objected :—(1) That the seamen must appear in evidence
to be Frenchmen born, for if they were Dutch, they are not *subditi
Gallici*; (2) That though he was said to adhere to the King's enemies,
it was not said to be against the King; (3) That this was not a
sufficient act of adhering, without fighting or some act of hostility.

PER CURIAM.   (1) If the [Dutch] States be in alliance with us, and
the French at war with us, and certain Dutchmen turn rebels to the
States and fight under command of the French King, they are *inimici*
to us and *Gallici subditi*. For their French subjection makes them
French subjects, in respect of all other nations but their own. And if
such cruise be at sea, and an Englishman assist them, he is a traitor;
but not a pirate, for none are pirates that act under the command of
a sovereign prince.   (2) Adhering to the King's enemies must of
necessity be against the King.   Therefore, if an Englishman assist
the French, being at war with us, and fight against the King of Spain
who is an ally of the King of England, this is treason, as adhering to
the King's enemies against the King; for the King's enemies are
thereby strengthened and encouraged. So it is within the express
words of 25 Edw. III. "adhering to the King's enemies." And it is
sufficient to allege the treason in the words of the Statute. (3) Cruising
is a sufficient overt act of adhering, comforting, and aiding; as, if
Englishmen enlist themselves and march, this is sufficient without
coming to battle; and there may be a "levying war" without actual
fighting.

LORD PRESTON'S CASE.

OLD BAILEY. 1691.   12 HOWELL'S STATE TRIALS 646.

[Sir Richard Grahame (Viscount Preston, of Scotland) was indicted, along with others, for compassing the death of William and Mary, King and Queen of England. One overt act laid was the hiring a ship for the conveyance of treasonable papers to the French Government (then at war with England). Another was the hiring a boat and boatman in order to proceed to that ship.]

In answer to an objection raised by Lord Preston,

ATKYNS, C.B. said :—Here are instructions given to the French King how to invade England, and carry on the war against us. These instructions are contained in several papers, and these papers in a packet are carried to the smack, which smack was hired to go to France. You are found taking water at Surrey-stairs, which is in the county of Middlesex, in order to go to the smack. You did go to the smack; the papers were taken in your company; and were seen, lying by your seals; and the witnesses swear they believe some of them to be your hand. You took care to desire to have them disposed of. Now how far the jury will believe this matter of fact (that is thus testified) is left to them. This seems to be the proof; and if the jury do believe it, here is plain evidence of an overt act in the county of Middlesex.

[See also REGINA *v.* DAVITT, *infra*, p. 380.]

HUGH PYNE Esq. ; HIS CASE.

A CONSULTATION A.D. 1628.   CROKE CAR. 117.

One William Collier, attending the said Mr Pyne at his house in the country, was demanded of him, whether he had seen the King at Hinton, or no? whereunto Collier answered, that he had seen the King there. Mr Pyne thereto replied, "Then hast thou seen as unwise a King as ever was, and so governed as never King was; for he is carried as a man would carry a child with an apple : therefore I, and divers more, did refuse to do our duties unto him....And Mr Pyne said aloud, " Before God, he is no more fit to be king than Hickwright." This Hickwright was an old simple fellow, who was then Mr Pyne's shepherd.

These words being thus proved by William Collier and George Morley, all the Judges were commanded to assemble themselves; to consider and resolve what offence the speaking of those words were. Whereupon Sir NICHOLAS HIDE, Chief Justice of the King's Bench, Sir THOMAS RICHARDSON, Chief Justice of the Common Bench, Sir JOHN WALTER, Chief Baron of the Exchequer, Sir WILLIAM JONES, one of the Justices of the King's Bench, Sir HENRY YELVERTON, one of the Justices of the Common Bench, Sir THOMAS TREVOR, and GEORGE VERNON, Barons of the Exchequer, none other of the Judges being then in town, met at Serjeants' Inn in Fleet Street, where they debated the case amongst themselves, in the presence of Sir ROBERT HEATH, the King's Attorney General : and divers precedents were then produced. *E.g.* ...Edward Peacham[1] was indicted of treason, for divers treasonable passages in a sermon, which was never preached, or intended to be preached, but only set down in writings, and found in his study : he was tried and found guilty, but not executed. Note, that many of the Judges were of opinion that it was not treason....

Upon consideration of all which precedents, and of the statutes of treason, it was resolved by all the Judges before named, and so certified to his Majesty, that the speaking of the words before mentioned, though they were as wicked as might be, was not treason. For they resolved, that unless it were by some particular statute, no words will be treason ; for there is no treason at this day, but by the Statute of 25 Edw. III.; for imagining the death of the King, &c. And the indictment must be framed upon one of the points in that Statute ; and the words spoken here can be but evidence to discover the corrupt heart of him that spake them : but of themselves they are not treason, neither can any indictment be framed upon them.

To charge the King with a personal vice, as to say of him that he is the greatest whoremonger or drunkard in the kingdom, is no treason, as YELVERTON said it was held by the Judges, upon debate of *Peacham's* case.

---

[1] EDITOR'S NOTE. For Peacham's case, A.D. 1615, see 2 State Trials 869, Foster 199, and Hallam's *Const. Hist.* I. 342.

[*When* words spoken *constitute an Overt Act.*]

REX *v.* CHARNOCK.

OLD BAILEY. 1694.   2 SALKELD 633.

The question at the trial was, whether words could be an overt act
of treason in compassing the death of the King. For Hale (Pleas of
the Crown, 13) says, " Words are not an overt act of treason unless set
down in writing."

HOLT, C.J. Loose words, spoken without relation to any act or
project, are not treason. But words of persuasion to kill the King are
overt acts of high treason. So is a consulting how to kill the King.
So, if two men agree together to kill the King. For the bare
imagination and compassing makes the treason ; and any external act
that is a sufficient manifestation of that compassing and imagining, is
an overt act. It was never yet doubted but that to meet and consult
how to kill the King, was an overt act of treason.

SECTION XV.

TREASON-FELONY.

[*What is Treason-Felony.*]

THE QUEEN *v.* CHARLES GAVAN DUFFY.

DUBLIN COMMISSION COURT. 1849.   7 STATE TRIALS (N.S) 950.

[This was the last of four indictments for treason-felony, against
C. G. Duffy, the publisher of the *Nation* newspaper (afterwards Sir
Charles Gavan Duffy, K.C.M.G., Speaker of the Legislative Assembly
of Victoria).]

BALL, J., in summing up, thus explained to the jury the nature of
the crime :—Divested of redundant phraseology, the 11 and 12 Vict.
c. 12 s. 3 [the Treason-Felony Act, 1848] appears, so far as the
prisoner is concerned, to amount to this. If any person shall entertain the intention of deposing Her Majesty from her sovereignty in
this country, or the intention of levying war against Her Majesty for
the purpose of coercing her to change her measures and counsels, and
shall in either case manifest such intention by any printing or writing,

he shall be guilty of felony. It is not the act of endeavouring to depose the Queen, and the act of levying war, that are made felonies by this Statute. Those acts amount by law to the crime of high treason, and do not constitute any part of the legislation of this Act. It is the intention to do such acts, proved to exist in the mind of the accused, that by this Statute is made a substantive felony. By the term 'intention' you are not to understand a mere passing thought, but, as the word imports, a settled and deliberate purpose. It is not the intention in the mind which alone constitutes the offence, and which will render a man amenable to the penalties of this Statute. He must be proved not only to have entertained the intention, but to have expressed or manifested it by some printing or writing. Again, gentlemen, an attempt to depose the Sovereign does not import any intention to injure the Queen, or even to treat her with any personal disrespect. Neither is a formal intention to deprive her of her title, position, and dignity, necessary. The offence has been perpetrated, if the prisoner has entertained and expressed the intention of constituting or setting up in this kingdom any body of persons who were to exercise the functions of the Government, and virtually to supersede the Queen's authority—still more so, if the prisoner has entertained and expressed an intention of severing this country from the British crown, and establishing either a republic or any other form of government. With regard to the other charge of compassing to levy war, you are further to understand that when the Statute uses the words "levying of war," such terms are not confined, in their legal construction, to the exhibition of warlike array. It is not necessary that the prisoner should have had present in his mind the idea of any military force or regularly-organized army. If he contemplated an extensive insurrection, or rising of the people, for the purpose of compelling Her Majesty to change her measures and counsels, the law holds him guilty of the offence of levying war within the meaning of this Act of Parliament....

[*How a Treason-Felony may be proved.*]

REGINA v. DAVITT AND WILSON.

CENTRAL CRIMINAL COURT. 1870. 11 Cox 676.

[Indictment for feloniously compassing and devising to deprive and depose the Queen from her style and title of the Imperial Crown of

the United Kingdom.   Thirty-three overt acts were set out; including
a conspiracy to subvert the constitution, and a conspiracy to provide
arms and ammunition for levying war within the realm.   At the conclusion of the evidence the Attorney General (Sir R. Collier) urged
that the numerous secret consignments of arms—especially to Ireland
—all emanating from the shop of one prisoner, Wilson, and conducted
by the other prisoner, were proofs of the complicity of both of them.]

COCKBURN, C.J.   Supposing the prisoner Wilson had had nothing to
do with Fenian designs, but was willing to supply men whom he knew
to be Fenians with arms, although indifferent to the purposes for which
they might be used, is it contended that he would have "conspired"
in the felony?   In such a case he would sell arms with a knowledge of
his customers, but without any intention of his own to aid in their
design.   Would he be liable to be charged with complicity in the
felony?

Sir R. Collier, A.G., said he apprehended that if the prisoner knew
the illegal purpose for which the arms were to be used, he would,
without any further complicity on his part than the mere sale, be
guilty of felony.   An accessory before the fact to a treason has been
held to be a principal.   In this case the prisoner had done more than
sell the arms—he had gone to Leeds to co-operate with Davitt in
using them.

COCKBURN, C.J.   It may be so [1]....

Afterwards, at the close of the case,

COCKBURN, C.J., in summing up to the jury, said:—The prisoners
are indicted for what in substance is high treason; but that is not the
crime for which they are indicted, as, under the Statute (11 and 12
Vict. c. 12), what would before have been high treason is now created
an offence for which, upon conviction, a lesser punishment than that of
treason is to be inflicted.   The substance of the charge against the
prisoners contained in this voluminous indictment may be thus stated:—
a conspiracy to depose the Queen (a charge which would be proved by
shewing an attempt to depose her from her State as sovereign in any
part of her dominions, *e.g.* Ireland), and with that object to levy war
against her.   And the overt acts relied upon in support of the conspiracy are the procuring and producing arms for the purpose of being
used in the intended insurrection against the royal authority in Ireland.
You will have to consider, first, whether arms were provided in this
country for the purpose of being sent to Ireland with the intention of
being used and employed in rebellion there; next, whether they were

---

[1] It will be seen that the Lord Chief Justice, after consideration, directed the
jury in accordance with this view of the case.

sent by the prisoners, or either of them, with the intention of their being so used and employed. We have the fact of the letter proved to be in the handwriting of the prisoner Davitt; and proved by a witness for the defence to refer to the Fenian conspiracy, and to traitors to it, and to the use of weapons against such traitors. We have the fact of large and repeated consignments of arms by the defendants to false addresses and fictitious persons in Ireland and other parts of the country; these arms coming from the workshop of one prisoner, Wilson, and secretly consigned to false addresses written in the handwriting of the other prisoner, Davitt.

The question naturally arises, for what purpose were all these consignments? And why were they thus made, not openly, but secretly, and by means of such devices and contrivances? The fact that strikes the mind most forcibly is that in all these cases there was concealment and contrivance; which must have been for some purpose. It is for you to exercise your own judgment as to whether it was an innocent purpose. In these consignments both prisoners take part; and finally one of them, Wilson, comes to London, evidently to meet the other; with his address, under a feigned name, in his pocket, and with fifty revolvers. And there, at Paddington, the other prisoner (Davitt) actually is, to meet him. As regards the prisoner Davitt, there is positive evidence (that of the informer) that he was engaged in the Fenian conspiracy. Whether the evidence is credible and reliable, and how far it is confirmed, it is for you to judge. There is the letter, which in terms appears to point to this conspiracy. As to it, you have heard explanations; which it is for you to judge of, and, if you are not satisfied with them, then from the terms of that letter you may infer the complicity of Davitt. But that is not the whole evidence; and even if you are not satisfied as to the evidence of the informer, and are satisfied with the explanation as to the letter, there will yet remain other evidence in the case fit for you to consider. There is the internal evidence, afforded by the nature of the acts themselves that are laid as overt acts of the alleged conspiracy. When you find men sending arms to a country in which disaffection and disloyalty exist—doing it secretly and by clandestine means, and under circumstances calculated to excite extreme suspicion and distrust—it will not be difficult for you, in the absence of any explanation of such conduct, to draw your own inferences as to the purpose and motive of such conduct. No doubt it is for the Crown to make out their case. But it is often impossible to give direct evidence of a man's motives or intentions in a particular matter; and a jury must often look at the act itself, and judge from the nature of the act as to the character of the motive. And when you find these clandestine consignments of arms to Ireland, the country where this treasonable conspiracy existed, and where it was to be attempted to effect its object, it is for you to form your own judgment as to the purpose of these consignments. And if you are satisfied, either from the letter or from the other facts proved, that the purpose in sending these arms was the furtherance of the Fenian conspiracy, and that the arms were intended to be used in subverting the Queen's authority in that country, then—although you may not be satisfied that the prisoner was at any of the Fenian meetings—you may draw your own inferences from the facts. Considering, as well as the circumstances under which the arms were sent, the character of the arms themselves, arms in a rough and unfinished state, not fitted for sale though just as well capable of being used—and bearing in mind the absence of any attempt at an explanation of these things—it is for you to judge what is the natural inference to be drawn. And if you believe that the prisoners sent these arms in order that they might be used in levying war against the Queen, then the case is established against them.

These remarks on the evidence in the case have applied more particularly to the prisoner Davitt, who directed the transmission of the arms. With regard to the other prisoner, Wilson, there can be no doubt the arms were made by him; but if he did no more than make and supply them, and merely shut his eyes to their destination, that is not sufficient to convict him. But if you believe that, in supplying the arms, he had a knowledge that they were about to be used for a traitorous purpose, and had the intention that they should be so used, then he is involved with the other prisoner in a common guilt. If he was indeed ignorant of their destination, then it would be otherwise; of this you must form your own judgment. And if, knowing the object, though himself not caring about it, he yet, for the sake of sordid gain, lent himself to that object, he would be guilty.

The great question is, whether the arms were sent with the traitorous purpose of exciting insurrection. If you are satisfied that they were sent for that purpose, then, if both the prisoners knew of it, both are guilty; or, if not, then such one of them as knew of it. It is necessary that an overt act should have been committed within the jurisdiction of this court, and if you are satisfied that the arms were brought by the prisoner Wilson to the Paddington station in pursuance of the traitorous object, then there would be such an act within the jurisdiction. Nothing has been proved to account for the arms being so brought. If you are satisfied that they were brought to be used for the traitorous purpose, and that one prisoner was bringing them in concert with the other for that purpose, then they would both be guilty upon this indictment. For there would be an overt act by both of them in furtherance of a common traitorous design. Consider, then, whether the prisoners, or either of them, sent these arms, and sent them secretly and clandestinely, for the purpose of aiding the treasonable conspiracy.

Verdict, Guilty. Davitt was sentenced to fifteen years' penal servitude, and Wilson to seven.

SECTION XVI.

RIOT AND UNLAWFUL ASSEMBLY.

[*The difference between statute law and common law as to* Riots.]

REX *v.* FURSEY.

OLD BAILEY.   1833.   6 CARRINGTON AND PAYNE 81.

[Indictment for stabbing and wounding John Brooke. Various intents were specified in various counts; amongst them an intent to do grievous bodily harm, and an intent to resist arrest for rioting.]

The prosecutor, Brooke, was a sergeant of the Metropolitan police force : and, on the 13th of May, 1833, was with a very considerable number of the police at a vacant space of ground adjacent to the west side of the Cold Bath Fields Prison. It appeared that there was a meeting there, consisting of a number of persons, and that there were four flags. The prisoner carried an American flag; which a police constable, named Redwood, tried to take from him, when he stabbed both the prosecutor and Redwood with a sort of dagger with a tri-angular blade, similar to that of a court sword....

For the defence, it was stated by Mr Stallwood, who had been a magistrate for the county of Middlesex, that a considerable number of the police constables behaved with considerable violence, striking everybody they met with. He also stated, that there was no order given to the people to disperse, nor was the proclamation from the Riot Act read. In answer to questions put by *Campbell*, S.G., Mr Stallwood stated that he saw a paper fixed up to the wall of Cold Bath Fields, cautioning persons "By order of the Secretary of State" not to attend an illegal meeting.

Campbell, S G., was proceeding to examine into the contents of this caution.

C. Phillips. As this was a printed paper the manuscript from which it was printed ought to be produced.

Campbell, S.G. We cannot bring the wall of Cold Bath Fields here; and there is no proof that there ever was any manuscript....

PARK, J. The usual way in such cases is to give a copy to the witness, and ask if it is a copy of what he saw. I do not say that parol evidence is inadmissible; the paper was affixed to a wall.

...It was also proved on the cross-examination of another of the witnesses for the defence, Mr Carpenter, that he knew of the intended meeting before he went to the ground, as he had seen it stated to be the intention of the meeting to establish a National Convention; that he had seen it stated in various publications, advertisements, and bills; and he further stated that it was notorious.

GASELEE, J. (in summing up). The question for you to consider will be, whether there was sufficient provocation to reduce the offence of the prisoner below the crime of murder, if death had ensued. And although it is not mentioned in the indictment, you are at liberty to inquire whether the meeting was an illegal meeting or not; for if it was, the police would be justified in taking away the flag; but if the meeting was not an illegal one, then they would have no right to take the flag away from the prisoner. Taking it that the meeting was a legal one, this question will arise, whether the taking away of the flag was a sufficient provocation to justify the prisoner in striking with such a deadly weapon; and it makes a great difference whether a man under provocation takes up a deadly weapon on the sudden, or whether he goes out with the weapon, intending to use it to prevent the taking away of the flag. It will be for you to say whether the conduct of the prisoner shewed that malignity of purpose which would, if death had ensued, have constituted the crime of murder. If you are of opinion, that he took this deadly weapon with an intention to resist, under all circumstances, the taking away of the flag, I feel justified in telling you, and I believe that my learned brother will agree with me, that, if death had ensued, the crime of the prisoner would not have been less than the crime of murder. However, you ought also to consider whether there was sufficient provocation before the blow was given, to reduce the offence, had death ensued, to the crime of manslaughter....

On the part of the prisoner a great deal of evidence has been given to shew that the conduct of the policemen was very violent and very outrageous. You will have, therefore, to consider whether their

K.   25

conduct was a sufficient provocation to the prisoner to resist as he did,
or whether, from the fact of his having taken the weapon out with
him, there was that malignity of purpose which would have made the
offence of the prisoner amount to murder, if death had ensued.

It appears, from the evidence of Mr Stallwood, that the proclamation contained in the Riot Act was not read. Now, a riot is not the
less a riot, nor an illegal meeting the less an illegal meeting, because
the proclamation of the Riot Act has not been read. The effect of
that proclamation is to make the parties guilty of a capital offence if
they do not disperse within an hour. But, if that proclamation be not
read, the common law offence remains, and it is a misdemeanor ; and
all magistrates, constables, and even private individuals, are justified
in dispersing the offenders ; and, if they cannot otherwise succeed in
doing so, they may use *force* [1]. I do not lay down this as the law for
the first time ; the law has been so laid down by the judges on the
special commissions [2]. There has also been given in evidence a proclamation issued by order of one of the Secretaries of State ; and in
that proclamation it is stated that printed papers have been posted up,
advertising that a public meeting would be held to adopt preparatory
measures for holding a National Convention. Now, that proclamation
is not evidence that the meeting was to be held for the purposes there
mentioned. It is, in effect, only a notice given by the Secretary of
State, and is evidence in this case in no other way. But if placards
convening the meeting were posted up, stating that the meeting was
for those purposes, then it is an illegal meeting. If it was intended
by force to make any alterations in the laws of the country, that would
be a much more serious offence ; as it would be high treason. The
proclamation states it to be an illegal meeting, and commands all constables and others to disperse it. If such a notice be given, and a party
chooses to treat it as of no effect, he does it at his own risk.

But without any proclamation at all, if a meeting is illegal, a party
who attends it, knowing it to be so, is guilty of an offence. There may
be a difficulty in saying in what way this meeting was illegal, but it
was either illegal as a misdemeanor or a higher offence ; and whichever
it was, it justifies the dispersion of the meeting. One of the witnesses
has stated that the purpose of the meeting was to adopt preparatory
measures for holding a National Convention ; and that that was generally known. If you think that the meeting was held for the purpose
of adopting preparatory measures for the holding of a National Convention, then the police had a right to interfere and arrest the parties.

---

[1] [EDITOR'S NOTE. I.e. blows, but not shots, in the first instance.]
[2] I.e. at Bristol and Nottingham, 1832. (3 St. Tr., N. S., 1.)

The first question will be, whether the prisoner was the person who gave the wound to the prosecutor Brooke? The question will then be, whether there was such provocation as would have reduced the offence to the crime of manslaughter, if death had ensued? If you are of opinion that the prisoner, having taken the flag in his hand, had prepared the weapon with a view of protecting it under all circumstances, then I own it appears to me, that there are not those circumstances which will so reduce the crime as that, if this person Brooke had died, it would not have amounted to murder. If you think that the prisoner, previous to his going out, prepared a deadly weapon to resist any attempt to defeat the object of the meeting, or to prevent himself from being deprived of the flag which he carried, I am bound to tell you that I think the offence has been proved....If the meeting was legal, then the arrest was improper. Then the question would become, whether the resistance to the arrest was proportioned to the attempt made to arrest. It is not merely because a man attempts to arrest you wrongfully, that you are to kill him....The question would be whether the instrument was prepared in order to resist at all hazards any attempt to oppose them.......

Verdict, Not guilty.

[*The difference, at common law, between a* Riot *and an* Unlawful Assembly.]

REX *v.* BIRT.

GLOUCESTER ASSIZES.   1831.   5 CARRINGTON AND PAYNE 154.

Indictment for a riot, with a second count for an unlawful assembly. Each count concluded ' in terrorem populi.'

It appeared that the prisoners, and a large number of persons, assembled to cut down the fences of the inclosures of the forest of Dean ; and that the surveyor-general of the forest, and his woodmen, did not think themselves strong enough to resist them , and that inclosure fences to the extent of a mile and more were destroyed.

Mr Justice PATTESON. The difference between a riot and an unlawful assembly is this : If the parties assemble in a tumultuous manner, and actually execute their purpose with violence, it is a riot ; but if they merely meet upon a purpose, which, if executed, would

make them rioters, and, having done nothing, they separate without
carrying their purpose into effect, it is an unlawful assembly[1]

[*What renders an Assembly* Unlawful.]

THE KING *v.* HENRY HUNT.

York Assizes.   1820.   1 State Trials (N. S.) 171.

[Henry Hunt and nine other persons were indicted for riot, unlawful assembly, and a conspiracy to assemble unlawfully. The
assembling took place on Aug. 16, 1819, in St Peter's Fields, at
Manchester; when about 60,000 persons attended, many of whom
arrived marching in military order. The meeting was dispersed by
the yeomanry cavalry, at the command of the magistrates. As between
three and four hundred persons were wounded in consequence, the
affair came to be called the "Peterloo Massacre." (See Molesworth's
Hist. Eng. I. 16.)]

BAYLEY, J., in summing up, said:—...In all cases of unlawful
assembly, you must look to the purpose for which they meet; you
must look to the manner in which they come; you must look to the
means which they are using[2]. All these are circumstances which you
must take into your consideration. I have no difficulty in stating to

---

[1] In *Reg.* v. *Williams* (6 St. Tr., N. S., 779) PARKE, B, said:—"If this was an
'unlawful assembly' then a resistance to constables, accompanied with personal
violence against them, was an act of 'riot' on the part of those persons who were
guilty of it."

[2] For illustrations of 'manner' and 'means,' reference may be made to what
was shortly afterwards said by the same learned judge in *Rex* v. *Dewhurst*
(1 St. Tr., N. S., 598, 601):—"Terror may be inspired by the arms, or the staves
and sticks;...or by the nature of the speeches....A man has a clear right to arms
to protect himself in his house. A man has a clear right to protect himself when
he is going singly or in a small party upon the road where he is travelling or going
for the ordinary purposes of business. But you have no right to carry arms to a
public meeting, if the number of arms which are so carried is calculated to produce
terror and alarm. If you could be at liberty to carry arms upon an expectation
that by possibility there might be an attack at the place, that would be an excuse
for carrying arms in every instance when you went to a public meeting. Therefore
I have no difficulty in saying that persons are not warranted in carrying arms to
a public meeting if they are calculated to create terror and alarm."

And again to what was said by PARKE, B., in *Reg.* v. *Williams* (6 St. Tr., N.S.,
779):—" The assembling at that hour of the night—seven o'clock and continuing
until twelve o'clock—the very large number of persons—varying from 3,000

you that it is not because a meeting consists of sixty thousand men, women, and children, a mixed multitude, that it is therefore necessarily an unlawful assembly. That number may meet under such circum. stances as by no means to raise public terror, or to raise fears and jealousies in the minds of the persons in the neighbourhood where they meet. But if in an assembly so constituted, met for perfectly legal purposes, any men introduced themselves illegally to give to that meeting an undue direction which would produce terror to His Majesty's subjects, although fifty-nine thousand out of that meeting would be perfectly innocent, there might be twelve or twenty illegally assembled; and those twelve or twenty would be liable to be tried upon the ground of illegally assembling there, although the assembly be perfectly legal as to the bulk of the people who are there. If any persons by plan amongst themselves contrive that there shall be such observations made to them by harangues, by placards, or by other means, as are likely to give to that large body of persons that direction which will be likely to endanger the public peace and strike terror into the minds of His Majesty's subjects, those persons will be liable to conviction of the offence of illegal conspiracy....

In conspiracy it is by no means necessary to prove actual meeting together. If the circumstances are such as imperiously call upon you to say that they could not have occurred but in pursuance of previous conspiracy and plan between the parties, then that implies that there must have been such previous plans, and, therefore, will entirely warrant the conclusion of conspiracy. For instance, in this case, if you should be of opinion that these persons could not have come together in that conformity of circumstances without a plan previously agreed upon between the parties—that would be evidence of previous plan....

In considering the question of unlawful assembly, you are, of course, to take into consideration all the accompanying circumstances. Those circumstances in this case are the banners; appearance as if the parties had been drilled; thirdly, actual evidence of drilling, perhaps. Now if the case is to be made illegal in respect of the banners, it is not necessarily illegal on that account as to every man present at the meeting, but would only be illegal as to that particular man or as to those particular persons who had adopted that banner, or who, with a full knowledge of the existence of that banner, had given their

at the commencement to 50,000 at the end—the circumstances under which the meeting took place, and the mode in which they marched—in the night-time. alarming the tradesmen and compelling them to shut their shops—beyond all doubt bring it within the description of an ‘unlawful assembly’.”

co-operation and countenance to the meeting....So in the case of drilling.   If the meeting is to be considered as illegal because the men
were drilled (drilled, I mean, for an illegal purpose), then it would only
be illegal as to those individuals who knew of the illegal drilling.   For
instance, if, knowing that a body of men, who will be there, have
been previously drilled in order to overawe, intimidate, and menace,
I yet go to that meeting, and give my countenance to that meeting,
I am guilty of giving my attendance at that meeting illegally.   At the
same time, if you go with me, countenancing the general objects of the
meeting, but being ignorant of the drilling, you would not be affected
by that fact..

In considering whether it was generally criminal as to the body of
those who met, when it was legal as to the purpose but illegal as to
the manner, did it or did it not produce terror ?   Was it or was it not
calculated to produce terror ?   As it seems to me, that terror ought to
be a terror to arise before the mob shall disperse.

Is there any evidence of general panic ?   There is no interruption
of business ; the circumstance of their meeting without any arms, the
circumstance of their taking with them women and children, the
circumstance of their demeanour from first to last—peaceable with
scarcely any exception—these are circumstances to enable you to form
a judgment whether either it did produce terror, or was in its nature
calculated to produce the supposition that mischief would result before
the meeting should separate[1]....

[EDITOR'S NOTE.   The summing up given in this case by Mr Justice BAYLEY was
approved by the Court of King's Bench on a motion being made for a new trial.
(See 3 Barnewall and Alderson 566.)]

[1] On the other hand, an absence of women and children was thus commented
upon by the same judge a few days later in *Rex* v. *Dewhurst* (1 St. Tr., N. S.,
600) :—"If I see an immense number of persons, all men ; and I see that women
and children are cautiously excluded ; that may produce terror.   Because I may
say, Why should it be confined to men alone ?"

[*What renders an Assembly* unlawful.]

REGINA *v.* VINCENT AND OTHERS.

MONMOUTH ASSIZES. 1839. 9 CARRINGTON AND PAYNE 91;
3 ST. TR. (N.S.) 1037.

[Indictment for conspiracy, and for unlawful assembly. The de
fendants had addressed meetings in the streets and open spaces of
Newport (Mon.), at which they had denounced the government of the
country, and had demanded the granting of the People's Charter;
threatening that, if necessary, they would have it without the consent
of the Government; and encouraging the people to use violence to
those who might be sent to interfere with them. The meetings attracted a crowd of about 1000 persons; who were in an excited state,
loudly cheering the speeches, and groaning when any of the magistrates passed by.]

ALDERSON, B., in summing up, said: I take it to be the law of the land
that any meeting assembled under such circumstances as, according to
the opinion of rational and firm men, are likely to produce danger to
the tranquillity and peace of the neighbourhood, is an unlawful
assembly. You will have to say whether, looking at all the circumstances, these defendants attended an unlawful assembly. For this
purpose you will take into your consideration the way in which the
meetings were held, the hour of the day at which the parties met, and
the language used by the persons assembled and by those who addressed them. Every one has a right to act in such cases as he may
judge right, provided it be not injurious to another; but no man or
number of men has a right to cause alarm to the body of persons who
are called the public. You will consider how far these meetings
partook of that character; and whether firm and rational men, having
their families and property there, would have reasonable ground to fear
a breach of the peace. For I quite agree with the learned counsel for
the defendant, that the alarm must not be merely such as would
frighten any foolish or timid person, but must be such as would alarm
persons of reasonable firmness and courage. The indictment also contains charges of conspiracy; which is a crime which consists either in
a combination and agreement by persons to do some illegal act, or
a combination and agreement to effect a legal purpose by illegal means.
The purpose which the defendants had in view as stated by the
prosecutors was to excite disaffection and discontent; but the defendants say that their purpose was by reasonable argument and proper
petitions to obtain the five points mentioned by their learned counsel.

If that were so, I think it is by no means illegal to petition on those points. The duration of parliaments and the extent of the elective franchise have undergone more than one change by the authority of Parliament itself; and with respect to the voting by ballot, persons whose opinions are entitled to the highest respect are found to differ. There can also be no illegality in petitioning that members of Parliament should be paid for their services by their constituents; indeed, they were so paid in ancient times. They were not required to have a property qualification till the reign of Queen Anne; and are now not required to have it in order to represent any part of Scotland or the English universities.

If, however, the defendants say that they will effect these changes by physical force, that is an offence against the law of the country. No civilized society can exist if changes are to be effected in the law by physical force.

You will say whether you are satisfied that the defendants conspired to excite disaffection; if you are so, you will find the defendants guilty of the conspiracy. You will also say whether you think that the nature of the meetings was such as would excite alarm in the minds of rational and constant men; for, if so, I am of opinion that they were illegal meetings, and then you ought to find the defendants guilty on the counts for attending unlawful assemblies.

The jury found all the defendants Not guilty of conspiracy, but Guilty of attending unlawful assemblies.

BEATTY AND OTHERS *v.* GILLBANKS.

QUEEN'S BENCH DIVISION. 1882.   L.R. 9 Q.B.D. 308.

[This was an appeal from an order made by the justices at a Petty Sessions held at Weston-super-Mare, whereby the appellants were severally bound over to keep the peace, upon an information for having on March the 26th unlawfully and tumultuously assembled with divers other persons in the public thoroughfares, to the disturbance of the public peace. The appellants were leading members of the Salvation Army; who were in the habit of parading the streets of Weston-super-Mare with flags and banners and a band, and thereby creating much noise and collecting a mob of persons. Another organised body of persons, antagonistic to the Salvation Army, called the "Skeleton

Army," similarly paraded the streets and disputed the passing of the Salvation Army. The two bodies frequently came into collision ; and on March 23rd, the Salvation Army as they paraded the streets were accompanied by a mob of over 2000 persons, and in the midst of the mob there was fighting, stone-throwing and noise. The police ultimately dispersed the crowd. These matters caused great terror in the minds of the inhabitants of the town. A public notice was then issued by two Justices of the Peace, stating that there were reasonable grounds for apprehending a repetition of these tumults and directing all persons to abstain from assembling to the disturbance of the public peace in the public streets. The appellants disregarded the notice, and as-sembled and marched as usual on the following Sunday morning (March 26th), with a crowd accompanying them. The serjeant of the police met them and required Beatty to desist from leading the pro-cession. On his refusing to comply, he was arrested. The other appellants then took command of the procession, whereupon they also were arrested. The question for the opinion of the Court was, whether the facts constituted an unlawful assembly.]

A. R. Poole, for the respondent. Any meeting assembled under such circumstances as, according to rational and firm men, are likely to produce danger to the tranquillity and peace of the neighbourhood, is an unlawful assembly. The justices were entitled to look to what had taken place on previous occasions. The object of the appellants was to collect a mob of persons, although they must have known that if they did so a disturbance would arise; and under these circumstances, whatever their ultimate object, the assembly was unlawful.

FIELD, J. The appellants have, with others, formed themselves into an association for religious exercises among themselves, and for a religious revival, if I may use that word, which they desire to further among certain classes of the community. No one imputes to this association any other object; and so far from wishing to carry that out with violence, their opinions seem to be opposed to such a course, and, at all events, in the present case, they made no opposition to the authorities. That being their lawful object, they assembled as they had done before and marched through the streets of Weston-super-Mare. No one can say that such an assembly is in itself an unlawful one. The appellants complain that in consequence of this assembly they have been found guilty of a crime of which there is no reasonable evidence that they have been guilty. The charge against them is, that they unlawfully and tumultuously assembled, with others, to the dis-turbance of the public peace and against the peace of the Queen. Before they can be convicted it must be shewn that this offence has been committed. There is no doubt that they, and with them others, assembled together in great numbers; but such an assembly to be unlawful must be tumultuous and against the peace. As far as these appellants are concerned, there was nothing in their conduct when they were assembled together which was either tumultuous or against the peace. But it is said that the conduct pursued by them on this occasion was such as, on several previous occasions, had produced riots and disturbance of the peace and terror to the inhabitants; and that the appellants, knowing when they assembled together that such consequences would again arise, are liable to this charge.

Now I entirely concede that every one must be taken to intend the natural consequences of his own acts, and it is clear to me that if this disturbance of the peace was the natural consequence of acts of the appellants they would be liable, and the justices would have been right in binding them over. But the evidence set forth in the case does not support this contention; on the contrary, it shews that the disturbances were caused by other people antagonistic to the appellants, and that no acts of violence were committed by them....

What has happened here is that an unlawful organization has assumed to itself the right to prevent the appellants and others from lawfully assembling together; and the finding of the justices amounts to this, that a man may be convicted for doing a lawful act, if he knows that his doing it may cause another to do an unlawful act. There is no authority for such a proposition. The question of the justices whether the facts stated in the case constituted the offence charged in the information must therefore be answered in the negative.

Judgment for the appellants.

[EDITOR'S NOTE. With this case the student may contrast the later one of *Wise* v. *Dunning* (L. R., 1902, 1 K. B. 167), which, however, should be read in the light of Prof. Dicey's comments. See his *Law of the Constitution*, 7th ed., p. 272.]

[*Magistrate's* power *of suppressing unlawful assemblies.*]

REGINA *v.* NEALE.

WARWICK ASSIZES. 1839. 9 CARRINGTON AND PAYNE 431.

[The defendants were indicted for a riot at Birmingham, which took place on July 4th, 1839. It appeared that previously to July 4th meetings had taken place at Birmingham which caused such alarm that some of the shops were closed; as the police force at Birmingham amounted to only 28 persons, and some of these were decrepit old men.

On July 4th a large and tumultuous meeting was held in the Bull-ring. Dr Booth, a magistrate, having obtained the attendance of 60 London policemen, proceeded to the Bull-ring and desired the mob to disperse. On a refusal, he directed the police to disperse the assembly and apprehend the leaders. A conflict took place, in which several of the police were wounded; and it was found necessary to read the Riot Act and send for the military.]

Miller, for the defence....It is not because large numbers are assembled that a meeting is illegal....Not a single inhabitant has been called to state that this meeting was conducting itself in a manner calculated to produce the slightest alarm; and what right has any magistrate to tell people in a public area in a town to disperse? And unless he has a right to do so, if he let loose a body of constables upon them, and the people resist in consequence of being assailed, they are justified by law; and the rioters are the men who are set upon them, and not those who are assailed. If the police or the magistrates had no authority to assail the people, and a riot ensued afterwards, the people were justified in repelling the assault, and were not guilty of any offence.

Littledale, J., in summing up, said :—...There was an assembly of persons; but up to the time that Dr Booth went in among them, I do not find that any riot had taken place on that day. It is, however, another question whether there had been an unlawful assembly; because if there was a meeting attended with circumstances calculated to excite alarm, that is an unlawful assembly. And whether there be an unlawful assembly, may also depend on the resistance made to the attempts to disperse it and prevent the persons remaining together. And it is not only in the power of magistrates, it is not only lawful for magistrates, to disperse any such meeting, but if they do not, and are guilty of criminal negligence in not putting down any unlawful assembly, they are liable to be prosecuted for a breach of their duty. The first question in the present case is, whether this meeting, constituted as it was before Dr Booth and the police made their appearance, was an unlawful assembly; if it was, then the magistrates had a right to disperse it. The modes of dispersing an unlawful assembly may be very different, according to the circumstances attending it. It might be an unlawful assembly in a very slight degree, parties might have got just within the pale of what is unlawful, and the appearance of one magistrate and two or three

constables might disperse them. If this assembly were of that description, there was no pretence for a magistrate's going with a great
police force to disperse the persons assembled. But all these cases
admit of a variety of shades; because an assembly may be such that
though, up to the time the magistrate goes to it, there may be no
breach of the peace, yet it may be so far verging towards a riot, that
it may be the bounden duty of the magistrates to take immediate
steps to disperse the assembly. If it was a slight matter, a magistrate
going with two or three constables would oblige the people to go away
at once. But if he were to go to a large and tumultuous meeting with
only two or three constables, it would be absurd, and he would only be
laughed at; and there may be cases where a magistrate would be
bound to use force to disperse the assembly. All these different cases
must depend on their own circumstances; and you would have to say
in each whether, under the particular circumstances, the magistrates
were justified in resorting to the means they did. If the meeting
about which we are now inquiring was an unlawful assembly, it was
the duty of the magistrate to disperse it; and you will then have to
consider whether the magistrates used more violent means than were
necessary to disperse the assembly. They are to use all lawful means,
and you must say whether or not they did more.

The jury found all the defendants guilty[1].

[*Magistrate's* duty *of suppressing them.*]

REX *v.* KENNETT.

King's Bench. 1781.   5 Carrington and Payne 282.

[This was an information filed by the Attorney General against Mr
Brackley Kennett for having, when Lord Mayor of London, wilfully
omitted to suppress a riot. The riot in question was Lord George
Gordon's "No Popery" riot of 1780; which lasted five days, and

---

[1] "A person who is accidentally present as an idle spectator is not necessarily
indictable for the offence of unlawful assembly...; but he cannot complain of any
act of force which is necessarily and properly used by the constables for the purpose
of dispersing that assembly. For by his own voluntary act he put himself into a
position of being mistaken for men who are guilty of a breach of law; and he
must take the consequences." (Per Parke, B., in *Reg.* v. *Williams*, 6 St. Tr.,
N. S., 780.)

involved the destruction of £180,000 worth of property. Dickens
describes it vividly in *Barnaby Rudge*. In the ultimate suppression,
210 rioters were killed.]

LORD MANSFIELD, C.J., in summing up to the jury, said :—The
common law and several statutes have invested Justices of the Peace
with great powers to quell riots, because, if not suppressed, they tend
to endanger the constitution of the country. And, as they may assemble
all the King's subjects, it is clear they may call in the soldiers, who
are subjects, and may act as such ; but this should be done with great
caution. It is well understood that magistrates may call in the
military. It would be a strange doctrine, if, in an insurrection rising
to rebellion, every subject had not a power to act, when he possesses
the power in a case of a mere breach of the peace. By the Act of the
1st George the First, a particular direction is given to every Justice for
his conduct; he is required to read the Act, and the consequences are
explained. It is a step in terrorem, and of gentleness ; and is not
made a necessary step, as he may instantly repel force by force. If the
insurgents are not doing any act, the reading of the proclamation
operates as notice. There never was a riot without by-standers, who go
off on reading the Act....

...This information does not charge any intent of favouring or con-
niving at the riots, but only a neglect of duty ; and every neglect of
duty depends upon circumstances. In this case the charge is proved.
In law, to say, "I was afraid," is not an excuse for a magistrate ; it
must be a fear arising from danger, which is reduced to a maxim in
law to be such danger as would affect a firm man. In this case the
neglect, at first view, is proved. The witnesses have sworn that the
defendant used none of the authorities vested in him by law ; he did
not read the proclamation, or restrain or apprehend the rioters, or give
orders to fire, or make any use of the military under his direction. But
this does not exclude a defence. The defence here relied on is—
"'Tis true, I did not restrain or apprehend any rioters, nor use the
military ; but, under all the circumstances, this was not a neglect."
It is primâ facie the duty of a magistrate to read the Act; but this
duty depends on circumstances ; he might be alone, and not able to do
it. If he did what a firm and constant man would have done, he must
be acquitted. If, rather than apprehend the rioters, his sole care was
for himself, this is neglect. The sole question is, under all the circumstances of the case—Has the defendant laid before you the justification
of a man of ordinary firmness?

                                        Verdict, Guilty.

SECTION XVII.

CONSPIRACY.

[*Mere* agreement *constitutes the offence.*]

THE KING *v.* GILL AND HENRY.

KING'S BENCH.   1818.   2 BARNEWALL AND ALDERSON 205.

The defendants were found guilty upon an indictment which charged that they unlawfully did conspire and combine together, by divers false pretences and subtle means and devices, to obtain and acquire to themselves, of and from *P. D.* and *G. D.*, divers large sums of money of the respective moneys of the said *P. D.* and *G. D.*, and to cheat and defraud them respectively thereof, to the great damage, &c. And, being now brought up for judgment,

Gurney moved in arrest of judgment, on the ground that the indictment was framed too generally; that the words, "by divers false pretences and subtle means and devices," gave no information to the defendants of the specific charge against which they were to defend themselves; that the overt acts of conspiracy should be stated, or at least so much of them as to shew the corpus delicti or transaction to which the charge was meant to be applied; and that in no instance hitherto had so general a count been supported.

ABBOTT, C.J. The indictment appears to me sufficient. The gist of the offence is the conspiracy; and although the nature of every offence must be laid with reasonable certainty, so as to apprise the defendant of the charge, yet I think that it is sufficiently done by the present indictment. It is objected that the particular means and devices are not stated. It is, however, possible to conceive that persons might meet together, and might determine and resolve that they would, by some trick and device, cheat and defraud another, without having at that time fixed and settled what the particular means and devices should be. Such a meeting and resolution would nevertheless constitute an offence.

*   *   *   *

HOLROYD, J. I am of the same opinion. The present case differs materially from the case of obtaining money under false pretences. There the false pretences constitute the offence; but here the conspiracy is the offence, and it is quite sufficient to state only the act of conspiring and the object of the conspiracy in the indictment. Here it is stated that the parties did conspire, and that the object was to obtain, by false pretences, money from a particular person. Now, a conspiracy to do that would be indictable, even where the parties had not settled the means to be employed. I therefore think that there is no ground for arresting the judgment.

Rule refused.

[See also REX v. STARLING, *infra*, p. 403.]

[*This agreement may be to commit a substantive* crime.]

[See REGINA v. DAVITT AND WILSON, *supra*, p. 380.]

[*Or this mere* agreement *to do an act may be* criminal, *although the act itself be not criminal or even actionable.*]

THE KING v. DE BERENGER AND OTHERS.

KING'S BENCH.   1814.   3 MAULE AND SELWYN 67.

[De Berenger and seven others, amongst them Lord Cochrane, the celebrated naval commander, were tried before Lord Ellenborough, C.J. upon an indictment for a conspiracy. The jury found them guilty upon counts alleging that, during the war then existing with France, they had conspired to make and propagate divers false reports and rumours that Napoleon Bonaparte was killed, and that thus a peace would soon be made between the king and his subjects and the people of France, and that the defendants would by such false reports and rumours, as far as in them lay, occasion an increase and rise in the prices of the public government funds and other government securities, with a wicked intention thereby to injure and aggrieve all the subjects of the king who should, on the 21st of February, purchase or buy any part or parts, share or shares of and in the said public government funds, and other government securities.]

Best, Serjt., moved in arrest of judgment....No adjudged case of conspiracy has gone so far as this; the crime alleged is a conspiracy to raise the price of the government funds of this country; but if it be not a crime in itself to raise the price of the government funds of this country, a conspiracy to do so will not carry it farther, unless some collateral object be stated to give it a criminal character. Generally speaking, the higher the price of the public funds, the better for the country; because the higher the state of public credit.

Lord Ellenborough, C.J. I am perfectly clear that there is not any ground for the motion in arrest of judgment. A public mischief is stated as the object of this conspiracy; the conspiracy is by false rumours to raise the price of the public funds and securities. The crime lies in the act of conspiracy and combination to effect that purpose; and would have been complete although it had not been pursued to its consequences, or the parties had not been able to carry it into effect. The purpose itself is mischievous; it strikes at the price of a vendible commodity in the market, and if it gives it a fictitious price by means of false rumours, it is a fraud levelled against all the public; for it is against all such as may possibly have anything to do with the funds on that particular day. It seems to me also not to be necessary to specify the persons, who became purchasers of stock, as the persons to be affected by the conspiracy; for the defendants could not, except by a spirit of prophecy, divine who would be the purchasers on a subsequent day. The excuse is, that it was impossible they should have known; and if it were possible, the multitude would be an excuse in point of law. But the statement is wholly unnecessary, the conspiracy being complete independently of any persons being purchasers.

Le Blanc, J. ...It may be admitted therefore that the raising or lowering the price of the public funds is not per se a crime. A man may have occasion to sell out a large sum, which may have the effect of depressing the price of stocks, or may buy in a large sum, and thereby raise the price on a particular day, and yet he will be guilty of no offence. But if a number of persons conspire by false rumours to raise the funds on a particular day, that is an offence; and the offence is, not in raising the funds simply, but in conspiring by false rumours to raise them on that particular day.

* * * * *

Dampier, J. I own I cannot raise a doubt but that this is a complete crime of conspiracy according to any definition of it. The

means used are wrong, they were false rumours; the object is wrong, it
was to give a false value to a commodity in the public market, which
was injurious to those who had to purchase. That disposes of the first
objection. The second objection is, that the persons injured ought
to have been named. To which one answer is, that the criminality is
complete when the concert to bring about a mischievous object by
illegal means is complete; it is not necessary that the object should be
attained. Therefore there was no need to set out the name of any
person, because no person need be injured. That is the first answer;
and the next is, that it was impossible the defendants could know who
those persons would be.

[EDITOR'S NOTE. See the very similar case of *Scott* v. *Brown* (L. R. [1892]
2 Q. B. 724), where the conspiracy was to raise the price of the shares in the Steam
Loop Company Limited by making sham sales and purchases of them at a high
price.]

[*Agreement merely to break a contract, if under circumstances
injurious to the public.*]

VERTUE *v.* LORD CLIVE.

KING'S BENCH. 1779.   4 BURROWS 2473.

[This was an action brought by an officer in the military service of
the East India Company against the defendant, who was commander-
in-chief of the Company's forces in India, for an assault and false
imprisonment committed in India. The transaction arose in the
East Indies upon a dispute about a perquisite called *Batta*; which had
been received by former military officers there, but which Lord Clive
thought proper to lessen considerably. The officers were exceedingly
dissatisfied with this reduction of their pay or perquisite; and resented
it so highly that 175 of them threw up their commissions and quitted
the service. Of these, Lieutenant Vertue was one. His colonel
refused to accept his resignation, and commanded him to stay in the
camp. He disobeyed; and quitted the camp in the sight of the officers
and men. He was arrested and tried by a court-martial; whose
sentence was approved by Lord Clive.

K.   26

At the trial, the question was whether the plaintiff was still subject to military law at the time of holding the court-martial. The jury found for the defendant. A motion was made for a new trial.]

Dunning, for plaintiff. Lieut. Vertue was not in a military character, or in a capacity to commit a military offence, at the time when this military jurisdiction was exercised upon him by the defendant. The commission which Mr Vertue had received contained no engagement or obligation upon the East India Company to keep him in their service a moment longer than they liked; nor upon him, to continue in their service longer than he liked. Either party was at liberty to put an end to the contract, under proper circumstances and in a proper situation. The reduction of the *batta* took away from the officers what induced them to enter into the Company's service; and the enemy [the Mahrattas] had been defeated before the plaintiff resigned his commission....

LORD MANSFIELD, C.J.... The officers of each brigade combined together to throw up their commissions; and all of them (about 200 in number) to resign at the same time. The plaintiff was one of those who thus combined...to throw up their commissions, in order to force the Company into allowing them the double *batta*. The very measure shews that it was meant to terrify and intimidate the Company into the allowance. And the danger of such a combination, and of all these officers quitting the service at once, is too obvious to be denied or doubted. There must, at the least, have been great danger of an insurrection amongst the sepoys and common soldiers; though there might not have been any from the Mahrattas....

YATES, J. This combination being a criminal act, it could not be a legal determination of the service.

*   *   *

New trial refused.

[*Agreements to pervert the course of justice are indictable as Conspiracies.*]

[See REX *v.* MACDANIEL, *supra,* p. 98.]

[*Conspiracy so to carry on trade as to diminish the revenue.*]

THE KING *v.* STARLING.

KING'S BENCH. 1663.　　　1 SIDERFIN 174; 1 LEVINZ 125.

An information was preferred against Sir Samuel Starling, an Alderman of the City, and fifteen other London brewers, for having confederated and conspired to brew no 'gallon beer'—which is that small-beer with which the poorer people are supplied—with intent to move the common people to pull down the Excise House. The information further charged that, whereas the farm-rents of the Excise (then £118,000 a year) were settled upon the King by Act of Parliament and formed part of his revenue, the defendants had endeavoured by combination and confederacy to impoverish the farmers of the Excise. [Starling had failed in his attempt to become one of the farmers, and was consequently envious of their prosperity.] The trial was at bar. The jury acquitted the defendants, except on the conspiracy to impoverish the farmers of the Excise.

*　　*　　*　　*　　*

A motion was made to quash the information on the ground that the only charge found by the verdict was not a criminal offence. It is no offence punishable by our laws to impoverish another for the purpose of enriching myself, as for instance by selling commodities at cheaper rates than his; 29 Lib. Ass. 45.

But after several discussions THE COURT adjudged that this is a good verdict, on which judgment may be given for the King. For the verdict refers to the information, and the information sets out that the Excise is parcel of the revenue of the King; and to impoverish the farmers of it may make them incapable of paying the King his revenue.... Starling was fined 500 marks and the other defendants 100 marks each.

HYDE, TWISDEN, and KEELING, JJ., held also that the bare conspiracy to diminish the King's revenue is punishable, though no overt act was done; 27 Ass. 44, 43 Ass. 26.

[*At common law*[1], *even an agreement* in restraint of trade
might amount to a Conspiracy.]

THE KING *v.* THE JOURNEYMEN TAILORS
OF CAMBRIDGE.

KING'S BENCH.   1721.   8 MODERN 11.

One *Wise* and several other journeymen tailors, of or in the town of
Cambridge, were indicted for a conspiracy amongst themselves to raise
their wages; and were found guilty.   Motion was made in arrest of
judgment, upon several errors in the record.

*   *   *   *   *

Thirdly, because no crime appears upon the face of this indictment;
for it only charges them with a conspiracy in a refusal to work at so
much *per diem*; whereas, they are not obliged at all to work by the
day, but by the year, by 5 Eliz. c. 4.

THE COURT....It is not for the refusing to work, but for conspiring, that they are indicted.   And a conspiracy of any kind is
illegal, although the matter about which they conspired might have
been lawful for them, or any of them, to do if they had not conspired
to do it.

Fourthly, that this fact is laid in the town of Cambridge, but
it doth not appear by the record in what county Cambridge is; which
it ought to do, because there are other towns of that name in England,
e.g. in Gloucestershire.   And so it is a mis-trial, for there is no more
reason...[to summon the jury from] Cambridgeshire than any other
county....

THE COURT....Cambridge being mentioned in several Acts of Parliament, the Court must take notice of such Acts, and will intend that
Cambridge is in the county of Cambridge.

Fifthly.   This indictment ought to conclude *contra formam statuti*,
for by the late statute, 7 Geo. I. c. 13, journeymen tailors [in London]
are prohibited to enter into any contract for advancing their wages..

It was answered that the omission...is not material, because this
indictment is for a conspiracy; which is an offence at common law.
It is true that the indictment sets forth that the defendants refused to
work under rates which were more than is enjoined [in London] by the
statute, for that is only two shillings a day.   But...it is not for this

---

[1] *I.e.* as the common law was understood until modern times.   But it is now
held (*Mogul Steamship Co.* v. *McGregor*, L. R. [1892] A. C. at pp. 45, 57, 58) that
contracts in restraint of trade, though so unlawful as to be unenforceable, are not
indictable as Crimes.

denial to work...but for a conspiracy to raise their wages, that these defendants are indicted. It is true it does not appear by the record that the wages demanded were excessive; but that is not material, because it may be given in evidence.

THE COURT. This indictment need not conclude *contra formam statuti*; because it is for a conspiracy, which is an offence at common law.

So the judgment was confirmed by the whole Court.

[EDITOR'S NOTE. See also the case of *Rex* v. *Hammond, infra*, p. 411. But the rules, (based partly on the common law doctrine of Conspiracy and partly upon statutes), by which it was made criminal for associations of workmen to attempt to affect the rate of wages and the course of the labour-market, have been brought to an end by s. 3 of the Conspiracy and Protection of Property Act, 1875 (38 and 39 Vict. c. 86). This provides that an agreement to do, or procure to be done, any act in contemplation or furtherance of a trade dispute between employers and workmen shall not be indictable as a conspiracy, if such act committed by one person would not be a crime punishable with imprisonment. See also the extension of this principle to civil proceedings by the Trade Disputes Act 1906, s. 1.]

[*What injurious agreements may not be indictable as Conspiracies.*]

THE KING *v.* SEWARD AND OTHERS.

KING'S BENCH. 1834.   1 ADOLPHUS AND ELLIS 706.

This was an indictment for conspiracy, found at the General Sessions of Oyer and Terminer and Gaol Delivery in and for the Isle of Ely, holden at Ely. [The conspiracy alleged was a combination by certain parishioners of Chatteris to give a poor man, who was legally settled in the parish of St Ives, a sum of three pounds to marry a female pauper then legally settled in, and actually chargeable to, the parish of Chatteris; and thereby throw her maintenance upon the parish of St Ives. The marriage had taken place, and the wife had been removed to St Ives, and had there received poor-law relief. The defendants having been convicted, a motion was made for a rule to shew cause why the judgment should not be arrested, because the indictment did not shew that the marriage had been procured by any violence, threat, contrivance, or other sinister means.]

Kelly. The objection here taken is founded on an erroneous view of the offence. The charge is, in substance, not a conspiracy to procure a marriage, but a conspiracy unlawfully to exonerate one parish from the maintenance of a pauper and throw it upon another. A conspiracy merely to procure a marriage would not be indictable; but it becomes an offence if the thing is to be done for an unlawful end or by unlawful means. Here an unlawful end is stated, viz. to transfer a burden wrongfully from one parish to another; hence if no means were stated, or no overt acts alleged, the indictment would still be good.

＊　　＊　　＊　　＊　　＊

LORD DENMAN, C.J. I am of opinion that this rule must be absolute. An indictment for conspiracy ought to shew that it was either for an unlawful purpose, or to effect a lawful purpose by unlawful means: that is not done here. To say that meeting together and combining to exonerate one parish from the burden of a poor person and throw it on another, amounts to an indictable conspiracy, is extravagant. If such a proposition could be maintained, it would apply to parishioners hiring out a poor boy from their own parish into another. Then when it is said that such a proceeding is a conspiracy, because it is to be carried into effect by unlawful means, we must see in the means stated something which amounts to an offence.

＊　　＊　　＊　　＊　　＊

TAUNTON, J. I am of the same opinion. Merely persuading an unmarried man and woman in poor circumstances to contract matrimony, is not an offence. If, indeed, it were done by unfair and undue means, it might be unlawful; but that is not stated. There is no averment that the parties were unwilling, or that the marriage was brought about by any fraud, stratagem, or concealment, or by duress or threat. No unlawful means are stated, and the thing in itself is not an offence: to call this a conspiracy, is giving a colour to the case which the facts do not admit of. As stated, it is nothing more than the case where the officers of a parish agree, after consultation, to apprentice out children from their own parish into another. No doubt, when that is done, the one parish may be exonerated and the other subjected to a charge; but no offence is committed.

[*A Conspiracy requires more than* one *conspirator.*]

THE KING AND QUEEN v. THORP AND OTHERS

KING'S BENCH. 1696.   5 MODERN 221; COMBERBACH 158.

Information against Thorp and others, setting forth that they and each of them, being persons of ill fame, did, on the tenth of October in the fifth year of William and Mary, and at divers other times as well before as after, wickedly, unlawfully, and deceitfully, conspire, at Winchester, to take one Edward Mitchell, being under the age of eighteen years, the only son and heir of Robert Mitchell, Esq., and to carry him out of the custody, counsel, and government of his said father, without his notice and against his will, and to marry him to Cornelia Holton, a person of ill name and of no fortune; that the defendants did unlawfully assemble themselves together to accomplish the said conspiracy and wicked intentions; that they, and every one of them, by divers false, malicious, and deceitful insinuations, did falsely, unjustly, maliciously, and deceitfully persuade the said Edward Mitchell to hate his father, and to leave Winchester School where he was placed by his father for his learning, and to frequent the house of the defendant Thorp at Winton, and did persuade the said Edward Mitchell, and by divers false allurements did compel him, to be drunk with strong waters and other liquors; and that they introduced Cornelia Holton into his company, and did unlawfully and deceitfully, by false speeches, persuade and solicit him to be married to her; that in further prosecution of their intentions the defendants, and every of them, on the sixteenth of October in the fifth of William and Mary, did, by divers false assurances and promises, solicit, invite, and procure the said Edward Mitchell to leave the said school, against the will and without the notice or consent of his father, and did receive, maintain, and keep him, with an intent to persuade him to marry the said Cornelia Holton; that the said Cornelia Holton did contract matrimony with the said Edward Mitchell, on the twentieth day of October, in the fifth year aforesaid, at Watlington, in the county of Oxford, by the abetting and false means of the said defendants, to the damage of the said father, &c.

Upon not guilty pleaded, this information was tried at the Assizes at Winchester, and all the defendants were found not guilty, except Thorp; and he was acquitted of compelling the said Mitchell to be drunk, and found guilty of all the rest in the information.

It was moved in arrest of judgment:—Firstly, that this information does not contain any matter of misdemeanor. As it is no crime in

him to marry, it is no crime to persuade him to marry. Secondly, it is
laid by way of a conspiracy; and the defendant Thorp being alone found
guilty, there can be no judgment against him. Because *one* cannot
conspire.

*   *   *   *   *

HOLT, C.J. It is a great crime and worthy to be punished; and so
it shall be, if we can any way come at it.

[But no judgment was ever given.]

[EDITOR'S NOTE. As to when conspiracies to bring about a marriage are
criminal, see the cases of *Wade* v. *Broughton*, 3 Ves. & B. 173, and *Rex* v. *Edward
Gibbon Wakefield*, 2 Lewin 1.]

[*How a Conspiracy is* proved.]

THE KING *v.* PARSONS AND ANOTHER.

KING'S BENCH.   1762.   1 WM BLACKSTONE 391.

The defendants were convicted on an information for a conspiracy
to take away the character of one Kempe, and accuse him of murder,
by pretended conversations and communications with a ghost, that
conversed by knocking and scratching in a place called Cock-lane[1].
When they were brought up for judgment, Lord MANSFIELD, who tried
the information, declared, that he had directed the jury that there was
no occasion to prove the actual fact of conspiring, but that it might be
collected from collateral circumstances[2]; and he should be glad to know
the opinion of his brethren, whether he was right in such direction.
Quod nemo negavit.

[See also REX *v.* HUNT *supra*, p. 388.]

---

[1] [In Smithfield. Parsons' daughter, a child of eleven, effected the deceptions.
For details, see Boswell's *Life of Dr Johnson*, under June 1763.]

[2] So where the defendants *severally* had bribed the prosecutor's apprentices to
put grease into his cards (he being a card-maker), their being all of one family, and
concerned in card-making, was held evidence of a conspiracy; *Rex* v. *Cope*, 1 Stra.
144; *infra*, p. 410.

[*What circumstances are* insufficient *proof.*]

REX *v.* PYWELL AND OTHERS.

WESTMINSTER NISI PRIUS SITTINGS.   1816.   1 STARKIE 102.

This was an indictment against the defendants for a conspiracy to cheat and defraud General Maclean, by selling him an unsound horse.

It appeared that the defendant Pywell had advertised the sale of horses, undertaking to warrant their soundness. Upon an application by General Maclean at Pywell's stables, Budgery, another of the defendants, stated to him that he had lived with the owner of a horse which was shewn to him, and that he knew the horse to be perfectly sound, and, as the agent of Pywell, he warranted him to be sound.

It was discovered, very soon after the sale, that the animal was nearly worthless.

LORD ELLENBOROUGH intimated that the case did not assume the shape of a conspiracy; the evidence would not warrant any proceeding beyond that of an action, on the warranty, for the breach of a civil contract. If this (he said) were to be considered to be an indictable offence, then instead of all the actions which had been brought on warranties, the defendants ought to have been indicted as cheats. And no indictment in a case like this could be maintained without evidence of concert between the parties to effectuate a fraud.

The defendants were accordingly acquitted.

[*Wide range of admissible evidence.*]

REX *v.* ROBERTS AND OTHERS.

WESTMINSTER NISI PRIUS SITTINGS.   1808.   1 CAMPBELL 399.

This was an indictment against the defendants, which charged that, being persons of evil fame and in low and indigent circumstances, they conspired together to cause themselves to be reputed persons of considerable property, and in opulent circumstances, for the purpose of defrauding one A. B., &c.

Evidence being given of their having hired a house in a fashionable street, and represented themselves to one tradesman employed to furnish it as people of large fortune, a witness was called to prove that, at a different time, they had made a similar representation to another tradesman.

Marryat objected that it was not competent to the prosecutor to give evidence of various acts of this sort; and that he was bound to select and confine himself to one. It was impossible for a man to come prepared to explain all the transactions of his life; and if this mode of fixing a crime were allowed, no one could be secure.

Lord Ellenborough. This is an indictment for a conspiracy to carry on the business of common cheats; and cumulative instances are necessary to prove the offence. The same sort of evidence is allowed in an indictment for barratry. In a prosecution for high treason itself, the gravest of all offences, if the indictment lays that the prisoner imagined the death of the King, and in pursuance of such imagination wrote divers letters to the enemies of our Lord the King, or held divers consults upon that subject, evidence may be given of the prisoner's having written any treasonable letter, or attended any meeting held for treasonable purposes. The objection is unfounded.

The defendants were all found guilty.

[*Wide range of admissible evidence.*]

REX *v.* COPE AND OTHERS.

Middlesex N.P. Sittings. 1718. 1 Strange 144.

The husband and wife and servants were indicted for a conspiracy to ruin the trade of the prosecutor, who was the king's card-maker. The evidence against them was, that they had at several times given money to the prosecutor's apprentices to put grease into the paste, which had spoiled the cards. But there was no account given that more than one at a time ever were present, though it was proved they had all given money in their turns.

It was objected that this could not be a conspiracy; for two men might do the same thing without having any previous communication with one another.

But Pratt, C.J. ruled that, all the defendants being of a family, and concerned in making of cards, it would amount to evidence of a conspiracy; and directed the jury accordingly.

[*Wide range of admissible evidence.*]

REX *v.* HAMMOND AND WEBB.

KING'S BENCH.   1799.   2 ESPINASSE 718.

This was an indictment against the defendants, who were journeymen shoemakers, for a conspiracy to raise their wages. [See note at
p. 405, *supra.*] It was stated, on the part of the prosecution, that a plan
for a combination amongst journeymen shoe-makers had been formed
and printed in the year 1792; regulating their meetings, the sub-
scriptions for their mutual support, and other matters for their mutual
government in forwarding their designs. The prosecutor's counsel
were going into evidence of this, when the defendants' counsel objected
to its being admitted until it had been brought home to the defendants,
and they had been proved parties to the combination stated.

LORD KENYON. If a general conspiracy exists, you may go into
general evidence of its nature and the conduct of its members, so as to
implicate men who stand charged with acting upon the terms of it
years after those terms have been established; and who may reside at
a great distance from the place where the general plan is carried on.
So it was done in the State Trials in the year 1745; where, from the
nature of the charge it was necessary to go into evidence of what was
going on at Manchester, in France, in Scotland, and in Ireland, at the
same time.

His Lordship therefore permitted a person, who was a member of
this society, to prove the printed regulations and rules of the society,
and that he and others acted under them in execution of the conspiracy
charged upon the defendants Hammond and Webb, as evidence intro-
ductory to the proof that they were members of this society, and
equally concerned. But he added that it would not be evidence to
affect the defendants, until they were shewn to be parties to the same
conspiracy.

In the course of the evidence, it was stated that the demands of the
journeymen had been occasioned by some of the masters giving wages
beyond what were the usual ones in the trade.

LORD KENYON said that masters should be cautious of conducting
themselves in that way, as they were as liable for a conspiracy as the
journeymen. There was a case where a master, from shewing too great
indulgence to his men, had become himself the object of a prosecution.

The defendants were found guilty.

[*The nature, and the evidence, of Conspiracy.*]

REGINA *v.* PARNELL AND OTHERS.

IRISH QUEEN'S BENCH DIVISION.   1881.   14 Cox 505.

Information by Her Majesty's Attorney General for Ireland against Charles Stewart Parnell, M.P., John Dillon, M.P., Joseph Gillis Biggar, M.P., Timothy Daniel Sullivan, M.P., Thomas Sexton, M.P., Patrick Egan, P. J. Sheridan, and others.

The first count of the information charged that "The traversers, intending, with others, to impoverish and injure owners of farms in Ireland let to tenants in consideration of the payment of rent, did conspire combine and confederate to solicit large numbers of tenants. in breach of their contracts of tenancy, to refuse to pay, and not to pay, to the owners of farms the rents which they the said tenants were and might become lawfully bound to pay; and which the said owners might become lawfully entitled to be paid under the said contracts of tenancy; to the great damage of the said owners, and to the evil example of others in the like case offending."

*   *   *   *   *

[The case came on for trial at the bar of the Queen's Bench Division, before FITZGERALD, J., and BARRY, J.]

FITZGERALD, J....A conspiracy consists in the agreement of two or more to do an unlawful act, or to do a lawful act by unlawful means. By the terms 'illegal' and 'unlawful' it is not intended to confine the definition to an act that would in itself be a crime or an offence. They extend to and may embrace many cases in which the purpose of a conspiracy, if effected by one person only, would not be a criminal act; as, for instance, if several persons combined to violate a private right, the violation of which, if done by one, would be wrongful but not in itself criminal. If, for instance, a tenant withholds his rent, that is a violation of the right of his landlord to receive it, but would not be a criminal act in the tenant, though it would be the violation of a right. But if two or more incite him to do that act, their agreement so to incite him is by the law of the land an offence. Conspiracy has been aptly described as divisible under three heads :—where the end to be attained is in itself a crime; where the object is to do injury to a third party or to a class, though if that injury were effected by a single individual it would be a civil wrong but not a crime; and where the object is lawful, but the means to be resorted to are unlawful. The first defini- tion, that is, where the end to be obtained is criminal, speaks for itself. One of the charges against the defendants is that they conspired to advise that to be done which in itself was a crime ; namely, forcibly to retake possession of the land which the law had awarded to the landlord. Of the third, the illustration commonly given is where a man has a right to real property, and two or three agree to support him in that right ; (so far their action is proper, to support him in the right which he really has;) but they agree to give him that support by unlawful means, *e.g.*, by the procuring of some fabricated evidence. The agreement to do this by unlawful means makes it an offence. As to the intermediate definition, it is not inaptly illustrated by *Reg.* v. *Druitt* (10 Cox C. C. 592). In that case Baron Bramwell says, "The public have an interest in the way in which a man disposes of his industry and his capital ; and if two or more persons conspire by threats, intimidation, or molestation, to deter or influence him in the way he should employ his talents or his capital, they become guilty of an indictable offence." And he adds emphatically, "that is the common law of the land." In such cases, the agreement by two or more persons to effect an injury or wrong to another is constituted an offence, because a wrong to be effected by a combination assumes a formidable character. When done by one alone, it is but a civil injury; but it assumes a formidable or aggravated character when it is to be effected by the powers of a combination. And it is justly so; because, though you may assert your rights against one individual, how can you defend your rights against a number of persons combined together to inflict a wrong on you?...

A great deal has been said as to conspiracies to effect objects which would not be criminal in themselves ; and you were, above all, referred to the action of Trades Unions. But the action of Trades Unions, which is now regulated by Statute [*supra*, p. 405], is totally different from the charge which is here made against the defendants. Workmen may agree in common not to work unless they are paid certain prices. The same in the case of the employers of labour. They may agree not to take men into their employment unless at certain rates. They are free to do that. But see how different the circumstances are. A man or a body of men may say, " We won't give our labour unless we are paid in a certain way "; or a body of employers may say, "We cannot give employment, profitably to ourselves, unless you work at a certain rate." How different to the case before us ! For the combination alleged here is an agreement to incite farmers, who have agreed to pay certain rents, not to pay them ; and not only not to pay the rents which they have contracted to pay, but to keep the farms by force and against the law of the country. There is no analogy between the two cases.

Some observations have been addressed to you in the course of this case, and have been often repeated, to the effect that there has been no proof given that the defendants ever met, or entered into or became parties to any agreement or confederacy or conspiracy....But I have now to inform you, as part of the law of conspiracy, that there is no necessity that there should be express proof of a conspiracy; such as proof that the parties actually met and laid their heads together, and then and there actually agreed to carry out a common purpose. Nor is such proof usually attempted. In *Mulcahy's case* (L. R. 3 H. of L. 306), a great judge (Mr Justice Willes) says, "So far as proof goes, conspiracy, as Grose, J., says in *Rex* v. *Brissac* (4 East 171), is generally a matter of inference, deduced from certain criminal acts of the parties accused, done in pursuance of an apparent criminal purpose in common between them." It may be that the alleged conspirators have never seen each other, and have never corresponded; one may have never heard the name of the other; and yet by the law they may be parties to the same common criminal agreement. Thus, in some of the Fenian cases tried in this country, it frequently happened that one of the conspirators was in America, the other in this country; that they had never seen each other; but that there were acts on both sides which led the jury to draw the inference that they were engaged in accomplishing the same common object. And when the jury had arrived at this conclusion, the acts of one conspirator became evidence against the other; as in a remarkable case at Cork (as singular and remarkable a case as I ever met with). It was a case in which two persons had been connected with the American service in the late war. One was a captain of cavalry on the Southern side, and the other was a captain on the Northern side. The one was a native of this country, the other a native of America. They had been opposed to each other during the war; they had never seen each other; and amongst the documents found upon them when arrested was a letter in which one complained of violence and murder committed by the commander on the other side. These two men had never seen each other. When they arrived at Queenstown they were arrested. The one had come to take command of a brigade of Fenian cavalry, and had brought with him as his whole equipment a saddle, a pair of spurs, and two long pistols. The other was returning to Ireland; and was alleged to be a party to the Fenian conspiracy. They were put upon trial in the same dock, upon the same indictment; and the first time they saw each other was when they thus stood face to face in the dock. I mention this case as illustrating that a charge of conspiracy may be well founded, even though the parties never saw each other....

Again, it has been suggested that secrecy is to some extent an

essential of conspiracy; and your attention has been repeatedly called
to the fact that all the proceedings of the defendants were above
board, that they were unconcealed, that they were not carried on in
the dark; and it was urged that there could be no guilty conspiracy,
because all was done openly and above board.   But I have to inform
you in point of law that, though secrecy is frequently a characteristic
of conspiracy, it forms no essential element of the crime.   The crime of
conspiracy may be complete though all the proceedings of the confederates have been open and above board and unconcealed.   In
point of law, secrecy or darkness forms no element in the crime of
conspiracy.

   This law of conspiracy is not an invention of modern times.   It
is part of our common law; it has existed from time immemorial.
It is necessary, to redress certain classes of injuries which at times
would be intolerable, and which, but for it, would go unpunished.   If
the defendants have broken the law in the manner alleged in the
information, there is no law of this land by which they could be
reached but by the law of conspiracy.   It has been said that in England
this law has become entirely disused.   But that is untrue; it is a law
repeatedly put in force.   It is seldom resorted to in political trials.
But in a political trial such as the present, if the defendants have
broken the law, their offence can only be reached by the common law
indictment for conspiracy.

SECTION XVIII.

PERJURY.

[Perjury declared to be criminal.]

REX v. ROWLAND AP ELIZA.

STAR CHAMBER.   1613.   COKE'S THIRD INSTITUTE 164.

   The King's attorney preferred an information in the Exchequer
against Hugh Nanny, Esq., the father, and Hugh Nanny, the son, and
others, for intrusion and cutting down a great number of trees, &c., in
Penrose, in the county of Merioneth.   The defendant pleaded not guilty,
and the trial being at the bar, Rowl. Ap Eliza was a witness produced
for the King, who deposed upon his oath to the jury, that Hugh, the

father, and Hugh, the son, joined in sale of the said trees, and commanded the vendees to cut them down. Upon which testimony the jury found for the King, and assessed great damages, and thereupon judgment and execution was had. Hugh Nanny, the father, exhibited his bill in the Star Chamber at the common law, and charged Rowland ap Eliza with perjury, and assigned the perjury in that he, the said Hugh, the father, never joined in sale, nor commanded the vendees to cut down the trees, &c. And it was resolved, first, that perjury in a witness was punishable by the common law. Secondly, that perjury in a witness for the King was punishable by the common law, either upon an indictment, or in an information.... And the said Rowland Ap Eliza was by the sentence of the Court convicted of wilful and corrupt perjury.

[EDITOR'S NOTE. Mr Justice Stephen pronounces this decision to have been "one of the boldest, and, it must be added, one of the most reasonable, acts of judicial legislation on record" (*Digest Cr. L.*, 1st ed., p. 345).]

[*Perjury can only be committed in a judicial proceeding.*]

THE KEEPERS OF THE LIBERTIES OF ENGLAND *v.* HOWELL GWINN.

UPPER BENCH. 1652. STYLE 336.

Howell Gwinn was indicted of perjury for taking of a false oath in an affidavit made before a Master of the Chancery, and was found guilty[1]. It was moved in arrest of judgment (i) that it doth not appear by the record that the oath made was anything material to the suit depending in that Court; and so it is but an extra-judicial oath, and is not perjury either by the common law or by statute; (ii) it doth not appear that the party took a false oath; for it appears not whether the Master of the Chancery had any power to take this oath.

* * * * *

ROLLE, C.J. Perjury at the common law is intended to be in some Court, and in legal proceedings. For a false oath, made before

---

1 p. 363. "Memorandum. Howell Gwinn cut off a dead man's hand, and put a pen and a seal in it; and so signed and sealed and delivered with the dead hand; and swore that he saw the deed sealed and delivered."

us, not touching a matter in question between parties, an indictment of perjury lies not....A false oath is one thing, and perjury is another; for one is judicial, and the other is extra-judicial. And the law inflicts greater punishment for a false oath made in a Court of justice than if it be made elsewhere; because of the preservation of justice.

THE COURT held the indictment ill; and gave judgment against the Custodes.

[EDITOR'S NOTE. Following this rule, the Perjury Act 1911 (1 and 2 Geo. V. c. 6, s. 1), limits the definition of Perjury to wilful material falsehoods told "in a judicial proceeding." But it extends Perjury to cases where the witness has affirmed or declared, and *not* taken a religious oath.]

[*But taking a false oath in a matter which, though* extra-judicial, *concerns the public, is indictable; although not as Perjury.*]

REX *v.* FOSTER.

CROWN CASE RESERVED. 1821.   RUSSELL AND RYAN 459.

The defendant was convicted before Mr JUSTICE BAYLEY, on an indictment for *perjury*, in falsely swearing before a surrogate (in order to obtain a marriage licence) that his intended wife had been residing in the parish of Sunderland.

The learned JUDGE, not being aware of any instance in which a false oath before a surrogate had been made the foundation of such an indictment, thought it right to reserve the case.

In Easter term, 1821, THE JUDGES met and were unanimously of opinion that perjury could not be charged upon an oath taken before a surrogate. THE JUDGES were also of opinion that, as the indictment in this case did not *charge* that the defendant took the oath to procure a licence, or that he did procure one, no punishment could be inflicted. THE JUDGES directed a pardon to be applied for.

[EDITOR'S NOTE. The Perjury Act 1911 (s. 2) now makes it not only a misdemeanor, but even one as severely punishable as Perjury itself, for any person, who (otherwise than in a judicial proceeding) is "authorised by law to make *any* statement on oath (or on affirmation or declaration) for *any* purpose," to make that statement with wilful and material falsity.]

[*The false statement must be* material *to the proceedings*[1].]

REGINA *v.* HOLDEN.

The prisoner was indicted for perjury committed by him at the hearing, before the Justices at Petty Sessions, of a summons taken out by him against the present prosecutor for using language calculated to incite him (Holden) to commit a breach of the peace....

The prisoner, who was a saddler at Colne, was removing his goods from his shop ; and, as he was standing on the top of the cart, arranging the goods, the horse moved slightly. This so enraged him that he jumped off the cart and kicked the horse and struck it on the head. The prosecutor, seeing the prisoner thus act, shouted to him, "That is nice conduct for a religious man ! If there was a Society here for the prevention of cruelty to animals, I would summon you." Whereupon the prisoner replied, "If you don't go into your own house, I will do the same to you." The prosecutor then retorted in these words :— "Thou can't ; thou art a squinting, lying devil." Next day the prisoner laid an information[2] against the prosecutor for using language calculated to incite him to commit a breach of the peace. The Justices heard the charge, and eventually dismissed it. During the case, several witnesses proved that they saw the prisoner kick and strike the horse. But the prisoner in cross-examination swore distinctly that he had not done anything of the kind. The magistrates thereupon committed the prisoner to the Assizes for having committed perjury.

MELLOR, J., said he doubted whether perjury could be assigned on the statement made by the prisoner that he had never kicked or struck the horse ; as he did not think the words were material to the issue.

Hawthorne, for the Crown, said that as it went to the credit of the witness, it was material....

MELLOR, J....My brother LUSH and I have considered this case. We are of opinion that there can be no assignment of perjury. The words used were merely collateral to the issue then before the Court.

Not guilty

---

[1] [EDITOR'S NOTE.] To the judicial " proceedings," in the case of Perjury ; to the "purpose" for which the statement is made, in extra-judicial cases. See the Perjury Act, 1911, ss. 1 (2), 2 (1). Cf. *Keepers* v. *Howell Gwinn*, *supra*, p. 416.

[2] [EDITOR'S NOTE.] As the spoken words were not a crime (though in a *London* street they would be, under 2 and 3 Vict. c. 47, s. 54, sub-s. 13) the information was probably only in order to have the utterer bound over to keep the peace.

[*What may be material.*]

THE QUEEN *v.* BAKER.

CROWN CASE RESERVED. 1895.   L.R. [1895] 1 Q.B. 797.

Case stated by His Honour Judge Chalmers, sitting as Commissioner of Assize.

The defendant Baker was tried on February 9, 1895, at the Glamorganshire Assizes, on a charge of wilful and corrupt perjury.

The substance of the indictment was that, on December 18, 1894, at the Petty Sessions held at Cardiff before the stipendiary magistrate, he, Baker, was charged with the offence of selling beer without a licence; and, having been duly sworn, deposed that he had never authorized the plea of guilty to be put in to a previous charge of selling beer without a licence, contrary to section 3 of the Licensing Act, 1872[1], on November 6, 1894, and that he had not authorized his solicitor to put in the plea of guilty to the charge, even by an indirect authority, and that he had no knowledge that his solicitor was going to plead guilty on his behalf, and that it was against his wish and will that the plea of guilty was put in.

Evidence was called on behalf of the Crown to shew that the defendant, after full explanation of the matter, had authorized his solicitor, Belcher, to plead guilty on his behalf; and that when he was informed of what had been done he expressed himself as perfectly satisfied with the result.

At the conclusion of the case for the Crown, counsel for the defendant took the objection that, even if the statements made by Baker were knowingly false, they could not amount to perjury, because they were not material to the issues then pending before the stipendiary magistrate.

The commissioner held that Baker, having tendered himself as a witness under 35 and 36 Vict. c. 94, s. 51, sub-s. 4, was properly examined at that stage of the proceedings concerning the circumstances of his previous conviction; and that his answers were material, inasmuch as, in the event of a conviction, the facts deposed to would be taken into consideration by the magistrate in the ultimate determination of the case. But he said he would state a case on the objections raised.

The jury found the defendant guilty.

The question for the opinion of the Court was, whether the above statements of the defendant were material to the issues then depending before the stipendiary magistrate.

[1] 35 and 36 Vict. c. 94.

LORD RUSSELL of KILLOWEN, C.J. The sole point for our consideration in this case is, whether the statements made by the defendant,
which the jury have found to have been made falsely and wilfully, were
material to the case which was before the stipendiary magistrate when
the defendant was charged for the second time with the offence of
selling beer without a licence. I will take the grounds relied on for
the defendant in the order in which they are stated in the case. The
first ground taken is that, as the defendant had admitted his previous
conviction, and had not appealed therefrom, it was immaterial to the
then pending inquiry whether the previous plea of guilty had been put
in by the defendant's consent or not. The answer to that contention is
that the defendant's answers would affect his credit as a witness, and
all false statements, wilfully and corruptly made, as to matters which
affect his credit, are material. The magistrate may be influenced, in
arriving at his decision, by the circumstances of the previous conviction,
and, if the defendant's solicitor had pleaded guilty on his behalf without his knowledge or consent, that circumstance might have been
taken into consideration as affecting the amount of punishment. The
second ground taken is that the previous conviction could only become
material when the magistrate decided to convict in the then pending
proceeding ; and that, as a fact, the proceedings had been adjourned to
await the result of the prosecution for perjury. I do not see the
relevance of that argument. The magistrate must consider the case on
the evidence given before him, and the circumstances may have an
influence on the punishment. If on the previous occasion the defendant
had, as he alleged, been convicted per incuriam, the magistrate might
have given him the benefit of that fact, and might have treated the
subsequent charge as if it had been a charge of a first offence. The
third ground taken is[1] that a previous conviction only affected the
amount of punishment to be awarded by a magistrate, and not any
issue to be determined by him, and further that the magistrate could
only take cognizance of the fact of the previous conviction, and not of
the circumstances under which it took place. But it is wrong to
suggest that the magistrate could only take cognizance of the fact of
the previous conviction. For these reasons I am of opinion that the
words stated in the case were material. I will deal shortly with the
authorities. In *Reg.* v. *Overton*[2] the date of a receipt which had been
given for the price was held material ; on the ground that every question
on cross-examination of a witness which goes to his credit is material.

[1] [EDITOR's NOTE.] Consider *Reg.* v. *Tate* (12 Cox 7). But is not this ground
now set aside by the wide words of the Perjury Act, 1911, s. 1 (1)—"material
in that proceeding"?   [2] Car. and Marsh. 655.

The case afterwards came before a Court consisting of eleven judges, who supported the view adopted by Parke, B., and Patteson, J. In *Reg.* v. *Lavey*[1], where a plaintiff in a county court had falsely sworn that she had never been tried at the Old Bailey, and had never been in custody at the Thames Police Station, the evidence was held to be material. This, again, was on the ground that it affected her credit. In *Reg.* v. *Gibbon*[2] it was held by eleven judges (Martin, B., and Crompton, J., doubting), that perjury might be assigned on evidence going to the credit of a material witness in a cause, although such evidence, being legally inadmissible, ought not to have been received. That is a very strong authority—much stronger than is needed to support the conviction in the present case. I am of opinion that the evidence was material; and the conviction was right, and ought to be affirmed.

The other four Judges concurred.

Conviction affirmed.

[*Mens rea is necessary.*]

[Self-contradiction *is not sufficient evidence for conviction.*]

REX *v.* MARY JACKSON.

YORK ASSIZES.   1823.   1 LEWIN 270.

Prisoner was indicted for perjury. It appeared that she had made two statements on oath, one of which was directly at variance with the other.

HOLROYD, J., to the jury :—Although you may believe that, on one or other occasion, she swore that which was not true, it is not a necessary consequence that she committed perjury[3]. For there are cases in which a person might very honestly and conscientiously swear to a particular fact from the best of his recollection and belief, and, from other circumstances at a subsequent time, be convinced that he was wrong, and swear to the reverse ; without meaning to swear falsely either time. Again, if a person swears one thing at one time, and another at another, you cannot convict if it is not possible to tell which was the true and which was the false.

---

[1] 3 C. and K. 26; and see 21 L. J. R. (M.C.) 10.   [2] L. and C. 109.

[3] [EDITOR'S NOTE.] And, on the other hand, a person may have committed perjury, although the fact which he swore to *was* true. For "where a man swears to a particular fact without knowing at the time whether the fact be true or false, it is as much Perjury as if he knew the fact to be false; and is equally indictable;" (6 T. R. 637). This rule is preserved by the Perjury Act, 1911, ss. 1 and 2.

[*What evidence is sufficient for conviction.*]

REGINA *v.* HOOK.

CROWN CASE RESERVED.   1858.   DEARSLY AND BELL 606.

[The prisoner had been convicted, at Chester Assizes, of a perjury. On the hearing of an information, at Petty Sessions, against a publican for keeping his house open during prohibited hours, Hook had sworn "I did not see any person leave the public-house that night after 11 p.m." To prove the falsehood of this statement, evidence was given (1) by three witnesses, that, to each of them separately, Hook had stated that he had seen one Williamson and three other men leave after eleven on the night in question, and by other witnesses (2) that the four men did so leave the house, and (3) that Hook asked the publican to give him a bribe to perjure himself. The question was reserved, whether this evidence was sufficient to support a conviction for perjury.]

M'Intyre, for the prisoner. It is clearly established that to support a conviction for perjury the falsity of the oath must be proved directly by two witnesses at least; or there must be one witness and strong corroborative evidence to confirm him. One witness is not sufficient, because there would be only one oath against another. Although it was proved that persons did leave the house after eleven, there is no evidence beyond the prisoner's own statement, when he was not upon his oath, that he saw any person leave, or that the statement he made when upon oath was false. Not only is there no oath that he did see, but none that he was there and could have seen. Here, there is the prisoner's statement not upon oath against his statement on oath; and the facts proved against him are consistent with his evidence on oath being true, and his statements not on oath being false.

*   *

BYLES, J. The rule requiring two[1] witnesses to prove perjury reposes on two reasons; first, that it would be unsatisfactory to convict when there is but the oath of one man against the oath of another: secondly, that all witnesses, even the most honest, would be exposed to the peril of indictments for perjury, if the single oath of another man, without any confirmatory evidence, might suffice to convict.

But the letter and spirit of the rule, and both the reasons for it, appear to me to be satisfied where, of two distinct admissions of the

---

[1] [EDITOR'S NOTE.] By s. 13 of the Perjury Act, 1911, no person can be convicted of any offence against it "solely on the evidence of one witness to the *falsity* of any statement alleged to be false."

defendant inconsistent with his innocence, one is proved by one witness, and one by another.

It has been already held that the testimony of one witness deposing to the defendant's admission on oath, if there is corroboration, is enough ; *Regina* v. *Wheatland*[1]. But if a single witness deposing to an admission of the defendant be one witness within the rule, then another witness, deposing to another admission, must surely be a second witness within the same rule

Conviction affirmed.

SECTION XIX.

BIGAMY.

[May be committed although the second marriage was invalid *on other grounds as well as that of the bigamy.*]

THE QUEEN *v.* ALLEN.

CROWN CASE RESERVED. 1872.   L.R. 1 C.C.C.R. 367.

*   *   *   *   *

COCKBURN, C.J., delivered the judgment of the Court :—This case came before us on a point reserved by Martin, B., at the last Assizes for the county of Hants. The prisoner was indicted for having married one Harriet Crouch, his first wife being still alive. The indictment was framed upon the statute 24 and 25 Vict. c. 100, s. 57, which enacts that "whosoever being married shall marry any other person, during the life of the former husband or wife, shall be guilty of felony." The facts of the case were clear. The prisoner had first married one Sarah Cunningham, and on her death he had married his present wife, Ann Pearson Gutteridge. The second wife being still living, he, on the 2nd of December, 1871, married one Harriet Crouch. So far the case would appear to be clearly one of bigamy within the statute ; but, it appearing that Harriet Crouch was a niece of the prisoner's first wife, it was objected, on his behalf, that since the passing of 5 and 6 Wm. IV. c. 54, s. 2, such a marriage was in itself void, and that to constitute an offence, within 24 and 25 Vict. c. 100, s. 57, the second marriage must be one which, independently of its bigamous character,

---

[1] 8 C. and P. 238.

would be valid, and, consequently, that the indictment could not be sustained. For the proposition that, to support an indictment for bigamy, the second marriage must be one which would have been otherwise valid, the case of *Reg.* v. *Fanning*[1], decided in the Court of Criminal Appeal in Ireland, was cited; and, in deference to the authority of the majority of the Judges in that Court, Martin, B., has stated this case for our decision....

The facts in *Reg.* v. *Fanning* were shortly these. The prisoner, being a Protestant and having within twelve months been a professing Protestant, was married, having a wife then living, to another woman, who was a Roman Catholic, the marriage being solemnized by a Roman Catholic priest.

Independently of the second marriage being bad as bigamous, it would have been void under the unrepealed statute of the 19 Geo. II. c. 13, which prohibits the solemnization of marriage by a Roman Catholic priest where either of the parties is a Protestant, and declares a marriage so solemnized null and void to all intents and purposes.

On an indictment against the prisoner for bigamy, the invalidity of the second marriage was insisted on as fatal to the prosecution. The point having been reserved, seven Judges against four in the Court of Criminal Appeal held the objection to be fatal, and quashed the conviction. After giving our best consideration to the reasoning of the learned Judges who constituted the majority of that Court, we find ourselves unable to concur with them, being unanimously of opinion that the view taken by the four dissentient Judges was the right one...

The ground on which such a marriage is very properly made penal is, that it involves an outrage on public decency and morals and creates a public scandal by the prostitution of a solemn ceremony, which the law allows to be applied only to a legitimate union, to a marriage at best but colourable and fictitious, and which may be made, and too often is made, the means of the most cruel and wicked deception. It is obvious that the outrage and scandal involved in such a proceeding will not be less, because the parties to the second marriage may be under some special incapacity to contract marriage. Now the words "shall marry another person" may well be taken to mean "shall go through the form and ceremony of marriage with another person." The words are fully capable of being so construed, without being forced or strained; and as a narrower construction would have the effect of leaving a portion of the mischief untouched, which it must have been the intention of the legislature to provide against, and thereby, as is fully admitted by those who contend for it, of bringing a grave reproach

[1] 17 Ir. C. L. 289; 10 Cox, Cr. C. 411.

on the law, we think we are warranted in inferring that the words were used in the sense we have referred to, and that we shall best give effect to the legislative intention by holding such a case as the present to be within their meaning. To assume that the words must have such a construction as would exclude it, because the second marriage must be one which, but for the bigamy, would have been as binding as the first, appears to us to be begging the entire question, and to be running directly counter to the wholesome canon of construction which prescribes that, where the language will admit of it, a statutory enactment shall be so construed as to make the remedy co-extensive with the mischief it is intended to prevent.

In thus holding, it is not at all necessary to say that forms of marriage unknown to the law, as was the case in *Burt* v. *Burt*[1], would suffice to bring a case within the operation of the statute. We must not be understood to mean that every fantastic form of marriage to which parties might think proper to resort, or that a marriage ceremony performed by an unauthorized person or in an unauthorized place, would be a marrying within the meaning of the 57th section of 24 and 25 Vict. c. 100. It will be time enough to deal with a case of this description when it arises. It is sufficient for the present purpose to hold, as we do, that where a person already bound by an existing marriage goes through a form of marriage known to and recognized by the law as capable of producing a valid marriage, for the purpose of a pretended and fictitious marriage, the case is not the less within the statute by reason of any special circumstances which, independently of the bigamous character of the marriage, may constitute a legal disability in the particular parties, or make the form of marriage resorted to specially inapplicable to their individual case.

[*Mistaken belief that first spouse was dead.*]

[See REGINA *v.* TOLSON, *supra*, p. 15.]

---

[1] 2 Sw. and Tr. 88; 20 L. J. R. (P. M. and A.) 133.

[*The evidence and the Burden of Proof.*]

THE QUEEN *v.* CURGERWEN.

CROWN CASE RESERVED.   1865.   L.R. 1 C.C.R. 1.

The following case was stated by Willes, J. :—

The accused was tried before me at the last Cornwall Assizes for bigamy; when the question arose whether, when a husband and wife have lived apart for seven years, and he marries again, there being no evidence to shew his knowledge of the existence of his first wife (so to speak), he is liable to be convicted of bigamy unless he can prove that, at the time of the second marriage, he did not know of his first wife being alive; in other words, whether the burden of proof of absence of such knowledge rests upon the prisoner; a question left undecided in *Reg.* v. *Briggs*[1].

The prisoner was a man-of-war's man. The first marriage was to one Charlotte Curgerwen, on the 1st day of September, 1852, at Buryan, in Cornwall. After the marriage the couple went to Ireland, where the prisoner was then in the Coast Guard service; and they lived together until June, 1853, when, in consequence of some disagreement, she left him, and returned to her father's house at Buryan. In January, 1854, the prisoner went to Portsmouth to join a ship of war which was proceeding to the Baltic, and was afterwards engaged in the Russian war. Upon that occasion the first wife went to Portsmouth to see the prisoner off; and, after doing so, she, in or about March, 1854, returned to her father's house, where she remained without seeing or corresponding with her husband, or, so far as the evidence went, knowing whether he was dead or alive, until shortly before the prosecution. There was no evidence that he had in the mean time ever been near where she lived, or had seen or heard of her or any member of her family, or known whether she was dead or alive. After the war, but at what precise time did not appear, the prisoner returned to England, and was again employed in the Coast Guard. On the 9th of July, 1862, the prisoner, being then at a Coast Guard station at a small place upon the coast of Devon, contracted the second marriage with one Eliza Hardy; and they lived together as man and wife undisturbed until this prosecution. A short time before the prosecution he was promoted, and sent to a station in Cornwall about twenty miles from where his first wife was living. This led to the proceedings. It appears, therefore, that the prisoner and his first wife had been living

---

[1] Dearsly and Bell, C. C. 98; 26 L. J. R. (M. C.) 7.

apart for more than eight years at the time of the second marriage; and
under circumstances in which it was at the least equally probable that
he did not know, as that he did know, of his first wife being alive, if
not, indeed, as I inclined to think, more probable that he did not know.
A statement of the prisoner before the magistrates was put in ; but,
fairly construed, it amounted only to an admission of having been
married twice, and of his then—that is, when before the magistrates—
knowing that his first wife was alive. *Prideaux*, for the prisoner,
contended that there was no evidence upon which a conviction could
properly take place, and that the burden of proving absence of know
ledge was not upon the prisoner.

Knowing that the question of burden of proof in these cases was
unsettled, I determined, in the event of a conviction, to reserve these
objections ; and I directed the jury, in substance, that the fact of the
second marriage whilst the first wife was alive made a primâ facie case,
and that the burden was upon the prisoner to bring himself within the
exception in the statute ; and, it being clear that the living apart for
seven years was proved, they ought to acquit him if they were satisfied
that he did not know of his wife being alive within the seven years,
and convict if the evidence did not so satisfy them.

The jury found the prisoner guilty ; and I let him out on bail, until
the opinion of the Court for Crown Cases Reserved was taken upon the
propriety of the conviction.

The case was considered on the 11th of November, 1865, by
POLLOCK, C.B., WILLES, J., PIGOTT, B., and SHEE and MONTAGUE
SMITH, JJ.

No counsel was instructed to argue on either side ; but

Prideaux, amicus curiœ, referred the Court to *Reg.* v. *Heaton*[1],
where it was held by Wightman, J., that the burden of proof that
a prisoner charged with bigamy has not been continually absent from
his wife for seven years, and that she was known by him to be living
within that time, is on the prosecution ; on the ground that the prisoner
cannot prove the negative. He also called the attention of the Court
to *Reg.* v. *Ellis*[2], in which Willes, J., said that, where the husband had
been living apart from his wife for seven years, under such circumstances as to raise a probability that he supposed that she was dead
when he re-married, it might be necessary on the part of the prosecution to offer evidence to shew that he knew that his first wife was
alive.

POLLOCK, C.B. This question has arisen more than once before ;
and we are now asked to settle the law on the subject. The term

---

[1] 3 Fost. and Fin. 819.　　　　[2] 1 Fost. and Fin. 309.

"burden of proof" is an inconvenient one, except when a person is called upon to prove an affirmative. Our attention has been called to a note by the editor of Russell on Crimes[1], known as a gentleman of great learning, ability, and research, who appears to have adopted the view that the burden of proof lies on the prisoner. We think, however, that it is contrary to the general spirit of the English law that the prisoner should be called on to prove a negative; and that it is better, and more in agreement with the general doctrine and principles of our criminal law, to adopt the rule laid down by Wightman, J., in *Reg. v. Heaton*[2].

Conviction quashed.

[*When the Burden of Proof is shifted to the prisoner.*]

THE QUEEN *v.* JONES.

CROWN CASE RESERVED. 1883.   L.R. 11 Q.B.D. 118.

The following case was stated by Stephen, J., for the opinion of the Court.

Thomas Jones was convicted before me at the last Stafford Assizes on a charge of bigamy.

It was proved that he was married to Winifred Dodds, on the 13th of March, 1865; and that he went through the ceremony of marriage with Phœbe Jones, on the 11th of September, 1882, Dodds being then alive. One witness said that the prisoner and his wife had lived together after marriage, but how long she did not know. There was no evidence at all as to their having ever separated; or as to when, if separated, they last saw each other.

In *Reg. v. Curgerwen*[3], it was proved that the prisoner and his wife had lived apart for many years before the second marriage, and it was held that in that state of facts the prosecution were bound to prove that the prisoner had known that his wife was alive within seven years of the second marriage. As there was no proof that Jones and his wife had ever separated, I thought that *Reg. v. Curgerwen*[3] did not apply, and directed the jury to convict the prisoner if they believed he had married a second time in his wife's lifetime.

---

[1] Russell on Crimes and Misdemeanors, 4th edition, by Greaves, vol. I. p. 270, note (*l*).

[2] 3 Fost. and Fin. 819.   [3] Law Rep. 1 C. C. R. 1; *supra*, p. 426.

He was found guilty; and I sentenced him to two months' imprisonment and hard labour, but suspended the execution of the sentence, and committed him, in default of bail, till this case should be determined.

The question for the Court is, whether in these circumstances, I ought to have directed an acquittal?

No counsel appeared.

LORD COLERIDGE, C.J. We are opinion that this conviction must be affirmed. There is nothing to shew that the parties ever separated so as to bring the facts within the case cited of *Reg.* v. *Curgerwen.* There is proof of the existence of a state of things, and no evidence of the cessation of that state of things, consequently, the presumption is that the existing state continued. That presumption could only have been displaced by evidence, and no evidence displacing it was forthcoming.

Conviction affirmed.

[*Conflict of Presumptions.*]

REGINA *v.* WILLSHIRE.

CROWN CASE RESERVED. 1881. L.R. 6 Q.B.D. 366.

Case stated by Sir W. T. Charley, Q.C., the Common Serjeant of the City of London. The prisoner was tried before me at the Session of the Central Criminal Court, held on the 31st of January last. The indictment charged that he married Charlotte Georgina Lavers on the 7th of September, 1879; and that he feloniously married Edith Maria Miller on the 23rd of September, 1880, his wife Charlotte Georgina being then alive. The indictment also charged that the prisoner had been previously convicted of felony at the Central Criminal Court in the month of June, 1868. A marriage between the prisoner and Charlotte Georgina Lavers on the 7th of September, 1879, and a subsequent marriage between the prisoner and Edith Maria Miller on the 23rd of September, 1880, were clearly proved. It was also proved that at the time of the prisoner's marriage to Edith Maria Miller his alleged wife Charlotte Georgina was alive. When the case for the prosecution was concluded, the prisoner's counsel asked the counsel for the prosecution to call a witness whose name appeared on the indictment, but the counsel for the prosecution declined to call him. The prisoner's counsel then himself called the witness, who produced a certificate of the previous conviction of the prisoner for felony in June, 1868. The indictment for this felony and caption were also produced in Court by the proper officer at the instance of the prisoner's counsel. The indictment was for bigamy, and alleged that the prisoner married Ellen Earle on the 31st of March, 1864, and feloniously married Ada Mary Susan Leslie on the 22nd of April, 1868, his wife Ellen Earle being then alive. The prisoner's counsel contended that he had proved that the prisoner had a wife living in June, 1868; and that, in order to convict the prisoner on the present indictment, it was incumbent on the prosecution to shew that this wife was dead on the 7th of September, 1879, when the prisoner married Charlotte Georgina Lavers. Counsel for the prosecution contended that there being no presumption of law that Ellen Earle was alive on the 7th of September, 1879, when the prisoner married Charlotte Georgina Lavers (the presumption, if any, after seven years, being, indeed, the other way), and a primâ facie case of bigamy having been clearly proved by the prosecution on the present indictment, the onus was thrown upon the prisoner of shewing that Ellen Earle was alive on the 7th of September, 1879, when the prisoner married Charlotte Georgina Lavers. I held that the burden of proof was on the prisoner. No evidence was offered by the prisoner's counsel that Ellen Earle was alive on the 7th of September, 1879. There was no evidence that the alleged marriage of the prisoner with Ellen Earle was declared void or dissolved by any Court of competent jurisdiction. The prisoner was found guilty. He was then arraigned on that part of the indictment which charged the previous conviction of felony in June, 1868, and pleaded guilty. I respited judgment. The prisoner remains in gaol. The question which I reserve for the opinion of the Court for the consideration of Crown Cases Reserved is: "Whether the prisoner has been properly convicted of feloniously marrying Edith Maria Miller, his wife Charlotte Georgina being then alive."

*   *   *   *   *

Poland, for the Crown. There was a clear primâ facie case made out by the prosecution. The prisoner described himself, when he married Charlotte Lavers, as a "bachelor," and by his act furnished evidence against himself that he was then free to marry. A primâ facie case thus being made, it was for the prisoner to displace it by evidence. The prisoner only shewed that in 1868 his first wife Ellen Earle was living, a fact which is equally consistent with her being alive or dead in 1879. Indeed the statute as to bigamy (24 and 25 Vict. c. 100,

s. 57) sanctions a presumption that a person not heard of for seven years is dead[1].

The marriage with Charlotte Lavers cannot be held invalid merely because eleven years before the time of such marriage the prisoner had a wife alive.

[LORD COLERIDGE, C.J. The learned Common Serjeant did not leave the question to the jury as to whether Ellen Earle was alive or dead at the time of the marriage with Charlotte Lavers.

HAWKINS, J. Ought not the direction to the jury to have been that it was proved that Ellen Earle was alive in 1868, and that there was no further evidence upon the point except that the prisoner had in 1879 presented himself to be married as one free to marry, which was, in effect, a representation by him that he was legally free so to do; and would it not then have been for the jury to find whether Ellen Earle had died before the marriage with Charlotte Lavers?]

It is submitted that, in substance, that was the course adopted. The facts were all left to the jury, with a direction that under the circumstances the burden of proving that Ellen Earle was alive in 1879 was on her husband, the prisoner.

LORD COLERIDGE, C.J. I am of opinion that this conviction cannot be sustained. The facts are short and are clearly stated in the case. There was a marriage, admitted to be valid, contracted by the prisoner in 1864; there was evidence that the woman then married to the prisoner was alive in 1868. In 1879, the prisoner went through the ceremony of marriage with another woman. It is said, and I think rightly, that there is a presumption in favour of the validity of this latter marriage, but the prisoner shewed that there was a valid marriage in 1864, and that the woman he then married was alive in 1868. He thus set up the existence of a life in 1868, which, in the absence of any evidence to the contrary will be presumed to have continued to 1879. It is urged, in effect, that the presumption in favour of innocence, a presumption which goes to establish the validity of the marriage of 1879, rebuts the presumption in favour of the duration of life. It is sufficient to raise a question of fact for the jury to determine. It was for the jury to decide whether the man told and acted a falsehood for the purpose of marrying in 1879, or whether his real wife was then dead. The Common Serjeant did not leave the question to the jury; but, on these conflicting presumptions, held that the burden of proof was on the prisoner, who was bound to adduce other or further evidence of the existence of his wife in 1879; thus withdrawing from the jury the determination of the fact from these conflicting presumptions. I

[1] *Reg.* v. *Lumley,* Law Rep. 1 C. C. R. 196, 199.

am clearly of opinion that in this the learned Common Serjeant went beyond the rules of law. The prisoner was only bound to set up the life; it was for the prosecution to prove his guilt.

The four other Judges concurred.

Conviction quashed.

SECTION XX.

LIBEL.

[The nature of the offence.]

THE QUEEN *v.* MUNSLOW.

CROWN CASE RESERVED.   1895.   L.R. [1895] 1 Q.B. 758.

Case stated for the opinion of the Court by Cave, J.

The defendant was tried at the Warwick Assizes upon an indictment for libel under 6 and 7 Vict. c. 96, s. 5. The indictment contained three counts, each setting out a separate libel; the language of each count, so far as it affected the question of law raised, was identical, and for the purpose of the case it was only necessary to set out the material words of the first count, which were as follows: "The jurors for our lady the Queen upon their oath present that George Munslow unlawfully did write and publish a certain defamatory libel of and concerning Henry Truslove, according to the tenor and effect following, that is to say" (here followed the specific words of the libel complained of). The prisoner pleaded not guilty; whereupon his counsel applied to quash the indictment, on the ground that it did not contain any averment that he published the libels or any of them 'maliciously,' and therefore did not sufficiently disclose any offence under the section. The application was refused, and the case proceeded, and, the defendant having been convicted on all the counts, his counsel again raised the same point by way of arrest of judgment. The learned Judge postponed sentence, and admitted the defendant to bail pending the hearing of this case. The question for the opinion of the Court was whether judgment ought to be arrested on the ground taken by the defendant's counsel.

Stanger, for the defendant....Malice must be found by the jury before they can convict the accused; and as it is necessary to be proved,

it must be alleged in the indictment. It is true that it may be proved
by inference from the fact of publication, which affords primâ facie
evidence of malice that must be disproved by the accused. But that is
a question of evidence, and does not affect the description of the offence
in the indictment.

*   *   *   *   *

LORD RUSSELL OF KILLOWEN, C.J....The Libel Act, 1843, provides
by section 5 that if any person maliciously publishes a defamatory
libel, he shall, being convicted thereof, be liable to fine or imprisonment
or both, such imprisonment not to exceed one year. The section does
not create a new offence, nor does it purport to give a definition of an
existing offence; it provides for the application, to that which was
already an offence at common law, of the appropriate punishment. The
word "maliciously" was introduced into the section in order to prevent
the section working great injustice. Any one who publishes defamatory
matter of another, tending to damage his reputation or expose him to
contempt and ridicule, is guilty of publishing a defamatory libel; and
the word "maliciously" was introduced in order to shew that, though
the accused might be primâ facie guilty of publishing a defamatory
libel, yet if he could rebut the presumption of malice attached to such
publication he would meet the charge. For example, upon the production of the alleged libel, it is for the judge to determine whether it is
capable of being regarded as a libel by the jury; his function is then
ended, and if the jury determine it to be a libel, then, in the absence of
evidence of the motive for publication, the law attaches to the fact of
publication the inference that the publication was malicious. But the
accused may be able to shew that, though the matter is defamatory, it
was published on a privileged occasion, or he may be able to avail himself of the statutory defence that the matter complained of was true,
and that its publication was for the public benefit; and those classes of
cases were meant to be excluded from the purview of the section by the
use of the word "maliciously."

Here the case went to the jury after the objection was taken; and
we must assume that the language was capable of bearing the innuendoes
placed on it and was capable of being a libel, that the jury found that
it was in fact a libel, and that there was no lawful excuse, such as
privilege, for its publication. In that state of facts, is the prisoner to
be absolved from the consequences of the verdict, and is the conviction
to be quashed, merely because the word "maliciously" has been omitted
from the indictment?.

In *Rex* v. *Harvey* (2 B. and C. 257) the defendants were indicted
for a libel imputing mental insanity to George the Fourth. The jury

K.   28

at the trial required to know from the Lord Chief Justice whether it was necessary that there should be a malicious intention in order to constitute a libel; and the answer given was, "The man who publishes slanderous matter, in its nature calculated to defame and vilify another,' must be presumed to have intended to do that which the publication is calculated to bring about, unless he can shew the contrary."...Upon the motion for a new trial, Holroyd, J., said: "It is not necessary to aver in such an indictment any direct malice, because the doing of such an act without any excuse is indictable."

WILLS, J....It is clear to me that this is a good indictment at common law. The use of the word "unlawfully" excludes all such cases as publication on a privileged occasion; and the words "libel" and "publish" exclude what is called an accidental publication. (Indeed, as I understand the judgment of Lord Esher, MR., in *Emmens* v. *Pottle*, L.R. 6 Q.B.D. 354, an accidental publication is no publication at all.)...It seems therefore that every case is excluded in which the law would not attach the epithet "malicious" to the publication. If that is so, the averment of malice cannot be the less effectively made because it is made inferentially, if the inference is inevitable.

*   *   *   *

The other three Judges concurred.

[*There may be a libel without the use of* words.]

MONSON *v.* TUSSAUDS LIMITED.

QUEEN'S BENCH DIVISION.   1894.   L.R. [1894] 1 Q.B. 671.

Application for an interim injunction to restrain the defendants from publishing or exhibiting a portrait model of the plaintiff until the trial of the action, or until further order....The plaintiff had been tried in Scotland upon a charge of having murdered a young man named Hambrough by shooting him with a gun, at a place called Ardlamont. The defence to the charge was that Hambrough was killed by the accidental discharge of his own gun. The jury returned a verdict of "Not proven." Shortly after the trial the defendants in the first action, who were the proprietors of an exhibition in London, consisting mainly of wax figures of celebrated and notorious personages, placed in their exhibition a portrait model of the plaintiff, bearing his

name, with a gun in close proximity thereto described as his gun. This
figure was exhibited in a room called the Napoleon Room, No. 2, within
a turnstile, at which an extra sixpence was charged for admission. In
this room there were four other figures. Of these one was a recumbent
figure of the Emperor Napoleon I., another that of a Mrs Maybrick,
who had been convicted of murder, another that of one Pigott, a witness
before the Parnell Commission, who had committed suicide to avoid
arrest, and another that of a man named Scott, who was charged with
having been concerned in the alleged murder with which the plaintiff
was charged, but who could not be found. There were some other
objects of interest in the room; for instance, relics of the Emperor
Napoleon and the Duke of Wellington. From this room access could
be obtained by descending some stairs, without further payment, to
a room known as the "Chamber of Horrors"; in which were exhibited
figures, the bulk of which represented murderers and malefactors, and
also relics connected with, and models of the scenes of, notorious
murders. In this room there was a representation of the place where
Hambrough's body was found; described by the words "Ardlamont
Mystery : Scene of the Tragedy."

*   *   *   *   *

COLLINS, J. The law is clearly settled that a person may be
defamed as well by a picture or effigy as by written or spoken words.
I do not wish to express any opinion on the question whether a private
person can restrain the publication of a portrait or effigy of himself
which has been obtained without his authority. That is quite a different
question. Applying the standard of a libel action to this application
to restrain the exhibition of an effigy of the plaintiff, we have to
consider first whether the libel is established, and, secondly, whether it
is such as to call for and justify the interference of the Court by an
interim injunction. When the matter comes to be analysed it falls
into a very small compass, and we are relieved in the present case from
difficulties which often exist. The counsel for both the defendants
have told us that the real question is whether the public exhibition of
an effigy of the plaintiff for money amounts to an injurious imputation
upon him. They both absolutely disclaim any intention to justify any
innuendo or imputation upon the plaintiff, and their case is that no
imputation of any kind is intended by such exhibition. We have to
consider the object for which the figure is exhibited and the manner in
which that object is carried out. The exhibitions are exhibitions for
money of the effigies of famous or infamous people, as the catalogue and
advertisements shew. No effigies of private persons are found there
unless such persons have obtained notoriety or fame. Why, then, is

the effigy of Monson placed there, and why is public attention invited to it? Is it because he was present at Ardlamont as a casual spectator when through an unfortunate accident Lieutenant Hambrough was shot? Can it be suggested that every person who was present at a grouse drive, for instance, when some member of the party was accidentally shot, would acquire a title to have his effigy placed in these exhibitions? Is the mere presence of the plaintiff at the tragedy a ground for the inclusion of his effigy? It is clear that it is not. The only ground for the exhibition of his effigy must be, therefore, that what happened at Ardlamont was not an accident but a crime, and that he was in some way or another mixed up with that crime.... Under these circumstances it seems to me that the inference which any reasonable jury would draw is inevitable, i.e., that an imputation is made on the plaintiff, and that the exhibition of the effigy is a libel upon him....

Application granted.

[The COURT OF APPEAL concurred in the reasoning of COLLINS, J.; but, in consequence of the production of fresh evidence, refused the injunction.]

[Oral *defamation is not a crime.*]

THE KING *v.* BURFORD.

KING'S BENCH.　1669.　　　　1 VENTRIS 16; 2 KEBLE 494.

He was indicted for that he scandalously and contemptuously uttered and published the following words, viz., "None of the justices of peace do understand the statutes for the Excise—unless Mr Hunt, and he understands but little of them. No, nor many Parliament-men do not understand them upon the reading of them."

And it was moved to quash the indictment, for that a man could not be indicted for speaking such words.

And THE COURT was of that opinion. But they said he might have been bound to his good behaviour.

[Oral *defamation is not a crime.*]

THE QUEEN *v.* LANGLEY.

QUEEN'S BENCH.   1704.   6 MODERN 125.

Langley was indicted for these words spoken to the Mayor of
Salisbury, "...You, Mr Mayor, are a rogue and a rascal."...

THE COURT...agreed that whatever is a breach of the peace is
indictable, as sending a challenge; but that these words were not
a breach of the peace, but only occasional and tending towards it.
And after great deliberation they adjudged the words were not indictable: for it is not as much as said that he was in the exercise of his
office, or a justice of the peace. If indeed they were put *in writing,*
they would be a libel, punishable either by indictment or action. But
they are but loose unmannerly words; like those spoke of an Alderman
of Hull—"When he puts on his gown, Satan enters into it"—which
were adjudged not indictable in Kelynge's time (1 Mod. 35). "You
are a forsworn mayor, and have broken your oath," is not indictable
(Style 251). And binding him to his good behaviour is sufficient to
secure the authority of mayors; [and even *it*] must be done instantly
(8 Coke 116, 118).

HOLT, C.J., said that words that directly tend to a breach of the
peace may be indictable[1]. But otherwise to encourage indictments for
words would make them as uncertain as actions for words are.

[*Publication to* the person libelled *suffices in* Criminal *Law.*]

BARROW *v.* LEWELLIN.

STAR CHAMBER.   1615.   HOBART 62.

Paul Barrow preferred a bill in the Star Chamber against Maurice
Lewellin for writing unto him a despiteful and reproachful letter, which
(for ought that appeared to the Court) was sealed, and delivered to his
own hands and never otherwise published. And it was resolved that
though the plaintiff in this case could not have an action of the case,
because it was not published and therefore could not be to his defamation without his own fault of divulging it,...yet the Star Chamber for

---

[1] [EDITOR'S NOTE. See *Rex* v. *Phillips* (6 East 464). The cases previously cited,
from 1 Mod. and from Style, scarcely went so far as the Court alleges.]

the King doth take knowledge of such cases and punish them. Whereof the reason is that such quarrellous letters tend to the breach of the peace and to the stirring of challenges and quarrels. And therefore the means of such evils, as well as the end, are to be prevented.

[*Publication merely to the person libelled.*]

CLUTTERBUCK *v.* CHAFFERS.

GUILDHALL N.P. SITTINGS. 1816.   1 STARKIE **471.**

This was an action for the publication of a libel.

The witness who was called to prove the publication of the libel (which was contained in a letter written by the defendant to the plaintiff) stated, on cross-examination, that the letter had been delivered to him, folded up, but unsealed ; and that, without reading it, or allowing any other person to read it, he had delivered it to the plaintiff himself, as he had been directed.

LORD ELLENBOROUGH held, that this did not amount to a publication which would support an action; although it would have sustained an indictment, since a publication to the party himself tends to a breach of the peace.

Verdict for the defendant.

[*In* Criminal *Law the* truth *of the libel is not always a defence.*]

THE QUEEN *v.* JOHN HENRY NEWMAN, D.D.

QUEEN'S BENCH. 1853.   1 ELLIS AND BLACKBURN 268, 558.

[This was a criminal information charging the defendant (the late Cardinal Newman) with composing and publishing a libel upon Giovanni Giacinto Achilli. The libel contained imputations of seduction, adultery and other offences, and that Dr Achilli had been prohibited from preaching and hearing confessions. The defendant pleaded (i) not guilty, (ii) the truth of the several imputations. The jury found that only one of the twenty-three criminatory matters charged in the libel had been proved to their satisfaction. A motion was made for a new trial on the ground that the verdict was against the weight of evidence.]

LORD CAMPBELL, C.J....Before the recent statute (6 and 7 Vict. c. 96, s. 6) the truth of the charges contained in a libel was no defence[1] to an indictment or criminal information for publishing it. The truth could not be given in evidence under a plea of Not guilty; and no special justification on the ground of truth could be pleaded. It was even said that "the greater the truth the greater the libel." The legislature, thinking that such a maxim misapplied brought discredit on the administration of justice, and that, under certain guards and modifications, the truth of the charges might advantageously be inquired into and might be permitted to constitute a complete defence, passed the statute referred to. But this statute provides that "to entitle the defendant to give evidence of the truth of such matters charged as a defence to such indictment or information, it shall be necessary for the defendant, in pleading to the said indictment or information, to allege the truth of the said matters charged," "and further to allege that it was for the public benefit that the said matters charged should be published"; "to which plea the prosecutor shall be at liberty to reply generally, denying the whole thereof." Thus it is quite clear that, when the prosecutor has replied, to such a plea, that the defendant wrongfully published the libel without the cause alleged, and issue has been joined upon this replication, the prosecutor is entitled to a verdict unless the defendant proves, to the satisfaction of the jury, the truth of all the material allegations in the plea. The only function allotted to the jury is to say whether the whole plea is proved or not. If they find that it is, the defendant is acquitted. If they think that it is not, they are to declare that the defendant wrongfully published the libel without the cause alleged; and he is convicted. The jury are then functi officio; and the legislature did not contemplate that any question would be put to them as to how much of the plea was proved, if the whole was not proved; for, without proof of the whole, a conviction must take place, to be followed by a sentence. Nevertheless, the legislature wisely thought that, although under such circumstances sentence must be passed, the just measure of punishment may materially depend upon the unsuccessful plea of justification and the evidence given under it. In some cases, the defendant may maliciously plead such a plea, when he has no substantial evidence to support it; or he may try to support it by false

---

[1] [EDITOR'S NOTE. See the *Case de Libellis famosis* (5 Coke 125).]

evidence. On the other hand, he may have had reasonable ground for believing that he could prove the whole of it; and he may have adduced sincere witnesses to substantiate a part of it, while without default of his own a material part of it is not substantiated by legal proof. Where there has been a conviction after a plea of justification, what course is to be followed, so that justice may be done, and a due measure of punishment meted out according to the real guilt of the defendant? It is quite clear that the legislature refers everything to the Court alone, after the finding of the jury upon the question whether the whole plea is proved; for it has enacted that "if after such plea the defendant shall be convicted on such indictment or information it shall be competent to the Court, in pronouncing sentence, to consider whether the guilt of the defendant is aggravated or mitigated by the said plea, and by the evidence given to prove or disprove the same...."

*   *   *   *   *

Erle, J....In a civil action for libel a plea of "justification" affords a ground for enhancing the damages. So here the plea, if pleaded without reasonable ground, would have the effect of aggravation.

*   *   *   *   *

The defendant was sentenced to pay a fine of £100, and to be imprisoned among the misdemeanants of the first class until the fine should be paid.

[*Publication in Parliament is privileged absolutely*]

THE KING *v.* LORD ABINGDON.

Westminster N.P. Sittings.   1794.   1 Espinasse 225.

This was an information for a libel. The libel was a paragraph in the public newspapers, stated to be part of a speech delivered by Lord Abingdon in the House of Lords....In giving notice of his intention to bring in a Bill to regulate the practice of attorneys, he, in the course of his speech, mentioned his having employed a Mr Sermon as his attorney; and, after much invective, he charged him with improper conduct in his profession and pettifogging practices. This speech his Lordship read in the House from a written paper; which paper he, at his own expense, sent and had printed in several of the public papers. This trial exhibited the novel spectacle in Westminster Hall of a peer, unassisted by counsel or attorney, appearing to plead his own cause.

*   *   *   *   *

LORD KENYON, C.J., said that had the words in question been spoken *in the House of Lords* only, and confined to its walls, the Court would have had no jurisdiction to call his Lordship before it to answer for them as an offence. But in the present case the offence was the subsequent publication, under his authority and sanction, and at his expense. A member of Parliament certainly has a right to publish his speech, but that speech should not be made the vehicle of slander against any individual.

*   *   *   *   *

Guilty. To be imprisoned for three months and fined £100.

[*Qualified[1] privilege for Fair Comments on any matter of* public concern.]

[See PARMITER *v.* COUPLAND, *infra* p. 444.]

[*Qualified privilege where persons by whom and to whom the defamation is published have a* common interest.]

[*Publication* invited *by the person libelled is not criminal.*]

THE KING *v.* HART.

KING'S BENCH.   1762.   1 WM. BLACKSTONE 386.

Motion for a new trial. It appeared that Mary Jerom, the prosecutrix, was a quaker; but, being less rigid than the rest of her sect, the brethren, according to their usual discipline, first admonished her

---

1 It is now established that this privilege is only Qualified. See *McQuire* v. *Western Morning News Co.,* L. R. [1903] 2 K. B. 100.

for frequenting balls and concerts; then sent deputies to her; and lastly expelled her; and entered as a reason in their books, "For not practising the duty of self-denial." This was signed by the defendant, their clerk. The prosecutrix sent her maid for a copy of the entry; which was delivered to her by the defendant, and was the only act of publication proved. She thereupon moved the Court for an information for a libel, which was denied: whereupon she preferred an indictment, which was found at Nottingham Sessions, and removed into B. R. by certiorari, and tried at last Nottingham Assizes before Mr Justice Clive, who left it to the jury, and they brought in the defendant guilty. It was argued to be irregular to leave it at all to the jury, upon such an evidence only of publication; 5 Mod. 167. But as the Judge was dissatisfied with the verdict, the whole transaction being merely a piece of discipline, (in which the Court strongly concurred), they for that reason granted the new trial in the first instance, without any rule to shew cause; Serjeant Hewit having attended to watch the motion on the part of the prosecutrix, and confessed the dissatisfaction of Mr Justice Clive at the verdict.

[*Qualified privilege for reports of* judicial proceedings.]

USILL *v.* HALES.

COMMON PLEAS DIVISION. 1878.   L.R. 3 C.P.D. 319.

Action for libel published in the *Daily News.* The publication complained of consisted of a report of an application, made in public to a police-magistrate in London, for a summons against the plaintiff under the following circumstances:—The persons by whom the application to the magistrate was made were respectively civil engineers or surveyors who had been employed under the plaintiff, a civil engineer, in making surveys, &c., for a projected railway in Ireland. The applicants having heard that the plaintiff had been paid by the promoters for his services, and conceiving that he had improperly withheld from them the money which was due to them for theirs, made an ex parte application under the Employers and Workmen Act (38 and 39 Vict. c. 90). The magistrate, after hearing the statement of the parties, came to the conclusion that he had no jurisdiction to entertain the matter, and declined to grant the summonses. A report of the proceeding appeared in the newspaper in question on the following morning, and it was in these terms,—

"Three gentlemen, civil engineers, were among the applicants to the magistrate yesterday, and they applied for criminal process against Mr Usill, a civil engineer, of Great Queen Street, Westminster. The spokesman stated that they had been engaged in the survey of an Irish railway by Mr Usill, and had not been paid what they had earned in their various capacities, although from time to time they had received small sums on account; and, as the person complained of had been paid, they considered that he had been guilty of a criminal offence in withholding their money. Mr Woolrych said it was a matter of contract between the parties; and, although, on the face of the application, they had been badly treated, he must refer them to the county court."

The cause was tried before Cockburn, C.J., at Westminster, on the 15th of November, 1877. The learned Judge told the jury that the only question for their consideration was whether or not the publication complained of was a fair and impartial report of what took place before the magistrate; and that, if they found that it was so, the publication was privileged.

The jury found that it was a fair report of what occurred, and accordingly returned a verdict for the defendant.

Ballantine, Serjt., moved for a new trial, contending that the publication being a report of an ex parte application made to a functionary who had no jurisdiction to entertain it, and made against one who had no means of answering the charges made against him, the privileges usually accorded to the publication of proceedings in a Court of justice did not attach to it.

*   *   *   *   *

LOPES, J. In this case three men who believed themselves aggrieved by the conduct of the plaintiff in respect of the payment of their wages, applied to a magistrate in open Court for a summons under the Employers and Workmen Act. The magistrate refused the application, considering it a matter for a civil, and not for a criminal, Court. The defendant afterwards published a report, which the jury have found was a fair report of what occurred.

On principles of public convenience, the ordinary rule is that no action can be maintained in respect of a fair and impartial report of a judicial proceeding, though the report contain matter of a defamatory kind and injurious to individuals.

It was urged that the matter in respect of which the application was made was not within the jurisdiction of the magistrate. But the cases are clear to shew that want of jurisdiction will not take away the privilege, if it is maintainable on other grounds. Nor do I think the privilege is confined to the superior Courts : it is not the tribunal, but the nature of the alleged judicial proceeding, which must be looked at.

The point mainly relied on by the plaintiff was, that the application to the magistrate was ex parte, and as such could not be privileged.

Had the matter before the magistrate been in the nature of a preliminary inquiry, and if the ultimate judicial determination was to remain in abeyance until a further investigation, I should have thought there was authority at any rate for the plaintiff's contention ; though how far those authorities might be followed in the present day I think doubtful[1]. But the matter of the application was *finally* disposed of by the magistrate ; and I can find no case where a fair report of a judicial proceeding *finally* dealing with the matter in open Court has been held libellous. There are authorities which, until they are carefully examined, would seem to support the contention that an ex parte proceeding in Court is not privileged. So far as I can ascertain, these are all cases where the proceeding was *preliminary,* and where there was no *final* determination at the time of the alleged libellous report.

Rule discharged.

[*Respective functions of* jury *and* Judge.]

PARMITER *v.* COUPLAND AND ANOTHER.

EXCHEQUER.   1840.   6 MEESON AND WELSBY 105.

This was an action on the case for a series of libels published of the plaintiff, the late mayor of the borough of Winchester, in the *Hampshire Advertiser* newspaper, between the 17th of November, 1838, and the 2nd of March, 1839, imputing to him partial and corrupt conduct and ignorance of his duties, as mayor and justice of the peace for the borough. The defendants pleaded not guilty. At the trial before Coleridge, J., at the last Winchester Assizes, the learned Judge, in the course of his summing up, stated to the jury that there was a difference with regard to censures on public and on private persons; that the character of persons acting in a public capacity was to a certain extent

---

[1] [EDITOR'S NOTE.] They are overruled by *Kimber* v. *Press Association,* L. R. [1893] 1 Q. B. 65, where privilege was conceded to the report of an ex parte application (for a summons for perjury) though the application had not been disposed of but only adjourned.

public property, and their conduct might be more freely commented on than that of other persons : and having told the jury what, in point of law, constituted a libel, he left it to them to say whether the publications in question were calculated to be injurious to the character of the plaintiff. The jury having found a verdict for the defendants, a motion was made for a new trial.

＊　　＊　　＊　　＊　　＊

PARKE, B. I think there was no misdirection on the part of the learned Judge. One of the grounds upon which this rule was obtained was, that the learned Judge ought to have told the jury that the terms of these papers were libellous, and not to have left that as a question of fact for them to determine. But it has been the course for a long time for a judge, in cases of libel, as in other cases of a criminal nature, first to give a legal definition of the offence, and then to leave it to the jury to say whether the facts necessary to constitute that offence are proved to their satisfaction ; and that, whether the libel is the subject of a criminal prosecution, or civil action. A publication, without justification or lawful excuse, which is calculated to injure the reputation of another, by exposing him to hatred, contempt, or ridicule, is a libel. Whether the particular publication, the subject of inquiry, is of that character, and would be likely to produce that effect, is a question upon which a jury are to exercise their judgment, and pronounce an opinion, as a question of fact. The Judge, as a matter of advice to them in deciding that question, might have given his own opinion as to the nature of the publication ; but was not bound to do so as a matter of law. Mr Fox's Libel Bill was a declaratory Act, and put prosecutions for libel on the same footing as other criminal cases (32 Geo. III. c. 60).

I also think that there was no misdirection in the other part of the learned Judge's summing up, to which an objection was raised. There is a difference between publications relating to public and private individuals. Every subject has a right to comment on those acts of public men which concern him as a subject of the realm, if he do not make his commentary a cloak for malice and slander. But any imputation of wicked or corrupt motives is unquestionably libellous ; and such appears to be the nature of the publications here. I do not find that the learned Judge stated otherwise : we cannot therefore grant a new trial as for a misdirection.

PART III.

MODES OF LEGAL PROOF.

SECTION I.

PRESUMPTIONS.

[(A) *There is so strong a presumption against the commission of any* Crime, *that it must be proved beyond* reasonable *doubt.*]

REGINA *v.* FREDERICK GEORGE MANNING AND MARIA MANNING.

CENTRAL CRIMINAL COURT. 1849. "THE TIMES" for Oct. 27, 1849.

[The two prisoners were indicted, before Pollock, L.C.B., Maule, J., and Cresswell, J., for the murder of Patrick J. O'Connor, a Customs Officer, who was the paramour of the female prisoner. The husband was charged as principal in the first degree, and the wife as aider and abettor. The crime was one of such cold-blooded treachery as to be, as the Lord Chief Baron said, "perhaps one of the most un-exampled ever recorded in the history of this country." On this account, and partly also because Mrs Manning (the Mademoiselle Hortense of Dickens' *Bleak House*) had been a lady's maid in the Duke of Sutherland's family, the case aroused extraordinary interest. At the prisoner's house, where O'Connor had gone to dine as a guest, he was killed by many blows and his body was buried under the kitchen floor. Both the prisoners then fled from London.

Wilkins, Serjt., for the male prisoner, urged that the wife had alone committed the murder; her object being robbery.

Ballantine, for the female prisoner, urged that the crime had been committed by the male prisoner alone, in a paroxysm of jealousy.]

POLLOCK, L.C.B., in the course of summing up to the jury, said:—
There can be no doubt that Patrick O'Connor was murdered. It has not been suggested by either of the learned counsel for the prisoners that anybody out of the house in which the body was found could

have committed the murder and brought the body and deposited it in the kitchen. There can be no doubt, then, that very grave suspicion must exist against the persons living in the house. The two prisoners appear by different counsel; and each attempts to throw the blame of this dreadful crime upon the other. You, however, must come to a conclusion as to where the guilt rests, and whether it belongs to one or the other or to both.

If you think that one is guilty, and the other innocent of participatiou in the murder, but cannot possibly decide which is the guilty party, you may be reduced to the alternative of returning a verdict of 'Not guilty' as regards both.

Yet, if you consider that one of them was guilty, it will be for you to consider whether, seeing that the murder was committed in the house where both the prisoners lived, it could possibly have been undertaken by the one without the knowledge of the other....With respect to any question of doubt, your duty is, calmly and gravely to investigate the case, and to see what is the conclusion impressed upon your minds as men of the world, as men of sense, as men of solid justice. If the conclusion to which you are conducted be that there is that degree of certainty in the case that you would act upon in your own grave and important concerns, that is the degree of certainty which the law requires, and which will justify you in returning a verdict of guilty against one or both of the prisoners. It is not necessary that a crime should be established beyond the possibility of doubt. There are crimes committed in darkness and secrecy, that can only be traced and brought to light by a comparison of circumstances, which press upon the mind more and more as they are increased in number. There are doubts involved, more or less, in every human transaction. We are frequently mistaken as to what we suppose we have seen— still oftener as to what we suppose we have heard. In all the transactions of life there is a certain degree of doubt mixed up. But these are not the doubts upon which you act in deciding upon a case so important as this; important for the public, on the one hand, and for the prisoners on the other. I doubt not that you will discharge your duty. You will consider that you have on the one hand a duty to the public—namely, to take care that the guilty shall not escape; and that, on the other, you have a duty to the prisoners—to take care that they shall not be convicted upon any mere surmises or suspicion, upon rash or light grounds, but only on grave and solid reasons presenting themselves to your understandings and leading you to a satisfactory conclusion that one, or that both, must be guilty of the crime.

[Both prisoners were convicted and executed.]

[*Hence the Crown must not only prove the crime, but also* identify *the criminal.*]

THE KING *v.* RICHARDSON AND ANOTHER.

OLD BAILEY SESSIONS.   1785.   LEACH 387.

At the Old Bailey, in June Session 1785, Daniel Richardson and Samuel Grenow were indicted before Mr Justice BULLER for a highway robbery on John Billings.

It appeared in evidence that the two prisoners accosted the prosecutor as he was walking along the street, by asking him, in a peremptory manner, what money he had in his pocket? Upon his replying that he had only two-pence half-penny, one of the prisoners immediately said to the other, "If he really has no more do not take that," and turned as if with an intention to go away; but the other prisoner stopped the prosecutor, and robbed him of the two-pence half-penny, which was all the money he had about him. But the prosecutor could not ascertain which of them it was that had used this expression, nor which of them had taken the half-pence from his pocket.

THE COURT. The point of law goes to the acquittal of both the prisoners. For if two men assault another with intent to rob him, and one of them, before any demand of money or offer to take it be made, repent of what he is doing, and desist from the prosecution of such intent, he cannot be involved in the guilt of his companion who afterwards takes the money; for he changed his evil intention before the act, which completes the offence, was committed. That prisoner therefore, whichever of the two it was who thus desisted, cannot be guilty of the present charge; and the prosecutor cannot ascertain who it was that took the property. One of them is certainly guilty, but which of them personally does not appear. It is like the Ipswich case, where five men were indicted for murder; and it appeared, on a special verdict, that it was murder in one, but not in the other four; but it did not appear which of the five had given the blow which caused the death. And the Court thereupon said that, as the man could not be clearly and positively ascertained, all of them must be discharged.

The two prisoners were accordingly acquitted.

[See also REG. *v.* MANNING, p. 446 *supra.*]

[*Hence in so grave a crime as Murder, mere* circumstantial *evidence is usually insufficient to prove the fact of* Death.]

ANONYMOUS.

STAFFORD ASSIZES. 16—.   HALE'S PLEAS OF THE CROWN cap. XXXIX.

I would never convict any person of murder or manslaughter unless the fact were proved to be done, or at the least the body found dead; for the sake of two cases. One is mentioned by my Lord Coke. [*Infra,* p. 449.] In the other, that happened in my remembrance, in Staffordshire, A. was long missing; and upon strong presumptions B. was supposed to have murdered him, and to have consumed him to ashes in an oven, that he should not be found. Thereupon B. was indicted of murder, and convicted and executed. And within one year after, A. returned; having indeed been sent beyond sea by B. against his will. So, though B. justly deserved death, yet he was really not guilty of that offence for which he suffered[1].

ANONYMOUS.

WARWICK ASSIZES. 1610.   COKE'S THIRD INSTITUTE cap. 104.

In the county of Warwick there were two brethren. The one, having issue a daughter, and being seised of lands in fee, devised the government of his daughter and his lands, until she came to her age of sixteen years, to his brother; and died. The uncle brought up his niece very well, both at her book and needle, &c., and she was about eight or nine years of age. Her uncle for some offence correcting her, she was heard to say, "Oh, good uncle, kill me not." After which time the child, after much inquiry, could not be heard of. Whereupon the uncle, being suspected of the murder of her, the rather for that he was her next heir, was upon examination (anno 8 Jac. regis) committed to the gaol for suspicion of murder, and was admonished by the Justices of Assize to find out the child, and thereupon bailed until the next Assizes. Against which time, for that he could not find her, and feared

---

[1] [EDITOR'S NOTE. Sir Matthew Hale proceeds to add that, in his opinion, witchcraft is one of the two crimes that give the greatest difficulty in point of evidence, inasmuch as "many times persons are really guilty of it, yet such an evidence as is satisfactory to prove it can hardly be found."]

what would fall out against him, he took another child as like to her both in person and years as he could find, and apparelled her like unto the true child, and brought her to the next Assizes.. But, upon view and examination, she was found not to be the true child ; and upon these presumptions he was indicted and found guilty, had judgment, and was hanged. But the truth of the case was, that the child, being beaten over night, the next morning when she should go to school, ran away into the next county : and, being well educated, was received and entertained of a stranger. And when she was sixteen years old, at what time she should come to her land, she came to demand it, and was directly proved to be the true child.

[*What is not sufficient evidence to rebut this presumption of innocence.*]

REGINA *v.* WALKER AND MORROD.

CROWN CASE RESERVED.　1854　　　　　DEARSLY 280.

The prisoners were indicted at the East Riding of Yorkshire Sessions, held at Beverley on the 3rd of January, 1854, for stealing six pounds weight of brass from Mr Crosskill ; with a count in the indictment for receiving.

It was proved at the trial that Walker had worked for Mr Crosskill and borne a good character for five or six years. That on the 9th of November he left Mr Crosskill's employment. That on the 9th of November, Morrod, who was brother to Walker's wife, offered for sale in Beverley six pounds weight of brass (being that charged in the indictment as being stolen from Mr Crosskill's) and a quantity of white metal similar to block tin. That the brass (which was of a peculiar kind, and was in ingots cast in moulds belonging to Mr Crosskill) was usually left in a shop the door of which opened on to the road leading into Mr Crosskill's works ; to which workmen on the premises might have access, the door not being kept locked. That block tin and white metal were only kept in the brass foundry within this outer shop, with a door between them. That Thomas Morrod was employed for one week on Mr Crosskill's premises in September last as a bricklayer's labourer, and that in such employment he would have to pass along the road into Mr Crosskill's works, and might have access to the outer shop (where the metal called brass was kept), but had never been seen there ; that he never had been seen in the brass foundry, and could not have gone in there without some of the workmen seeing him. That Walker was employed as an iron moulder at works on the other side of Mr Crosskill's yard. That he frequently went into the brass foundry to borrow tools, and had at.times borrowed white metal, saying that he wanted it for purposes of casting. Walker was apprehended in November, at Wakefield. Morrod, when he sold the brass on the 9th of November, stated to the person to whom he sold it that Walker's wife had given it to him to sell, and that Walker had that day left her and gone into the West Riding ; which he also stated to the jury in his defence, telling them that he did not know but that it was honestly obtained. It was proved that he had given his name and address to the person to whom he sold the brass, and immediately he heard that it had been stolen from Mr Crosskill had gone to see him about it.

The Chairman told the jury they were not to take what Morrod said as to the way he obtained the brass as evidence against Walker, drawing their attention to the fact that it was easy for a man who had himself stolen it to invent such a story, and that it was therefore not fair to take such into account as evidence against the other prisoner.

The jury believing that Walker had stolen the metal, and that Morrod had received it not knowing it to have been stolen, found Walker guilty of stealing, and acquitted Morrod.

Mr Dearsly, on behalf of Walker, objected that there was no evidence whatever to go to a jury of Walker having stolen the brass, and requested the Chairman to reserve a case for the consideration of the Court of Criminal Appeal, and the case was therefore reserved upon this point. The jury were probably partly influenced in their finding by the facts which it was omitted to prove distinctly by the prosecution, but which were nevertheless apparent in the case, that Walker and his wife and her brother Morrod lived in one house together, and that Walker had left Beverley on the 9th of November, and also by the general demeanour of the prisoners. It is also impossible that they should not give some weight to what Morrod had said at different times as against Walker, believing as they did that he had sold the metal innocently, and was speaking the truth for himself.

C. W. Strickland,
Chairman.

This case was argued on the 28th of January, 1854, before JERVIS, C.J., MAULE, J., WIGHTMAN, J., WILLIAMS, J., and PLATT, B.

Dearsly for the prisoner. This conviction is wrong. There was not a particle of evidence to be left to the jury.

MAULE, J. Not a scintilla.

JERVIS, C.J. This conviction must be quashed.

Conviction quashed.

[*Not sufficient evidence to rebut this presumption.*]

REGINA *v.* SLINGSBY.

KENT ASSIZES.   1864.   4 FOSTER AND FINLASON 61.

The prisoner was indicted for that she, on the 7th of January, 1864, a certain cheque, drawn by one Langley for the sum of £18, feloniously did steal.   She was also indicted for that she, on the 7th of January, feloniously forged and altered an indorsement upon the cheque with intent to defraud Langley.   But she was first arraigned on the indictment for larceny; and pleaded not guilty.

The prisoner lived as a general servant with a lady named Carley. On the 5th of January, 1864, Langley, who owed the mistress money, sent her his cheque for £18, enclosed in a letter and drawn to her order.   The lady was then unwell   On the 7th of January the cheque was cashed by the prisoner, with an indorsement on it of her mistress's name, which her mistress's relatives believed not to be hers.   On the 9th her mistress rather suddenly died.   Being then asked if she had received any letters for her mistress during her illness, she said she had not.   It turned out that she had, after cashing the cheque, paid £14 to a tradesman, to whom her mistress owed that sum for a bill, payment of which he had pressed for and been promised.   The prisoner being taxed with this, as proof that she must have received the cheque, still denied it, and had retained and never accounted for the surplus.   But there was no count for stealing the £4.   Nor was there opened any evidence of the forgery, and none was given beyond the belief above mentioned.

POLLOCK, C.B. (to the jury).   You cannot properly convict the prisoner of stealing the cheque.   Indeed, considering how short the interval which elapsed between the cashing of it and her mistress's death, it is doubtful whether you could convict her of stealing the £4, the surplus of the proceeds; but there is no count for that.   Neither is there any evidence of the forgery of the indorsement; and the cheque could not have been paid without an indorsement which appears upon it, and which, for anything that has been proved, may have been genuine.   Perhaps, in the absence of any proof of a forgery, the prisoner is entitled to have it presumed that it is genuine.   At all events it cannot be taken that it is not so; and if it were so, then that, coupled with the undoubted fact that the prisoner applied almost all the proceeds to the payment of her mistress's debt, would negative any felony as to the cheque.   And, on the other hand, the appropriation of the proceeds to what must be deemed to have been a purpose of the mistress, and may fairly be presumed to have been directed by her, tends strongly to show that the cheque was entrusted to the prisoner and not feloniously taken.

Not guilty.

[*But the evidence given by Crown may suffice to reverse the presumption and throw on prisoner the necessity of an explanation.*]

[*See* REGINA *v.* FROST, *supra* p. 374.]

[*What* is *sufficient evidence to rebut the presumption of innocence.*]

REGINA *v.* HOBSON.

CROWN CASE RESERVED. 1854. DEARSLY 400.

The prisoner, George Hobson, was tried at the West Riding Quarter Sessions, held at Rotherham, on the 30th of June, 1854, upon a charge of feloniously receiving from William Levick, one watch, one hat, and one shilling, the property of James Birkenshaw, and was found guilty and sentenced to be imprisoned and kept to hard labour in the House of Correction at Wakefield for twelve calendar months. William Levick had previously at the same Sessions pleaded guilty to the theft. Upon the trial William Laughton, a policeman, proved that on the 8th day of June, 1854, he went to the prisoner's house in consequence of something he had heard from William Levick, the party charged in the indictment as the thief—that Levick took witness there—that witness asked the prisoner, who was in bed, if Levick had brought a hat there —that the prisoner said "Yes"—that the prisoner then got out of bed and took the hat out of a box in a corner of the room, and gave the hat to witness—that witness asked the prisoner if he knew anything about the watch—that the prisoner said he did not—that witness went the next day to the prisoner's house and took him into custody—that witness told the prisoner that he (witness) would most likely trace the watch and who had it—that when witness and the prisoner got outside the house, the prisoner said he did not like to say anything about the watch before the folks in the house, but he knew where it was, that it was planted, that it was at Mr Wastenholmes'—that witness and the prisoner went to Mr Wastenholmes', but could not find a watch there— that the prisoner then called for a boy and asked him to get the watch —that the watch was afterwards brought by the boy to the prisoner, who gave it to witness. On cross-examination, the witness said that the house where the prisoner lived was a lodging-house—that witness did not know whether the thief (Levick) lived there or not, or whether or not the prisoner had exclusive possession of the room where the hat was found—that witness did not notice how many beds were in the room where the hat was found—that when the prisoner said he knew nothing about the watch, there were several people in the house stand- ing round him. It was objected by the prisoner's counsel that there was no evidence to go to the jury; first, as to the hat, because there was not sufficient evidence of the prisoner's possession of it, the house where the hat was found being a lodging-house, and the prisoner having no exclusive possession of the room; secondly, as to the watch, because the prisoner was not shewn to have had possession of it—all the evidence was, that the prisoner knew where the watch was. The Court overruled the objection, being of opinion that there was sufficient evidence to go to the jury, but granted a case for the opinion of the Judges.

This case was considered on the 11th of November, 1854, by JERVIS, C.J., ALDERSON, B., COLERIDGE, J., MARTIN, B., and CROWDER, J.

No counsel appeared either for the Crown or for the prisoner.

JERVIS, C.J. We all think that in this case there was evidence to go to the jury.

Conviction affirmed.

[*But in some* statutory *offences, the burden of disproving the* Mens Rea *is thrown on the accused.*]

[E.g., *exceptional cases of a master's being prima facie liable for a servant's criminal acts even though unauthorized.*]

COPPEN *v.* MOORE.

QUEEN'S BENCH DIVISION.   1898.   L.R. [1898.]   2 Q.B.D. 306.

Case stated by justices of Richmond, in the county of Surrey, for the opinion of a Divisional Court.

* * * * * *

Lord Russell of Killowen, C.J. This is a case stated by justices, who summarily convicted the appellant of an offence against the Merchandise Marks Act, 1887 (50 and 51 Vict. c. 28)[1]

The appellant was charged under s. 2, sub-s. 2, with having sold goods to which a "false trade description" was applied. The facts were as follows:—

On September 4, 1897, the respondent, at the London Supply Stores, 42, George Street, Richmond (one of several places of business of the appellant), asked the salesman at the door of the shop for a small English ham. The salesman pointed to a number of hams on a shelf, and said they were Scotch hams. In fact they were long-cut American hams. The salesman stated the price, $8\frac{1}{2}d$. per lb., and the respondent said he would take one, which was then produced. The salesman then passed the ham selected through the open window to a shop assistant inside, saying, "Weigh up Scotch ham, $8\frac{1}{2}d$." The respondent, before paying, asked the assistant to make him out an account and put on it "Scotch ham," as he had bought it as such. The assistant at first handed the respondent an invoice without the word "Scotch" on it. The respondent did not accept it so written, but told the assistant to put the word "Scotch," "as he had bought it as such." The assistant then did so, and handed the invoice to the respondent, who then paid the price, $5s. 5\frac{1}{2}d$. Upon this being done, the respondent asked the assistant whether he still said it was a Scotch ham whereupon the assistant admitted it was not, but was an American ham. The salesman, in like manner, was asked, and he at once admitted it was an American ham.

On the part of the appellant evidence was given that he had

---

[1] By s. 2, sub-s. 2, of the Act, "Every person who sells, or exposes for, or has in his possession for, sale, or any purpose of trade or manufacture, any goods or things to which any forged trade-mark or false trade description is applied, or to which any trade-mark or mark so nearly resembling a trade-mark as to be calculated to deceive is falsely applied, as the case may be, shall, unless he proves—

(a) That having taken all reasonable precautions against committing an offence against this Act, he had at the time of the commission of the alleged offence no reason to suspect the genuineness of the trade-mark, mark, or trade description; and

(b) That on demand made by or on behalf of the prosecutor he gave all the information in his power with respect to the persons from whom he obtained such goods or things; or

(c) That otherwise he had acted innocently;
be guilty of an offence against this Act."

sent out a notice to all his branch places of business, including that in question, in the following terms :—

"February 25th, 1897.

"Most important.

"Please instruct your assistants most explicitly that the hams described in list as breakfast hams must not be sold under any specific name of place or origin. That is to say, they must not be described as 'Bristol,' 'Bath,' 'Wiltshire,' or any such title, but simply as breakfast hams. Please sign and return.

"H. W. Coppen."

The ham in question would come within the category of breakfast hams. Evidence was given that the terms of this notice were communicated to the manager and assistants, and the appellant stated that he had no reason to believe that his instructions were not being carried out....

It was admitted that the description "Scotch ham" was a trade description, and it is found that it was applied to the ham sold by the appellant's employees, and it was admittedly false. It was not contended that it was not material. In these circumstances it is clear that an offence against the Act was committed by the salesman and by the assistant of the appellant. But the question which the Court is now called upon to decide is whether the appellant also is not personally liable to be convicted. This was the question argued.

The appellant's contention was that the charge here preferred was a criminal charge, and that the general principle of law applied, "Nemo reus est nisi mens sit rea." There is no doubt that this is the general rule, but it is subject to exceptions, and the question here is whether the present case falls within the rule or within the exception. Apart from statute, exceptions have been engrafted upon the rule: for example, in the case of *Reg.* v. *Stephens*[1] the defendant was held liable on an indictment for obstructing navigation by throwing rubbish into a river from a quarry owned by him but managed by his son, although it was proved that the men employed at the quarry had been by order prohibited from doing the acts complained of. No doubt in that case the fact that the proceedings were only in form criminal was adverted to by the judges who decided it, but the fact remains that the defendant was criminally indicted. But by far the greater number of exceptions engrafted upon the general rule are cases in which it has been decided that by various statutes criminal responsibility has been put upon masters for the acts of their servants. Amongst such cases is *Mullins* v. *Collins*[2], where a licensed victualler was convicted of an

---

[1] L. R. 1 Q. B. 702. [2] L. R. 9 Q. B. 292.

offence under s. 16 of the Licensing Act, 1872, for supplying liquor to a constable on duty, although this was done by his servant without the knowledge of the master. Again, in *Bond* v. *Evans*[1], a licensed victualler was convicted of an offence against s. 17 of the same Act, · where gaming had been allowed in the licensed premises by the servant in charge of the premises although without the knowledge of his master. The decisions in these and in other like cases were based upon the construction of the statute in question. The Court in fact came to the conclusion that, having regard to the language, scope, and objects of those Acts, the legislature intended to fix criminal responsibility upon the master for acts done by his servant in the course of his employment, although such acts were not authorized by the master, and might even have been expressly prohibited by him.

The question, then, in this case, comes to be narrowed to the simple point, whether upon the true construction of the statute here in question the master was intended to be made criminally responsible for acts done by his servants in contravention of the Act, where such acts were done, as in this case, within the scope or in the course of their employment. In our judgment it was clearly the intention of the legislature to make the master criminally liable for such acts, unless he was able to rebut the primâ facie presumption of guilt by one or other of the methods pointed out in the Act. Take the facts here, and apply the Act to them. To begin with, it cannot be doubted that the appellant sold the ham in question, although the transaction was carried out by his servants. In other words, he was the seller, although not the actual salesman. It is clear also, as already stated, that the ham was sold with a "false trade description," which was material. If so, there is evidence establishing a primâ facie case of an offence against the Act having been committed by the appellant. But it is only a primâ facie case. The burden of proof is shifted upon the appellant....

In the present case there was ample evidence to justify the conclusion of the magistrates that the appellant was primâ facie guilty of the offence charged, and that primâ facie case has not been met in the manner required by the Act....

In answer, then, to the question which alone is put to us, namely, whether upon the facts stated the decision of the magistrates convicting the appellant was in point of law correct, our answer is that in our judgment it was. When the scope and object of the Act are borne in mind, any other conclusion would to a large extent render the Act ineffective for its avowed purposes. The circumstances of the present

[1] 21 Q. B. D. 249.

case afford a convenient illustration of this. The appellant, under the style of the "London Supply Stores," carries on an extensive business as grocer and provision dealer, having, it appears, six shops, or branch establishments, and having also a wholesale warehouse. It is obvious that, if sales with false trade descriptions could be carried out in these establishments with impunity so far as the principal is concerned, the Act would to a large extent be nugatory. We conceive the effect of the Act to be to make the master or principal liable criminally (as he is already, by law, civilly) for the acts of his agents and servants in all cases within the sections with which we are dealing where the conduct constituting the offence was pursued by such servants and agents within the scope or in the course of their employment, subject to this : that the master or principal may be relieved from criminal responsibility where he can prove that he had acted in good faith and had done all that it was reasonably possible to do to prevent the commission by his agents and servants of offences against the Act. The result, therefore, is that the conviction will be affirmed, and with costs.

We wish to add that the form in which this case is stated is not satisfactory. It does not throughout clearly distinguish between what was merely evidence and what was proved to the satisfaction of the magistrates. It is important that it should be borne in mind that when a case is submitted to the Court it ought to state clearly what the facts proved were, and not merely what the evidence was.

[Sir F. H. JEUNE, P., CHITTY, L.J., WRIGHT, DARLING, and CHANNELL, JJ., concurred.]

Conviction affirmed.

[(B)   *There is a presumption against the commission of an immoral act.*]
[*Hence cohabitation is evidence of marriage.*]

DOE dem. FLEMING *v.* FLEMING.

COMMON PLEAS.   1827.   4 BINGHAM 266.

The lessor of the plaintiff claimed the premises sought to be recovered in this ejectment as heir at law to his brother, the person last seised.

His father was still alive, and the only evidence of the lessor of the plaintiff's having been born in lawful wedlock was the reputation of his parents having lived together as husband and wife.

A verdict having been found for the plaintiff at the trial before Best, C.J., at Middlesex sittings after last term,

Wilde, Serjt., moved for a new trial, on the ground that though reputation was evidence of marriage in ordinary cases, yet where the plaintiff was to recover as heir at law, where his being such was the sole question to be tried, and his father was still alive, direct evidence of the marriage ought to have been furnished.

PARK, J. The general rule is, that reputation is sufficient evidence of marriage, and a party who seeks to impugn a principle so well established, ought, at least, to furnish cases in support of his position ; as we have heard none, I see no reason for disturbing the verdict.

BEST, C.J. The rule has never been doubted. It appeared on the trial that the mother of the lessor of the plaintiff was received into society as a respectable woman, and under such circumstances improper conduct ought not to be presumed.

Rule refused.

[*But this presumption against* moral *wrong-doing is counterbalanced by the stronger presumption against* criminal *wrong-doing.*]

MORRIS *v.* MILLER.

KING'S BENCH.   1767.   1 W. BLACKSTONE 632.

Action for criminal conversation with the plaintiff's wife. The only proof of the marriage was by reputation and cohabitation of the parties.

Per Lord MANSFIELD, C.J., and *tot. Cur.* In these actions there must be proof of a marriage in fact ; as contrasted to cohabitation and reputation of marriage arising from thence. Perhaps there need not be strict proof from the register, or by a person present, but strong evidence must be had of the fact: as by a person present at the wedding dinner, if the register be burnt and the parson and clerk be dead. This action is by way of punishment : therefore the Court never interfere as to the quantum of damages. No proof in such a case shall arise from the parties' own act of cohabitation. The case of bigamy is stronger than this : and on an indictment for that offence, Dennison, J., on the Norfolk Circuit, ruled, that though a lawful canonical marriage need not be proved, yet a marriage in fact (whether regular or not), must be shewn. Except in these two cases, I know of none where reputation is not a good proof of marriage.

Plaintiff nonsuited.

[(C) *Omnia praesumuntur ritè ac solenniter esse acta.*]

[See WARREN *v.* GREENVILLE, *infra.*]

[E.g., *a due* Licence *presumed.*]

THE QUEEN *v.* CRESSWELL.

CROWN CASE RESERVED.   1876.   L.R. 1 Q.B.D. 446.

Case stated by Kelly, C.B.

The prisoner was tried at the last Summer Assizes at Chelmsford for bigamy and convicted. It was proved that he married one Sarah Hill in 1868, and that she was still alive; and that he married his present wife, the prosecutrix, in October, 1874, at St Mary, Islington. It was, however, objected for the prisoner that the first marriage was void, on the ground that it was solemnised not in a church, but in a chamber at South Weald Hall, in Essex, which was situate some yards from the parish church, and that the marriage took place while the church was under repair. Divine service had been several times performed in the building in question, from which it was for the Court to consider whether the presumption might be raised which would give validity to the marriage. The statutes 4 Geo. IV. c. 76, ss. 21, 22, and 6 Wm. IV. c. 85, were quoted. The learned Judge reserved the point; and the question for the opinion of the Court was, whether upon the above facts this was a valid marriage. If not, the conviction was to be set aside; otherwise affirmed.

No counsel appeared for the prisoner.

C. E. Jones, for the prosecution, was not called upon.

LORD COLERIDGE, C.J. This conviction must be affirmed. The case states that divine service had been several times celebrated in the place where the marriage in question was solemnised. This is sufficient, in accordance with the maxim omnia presumuntur rite esse acta, to give rise to the presumption that the building was licensed. The presumption is the stronger because the clergyman who celebrated the marriage might, by 6 and 7 Wm. IV. c. 85, s. 3, have been indicted for felony if he knowingly did so, in an unlicensed place.

[MELLOR, LUSH, and GROVE, JJ. and AMPHLETT, B., concurred.]

Conviction affirmed.

[E.g., *a due* appointment *of an official presumed.*]

REX *v.* BORRETT.

OLD BAILEY SESSIONS.   1833.   6 CARRINGTON AND PAYNE 124.

The prisoner was indicted upon stat. 2 Will. IV. c. 4, as a '' person employed in the public service of his Majesty," for embezzling the overcharge of a letter which came to his hands as a letter-carrier. The letter was charged as a treble letter, but was, in fact, only a double one.

It was directed to Mr Collins; but Mrs Collins had taken it in, and paid the postage of it, and she alone had made any demand upon the prisoner for repayment of the overcharge.

No evidence was offered of the prisoner's appointment as a letter-carrier; but one of the witnesses proved incidentally that he acted as such.

Stammers, for the prisoner, contended (1) that the prisoner's appointment ought to have been proved; and (2) that the letter being directed to Mr Collins, he was the only person authorized to receive the overcharge, and that, consequently, as there had been no refusal to account to him, the embezzlement was not proved.

Adolphus, contended that it was not necessary to prove the prisoner's appointment; that he had been proved to have been acting as a letter-carrier, and was therefore within the terms of the statute. With regard to the second objection, Mrs Collins was the person who paid the postage of the letter, and, therefore, she was authorized to receive the rebate.

The Judges present (LITTLEDALE, J., BOLLAND, B., and BOSANQUET, J.) were of this opinion. The case went to the jury; and the prisoner was convicted.

[E.g., *due fulfilment of a statutory condition presumed.*]

BENNETT *v.* CLOUGH AND ANOTHER.

KING'S BENCH.   1818.   1 BARNEWALL AND ALDERSON 461.

Action by plaintiff, a sub-distributor of stamps at Chorley in Lancashire, against the defendants, who were proprietors of a coach running from Manchester through Chorley and Preston to Carlisle, for £140 being the value of a parcel which had been sent by that con-

veyance and which had been lost by the way. The parcel was directed
to Samuel Staniforth, Esq., Liverpool (the stamp distributor there),
and contained two Bank post bills of £50 each, £40 in Bank of
England notes, and some stamps. In the cross-examination of Mr
Henry Bennett, the plaintiff's son, who proved the value and contents
of the parcel, it further appeared that there was contained in the
parcel a letter sealed and directed to Mr Staniforth, but of the contents of which he could give no account, not having ever seen them.
Bayley, J., who tried the cause at the last Assizes for the county of
Lancaster, thought that this did not prevent the plaintiff from recovering for the value of the parcel, but gave the defendant leave to move
to enter a nonsuit if the Court should be of a different opinion. And
now

Scarlett moved to enter a nonsuit. The question depends on
42 G. III. c. 81, by the fifth section of which it is enacted, "that no one
shall send any letter or letters, packet or packets of letters otherwise
than by the post, or by and with the authority of the Post-Master
General, on pain of forfeiting £5." It was therefore illegal to send
this packet, being within the express prohibition of the Act; and the
plaintiff cannot recover for its loss, unless in the opinion of the Court
it falls within the proviso mentioned in that Act. That proviso is[1],
"that the Act shall not extend to subject any person to any such
penalty or forfeiture as aforesaid, for sending or causing to be sent or
conveyed, or for tendering or delivering in order to be sent or conveyed, any letter or letters which shall respectively concern goods sent
by any common carrier of goods, and which shall be sent with, and for
the purpose of being delivered with, the goods that such letter or letters
do concern, without hire or reward, profit or advantage, for the
receiving or delivering the same." Now this was not a letter accompanying goods: for the principal contents of the parcel were bank
notes, and though there were certainly a few stamps also in it, yet the
plaintiff did not seek to recover any thing for them. At any rate it
must be a letter concerning the goods to bring it within the proviso,
and the plaintiff therefore ought to have proved this by giving some
evidence of its contents, which was not done. But

THE COURT thought that the defendant ought to have given primâ
facie evidence that the letter did not concern the goods sent in the
parcel in order to have laid a foundation for his objection. The parcel
contained stamps, and the letter was directed to the stamp distributor
at Liverpool, the presumption therefore is, that this letter which

[1] For the similar exemption in force under the present Post Office Act, see
1 Vict. c. 32, s. 2.

accompanied the stamps related to them. Illegality is never presumed:
on the contrary, everything must be presumed to have been legally
done till the contrary is proved.

Rule refused.

[(D) *There is a presumption that a man who does any act*
intends its natural consequences.]

REX *v.* SHEPPARD.

CROWN CASE RESERVED.   1810.   RUSSELL AND RYAN 169.

The prisoner was tried before Mr JUSTICE HEATH, at the Old
Bailey September Sessions, in the year 1809, on an indictment consisting of four counts. The first count charged the prisoner with forging
a receipt for £19. 16s. 6d., purporting to be signed by W. S. West,
for certain stock therein mentioned, with intent to defraud the
Governors and Company of the Bank of England. The second count
was for uttering the same knowing it to be forged, with the like intent.
The third and fourth counts varied from the first and second, in
charging the intent to have been to defraud Richard Morley.

It appeared in evidence at the trial, that Richard Morley gave £20
to his brother Thomas Morley in the month of January, 1809, to buy
stock in the five per cent. Navy. In February following, Thomas Morley
gave the £20 to the prisoner, for the purchase of the said stock, on the
prisoner's delivering to him the receipt stated in the indictment. The
prisoner being examined at the bank, confessed that the receipt was
a forgery, that there was no such person as W. S. West, whose
signature appeared subscribed to the receipt, and that he being pressed
for money forged that name, but had no intention of defrauding
Richard Morley. Richard Morley and Thomas Morley swore they
believed that the prisoner had no such intent. On examining the
bank books, no transaction corresponding with this could be found.

The learned Judge told the jury that the prisoner was entitled to
an acquittal on the first and second counts, because the receipt in
question could not operate in fraud of the governor and company of the
Bank. That as to the third and fourth counts, although the Morleys
swore that they did not believe the forgery to have been committed
with an intent to defraud Richard Morley, yet as it was the necessary

effect and consequence of the forgery (if the prisoner could not repay the money), it was sufficient evidence of the intent for them to convict the prisoner.

The jury acquitted the prisoner on the first and second counts, and found him guilty on the third and fourth counts; and the learned Judge reserved this case for the opinion of the Judges, to determine whether this direction to the jury was right and proper.

In Easter term, 31st of May, 1810, ALL THE JUDGES were present, and they were all of opinion that the conviction was right, as the immediate effect of the act was the defrauding Richard Morley of his money.

[See also REGINA *v.* DAVITT, *supra* p. 380; and BEATTY *v.* GILL-BANKS, *supra* p. 392.]

[(E)   *There is a presumption that any existing state of things
will* continue *for some time further.*]

[See REGINA *v.* JONES, *supra* p. 428.]

[E.g., *that a man survived for some time after being last heard of.*]

[See REGINA *v.* WILLSHIRE, *supra* p. 429.]

(F)| *There is a presumption that the* possessor *of goods* recently
stolen *is either the thief or a guilty receiver.*]

REGINA *v.* LANGMEAD.

CROWN CASE RESERVED. 1864.   LEIGH AND CAVE 427.

[At the Devonshire Quarter Sessions, James Langmead was charged, in the first count of the indictment with stealing certain sheep, and in

the second count with feloniously receiving the same, knowing them to
have been stolen. It was proved that, a few days after the theft, he
was in possession of the sheep. He gave the jury no explanation to
account for this possession. The circumstances given in evidence
seemed, however, to shew that he had not himself committed the theft.]

The jury found the prisoner guilty of feloniously receiving the
sheep, knowing them to have been stolen. Whereupon the counsel
for the prisoner objected that there was no evidence before the Court
to support the second count, and that the jury should have been
directed that they could not find the prisoner guilty on that count; for
the evidence proved no more than recent possession by the prisoner
after the loss, unaccounted for. He contended that (although a
presumption of guilt might legally be inferred from recent possession,
unaccounted for, alone, if the offence of which the jury found the
prisoner guilty had been theft, yet) guilt could not be thus inferred
from recent possession, unaccounted for, alone, in considering whether
the prisoner were guilty of feloniously receiving the sheep, knowing
them to have been stolen. The Court were of opinion that there was
sufficient evidence to support the verdict; but, at the request of the
prisoner's counsel, they granted a case on the following question:

Whether, upon the whole case, the jury should have been directed
that they could not lawfully find the prisoner guilty upon the second
count?

S. Carter, for the prisoner. In this case it was proved to have
been impossible for either the prisoner or his sons to have stolen the
sheep; and therefore the prisoner should have been acquitted. For
recent possession is evidence of stealing only, and not of receiving..

BLACKBURN, J. The prisoner was in possession of the sheep, and
gave no satisfactory account of them. He had possession of them,
therefore, dishonestly; and that dishonest possession might arise from
his being either the thief or the receiver.

Carter. Four things were wanting to prove that the prisoner was
guilty of receiving the sheep knowing them to have been stolen, viz.:—
first, evidence that sheep had been stolen; secondly, evidence that
sheep had been received by the prisoner; thirdly, evidence that the
sheep stolen and those received were the same; fourthly, evidence of
guilty knowledge.

POLLOCK, C.B. Here, first, the sheep were lost; secondly and
thirdly, the lost sheep were traced to the prisoner; and, fourthly, he
gave no satisfactory account of them.

*   *   *   *

BYLES, J. There are three ways in which the prisoner may have

K.   30

received these sheep with a guilty knowledge. First, the boys may have stolen them independently of their father, who may have received the sheep from them. Secondly, the father may have sent the boys as innocent agents to receive the sheep from the actual thief; in which case the father would be guilty of receiving as a principal, the boys being, as it were, merely the long arms with which he took the sheep. Thirdly, he may have sent the boys for the same purpose, as guilty agents; in which case, although the boys would be the principals in the felony, yet the father would be an accessory before the fact, and might be indicted and convicted as a principal. The jury may fairly have drawn any one of these conclusions from the facts before them. Whether they were right or wrong in their conclusion is not a question for us. Where there has been a burglary, and some men and a woman are found in possession of the property stolen, although the evidence may be the same against all, the jury almost universally find the men guilty of the burglary and the woman only of receiving; the consideration of her sex inclining their minds to the belief that she did not take any part in the burglary.

BLACKBURN, J. I am of the same opinion. I do not agree with Mr Carter in thinking that recent possession is not as vehement evidence of receiving as of stealing. When it has been shewn that property has been stolen, and has been found recently after its loss in the possession of the prisoner, he is called upon to account for having it; and, on his failing to do so, the jury may very well infer that his possession was dishonest, and that he was either the thief or the receiver according to the circumstances. If he had been seen near the place where the property was kept before it was stolen, they may fairly suppose that he was the thief. If other circumstances shew that it is more probable that he was not the thief, the presumption would be that he was the receiver. The jury should not convict the prisoner of receiving, unless they are satisfied that he is not the actual thief. At first I was inclined to suppose that in this case the jury came to the wrong conclusion; but I now think that they were right. The prisoner is found at Exeter dealing with the sheep which are brought to him there by the boys. Now, he had set out with the boys that same morning; and the distance from the place where the sheep were kept to Exeter was too great for the boys to have travelled on foot. It is more probable, therefore, that the sheep had been stolen previously by some other person and driven to some place near Exeter, where they were picked up by the boys. If that was so, the inference would be irresistible that the person from whom the boys received them was the actual thief. Then, that being so, the father was, no doubt, an accessory before the fact, and there was, therefore, evidence for the jury on which they might convict him of receiving.

MELLOR, J. I am of the same opinion. In theory the jury ought to agree in their opinion; but in practice they often do not. Some think that the prisoner was the actual thief, and others that he was the receiver only. It has been proposed to find some form of indict. ment in which both parties might consistently concur in a verdict of Guilty. That, however, has not been done; but instead two counts— one for stealing and the other for receiving—are joined in the same indictment. It is clear that, whatever was the mode in which the jury in this case arrived at their verdict, there was evidence from which they might safely have drawn either conclusion.

Conviction affirmed.

[*But this presumption does not arise until the goods are proved to have been actually* stolen.]

ANONYMOUS.

OXFORD ASSIZES. 16—. 2 HALE'S PLEAS OF THE CROWN cap. xxxix.

In some cases presumptive evidences go far to prove a person guilty, though there be no express proof of the fact to be committed by him; but then it must be very warily pressed, for it is better five guilty persons should escape unpunished than one innocent person should die.

If a horse be stolen from A., and, the same day, B. be found upon him, it is a strong presumption that B. stole him. Yet I do remember, before a very wary and learned judge, in such an instance, B. was condemned and executed at Oxford Assizes; and yet within two Assizes after, C., being apprehended for another robbery and convicted, upon his judgment and execution, confessed he was the man that stole the horse. He, being closely pursued, desired B., a stranger, to walk his horse for him while he turned aside upon a necessary occasion; and escaped; and B. was apprehended with the horse, and died innocently.

I would never convict any person for stealing the goods 'cujusdam ignoti' merely because he would not give an account how he came by them, unless there were due proof made that a felony was committed of these goods.

[*An actual* stealing *must first be proved.*]

REX *v.* YEND AND HAINES.

GLOUCESTER ASSIZES.   1833.   6 CARRINGTON AND PAYNE 176.

Horse-stealing.   The prisoners were indicted for stealing a horse, the property of Mr Lord.   The prosecutor proved that he had put the stolen horse to be agisted with a person who resided twelve miles distance from his own residence ; and, in consequence of hearing of its loss from that person, he went to the field where the horse had been put to feed, and discovered that it was gone.

GURNEY, B.   I think you should prove the loss more distinctly, because non constat but the prisoners might have obtained possession of the horse honestly.   I do not see how we can get at that, without the person with whom it was put to agist, or his servant.   It is perfectly consistent with what has been proved, that the horse might have got out of this person's possession in some other way, and not by felony.

Verdict, Not guilty.

[*The degree of recentness required varies with the kind of property.*]

REX *v.* PARTRIDGE.

GLOUCESTER ASSIZES.   1836.   7 CARRINGTON AND PAYNE 551.

Larceny.   The prisoner was indicted for stealing two ends of woollen cloth (pieces consisting of about 20 yards each), the property of John Figgins Marling.

It appeared that the cloth was missed on the 23rd of January, 1836, it then being in an unfinished state; and that part of it was, on the 21st of March, left by the prisoner at the house of a person named Porter ; and that on the 30th of the same month the prisoner sent the residue of it to be shorn.   It further appeared that, the prisoner being in the custody of a constable, the latter said to the prosecutor, Mr Marling, "You must not use any threat or promise to the prisoner": and immediately after this Mr Marling said to the prisoner, "I should be obliged to you if you would tell us what you know about it ; if you will not, we of course can do nothing ; I shall be glad if you will."

C. *Phillips*, for the prisoner, submitted that anything said by the prisoner after this was not receivable.

PATTESON, J. I think this is a distinct promise; what could the prosecutor mean by saying that if the prisoner would not tell they could do nothing, but that, if the prisoner would tell, they would do something for him?

The statement of the prisoner was not given in evidence.

C. Phillips. I submit that the length of time that has elapsed since the loss of the cloth is so great that there is no presumption of guilt raised against the prisoner by the possession of it.

PATTESON, J. I think the length of time is to be considered with reference to the nature of the articles which are stolen. If they are such as pass from hand to hand readily, two months would be a long time; but here that is not so. It is a question for the jury.

Verdict, Guilty.

[*A possession which is* not *sufficiently recent.*]

ANONYMOUS.

BUCKINGHAM ASSIZES.   1826.   2 CARRINGTON AND PAYNE 459.

Larceny. Goods, which had been lost sixteen months before, were found in the house of the prisoner. This was the whole of the evidence against him.

BAYLEY, J. The rule of law is that if stolen property be found, *recently* after its loss, in the possession of a person, he must give an account of the manner in which he became possessed of it; otherwise the presumption attaches that he is the thief. But I think that, after so long a period as sixteen months had elapsed, it would not be reasonable to call upon a prisoner to account for the manner in which property supposed to be stolen came into his possession.

Verdict, Not guilty.

[*A possession not sufficiently recent.*]

REGINA *v.* COOPER.

ESSEX ASSIZES.   1852.   3 CARRINGTON AND KIRWAN 318.

The prisoner was indicted for stealing a mare. It appeared that the mare had been lost on Dec. 17, 1849, and was found in the possession of the prisoner on June 20, 1850.

MAULE, J., said he thought there was no case to go to the jury, the possession not being sufficiently recent. Where a man is found in possession of a horse six or seven months after it is lost, and there is no other evidence against him except this possession, he ought not to be called on to account for it.

Verdict, Not guilty.

[*But the possessor can rebut the presumption by merely* giving *an explanation without* proving *it.*]

REGINA *v.* CROWHURST.

KENT ASSIZES.   1844.   1 CARRINGTON AND KIRWAN 370.

Larceny. The prisoner was indicted for stealing a piece of wood, the property of a person named Harman.

It appeared from the evidence given on the part of the prosecution that, on the piece of wood being found by a police-constable in the prisoner's shop, about five days after it was lost, he stated that he bought it from a person named Nash, who lived about two miles off. Nash was not produced as a witness for the prosecution, and the prisoner did not call any witness.

ALDERSON, B. (in summing up). In cases of this nature you should take it as a general principle that where a man, in whose possession stolen property is found, gives a reasonable account of how he came by it, (as by telling the name of the person from whom he received it, and who is known to be a real person,) it is incumbent on the prosecutor to shew that that account is false. But if the account given by the prisoner be unreasonable or improbable on the face of it, the onus of proving its truth lies on him. Suppose, for instance, a person were to charge me with stealing this watch, and I were to say I bought it from a particular tradesman, whom I name, that is primâ facie a reasonable account, and I ought not to be convicted of felony unless it is shewn that that account is a false one.

Verdict, Not guilty.

SECTION II.

THE BURDEN OF PROOF.

[*Ei incumbit probatio qui* dicit, *non qui* negat (Dig. 22. 3. 2).]

[See REGINA v. CURGERWEN, *supra* p. 426.]

[*But in accusations of* crime *the Presumption of Innocence throws back upon the accuser the burden of proving even* negative *averments of guilt.*]

REX v. HAZY AND COLLINS.

BUCKS ASSIZES.   1826.   2 CARRINGTON AND PAYNE 458.

Indictment on the stat. 6 Geo. III. c. 36, for lopping and topping an ash timber tree, "without the consent of the owner." The owner (Sir J. Aubrey) had died before the trial. The offence was committed at 11 o'clock at night on the 18th of February. Sir J. Aubrey died on the 1st of March following, having given orders for apprehending the prisoners on suspicion.

The land-steward was called to prove that he himself never gave any consent; and, from all he had heard his master say, he believed that he never did.

BAYLEY, J., told the jury that they must be perfectly satisfied that the prisoners had not obtained the consent of the owner of the tree (namely, Sir J. Aubrey) that they might lop and top it; and left it to them to say, whether they thought there was reasonable evidence to shew that in fact he had not given any such permission. His Lordship adverted to the time of night when the offence was committed, and to the circumstance of the prisoners running away when detected, as evidence to shew that the consent required had not in fact been given.

Verdict, Guilty.

[*Negative averments in accusations of* Crime.]

WILLIAMS *v.* EAST INDIA COMPANY.

KING'S BENCH.   1802.   3 EAST 192.

[Action by owner of a ship called the *Princess Amelia*, which
had been let to freight to the East India Company by charter-party,
for the destruction of the said ship by fire through the negligence of
the company. The negligence complained of was that the E.I.
Company, as charterers, had loaded on board the said ship certain
oil and varnish of a combustible and inflammable nature, without
giving "due or sufficient notice or intimation thereof" to the persons
concerned in the navigation of the said ship, in order that they might
so stow the same as not to endanger the safety of the ship.   Upon
a plea of not guilty it was proved at the trial before Lord Ellenborough
that a jar of a certain oil or varnish called by the natives in India
"Roghan," supposed to be a composition of gum-gopal and linseed oil,
of a very inflammable nature was put on board at Bombay amongst
a quantity of other military stores.   In the written order to receive the
package on board it was simply called "Roghan" without any specifi-
cation of its nature.   Evidence was given that neither the nature nor
the name of it was known generally.   By its oozing out of the jar the
ship was set on fire, on the fourth day after putting out to sea, and
totally destroyed.   The captain of the ship and the second mate proved
that no communication had been made to them or, so far as they knew,
to any other person on board the ship concerning the inflammable
nature of the article.   The chief mate, the person who actually received
the "Roghan" on board, was dead; and no evidence was given of what
passed between him and the Company's officer who delivered the
military stores on board.

   LORD ELLENBOROUGH, C.J., non-suited the plaintiff on the ground
that he had failed to prove an allegation which was material to support
the action; viz. that no notice was given to the chief mate, as to
the dangerous nature of the commodity, when it was received on
board; for non constat but that the fullest notice had been given.]

   Adam shewed cause against granting a new trial.   Supposing it to
have been the duty of the Company's officer to give notice of the
dangerous nature of the commodity when it was delivered on board the
plaintiff's ship, it must be presumed, in the absence of all proof to the
contrary, that such notice was given; as it cannot be presumed that the
officer acted contrary to his duty.   It was therefore a necessary part of
the plaintiff's case to shew that no such notice had been given; that

being the gist of the action, the wrong complained of; without which the action cannot be sustained, being damnum sine injuriâ. The plaintiff having averred the want of such notice in his declaration, and made it the foundation of his complaint, it was incumbent on him to prove it; the subject-matter of the allegation, though conveying a negative in terms, being capable of affirmative proof, by calling either of the persons by or to whom the commodity was delivered on board, or any other who might happen to have been present at the time, to speak to what passed on the occasion....

Erskine, for plaintiff. This being a negative averment on the part of the plaintiff, the affirmative of which was the ground of defence to the action, it lay upon the defendant, whose duty it was to give the notice, to prove affirmatively that it was in fact given. The general rule is, that the party on whom the affirmative of the issue lies is to begin by proving it. Now upon the plea of not guilty to an action on the case, which puts in issue every material fact, the same rule must prevail....

LORD ELLENBOROUGH, C.J., delivered the opinion of the Court The rule of law is that where any act is required to be done on the one part, so that the party neglecting it would be guilty of a criminal neglect of duty in not having done it, the law presumes the affirmative, and throws the burden of proving the contrary, that is, in such case, of proving a negative, on the other side. *Monke* v. *Butler,* 1 Rol. Rep. 83. "In a suit for tythes in the spiritual court, the defendant pleaded, that the plaintiff had *not* read the XXXIX. Articles; and the Court put the defendant to prove it, though a negative. Whereupon he moved the Court for a prohibition; which was denied: for in this case the law will presume that a parson had read the Articles; for otherwise he is to lose his benefice. And when the law presumes the affirmative, then the negative is to be proved." This, it will be observed, was in a civil suit. So upon the same principle in Lord Halifax's case, Bull. N. P. 298, upon an information against Lord Halifax for refusing to deliver up the rolls of the auditor of the Court of Exchequer, the Court of Exchequer put the plaintiff upon proving the negative, viz. that he did not deliver them: for "a person shall be presumed duly to execute his office until the contrary appear.".. Where the law supposes the matter contained in the issue, there the opposite party (that is, the party who contends for the contrary of that which the law supposes) must be put into proof of it by a negative. That the declaration, in imputing to the defendants the having wrongfully put on board a ship, without notice to those concerned in the management of the ship, an article of a highly dangerous combustible nature, imputes to the defendants a criminal negligence, cannot well be questioned. In order to make the putting on board wrongful, the defendants must be conusant of the dangerous quality of the article put on board ; and if being so, they yet gave no notice, considering the probable danger thereby occasioned to the lives of those on board, it amounts to a species of delinquency in the persons concerned in so putting such dangerous article on board, for which they are criminally liable, and punishable as for a misdemeanor at least. We are therefore of opinion, upon the principle and the authorities above stated, that the burden of proving that the dangerous article was put on board without notice, rested upon the plaintiff, alleging it to have been wrongfully put on board without notice of its nature and quality. The next question is, Whether the plaintiff have given sufficient primâ facie evidence of the want of notice to have gone to a jury. And we are of opinion that he has not. The best evidence should have been given of which the nature of the thing was capable. The best evidence was to have been had by calling in the first instance upon the persons immediately and officially employed in the delivery and in the receiving the goods on board, who appear in this case to have been the first mate on the one side, and the military conductor on the other. And though the one of these persons, the mate, was dead, it did not warrant the plaintiff in resorting to an inferior and secondary species of testimony, viz. the presumption and inference arising from a non-communication to other persons on board, as long as the military conductor, the other living witness immediately and primarily concerned in the transaction of shipping the goods on board, could be resorted to: and no impossibility of resorting to this evidence of the military conductor, the proper and primary evidence on the subject, is suggested to exist in this case. We are therefore of opinion that the nonsuit was proper, and that the rule for setting it aside must be discharged.

Rule discharged.

[*Unless apparent guilt has been proved, and the* affirmative *fact which would disprove guilt lies peculiarly within* prisoner's own *knowledge.*]

REX *v.* TURNER.

Kıng's Bench.   1816.   5 Maule and Selwyn 206.

[Conviction by two justices, under 5 Anne c. 14, s. 2, against a carrier for having pheasants and hares in his possession ; he not being a person in any manner qualified or authorised by the laws of this realm to kill game.   Against the validity of the conviction, it was argued (inter alia) that no evidence had been given by the prosecution to prove that the defendant possessed none of the ten forms of qualification recognised by the game-laws then in force.]

*   *   *   *   *

HOLROYD, J.   It is a general rule, that the affirmative is to be proved, and not the negative, of any fact which is stated; unless under peculiar circumstances, where the general rule does not apply.   Therefore it must be shewn that this is a case which ought to form an exception to the general rule.   Now all the qualifications mentioned in the statute are peculiarly within the knowledge of the party qualified. If he be entitled to any such estate, as the statute requires, he may prove it by his title deeds, or by receipt of the rents and profits: or if he is son and heir apparent, or servant, to any lord or lady of a manor appointed to kill game, it will be a defence.   All these qualifications are peculiarly within the knowledge of the party himself, whereas the prosecutor has, probably, no means whatever of proving a disqualification.   It seems to be the very case to which the rule ought to apply.

Conviction affirmed.

SECTION III.

EVIDENCE.

CHAPTER I.   IMPORTANCE OF OBSERVING THE RULES OF EVIDENCE.

[*In* criminal *proceedings rigid adherence to the rules of evidence is necessary ; as Consent* cannot[1] *waive them.*]

[*A conviction will be set aside if evidence wrongly admitted* may *have influenced the jury.*]

REX *v.* FISHER.

COURT OF CRIMINAL APPEAL.   L.R. [1910] 1 K.B. 149.

[Appeal against a conviction for obtaining a pony and cart by false pretences on June 4, 1909.   The prosecution had been allowed to give

---

[1] In *civil* actions, if all parties are sui juris, " the technical rules of Evidence can of course be dispensed with "; (see Lindley, L.J., L.R. [1895] 2 Ch. at p. 492) On the other hand, "jus *publicum* privatorum pactis mutari non potest";

evidence not only of this particular offence, but also of the defendant's having, by various dissimilar false pretences, obtained provender on May 14, 1909 and July 3, 1909, and a horse on June 1, 1909. The jury convicted: but disbelieved this last charge, the one about the horse.

Marshall, for appellant. The evidence as to the three other cases was inadmissible. There was no special connexion between them and the case charged on the indictment; nor were the goods the same; nor the pretences the same. The cases would only prove that the defendant had a generally fraudulent disposition; and such proof is inadmissible.

Lawrie, for prosecution. They do shew a systematic course of conduct in obtaining horses and provender by false pretences.]

CHANNELL, J....The evidence was amply sufficient to enable the prosecution to ask the jury to convict the appellant. But the prosecution proceeded to call witnesses to speak to other cases in which the appellant was alleged to have obtained goods by false pretences. In one the circumstances were very similar to those of the present case; but the jury were not satisfied that the appellant was the man concerned in that case; otherwise I should have been inclined to think that the evidence as to that case was admissible..

The principle is, that the prosecution are not allowed to prove that a prisoner has committed the offence with which he is charged by giving evidence that he is in the habit of committing crimes....

The evidence as to the other cases was inadmissible because it only amounted to a suggestion that he was of a generally fraudulent disposition. If all the cases had been frauds of a similar character, shewing a systematic course of swindling by the same method, then it would have been admissible.

In the circumstances of this case we cannot come to any other conclusion but that the jury *may* have been influenced by the evidence of the other cases; and therefore, (although there was sufficient evidence

---

(Papinian, in *Digest,* II. 14. 38). And the public interests are so deeply concerned in every instance of the administration of criminal justice that this maxim applies with full force to each fundamental rule in criminal procedure; and not least to those relating to Evidence. "We cannot, in a criminal case, take anything as admitted"; as Erle, C.J. said, (see p. 191 *supra*). Hence in every criminal trial "it is the duty of the judge to see that the accused is condemned *according to law*; and the rules of Evidence form part of that law....(Still, much latitude is given—*de facto* though not *de jure*—to prisoners who are not defended by counsel)"; (Best on Evidence, § 97).

to convict the prisoner without the evidence as to the other cases), in accordance with the rule laid down in this Court, the conviction cannot stand.

[EDITOR'S NOTE. Until lately a still more stringent rule prevailed in criminal courts; (though, since the Judicature Acts, not in civil ones). If any item of evidence, however unimportant, was illegally admitted or illegally excluded, a conviction would be vitiated; for the courts declined the task of deciding whether or not the evidence rightfully admitted must have been sufficient to convince the jury of the prisoner's guilt. See *Reg.* v. *Gibson* (L.R. 18 Q.B.D. 537). But under the Criminal Appeal Act, 1907, s. 4 (1), "the Court may, notwithstanding that they are of opinion that the point...might be decided in favour of the appellant, dismiss an appeal if they consider that no substantial miscarriage of justice has actually occurred." Hence a conviction will now be upheld, in spite of a wrong ruling as to evidence, if the Court sees that the jury (not merely *might* but) unmistakeably "*would* have come to the same verdict even if the case had been tried in the proper manner"; *Rex* v. *Atherton*, 5 Cr. App. R. at p. 237.]

CHAPTER II. THE RELEVANCY OF EVIDENCE.

[*Evidence must be confined to the points in issue.*]

BOLDRON *v.* WIDDOWS.

WESTMINSTER N. P. SITTINGS. 1824. 1 CARRINGTON AND PAYNE 65.

This was an action for defamation of the plaintiff in his business of a schoolmaster. The words were, in substance, that the scholars were ill fed, and badly lodged, had had the itch, and were full of vermin. Plea—that the whole of the words were true.

For the plaintiff, several witnesses proved the speaking of the words, and that the boys were boarded, educated, and clothed, by the plaintiff, at £20 a year each, near Richmond in Yorkshire : and the usher of the school was called to prove that the boys were well fed and

well lodged, and had no itch. In his cross-examination it appeared
that there were between eighty and ninety boys; that about seventy
of them had had a cutaneous disease; and that they all slept in three
rooms close to the roof, with no ceiling; and that there was a general
combing of the heads of the whole school every morning over a pewter
dish, and that the vermin combed out were thrown into the yard; no
boy was free from them. A piece of bread of a perfectly black hue
was shewn him: he did not think the bread in the school so black as
that.

The witness having stated that he had himself been at the Appleby
grammar-school, the plaintiff's counsel wished to ask him what was the
quality of the provisions used by the plaintiff's school, compared with
those consumed by the Appleby grammar-school.

The defendant's counsel objected to this.

Abbott, C.J. That cannot be asked; what is done at any particular
school is not evidence. You may shew the general treatment of boys
at schools, and shew that the plaintiff treated the boys here as well as
they could be treated for £20 a year each, for board, education, and
clothes.

One of the plaintiff's scholars was then called to prove the plaintiff's
good treatment of them.

In cross-examination, the defendant's counsel wished to ask him
whether the plaintiff did not set the boys to plant potatoes in school
hours?

Abbott, C.J. I do not think you can ask this; the issue here
being whether the plaintiff's scholars were ill fed, badly lodged, had the
itch, and had vermin. Nothing has been said as to their being badly
educated. Their education is not in question here.

Gurney, for the defendant, addressed the jury, and called witnesses
to prove the truth of the words.

Verdict for the plaintiff, damages £120.

[See also Rex *v.* Vaughan, *supra* p. 375.]

[As to the application of this rule on trials for Conspiracy, see Rex *v.*
Roberts, Rex *v.* Cope, and Rex *v.* Hammond, *supra* pp. 409–411.]

[Hence evidence of other crimes, though similar and committed by the same prisoner, is usually irrelevant.]

REX v. BIRDSEYE.

BEDFORD ASSIZES.   1830.   4 CARRINGTON AND PAYNE 386.

Indictment for stealing pickled pork, a bowl, some knives, and a loaf of bread.

It appeared that the prisoner entered the shop of the prosecutor, and ran away with the pork.   In about two minutes he returned, replaced the pork in a bowl, which contained the knives, and took away the whole together, threatening destruction to any one who followed him.   In about half an hour after, he came back to the prosecutor's shop, and took away the loaf.

Mr Justice LITTLEDALE.   This taking away the loaf cannot be given in evidence upon this indictment.   I think that the prisoner's taking the pork, and returning in two minutes, and then running off with the bowl, must be taken to be one continuing transaction, but I think that half an hour is too long a period to admit of that construction   The taking of the loaf, therefore, is a distinct offence.

The prisoner was acquitted, the learned Judge telling the jury, that the felonious intent was not sufficiently made out.

Cf. REX v. FISHER, *supra*, p. 475.

[But becomes relevant if those crimes are so connected with the one now charged as to shew its character.]

THE KING v. ELLIS.

KING'S BENCH.   1826.   6 BARNEWALL AND CRESSWELL 145.

An indictment, charging the prisoner with feloniously stealing six shillings, the property of S. Newman, was found at a gaol delivery for the city of Exeter, and was afterwards, on the motion of the prisoner, supported by affidavits that great prejudice existed against him at Exeter, removed into this Court by certiorari ; and an order was made that the jury, to try the indictment, should be drawn from the body of the county of Devon.   The prisoner was accordingly tried before Littledale, J., sitting at Nisi Prius at the last Summer Assizes for Devon; and found guilty.   At the trial the following facts were proved. The prisoner was a shopman in the employ of the prosecutrix, and, his honesty being suspected, on a particular day the son of the prosecutrix put seven shillings, one half crown, and one sixpence, marked in a particular manner, into a till in the shop, in which there was no other silver at that time. The prisoner was watched by the prosecutrix's son, who from time to time went in and out of the shop, occasionally looking into and examining the till, while customers came into the shop and purchased goods. Upon the first examination of the till it contained 11s. 6d. After that the son of the prosecutrix received one shilling from a customer and put it into the till; afterwards another person paid one shilling to the prisoner, who was observed to go with it to the till, to put his hand in and to withdraw it clenched. He then left the counter, and was seen to raise his hand clenched to his waistcoat pocket. The till was examined by the witness, and 11s. 6d. was found in it, instead of 13s. 6d., which ought to have been there. The prosecutor was proceeding to prove other acts of the prisoner, in going to the till and taking money; when Wilde, Serjt. objected that evidence of one felony had already been given, and that the prosecutrix ought not to be allowed to prove several felonies. The learned Judge overruled the objection, and the son of the prosecutrix proved that, upon each of several inspections of the till after the prisoner had opened it, he found a smaller sum than ought to have been there. Upon one occasion there was 8s. 6d. in it, and the witness observed that most of that money was marked; he then put in 1s. 6d. more, and upon examining again found only 6s. 6d. He then caused the prisoner to be apprehended and searched, and 14s. 6d. was found upon him, six of the shillings being part of the money marked by the witness and placed in the till the same morning. The counsel for the prosecution said that he relied upon the taking of the 3s. 6d. after the witness had added 1s. 6d. to the 8s. 6d. which was then in the till; and desired that the other takings might be excluded from the consideration of the jury. The prisoner having been found guilty,

Praed, within the first four days of the term, had moved for a rule for staying the judgment ; and it was then intimated by the Lord Chief Justice that, although it was usual to confine the prosecutor to the proof of one single act of felony, yet where the character of the particular act with which the prisoner was charged was to be collected from other acts done by him, all of them constituting one entire transaction, it was discretionary in the Judge to allow the prosecutor to go into the whole ; but it would, however, be competent to the prisoner's counsel, when he was brought up for judgment, to urge any matter to the Court to induce them to stay the judgment. The prisoner upon a subsequent day being brought up for judgment, Chitty and Praed renewed the application. They urged that, as at the different times when the witness went to the till it appeared money had been taken from it, if the money taken each time was part of the marked money, each taking would be a distinct felony; and the prosecutor ought to have been confined in proof to one felony, otherwise the prisoner, if afterwards indicted for any of those felonies, could not possibly plead auterfois convict. If, on the other hand, all the marked money was taken at one time, the other takings amounted to embezzlement; and in that case evidence of an offence different from that which was the subject of the indictment had been received. The prosecutrix ought to have been compelled to make her election; and in consequence of that not having been done, the prisoner has been injured by the evidence which has been given.

BAYLEY, J. I think that it was in the discretion of the Judge to confine the prosecutor to the proof of one felony, or to allow him to give evidence of other acts which were all part of one entire transaction. Generally speaking, it is not competent to a prosecutor to prove a man guilty of one felony, by proving him guilty of another unconnected felony; but where several felonies are connected together, and form part of one entire transaction, then the one is evidence to shew the character of the other. Now all the evidence in this case tended to shew that the prisoner was guilty of the felony charged in the indictment. It went to shew the history of the till, from the time when the marked money was put into it, up to the time when it was found in the possession of the prisoner. The evidence was properly received.

* * * *

[*Or if they shew the prisoner's* mens rea.]

See REGINA v. FRANCIS, *infra,* p. 492.

REGINA v. NEILL.

CENTRAL CRIMINAL COURT. 1892. SESSIONS PAPERS CXVI. 1417.

[A surgeon named Thomas Neill[1] was indicted for (and charged on the coroner's inquisition with) the wilful murder of Matilda Clover. A witness named Lucy Rose gave evidence thus: "I found the deceased

1 See the biography of Sir Wm. Broadbent, M.D., for Neill's scheme for blackmailing, by accusing others of having murdered these women.

lying across the foot of the bed, screaming, and apparently in great agony. She said she had been poisoned by pills. She said once she thought she was going to die, and that she would like to see her baby then because she thought she was going to die."]

Sir Chas. Russell, Att. Gen., submitted that he had laid the foundation for asking what statement the deceased had made as to how she had been poisoned.

Geoghegan contended that the mere fact that a person said, when in great pain, that she thought she was going to die, did not imply such a settled sure feeling that there was no possible chance of recovery as could render a dying declaration admissible.

HAWKINS, J. Before a dying declaration can be admitted, it must be proved that at the moment the person made the statement she was in such a condition that her immediate death was probable ; she must be labouring under a mortal disorder, which mortal disorder she believes will be the immediate cause of death.

[The question was accordingly not asked.]

*   *   *   *   *

At a subsequent stage of the case, the Attorney-General said that he proposed to prove the prisoner's possession of strychnine, and to shew that strychnine was the cause of death ; and thereupon to give evidence of his having caused the deaths of three other women by strychnine, and having attempted to administer it to a fourth. He urged that these latter facts would be admissible (1) as evidence of identity, (2) as evidence of motive, (3) as negativing any suggestion of mistake or accident, and shewing that prisoner understood the nature and quality of his act.

Warburton. The proposed evidence is not relevant to the issue. Moreover it is the subject of other indictments against the prisoner. In all the cases cited by the Attorney-General, the prisoners had lived under the same roof with the deceased persons, and had admittedly prepared the food by which they were poisoned. Strychnine is a common drug, to which all doctors and chemists have access, so that the possession of it by the prisoner was not an exceptional circumstance. The kind of evidence proposed might be admissible to negative an obvious defence of accident, but in the present case no such defence is possible. It is equivalent to trying the prisoner on several indictments at the same time ; and it can only have the effect of prejudicing the case against him.

HAWKINS, J. I am of opinion that I must admit the evidence. What the weight of it may be, is another question. As to its admissibility I entertain no doubt, and therefore I shall not consent to reserve a case.

JOHN MAKIN AND SARAH MAKIN *v.* THE ATTORNEY
GENERAL FOR NEW SOUTH WALES.

JUDICIAL COMMITTEE OF THE PRIVY COUNCIL.   1893.   L.R. [1894]
A.C. 57.

[Appeal from a judgment of the Supreme Court of New South
Wales, sustaining a verdict of guilty on an indictment for the murder
of an infant named Horace Amber Murray.]

The special case contained the following statement: "On the 9th of
November some constables found the remains of four infants in the
back yard of 109, George Street, among which was the body of a male
child, from two to nine weeks old. It was clothed with a long white
baby's gown and underneath a baby's small white shirt, both of which
were identified as being the gown and shirt in which Murray's baby
had been dressed. A minute portion of the infant's hair resembled
the hair of Murray's child. Previous to the finding of the four infants
in George Street, Redfern (on the 9th of November), two bodies of
infants had been discovered, one on the 11th and the other on the 12th
of October, on the premises in Burren Street, McDonaldtown, where
the prisoners had, it appears, resided from the end of June until about
the middle of August. During the adjournment of an inquest on one
of those bodies, held in October, the prisoner Sarah came to her former
residence in George Street, Redfern, and said to a witness, residing
there, that she had called to see about those people that had lived
there before her, that she was a great friend of theirs, and asked if the
police had dug the yard up, and further asked if any bodies had been
found in the yard. At this inquest both prisoners were examined, no
charge at that time having been made against them. They both swore
that the only child that they had ever received to nurse was the one
which they had in Burren Street, and which was given them after they
arrived there. The prisoner Sarah swore that none but her own family
had removed from George Street to Burren Street. On the 2nd of
November one body, and on the 3rd four more, were discovered
buried in Burren Street; and on the 3rd of November the prisoners
were arrested. On the night of that day prisoner John was placed in
a cell with a witness, who deposed that prisoner said to him that he
(Makin) was there for baby-farming, that there were seven found
and there was another to be found, and when that was found he would
never see daylight any more; that is what a man gets for obliging
people; that he could do nothing outside as they were watching the
ground too close; that there was no doctor could prove that he ever
31—2

gave them anything; that he did not care for himself, but that his children were innocent. On the 12th of November the bodies of two infants, bones only, were found on the premises of Levy Street, Chippendale, where prisoners had resided some time previous to their residence in Kettle Street. The prisoners had moved from Kettle Street to George Street, and thence to Burren Street.

*   *   *   *   *

Fullarton, Q.C., and *Cunynghame,* for the appellants, contended that evidence as to finding of bodies other than the body the subject of the issue to be tried, and the evidence of five women to the effect that they had intrusted other children to the prisoners, which children had never been seen again, was inadmissible and vitiated the verdict. The general rule and practice of the Courts in criminal cases confined the evidence strictly to direct evidence of the commission of the particular act charged, and excluded evidence of similar acts committed, or supposed to have been committed, by the same prisoner on other occasions, not as being wholly irrelevant, but as inconvenient and dangerous. To admit this latter class of evidence was apt to take the prisoner by surprise, and raised issues as to other alleged acts, which were confused with the true issue and which tended both to confuse and unduly to prejudice the jury. The rule in cases of forgery and of receiving stolen goods was an exception to the general rule for special reasons, and should not be extended. Even in forgery cases such evidence is only admitted after proof of the actual uttering of forged notes or base coin by the prisoner, and where the only issue left is as to the guilty intent, there being in these cases no presumption of guilty knowledge or intent; but in murder this presumption is made by law upon mere proof of the killing. In this case, moreover, there is no proof of the killing; the evidence objected to is introduced to induce the jury to believe the prisoners killed the child the subject of indictment, and not merely to prove a felonious killing....Then there is no identification of any of the bodies except the one which is the subject of indictment. Even if the cases in George Street and Burren Street were admissible, the Levy Street evidence was wrongly admitted. There was no proof that any children had ever been in the keeping of the prisoners before or in Levy Street, and nothing to connect them with the remains found there...

Sir E. Clarke, Q.C., *Poland,* Q.C., *Cluer,* and *R. H. Long Innes,* for the respondent, contended that the evidence in question was not wrongly received. With regard to the evidence as to the finding in Levy Street, that stood on a different footing from the evidence as to George Street and Burren Street. The strongest evidence, as regards admissibility, was that relating to George Street. The evidence of finding bodies other than the subject of indictment was of necessity admitted in that instance because they were all found at the same time and place. Then, in order to rebut the defence set up of bonâ fide intention to adopt and maintain and of accidental death, the evidence of the mothers of babies having delivered their children to the prisoners at similar places and under similar circumstances, including insufficiency of premium, was admissible. That brought in the evidence with regard to the finding of bodies at Burren Street, because the child of one of these mothers was traced to and seen at the house in Burren Street, but not seen elsewhere nor accounted for. All the children of the mothers called disappeared and were not heard of again since the prisoners left Burren Street; and the presumption arose that the bodies found were identical with those of the missing children unless the prisoners shewed to the contrary. The Levy Street evidence was admissible because the evidence with regard to the finding of the bodies at George Street and Burren Street, joined with the evidence of the mothers called, led to the inference that the prisoners had pursued a similar course of conduct for some time previously. Evidence was therefore admissible to support this inference by the recurrence of the unusual phenomena of bodies of babies having been buried in an unexplained manner in a similar part of premises previously occupied by the prisoners. It was not merely in exceptional cases that evidence of the kind objected to was receivable. It was the general, and not the exceptional, rule of law to admit such evidence to rebut defence of accident, and to shew existence of motive and a systematic course of conduct....

The LORD CHANCELLOR delivered the judgment of their Lordships[1]:

...In their Lordships' opinion, there can be no doubt that there was ample evidence to go to the jury that the infant was murdered. The question which their Lordships had to determine was the admissibility of the evidence relating to the finding of other bodies, and to the fact that other children had been entrusted to the appellants.

In their Lordships' opinion the principles which must govern the decision of the case are clear, though the application of them is by no means free from difficulty. It is undoubtedly not competent for the prosecution to adduce evidence tending to shew that the accused has been guilty of criminal acts, other than those covered by the indictment, for the purpose of leading to the conclusion that the accused is a person likely from his criminal conduct or character to have com-

[1] The Lord Chancellor (Lord Herschell), Lord Watson, Lord Halsbury, Lord Ashbourne, Lord Macnaghten, Lord Morris, Lord Shand.

mitted the offence for which he is being tried. On the other hand, the mere fact that the evidence adduced tends to shew the commission of other crimes does not render it inadmissible if it be relevant to an issue before the jury; and it may be so relevant if it bears upon the question whether the acts alleged to constitute the crime charged in the indictment were designed or accidental, or to rebut a defence which would otherwise be open to the accused. The statement of these general principles is easy, but it is obvious that it may often be very difficult to draw the line and to decide whether a particular piece of evidence is on the one side or the other.

The principles which their Lordships have indicated appear to be on the whole consistent with the current of authority bearing on the point, though it cannot be denied that the decisions have not always been completely in accord.

The leading authority relied on by the Crown was the case of *Reg.* v. *Geering*[1], where, on the trial of a prisoner for the murder of her husband by administering arsenic, evidence was tendered with the view of shewing that two sons of the prisoner who had formed part of the same family, and for whom as well as for her husband the prisoner had cooked their food, had died of poison, the symptoms in all these cases being the same. The evidence was admitted by Pollock, C.B., who tried the case; he held that it was admissible inasmuch as its tendency was to prove that the death of the husband was occasioned by arsenic, and was relevant to the question whether such taking was accidental or not. The Chief Baron refused to reserve the point for the consideration of the judges; intimating that Alderson, B., and Talfourd, J., concurred with him in his opinion.

This authority has been followed in several subsequent cases. And in the case of *Reg.* v. *Dossett*[2], which was tried a few years previously, the same view was acted upon by Maule, J., on a trial for arson, where it appeared that a rick of wheat-straw was set on fire by the prisoner having fired a gun near to it. Evidence was admitted to shew that the rick had been on fire the previous day, and that the prisoner was then close to it with a gun in his hand. Maule, J., said: "Although the evidence offered may be proof of another felony, that circumstance does not render it inadmissible, if the evidence be otherwise receivable. In many cases it is an important question whether a thing was done accidentally or wilfully."

The only subsequent case to which their Lordships think it necessary to refer to specifically is that of *Reg.* v. *Gray*[3], where on a trial for arson with intent to defraud an insurance company, Willes, J.,

---

[1] 18 L. J. R. (N.S.) (M.C.) 215.   [2] 3 C. and K. 306.   [3] 4 F. and F. 1102.

admitted evidence that the prisoner had made claims on two other insurance companies, in respect of fires which had occurred in two other houses which he had occupied previously and in succession, for the purpose of shewing that the fire which formed the subject of the trial was the result of design and not of accident....

Their Lordships do not think it necessary to enter upon a detailed examination of the evidence in the present case. The prisoners had alleged that they had received only one child to nurse; that they had received 10s. a week while it was under their care, and that after a few weeks it was given back to the parents. When the infant with whose murder the appellants were charged was received from the mother she stated that she had a child for them to adopt. Mrs Makin said that she would take the child, and Makin said that they would bring it up as their own and educate it, and that he would take it because Mrs Makin had lost a child of her own two years old. Makin said that he did not want any clothing; they had plenty of their own. The mother said that she did not mind his getting £3 premium so long as he took care of the child. The representation was that the prisoners were willing to take the child on payment of the small sum of £3, inasmuch as they desired to adopt it as their own.

Under these circumstances their Lordships cannot see that it was irrelevant to the issue to be tried by the jury that several other infants had been received from their mothers on like representations and upon payment of a sum inadequate for the support of the child for more than a very limited period, or that the bodies of infants had been found buried in a similar manner in the gardens of several houses occupied by the prisoners.

*   *   *   *   *

Appeal dismissed.

[EDITOR'S NOTE. Important though Makin's case is, its *ratio decidendi* is not very clearly expressed. Hence it has often been regarded—e.g., by the present Lord Coleridge (5 Cr. App. R. at p. 240)—as having declared the evidence about the other deceased children to be admissible merely for the familiar purpose of establishing *mens rea*, by tending to shew that the prisoners, when they accepted possession of the child Murray, must have had the intention of making away with him. But there is now a great weight of authority for regarding it as having pronounced the evidence admissible even for the purpose of establishing the *actus reus* itself. Thus in *Rex* v. *Ball* (*infra*, p. 489) Scrutton, J., told the jury (L.R. [1911] A.C. at p. 52) that this evidence "must have been" admitted to prove the act of killing: for until the killing itself was proved,—and this evidence was the only proof of it—no question of *mens rea* could arise. Similar views were expressed in the same case, during the course of the appeal, by Pickford, J. (5 Cr. App. R. 240) and by Lord Atkinson (6 Cr. App. R. 37). And Lord Loreburn, L.C., in delivering judgment in *Rex* v. *Ball*, would seem to indicate, by the use he made of Makin's case, that he, too, regarded the disputed evidence in it to have been used for just the same purpose as the disputed evidence in the case he was deciding—viz. for affording proof of the *actus reus*.

A curious counterpart to Makin's case is afforded by another Australian prose-cution, very similar in its facts yet sufficiently different to have justified the Court in giving an opposite ruling. In *Reg.* v. *Smith* (1 West Australian Reports 43, A.D. 1898), at the trial of a midwife on a charge of murder by an unlawful operation for abortion, evidence was tendered that there had been found buried in her garden the bodies of three *very immature* infants. It was held that, as there was nothing to shew that the premature birth of these was due to any unlawful act, and as her lawful calling was one in the course of which she might naturally become possessed of such fœtuses and bury them secretly, the evidence was *not* admissible against her.]

[*Or even shew the prisoner's* Motive, *e.g. Malice.*]

REX *v.* VOKE.

CROWN CASE RESERVED. 1823.   RUSSELL AND RYAN 531.

[Indictment for maliciously shooting at Thomas Pearce. At the trial the prosecutor gave evidence that he was a gamekeeper; and, having caught the prisoner poaching, suggested to him to go to the steward's office and ask for forgiveness. They accordingly walked along together; but when Pearce had got a little in front of Voke, Voke fired at his back, and then ran away. Pearce went to where his horse was, and rode off. Half a mile further on, he came upon the prisoner lurking in a hedge; and the latter, when four yards off him, fired a shot which put out one of Pearce's eyes. This was about a quarter of an hour after the previous shot.]

[Counsel for the prisoner objected] that the prosecutor ought not to give evidence of two distinct felonies. But BURROUGH, J., thought it unavoidable in this case; as it seemed to him to be one continued transaction in the prosecution of the general malicious intent of the prisoner. Upon another ground, also, the learned Judge thought such evidence proper. The counsel for the prisoner, by his cross examination of Pearce, had endeavoured to shew that the gun might have gone off the first time by accident: and, although the learned Judge was satisfied that this was not the case, he thought the second firing was evidence to shew that the first (which had preceded it only one quarter of an hour) was wilful, and to remove the doubt (if any existed) in the minds of the jury.

[The Judges, on a case reserved, were of opinion that the evidence was properly received.]

[*The prisoner's Motive, e.g. a guilty* sexual attachment.]

REX *v.* BALL.

HOUSE OF LORDS.   L.R. [1911] A.C. 47.

[Wm. Hy. Ball and Edith L. Ball, a brother and sister, were convicted of two acts of incest committed in July and September of 1910. Evidence had been admitted at the trial not only as to these two acts, but also as to previous similar ones.

The Court of Criminal Appeal held this latter evidence to be inadmissible. In consequence of the "exceptional public importance" of the question, the Attorney-General permitted an appeal to the House of Lords, under s. 1 (6) of the Criminal Appeal Act, 1907.

Gregory, K.C., for the prisoners. The physical Act, and not the Intent, is in question; and the act must be established by evidence of what occurred at the time at which it is alleged to have occurred.

LORD ATKINSON. In a prosecution for murder...you can give in evidence the enmity of the accused towards the deceased, to prove that he took the deceased's life. Evidence of Motive necessarily goes to prove the fact of homicide as well as the malice aforethought.

Sir Rufus Isaacs, for Crown. We admit that evidence of W. H. Ball's intercourse with *another* of his sisters would not be admissible. But proof that he had a guilty desire for *this* particular person is relevant. Antecedent letters of an illicit amatory character would have been evidence.]

LORD LOREBURN, L.C....In accordance with the law laid down in Makin's case (*supra*, p. 483),—which is daily applied in the Divorce Court[1]—I consider that this evidence was clearly admissible on the issue that this crime was committed; not to prove a *mens rea*, as Mr Justice Darling considered, but to establish the guilty relations

------

[1] [EDITOR'S NOTE.] See *Wales* v. *Wales and Cullen*, L.R. [1900] Prob. 63.

between the parties, and the existence of a sexual passion between them, as elements in proving that they had illicit connexion *in fact* on or between the dates charged. Their passion for each other was evidence, as much as was their presence together in the bed, of the fact that when there they had guilty relations with each other. I agree that the courts of law ought to be very careful to preserve the time-honoured law of England that you cannot convict a man of one crime by proving that he has committed some other crime. That, and all other safeguards of our criminal law, will be jealously guarded; but here I think the evidence went directly to prove the actual crime for which these parties were indicted.

[All the eight other Lords who sat, expressed their concurrence.]

Conviction restored.

[EDITOR'S NOTE. The principle of this decision has since been carried further by the Court of Criminal Appeal; which, in a subsequent case of Incest, intimated the admissibility of evidence of sexual acts committed even *after* the act for which the parties stood indicted; *Rex* v. *Stone*, 6 Cr. App. R. 91, 94, 97.]

CHAPTER III.   LEADING QUESTIONS.

[*Leading questions are inadmissible.*]

LINCOLN *v.* WRIGHT.

ROLLS COURT.   1841.   4 BEAVAN 167.

[The plaintiffs had obtained an order for a commission to examine witnesses, and had exhibited written interrogatories for their examination. The fourth interrogatory was:—"Was it at any, and what, time after the decease of the testator, agreed by any, and what, persons...that any, and which, of them should be the chief acting executor and trustee under the will of the said testator"...? It was objected that this interrogatory was a leading one.]

LORD LANGDALE, M.R. All interrogatories must to some extent make a suggestion to the witness; it would be perfectly nugatory to ask a witness if he knew 'anything about something.'...One objection to the depositions was that they were taken under interrogatories, which were "leading." They are said to be leading, on the ground that they ask the witnesses whether it was agreed to the effect suggested in the interrogatories. In the argument, it was contended that the interrogatories ought to have asked, not simply whether it was so agreed, but whether it was or was not so agreed. Now it has been held that the interrogatories ought not to be in the form, "was it not so agreed?" that is considered to be leading. But the form "was it so agreed?" does not appear to me to be suggestive of the answer. It is impossible to examine a witness without referring to, or suggesting, the subject upon which he is to answer. If the question suggests a particular answer, it is leading and improper. Questions have also been held to be improper if, suggesting the subject, they are capable of being answered by a simple affirmative or negative without any circumstances. But a question 'whether such an event happened?' does not suggest the answer that it did happen. Having read the interrogatories in this case, I think that they are not capable of being answered in the affirmative or negative without circumstances.

[*Leading questions.*]

PARKIN *v.* MOON.

Westminster N.P. Sittings. 1836. 7 Carrington and Payne 409.

Action on a bill of exchange, by indorsee against drawers....

Platt, for the plaintiff, in the course of the cause, was cross-examining one of the defendant's witnesses (who it seemed was an unwilling witness for the defendant, but a willing one on the part of the plaintiff), by putting leading questions in the usual way, when

E. V. Williams, for the defendant, objected to this course; and submitted, that, under the circumstances, leading questions ought not to be allowed to be put even on cross-examination.

Alderson, B. I apprehend you may put a leading question to an unwilling witness on the examination in chief at the discretion of the judge; but you may always put a leading question in cross-examination, whether a witness be unwilling or not.

CHAPTER IV. WRITINGS.

[The contents of a writing should be proved by producing it in Court.]

McDONNELL *v.* EVANS.

LONDON N.P. SITTINGS.   1851.   3 CARRINGTON AND KIRWAN 51.

Assumpsit on a bill of exchange. The defence relied on was the forgery of the acceptance by one Peter Scott. Scott was called by plaintiff to prove that the acceptance was in the writing of the defendant. On cross-examination,

Bramwell, for defendant, put into Scott's hand a letter, and asked, "Did you not write this letter in answer to a letter charging you with forgery ?"

Byles, for plaintiff, objected to the question. The earlier letter referred to should be produced.

Bramwell. The question may be put without producing the letter; for the only object in asking it is to test the credibility of the witness and not to establish any fact in the case..

JERVIS, C.J. The question is inadmissible unless the letter referred to be produced, or its absence duly accounted for. The rule of law is that the best evidence must be produced; but the answer to the question would be giving secondary evidence of the contents of the letter. As to allowing the question to be put with the view merely of testing the veracity of the witness, *The Queen's case* (2 Br. and B. 286) decides that such a course cannot be pursued.

[See, for an *exception* to this rule, REX *v.* FURSEY, *supra,* p. 384.]

[Though the existence or condition of all other chattels may be proved by oral evidence.]

THE QUEEN *v.* FRANCIS.

CROWN CASE RESERVED.   1874.   L.R. 2 C.C.R. 128.

[On an indictment for attempting to obtain an advance of money upon a hoop ring, from a pawnbroker, by the false pretence that it was a diamond ring, evidence was admitted (for the purpose of shewing guilty knowledge of the spuriousness of the ring), from two other pawn-brokers, of the prisoner's having previously attempted to obtain similar advances from them upon a cluster ring, which he said was a diamond ring. This cluster ring was not produced in Court, and the only evidence that its stones were not genuine diamonds was the opinion of these two witnesses. The question for the Court was whether the evidence of these witnesses was properly admissible.]

Hensman for the prisoner. Evidence of previous specific criminal acts is not admissible on the trial of a criminal charge, according to the general rules of evidence....And, even if such evidence were admissible, it ought not to have been received without the production of the alleged fraudulent articles.

*   *   *   *   *

Lord Coleridge, C.J., delivered the judgment of the Court....It seems clear upon principle that when the fact of the prisoner having done the thing charged is proved, and the only remaining question is, whether at the time he did it he had guilty knowledge of the quality of his act or acted under a mistake, evidence of the class received must be admissible. It tends to shew that he was pursuing a course of similar acts, and thereby it raises a presumption that he was not acting under a mistake.

It was objected that the evidence of what took place at Leicester was not properly received, because the cluster ring which he there attempted to pass was not produced in Court; and that the evidence of two witnesses who saw it, and swore to its being false, was not admissible. No doubt if there was not admissible evidence that this ring was false it ought not to have been left to the jury; but though the non-production of the article may afford ground for observation more or less weighty, according to circumstances, it only goes to the weight, not to the admissibility, of the evidence; and no question as to the weight of this evidence is now before us. Where the question is as to the effect of a written instrument, the instrument itself is primary evidence of its contents; and until it is produced, or the non-production is excused, no secondary evidence can be received. But there is no case whatever deciding that, when the issue is as to the state of a chattel, (*e.g.* the soundness of a horse, or the equality of the bulk of the goods to the sample), the production of the chattel is primary evidence; and that no other evidence can be given till the chattel is produced in Court for the inspection of the jury. The law of evidence is the same in criminal and civil suits. The conviction, therefore, should be affirmed.

Conviction affirmed.

[*And so may the mere* existence or condition *of even a Writing.*]

JOLLEY *v.* TAYLOR.

COMMON PLEAS.　1807.　　　　　　　　　1 CAMPBELL 143.

Assumpsit against the proprietor of a stage coach, on a promise to carry three promissory notes of £5 each from Ware to London ; with the common money counts.

To prove the delivery of the notes, a witness was called who was stated to have remitted them to the plaintiff, in discharge of a debt. Being released[1], he was proceeding to describe the notes, when—

Best, Serjt., for the defendant, objected that the plaintiff must previously prove a notice to produce them. Promissory notes, like all written instruments, should speak for themselves, and are not to be described according to the loose recollection of witnesses....

SIR JAMES MANSFIELD, C.J.　A notice here appears to me to be unnecessary. I can make no distinction as to this purpose between written instruments and other articles ; between trover for a promissory note, and trover for a waggon and horses.

The witness then proved the delivery of three £5 notes of the Hertford bank to the defendant. For the amount of which, the plaintiff recovered a verdict.

CHAPTER V.　HEARSAY.

["Hearsay is no evidence." *I.e., a witness who has received from some one a narrative, whether oral or written, describing some of the Facts in Issue, is not allowed to give that narrative in evidence.*]

SAMSON *v.* YARDLEY AND TOTTILL.

KING'S BENCH.　1667.　　　　　　　　　2 KEBLE 223.

In an appeal .of murder.... *Wild*, Serjt., for the defendant, offered evidence of what a witness, [who had been] sworn on the trial on the

---

[1] [EDITOR'S NOTE. *I.e.*, released by the plaintiff from all liability for this debt. The object of this release would be to avoid the operation of the common law rule which rendered persons incompetent to give evidence in a litigation which concerned any matter in which they had an interest. Incompetency on the ground of interest was removed by Lord Denman's Act of 1843 (6 and 7 Vict. c. 85), and Lord Brougham's Act of 1851 (14 and 15 Vict. c. 99).]

indictment, said then, being now dead; also of what the now appellant confessed then....

ALL THE JUDGES admitted proof of what the appellant had said at any time before, generally....But what the dead witness had said, generally, they would not admit; it being but hearsay of a stranger (and not of a party interested), which might be true or false[1]

--- --- ---

THE KING *v.* THE INHABITANTS OF ERISWELL.

KING'S BENCH. 1790.   3 TERM REPORTS 707.

[Appeal against an order of Justices removing a pauper, John Sharpe, from the parish of Icklingham to that of Eriswell. Down to the time of the order being made he had been resident, since the year 1767, in the parish of Icklingham; but, on his becoming insane, an order was made at Petty Sessions for his removal to Eriswell. On an appeal to the Quarter Sessions the order was supported by tendering in evidence a statement which in the year 1779 had been made, upon oath and duly signed, by him before two Justices of the Peace when examined by them as to the place of his last legal settlement; in which he stated "that about 24 years ago he served for a year in Eriswell and received his year's wages; since which time he has done no act whereby to gain a settlement elsewhere." This evidence was objected to on the part of the appellants. But it was received by the Court of Quarter Sessions; who confirmed the order, but stated that in their opinion there would not be sufficient evidence to warrant a confirmation apart from this examination which had been objected to.]

*   *   *   *

[1] [EDITOR'S NOTE. "By the general rule of law, nothing that is said by any person can be used as evidence between contending parties, unless it be delivered on oath in the presence of these parties. Some inconvenience no doubt arises from such rigour. If material witnesses happen to die before the trial, the person whose case they would have established, may fail in the suit. But although all the Bishops on the Bench should be ready to swear to what they had heard these witnesses declare (and should add their own belief in the truth of the declarations), the evidence could not be received. The laws of other countries are quite different; they admit evidence of hearsay without scruple; there is not an appeal from Scotland in which you will not find a great deal of hearsay evidence." Per Mansfield, C.J., in the *Berkeley Peerage Case*, A.D. 1811; (4 Camp. 413).]

GROSE, J. It is a general rule that hearsay evidence is not admissible; except in some few particular cases where the exception (for aught we know) is as ancient as the rule. A pedigree may be proved by reputation; prescriptive rights may be so proved; and yet in cases of prescription those very persons who are permitted to give evidence of what they may have heard from dead persons respecting the reputation of the right, are not permitted to state instances of the exercise of the right, which the deceased persons said they had seen....No one ever conceived that an agreement could be proved .by a witness swearing that he had heard another say that such an agreement was made. Is the evidence better upon the ground that it was upon oath administered by two justices? Evidence, though upon oath, to affect an absent person, is incompetent, because he cannot cross-examine; as nothing can be more unjust than that a person should be bound by evidence which he is not permitted to hear. Before the statute of Philip and Mary (1 and 2 P. and M. c. 13; and 2 and 3 P. and M. c. 10), a deposition taken before the justice of the county where the murder was committed was not evidence, even though the party died or was unable to travel. Why? Because although the justice had jurisdiction to enquire into the fact, the common law did not permit a person accused to be affected by an examination taken in his absence, because he could not cross-examine; and therefore that statute was made.

*   *   *   *   *

LORD KENYON....Evidence should be given under the sanction of an oath legally administered; and in a judicial proceeding depending either between the parties affected by the evidence or those who stand in privity of interest with them....Examinations upon oath (except in the excepted cases) are of no avail unless they are made in a proceeding depending between the parties to be affected by them, and where each of those parties has an opportunity of cross-examining the witness... which was not the case with the parish now to be affected, as to whom it was altogether res inter alios acta....It has been said that there are cases where examinations are admitted, viz. before the coroner, and before magistrates in cases of felony. That observation appears to me to go rather in support of the general rule than in destruction of it. Every exception that can be accounted for is so much a confirmation of the rule that it has become a maxim, "exceptio probat regulam." Those exceptions alluded to are founded on the statutes of Philip and Mary, and that they go no further is abundantly proved.

...I am most clearly of opinion that this examination was not admissible in evidence. It was ex parte, obtained at the instance of those overseers whose parish was to be benefited by it, and behind the backs of the parish against whom it has now been used, without their having an opportunity of knowing what was going on or attending to have the benefit of a cross-examination.

[The other two Judges dissented; but the opinion of Lord Kenyon and Grose, J., was afterwards approved in the case of *Rex* v. *Ferry Frystone,* 2 East 54.]

[*But a witness may give evidence of any utterance he has heard which does not merely* describe, *but itself actually* is, *or* qualifies, *a Relevant Fact.*]

[*E.g., Utterances explanatory of the* "res gestae" *in which the speaker was concerned at the time of utterance.*]

THOMPSON AND WIFE *v.* TREVANION.

MIDDLESEX N.P. SITTINGS. 1692. SKINNER 402.

In an action of trespass for assault, battery and wounding of the wife of the plaintiff...HOLT, C.J., allowed that what the wife said immediately upon the hurt received, and before that she had time to devise or contrive anything for her own advantage, might be given in evidence.

DU BOST *v.* BERESFORD.

WESTMINSTER N.P. SITTINGS. 1810. 2 CAMPBELL 511.

Trespass for cutting and destroying a picture of great value, which the plaintiff had publicly exhibited; per quod he had not only lost the picture, but the profits he would have derived from the exhibition. Plea, Not guilty.

It appeared that the plaintiff is an artist of considerable eminence, but that the picture in question, entitled "La Belle et la Bête," or "Beauty and the Beast," was a scandalous libel upon a gentleman of fashion and his lady, who was the sister of the defendant. It was exhibited in a house in Pall Mall for money, and great crowds went daily to see it, till the defendant one morning cut it in pieces. Some of the witnesses estimated it at several hundred pounds.

*   *

In the course of the trial, LORD ELLENBOROUGH, C.J., held upon argument that the declarations of the spectators, while they looked at the picture in the exhibition room, were evidence to shew that the figures pourtrayed were meant to represent the defendant's sister and brother-in-law....

Verdict for the plaintiff. Damages £5.

[*Or which* describes *the speaker's own* feelings, *bodily or mental, at the time of utterance.*]

REGINA *v.* JOHNSON.

LIVERPOOL ASSIZES.   1847.   2 CARRINGTON AND KIR. 354.

Murder. The indictment charged the prisoner with having caused the death of her husband by poison....In order to prove the state of health of the deceased prior to the day of his death, a witness was called, who had seen him a day or two before that time ; and on this witness being asked by the counsel for the prosecution in what state of health the deceased seemed to be when he last saw him, he began to state a conversation which had then taken place between the deceased and himself on this subject.

Wilkins, Serjt., objected.

ALDERSON, B. I think that what the deceased said to the witness is reasonable evidence to prove his state of health at the time[1]....

AVESON *v.* LORD KINNAIRD AND OTHERS.

KING'S BENCH.   1805.   6 EAST 188.

This was an action on a policy of insurance, dated 22nd November, 1802, whereby the defendants, for a certain consideration, insured the

[1] [EDITOR'S NOTE. "If a man says to his surgeon, 'I have a pain in the head,' or a pain in such a part of the body, that is evidence ; but if he says to his surgeon, 'I have a wound,' and was to add, 'I met John Thomas, who had a sword and ran me through the body with it,' that would be no evidence against John Thomas"; (per Pollock, C.B., in *Reg.* v. *Nicholas,* 2 Car. and Kir. 248, A.D. 1846).]

life of the plaintiff's wife, then warranted in good health, and of the description set forth in a certain certificate signed &c. and dated the 9th of November, 1802; and engaged to pay to the plaintiff £1500 within three months after her death: and the plaintiff averred that she died on the 29th of April, 1803.

The defendant pleaded, 1st, That the plaintiff's wife was not in good health, nor of the description set forth in the said certificate at the time of making the policy....

...At the trial at Lancaster Assizes the plaintiff called the surgeon from whom he had obtained the certificate of his wife's health on the 9th of November, 1802, who swore positively to his belief of her good health on that day, though before a stranger to her; and stated that he observed her very minutely on that account, and formed his opinion from an examination of her general appearance, her pulse, complexion and other circumstances, and principally from the satisfactory answers she gave to his inquiries....

The principal question, however, arose on the evidence of one Susannah Lees; who, being an intimate acquaintance of Mrs Aveson, called accidentally upon her in November, 1802, soon after her return from Manchester (where she went to obtain the certificate of her health, on which the policy was afterwards effected). She found her in bed at 11 o'clock in the forenoon. Mrs Aveson then said she was very poorly; that she had been to Manchester the Tuesday before; that her husband had been insuring her life; and that she was not well when she went. She spoke in a faint way. It was then objected by the plaintiff's counsel that what she said was not evidence; but the learned Judge admitted the evidence....The witness then proceeded to state that Mrs Aveson then told her that she was poorly when she went to Manchester and not fit to go; that it would be ten days before the policy could be returned; and that she was afraid she could not live till it was made, and then her husband could not get the money....The jury having found a verdict for the defendants, a rule nisi was obtained for granting a new trial on the ground that the evidence of Susannah Lees was improperly admitted, being no more than evidence of hearsay.

Park, for the defendants....The question being her own state of health, of which no one could have so competent a knowledge as herself, whatever was said by her on that subject, at times and under circumstances when collusion could not be suspected, formed part of the res gestae of the subject of inquiry....When an act is done to which it is necessary to ascribe a motive, it is always considered that what is said at the time, whence the motive may be collected, is part of the

32—2

fact—part of the res gestae. As where the question is whether a trader ordered himself to be denied when at home, or left his house in order to delay creditors; what he said at the time of the act done must necessarily be admitted to explain it, though not what he said at another time; *Bateman* v. *Bailey* (5 T.R. 512)....

Cockell, Serjt., for plaintiff....The evidence is open to the general objection of hearsay; much, at least, of it being no part of the res gestae, as it is said to be. Her reason for being found in bed at the time, that she was then unwell, might perhaps be admissible as a declaration accompanying an act; but what happened at Manchester, the motives of herself and her husband in going there, and how she was at that time, and her future apprehensions concerning the policy, were no part of the res gestae, nor capable of being proved by hearsay. Declarations by the wife upon her elopement from her husband, accusing him of misconduct, could not be given in evidence against him in an action against the adulterer; and yet the character of the wife and husband are as much implicated in the inquiry of damages there as the health of the wife was in this case....

LORD ELLENBOROUGH. It is not so clear that her declarations made at the time would not be evidence under any circumstances. If she declared, at the time, that she fled from immediate terror of personal violence from the husband, I should admit the evidence; though not if it were a collateral declaration of some matter which happened at another time. His lordship also referred to the case of *Thompson et Uxor* v. *Trevanion*, (*supra* p. 497).

*   *   *

GROSE, J. The question in the cause was concerning her state of health at the time of the insurance effected; and, in order to ascertain that, it became material to inquire what the state of her health was between the time of her first examination by the surgeon and the time when she was seen by the witness who conversed with her. The first question put to the witness was, in what situation she found Mrs Aveson when she called? The answer was, in bed. To that there could be no objection. The next question was, why was she in bed? Now who could possibly give so good an account of that as the party herself? It is not only *good* evidence, but the best evidence which the nature of the case afforded. It is true that she added something about the insurance of her life in the course of explaining what the state of her health really was at the time, but the whole taken together is evidence to shew what her own opinion of her health was at the time of the insurance: and on that ground I think it was evidence. But I also think the evidence was properly admitted on the other ground stated by my lord. For she had been examined by the surgeon as to her state of health on the 9th of November, and the surgeon was called as a witness by the plaintiff to prove what in his judgment was the state of her health when he examined her, which judgment was in course formed in part from her answers to his inquiries. Then her subsequent declarations were evidence to shew, that in truth she was not in the state, at the time, which she represented herself to be in to him. In strictness such declarations are admissible not so much as evidence of confession of the wife against her husband, as of the actual state of her health in her own opinion at the time. But in getting at this opinion it is impossible to help particular expressions mingling with it and coming out from the witness to explain that fact, which are not evidence of the particular facts alluded to. But they were not tendered, or received, as evidence of such particular facts.

[The other two Judges concurred.]

[*But not one which narrates* past *conduct, however recent.*]

REGINA *v.* BEDINGFIELD.

NORWICH ASSIZES. 1879.   14 Cox 341.

Henry Bedingfield was indicted for the murder of a woman at Ipswich. It appeared that he had conceived a violent resentment against the deceased woman, on account of her...wish to put an end to her relations with him. He had uttered violent threats against her, and had distinctly threatened to kill her by cutting her throat. She carried on the business of a laundress, with two women as assistants; the prisoner living a little distance from her. On the night before the day on which the act in question occurred, the deceased, from something that had been said, entertained apprehensions about him, and desired a policeman to keep his eye on her house. At ten at night, he, being near, heard the voice of a man in great anger. Early next morning the prisoner came to her house, earlier than he had ever been there before; and they were together in a room some time. He went out; and she was found by one of the assistants lying senseless on the floor, her head resting on a footstool. He went to a spirit shop and bought some spirits, which he took to the house, and went again into the room where she was, both the assistants being at that time in the yard. In a minute or two the deceased came suddenly out of the house towards the women, with her throat cut; and on meeting one of them she said something, pointing backwards to the house. In a few minutes she was dead. In the course of the opening speech on the part of the prosecution it was proposed to state what she said. It was objected on the part of the prisoner that it was not admissible.

COCKBURN, C.J. I have carefully considered the question, and am clear that it cannot be admitted; and therefore ought not to be stated, as it might have a fatal effect. I regret that, according to the law of England, any statement made by the deceased should not be admissible. Although made in the absence of the prisoner, could it be admissible as part of the res gestae? It is not so admissible; for it was neither part of anything done, nor was it something said while something was being done. It was something said after something done. It was not as if, while still in the room, and while the act was being done, she had said something which was overheard.

Counsel for the prosecution consequently did not state what the deceased said, but said they should tender it in evidence. Accordingly, when one of the assistants who heard the statement was called as a witness, she was asked as to the circumstances. She stated that "the deceased came out of the house, bleeding very much at the throat, and seeming very much frightened, and then said something, and died in ten minutes."

It was then proposed to ask what she said.

COCKBURN, C.J. It is not admissible. Anything uttered by the deceased at the time the act was being done would be admissible; as, for instance, if she had been heard to say "Don't, Harry!" But here it is something stated by her after it was all over, whatever it was, and after the act was completed.

It was submitted, on the part of the prosecution, that the statement was admissible as a dying declaration, the case being that the woman's throat was cut completely and the artery severed, so that she was dying, and was actually dead in a few minutes; but

COCKBURN, C.J., said the statement was not admissible as a dying declaration, because it did not appear that the woman was aware that she was dying.

[See also REGINA *v.* GLOSTER, *infra* p. 518.]

[*There are, moreover, some* exceptional *cases in which even mere Hearsay* (i.e. *a narrative of the past*) *can be given in evidence.*]

[Exception 1. *In sexual crimes against Females, complaints (made even subsequently to the crime) are admissible to corroborate the sufferer's story, as shewing a consistency of conduct.*

REGINA *v.* LILLYMAN.

CROWN CASE RESERVED. 1896.   L.R. [1896] 2 Q.B. 167.

Case stated by Hawkins, J. The prisoner was tried at the Nottingham Assizes upon an indictment containing three counts : the first count charged him with an attempt to have carnal knowledge of the prosecutrix, a girl above the age of thirteen and under the age of sixteen years; the second with an assault upon her with intent to ravish and carnally know her ; and the third with an indecent assault upon her.

The prosecutrix was called as a witness, and deposed to the acts complained of having been done without her consent. Counsel for the prosecution tendered evidence in chief of a complaint made by her to her mistress, in the absence of the prisoner, very shortly after the commission of the acts, and proposed to ask the details of the complaint as made by the prosecutrix. The admission of the evidence was objected to by the prisoner's counsel ; but the learned Judge overruled the objection and admitted the evidence. The mistress then deposed to all that the prosecutrix had said respecting the prisoner's conduct towards her. The jury found the prisoner guilty, and he was sentenced to one month's imprisonment with hard labour, subject to the opinion of the Court upon the question whether the evidence so admitted was rightly admitted. If the evidence was rightly admitted, the conviction was to be affirmed ; if otherwise, to be quashed.

The learned Judge stated that, the authorities being conflicting, he had reserved the case in the hope that the law might be settled upon a point of daily occurrence.

Fox, for the prisoner. The evidence was improperly admitted. Upon principle, the fact of a complaint having been made is not admissible in evidence, but it has been the universal practice to admit it ; the particulars of the complaint, however, cannot be given in evidence. What is then said by the prosecutrix is not part of the res gestae, and its admission must seriously prejudice the prisoner, who has no means of contradicting it. The authorities shew a large balance of judicial opinion against admitting the evidence.

The judgment of the Court (Lord Russell of Killowen, C.J., Pollock, B., Hawkins, Cave, and Wills, JJ.) was delivered by

HAWKINS, J....It is necessary, in the first place, to have a clear understanding as to the principles upon which evidence of such a complaint, not on oath, nor made in the presence of the prisoner, nor forming part of the res gestae, can be admitted. It clearly is not admissible as evidence of the facts complained of : those facts must therefore be established, if at all, upon oath by the prosecutrix or other credible witness ; and, strictly speaking, evidence of them ought to be given before evidence of the complaint is admitted. The complaint can only be used as evidence of the consistency of the conduct of the prosecutrix with the story told by her in the witness-box, and as being inconsistent with her consent[1] to that of which she complains.

In every one of the old text-books proof of complaint is treated as a most material element in the establishment of a charge of rape or other kindred charge

...It is too late, therefore, now to make serious objection to the admissibility of evidence of the fact that a complaint was made, provided it was made as speedily after the acts complained of as could reasonably be expected.

We proceed to consider the second objection, which is that the evidence of complaint should be limited to the fact that *a complaint* was made without giving any of the particulars of it. No authority binding upon us was cited during the argument, either in support of or against this objection. We must therefore determine this matter upon principle. That the *general usage* has been substantially to limit the evidence of the complaint to proof that the woman made a complaint of something done to her, and that she mentioned in connection with it the name of a particular person cannot be denied ; but it is equally true that judges of great experience have dissented from this limitation, and of those who have adopted the usage none have ever carefully discussed or satisfactorily expressed the grounds upon which their views have been based....

After very careful consideration we have arrived at the conclusion that we are bound by no authority to support the existing usage of limiting evidence of the complaint to the bare fact that a complaint was made; and that reason and good sense are against our doing so. The evidence is admissible only upon the ground that it was a complaint of that which is charged against the prisoner; it can be legiti-

---

[1] [EDITOR'S NOTE. But it is now settled, (see *Rex* v. *Osborne*, L. R. [1905] 1 K. B. 551), that the exception thus established by *Reg.* v. *Lillyman* is *not* to be confined to those offences in which the absence of Consent is an essential element.]

mately used only for the purpose of enabling the jury to judge for themselves whether the conduct of the woman was consistent with her testimony on oath given in the witness-box (negativing her consent and affirming that the acts complained of were against her will) and in accordance with the conduct they would expect in a truthful woman under the circumstances detailed by her. The jury, and they only, are the persons to be satisfied whether the woman's conduct was so consistent or not. Without proof of her condition, demeanour, and verbal expressions, all of which are of vital importance in the consideration of that question, how is it possible for them satisfactorily to determine it? Is it to be left to the witness to whom the statement is made to determine and report to the jury whether what the woman said amounted to a real complaint? And are the jury bound to accept the witness's interpretation of her words as binding upon them without having the whole statement before them, and without having the power to require it to be disclosed to them, even though they may feel it essential to enable them to form a reliable opinion? For it must be borne in mind that if such evidence is inadmissible when offered by the prosecution, the jury cannot alter the rule of evidence and make it admissible by asking for it themselves.

In reality, affirmative answers to such stereotyped questions as these, "Did the prosecutrix make a complaint" (a very leading question, by the way) "of something done to herself?" "Did she mention a name?" amount to nothing to which any weight ought to be attached; they tend rather to embarrass than assist a thoughtful jury, for they are consistent either with there having been a complaint or no complaint of the prisoner's conduct. To limit the evidence of the complaint to such questions and answers is to ask the jury to draw important inferences from imperfect materials, perfect materials being at hand and in the cognizance of the witness in the box. In our opinion, nothing ought unnecessarily to be left to speculation or surmise.

It has been sometimes urged that to allow the particulars of the complaint would be calculated to prejudice the interests of the accused, and that the jury would be apt to treat the complaint as evidence of the facts complained of. Of course, if it were so left to the jury they would naturally so treat it. But it never could be legally so left; and we think it is the duty of the judge to impress upon the jury in every case that they are not entitled to make use of the complaint as any evidence whatever of those facts, or for any other purpose than that we have stated. With such a direction, we think the interests of an innocent accused would be more protected than they are under the present usage. For when the whole statement is laid before the jury they are less likely to draw wrong and adverse inferences, and may sometimes come to the conclusion that what the woman said amounted to no real complaint of any offence committed by the accused. Moreover, the present usage and consequent uncertainty in practice (for the usage is not universal) provokes many objections to the evidence on the part of the prisoner's counsel, and these are generally looked upon with disfavour by the jury; and the very object of confining the evidence of the complaint to the few stereotyped questions we have referred to is often defeated by a device, not to be encouraged, by which the name of the accused, though carefully concealed as an inadmissible particular of the complaint, is studiously revealed to the jury by some such question and answer as the following: "*Q.* In consequence of that complaint did you do anything? *A.* Yes, I went to the house of the prisoner's mother, where he lives, and accused him." This seems to us to be an objectionable mode of introducing evidence indirectly, which, if tendered directly, would be inadmissible.

In the result, our judgment is that the whole statement of a woman containing her alleged complaint should, so far as it relates to the charge against the accused, be submitted to the jury as a part of the case for the prosecution, and that the evidence in this case was, therefore, properly admitted. The conviction must be affirmed.

Conviction affirmed

[Exception 2. Admissions *made by, or by authority of, the* party against *whom they are produced.*]

MALTBY *v.* CHRISTIE.

GUILDHALL N.P. SITTINGS. 1795.   1 ESPINASSE 340.

The declaration stated that, the defendant being an auctioneer, a bankrupt, Durouveray, whose assignee the plaintiff was, had, before the bankruptcy, delivered to him a certain quantity of French plate-glass to sell. The action was brought to recover the sum for which it had been sold.

*   *   *   *   *

Garrow, for plaintiff, in proving his case, found some difficulty in proving the bankruptcy of Durouveray. He then produced the defendant's catalogue of the sale of the glasses in question; in this, they were stated to be "the property of Durouveray, a bankrupt."

LORD KENYON, C.J., held that this superseded the necessity of going through the different steps; the defendant being thereby precluded from disputing the bankruptcy of Durouveray.

WILLIAMS *v.* INNES AND OTHERS, EXECUTORS.

WESTMINSTER N.P. SITTINGS. 1808.   1 CAMPBELL 364

Covenant on an indenture, whereby the defendant's testator covenanted to marry the plaintiff within a certain time, or to pay her an annuity. The defendants (inter alia) pleaded that they had fully administered. To prove assets in their hands, an account rendered by them to the plaintiff was given in evidence, in which they stated that £1000 had been awarded as due to the testator's estate from a person who had been jointly concerned with him in underwriting policies of insurance.

LORD ELLENBOROUGH held this not to be sufficient proof of assets, as it did not shew that any part of the sum awarded had been received by the executors.

A letter from the defendants to the plaintiff was then put in, stating to her, that if she wanted any farther information concerning the affairs of the deceased, she should apply to a Mr Ross, a merchant in the city. It was next proposed to adduce the plaintiff's attorney, to prove that by her desire he had called upon Mr Ross, who informed him that the whole of the £1000 had actually been received by the defendants.

Scarlett objected to the admissibility of this evidence as not being the best which the nature of the case admitted of, and contended that Ross himself should be called, who would then state upon his oath what he knew concerning this matter, and might be cross-examined as to the means of knowledge which he possessed. But—

Per LORD ELLENBOROUGH. If a man refers another upon any particular business to a third person, he is bound by what this third person says or does concerning it, as much as if that had been said or done by himself. This was agreed to be law by all the judges on the trial of Mr Hastings.

[*Even though the admission be made during* infancy.

O'NEILL *v.* REED.

IRISH COURT OF COMMON PLEAS. 1845.　　　7 IRISH L.R. 434.

Action to recover the price of a horse sold and delivered by the plaintiff to the defendant....The defendant pleaded infancy; and the plaintiff replied that the horse was a necessary, suitable to the degree, estate and condition of the defendant....At the trial, at Cork Assizes, the plaintiff produced and examined a witness who deposed that he had a conversation with the defendant. The latter, who then was still under age, told him that he wished to buy a horse from the plaintiff; and requested the witness (who was the plaintiff's attorney) not to throw obstacles in the way, as his health was delicate, and he required horse exercise. He also told witness that his allowance as a minor was £300 per annum; and that, on attaining his majority, he would have £1000 per annum. Counsel for the defendant objected to the reception in evidence of these declarations. BALL, J., admitted them. The jury found a verdict for the plaintiff for £100, the price of the horse....

O'Shaughnessy moved for a new trial, on the ground of the reception of illegal evidence. If the admissions of infants are to be received in evidence against themselves, an infant may in all cases represent his circumstances to be such that the plaintiff may safely contract with him, without further inquiry; and so the protection which the law affords the infant will be neutralized....

Henn, Q.C., for plaintiff. The testimony of an infant (if he is old enough to be capable of knowing the nature of an oath) is receivable against others, so why should it not be received as against himself? In criminal cases the confessions of infants are receivable to convict them, *Wilde's Case* (1 Moody 452); so their admissions should be equally receivable in civil cases

*　　*　　*　　*　　*

JACKSON, J....If the argument for the defendant were well founded, it would go the entire length of excluding from evidence all matters connected with the contracts of a party while under age. But it is well settled that some of these contracts are capable of confirmation by him after attaining age; which confirmation could in few cases, if any, be rendered effectual, if such evidence was held to be wholly inadmissible....The Judge was right, and the verdict must stand.

[The three other Judges concurred.]

[Admission by silent conduct is sufficient.]

NEILE *v.* JAKLE.

WESTMINSTER N.P. SITTINGS. 1849. 2 CARRINGTON AND KIRWAN 709.

Case for false imprisonment and malicious prosecution. In the course of the cause a witness stated that, on one occasion, the plaintiff was in the kitchen of the defendant's house, that no one else was there, and that the defendant's wife stood at the head of the kitchen-stairs, and said something in a tone of voice loud enough for the plaintiff to hear.

On *Wilkins*, Serjt., proposing to ask what it was the defendant's wife said—

Whitehurst, for the plaintiff, objected to the question, on the ground that the only principle on which such questions were allowed was, that if statements were made in the presence of a party, he had an opportunity of contradicting them if untrue ; in this case the plaintiff was not present.

Wilkins, Serjt., contended that as the plaintiff could hear what was said, she might have contradicted it if untrue, although she was not actually present.

MAULE, J., held that the question might be put.

REGINA *v.* SMITH.

CENTRAL CRIMINAL COURT. 1897. SESSIONS PAPERS CXXV. 266.

Arthur Greatorex Smith was indicted for feloniously using an instrument upon the person of Constance Fletcher, with intent to procure a miscarriage.

In the course of the case, evidence was given that two Inspectors, Russell and Fox, went to the residence of the deceased, who at the time was lying in bed very seriously ill. They obtained from her, in the presence of the girl's mother and sister, and of the prisoner, a statement, which was made in answer to questions put by Fox. It was taken down in writing by Russell. It was shewn that, at the time, the prisoner had immediately denied the truth of the material part of this statement....

Avory, for the crown, proposed to ask the witness what passed between the deceased and the Inspectors, in the prisoner's presence.

He submitted that it was evidence, upon the ground that any state-ment made in the presence of a prisoner was evidence against him.

HAWKINS, J. A mere statement of the girl would clearly be inadmissible if made in the absence of the prisoner. It could only become admissible if evidence were given that the prisoner was present, and moreover that he assented to it, whether by his words or by his acts, or by his demeanour ; but, even then, only to the extent of that assent. And, even then, it would become admissible, not because of the girl's having so stated, but because of the prisoner's having by his con-duct, tacitly or expressly, admitted its truth. The value of a statement made in the prisoner's presence is nothing, unless the prisoner, by what he said or did, or omitted to say or do, afforded evidence from which the jury may reasonably draw the inference that he assented to the truth of the statement. Hence, à fortiori, it will not¹ be admissible if the prisoner denied the truth of the statement. If the prisoner dis-sented from a statement made in his presence, it will not be evidence. The affirmative ought not to be assumed without evidence from which the jury might, if they think fit, draw the inference that the prisoner had assented to it. And it is for the Court to decide whether there is any evidence from which such an inference could properly be drawn. There is no such evidence in the present case, for the prisoner has positively denied the material part of the statement. Therefore, the statement ought to be rejected. In short, the statement of the girl is inadmissible per se ; and it can only be made admissible by evidence that the prisoner heard it, understood it, and by his words or conduct afforded some reasonable evidence that he admitted its truth. If with-out such evidence a statement were to be admitted, the only effect of it would be to prejudice the prisoner unfairly.

Mathews, for the Crown, withdrew the statement.

[*Thus, if a document be found in your possession, your conduct, in having kept it, is evidence of your knowledge of its contents.*]

COTTON *v.* JAMES.

WESTMINSTER N.P. SITTINGS. 1829.   MOODY AND MALKIN 273.

[Action of trespass for breaking and entering the plaintiff's house and taking his goods. Plea that the plaintiff was a bankrupt, and that

----

¹ [EDITOR'S NOTE.] *Usually* not; but a denial in words may, conceivably, be neutralized by the prisoner's demeanour. See the whole doctrine considered in *Rex* v. *Norton,* 5 Cr. App. R. at p. 74.

the seizure was under the warrant of the commissioners in the bank-ruptcy. Replication by the plaintiff denying the bankruptcy. The only question being as to the existence of the bankruptcy, and the affirmative of this issue being upon the defendant, he was held entitled to begin. The act of bankruptcy relied upon was a fraudulent delivery of part of the plaintiff's goods with intent to defeat a creditor.]

To prove this, *Pollock*, for the defendant, offered in evidence letters of the plaintiff's son, who principally carried on the business, addressed to the plaintiff and giving accounts of the manner in which he intended to bestow different parts of the property, and of other circumstances relating to the condition of the plaintiff's affairs. The letters had post-marks antecedent to the act of bankruptcy; and the messenger under the commission found them among the plaintiff's papers, took possession of them, and produced them.

Sir James Scarlett, for the plaintiff, objected to their being received; the plaintiff's son himself ought to prove the facts.

LORD TENTERDEN, C.J. I must receive the evidence. Being found in the plaintiff's possession after the bankruptcy, with postmarks of a time before it, I must take it that he received them before it; and then they are evidence to shew, in explanation of the plaintiff's con-duct, that he received intimation that such facts as those mentioned in the letters took place. Of course they are not evidence that the facts stated really did occur.

[Exception 3. *Statements made by a person, now deceased, against his pecuniary interest.*]

WARREN *v.* GREENVILLE.

KING'S BENCH. 1740. 2 STRANGE 1129.

Action of ejectment. Upon a trial at bar, the lessor of the plaintiff claimed under an old entail in a family settlement, by which part of the estate appeared to be in jointure to a widow at the time her son suffered a common recovery, which was in 1699. And the defendants not being able to shew a surrender of the mother's estate for life, it was insisted that there was no tenant to the praecipe for that part, and the remainder under which the lessor claimed was not barred.

To obviate this, it was insisted by the defendant that, at this distance of time, a surrender should be presumed; and to fortify this presumption they offered to produce the debt book of Mr Edwards, an attorney at Bristol, long since deceased, where he charges £32 for suffering the recovery; two articles of which are—for drawing a surrender of the mother 20*s.*, and for ingrossing two parts thereof 20*s.* more; and that it appeared by the book the bill was paid.

And this being objected to as improper evidence, the Court was of opinion to allow it; for it was a circumstance material upon the inquiry into the reasonableness of presuming a surrender, and could not be suspected to be done for this purpose; and if Edwards was living he might undoubtedly be examined to it; and this was now the next best evidence. And it was accordingly read. After which the Court declared that, without this circumstance, they would have presumed a surrender; and desired that it might be taken notice of, that they did not require any evidence to fortify the presumption after such a length of time.

THE QUEEN *v.* THE CHURCHWARDENS &c. OF BIRMINGHAM.

QUEEN'S BENCH. 1861. 1 BEST AND SMITH 763.

[Case stated by the Birmingham Quarter Sessions, who had quashed an order for the removal of a pauper to the parish of Kingswood, on the ground that there was no legal evidence that the tenement which her husband's father had occupied in Kingswood was of the amount sufficient to confer a settlement in the parish. The evidence tendered to prove the amount of that rent was a statement, uttered by the deceased man whilst in occupation of the tenement, to the effect that he occupied it as tenant at a rent of £20 a year.]

O'Brien for respondent. This declaration is clearly hearsay, and does not fall within any of the recognised exceptions to the rule rejecting that kind of evidence. Declarations by which a party in occupation cuts down his interest are admissible to prove the fact of tenancy, but not to prove collateral facts, such as the amount of rent, as here....

COCKBURN, C.J. I have seen many cases where facts have been proved by written entries against interest, of the truth of which no one could entertain a doubt, and justice would have been defeated if they had not been received. A judge can always tell a jury that anything extraneous in such statements may be disregarded. People were formerly frightened out of their wits about admitting evidence, lest juries should go wrong. In modern times we admit the evidence, and discuss its weight. If a man says, "I pay £20 a year rent," there is no more reason to doubt that he is telling the truth than when he says he is paying rent at all.

* * * * *

COCKBURN, C.J. I am of opinion that this evidence ought to have been received. It is well established that a declaration made by a person in occupation of real estate that he holds as tenant, is admissible after his decease to rebut the presumption of law, arising from the fact of occupation, that he was owner in fee simple. The question here is, whether, if a person, at the time he admits that he is not the owner in fee but is only tenant of the property, states also the amount of rent which he pays for it, that declaration is admissible, not merely to shew that his occupation is an occupation as tenant, as distinguished from that as owner, but to shew what in fact was the amount of rent which he paid as tenant.

Now, it has been held, over and over again, in the analogous case of declarations against pecuniary interest, that the declaration of the deceased person may be received not only to prove so much contained in it as is adverse to his pecuniary interest, but to prove collateral facts stated in it; at all events, so far as relates to facts which are not foreign to the declaration, and may be taken to have formed a substantial part of it. That being settled, I cannot see in principle any reason why the same effect should not be given to declarations against *proprietary* as to declarations against *pecuniary* interest. It is true that in this case the declaration was oral, and it has been pressed upon us that a declaration of that kind does not stand on the same footing as an entry made in the course of business, which was the evidence in *Higham* v. *Ridgway*[1]. And I quite admit that, as regards the *effect* of the evidence, there is a great difference between them ; but that goes rather to the weight, than the admissibility, of the evidence. I am disposed to hold that there is no distinction in principle between written and oral declarations if the other element of admissibility is present, i.e., that the declaration was against pecuniary or proprietary interest ; and either is admissible to prove what are, not very properly, called collateral facts.

* * * *

[1] 10 East, 109.

[Exception 4. *Statements made by a person now* deceased, *in
the course of his* duty, *either public or private.*]

PRICE *v.* THE EARL OF TORRINGTON.

GUILDHALL N.P. SITTINGS.   1704.   1 SALKELD 283.

The plaintiff, being a brewer, brought an action against the Earl of
Torrington for beer sold and delivered; and the evidence given to
charge the defendant was that the usual way of the plaintiff's dealing
was that the draymen came every night to the clerk of the brewhouse,
and gave him an account of the beer they had delivered out, which he
set down in a book kept for that purpose, to which the draymen set
their hands; and that the drayman was dead, but that this was his
hand set to the book.   And this was held by HOLT, C.J., good evidence
of a delivery; otherwise of the shop book if left singly, without more.

[*Statement made in the course of duty*]

POOLE *v.* DICAS.

COMMON PLEAS.   1835.   1 BINGHAM (N.C.) 649.

[Action on bill of exchange by indorsee against drawer.   To prove
the dishonour, a notary's clerk produced at the trial a book containing
by the side of a copy of this bill the entry, "No effects," made by
another clerk named Manning, since deceased, who had gone, on the
day when the bill fell due, to demand payment of the acceptor.
A verdict having been given for the plaintiff, a motion was made to set
it aside, on the ground that the entry made by Manning ought not to
have been received in evidence, and that the person who gave the
answer at the place of presentment ought to have been called.]

Kelly, for defendant....The entry was not the best evidence; for the
person who gave the answer at the place of presentment might have
been called.

*   *   *   *   *

TINDAL, C.J....We think the evidence admissible; on the ground that
it was an entry made at the time of the transaction, and made in the
usual course and routine of business, by a person who had no interest
to misstate what had occurred.   If there were any doubt whether it
were made at the time of the transaction, the case ought to go down to

trial again : but according to my impression of the testimony in the cause, the entry *was* made at the time. Had any ambiguity existed on that head, a single question to the witness, on cross-examination, would have cleared it up....The clerk had no interest to make a false entry: if he had any interest, it was rather to make a true entry: it is easier to state what is true than what is false; the process of invention implies trouble, in such a case unnecessarily incurred; and a false entry would be likely to bring him into disgrace with his employer. Again, the book in which the entry was made was open to all the clerks in the office, so that an entry if false would be exposed to speedy discovery....In the present case, it would operate as a great hardship to require the testimony of the persons who might have been present. The clerk who presented the bill could scarcely, at the distance of two years, point out who it was that answered his application ; and if it were necessary to call all the persons who resided at the place of presentment, the expense and inconvenience would be enormous....

[Exception 5. *On trials for* homicide, *declarations are admissible which were made by the slain person after he had lost all hope of recovery.*]

THE QUEEN *v.* JENKINS.

CROWN CASE RESERVED.   1869.   L.R. 1 C.C.R. 187.

Case stated by BYLES, J. :—

The prisoner was convicted at the last Bristol Assizes of the murder of Fanny Reeves, and is now under sentence of death, subject to the decision of the Court of Criminal Appeal as to the admissibility of the dying declaration of the deceased woman.

On the night of the 16th of October, between 8 and 9 o'clock, the deceased was found in the river Avon, at a place where the river is very deep. She was rescued from the water, but in an exhausted condition, and she became, according to the medical evidence, in great danger. On the next day, the 17th, she said she did not think she should get over it, and desired that some one should be sent for to pray with her. A neighbour accordingly visited her about 8 o'clock P.M., who prayed with her, and, as her mother said, talked seriously to her.

At 10 o'clock the same evening the magistrates' clerk came. He found her in bed, breathing with considerable difficulty and moaning occasionally. He administered an oath and she made a written statement as hereinafter set forth. He asked her if she felt she was in a dangerous state, whether she felt she was likely to die? She said, "I think so." He said, "Why?"—She replied, "From the shortness of my breath." Her breath was extremely short; the answers were disjointed from its shortness. Some intervals elapsed between her answers. The magistrates' clerk said, "Is it with the fear of death before you that you make these statements?" and added, "Have you any present hope of your recovery?"—She said, "None."

The counsel for the defendant pointed out that in the statement the words "at present" were interlined. The magistrates' clerk was recalled. He said, that after he had taken the deposition he read it over to her, and asked her to correct any mistake that he might have made. She then suggested the words "at present." She said "no hope at present of my recovery." He then interlined the words "at present." She died about 11 o'clock the next morning....

...The examination of the deceased gave a detailed account of a walk she had taken with the prisoner on the evening of the 16th of October, and stated that he had induced her to go to the edge of the river Avon, and had then pushed her in. After describing how she was saved from being drowned, the declaration continued:—"After being so taken out I became insensible, and did not recover till I found myself in bed in this house. Since then I have felt great pain in my chest, bosom, and back. From the shortness of my breath I feel that I am likely to die, and I have made the above statement with the fear of death before me, and with no hope *at present* of my recovery. Dr Smart has been to see me twice to-day."

"The mark X of Fanny Reeves."

The jury found the prisoner guilty.

Sentence of death was passed, but execution stayed, that the opinion of this Court might be taken on the admissibility of the declaration.

Collins, for prisoner. The declaration of the deceased was not admissible in evidence, as it does not appear that she had absolutely no hope of recovery. The general principle on which declarations of this kind are admitted is that "they are made in extremity, when the party is at the point of death, and when every hope of this world is gone, when every motive to falsehood is silenced, and the mind is induced by the most powerful considerations to speak the truth.

A situation so awful is considered by the law as...equal to an oath," per EYRE, L.C.B., in *Woodcock's Case* (1 Leach 502)

T. W. Saunders, for the prosecution. It is admitted that to make the declaration evidence, it must be shewn that it was made in the fear of impending death, under immediate expectation of death, and when there was no hope of recovery....But the words "at present" do not really alter the meaning of the sentence. The sentiment of hope, or of want of hope, must necessarily refer to the time when the feeling is expressed....And while there is life, there is hope; and therefore there can never be absolutely no hope of recovery.

KELLY, C.B....The result of the decisions is that there must be an unqualified belief in the nearness of death, a belief without hope that the declarant is about to die. If we look at reported cases, and at the language of learned judges, we find that one has used the expression "every hope of this world gone[1]"; another "settled hopeless expectation of death[2]"; another "any hope of recovery, however slight, renders the evidence of such declarations inadmissible[3]." We, as Judges, must be perfectly satisfied beyond any reasonable doubt that there was no hope of avoiding death; and it is not unimportant to observe that the burden of proving the facts that render the declaration admissible is upon the prosecution.

If the present case had rested upon the expression, "I have made the above statement with the fear of death before me, and with no hope of my recovery," a difficult question might have been raised. But when these words were read over to the declarant, she desired to put in the important words "at present"; and the statement so amended is "with no hope at present of my recovery." We are now called upon to say what is the effect of these words, taking into consideration all the circumstances under which they were put in. The counsel for the prosecution has argued that the words "at present" do not alter the sense of the statement. We think, that they must have been intended to convey some meaning, and we must endeavour to give effect to that meaning....If they have any meaning at all, they must qualify the absolute meaning (which the declaration must contain in order to render it admissible evidence). The conviction must therefore be quashed.

BYLES, J. As I tried the case, I wish to state that I entertain no doubt that the declaration was not admissible. There being no other

---

[1] Per Eyre, C.B., *Woodcock's Case*, 1 Leach, C. C. at p. 502.

[2] Per Willes, J., *Reg.* v. *Peel*, 2 F. and F. at p. 22.

[3] Per Tindal, C.J., *Rex* v. *Hayward*, 6 C. and P. at p. 160.

evidence against the prisoner, I thought it best to admit the declaration, and reserve the point whether it was admissible evidence.

Dying declarations ought to be admitted with scrupulous, and I had almost said with superstitious, care.   They have not necessarily the sanction of an oath; they are made in the absence of the prisoner; the person making them is not subjected to cross-examination, and is in no peril of prosecution for perjury.   There is also great danger of omissions, and of unintentional misrepresentations, both by the declarant and the witness, as this case shews.   In order to make a dying declaration admissible, there must be an expectation of impending and almost immediate death, from the causes then operating. The authorities shew that there must be no hope whatever....

[The other three Judges concurred.]

Conviction quashed.

REGINA *v.* GLOSTER.

CENTRAL CRIMINAL COURT.   1888.   SESSIONS PAPERS CVIII. 647.

[James Gloster was indicted for (and charged on the Coroner's inquisition with) the wilful murder of Eliza Jane Schumacher.   The prisoner, a medical man, was alleged to have caused the death of the deceased by an unlawful operation, performed with intent to procure abortion....The deceased woman had, from time to time during her illness, made statements as to her bodily sufferings and their cause; but not under such circumstances as would render them admissible as dying declarations.]

Poland, for the Crown, offered these statements as expressions of the deceased's bodily feelings.   He cited *Reg.* v. *Palmer* (shorthand report), *Aveson* v. *Lord Kinnaird (supra,* p. 498).

Gill and *Avory,* for the prisoner, contended that such evidence must be restricted to expressions of the deceased's feelings and symptoms at the time of making the complaint; thus excluding all statements as to their cause and the mention of any name.   They cited *Reg.* v. *Gutteridge* 9 C. and P. 472; *Reg.* v. *Osborne* Car. and M. 622; *Reg.* v. *Megson* 9 C. and P. 420.

CHARLES, J., decided that the statements must be limited to contemporaneous symptoms; and that nothing in the nature of a narrative was admissible; as, for instance, how the bodily condition was caused, or who occasioned it. With these limitations, the evidence was admitted.

The Crown tendered in evidence a written statement, which had been taken down from the dictation of the deceased (and afterwards signed by her) shortly before her death. On the admissibility of this as a dying declaration, the counsel for the Crown asked the Court to decide whether it was sufficiently shown to have been made in expectation of impending death. The woman's expressions were: "I do not think I shall recover, and "I shall not be long here."

Gill objected to its admission; and quoted the dictum of Byles, J., in *Reg.* v. *Jenkins* (*supra*, p. 515) that "dying declarations ought to be admitted with scrupulous and almost superstitious care."

CHARLES, J. The result of the decisions is that there must be an unqualified belief in the nearness of death, every hope of this world must be gone; and in the words of Mr Justice Willes, in *Reg.* v. *Peele* (2 F. and F. 21) there must be "a settled hopeless expectation of death." Taking all the circumstances of the case together, I cannot come to the conclusion that the deceased was in that condition. The statement, therefore, cannot be admitted.

Poland stated that, the declaration being excluded, he could not proceed further.

Not guilty.

[See also REGINA *v.* NEILL, *supra*, p. 483,
and REGINA *v.* BEDINGFIELD, *supra*, p. 501.]

[*But only on trials for* homicide.]

REX *v.* MEAD.

KING'S BENCH.   1824.   2 BARNEWELL AND CRESSWELL 605.

The defendant was indicted for perjury; and at the Middlesex sittings, before ABBOTT, C.J., was found guilty. The perjury, of which the defendant was convicted, consisted in Mead's swearing, upon the trial of an information in the Exchequer, that one James Law had been present at and engaged in a smuggling transaction, at a place

called the Salt-Pans, in the parish of Scalby, in the county of York, on
the 20th of August, 1820 ; upon the trial of which information Law
was acquitted. A rule for a new trial was obtained by the Attorney
General, on the ground of the verdict having been against the weight
of evidence. [Counsel for the Crown now shewed cause against a new
trial. They tendered affidavits, some of which stated a dying declaration of the above-mentioned James Law ; who had been the prosecutor
on the indictment for perjury, and had been shot by the defendant
Mead, after the conviction of the latter. The dying declaration of
Law, after giving an account of the circumstances under which he was
shot by Mead, proceeded to negative his having been present at, or
having had any concern whatever in, the smuggling transaction which
Mead had deposed to in the Court of Exchequer.

The *Attorney General* objected to these affidavits of the dying
declaration being received. Dying declarations are only admissible in
criminal prosecutions where the death of the deceased and the circumstances of the death are the subject of the charge against a prisoner.
Whereas here the statement, disclosed by the affidavits tendered, was
not made with reference to the death of the dying man, but with reference to the antecedent charge of perjury. In *Doe dem. Sutton* v.
Ridgeway (4 B. and A. 53), it was held that the dying declarations of
a person as to the relationship between the lessor of the plaintiff and
the person last seised, could not be received in evidence.

D. F. Jones and *Chitty*, for the Crown, contended that the affidavits
as to the dying declarations were admissible. The general principle
upon which such evidence is competent is founded partly on the situation of the dying man, which must be taken to have as much power
over his conscience as the sanction of any oath could have, and partly
on the manifest absence of any interest, when he is on the point of
passing into another world. *Lord Mohun's* case, 12 St. Tr. 949 ; *Rex*
v. *Reason*, 1 Strange 499....

ABBOTT, C.J. We are all of opinion that the evidence cannot be
received....The dying declaration of Law was for the purpose, not of
accusing but, of clearing himself. It therefore falls within the general
rule that evidence of this description is only admissible where the death
of the deceased is the subject of the charge, and the circumstances of
the death are the subject of the dying declaration.

CHAPTER VI.　CONFESSIONS.

[*In* criminal *trials, an admission made by the accused cannot be given
in evidence if it were induced by any threat or promise, connected
with the prosecution.*]

THE QUEEN *v.* THOMPSON.

CROWN CASE RESERVED.　1893.　　　L.R. [1893] 2 Q.B. 12.

At the Westmoreland Quarter Sessions, held at Kendal on
October 21, 1892, Marcellus Thompson was tried for embezzling
certain moneys belonging to the Kendal Union Gas and Water Company, his masters. Mr Crewdson, the chairman of the Company, at
whose instance the warrant for the prisoner's apprehension had been
issued, was called as a witness by the prosecution to prove among other
things a confession by the prisoner. As soon as this confession was
sought to be put in evidence, objection was taken to its admissibility,
and we therefore, before receiving further proof, allowed the witness to
be cross-examined by the prisoner's counsel. In answer to the latter's
questions, the witness stated that, prior to the confession being made,
the prisoner's brother and brother-in-law had come to see him, and that
at this interview he said to the prisoner's brother, "It will be the right
thing for Marcellus to make a clean breast of it." The witness added,
"I won't swear I did not say 'It will be better for him to make a clean
breast of it.' I may have done so. I don't think I did. I expected
what I said would be communicated to the prisoner. I won't swear I
did not intend it should be conveyed to the prisoner. I should expect
it would. I made no threat or promise to induce the prisoner to make
a confession. I held out no hope that criminal proceedings would not
be taken." No evidence was produced to the Court tending to prove
that the details of the interview had been communicated to the
prisoner, or to rebut the evidence of Mr Crewdson as to what took
place at the interview. It was then contended by the prisoner's counsel
that the above statements to the prisoner's brother were inducements to
the prisoner to confess, held out by a person in authority, and that
evidence of the confession was therefore inadmissible. We found that
Mr Crewdson was a person in authority, and we found, as a fact, that
the statements made by him were calculated to elicit the truth, and
that the confession was voluntary, and we accordingly admitted the
evidence. The witness then proved that after the interview he charged
the prisoner with embezzling the Company's money, and one of the
directors told the prisoner that he was in a very embarrassing position.

The prisoner replied, "I know that; I will give the Company all the assistance I can." He said, in answer to witness's charge, "Yes, I took it; but I do not think it is more than £1000. It might be a few pounds more." No statement was made to the prisoner that the confession would save him from prosecution; there was no threat or promise. Subsequently the prisoner made out a list of moneys which he admitted had not been accounted for by him. This list we also admitted in evidence. The prisoner was convicted and sentenced to three years' penal servitude. The question for the opinion of the Court is whether the evidence of the confession was properly admitted. The case having been sent down for amendment, the following statement was added:—At a meeting of the directors a question was asked by one of the directors as to the value of the stock on a farm occupied by the prisoner's brother, and it was suggested that a bill of sale over the stock should be given. The prisoner stated that the worth of the stock was over £1000, but that he could not accept the suggestion about the security without telling his brother. At the same meeting the prisoner said, "My brothers have got it" (meaning the money); "it has gone to pay interest on mortgages." Mr Crewdson said, "I never agreed not to prosecute, if a bill of sale were given." After the charge was made, £340 was received from the prisoner, together with some money and an I.O.U. for £25, which were found in the cash-box. Of the sum of £340, £90 was paid into the bank by the prisoner, and £250 by his brother. Mr Crewdson stated that no arrangement was made as to the discrepancy being treated as a debt, and that the sum paid was simply by way of restitution.

*   *   *   *   *

Segar for the prosecution. Evidence of the confession was admissible. It is not shewn that what passed between the prisoner's brother and the prosecutor was communicated to the prisoner. The words used were also advice on moral grounds. Confessions preceded by exhortations of this kind were held admissible in *Reg.* v. *Jarvis*[1], and *Reg.* v. *Reeve*[2]. The justices have found that the confession was voluntary; and it was for them to decide what words were used, and whether they were repeated to the prisoner in such a manner as to convey a promise or threat. Evidence of a confession is primâ facie admissible, and can only be excluded upon proof by the prisoner that the confession was not voluntary.

CAVE, J. . Many reasons may be urged in favour of the admissibility of all confessions, subject of course to their being tested by the cross-examination of those who heard and testify of them; and Bentham

---

[1] L. R. 1 C. C. R. 96; *infra*, p. 525.   [2] L. R. 1 C. C. R. 362.

seems to have been of this opinion (Rationale of Judicial Evidence, Bk. v., ch. vi., s. 3). But this is not the law of England. By that law, to be admissible, a confession must be free and voluntary. If it proceeds from remorse and a desire to make reparation for the crime, it is admissible. If it flows from hope or fear, excited by a person in authority, it is inadmissible. On this point the authorities are unan - mous....

In *Reg.* v. *Baldry*[1] it is said by Pollock, C.B., that the true ground of the exclusion is not that there is any presumption of law that a confession not free and voluntary is false, but that "it would not be safe to receive a statement made under any influence or fear." He also explains that the objection to telling the prisoner that it would be better to speak the truth is that the words import that it would be better for him to say *something*. With this view the statutory caution agrees, which commences with the words : "You are not obliged to say anything unless you desire to do so[2]."...

If these principles and the reasons for them are, as it seems impossible to doubt, well founded, they afford to magistrates a simple test by which the admissibility of a confession may be decided. They have to ask, Is it proved affirmatively that the confession was free and voluntary—that is, Was it preceded by any inducement to make a statement held out by a person in authority? If so, and the inducement has not clearly been removed before the statement was made, evidence of the statement is inadmissible.

In the present case the magistrates appear to have intended to state the evidence which was before them, and to ask our opinion whether on that evidence they did right in admitting the confession. Now there was obviously some ground for suspecting that the confession might not have been free and voluntary ; and the question is whether the evidence was such as ought to have satisfied their minds that it was free and voluntary. Unfortunately, in my judgment, the magistrates do not seem to have understood what the precise point to be determined was, or what evidence was necessary to elicit it. The new evidence now before us throws a strong light on what was the object of the interview between Mr Crewdson and the prisoner's brother and brother-in-law, why he made any communication to them, and why he expected that what he said would be communicated to the prisoner. There is, indeed, no evidence that any communication was made to the prisoner at all ; but it seems to me that after Mr Crewdson's statement, that he had spoken to the prisoner's brother and ·brother-in-law about

---

[1] 2 Den. C. C. 430, at p. 442.
[2] See the Indictable Offences Act, 1848 (11 and 12 Vict. c. 42), s. 18.

the desirability of the prisoner making a clean breast of it, with the expectation that what he had said would be communicated to the prisoner, it was incumbent on the prosecution to prove whether any, and if so, what, communication was actually made to the prisoner, before the magistrates could properly be satisfied that the confession was free and voluntary.

The magistrates go on to say that they inferred that the details of the interview would be (by which I suppose they intend to say that they inferred they were) communicated to the prisoner, which seems to have been the right inference to draw under the circumstances. They add that they found, as a fact, (1) that the statements made by Crewdson were calculated to elicit the truth, and (2) that the confession was voluntary. The first of these findings, if the ruling of Pollock, C.B., in *Reg.* v. *Baldry*[1] is, as I take it to be, correct, is entirely immaterial. The second finding, if it is a corollary from the first, does not follow from it, and, if it is an independent finding, is not warranted by the evidence; and, as the question for us is whether this finding was warranted by the evidence, I feel compelled to say that in my judgment it was not. Taking the words of Mr Crewdson to have been, "It will be the right thing for Marcellus to make a statement," and that those words were communicated to the prisoner, I should say that that communication was calculated in the language of Pollock, C.B., to lead the prisoner to believe that it would be better for him to say *something*. All this, however, is matter of conjecture; and I prefer to put my judgment on the ground that it is the duty of the prosecution to prove, in case of doubt, that the prisoner's statement was free and voluntary; and that they did not discharge themselves of this obligation..

[The other four Judges concurred.]

Conviction quashed.

[See also Rex v. Partridge, *supra*, p. 468.]

[*But not if the person who induced the confession had no share of* authority *in the prosecution.*]

REX v. GIBBONS.

Worcester Assizes.   1823.   1 Carrington and Payne 97.

The prisoner was indicted for the murder of her bastard child.

[1] 2 Den. C. C. 430, at p. 442.

Mr Cozens, a surgeon, was called to prove certain confessions made by the prisoner to him. The witness objected to giving such evidence, on the ground, that, at the time of the statement, he was attending the prisoner in the capacity of a surgeon.

PARK, J. That is no sufficient reason to prevent a disclosure for the purposes of justice.

The witness also stated that he had held out no threat or promise to induce her to confess; but a woman who was present said, that she had told the prisoner she had better tell all; and then the prisoner made certain confessions to the witness.

Campbell objected, that, as the confession was made after an inducement held out, it could not be received in evidence.

PARK, J., after consulting with HULLOCK, B., laid down that, as no inducement had been held out by Mr Cozens, to whom the confession was made; and the only inducement had been held out (as was alleged) by a person having no sort of authority; it must be presumed that the confession to Mr Cozens was a free and voluntary confession. If the promise had been held out by any person having any office or authority, as the prosecutor, constable, &c., the case would be different; but here some person, having no authority of any sort, officiously says, you had better confess. No confession follows; but, some time afterwards, to another person (the witness), the prisoner, without any inducement held out, confesses. They (the Judges) had not the least doubt that the present evidence was admissible.

It was accordingly admitted.

The prisoner was acquitted on other grounds.

[*Or if he induced it by an appeal made solely to* moral or religious *considerations.*]

THE QUEEN *v.* JARVIS.

CROWN CASE RESERVED.   1867.   L.R. 1 C.C.R. 96.

The following case was stated by the Recorder of London :—

At a Session of the Central Criminal Court, held on the 8th of July, 1867, and following days, Frank Jarvis, Richard Bulkley, and Wilford Bulkley, were tried before me on an indictment for feloniously stealing 138 yards of silk and other property of William Leaf and others, the masters of Jarvis. There was a second count in the indictment for

feloniously receiving the same goods. William Laidler Leaf was
examined, and said : The prisoner Jarvis was in my employ. On the
13th of May we called him up, when the officers were there, into our
private counting house. I said to him, "Jarvis, I think it is right that
I should tell you that, besides being in the presence of my brother and
myself, you are in the presence of two officers of the police ; and I
should advise you that to any question that may be put to you you will
answer truthfully, so that, if you have committed a fault, you may not
add to it by stating what is untrue." I produced a letter to him,
which he said he had not written ; and I then said, "Take care,
Jarvis ; we know more than you think we know." I do not believe I
said to him, "You had better tell the truth."

Counsel for the prisoner Jarvis objected to any statement of his
made after the above was said being received in evidence; and referred
to *Rex* v. *Williams*[1], *Reg.* v. *Warringham*[2], *Reg.* v. *Garner*[3], *Rex* v.
Shepherd[4], and *Reg.* v. *Millen*[5]

Counsel for the prosecution referred to *Reg.* v. *Baldry*[6], *Reg.* v.
Sleeman[7], and *Reg.* v. *Parker*[8]. I decided that the statement was
admissible.

The jury found Jarvis guilty, adding that they so found upon his
own confession, but they thought that confession prompted by the
inquiries put to him. They acquitted the other two. At the request
of counsel for Jarvis I reserved for the Court for the consideration of
Crown Cases Reserved the question,—Whether I ought to have
admitted the statements of the prisoner in evidence against him?

Coleridge, Q.C. (*Straight* with him) for the prisoner. In the case
of *Reg.* v. *Baldry*[6], all the cases with reference to the admissibility of
confessions are reviewed. The principles arrived at in that case were,
first, that a confession must be free and voluntary, and that the onus
of shewing this lies on the prosecution ; secondly, that any inducement
or threat of a temporal kind prevents the confession from being free or
voluntary ; thirdly, that it is immaterial what impression the person
who made use of the inducement or threat intended to convey. The
ground for not receiving such evidence is that it would not be safe to
receive a statement made under any influence, whether of hope or fear.
If in this case the words had been, "You had better answer truthfully," there would have been no doubt about the inadmissibility of the
statement ; and yet the words actually used are substantially the same.
It is playing with language, considering the position of the parties, to

[1] 2 Den. C. C. 433.   [2] 15 Jur. 318; 2 Den. C. C. 447, note.
[3] 1 Den. C. C. 329.   [4] 7 C. and P. 579.   [5] 3 Cox's Crim. Cas. 507.
[6] 2 Den. C. C. 430.   [7] Dears. C. C. 249.   [8] Leigh and Cave C. C. 42.

say there was no inducement. It was equivalent to saying, "I should advise you to say what is better for you"; or, in other words, "You had better tell the truth." The law cannot measure the extent of the influence used, if any has been used and exercised on the mind.

*　　*　　*　　*　　*

KELLY, C.B....In this case, do the words fairly considered import either a threat of evil or a promise of good? They are these: "Jarvis, I think it is right that I should tell you that, besides being in the presence of my brother and myself, you are in the presence of two officers of the police; and I should advise you that to any question that may be put to you you will answer truthfully." Pausing at these words, they would seem to operate as a warning rather than a threat, as advice given by a master to a servant. What follows?—"So that, if you have committed a fault you may not add to it by stating what is untrue." These words appear to have been added on moral grounds alone; there was no inducement of advantage. Under these circumstances, putting no strain one way or the other, the words amount only to this: "We put certain questions to you; I advise you to answer truthfully, only that you may not add a fault to an offence committed, if any has been committed." With reference to the last words, "Take care; we know more than you think we know"—these amount only to a caution. The words, "You had better tell the truth," seem to have acquired a sort of technical meaning, importing either a threat or a benefit; but they were not used in this case. The words that have been used import only advice on moral grounds.

[The other four Judges concurred.]

Conviction affirmed.

[*Or made even to temporal considerations if they are unconnected with the result of the prosecution.*]

REX v. WM. LLOYD AND GEORGE LLOYD.

GLOUCESTER ASSIZES. 1834.　　　6 CARRINGTON AND PAYNE 393.

The prisoner, William Lloyd, was indicted for stealing bank notes and money in the dwelling-house of Frances Gurner; and the prisoner George Lloyd was charged with receiving the stolen property, knowing it to have been stolen.

It appeared that the prisoner, George Lloyd, and his wife, were both in custody on this charge, but in separate rooms. A person, who was in the room where the former was in custody, said—"I hope you will tell, because Mrs Gurner can ill afford to lose the money"; and that the constable said—"If you will tell where the property is, you shall see your wife."

Greaves, for the prisoner, objected to evidence being given of any thing that was said after this.

PATTESON, J. I think that this is not such an inducement to confess as will exclude the evidence of what the prisoner said. It amounts only to this, that, if he would tell where the money was, he should see his wife[1]

The evidence was received.

CHAPTER VII. EVIDENCE OF CHARACTER.

[*'Character'* *does not mean* disposition *but* reputation.]

[*In criminal cases, evidence of the defendant's good character is always admissible.*]

REGINA *v.* ROWTON.

CROWN CASE RESERVED. 1865.   LEIGH AND CAVE 520.

The following case was stated by the Deputy Assistant Judge of the county of Middlesex.

James Rowton was tried before me, at the Middlesex Sessions, on the 30th of September, 1864, on an indictment which charged him with having committed an indecent assault upon George Low, a lad about fourteen years of age.

On the part of the defendant, several witnesses were called, who had known him at different periods of his life; and they gave him an excellent character, as a moral and well conducted man.

On the part of the prosecution, it was proposed to contradict this testimony; and a witness was called for that purpose. This was

---

[1] [EDITOR'S NOTE. "I take it no man ever makes a confession voluntarily without proposing to himself in his own mind *some* advantage to be derived from it"; per TAUNTON, J., in *Rex* v. *Green* (6 C. and P. 656), where the removal of the arrested prisoner's handcuffs was held not to be such an inducement as would exclude.]

objected to by the defendant's counsel, who contended that no such evidence was receivable, and cited the case of *Regina* v. *Burt*[1].

I thought the evidence was admissible; and, after the witness had stated that he knew the defendant, the following question was put to him:—"What is the defendant's general character for decency and morality of conduct?" His reply was, "I know nothing of the neighbourhood's opinion, because I was only a boy at school when I knew him; but my own opinion, and the opinion of my brothers who were also pupils of his, is that his character is that of a man capable of the grossest indecency and the most flagrant immorality."

It was objected that this was not legal evidence at all of bad moral character.

I considered that it was some evidence; and I left the weight and effect of it, as an answer to the evidence of good character, to be determined by the jury.

The defendant was convicted, and is now in prison awaiting the judgment of your Lordships.

The questions upon which I respectfully request your decision are:—

First. Whether, when witnesses have given a defendant a good character, any evidence is admissible to contradict?

Secondly. Whether the answer made by the witness in this case was properly left to the jury?

Sleigh, for prisoner. Firstly; evidence is not admissible in reply to evidence of good character. Character forms no part of the issue on the record. [COCKBURN, C.J. Then why is evidence of character admitted at all?]...Secondly; assuming that evidence of general bad character can be given in reply, this evidence was wrongly admitted, on the ground that evidence of general reputation only can be given, and that nothing which amounts to an individual opinion can be received. Character and reputation both mean credit derived from public opinion or esteem. When the witness in this case said that he knew nothing of the opinion of the neighbourhood, he should have been stopped. The best definition of character is to be found in a speech of Erskine's, when he was counsel for Hardy[2], "You cannot," he says, "when asking to character, ask what has A., B., C. told you about this man's character. No; but what is the general opinion concerning him. Character is the slow-spreading influence of opinion, arising from the deportment of a man in society. As a man's deportment, good or bad, necessarily produces one circle without another, and so extends itself till it unites in one general opinion, that general

_____

[1] 5 Cox Crim. Cas. 284.　　　　　[2] 24 St. Tr. 1079.

opinion is allowed to be given in evidence." In *Rex* v. *Jones*[1] the following passage occurs :—

"Mr *Park* (to the witness). 'During the time you did know him (the prisoner), what was his general character for integrity?'

"Answer. 'During the whole time I knew him I considered him man not only of unexceptionable but of most honourable character.'

"LORD ELLENBOROUGH. 'It is reputation; it is not what a person knows. There is hardly one question in ten applicable to the point; it is very remarkable, but there is no branch of evidence so little attended to.'" Individual opinion can only be given so far as it goes to general reputation; and a witness who has known the defendant longest will have the best chance of knowing what his general reputation is.

Tayler, for the Crown....The prisoner, by giving evidence of character, raises the issue that he is of such a disposition as to make it more than ordinarily improbable that he should have committed the offence charged against him. Character, in that sense, and reputation do not stand on the same basis. The latter should rather be defined as estimated character. There is no rule of law that, to make evidence of reputation admissible, it must be founded upon the judgment of a definite number. If, then, the judgment of ten or a less number of men is admissible under the name of reputation, how can the judgment of one only (that is, how can the estimate of disposition formed by one man only, or, in other words, individual opinion) be excluded?...

COCKBURN, C. J....There are two questions to be decided. The first is whether, when evidence of good character has been given in favour of a prisoner, evidence of his general bad character can be called in reply. I am clearly of opinion that it can be. It is true that I do not remember any case in my own experience where such evidence has been given; but that is easily explainable by the fact that evidence of good character is not given when it is known that it can be rebutted; and it frequently happens that the prosecuting counsel, from a spirit of fairness, gives notice to the other side, when he is in a position to contradict such evidence. But, when we come to consider whether the evidence is admissible, it is only possible to come to one conclusion. It is said that evidence of good character raises only a collateral issue; but I think that, if the prisoner thinks proper to raise that issue as one of the elements for the consideration of the jury, nothing could be more unjust than that he should have the advantage of a character which, in point of fact, may be the very reverse of that which he really deserves.

[1] 31 St. Tr. 310.

Assuming, then, that evidence was receivable to rebut the evidence of good character, the second question is, was the answer which was given in this case, in reply to a perfectly legitimate question, such an answer as could properly be left to the jury? Now, in determining this point, it is necessary to consider what is the meaning of evidence of character. Does it mean evidence of general reputation or evidence of disposition? I am of opinion that it means evidence of general reputation. What you want to get at is the tendency and disposition of the man's mind towards committing or abstaining from committing the class of crime with which he stands charged; but no one has ever heard the question—what is the tendency and disposition of the prisoner's mind?—put directly. The only way of getting at it is by giving evidence of his general character founded on his general reputation in the neighbourhood in which he lives. That, in my opinion, is the sense in which the word "character" is to be taken, when evidence of character is spoken of. The fact that a man has an unblemished reputation leads to the presumption that he is incapable of committing the crime for which he is being tried. We are not now considering whether it is desirable that the law of England should be altered whether it is expedient to import the practice of other countries and go into the prisoner's antecedents for the purpose of shewing that he is likely to commit the crime with which he is charged, or, stopping short of that, whether it would be wise to allow the prisoner to go into facts for the purpose of shewing that he is incapable of committing the crime charged against him. It is quite clear that, as the law now stands, the prisoner cannot give evidence of particular facts, although one fact would weigh more than the opinion of all his friends and neighbours. So, too, evidence of antecedent bad conduct would form equally good ground for inferring the prisoner's guilt, yet it is quite clear evidence of that kind is inadmissible. The allowing evidence of good character has arisen from the fairness of our laws, and is an anomalous exception to the general rule. It is quite true that evidence of character is most cogent when it is preceded by a statement shewing that the witness has had opportunities of acquiring information upon the subject beyond what the man's neighbours in general would have; and in practice the admission of such statements is often carried beyond the letter of the law in favour of the prisoner. It is, moreover, most essential that a witness who comes forward to give a man a good character should himself have a good opinion of him, for otherwise he would only be deceiving the jury; and so the strict rule is often exceeded. But when we consider what, in the strict interpretation of the law, is the limit of such evidence, in my judgment it must be restricted to the man's general reputation, and must not extend to the individual opinion of the witness. Some time back, I put this question—Suppose a witness is called who says that he knows nothing of the general character of the accused, but that he has had abundant opportunities of forming an individual opinion as to his honesty or the particular moral quality that may be in question in the particular case. Surely, if such evidence were objected to, it would be inadmissible.

, If that be the true doctrine as to the admissibility of evidence to character in favour of the prisoner, the next question is, within what limits must the rebutting evidence be confined? I think that that evidence must be of the same character and confined within the same limits—that, as the prisoner can only give evidence of general good character, so the evidence called to rebut it must be evidence of the same general description, shewing that the evidence which has been given in favour of the prisoner is not true, but that the man's general reputation is bad. In this case the witness disclaims all knowledge of the gen reputation of the accused. I take his meaning to be this—"I know nothing of the opinion of those with whom the man has in the ordinary occupations of life been brought into contact. I knew him; and so did two brothers of mine, when we were at school; and in my opinion his disposition" (for that is the sense in which the word "character" is used by the witness) "is such that he is capable of committing the class of offences with which he stands charged." I am strongly of opinion that that answer was not admissible. As, when a witness is called to speak to the character of the accused, he cannot say, "I know nothing of his general character, but I have had an opportunity of forming an opinion as to his disposition, and I consider him incapable of committing this offence:" so here, when the witness declared that he knew nothing of the general character of the accused, but that in his opinion the prisoner's disposition was such as to make it likely that he would commit the offence in question—applying the same principle—the answer was inadmissible. But, if an objectionable answer is given to an unobjectionable question, the judge who presides at the trial should stop the answer before it is completed, or, if that is impossible, should tell the jury that they must withdraw it from their consideration; and then the answer would not prejudice the case. Here, however, it was not so. The learned Judge expressly left the answer to the jury, and directed them to take it into account and balance it against the evidence of character given in favour of the prisoner. That being so, the answer became a part of the case, and cannot be treated as an objectionable answer inadvertently given to an unexceptionable question....

I admit that negative evidence, such as "I never heard anything against the character of the man," is the most cogent evidence of a man's good character and reputation; because a man's character is not talked about till there is some fault to be found with it. It is the best evidence of his character that he is not talked about at all[1]; and in that sense such evidence is admissible.

*   *   *   *

WILLES, J. Only the prisoner can raise the question of character. Such evidence is strictly relevant to the issue; but it is not admissible on the part of the prosecution. Because, if the prosecution were allowed to go into such evidence, we should have the whole life of the prisoner ripped up; and upon a trial for murder you might begin by shewing that, when a boy at school, the prisoner had robbed an orchard, and so on through the whole of his life; and the result would be that the man on his trial might be overwhelmed by prejudice....The ultimate fact to be arrived at by such evidence is that the prisoner's disposition is good and not evil. You can, no doubt, go into the question of reputation, and inquire as to the opinion of others concerning the man. But I apprehend that his disposition is the principal matter to be inquired into; and that his reputation is merely accessory and admissible only as evidence of disposition. And, when it is stated that general evidence is alone admissible, that, in my opinion, does not mean merely general evidence of the opinion of others as to the prisoner's character, but general evidence of the disposition of the man. (Evidence of particular facts is excluded, because a robber may do acts of generosity; and the proof of such acts is therefore irrelevant to the question whether he was likely to have committed a particular act of robbery.)...

According to the experience of mankind one would ordinarily rely rather on the information and judgment of a man's intimates than on general report; and why not in a court of law? It is said in answer that we are to be guided by the practice. But I apprehend that the practice is not merely to call persons to say that a man has a good character in the neighbourhood, but also to call his master or the people with whom he has been acquainted to say what character he has borne in their judgment and what is his disposition.

[Of the thirteen Judges who heard the appeal, all except ERLE, C.J., and WILLES, J. concurred in the opinion of COCKBURN, C.J.]

Conviction quashed.

---

[1] [EDITOR'S NOTE. "Hers is the greatest glory whose name is least talked of by men either ill or well"; Pericles, in Thucyd. II. 45.]

CHAPTER VIII. PRIVILEGE.

*[Counsel and solicitors are not even permitted to disclose matters
confided to them by their clients.]*

REX *v.* WITHERS AND OTHERS.

WESTMINSTER N. P. SITTINGS. 1811.   2 CAMPBELL 578.

This was an indictment for breaking open the house of one Copland,
the prosecutor, and assaulting and imprisoning his person.

On the part of the defendants, Mr Phillipson, an attorney, was called
to state that, the same day the assault was committed, the prosecutor
consulted him professionally and gave an account of the transaction
materially at variance with his testimony in the witness-box; and
that on the same occasion a Mr Bruce, who accompanied him, had
in his hearing directed Mr Phillipson to bring an action of trespass
against the defendants, for breaking and entering the house now
represented to be the prosecutor's, as the house of him Mr Bruce.

It was objected that the whole that passed between Mr Phillipson,
and the prosecutor and Bruce, on this occasion, was privileged on the
score of professional confidence.

Garrow, for the defendants, insisted that at any rate the privilege
could not extend to what was said by Bruce, in the prosecutor's
hearing; that this was a communication by a third person to his
attorney; and as Bruce was no party to this prosecution, no objection
could be made on his behalf to the disclosure.   But

LORD ELLENBOROUGH said, that an attorney is not at liberty to
disclose what is communicated to him confidentially by a client,
although the latter be not in any shape before the Court; and
Mr Phillipson was not permitted to be examined.

[EDITOR'S NOTE. In the case of *Wilson v. Rastall* (4 T. R. 759) BULLER, J.,
says:—" The privilege is confined to the cases of Counsel, Solicitor, and Attorney;
and, in order to raise the privilege, it must be proved that the information, which
the adverse party wishes to learn, was communicated to the witness in one of
those characters; for if he be employed merely as a *steward*, he may be examined.
It is indeed hard in many cases to compel a friend to disclose a confidential
conversation; and I should be glad if by law such evidence could be excluded.
It is a subject of just indignation where persons are anxious to reveal what has
been communicated to them in a confidential manner; and in the case of Mr
Petrie's trial at Salisbury for bribery, where Reynolds, who had formerly been the
attorney of Mr Petrie but who was dismissed before the trial of the cause, wished
to give evidence of what he knew relative to the subject *while he was concerned as
the attorney,* I strongly animadverted on his conduct, and would not suffer him to
be examined. He had acquired his information during the time that he acted as

attorney; and I thought that the privilege of not being examined to such points was the privilege of the party, and not of the attorney: and that the privilege never ceased at any period of time. In such a case it is not sufficient to say that the cause is at an end. The mouth of such a person is shut for ever. I take the distinction to be now well settled, that the privilege extends to those three enumerated cases at all times, but that it is confined to these cases only. There are cases, to which it is much to be lamented that the law of privilege is not extended; those in which medical persons are obliged to disclose the information which they acquire by attending in their professional character."]

[*Witnesses have the privilege of refusing to answer any question which tends to* criminate *themselves.*]

THE QUEEN *v.* BOYES.

QUEEN'S BENCH. 1861.   1 BEST AND SMITH 311.

[This was an information filed by the Attorney General in pursuance of a resolution of the House of Commons, for bribery at a Parliamentary election at Beverley.]

On the trial, before MARTIN, B., at the Yorkshire Summer Assizes in 1860, the Solicitor General, in opening the case for the Crown, stated that the evidence upon which the case for the prosecution rested would be the evidence of the persons who had received the bribes, whom he should call as witnesses. Accordingly John Best, mentioned in the first count, was called; and the learned Judge told him that, by the law of England, no man was bound to state anything which subjected him to a criminal prosecution; and, if he was asked any question with respect to the alleged bribery, he might say whether he would or would not answer it, at his pleasure. The witness, upon being asked whether he knew the defendant, declined answering the question. The Solicitor General then produced a pardon of the witness, under the Great Seal, and handed it to him....Similar pardons were also given to the other witnesses. It appeared from the evidence of the witnesses that on the day of the election they came to the front of a house which stood between and opened into two parallel streets of the town of Beverley, and went in succession into the house, and into a back room, in which the defendant was seated; after an interview with the defendant each of them passed into another room, in which another person was seated, from whom each received the sums mentioned in the several counts of the information; they then passed into

the other street, and so to the hustings, and voted. At the close of
the case for the prosecution, the counsel for the defendant took several
objections; and, among others, that there was no corroborative evidence of the witnesses, who were all accomplices with the defendant,
and that the Judge ought to tell the jury that they ought not to
convict on the uncorroborated testimony of the accomplices, citing
Regina v. Stubbs[1]. The learned Judge said that he was not prepared
to take that course, but that he would reserve leave to the defendant
to move for a new trial, on the ground that he was wrong in
compelling the witnesses to answer, and on the ground of the absence
of corroboration.

The jury found a verdict of guilty on the third count, and not
guilty on the others.

*   *   *   *   *

Edward James moved for a new trial. The other side assume
that a pardon restores the party to the same state as he was in
before any offence committed. But the pardoned man may be indicted and put to the inconvenience of pleading his pardon; for
unless pleaded it is of no avail; Com. Dig. Pardon H. Moreover
a pardon may be revoked. Besides, although the Crown may pardon
an offence as regards itself, it cannot take away the right of a subject
to prosecute for the offence. It is for this reason that the Crown
could not pardon in appeals of murder, and the like, for the appeal
was the suit of a subject. Supposing, however, that the pardon
makes the party a new man so far as prosecution by or in the name of
the Crown is concerned, he is still liable to be proceeded against by
impeachment, at the suit of the House of Commons, before the House
of Lords. When the House of Commons impeached Lord Danby, the
Crown, pending the impeachment, granted him a pardon; but the
Commons denied the right of the Crown to do so (2 Hallam's Const.
Hist. vol. 2, p. 411, 7th ed.); and afterwards it was enacted by the Act
of Settlement, 12 and 13 W. III. c. 2, s. 3, entitled "An Act for the
further limitation of the Crown, and better securing the rights and
liberties of the subject," that no pardon of the Crown should be plead-
able to an impeachment by the Commons in Parliament; 4 Blackst. C.
399. A pardon from the Crown, in order to be available in such
a case, must be granted after trial of the impeachment, not while the
impeachment is pending.

As to the point relating to accomplices, the Judge should have
advised the jury to acquit unless the accomplice was corroborated;
Regina v. Stubbs[1].

[1] Dears C. C. 555.

WIGHTMAN, J. With respect to the questions relative to the accomplice; even supposing that the witness here could be considered as an accomplice of the defendant, I think the learned Judge's direction at the trial was quite right. The law on this subject is correctly laid down in *Regina* v. *Stubbs* [1],—it is not a rule of *law* that an accomplice must be corroborated in order to render a conviction valid; but it is a rule of general and usual *practice* to advise juries not to convict on the evidence of an accomplice alone. The application of that rule, however, is a matter for the discretion of the Judge by whom the case is tried, and here he appears to have drawn the attention of the jury to the point. Moreover I think there was corroborative evidence here, if corroborative evidence is requisite. It is not necessary that there should be corroborative evidence as to the very fact; it is enough that there be such as shall confirm the jury in the belief that the accomplice is speaking truth....

HILL, J. I am of the same opinion. In the application of the rule respecting accomplices much depends on the nature of the crime and the extent of the complicity of the witnesses in it. If the crime is a very deep one, and the witness so far involved in it as to render him apparently unworthy of credit, he ought to be corroborated. On the other hand, if the offence be a light one, as in *Rex* v. *Hargrave* [2], which has been referred to, where the nature of the offence and extent of the complicity would not much shake his credit, it is otherwise....

COCKBURN, C.J....The pardon took away the privilege of the witness so far as regarded any risk of prosecution at the suit of the Crown; but it was objected...that the privilege of the witness still existed in this case, on the ground that the witness, though protected by the pardon against every other form of prosecution, might possibly be subject to parliamentary impeachment. In support of this proposition it was urged, on behalf of the defendant, that bribery at the election of members to serve in Parliament being a matter in which the House of Commons would be likely to take a peculiar interest as immediately affecting its own privileges, it was not impossible that, if other remedies proved ineffectual, proceedings by impeachment might be resorted to. It was also contended that a bare possibility of legal peril was sufficient to entitle a witness to protection: nay, further, that the witness was the sole judge as to whether his evidence would bring him into danger of the law: and that the statement of his belief to that effect, if not manifestly made malâ fide, should be received as conclusive.

With the latter of these propositions we are altogether unable to concur. Upon a review of the authorities, we are clearly of opinion

---

[1] Dears C. C. 555.   [2] 5 C. and P. 170.

34—5

that the view of the law propounded by Lord Wensleydale, in *Osborn* v. *The London Dock Company*[1], and acted upon by V. C. Stuart, in *Sidebottom* v. *Atkins*[2], is the correct one; and that, to entitle a party called as a witness to the privilege of silence, the Court must see, from the circumstances of the case and the nature of the evidence which the witness is called to give, that there is reasonable ground to apprehend danger to the witness from his being compelled to answer. We indeed quite agree that, if the fact of the witness being in danger be once made to appear, great latitude should be allowed to him in judging for himself of the effect of any particular question : there being no doubt, as observed by Alderson, B., in *Osborn* v. *The London Dock Company*, that a question which might appear at first sight a very innocent one, might, by affording a link in a chain of evidence, become the means of bringing home an offence to the party answering[3]. Subject to this reservation, a judge is, in our opinion, bound to insist on a witness answering unless he is satisfied that the answer will tend to place the witness in peril.

Further than this, we are of opinion that the danger to be apprehended must be real and appreciable, with reference to the ordinary operation of law in the ordinary course of things—not a danger of an imaginary and unsubstantial character, having reference to some extraordinary and barely possible contingency, so improbable that no reasonable man would suffer it to influence his conduct. We think that a merely remote and naked possibility, out of the ordinary course of the law and such as no reasonable man would be affected by, should not be suffered to obstruct the administration of justice. The object of the law is to afford to a party, called upon to give evidence in a proceeding inter alios, protection against being brought by means of his own evidence within the penalties of the law. But it would be to convert a salutary protection into a means of abuse if it were to be held that a mere imaginary possibility of danger, however remote and improbable, was sufficient to justify the withholding of evidence essential to the ends of justice.

Now, in the present case, no one seriously supposes that the witness runs the slightest risk of an impeachment by the House of Commons. No instance of such a proceeding in the unhappily too numerous cases

---

[1] 10 Exch. 698, 701.   [2] 3 Jur. N. S. 631.

[3] [EDITOR'S NOTE. So in *Fisher* v. *Ronalds* (12 C. B. 765) MAULE, J., says:— "The witness might be asked, 'Were you in London on such a day?' and though apparently a very simple question, he might have good reason to object to answer it, knowing that, if he admitted that he was in London on that day, his admission might complete a chain of evidence against him which would lead to his conviction."]

of bribery which have engaged the attention of the House of Commons has ever occurred, or, so far as we are aware, has ever been thought of. To suppose that such a proceeding would be applied to the case of this witness would be simply ridiculous ; more especially as the proceeding by information was undertaken by the Attorney General by the direction of the House itself, and it would therefore be contrary to all justice to treat the pardon (provided in the interest of the prosecution to ensure the evidence of the witness) as a nullity, and to subject him to a proceeding by impeachment.

It appears to us, therefore, that the witness in this case was not, in a rational point of view, in any the slightest real danger from the evidence he was called upon to give, when protected by the pardon from all ordinary legal proceedings ; and that it was therefore the duty of the presiding Judge to compel him to answer.

[EDITOR'S NOTE. The ruling in this case—that the Judge is not bound to accept the witness's statement, but may decide for himself whether under all the circumstances of the case the proposed question has really a tendency to criminate him—was considered and confirmed in *Ex parte Reynolds*, L.R. 20 Ch. D. 294.]

[*But* medical *advisers have no privilege of refusing to disclose matters confided to them by their patients.*]

[See REX *v.* GIBBONS, *supra* p. 524.]

CHAPTER IX.　ACCOMPLICES.

[*It is* usually *desirable that the evidence of an* Accomplice *should be corroborated.*]

[See REGINA *v.* BOYES, *supra* p. 535.]

[*Though such corroboration is never* absolutely *necessary.*]

THE KING *v.* ATWOOD AND ROBBINS.

CROWN CASE RESERVED. 1787.   1 LEACH 464.

At the Summer Assizes at Bridgewater, in the county of Somerset, in the year 1788, James Atwood and Thomas Robbins were tried before Mr Justice BULLER for a robbery on the highway.

The prosecutor deposed that on the day laid in the indictment he was met by three men, who, after using him with violence and threatening his life, demanded his money; and that in consequence of their threats he delivered to them the property mentioned in the indictment; but that it was so dark at the time, he could not swear that the prisoners at the bar were two of the men who robbed him.

An accomplice was, under this circumstance, admitted to give his testimony; and he deposed that he and the two prisoners at the bar had, in the company of each other, committed this robbery.

The jury, upon the evidence of these two witnesses, found the prisoners guilty; but the judgment was respited, and the case submitted to the consideration of the TWELVE JUDGES.

On the first day of Michaelmas Term, 1788, the Judges assembled at Serjeants' Inn Hall to consider of the propriety of this conviction.

Mr Justice BULLER, at the next Spring Assizes, held at Taunton, ordered the two prisoners to be put to the bar; and addressed them, in substance, as follows: " Prisoners, you were convicted of a highway robbery at the last Summer Assizes....My doubt was, whether the evidence of an accomplice, unconfirmed by any other evidence that could materially affect the case, was sufficient to warrant a conviction[1]? —And the Judges are unanimously of opinion that an accomplice alone is a competent witness; and that, if the jury, weighing the probability of his testimony, think him worthy of belief, a conviction supported by such testimony alone is perfectly legal. The distinction between the *competency* and the *credit* of a witness has been long settled. If a question be made respecting his *competency,* the decision of that question is the exclusive province of the Judge; but if the ground of the objection go to his *credit* only, his testimony must be received and left with the jury, under such directions and observations from the Court as the circumstances of the case may require, to say whether they think it sufficiently credible to guide their decision on the case. An accomplice, therefore, being a competent witness, and the jury in the present case having thought him worthy of credit, the verdict of

[1] See the case of *The King v. Durham and Crowder,* 1 Leach 478.

Guilty, which has been found, is strictly legal, though found on the testimony of the accomplice only.

[*What* kind *of confirmation is effective.*]

REX *v.* WILKES AND EDWARDS.

OXFORD ASSIZES.   1836.   7 CARRINGTON AND PAYNE 272.

The prisoners were charged with stealing a lamb, the property of Robert Pratt.

On the part of the prosecution an accomplice, named Gardner, was called. He proved the case against both prisoners, and stated that they threw the skin of the lamb into a whirley hole, the situation of which he described.

To confirm his evidence a constable, named Hutchinson, was called, who proved that he found the skin in the whirley hole.

ALDERSON, B.   There is a great difference between confirmations as to the circumstances of the felony, and those which apply to the individuals charged; the former only prove that the accomplice was present at the commission of the offence; the latter shew that the prisoner was connected with it. This distinction ought always to be attended to.

It was proved that in the house of the prisoner Edwards, a quantity of meat was found of a kind corresponding with that of the stolen lamb, but could not be positively identified; and it was proved by a witness named Meek, that the prisoner Wilkes had come to him to borrow a pair of shears, and had then made a statement to him to the same effect as the evidence of the accomplice.

ALDERSON, B. (in summing up). (1) The confirmation of the accomplice as to the *commission* of the felony is really no confirmation at all; because it would be a confirmation as much if the accusation were against you and me, as it would be as to those prisoners who are now upon their trial. The confirmation which I always advise juries to require, is a confirmation of the accomplice in some fact which goes to fix the guilt on the particular person charged. You may legally convict on the evidence of an accomplice only, if you can safely rely on his testimony; but I advise juries never to act on the evidence of an accomplice, unless he is confirmed as to the particular person who is charged with the offence. (2) With respect to the prisoner Edwards, it is proved that meat of a similar kind was found in his house. The meat cannot be identified, but it is similar: that is, therefore, some confirmation of the accomplice as to Edwards more than any one else. It is also proved that the skin was found in a whirley hole: that is no confirmation, because it does not affect the prisoners more than it affects any other persons. (3) With respect to the prisoner Wilkes, it is proved, by the witness Meek, that the prisoner Wilkes told him nearly the same story as the accomplice has told you to-day. If you believe that witness, there is confirmation of the accomplice as to the prisoner Wilkes.

You will say whether, with these confirmations, you believe the accomplice or not. If you think that his evidence is not sufficiently confirmed as to one of the prisoners, you will acquit that one; if you think he is confirmed as to neither, you will acquit both; and if you think that he is confirmed as to both, you will find both guilty.

The jury found both the prisoners guilty.

[*What kind of confirmation is useless.*]

REGINA *v.* PRATT.

HERTFORD ASSIZES.   1865.   4 FOSTER AND FINLASON 315.

Indictment for feloniously receiving certain goods, knowing them to have been stolen.

Two bushels of wheat were stolen on January 21st, 1865. On the same day the property was found on prisoner's premises, who was a carpenter, living near to the prosecutor. The only express evidence to prove the rest of the case was that of the thief; who was called for the prosecution.

POLLOCK, C.B. There is no evidence here, either of the theft, or of the guilty knowledge, except that of the thief. He proves the theft; he proves the possession (for the mere fact of the goods being on the prisoner's premises, which might be without his knowledge or assent, does not prove *possession*, much less receiving by him); and he proves the guilty knowledge. There is nothing to confirm him, except a fact which is quite consistent with the falsity of his story; for he might have put the goods on the prisoner's premises without his knowledge. The evidence, therefore, is not such as would make it safe or proper to convict, and the jury ought to acquit.

CHAPTER X.   DISCREDITING A WITNESS.

[*When cross-examined as to his own* discreditable conduct, *his answers
are final.*]

REX *v.* YEWIN.

MONMOUTH ASSIZES.   1811.   2 CAMPBELL 637.

Yewin was indicted for stealing wheat.   The principal witness
against him was a boy of the name of Thomas, his apprentice.

The prisoner's counsel asked Thomas, in cross-examination
(1) whether he had not been charged with robbing his master; and
(2) whether he had not afterwards said he would be revenged of him
and would soon fix him in Monmouth gaol.   He denied both.   The
prisoner's counsel then proposed to prove that he had been charged
with robbing his master, and had spoken the words imputed to him.

LAWRENCE, J.   His answer as to the former fact must be taken[1];
but [as to the latter], as the words alleged are material to the guilt or
innocence of the prisoner, evidence may be adduced that they were
spoken by the witness.

---

[1] [EDITOR'S NOTE.   "Had this been a matter in issue, I would have allowed
you to call witnesses to contradict him.   But it is entirely collateral, and you
must take his answer.   I will permit questions to be put to a witness as to any
improper conduct of which he may have been guilty, for the purpose of trying
his credit; but when these questions are irrelevant to the issue on the record, you
cannot call other witnesses to contradict the answers he gives.   No witness can be
prepared to support his character as to particular facts; and such collateral inquiries would lead to endless confusion."   Per LAWRENCE, J., in *Harris* v. *Tippett*
(2 Camp. 637); a case in which, however, the accepted rule, thus admirably laid
down, was applied to an answer that perhaps fell more properly within the doctrine
of *Thomas* v. *David, infra,* p. 544.]

[*But not when cross-examined as to his* bias *in the particular litigation.*]

THOMAS *v.* DAVID.

CARMARTHEN ASSIZES.   1836.   7 CARRINGTON AND PAYNE 350.

Action against the defendant as the maker of a promissory note. Plea—that the defendant did not make the note.

A witness on the part of the plaintiff, who was his female servant, and who was one of the attesting witnesses to the defendant's signature of the promissory note, was asked on cross-examination whether she did not constantly sleep with the plaintiff. She said that she did not. On the part of the defendant several witnesses were called ; and one of them (Edward Lloyd) was tendered to prove the fact which the servant had denied....

Evans, for plaintiff. I submit that the evidence of this witness is not admissible; because the point upon which he is called to contradict the witness for the plaintiff is collateral to the issue.

COLERIDGE, J. Is it not material to the issue, whether the principal witness who comes to support the plaintiff's case is his kept mistress ? If the question had been whether the witness had walked the streets as a common prostitute, I think that that would have been collateral to the issue, and that, had the witness denied such a charge, she could not have been contradicted. But here the question is, whether the witness had contracted such a relation with the plaintiff as might induce her the more readily to conspire with him to support a forgery ; just in the same way as if she had been asked if she was the sister or daughter of the plaintiff, and had denied that. I think that the contradiction is admissible.

The witness Edward Lloyd was examined, and stated that the witness in question slept constantly with her master.

Verdict for the defendant.

INDEX

315

Lightning Source UK Ltd.
Milton Keynes UK
UKOW06f1917171217
314644UK00006B/177/P